GLOBAL MARKETING STRATEGY

McGRAW-HILL SERIES IN MARKETING

GLOBAL MARKETING STRATEGY

SUSAN P. DOUGLAS
Stern School of Business

C. SAMUEL CRAIG
Stern School of Business

McGraw-Hill, Inc.
New York   St. Louis   San Francisco   Auckland   Bogotá   Caracas
Lisbon   London   Madrid   Mexico City   Milan   Montreal   New Delhi
San Juan   Singapore   Sydney   Tokyo   Toronto

This book was set in New Baskerville by Better Graphics, Inc.
The editor was Bonnie K. Binkert;
the production supervisor was Elizabeth J. Strange.
The cover was designed by Carol A. Couch.
Project supervision was done by Tage Publishing Service, Inc.
R. R. Donnelley & Sons Company was printer and binder.

GLOBAL MARKETING STRATEGY

This book is printed on recycled, acid-free paper
containing 10% postconsumer waste.

1 2 3 4 5 6 7 8 9 0 DOH DOH 9 0 9 8 7 6 5 4

ISBN 0-07-013447-2

Library of Congress Cataloging-in-Publication Data

Douglas, Susan P.
   Global marketing strategy / Susan P. Douglas, C. Samuel Craig.
      p.   cm. — (McGraw-Hill series in marketing)
    ISBN 0-07-013447-2
     1. Export marketing—Management.   2. Export marketing—Management—
Case studies.   I. Craig, C. Samuel.   II. Title.   III. Series.
   HF1416.D68   1995
   658.8'48—dc20   94-22706

ABOUT THE AUTHORS

SUSAN P. DOUGLAS is Professor of Marketing and International Business at New York University's Stern School of Business. She received her Ph.D. from the University of Pennsylvania. Prior to joining New York University in 1978, Professor Douglas taught at Centre-HEC, Jouy-en-Josas, France, and was a faculty member of the European Institute for Advanced Studies in Management in Brussels. She has also taught international marketing in executive programs in France, Belgium, Italy, Taiwan, Singapore, India, South Africa and the former Yugoslavia.

A past president of the European Marketing Academy, and former vice president of the Academy of International Business, Professor Douglas was elected a fellow of the Academy of International Business in 1991.

Professor Douglas co-authored *International Marketing Research* with Professor Craig. She has published over fifty articles on international marketing strategy and cross-national consumer behavior, which have appeared in the *Journal of Marketing, Journal of Consumer Research, Journal of International Business Studies, Columbia Journal of World Business, International Journal of Research in Marketing* and other publications.

C. SAMUEL CRAIG is Professor of Marketing and International Business and Chairman of the Marketing Department at New York University's Stern School of Business. He received his Ph.D. from the Ohio State University. Prior to joining New York University, Professor Craig taught at Cornell University. He has taught marketing for executive programs in the United States as well as France, Thailand, Singapore, Greece and the former Yugoslavia.

Professor Craig has co-authored two books; *Consumer Behavior: An Information Processing Perspective* (Prentice-Hall) and *International Marketing Research* (Prentice-Hall). His research has appeared in the *Journal of Marketing Research, Journal of Marketing, Journal of Consumer Research, Journal of International Business Studies, Columbia Journal of World Business, International Journal of Research in Marketing* and other publications.

To Nicholas and Stephanie,
(S.P.D.)

To Liz, Mary Catherine, and Caroline,
(C.S.C.)

CONTENTS

PREFACE

Developing a global marketing strategy to compete effectively in world markets is one of the most critical challenges facing firms today. Whether the firm concentrates on a few markets close to home or targets many markets throughout the world, a long run dynamic strategy must be formulated to provide the firm with a sustainable competitive advantage. This strategy should, at the same time, enable the firm to anticipate, respond and adapt to the complexity and rapid pace of change in the global market place.

Global Marketing Strategy deals directly with the issues that today's global marketers face. Currently available books on international marketing typically examine the various aspects of the international marketing environment, and the tactical decisions made by a marketing manager. However, limited attention is paid to strategic issues, and in particular, the need to consider the impact of regional market integration and the growing interdependence of markets worldwide on the formulation of global market strategy. Yet, with increasing recognition of the importance of global markets, there is a need to address global marketing issues in all their complexity.

THE STRATEGIC FRAMEWORK

This book develops an evolutionary framework for formulating global marketing strategy. A fundamental assumption is that, depending on the extent of the firm's involvement and experience in international markets, the challenges that a firm faces and hence the appropriate strategy will vary. Three stages in this evolution are identified: initial entry, local market expansion, and global rationalization. In initially entering international markets, a firm's primary concern is to assess and select the countries which provide the most attractive opportunities for its products and services, and to devise effective competitive strategies to enter and take advantage of these opportunities. Once a foothold has been successfully established in international markets, a firm's attention typically turns to expanding its local market presence. Often this entails broadening the product line, adding new variants and developing new products, and adapting marketing tactics to compete more effectively in local markets. As the firm's international operations develop and evolve over time, pressures arise to rationalize and consolidate operations across country markets so as to improve global efficiency and facilitate transfer of learning. Establishment of a global portfolio of countries,

xvii

products and market segments, charts a firm's direction and guides allocation of resources in global markets. A strategy then has to be developed to leverage its competitive position in global markets so as to take advantage of potential synergies that arise from international market operations. More details on the plan of the book and how these different topics are treated can be found on pages 21 to 24 of Chapter 1.

The approach provides an appropriate framework to guide the strategic activities of all types of firms irrespective of their size, national origin, and degree of experience in international markets. It can be a helpful approach to guide small and medium sized manufacturers or multi-nationals from emerging countries who are taking their first steps into international markets. Equally, issues facing firms already involved in international markets and seeking ways to expand and broaden their market base in different countries are discussed. Guidelines for developing an effective global marketing strategy are also outlined for firms seeking to improve efficiency through better coordination and integration of marketing strategies across country markets. The final chapter of the book discusses the challenges facing firms in each of these phases, and suggests appropriate response strategies to these challenges.

TEXT CASES

In addition to the 16 chapters of text, there are seven cases at the end of the book. These have been selected to illustrate various aspects of the concepts discussed in the text as well as to show the complexity of marketing in a multi-country environment. These seven cases, along with others suggested in the instructor's manual, provide an opportunity to apply the ideas developed in this book and explore the formulation of global marketing strategy.

The first two cases, Sterling Marking Products and Mary Kay Cosmetics, provide a close look at the issues facing firms entering international markets. The Sterling Marking case examines a firm that has been successful in its home market (Canada) and is seeking to expand into other markets. The Mary Kay case, in addition to looking at market entry issues, provides rich insights into consumer behavior and the industry structure of the cosmetics business in China and Japan. The second two cases, Heineken N.V. and Levi Strauss Japan K.K., deal with issues related to international market expansion. Heineken is seeking to develop a Pan-European strategy for Buckler, a non-alcoholic beer. It faces issues related to formulation of the marketing mix and coordination across countries. Levis is trying to expand its presence in the lucrative Japanese market in the face of increased competition in the market and structural changes in distribution channels. The last cases, ICI Paints (A,B) and Air BP, focus on the issue facing firms attempting to forge a global strategy. Air BP is struggling to be more competitive and more profitable in the market to supply fuel and service to aircraft. ICI Paints competes in a number of segments and regions worldwide and is attempting to develop an appropriate global strategy. Both firms are facing complex competitive and organizational challenges as they try to rationalize their strategies.

INTENDED AUDIENCE

This book is best suited for an advanced course in international marketing. The book is intended either for a global marketing strategy/international marketing course in a curriculum where substantial international material has already been integrated into the introductory course in marketing or where students have already taken an introductory international business course; or alternatively, for a second-level or advanced course in international marketing strategy at a school where the basic international marketing course focuses on the environment of international marketing and marketing mix decisions. It assumes that the reader has some appreciation of the environment for international business decisions and some familiarity with marketing mix decisions.

An important aspect of global strategy development is the environment that global marketers face. Topics such as the economic, sociocultural, political, and technological environments are covered in Chapter 1 as they relate to the context in which global marketing is carried out. Instructors who typically spend more time on these topics, will want to assign additional readings and devote more class time to these topics. Issues related to development of the marketing mix are covered in Chapter 10. Again, instructors wishing to spend more time on each of the mix components can expand on these topics. The cases included at the end of the text provide considerable additional information on marketing mix formulation. In addition, in the instructor's manual, we suggest additional reading, as well as soft cover books that deal with marketing mix and contextual issues.

INSTRUCTIONAL SUPPORT

A course in international/global marketing can be taught in a variety of ways depending on the instructor's preference and the students' backgrounds. For those interested in a lecture style course augmented with a few cases, this text along with the suggested supplemental reading would be appropriate. For those who prefer a more case oriented approach, we have keyed over 20 cases that are available through PRIMIS to the text. For those who like to use student projects, we have provided outlines for four different projects in the instructors manual. The first two projects deal with assessing international market potential and developing an initial entry strategy for a specific market. These have been used successfully by the senior author for over 15 years. The other two projects deal with industry structure and competitive strategy analysis and the evolution of a specific firm's strategy over time. In addition, the instructor's manual contains suggestions for supplemental materials that can be used to enrich any course, as well as questions that augment the text materials.

ACKNOWLEDGMENTS

We would like to thank all those who have contributed to the development of this book. We are particularly indebted to our colleagues both at New York University and other institutions with whom we have discussed many of the ideas in this book and whose encouragement and helpful comments contributed immeasurably to its development.

We are very grateful to Professors Roger Calantone, Michigan State University; Thomas Greer, University of Maryland; Hari Hariharan, University of Wisconsin; Michael J. Houston, University of Minnesota; Saul Klein, Wake Forest; Lynn Metcalf, California Polytechnic; and John Quelch, Harvard Business School, who reviewed the manuscript and provided many helpful and insightful comments.

The text is enriched by the seven cases that appear at the end of the book. These illustrate how firms are dealing with the issues they face at various stages of global development. We are indebted to the authors of these cases for granting us permission to use their materials.

Professor Franklyn Manu provided invaluable assistance in the preparation of the instructor's manual. His efforts greatly enriched the support materials available to instructors using the book.

We would also like to acknowledge the assistance received from the capable people at McGraw-Hill in guiding us through the steps in the writing and production process. In particular, Jim Nageotte provided helpful suggestions at the copy editing stage, and Tony Caruso oversaw the final production. A special thanks is due Bonnie Binkert, Senior Marketing Editor at McGraw-Hill, whose persistence and good humor kept us on schedule and helped shape the final manuscript.

Finally, last and by no means least, we want to thank Sylvia Santiago-Feliciano, who cheerfully and competently typed her way through the various chapter drafts, and Jenny Ryan who made the numerous corrections to the final drafts.

Susan P. Douglas
C. Samuel Craig

GLOBAL MARKETING STRATEGY

PART I

INTRODUCTION

CHAPTER 1

GLOBAL MARKETING STRATEGY
The Trend Toward Globalization

INTRODUCTION

The most striking trend in business today is the growing globalization of markets worldwide for goods and services. This is true for everything from airlines to automobiles, banking to burgers, clothing to computers, detergents to diapers, electronics to elevators . . . soft drinks to software, toothpaste to tacos. . . . Corporations whether of U.S., Japanese, European, or other national origin are drawing an increasing proportion of their sales from international markets. The 100 largest U.S. multinationals, derive 39 percent of their sales from operations overseas.[1] Companies such as Exxon, IBM, Colgate-Palmolive CPC International, and Coca-Cola draw more than 60 percent of their sales from international markets. International markets are critical for companies such as Unilever, the Anglo-Dutch conglomerate; Philips, the electronics giant; and Nestlé, the Swiss food mammoth, who have relatively small domestic markets. Vast multinational empires are emerging, whose total sales volume is often greater than the G.N.P. of many countries.

Yet globalization is not confined to large multinationals. A new breed of "mininationals" is emerging, opening factories, research labs, and sales units around the world.[2] These are typically mid-size manufacturing companies with sales of $200 million to $1 billion, which target specialty niche markets worldwide in areas such as precision instruments, medical equipment, or computer peripherals. Taking advantage of the opening up of markets and new technologies, they are able to serve customers from a limited number of manufacturing bases and keep a lean corporate profile to compete more effectively in world markets. Medtronic, a U.S. manufacturer of pacemakers, has opened plants in Japan and Europe for research and manufacturing to serve these markets and tap into new technology in micromachining and miniaturization.

Japanese and European companies have entered world markets and constitute a major challenge in many industries traditionally dominated by U.S. firms. Many companies from the newly industrializing and developing economies are also beginning to spread their wings and to assume increasing importance in fields such as electronics, textiles, shipbuilding, and steel.

Furthermore, the trend toward globalization is occurring, not only downstream in end markets for consumer or industrial goods, but also upstream in markets for raw materials, technology, and other resources. In many industries, global sourcing is on the increase, resulting in the development of complex logistical systems designed to take advantage of differential labor, production, and raw material costs in different countries, as well as the increased efficiency in international transportation and communication networks.

Thomson Consumer Electronics of France, for example, makes components in Malaysia and Indonesia that go into T.V. sets assembled in its highly automated plant in Singapore.[3] Indonesia has now become a favorite place for making expensive running shoes. Numerous U.S. and Japanese automobile companies are setting up operations in Mexico. Ford is investing $750 million in a plant in Chihuahua to manufacture two engines for North America. Nissan is spending $1 billion on a new assembly plant at Aguas Calientes to make Sentras, some of which are to be re-exported to Japan.[4]

Such developments imply that all companies need to adopt a global perspective in their strategic marketing planning, irrespective of their interest in international markets. Companies already involved in, or contemplating entry into, international markets need to identify the most attractive opportunities worldwide and to determine their global strategic thrust, or key competitive advantage and investment strategy relative to these markets. Even companies not considering international operations need to develop strategy with an eye to international developments and potential entry of foreign competition into the domestic market.

THE TREND TOWARDS GLOBALIZATION

Although multinationals such as Unilever and Nestlé have long been established features of the international business scene, the current trend toward globalization and the emergence of global markets essentially spans the last four decades. In the '60s many U.S. companies expanded overseas, attracted by higher rates of growth and opportunities in maturing markets in Europe, Latin America, and Asia. The '70s witnessed the entry of Japanese companies into foreign markets, notably the United States, as well as the retaliation of European companies to the American challenge. The '80s saw the growth of companies from the newly industrializing nations, entering, not only the U.S. and European markets, but also countries in Asia and Africa. The '90s have been characterized by major changes in spatial market boundaries. Some markets, such as Europe and North America, are becoming increasingly integrated, while others, notably the former Soviet Union and Yugoslavia, are becoming more fragmented. In addition, huge new markets are opening up in countries such as China, India, and Indonesia, as a result of changing geopolitics. As a result, many markets are becoming global in scope, and national boundaries are giving way to global pressures.

The '60s: The Movement of U.S. Companies Abroad

The initial impetus towards the globalization of business came from the movement overseas of U.S. companies in the early and mid '60s. Slackening rates of growth in their domestic markets led many companies to investigate opportunities in the increasingly affluent markets outside the United States. Polaroid, for example, faced with a stagnant market for instant photography in the United States, began to look to European markets for growth potential.

During this period, direct investment abroad by U.S. companies more than doubled, from $31 to $70 billion, according to U.S. Department of Commerce estimates. Other forms of international activity, including licensing and, other contractual agreements, and sourcing from other countries, also expanded rapidly, though their exact size is difficult to quantify. In addition, exports from the United States grew from $80 to over $140 billion.

For companies already established overseas, rates of growth in foreign markets often far outstripped growth in their domestic market. Coca-Cola, for example, hurt by a slow domestic economy and a decline in away-from-home eating in the United States, was nonetheless able to expand rapidly on the international front. Similarly, Kelloggs, by introducing the breakfast habit in many countries throughout the world, was able to sustain a rapid rate of growth in international markets.

The '70s: The Growth of the Japanese Challenge

The shift of U.S. companies into world markets did not go unchallenged, however. In the '70s Japanese companies became major contenders creating a serious threat to U.S. supremacy in markets ranging from consumer electronics to heavy construction equipment. Komatsu became a major force and challenged Caterpillar's dominance in world markets. Casio and Seiko began to dominate the market for low-priced watches and calculators, competing, not only on quality and price, but also in producing multifunction products, combining watches, calculators, and alarms.

Thus, while in 1960 Japan accounted for only 6.5% of world exports of manufactured goods, by 1970 it accounted for 11.2%, and by 1973, for 13%. Paralleling the growth of U.S. direct investment overseas, by the end of 1978 Japanese direct investment totalled over $26.8 billion, more than seven times its level in 1970. In addition, European companies that had been attacked in their domestic markets retaliated by entering the U.S. market. Initially, many hesitated to enter the U.S. market, due to its size and competitiveness. When it became evident that competition was developing on a worldwide scale, however, they concluded they had no option but to enter world markets. Olivetti, a major Italian manufacturer of office equipment, entered the U.S. market in order to keep abreast of the rapidly changing technology in the industry and to maintain its supremacy in European markets.

The '80s: The Emergence of Third World Multinationals

During the '80s yet another force in world markets emerged, multinationals from industrializing and developing countries. Often these were companies whose home base was in industrializing countries in the Far East, such as South Korea, Taiwan, Singapore, and Hong Kong, or in growing economies in Latin America, such as Brazil and Venezuela.

Some of these multinationals predominantly focused on establishing operations in countries at comparable levels of development. Their levels of technological sophistication and management culture were frequently better adapted to such countries than were those of companies from highly industrialized western nations. This was found to be a significant advantage in industries such as tropical agriculture, aquaculture, engineering, consulting, rural construction, and housing.

Other multinationals, in particular those from Taiwan, South Korea, Hong Kong, and Singapore (the four Asian Tigers), started by supplying parts and components to companies in highly industrialized nations, and then shifted to a direct frontal attack on these markets, often using price as a major competitive weapon. For example, Lucky Goldstar, a South Korean company, once a major supplier of components to U.S. television manufacturers such as Motorola, launched its own brand of consumer items such as microwave ovens, T.V.s, and refrigerators in the United States, targeting the lower end of the market.[5] The company also entered into a joint venture with Honeywell to make computer control systems, to provide it with the technology to move into factory automation and the market for industrial robots.

The '90s: Global Restructuring

The '90s reflect the continuation of changes undertaken in the previous three decades. The movement abroad by U.S. companies that began in the '60s left many firms with an extensive patchwork of loosely linked international operations vulnerable to increased competition from Japan and other industrializing nations. As a result, many have moved toward streamlining international operations and improving global efficiencies in order to survive.

Even Japanese firms are feeling increased pressure from new sources of global competition. The latest competitor in the automobile market is the South Korean company Kia Motors. Kia has launched the Sephia compact sedan into the U.S. market, aggressively positioning it as a low-priced, quality car.[6] Despite the risks entailed and the failure of other moderately priced foreign auto models such as Renault, Daihatsu, and Yugo in the United States, Kia views this strategy as key to its ambition of becoming a global player in the market. By the end of 1996 Kia hopes to sell 250,000 units annually, with several other models, including a sports utility vehicle, the Sportage. The ad copy stresses reliability, dependability, and affordability through the tag line, "It's about time everyone had a well-made car."

Further intensifying competition has been the movement toward regional trading blocs, such as ASEAN (Association of South East Asian Nations) and SAFTA (South American Free Trade), and the formal integration of markets, specifically the EU (European Union) and NAFTA (North American Free Trade Agreement). These groupings not only affect market access, but increasingly require that strategy be developed, implemented, and coordinated on a regional basis. Such market blocs, whether formally or loosely integrated, pose unique challenges to the marketing strategist, since they rarely have identical customer needs and operational requirements and there is often considerable variation among countries within a bloc. This means that firms must be flexible and design strategies that are not only viable across markets but at the same time recognize the diversity within market blocs. Additional complexity is created by the existence of interdependencies between these blocs.

In sharp contrast to such market integration is the uncertainty and turmoil of market fragmentation. The countries of the former Soviet Union and Eastern Europe have gone from being strongly linked to a loose and somewhat unstable confederation of individual markets. The breakup of the Soviet Union has also resulted in markets opening up in its former trading partners, such as India, Cambodia, and Vietnam. China has also emerged as a major force in world markets, both as a source of low-cost labor and manufacturing and as a market for products ranging from personal computers and telecommunications equipment to gold jewelry, razor blades, and Coca-Cola.[7] These changes pose unique challenges for the marketing strategist, as years of central control have hampered development of the necessary market mechanisms and infrastructure to support the implementation of marketing strategies. Such changes are creating a new dynamic in world markets as attention shifts away from focus on markets within the Industrial Triad (the United States, Europe, and Japan) to a broad and more complex pattern of interrelations among markets worldwide.

THE GLOBALIZATION OF MARKETS

Widespread movement into international markets by companies of all types has made an increasing number of product markets global or regional rather than domestic in scope. These include consumer and industrial electronics, semiconductors, computers, telecommunications equipment, plastics, organic chemicals, agricultural machinery, automobiles, motorcycles, and bicycles, to mention only a few. Markets that once were bounded by national limits today have assumed international dimensions.

In the United States, for example, the share of imports in the automobile market has climbed dramatically over the last three decades, particularly in the compact car segment. While in 1960, 96 percent of new cars purchased in the United States were supplied by the Big Three, by 1970 this had dropped to 82 percent, and from 1980 to 1993 it has stabilized at around 74 percent.[8] Much of this has been due to Japanese competition, though, as noted earlier, South Korean companies also have global ambitions. Such competition has also begun to pose an increasing threat to European markets. Here again, Japanese companies are making inroads into markets such as France, Germany, and the U.K., which were once the sole domain of national automobile makers.[9]

The trend toward globalization has not been confined to manufacturing industries but encompasses many other industries such as services and retailing. Many of the service industries that form an integral part of the business infrastructure, such as banks, insurance companies and other financial institutions, advertising agencies, and market research organizations, have become increasingly global in scope. Here, the momentum has largely been created by the movement of key clients into foreign markets, generating demand for the provision of services on a global scale. The development of a global marketing infrastructure has in turn played a key role in encouraging the development of global business operations.

Increased communication and travel by consumers across national boundaries, whether business related or not, has resulted in the emergence of global market segments with similar needs and interests worldwide. Industries such as fast foods, soft drinks, clothing, hotels and motels, and car rentals have expanded internationally in response to this demand. Fast food chains such as McDonald's, Pizza Hut, and KFC target hungry consumers worldwide, who desire to fulfill their food needs quickly, on the run; while the hotel chains such as Hilton, Nikko, Oberoi, and Meridien, and car rental companies such as Avis and Hertz, target travelling executives who wish to be assured of consistent service and comfort wherever they go.

Retailers are also moving into international markets. U.S. retailers such as Toys R Us and Pier I are expanding in markets from Japan and Europe to Mexico and Central and South America, exporting their distinctive retailing formulas and merchandising skills with the adaptation to local market tastes.[10] Discount retailers such as the Costco Wholesale Club, Kmart, and Walmart are chasing fat retail margins in European countries from Britain to Slovakia,[11] while Japanese department stores such as Isetan and Seibu are setting up outlets in Taiwan, Singapore, Thailand, and Hong Kong.

Even national sports and cable networks are going global. The National Basketball Association has already expanded into Europe and is now targeting the Pacific Rim, where sales from games and licensed merchandise are expected to grow rapidly.[12] A group of Pittsburgh investors has purchased 50 percent of the Russian Army hockey team, introduced new American-style marketing techniques to improve attendance, and is planning a new promotional tour through the United States.[13] U.S. cable networks such as MTV, QVC, and TNT are flooding into Europe. MTV, for example, has been highly successful with its pop-music format and has been able to generate millions in revenues from pan-European advertisers.[14]

MOTIVATION FOR GLOBAL INVOLVEMENT

Yet the motivations that underlie globalization are highly diverse and vary from market to market in their significance and role. An important spur to globalization in many consumer goods markets, particularly for personal items, such as moderate to high-priced cosmetics, expensive perfume and watches, clothing and leather goods, as well as pop music and records, has been increased communication and travel across national boundaries. This has stimulated the emergence of transnational or global market segments such as teenagers and young adults, business executives, or upscale consumers who often have tastes and interests closer to those of their counterparts in other countries than to other types of consumers in their own countries. As a result, opportunities have opened up for developing products and services targeted to these segments worldwide: for example, Cartier watches and handbags, Burberry raincoats, Sony Walkmans, MTV, and Nike running shoes.

The desire to exploit good ideas for products or services on a broader geographic scale may also lead firms to enter international markets. Thus, for example, Bic's initiative in marketing its disposable lighters and razors worldwide has been an important element stimulating the globalization of markets for these products.

Identifying sourcing opportunities in other countries has also encouraged the trend toward globalization. In some cases, the location of production has shifted to take advantage of differences in relative labor costs or natural resources. Much of the textile industry, for example, shifted to Southeast Asia to take advantage of lower wage rates in areas such as Indonesia and the Guangdong province in Southern China.[3] In the electronics industry global sourcing is rampant. Singapore produces over half the world's disc drives, while Japan has 95 percent of the world market for active-matrix LCDs.[15]

Yet another key factor is the growth of global competition. In some industries such as automobiles, electronics, steel, textiles, and computer chips, the major players compete in markets worldwide. Meeting competition in world markets is crucial to keep abreast of developments in technology, distribution, etc., or simply to retain global customers in these markets. Substantial economies of scale and operational efficiencies can also be realized through operation on a global scale. Consequently, in such industries, the key to success is market share on a worldwide scale.

The desire to diversify and to spread risk over a wider geographic area can also motivate firms to enter international markets. Recession in one country may be counterbalanced by growth in another. The movement of U.S. construction companies into Middle Eastern markets in the 1980s, for example, was motivated by the recession and decline in building starts in the United States. Declining birth rates in the United States prompted companies marketing baby products to seek new markets in Mexico, where, on the contrary, the birth rate is rising. Gerber, for example, expanded its baby food operations in Mexico.

Recent developments in communications technology and in electronic information-processing capabilities are a powerful factor encouraging the growth of international business. Improvements in the international telephone network and satellite linkages make possible rapid intercountry communications, bridging geographic barriers. More recent developments such as teleconferencing, view-data, electronic mail, faxes, international courier services, and international linkage of computer networks further contribute to the shrinking of distances. Consequently, conducting business between New York and Jakarta is almost as easy as doing so between New York and Los Angeles.

The much-heralded information superhighway, in addition to dramatically altering communication networks and ways of doing business in domestic markets, also promises to bring radical change in the global marketplace. Improved communication and more rapid interchange of information between markets will help to make the global village a reality. While much remains to be developed, Internet currently ties together over 25,000 computer networks worldwide. This links an estimated 20 million people and includes such firms as IBM, GE, JP Morgan, Merrill Lynch, and Xerox.[16]

Improvements in transportation systems and physical logistics have also encouraged the expansion of international operations. Containerization and specialized cargo ships for transporting raw materials, steel, and automobiles have reduced costs as well as the time required to move goods across major distances. Similarly, computer-aided design and manufacturing systems enable engineers in different parts of the world to work together on designing products and production systems, as in the case of Ford's Mondeo. Production logistics can also be more easily coordinated on a global or regional scale through the use of computerized information systems.

The development of a global market infrastructure has also made managing operations on an international scale easier. Not only has the growth of international business encouraged the development of communication and transportation networks that facilitate growth, but companies supplying services to corporations have followed their customers abroad. Accounting firms, advertising agencies, and market research companies have established branches or become tied into networks in other countries so as to provide services on a worldwide basis.

Some banks and financial institutions such as Citibank and Morgan Guaranty have long traditions of international operations and extensive international networks. With the explosion of international business, the scope of these operations has expanded considerably in recent years. The rapid growth of many

Asian economies has resulted in a substantial increase in investment and retail banking in these areas.

Advertising agencies have expanded operations internationally to meet the needs of their global clients. Saatchi & Saatchi, McCann-Erickson, J. Walter Thompson, Ogilvy & Mather Worldwide, and Young & Rubicam have established offices to service clients worldwide. Developments in communications have facilitated this trend, since advertising copy can be developed and transmitted via video networks almost instantaneously throughout the world.

Thus, globalization now touches all spheres of business activity from resource markets to markets for consumer and industrial goods. Furthermore, it has wrought profound changes in the organization of business. On the one hand, the broadened scope of operations has enabled an increased specialization of management skills such as export management, international sales, and foreign exchange prediction and management. At the same time, the geographic diversity of operations, and the scope of the resources required to manage these operations, have encouraged the development of complex organizational networks including, for example, alliances for R&D, production, marketing or distributing activities, a spread in the licensing of technology or brand names, and out-sourcing of services. Such arrangements require an increasing degree of cooperation and coordination with other organizations.

THE FORCES SHAPING GLOBAL MARKETING STRATEGIES

Articulating an effective global marketing strategy must begin with an understanding of the myriad of intertwined forces that continually shape and change the context in which global competitive strategies are played out. While one can identify a host of different environmental forces having an impact on global marketing strategy, for the sake of clarity they can be categorized into four main spheres of influence—*economic, technological, political,* and *sociocultural* (see Figure 1-1). This categorization is of necessity arbitrary but nonetheless provides a convenient grouping for the purposes of discussion. These spheres of influence are not independent, but rather intertwined. Often a particular force will be the product of a complex pattern of interaction and interplay among the different spheres of influence. For example, emerging concern for the environment is causing firms to rethink the underlying technology and resources used to produce and package new and existing products. This is stimulated in part by changing sociocultural values and heightened awareness of environmental issues, and further reinforced by political moves to exploit these concerns and halt environmental destruction. Bolstering both social concern and political action is the economic argument of the need to conserve scarce resources.

The forces influencing global strategy provide the backdrop for the formulation and implementation of global strategy. These forces are complex in and of themselves and interact both with one another and with strategies of firms.

FIGURE 1-1
Forces shaping global marketing strategy.

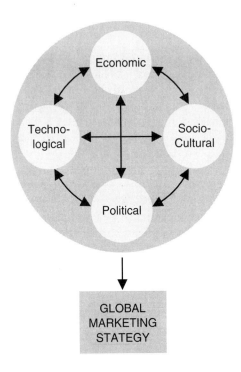

While these forces act in concert, in the following section they will be discussed separately.

Economic Forces

Economic forces impact global marketing strategies at both a macro and microeconomic level. At a macroeconomic level, they impact the nature and location of global marketing opportunities, as well as the spatial configuration of markets. Often macroeconomic forces are closely interlinked with political initiatives designed to stimulate or restrict natural economic flow and growth. Such forces are important factors in determining the direction of the firm's strategic thrust and, in particular, where and how it decides to focus its efforts. Microeconomic forces, on the other hand, impact the organization and efficiency of the firm's operations. The cost and availability of resources in different geographic locations impacts production and sourcing logistics as well as capital or labor substitution. Economic forces also underlie capital intensity of operations and potential for economies of scale and scope.

One of the dominant forces molding the world economy is the dramatic growth in global trade throughout the world and the increasing internationalization of business. No longer is the focus predominantly on markets within the Industrial Triad, but huge new markets such as China, India, Russia, and Eastern

Europe are opening up, as both customers and suppliers of resources, components, finished goods, and services. As a result, a firm can prosper in a wide range of different countries. These markets are thus beginning to exert a major influence on patterns of world trade. Consequently, a firm continually has to assess the changing nature of world markets and respond to emerging new opportunities and threats.

Links and trade flows between neighboring markets are also on the increase. For example, trade and business links among the Southeast Asian markets are expanding as Japanese companies invest or establish operations in Thailand, Malaysia, and Indonesia, while South Korean companies establish positions in southern Vietnam, northern China, and eastern Russia, and Taiwanese companies funnel investment into Hong Kong and the Pearl River Delta in southern China. Similarly, investment by French and German companies in the former Eastern European economy is on the increase, while U.S. companies are expanding operations in Mexico and Latin America. National boundaries are thus beginning to disappear and be replaced by new market configurations.

Economic volatility, and, in particular, rapidly accelerating (or falling) rates of inflation in various countries, together with sharp swings in foreign exchange, add to the uncertainty and unpredictability of market trends. For example, while China is a huge market, according to some estimates the third largest in the world, its rapid rate of growth appears highly unstable.[17] Similarly, trends in Latin America are precarious. As a result, it becomes increasingly critical for firms to diversify operations worldwide, to counterbalance fluctuations in different markets or geographic regions, and to develop strategic flexibility to respond to changing economic conditions.

Economic conditions also impact a firm's ability to compete in world markets and can create pressure to improve efficiency. For example, with the rising value of the yen, Japanese automobile manufacturers find their models increasingly less price-competitive in world markets.[18] Consequently, they are continually seeking to improve production efficiency and locating plants in important markets, such as the United States and Europe.

Patterns of national economic development and growth also influence production and sourcing logistics. As countries develop, wage levels rise, making them less attractive locations for production or sourcing of components. For example, rising wage levels in South Korea made companies there no longer competitive in athletic shoe and leather goods production. As a result, some South Korean companies are establishing production outlets overseas, in northern China or Indonesia, where wage levels are as much as four times lower.[19] Others are specializing in high technology hiking shoes and inline roller skates, which require skills Chinese and Indonesian workers have yet to master.

Recession in many industries in the United States and Europe, coupled with mounting unemployment, has encouraged many companies to prune layers of management, retrain employees, and operate under tight cost controls to sustain profitability.[20] There is also mounting competitive pressure to eliminate redundancy and duplication of effort in operations. Similarly, increasing capital intensity in many industries due to use of more sophisticated technology creates a need for sizable capital investments. Companies willing and able to make such investments can thus outdistance their competitors. Japanese firms such as Sharp, Seiko, and Toshiba, having invested heavily in improving manufacturing techniques for active-matrix LCDs, which are a big component in portable computers, camcorders, video games, and visual reality devices, as a result now control 95 percent of the world market for such devices.[15]

The cost and scarcity of natural resources such as water, energy, land, etc.[15], are also important issues, especially in view of increasing concern about the deterioration of the global environment. Firms are under growing pressure to conserve natural resources and to adapt production and manufacturing processes to prevent further deterioration.[21] Political actions to regulate environmental pollution, such as use of pesticides, waste emission, and creation of toxic gases, and to foster conservation of resources, reinforce the need for firms to respond to this heightened social concern.

Technological Forces

Technological forces are often closely intertwined with economic forces, especially insofar as technological developments impact the economic scale of operations and efficiency of production. Technological advances in communications have not only facilitated the development of international business operations but also have fostered greater awareness of and exposure to events and life-styles in other countries. Technological developments are important forces that help link and integrate markets while at the same time spawning increasing heterogeneity and market fragmentation.

Introduction of modular production techniques, for example, enables a firm to design a basic model for world or regional markets and make minor modifications in style or specific components, adapted to specific country markets or market segments.[22] Companies can thus supply smaller markets or market segments, or make minor changes in products to meet local market demand without substantially increasing costs. Electrolux, for example, has consolidated production of refrigerators worldwide. Production of compressors is centralized in a few locations, resulting in substantial cost savings due to scale economies. Production of the casing is modularized, allowing adaptation of size and design (i.e., number of inner compartments, door shelving, addition of items such as an ice-maker) to specific local market demand.

The rapid evolution of technology, especially marked in industries such as computers, consumer electronics, home entertainment, and communications, requires continual adaptation and retooling for a firm to keep pace. Rapid product and knowledge obsolescence shortens the life cycle of products and heightens the pace of competition. No longer can a firm expect to maintain a substantial lead over a competitor in introducing a new product. On the contrary, fast-followers may be able to leapfrog their competitors as technology evolves, introducing a superior product incorporating the latest technology.

Technological advances in communications have also revolutionized business operations and allowed the management of operations on a much broader geographic scope.[23] The development of computerized global information systems, for example, has dramatically expanded and improved coordination of global production and distribution logistics. Inventory, ordering, and delivery systems can be established on a worldwide scale, minimizing inventory levels, while at the same time ensuring rapid filling of customer orders. At the same time, market developments, such as changes in customer demand and competitor initiatives, can be monitored worldwide, to enable the firm to adapt and respond more rapidly to them. Performance, measured in terms of market share, profitability, advertising/sales ratios, or sales production levels, can also be monitored, and marketing tactics adapted and resources shifted from one market to another to meet target objectives.

The communications revolution has generated increased awareness of, and exposure to, interests, behavior, and markets in other parts of the world. Companies thus have become increasingly aware of potential opportunities as well as alternative production and distribution techniques, or technology and equipment, used by their counterparts in other countries. Advances in communications technology, and in particular the growth of satellite communications and the emergence of global media, have accelerated the rapid diffusion of innovations and ideas. In Asia, for example, the growth of satellite and cable systems such as Star TV and the Gang of Five are reaching a vast and previously untapped audience with a range of U.S., European, and Asian programs, dramatically increasing local residents' exposure to life-styles, entertainment, and events taking place in other parts of the world.[24]

Political Forces

Political actions are often closely linked with macroeconomic and technological conditions. These can be designed either to encourage or hamper the internationalization of business. Government policy, for example, can foster the growth of international trade and market integration by removing barriers to trade and establishing linkages in the market infrastructure. Alternatively, government policy can be designed to protect national competitors and national markets through erecting barriers to international competitors and establishing industrial policies favoring local companies. Similarly, political instability or insurgence will dampen economic growth and stifle technological progress. The breakup of the former Soviet Union, and the resulting economic disorder, led to the rapid demise of the American Trade Consortium, which had planned to invest $5–$10 billion there. Yet, despite continuing chaos, investment in Russia has begun to increase, buoyed by the size of the market and potential payoff.[25]

The advantages stemming from the creation of larger market areas, together with economic pressures toward the internationalization of markets, have encouraged a number of governments to dismantle or simplify trade barriers, such as customs regulations, border formalities, and other administrative restrictions, as well as to lower tariffs and quotas. In many cases, regional trade agreements have been established to create larger regional markets and trading areas, such as NAFTA, ASEAN and Mercosur.

The establishment of the European Union aims not only to create a free-trading area among the member nations but has also dismantled trade barriers. Product standards media regulation, and conditions of employment (i.e., through the Social Charter) are being harmonized throughout the community, and the development of a common fiscal policy and monetary union is envisaged for some future date.

Such initiatives have important implications for the spatial configuration of operations and the integration or coordination of marketing mix strategies. Many firms, such as Scott Paper, are consolidating production or marketing operations within the European Union. Others, such as Danone, the French food company, are expanding operations to reduce dependency on a single market, and to ensure widespread market coverage. Similarly, as a result of NAFTA, U.S. and Japanese automobile firms are shifting sourcing of components from Southeast Asian countries to Mexico, and establishing assembly operations in North American markets.

Increasingly widespread belief in the advantages and superiority of a free market system over central planning or state intervention as a means of fostering economic growth has resulted in the movement towards free market systems in mixed or centrally planned economies. Former centrally planned economies such as those of China, the former Soviet Union, and India are shifting toward free market economies, allowing the establishment of private enterprise, and opening up markets to the entry of foreign businesses. In some instances, state-owned enterprises are being sold or auctioned off, and in other instances, reformed and reorganized to operate along the lines of private enterprise.[26] Price supports and price-fixing structures are being removed to give way to free market pricing mechanisms. Similarly, in formerly mixed economies such as those of the U.K. and France, state-owned enterprises such as airlines, banks, steel companies, and utilities are being sold to private investors. Such changes have a dramatic impact on the intensity of competition in world markets and open up new opportunities in previously restricted markets.

On the other hand, political unrest and insurgency has grown in many parts of the world. The countries belonging to the former Soviet Union, African countries such as Nigeria and Rwanda, as well as some Middle Eastern countries provide examples. This unrest is often fomented by internal social conflict and creates unstable economic conditions that are often unfavorable to ventures or investment by foreign enterprises. Often, instability causes firms to halt business activities as they reassess market opportunities, and to allocate resources to ventures in other parts of the world.

Nationalist sentiment and economic recession also create pressures for the protection of domestic business in order to maintain employment and the erection of barriers, either direct or indirect, to bar the entry of foreign competition. In some cases, formation of regional trading blocs and regional market integration results either advertently or inadvertently in the erection of barriers to the entry of foreign competition. The EU, for example, has enacted rigorous product standards and regulation.[27] In particular, the ISO 9000 standards of quality management in a number of industries, as, for example, food and pharmaceuticals, have created barriers to the entry of products from many Third World countries.[28] At the same time, the EU has given support to various industries, as for example, subsidies to farmers to enable them to compete more effectively with foreign competition.

Concern with the ability of freely operating market forces to achieve social welfare goals has also led to increasing regulation of competitive market conditions. In many countries, as in the EU, increasingly strict standards relating to product quality, safety, labelling, terms of sale, and environmental concerns are being established. Regulation of advertising and other promotional activity is also increasing, particularly in North America and Europe. This includes prohibition of cigarette and alcohol advertising, and regulation of pharmaceutical advertising, advertising to children, promotional premiums, and gifts. Increased regulation reflects concern regarding protection of consumer welfare, and a belief that the freeplay of economic forces will not necessarily achieve desired social goals.

Thus, while political forces may operate to expand the geographic scope of markets and open up new opportunities, at the same time they may impose constraints on the firm's ability to exploit these opportunities and operate freely within world markets.

Sociocultural Forces

Social and cultural forces shape patterns of market demand and underlie the emergence of new interests and tastes, as well as the growth of new market segments. At the same time, sociocultural trends often reflect the impact of changing economic and technological conditions.

As noted earlier, the spread of satellite communications systems, cable TV, and international mass media has dramatically increased exposure to ideas, products, attitudes, life-styles, and events in other countries. This exposure has broadened horizons and generated awareness and interest in the products and artifacts of other cultures. As noted earlier, the impact has been particularly powerful in countries such as Russia and throughout Asia, where consumers have been starved for exposure to entertainment, and to Western life-styles and affluence.[24] In some cases, this exposure sparks desire for foreign products, viewed as symbols of a more affluent life-style, or results in a greater international sophistication in preferences and consumption patterns.

The response of international marketers to evolving consumer tastes has further expanded the range of alternative consumption styles available to consumers in countries throughout the world.[29] As a result, life-styles have become more diverse and less indigenous in orientation, incorporating products and behavior patterns from other cultures and countries. In some cases, products and ideas are modified to local preferences and market conditions in other countries, as, for example, in the variations of Italian pizza available. As a result, rather than becoming more homogeneous, as proposed by Levitt,[30] consumer tastes, preferences, and consumption patterns in many countries are becoming more diverse, incorporating a variety of elements borrowed from other countries around the world, some modified, others not. This is further compounded by increasing sophistication and higher levels of education among consumers making it difficult to follow broad-based market strategies, notably in industrialized countries.

This internationalization of life-styles is further fuelled by tidal waves of migration from one country to another. Immigrants from Mexico and other Latin American countries are moving into Florida and southwestern states in the United States; Turks and East Germans are finding work in the former West Germany; Arabs from Northern African countries such as Algeria, Morocco, and Tunisia are migrating to France; Chinese from Hong Kong are moving to Toronto and the U.K.; and Russian and Ukrainian Jews are migrating to Israel. Often these immigrants bring with them the products, tastes, and consumption patterns characteristics of their ethnic origin and thus contribute to the increasing cultural diversity of life-styles. Sometimes, they play a key role in introducing foreign products and consumption patterns into other countries, and in stimulating their adoption by a broader market base.

Increased ethnic awareness and concern with ethnic identity also results in greater market fragmentation and provides opportunities for market segmentation. This reinforces the impact of internationalization and further fragments markets. Broad-based market strategies are increasingly difficult to pursue and often require modification of products or marketing mix tactics in order to reach different ethnic market segments. At the same time, ethnic segments also create opportunities for niche marketing and can provide appropriate targets for international market expansion strategies.

As is apparent from the preceding discussion, the various spheres of influence are closely intertwined. Sometimes, different forces work together, reinforcing each other. For example, technological advances in communication result in rapid diffusion of innovations and ideas and encourage globalization of markets. In other cases, they may work in opposition: political actions to erect barriers to international trade protect domestic competition and foster market isolation.

HOW GLOBAL MARKETING DIFFERS

In developing a global marketing strategy relative to international markets, the firm must consider how far, and in what way, developing strategy on a global scale differs from formulating strategy for domestic markets. A key difference arises from the complexity of managing operations in multiple and diverse environments. How far, and in what way, should the strategies developed for the domestic market, be adapted to international markets? Several factors influence these decisions. First, host government attitudes and policies towards foreign enterprise have to be considered. These may constitute either a barrier or incentive to operations. Second, investment and resource allocation decisions are rendered more complex by differences in rates of economic growth and volatility in different countries, which make the consequences of such decisions more difficult to predict. This is further compounded by the growing interdependence of many national economies. Third, countries are characterized by different sociocultural and technological environments and by different market response patterns. As a result, what marketing strategies are appropriate or most effective will differ. Finally, the nature and strength of competition may differ from one market to another, implying that the firm's competitive advantage and what constitutes a desirable strategic thrust may differ.

Governments attitudes can be hostile, encouraging, or neutral to foreign enterprise. For example, governments can restrict investment options in a country, requiring joint venture and local participation, or increase the risk of investment due to possible hostile acts such as taxation or regulation of foreign enterprises. Alternatively, they may encourage foreign investment by providing location opportunities or tax exemption. Governments can also adopt measures to protect local enterprise, such as tariff barriers, subsidies, quotas, or product regulation, all of which may lessen the attractiveness of a particular market. Other measures that apply to both foreign and domestic enterprises, such as regulation of competition, pricing practices, product composition and labelling, and advertising and promotional content, as well as media availability, can also affect a firm's ability to exploit market potential. In addition, such factors impede adoption of standardized strategies and integration of marketing operations across national boundaries.

Differences in rates of economic growth from one country to another, as well as in their stability, also increase the complexity of evaluating and comparing alternative resource allocation strategies and investment options in different countries: production and marketing operations, such as establishing plants or sales networks, or sourcing of raw materials, technology, capital, and labor. Insofar as foreign exchange movements and capital flows influence these decisions, and the economies of different countries are interrelated, the situation becomes even more complex.

Different sociocultural environments often underlie different market response patterns. For example, cultural norms and lifestyle patterns vary markedly from one country to another and are reflected in areas such as food consumption habits, leisure activities, aesthetic values, and patterns of social interaction and communication. For example, in many European and Latin American countries, soccer is a key sport, while in Mexico and Spain bull fights, and in Japan sumo wrestling, are major national sports. Similarly, food consumption is highly "culture specific." While the staple food in the United States has traditionally been meat and potatoes, in China and the Far East rice is a key staple, garnished with fish or vegetables, and in Brazil and many other Latin

American countries beans often form the basis of a meal. Customer tastes often differ significantly from one country to another, requiring adaptation of strategies to each specific context and limiting potential for utilizing standardized strategies across national markets.

The nature of competition and key competitors often varies from one country to another. Two major types of competitors can typically be distinguished: multinational or global companies, and local competitors. In the razor blade market, for example, Gillette typically encounters competition from Wilkinson and Bic in all major international markets. Similarly, in detergents, P&G, Colgate, and Unilever are present in most major foreign markets. The resources and international commitment of such competitors tend to be similar. Competition may also, however, be encountered from local firms. In India, for example, major competitors in the razor blade market include Tata Industries, as well as other local firms. Similarly, a major contender in the detergent industry in Europe is the German company Henkel, while in Japan and Taiwan, Kao is a key player. Competitors may enjoy certain advantages, especially in their domestic markets—for example, government subsidies, tendencies to "buy national," or simply entrenched local positions.

The heterogeneity and complexity of national environmental conditions, together with the far-flung character of international operations, imply that planning strategy for global markets is considerably more complex than for domestic markets. Strategy has to be adapted to diverse political, economic, and sociocultural contexts, marketing response patterns, and marketing infrastructures. In addition, strategy needs to be coordinated and integrated across countries, in order to take advantage of potential synergies arising from operating on a global scale.

KEY TERMS

Various terms have been used to refer to marketing activities that take place in more than one country. These include: *international, multinational, multidomestic, transnational,* and *global.* At times, these terms appear to be used interchangeably, which can be confusing. Since there is considerable ambiguity and lack of agreement surrounding them, we will define here how they will be used in this book. The terms refer to either: (1) the geographic scope of operation, or (2) the way in which a business is run.

Geographic Scope of Marketing Operations

The terms *international, multinational,* and *global* establish a continuum relative to the geographic scope of the firm's operations. *International marketing* refers to marketing activities in one or more countries outside of the domestic base of operations. The term *international marketing* will also be used in a very general sense to refer to all types of involvement in markets beyond the firm's domestic market. *Multinational* suggests extensive international operations. A particular type of multinational marketing is *regional* marketing, under which a company operates outside the boundaries of the domestic market but confines its activities to adjacent markets. Regional marketing is particularly likely to occur in parts of Europe, the Middle East and Asia where markets for certain products cross national boundaries but are not truly multinational. *Global marketing* refers to situations where the company has extensive international operations throughout the world.

Management of Marketing Operations

In addition to the geographic scope of operations, the terms *international, multidomestic, transnational,* and *global* can be used to refer to different organizational arrangements and the management of marketing activities outside the firm's domestic market. *International* typically refers to a situation in which the domestic parent establishes a separate organization to deal with marketing in one or more countries. Often the international division is fully autonomous, operating as if it were a totally separate entity. *Multidomestic* refers to a situation where the parent establishes separate organizations in each country. There is direction from headquarters, but operational decisions are made at the local level. Finally, there is *transnational* and *global* management of marketing. In both cases, management attempts to coordinate and integrate operations across national boundaries so as to achieve potential synergies on a global scale. The concept of domestic markets disappears, as management views the world as a series of interrelated and interlinked markets.

PLAN OF THE BOOK

A firm rarely marches into international markets armed with a strong, globally oriented strategy. Rather, the firm's strategy emerges as a result of careful planning and marginal adjustments over an extended period of time. The organization of this book reflects this underlying developmental process. It is divided into six parts. Part I introduces the evolutionary perspective of global market development. It identifies three phases in the development of a firm's global marketing strategy, which are covered in more depth in each of the next three parts. The fifth part of the book identifies the four key challenges that global marketers face and suggests appropriate responses to achieve success in world markets. The sixth part of the book contains cases which show firms in different stages of global market development.

The first part of the book examines the nature of global marketing strategy. In Chapter 2, the three key phases in the evolution of global marketing strategy—(1) initial market entry, (2) market expansion, and (3) global rationalization—are identified, together with the forces that trigger movement from one phase to another. The key strategic issues facing the firm, and levers guiding strategy formulation in each of the phases, are examined. Chapter 3 discusses information needs common to all three phases of international development. This includes issues relating to both secondary data and primary data collection.

Part II is devoted to an examination of the key issues and decisions facing the firm as it first enters international markets. Chapter 4 deals with the establishment of goals and objectives relative to international markets, including the degree of involvement and level of risk the firm is willing to bear. The definition of the business in international markets, and assessment of its core competencies relative to those markets, also form important parameters determining the firm's global strategic thrust. Chapter 5 analyzes the basis of competitive advantage in international markets. First, the extent to which national environmental conditions in the domestic market mold the firm's competitive advantage is considered. Then, the bases of firm-specific competitive advantage are examined, as also the ease with which these can be leveraged in international markets.

Chapter 6 reviews country/market choice decisions and the underlying competitive dynamics. Central to this discussion is a strategic orientation that views market choice as the cornerstone of any strategic initiative. This underscores the importance of considering the timing and sequencing of market entry, as well as the role of competitive factors in such decisions. The final chapter of this section looks at alternative modes of entry into international markets and the factors underlying this choice, as well as the advantages and limitations associated with particular modes of operations.

Part III of the book focuses on issues relating to the second phase of globalization—international market expansion. Once a firm has set up operations in international markets it must plan to expand and consolidate its local market position if it is to continue to grow and compete successfully. Chapter 8 looks at how the firm redefines the business and its core competence and establishes goals and objectives to meet the new challenges. This also requires reformulating the firm's competitive posture and its strategic thrust in international markets. In Chapter 9, the implications of this new direction for product positioning strategies are examined. This involves analyzing the product market structure and competing products, as well as identifying target markets and segments and assessing their similarity across countries. Based on this analysis, alternative positioning strategies are identified and their implications assessed.

Strategies and tactics developed in one market are not necessarily appropriate in others. Chapter 10 covers issues relating to product modification, adapting communications strategy—e.g., advertising copy, media plans, and sales promotion—as well as tailoring price and distribution. Chapter 11 covers the implementation of market expansion strategies, focusing on establishing organizational networks to orchestrate the flow of goods, materials, and components, together with the companion flows of financing and information from points of supply to end customers.

Part IV of the book is devoted to issues arising in phase three—global rationalization. As at the onset of the second phase, the drive to consolidate operations across country markets and to improve global efficiency requires reassessing the appropriate business definition and establishing goals and objectives reflecting a global rather than a multidomestic orientation. These issues are covered in Chapter 12, together with the implications for leveraging core competencies and competitive posture in global markets.

Chapter 13 addresses the critical issue of portfolio analysis to chart direction and allocation of resources across countries, products, and target segments. International markets vary in terms of potential size, stage of development, rate of growth, and interconnectedness. Consequently, they require different levels of investment and vary in terms of short- and long-run profitability. Expansion, retraction, and reallocation decisions among countries, products, and segments have to be designed to balance the global portfolio and achieve long-run growth and profit goals.

Competition on a global scale is the subject of Chapter 14. This is examined first in terms of how global markets should be configured, both in terms of market scope and target segments. Once this has been determined, the firm must see how it can leverage assets and its position in global markets, while at the same time, finding ways to maintain strategic flexibility. Finally, the firm must determine whether its strategy will be broad-based, focused on a particular segment, or a hybrid combination of the two.

Implementation of global marketing strategy hinges on development of an infrastructure. This is the topic of Chapter 15. First, a careful assessment of the value chain and the interfunctional linkages with the firm and its suppliers and customers must be made. Not only are the traditional marketing aspects of global strategy important, but also issues related to sourcing, production, logistics, and information technology. As pointed out in Chapter 14, competitive strategy is not formulated in isolation. The firm must take into account competition as well as customer and market dynamics. Chapter 15 examines how to work with competitors through the formation of strategic alliances, and how to develop effective linkages with customers.

The final chapter, Part V, examines the challenges that global marketers face in the future. The 1990s are proving to be turbulent times, and firms that want to prosper into the twenty-first century must formulate strategies that are adaptive as well as impactful. Many forces, largely beyond the control of the firm, cause dramatic changes in world markets. As it attempts to formulate global marketing strategy, the firm must deal, not only with these forces, but also with the challenges of rapid change, increased complexity, intensified competition, and the need to conform to societal expectations for responsible behavior. Depending on its degree of involvement in international markets, the appropriate strategic response from the firm differs.

Part VI of the book contains seven cases which illustrate the different challenges that global marketers face. These provide an opportunity to apply the concepts developed in the book to situations facing firms. The first two cases, Sterling Marking Products and Mary Kay Cosmetics, provide the opportunity to discuss phase one issues—market entry. The next two case, Heineken N.V. Buckler and Levi Strauss Japan, illustrate firms that are looking to expand their presence in international markets and coping with issues that firms typically face in phase two—international market expansion. The final cases, ICI Paints (A, B) and Air BP, involve firms attempting to formulate a global strategy. The issues they face illustrate the complexity of phase three—global rationalization.

After reading and discussing these cases it will become clear that certain issues transcend the three phases identified in this book. There are certain issues, such as assessing international market potential that are more important in phase one, but that carry through to phase three. Tailoring marketing programs and developing new products to meet specific needs is a primary concern in phase two, but they continue to be important in phase three. Also, issues related to coordination and control of international operations are far more critical in phase three, but begin to emerge once a firm enters international markets. Collectively, these cases as well as others dealing with international issues enrich understanding of global markets as well as illustrate the complexity of developing a global marketing strategy.

REFERENCES

1. "The 100 Largest U.S. Multinationals," (1993) *Forbes*, July 19, pp. 182–186.
2. "Mininationals Are Making Maximum Impact," (1993) *Business Week*, September 6, pp. 66–69.
3. Kraar, Louis (1992) "Asia's New Growth Triangle," *Fortune*, October 5, pp. 136–142.
4. "Detroit South," (1992) *Business Week*, March 16, pp. 98–103.
5. "The Koreans Are Coming," (1985) *Business Week*, December 23, pp. 46–52.
6. Darlin, Damon (1993) "The Keep-It-Simple Strategy," *Forbes*, August 16, pp. 98–100.
7. Kraar, Louis (1993a) "Now Comes the Hard Part for China," *Fortune*, July 26, pp. 130–134.
8. "Besting Japan," (1993) *Business Week*, June 7, pp. 26–28.
9. Rapoport, Carla (1993) "The Europeans Take on Japan," *Fortune*, January 11, pp. 82–84.
10. "A Pier I in Every Port," (1993) *Business Week*, May 31, p. 88.
11. "U.S. Discount Retailers Are Targeting Europe and the Fat Margins," (1993) *Wall Street Journal*, September 20.
12. "The NBA's Global Marketing Machine Is Launching a Drive to the Pacific Rim," (1993) *Wall Street Journal*, September 19.
13. "Red Penguins, Free Beer and Hard Rock," (1993) *Business Week*, October 11, pp. 144–146.
14. "Cable Has a New Frontier: The Old World," (1993) *Business Week*, June 28, p. 74.
15. "Japan's Liquid-Crystal Gold Rush," (1994) *Business Week*, January 17, pp. 76–77.

16. Tetzeli, Rick, (1994) "The Internet and Your Business," *Fortune*, March 7, pp. 86–96.

17. Kraar, Louis (1993b) "China, Struggle for Control," *Fortune*, November 1, pp. 137–142.

18. Woods, Wilton (1993) "The World's Top Automakers Change Lanes," *Forbes*, October 4, pp. 13–75.

19. "Korea Is Overthrown As Sneakers Champ," (1993) *Wall Street Journal*, Thursday, October 7, 1993, p. A3.

20. "Europe's Shake-Out," (1992) *Business Week*, September 14, pp. 44–51.

21. Gladwin, Thomas N. (1993) "Envisioning the Sustainable Corporation," Emily T. Sheelth *Managing for Environmental Excellence, the Next Business Frontier*, Washington, DC: Island Press.

22. Tully, Shawn (1993) "The Modular Corporation," *Fortune*, February 8, pp. 106–114.

23. Roche, Edward (1992) *Managing Information Technology in Multinational Corporations*, New York: Macmillan.

24. Kraar, Louis (1994), "TV Is Exploding All Over Asia," *Fortune*, January 24, pp. 98–101.

25. Hofheinz, Paul (1994) "Rising in Russia," *Fortune*, January 24, pp. 92–97.

26. "China, the Emerging Economic Powerhouse of the 21st Century," (1993) *Business Week*, May 17, pp. 20–30.

27. Henkoff, Ronald (1993) "The Hot New Seal of Quality," *Fortune*, June 28, pp. 116–120.

28. "10,000 New EC Rules," (1992) *Business Week*, September 7, pp. 48–50.

29. Saporito, Bill (1993) "Where the Global Action Is," *Fortune* Autumn/Winter, pp. 62–65.

30. Levitt, Theodore (1983) "The Globalization of Markets," *Harvard Business Review*, May/June, pp. 92–102.

CHAPTER 2

PHASES IN THE EVOLUTION OF GLOBAL MARKETING STRATEGY[1]

INTRODUCTION

A prevalent view is that success in the new international order requires presence in markets worldwide and competition on a global scale. Some[2] have even argued that firms that ignore the new reality of global markets will be devastated by their globally oriented competitors.[2] This is true in some highly visible industries, such as automobiles, consumer electronics, and watches, which are dominated by global competition. However, in many other industries and even sectors of global industries, the alternative competitive strategies facing the typical firm are inherently more complex.

All firms must monitor international developments, since these may hold portent for domestically oriented strategies, signalling future market developments and the emergence of new foreign competitors. Deciding how to respond to such trends and developments depends largely on key success factors in a given industry, the firm's goals and objectives with respect to international markets, its size and resources, and its competitive thrust, as well as the nature of its existing operations and the degree of its involvement and experience in international markets.

While some industries are global in scope, in others, such as laundries or auto repair, the dominant imperative is inherently local. Similarly, firms vary considerably in their goals and objectives in international markets, and in their willingness to commit resources to international operations. Some have limited exposure and experience in international markets and lack the resources to expand on an international scale. Their main thrust is the development of prod-

[1] From "Evolution of Global Marketing Strategy: Sale, Scope and Synergy," Vol. 24, No. 3 by Susan P. Douglas and C. Samuel Craig. Copyright 1989. *Columbia Journal of World Business*. Reprinted with permission.

ucts and services targeted to the domestic market. Others already have operations and commitments in other countries and are concerned with expanding internationally.

The beer industry provides an interesting example of the range of strategies that can be adopted by companies in the same industry. The large European brewers such as the Dutch company Heineken, BSN in France, and the British company Guinness, expanded early outside their domestic markets, seeking to establish themselves as strong European or global brands. Often this focused primarily on increasing sales in the wine-drinking countries of Southern Europe, or establishing a specialty premium brand. Heineken targeted the premium beer segment worldwide and became the third largest brewer in the world with 85 percent of sales outside its domestic market.

U.S. companies, such as Anheuser-Busch and Miller, on the other hand, remained for a long time focused on their domestic market, roughly equivalent in size to that of Western Europe. Stagnant domestic growth has, however, recently led these giants to look overseas for expansion opportunities, often through acquisitions and deals with strong domestic brewers.[3] Anheuser-Busch, for example, has bought 18% of Grupo Modelo, the Mexican brewer, and 5% of Tsing Tao Brewery in China, as well as developing agreements with Kirin Brewery of Japan and Birra Peroni in Italy. It is also planning to buy a stake in the Czech brewer Budvar, which owns the rights to the Budweiser name in a number of European markets including Germany and Austria.[4,5] As a result of its efforts, Anheuser-Busch has increased international sales to 3.3 million barrels, still only about 4 percent of its total volume. Miller has also acquired a stake in Molson of Canada, which is itself a joint venture with Fosters of Australia.

Other brewers remain domestic and in some cases regional in focus. The Belgian beer industry remains highly fragmented, and few brands are known outside the country.[6] The only Belgian company with the resources to develop its brands internationally is Interbrew, which markets its Stella Artois brand of lager throughout Europe, as well as in Canada and Australia, and has launched its specialty beers, Hoegaarden Blanche and Leffe Blonde, in California.

The different strategies taken by firms in the brewing industry suggest that a firm's international strategy must be defined in the context of its existing operations, its objectives relative to international expansion, and its competitive position in world markets. International strategy development is typically an evolutionary process. Often a firm expands gradually from its domestic base, at first emphasizing geographic extension of existing products and services. If international operations prosper, the firm expands its presence in foreign markets and seeks to enter new markets. As this process continues, the firm develops a growing international presence and moves toward operating and planning strategy on a global scale. As markets globalize and become more integrated, the opportunities to transfer products and brands from one country to another and improved coordination across markets of strategies are emphasized.

Procter and Gamble, for example, initially entered into international markets with its core brands such as Mr. Clean, Camay, Tide, and Pampers. Operations were organized and managed on a country-by-country basis. As markets developed, the company acquired brands such as Domestos, an all-purpose household cleanser in the U.K., and developed new products such as Ariel, a low-temperature detergent, and Vizir, a heavy-duty liquid detergent, in response to specific local needs in Europe.

The key issues and strategic imperatives vary from firm to firm, depending on the stage of involvement in international markets. In the initial phase of entry into international markets, a key objective is the geographic expansion of operations, to identify markets in other countries for existing products and services and to leverage potential *economies of scale* in production and marketing. Once a beachhead has been established, emphasis shifts to developing local markets and exploiting potential *economies of scope*, building upon the existing geographic base. The third phase focuses on global rationalization, through consolidation of international activities and improved coordination and integration of operations, to take advantage of potential *synergies* arising from multinational operations.

This chapter examines each of the three phases of involvement in international markets, together with their underlying dynamics and the forces that trigger movement from one phase to another. The issues and levers that characterize each phase are highlighted, and the implications for the formulation of global marketing strategy discussed. This discussion also establishes the framework for the remainder of the book.

FORMULATING STRATEGY IN INTERNATIONAL MARKETS

An evolutionary perspective on internationalization is widespread in international economics and international management. Examination of international trade patterns in the 1960s and 1970s, for example, led to the theory of the international product life cycle, which identified a number of phases in the international expansion of an industry.[7] The underlying premise of this model is that many products go through a trade cycle analogous to the product life cycle. Initially, an industralized nation is an exporter of innovative high-technology products; then it loses its export markets to local competition and finally becomes a net importer of such products. In contrast to traditional theories of comparative advantage, this approach emphasizes the role of demand stimulation in the formation of international trade patterns.

Another approach emphasizes the incremental acquisition of information underlying the internationalization of the firm.[8] The basic assumption is that lack of knowledge, together with management hesitancy and limited resources, lead to high perceived risk and constitute major obstacles to international market entry. Consequently, a firm will often start by exporting to neighboring countries or countries perceived to be similar to the domestic market, using independent sales agents.[9] As the firm acquires experience and information relative to foreign markets, involvement and resource commitment in international markets increases through the establishment of a foreign sales subsidiary, and then foreign production and manufacturing facilities.

Another widely held view, the E.P.R.G. framework, emphasizes the role of management attitudes and orientation in shaping the evolution of international operations. This framework identifies four stages in the growth of the multinational corporation—ethnocentrism, polycentrism, regiocentrism, and geocentrism.[10] Each stage is characterized by distinct management attitudes. In the first stage, characterized by *ethnocentric* attitudes, operations in other countries are viewed as subsidiary to domestic operations. Mistakes resulting from such attitudes lead to the adoption of a *polycentric* or host-country orientation. This stage emphasizes national market differences. Products and strategy are adapted to local market conditions, with each subsidiary operating as a local profit center. Control and coordination problems associated with this approach, coupled with increasing regional integration of markets, fosters a *regiocentric* orientation. At this stage, regional product and brand management teams are established, often the aegis of a regional headquarters. In the fourth stage, a *geocentric* or world orientation emerges, the concept of national markets disappears, and operations are integrated and coordinated worldwide.

Importance of Strategy Formulation

Development of a coherent strategy to provide direction for the firm's activities in international markets is especially crucial for a number of reasons. Initial forays into international markets are often unsystematic and somewhat haphazard, resulting from an unsolicited export order from a foreign buyer, an order from a domestic customer for its international operations, or an interest expressed by an importer or potential business partner in a foreign market. Consequently, it is important to establish international marketing objectives, especially in terms of the level of involvement and degree of risk, in order to guide systematic evaluation of opportunities worldwide. Otherwise, international activities will lack direction. Choice of countries will be haphazard, resulting from creeping commitment and sporadic efforts, and will not necessarily be targeted to the most attractive opportunities for the firm in world markets.

Strategy formulation in international markets involves a number of key parameters which vary depending on the phase of internationalization.[11] These are shown diagrammatically in Figure 2-1. In each phase a number of triggers will prompt movement into a new phase, stimulating generation of a new strategic thrust, channelled by the international levers associated with that phase. The nature of this thrust defines investment and resource allocation priorities and establishes the key strategic decisions the firm has to make.

THE TRIGGERS

The triggers that propel a firm from one phase to another are both external and internal. External triggers, such as environmental or industry trends, technological change, or competitive pressures, cause the firm to reassess its current strategy. Internal triggers, on the other hand, consist of factors such as sales growth, profitability, management attitudes, or initiatives. Sometimes an internal trigger, for example, declining sales volume, results from or interacts with

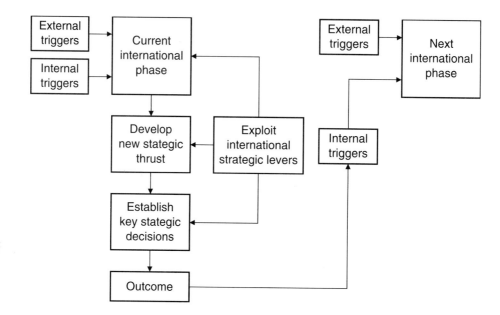

FIGURE 2-1

The Dynamics of global strategy development.

external factors, such as increased competition from foreign firms or changes in customer demand. Both internal and external factors thus create a climate that stimulates a new strategic thrust.

THE STRATEGIC THRUST

The strategic thrust determines the firm's direction in international markets and defines the arenas in which the firm will compete, as well as its strategic priorities. First, management must define the geographic scope of operations and desired direction for expansion. As noted earlier, direction varies with the phase of internationalization. In initial entry, emphasis is placed on extending the geographic boundaries of operations, and management must select which countries to target. The second phase is one of geographic consolidation as growth takes place within those countries, focusing on product market development. In the third phase, management becomes concerned with rationalization of product lines and transfer of product ideas across national boundaries. The significance of domestic or national markets fades and is replaced by planning relative to markets worldwide.

LEVERAGING THE FIRM'S STRENGTHS

Concern to leverage the firm's strengths provides direction for the firm's efforts and determines investment priorities at successive stages of internationalization. In the initial phase, lacking experience or familiarity with markets in other countries, a firm seeks to leverage its domestic position internationally, in order to achieve *economies of scale*. A firm's strength might be grounded, for example, in superior product quality or technological expertise, cost efficiency, a strong corporate or brand image, or mass-merchandising expertise. As familiarity with the local market environment builds up, and a marketing-and-distribution infrastructure and contacts with local distributors and other organizations are developed, a firm will leverage these assets across a broader range of products and services in order to achieve *economies of scope*. In the final phase, a firm tries to leverage both internal skills and environment-related knowledge, transferring learning and experience across national boundaries, so as to take maximum advantage of potential *synergies* in multinational operations.

STRATEGIC DECISIONS: DETERMINING THE NEXT MOVE

The key moves and strategic decisions vary depending on the phase of internationalization. In the initial phase, management must choose which countries to enter, how to enter or the mode of operation, and the timing and sequencing of entry. Once initial entry has been successfully achieved, the focus shifts to development of local market potential through product modification, product line extension, and development of new products tailored to specific local market needs. Often, a patchwork of local operations develops, resulting in the need to improve efficiency and to establish mechanisms to coordinate and integrate strategy across national markets. Learning and experience can be exchanged and transferred from one part of the world to another, and strategy developed relative to regional and global markets rather than on a country-by-country basis.

PHASES OF INTERNATIONAL MARKET DEVELOPMENT

Strategic decision making evolves with the degree of experience and stage of involvement in international markets. While, in practice, this evolution is a continuous process, for the purposes of analytical simplicity, three phases may be identified: (1) initial foreign market entry, (2) local or national market expansion, and (3) global rationalization. (Figure 2-2 models this evolutionary process.)

Preinternationalization

Prior to the firm's entry into international markets, the domestic market is the focal point of strategy development and defines the boundaries of operations. Strategy is designed based on information relating to customer needs and interests, industry trends, and on economic, sociocultural, and technological trends in the domestic market. At the same time, domestic competitors are viewed as the major threat to the firm.

In some cases a firm may deliberately decide *not* to enter international markets and to concentrate on serving its domestic market. Often a domestically oriented firm is likely to be focused inwards, bounded by narrow horizons, with limited interest in events outside its immediate sphere of operation. Such a firm will

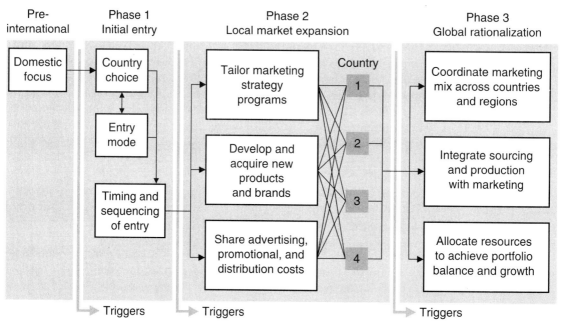

FIGURE 2-2

Phases in global marketing evolution.

be characterized by a lack of dynamism, content to supply its traditional cus-tomer base with existing technology through established marketing channels. Such attitudes may well be tinged with a certain complacency and satisfaction with present performance, with few ambitions to meet new challenges—essen-tial prerequisites to effective competition in an increasingly dynamic and rapid-ly evolving market place.

A domestic orientation often leads to lack of attention to changes taking place in the global marketplace—emerging new life-styles or target segments, new customer needs, growth of new competition, and the restructuring of mar-ket forces worldwide. A firm with that orientation will become vulnerable to the emergence of new technology or the advent of foreign competition armed with a better product, superior customer service, or lower price strategy. Other com-petitors may be quicker to respond to new challenges and opportunities in the marketplace. The failure of U.S. television manufacturers to monitor develop-ments in the Japanese T.V. industry in the 1960s and '70s, and to respond to the entry of low-cost Japanese T.V. sets into the U.S. market by moving to low-cost offshore production locations, led to their ultimate demise.[12] As a result, Zenith is the sole remaining U.S. manufacturer with a significant market share.[13]

TRIGGERS TO INITIAL INTERNATIONAL MARKET ENTRY

A variety of factors may prompt the domestically oriented firm to reexamine its position (see Table 2.1 for some typical events). Trends within the industry or product market, changes in demand or supply conditions, competitive developments, and other events all can open up new opportunities in markets abroad. Any of the following, alone or in concert, can provide impetus for the firm to venture into international markets:

- *Saturation of the domestic market* resulting from slackening rates of growth or limited potential for expansion
- *Movement of customers into international markets,* stimulating interest in following suit in order to retain the account
- Desire to *diversify risk* across a range of countries and product markets
- Identification of *advantageous sourcing opportunities,* such as lower labor or production costs in other countries
- Retaliation to the *entry of foreign competition* into the firm's domestic market
- Concern to keep abreast of *technological change* in world markets
- *Government incentives* such as information and research services, credit insurance, tax exemptions, and rent-free development zones

TABLE 2-1

TRIGGERS TO EACH STAGE OF INTERNATIONALIZATION

INITIAL MARKET ENTRY	LOCAL MARKET EXPANSION	GLOBALIZATION
1. Saturation of domestic market	1. Local market growth	1. Cost inefficiencies and duplication of efforts between countries
2. Movement of customers into foreign markets	2. Meeting local competition	2. Learning via transfer of ideas and experience
3. Diversification of risk	3. Local management initiative and motivation	3. Emergence of global customers
4. Sourcing opportunities in foreign markets	4. Desire to utilize local assets more effectively	4. Emergence of global competition
5. Entry of foreign competition in home market	5. Natural market boundaries	5. Development of global marketing infrastructure
6. Desire to keep abreast of technological changes		
7. Government incentives to export		
8. Advances in communications technology and marketing infrastructure		

■ *Advances in transportation and communication technology*, such as the growth of international telephone linkages, facsimile systems, satellite networks, and containerization

Once the firm decides to investigate opportunities for sourcing and/or marketing products and services in other countries, and to consider entry into these markets, it will face new challenges. These new challenges require a fundamental change in the way the firm thinks about its business, what activities are important and how it conducts itself.

Phase 1: Initial International Market Entry

Moving into international markets opens up new opportunities throughout the world for expansion and growth. At the same time, lack of experience and of familiarity with conditions in international markets create a considerable strain on management resources to acquire the knowledge and skills necessary to operate effectively in these markets.[9] Information relating to differences in environmental conditions, market demand, and the degree of competition has to be collected in order to select the most attractive country markets and develop a strategy to guide the firm's thrust into international markets.

A company that typifies the problems facing firms in phase 1, international market entry, is Sterling Marking Products, Inc., a small Canadian firm that makes embossers. Sterling is an innovative company in a relatively mature market. They have developed a modern functional embosser providing good impression quality which has captured over 60 percent of the Canadian market. In addition to having a superior product, Sterling has developed a highly computerized ordering system providing better quality and faster service. They have received inquiries from firms in Australia, Japan, Sweden, Italy, France, Barbados, Spain, and Indonesia. In addition, they have begun to export subassemblies to a firm in the United Kingdom and have an exclusive agreement with an agent in the United States market, for a 7-month period.

In planning its international expansion Sterling has to decide which countries to enter, what modes of entry to employ, and how rapidly to expand. They have some macroenvironmental data to assess the market potential of the various countries and some information on the competitive market structure in the U.K. While their initial forays into the United States and the U.K. involved exporting, they also have to consider whether to license, acquire or establish their own facilities. They also have to wrestle with whether they should develop an overall plan for international market expansion or proceed on a market by market basis.

The initial entry stage is especially crucial, since a false move may result in withdrawal or retreat from international markets. Mistakes made in initial entry can damage a firm's reputation and be difficult to surmount. Careful formulation of initial entry strategy is thus crucial in shaping the pattern of international market evolution.

KEY STRATEGIC THRUST: GEOGRAPHIC MARKET EXTENSION

First, management must identify the most attractive international market opportunities for its existing (i.e., domestic) products and services. Pinpointing the closest possible match between the firm's current offerings and markets in the other countries means that minimal adaptation of products or marketing strategies is needed. The guiding principle is to extend the geographic base of operations without incurring major incremental production or marketing costs, other than those needed to ensure adequate distribution of the product or service.

LEVERAGING THE FIRM'S DOMESTIC POSITION

Given lack of experience and knowledge of international markets, management aims to leverage the firm's domestic position and core competencies internationally in order to realize economies of scale (see Figure 2-3). Product- or skill-related assets that might be leveraged internationally include innovative or high-quality products, a patented process, a brand name, or other proprietary assets. In industries such as computers and medical equipment, international success has often resulted from the introduction of innovative products into other countries. High quality/price ratios, and the development of superior production skills, have been key elements in the penetration of world markets for consumer electronics and compact cars by Japanese companies. Patented processes may also be leveraged internationally, as demonstrated by the expansion of Xerox and Polaroid into international markets in the 1960s. In consumer markets, well-known brand names such as Coca-Cola, Levis, or Benetton are often important proprietary assets that can be exploited in international markets. Management expertise in mass merchandising and managing distribution channels has enabled companies such as P&G and Colgate to outpace competitors in markets

FIGURE 2-3

Economies of scale in international markets.

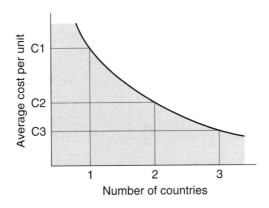

throughout the world. Such skills are often more difficult to leverage directly, especially in initial entry, as they typically require knowledge of and adaptation to local market conditions and are less susceptible to scale economies.

Many firms from countries within the Industrial Triad have already entered international markets. They still have to make decisions about entering new countries but have experience in making such decisions and should evaluate entry into additional markets in the context of existing international operations. Firms currently in the initial entry phase are more typically either small and medium-sized manufacturers or large firms from Third World markets. As noted in Chapter 1, small and medium-sized manufacturers often target niche markets which they can now serve effectively due to developments in communications technology. Large Third World firms, on the other hand, target either similar markets in other Third World countries such as Africa, Indonesia, or the Gulf states, or markets in the United States, Japan, and Europe with a low price or cost leadership strategy.

Kia, the South Korean automobile manufacturer, plans to enter the U.S. market with the Kia Sephia sedan and the four-wheel-drive Sportage, both priced below comparable Hyundai models.[14] Quality will be emphasized, based on engineering links with Ford, as well as experience in building Ford models such as Festiva and Aspire.

KEY DECISIONS

Initial entry decisions are especially crucial, because they entail commitments to locations and to other firms that are difficult to change in the short run and set the pattern for future market development. A false move here can cost a firm dearly in its bid for international market penetration. Decisions based on familiarity or ties with a particular country, a chance contact, or an unsolicited order from another firm can result in haphazard entry with little thought concerning future developments or selection of the most appropriate base for future international expansion. Systematic evaluation of alternative market opportunities worldwide, and the risks entailed in entering a given country, is therefore crucial prior to making entry decisions.

Such an evaluation provides the basis for three key decisions:

1. the choice of countries to enter,
2. the timing of entry, and
3. how operations are to be conducted in these countries.

While each of these decisions is discussed separately here, they are, nonetheless, highly interrelated. Choice of the mode of operation or entry, and the timing of entry, should take into consideration perceived opportunities and risks in a given country. Similarly, the timing of entry will affect the choice of mode of entry.

Choice of Countries. In choosing which countries to enter, opportunities and perceived threats are assessed at two different levels, (1) the general business climate of a country, and (2) the specific product market or service. At the country levels, the stability and rate of economic growth of a country should be examined, as well as its political, financial, and legal climate, and attitudes toward foreign investment. Similarly, at the product market level the size and growth of market potential have to be considered relative to the level of competition and costs of market entry. Often a trade-off has to be made between risk and return. Countries with high growth potential or large markets frequently are characterized by severe competition and may entail a high degree of risk.

For the novice entering international markets, familiarity or knowledge about a foreign market, and its perceived similarity to the domestic market, are often key factors in influencing country choice. Countries that are perceived as similar in terms of language, culture, education, business practices, or industrial development are often considered more likely to offer a more favorable climate for entry than those where the *psychic* distance is high. Davidson,[15] in examining foreign investment patterns of U.S. firms, found close to two-thirds chose to enter Canada first, followed by the U.K., though such choices were clearly not warranted by their size and growth potential relative to other countries such as West Germany or France. Similarly, Australia ranked considerably higher in investment priorities than its size would suggest.

Knowledge and familiarity with a country are often important factors influencing perceived risk and uncertainty of market entry. Both objective information and experimental knowledge affect this uncertainty. Thus, proximity and prior contact or experience in a country will influence market choice. Swedish companies, for example, have been found to enter neighboring countries such as Denmark, Norway, and Finland first, and more distant countries such as Brazil, Argentina, and Australia last.[16]

Timing of Entry. Another important issue is whether to enter several country markets simultaneously versus entering first one, and then, building on this experience, entering other country markets sequentially.[15,17,18] Here, much depends on the resources needed to enter international markets. If substantial financial, managerial, and other resources are required, for example, to build a marketing or sales organization and/or production facilities, management may prefer to enter markets sequentially. On the other hand, simultaneous entry enables the firm to preempt competition by establishing a beachhead in all major markets, and limits opportunities for imitation. Potential scale economies and experience effects may also be realized more rapidly, thus lowering unit costs.[19]

Mode of Entry. Each mode of entry varies in terms of resource or equity commitment to foreign markets. Companies can limit their equity exposure in high-risk countries by adopting low-commitment modes such as licensing, contract manufacturing, or minority joint ventures. Such modes may also be preferable in countries perceived as socioculturally different, or with limited market potential.[20,21]

If a firm is unfamiliar with the operating environment in a country, entry into a joint venture with a local partner, who can provide knowledge and contacts with the local market, can be advantageous. U.S. and European companies have often adopted this strategy in entering the Japanese market. For example, Wella, the German manufacturer of hair care products, initially entered the Japanese market through a joint venture with a local manufacturer of beauty salon chairs. Subsequently, as Wella acquired familiarity and understanding of the market, it bought out its Japanese partners.

The desired degree of control over international operations also influences choice of mode of operations.[20] Nonequity modes such as licensing or contract manufacturing entail minimal risk and commitment, but at the same time afford little control and limited returns. Majority joint ventures and wholly owned subsidiaries provide greater control and potential returns. Companies that desire to retain control over operations and are willing to commit resources to developing the market typically do so through establishing wholly owned subsidiaries. For example, P&G, Scott Paper, Bristol-Myers, and Ore-Ida all established subsidiaries rather than joint ventures in Japan.

Mode of entry decisions also depend on the size of the market and its growth potential, as well as factors such as local production costs, shipping costs, tariffs, and other barriers. Small markets or those surrounded by tariff barriers are typically supplied most cost effectively through licensing or contract manufacturing. Where there are substantial scale economies, however, exporting may be preferred. Then, as local market potential builds up and the minimum economic scale is reached, local production and marketing operations can be established.

The choice of mode of entry is often an important factor underlying the firm's rate of international growth. Such decisions not only reflect the commitment of resources to international markets, but also determine the degree of control exercised over operations and strategy in these markets and the firm's ability to adjust to changes in market conditions.

TRIGGERS TO LOCAL MARKET EXPANSION

Once the firm has established operations in a number of markets, attention shifts to developing local market potential. Strategies to combat competition effectively in these markets, and to expand demand through targeting new segments or developing new products, are needed. Consequently, the focus swings away from "exporting" domestic market know-how and strategies to greater reliance on local market know-how and expertise in local market conditions.

Among the triggers that prompt this new locally oriented focus are:

- *Concern with increasing market penetration* and adapting or developing new products for the local market

- *Need to meet local competition,* and to respond to local competitive initiatives in pricing and promotion
- *Desire to foster local management initiative and motivation*
- *Concern for more effective utilization of local assets,* e.g., the sales organization and distribution infrastructure, or contacts with local organizations
- *Constraints imposed by natural market boundaries and barriers* such as transportation systems, media networks, distribution systems, and financial and other institutions

Such pressures lead to adoption of a nationally oriented approach to strategy planning and development. Operations are organized on a country by country basis or as a series of multidomestic markets or businesses.

Phase 2: Local Market Expansion

In the second phase of internationalization, local market expansion, management begins to seek new directions for growth and expansion in countries where a base of operations has already been established. In some cases this thrust is initiated by local management, while in others it results from corporate headquarter's desire to transfer strategies that have been successful in one market to another. When the impetus is local, the result will often be a patchwork of different products, each adapted to its own particular local market. Here, the challenge is to identify new product opportunities that make use of existing local competencies and assets so as to realize economies of scope.

Often corporate management will want to take a successful product developed in a particular market and transfer that success elsewhere. Market expansion along these lines requires, not only that corporate management persuade local management to accept and market the product, but also that it develop strategies to ensure success in each additional market. The problems faced by Heineken N.V. as it attempted to expand the market for Buckler nonalcoholic beer are typical. In 1988, Buckler was successfully introduced into Spain and France, and Heineken's management was interested in extending this success to other European countries.

Market expansion did not progress smoothly, for country managers did not support it. The Netherlands manager felt that the launch of Buckler would conflict with other programs. Managers of Italy and Greece did not feel there was a market for nonalcoholic beer. Expansion became even more difficult because Heineken had different modes of operation in different markets, ranging from licensing in the U.K. and most of Scandinavia to exporting in Germany, Switzerland, and Belgium. In addition, Heineken had to meet increasing competition from BSN's Tourtel and other brands of nonalcoholic beer.

KEY STRATEGIC THRUST

The driving force underlying local market expansion is to expand *within* markets already entered. Attention is directed to making product and strategy modifications to broaden the local customer base and tap new segments. Product line extensions, and new product variants, are added, as well as new products and services geared to specific local preferences. In some cases, new product businesses are added or acquired, which share common management or marketing skills or are interrelated upstream or downstream to existing activities.

LEVERAGING COMPETENCIES ACROSS PRODUCTS AND PRODUCT BUSINESS

In this phase, in order to achieve economies of scope and to leverage core competencies across a broader market base, building on the organizational structure and assets established in each country become key priorities. Opportunities are investigated for adding product lines and businesses that share marketing expenditures, as well as production and distribution facilities, with existing lines and businesses.

Administrative overhead is then spread across a higher sales volume, reducing unit operating costs (see Figure 2-4). Such opportunities include sharing, not only physical assets such as production facilities, or a distribution network, but also intangible assets such as goodwill or market familiarity.[22] Often the costs and effort associated with country entry are substantial, such as developing familiarity with local market conditions and competition, and establishing relations with distributors, agents, or regulatory bodies and officials. Consequently, it may be advantageous to amortize such costs across a broad range of products. Coca-Cola, for example, has leveraged its knowledge of the Japanese market and its distribution system by developing new soft drinks specifically geared to Japanese tastes. These include Georgia, a highly successful canned cold coffee drink, and Aquarius, a sports drink.

Proprietary assets such as brand names, and specific skills such as technological expertise, can also be leveraged to expand the product line. A well-known brand name or company image can be utilized by marketing new products or

FIGURE 2-4
Economies of scope in international markets.

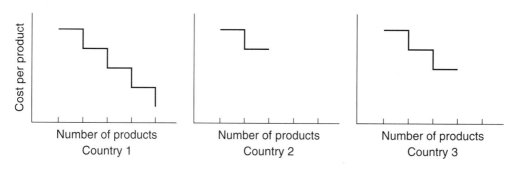

product variants under the same brand name. For example, Swatch, the Swiss fashion watch manufacturer, has leveraged its chic fashion image in the U.S. market to other products, marketing an extensive live of inexpensive sunglasses as collectible fashion accessories.[23] Similarly, a corporate reputation for product quality, reliability, and service can be leveraged in the promotion of new products and product lines, either to end customers or to distributors. Caterpillar, for example, has leveraged its reputation for sturdy, reliable construction, equipment to marketing boots and socks to trendy young consumers.

Marketing and mass-merchandising skills can also spread over a broader range of products or product lines, or be applied to the development of new product businesses. P&G, for example, has added a line of bubble baths and bath oils in the U.K. and France, marketed under the Camay name. In some cases, brands or product businesses may be acquired from local companies. CPC, for example, acquired Marmite and Bovril, a vegetable and a beef spread, respectively, highly popular in the U.K., together with the Ambrosia line of rice pudding and other milk desserts, in order to strengthen its position in these U.K. markets.[24] Thus, the firm can capitalize on the goodwill or customer franchise associated with an established local brand or local company, while applying its management expertise and marketing skills to manage the business.

KEY DECISIONS

Desire for local market growth drives the key decisions to center on the development of appropriate products, product lines, and product businesses in each country, as well as strategies to market them effectively. This includes adaptation and modification of products, product line extensions, and acquisition of new products and brands. Following the firm's strategic thrust, the key criteria in making these decisions are the potential for local market development and realization of economies of scope.

Product modification and adaptation may help to expand the potential market base. In developing countries, machine tool manufacturers may consider streamlining and simplifying their products and making them easy to maintain so as to tap less sophisticated customer segments. Nabisco, in order to adapt to local tastes in Japan, reduced the salt content of its snack products and increased the sugar content of its cookies. Similarly, McDonald's added chicken teriyaki to its menu in Japan.

A firm in this phase may also consider opportunities for developing product variants, extending the product line or developing new products specifically adapted to local market preferences. Canada Dry, for example, adds different flavors to its soft drinks in different countries, such as melon in the Far East, orange pineapple and bitter orange in the U.K., and strong ginger in Japan. Heinz developed a special line of rice-based baby foods as well as nutritious sweet and savory baby cereals for the Chinese market, and a fruit-based drink for children called Frutsi for Mexico, which was subsequently rolled out in a number of other Latin American markets. Nabisco developed "Parfait," a line of thumb-sized chocolate cupcakes for the Japanese market, as well as Chipstar, a Pringles-type potato chip (packaged in a tall can) in two flavors, natural and spinach.

Concern with economies of scope means addition of new products or product variants within a country is especially attractive if it enables more effective utilization of the existing operational structure, as, for example, the distribution network or the sales force, or if it capitalizes on experience acquired in operating in a specific market environment, or on contacts and relations established with distributors, advertising agencies, and other external organizations. For example, soft drink brands added by Coca-Cola utilize its existing distribution network, including its experience of managing and stocking vending machines in different countries.

Marketing tactics including advertising, sales promotion to trade and end users, pricing, and distribution channels should also be geared to local market development. Adaptation of advertising copy, and development of new themes should be undertaken whenever the costs are outweighed by the potential increase in sales. Similarly, pricing decisions should be designed to stimulate local market penetration. In many instances this implies greater attention to pricing based on evaluation of price elasticities in local markets and prices of competing and substitute products, rather than on a cost plus basis.

TRIGGERS TO GLOBAL RATIONALIZATION

The country-by-country orientation associated with this phase, while enabling the firm to consolidate operations within countries, often results in fragmentation of world markets. Operations in each country function as independent profit centers and gradually evolve into a patchwork of diverse national businesses. Each national business markets a range of different products and services targeted to different customer segments, utilizing different marketing strategies with little or no coordination of operations between countries. The inefficiencies generated by this system, as well as external forces toward the integration of markets worldwide, create pressures to improve coordination across countries.

Forces that trigger concern for global rationalization include:

- *Cost inefficiencies and duplication of effort* among country organizations
- *Opportunities for transferring products, brands, and other ideas,* and of learning from experience, in one country to another
- *Emergence of global customers* in both consumer and industrial markets
- *Growth of competition* on a global scale
- *Improved linkages* among national marketing infrastructures, leading to the development of a global marketing infrastructure

Once again both internal factors and changes in the external environment trigger the shift towards a global strategic orientation. Pressures develop to eliminate inefficiencies generated by a multiplicity of domestic businesses, and also to improve coordination and integration of strategy across national boundaries, moving toward the development of strategy on a global rather than on a country-by-country basis. (It should, however, be noted that this does not necessarily imply standardization of the marketing mix worldwide, but rather adoption of a global rather than a multidomestic perspective in designing strategy.)

Phase 3: Global Rationalization

The final phase of internationalization—global rationalization—is characterized by the adoption of a global orientation in strategy development and implementation. Attention focuses on improving global efficiency without losing local responsiveness. Mechanisms are developed to ensure transfer of ideas, experience, and skills and to improve coordination of operations across countries. The multidomestic orientation disappears, and strategy is developed in relation to country and product markets, which are viewed as a set of interrelated, interdependent entities that are becoming ever more integrated and interlinked worldwide.

Global rationalization concerns a wide range of companies. Air BP, the aviation fuel arm of British Petroleum, provides an interesting example of the difficulties a firm faces in trying to plan and implement a strategy on several continents. Faced by pressure on commercial aviation fuel prices, Air BP decided to invest in several aviation service centers or FBOs (fixed base operations). These provide fuel and other services, including maintenance and avionics, as well as rest and conference facilities. The margins obtained from selling fuel through FBOs are considerably higher than from selling fuel to commercial aircraft or independent traders for rebranding. In addition, company-owned or franchised FBOs help to develop Air BP's image as they sell fuel under the BP brand name and accept the BP credit card.

In 1986, Air BP decided to enter a joint venture with Field Aviation Enterprises in the U.K. to develop an international chain of FBOs. The flagship FBO was Field's Executive Jet Center at Heathrow. In addition, the venture developed a second FBO at Stansted, London's designated long-term general aviation airport, and acquired another at Cologne, Germany. Air BP inherited a highly profitable FBO at Cleveland, Ohio, as a result of its acquisition of Sohio in 1987.

In 1988, interest in FBO acquisitions mounted on both sides of the Atlantic, and Air BP decided on a global strategy of FBO development. The goal was to establish an international network of FBOs with a strong image of quality fuel and service. In the United States, this was designed to develop Air BP's image and capture higher margins at retail. In Europe, the goal was to secure BP's market position and create entry barriers. A total investment of $80 million over 5 years was allocated to develop 15 new sites. An FBO at Atlanta, Georgia was purchased, and equity participation was taken in a new FBO being constructed at Melbourne, Australia. However, by mid-1991, of the six FBOs owned by Air BP, only Cleveland and Heathrow were profitable. As a result, management had to decide whether to continue its strategy of creating an international network of FBOs and whether the same strategy should be pursued worldwide or should vary by continent.

KEY STRATEGIC THRUST

Moving into this phase, the firm seeks to capitalize on potential synergies arising from operating on a global scale, and to take maximum advantage of the multinational character of its operations. Attention centers on optimal allocation of resources across countries, product businesses, market segments, and business functions so as to maximize profits on a global rather than a country by country basis.[25]

A dual thrust is thus adopted, combining a drive to improve the efficiency of operations worldwide with a search for opportunities for global expansion and growth. Greater efficiency may be obtained through improved coordination and integration of marketing activities across countries, such as product development, advertising, distribution, and pricing.[26] This coordination in turn will unleash opportunities for rationalization of production, sourcing, management, and other functions. Standardization of product lines across countries may, for example, facilitate improved coordination of production, global sourcing, and the establishment of a global production and logistical system, resulting in greater cost efficiencies.

At the same time, global market expansion becomes a key principle guiding strategy formulation. Opportunities are explored for transferring products, brand names, successful marketing ideas, or specific skills and expertise acquired or developed in one country to operations in other countries. Global and regional market segments or target customers are identified, and products and services geared to their specific needs are developed and marketed on a regional or global basis.

OBTAINING GLOBAL SYNERGIES

In the global rationalization phase, management's goal is to realize potential synergies arising from operating on a global scale. Skills or assets that are transferable across national boundaries, such as R&D or production know-how, management expertise, and brand or company image, are, for example, leveraged globally across product businesses and geographic areas (see Figure 2-5). In the initial entry phase the firm seeks to leverage its domestic position in international markets. In the global market rationalization phase, the firm seeks to leverage position and assets in different countries and markets worldwide so as to obtain global synergies.

Adoption of a global perspective in planning strategy facilitates realization of potential economies of scale in production and logistics, as well as the employment of specialized skills and expertise that would not otherwise be feasible.[27] Leverage can also be achieved horizontally through the transfer of experience, skills, and resources from one country or product business to another. R&D

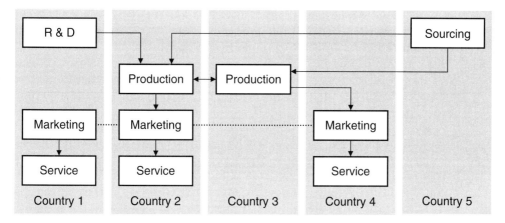

FIGURE 2-5
Synergies in international markets.

knowledge, products, or marketing ideas developed in one country may, for example, be transferred to another, just as cash or profits from one business or country may be used to grow another business or compete aggressively in another country.

MOVING TOWARDS GLOBAL RATIONALIZATION

Following the dual strategic thrust, management focuses attention on two principal areas: (1) improving the efficiency of the existing network of operations worldwide, and (2) developing a global strategy that identifies the market segments and customers to be targeted in world markets, and marketing strategies to compete successfully in these markets.

Improving Efficiency. As noted earlier, efficiency may be increased by improved coordination and rationalization of operations across countries and between different functional areas. Upstream activities such as R&D, production, sourcing, and other activities may be consolidated to eliminate duplication of effort and allow for realization of potential economies of scale. Alternatively, operations in different countries and parts of the world may be linked by a global logistical system, allowing different parts or components to be produced in one or more locations, and shipped to production or assembly locations in other parts of the world, while R&D know-how, production, and management expertise are shared and transferred across operations worldwide.

For example, in 1982, Black and Decker operated 25 plants in 13 countries on six continents. International operations were organized into three operating groups, below which were individual companies that operated autonomously in more than 50 countries, with little or no communication among them. This led to considerable duplication of effort. For example, Black and Decker's eight design centers produced 260 different motor sizes. A global restructuring of operations resulted in the reduction of this number to 10.

Rationalization can also take place on a regional rather than global basis. With the trend towards regional integration, numerous firms have opted to rationalize region by region. For example, in the light of European market integration, Scott Paper has developed a pan-European strategy, which extends beyond production and logistics to marketing and financial operations. Plants in the U.K., France, Spain, Italy, and Belgium still primarily supply local markets, since tissue and paper towels are high volume/low price items where transportation costs outweigh gains from a high degree of production centralization. Brand names such as Scottex, are, however, used throughout Europe (with the exception of the U.K.), and experience in product launches, brand positioning, and advertising in one market are applied in others. Three new plants have been constructed in France, Italy, and Spain, and all use the same technology, allowing sharing and transfer of experience in plant management. Capital is borrowed globally, rather than raised locally on a country-by-country basis.

Similarly, many automobile manufacturers are rationalizing their operations in North America. GM, for example, has established plants at Ramos Arizpe as well as at Toluca, close to Mexico City. Ford is retooling its plant at Chihuahua and expanding production at other facilities in Mexico.[28]

The speed with which companies can successfully move towards global rationalization does, however, vary with the industry and region of the world. In the appliance industry, for example, Whirlpool has successfully rationalized operations in North America, where two plants make more than 50 percent of all washers and dryers sold. In Europe, Electrolux has encountered difficulty in moving toward a pan-European operation. There are dramatic differences in consumer preferences for refrigerators. In Northern Europe, consumers tend to shop once a week and prefer large refrigerators with freezers on the bottom. In Southern Europe, where shopping is a daily event, consumers prefer small refrigerators with freezers on the top. In the U.K., where frozen foods are popular, consumers want units with 60 percent freezer space. As a consequence, Electrolux produces 120 basic refrigerator designs with 1,500 variants.[29]

The firm can improve its coordination of marketing strategies, advertising themes across countries, and standardization of products and product lines by establishing coordinating mechanisms between country management groups. These may take the form of coordinating committees that facilitate transfer of information and ideas across groups and are responsible for coordinating and integrating their activities, such as the widely publicized Eurobrand teams developed by P&G, or by establishing regional marketing or sales organizations such as those of Sony to direct activities within the region.

Global Strategy Development. In addition to improving the efficiency of existing operations, a global strategy should be established to guide the direction of the firm's efforts and the allocation of resources across countries, product businesses, target segments, and modes of operation worldwide. This strategy should combine a global vision and focus on global market opportunities with responsiveness to local market conditions and demand.

A global strategy should establish the customers and segments to be targeted, their specific needs and interests, and their geographic configuration. As markets for both industrial and consumer products become increasingly international, opportunities for identifying segments that are regional or global, rather than national in scope, are on the increase. Thus, for example, Whirlpool is targeting young professional couples in emerging nations such as India, Brazil, and Mexico with its compact World Washer.[30] Ericsson is grabbing share worldwide in the surging market for digital cellular phone networks, doubling its profits in 1993.[31] In the advertising industry, Saatchi & Saatchi target corporations with multinational operations, supplying services and meeting their needs worldwide.

Marketing programs to meet the specific needs of these regional and global targets also have to be established. The firm will have to put into place an organization to implement these programs, in some instances establishing an organizational infrastructure that matches that of potential customers. Companies servicing the needs of multinational corporations may establish a system of global account executives, such as that of Saatchi & Saatchi, with an executive specifically responsible for ensuring that the needs of a given client are satisfied worldwide.

Another decision is the appropriate mix of product businesses worldwide. Here, interdependence in their production, resource requirement, or cashflows on an international basis needs to be considered. For example, Thompson has retained a semiconductor business in France in order to supply its consumer electronics businesses worldwide. Due to increased price competition in the traditional wired phone network business and growth in cellular phones worldwide, Ericsson has shifted emphasis away from its wire-based public-network phone switch business, its cash cow, to cellular mobile phone networks and to linking cellular with fixed systems.[31]

Effective implementation of a global rationalization strategy thus necessitates establishment of mechanisms to coordinate and control activities and flows of information, resources, etc., across both national boundaries and product businesses.[27,32] In addition, other functional areas such as production, logistics, and finance need to be coordinated. Thus, in some cases, a radical restructuring of the organizational structure and management system, including lines of responsibility and communication, may be required to achieve globalization.

SUMMARY

Strategy formulation in international markets is a dynamic, evolutionary process in which the dominant strategic thrust, the international levers, and the key decisions vary at each successive phase. The major strategic challenges facing the firm—how to transfer strategies and skills developed in response to local market conditions to international markets, how to acquire and build on local market knowledge and experience, and how to take advantage of potential synergies of multinational operations—differ in each phase.

The dynamic character of international operations implies that strategic priorities must be tailored to the stage of evolution in international markets. Rather than assuming, as is commonly the case, that the basic parameters underlying strategy formulation, and, specifically, the key decisions, will be the same for all firms, recognition that these will depend on the nature and evolution of international operations is imperative. Strategy should thus be formulated in light of the firm's current position in international markets and geared to its vision of growth and future position in markets worldwide.

In the initial phase of international market entry, the firm's key strength is likely to lie in its existing (domestic) product line. Attention should be focused on acquiring experience in marketing that line internationally. As this experience is built up, emphasis should shift to new product development geared to specific local market needs. Only in the final stage, once experience in both marketing and new product development for international markets has been acquired, should the more complex issue of strategy integration and coordination across country markets be addressed.

Global strategy development should seek to maximize both potential economies of scale and scope. Economies of scale can be realized through attention to opportunities for marketing existing product lines on a broader geographic scale, enabling interlinking and consolidation of production and sourcing operations, management, and logistical systems across global markets. Economies of scope, on the other hand, will be achieved through identification of opportunities for shared production, marketing and distribution facilities, and utilization of the same management and logistical systems by different product lines or product businesses.

At the same time, marketing strategy, especially relating to product line decisions and product standardization, should be closely coordinated with production and sourcing operations. This establishes guidelines for the design of management, information, and logistical systems to direct these operations. Effective coordination of the various business functions becomes especially crucial as the scope and complexity of international operations expands and management faces new competitive challenges in markets worldwide.

The ultimate goal of global strategy should be to achieve optimal integration and rationalization of operations and decision systems on a global scale. Potential synergies arising from coordination and integration of strategy and of decision systems across country and product markets will be captured, and maximal efficiency in the allocation of resources worldwide achieved. Focus on the unique competitive advantages provided by the multinational character of operations is thus the key to success in a global marketplace.

REFERENCES

1. Douglas, Susan P., and C. Samuel Craig (1989) "Evolution of Global Marketing Strategy: Scale, Scope and Synergy," *Columbia Journal of World Business*, (Fall), pp. 47–59. This chapter is based on our article.
2. Levitt, T. (1983) "The Globalization of Markets," *Harvard Business Review*, (May–June), pp. 92–102.
3. "This Bud's for Them" (1993) *Fortune*, August 9, p. 12.
4. "Anheuser May Buy Czech Brewer Stake," (1993) *Wall Street Journal*, September 20.
5. "U.S. Brewer Woos Czech Bride-to-be," (1994) *Financial Times*, February 9.
6. Clarke, Hilary (1992). "Belgium's Strong Drinks," *International Management*, (June), pp. 62–65.
7. Vernon, Raymond (1966) "International Investment and International Trade in the Product Cycle," *Quarterly Journal of Economics*, (May), pp. 190–207.
8. Johanson, Jan, and Jan-Erik Vahlne (1990) "The Mechanism of Internationalism," *International Marketing Review* 7(4), pp. 11–24.
9. Cavusgil, S. Tamer (1980) "On the Internationalization Process of Firms," *European Research*, (November), pp. 273–80.
10. Perlmutter, Howard (1969) "The Tortuous Evolution of the Multinational Corporation," *Columbia Journal of World Business*, (January/February), pp. 9–18.
11. Douglas, Susan P., and C. Samuel Craig (1989) "Evolution of Global Marketing Strategy: Scale, Scope and Synergy," *Columbia Journal of World Business*, (Fall), pp. 47–59.
12. Rapp, W. V. (1973) "Strategy Formulation and International Competition," *Columbia Journal of World Business*, (Summer), pp. 98–112.
13. "Alain Gomez, France's High Tech Warrior," (1989) *Business Week*, May 15, pp. 100–106.
14. Darlin, Darren (1993) "The Keep It Simple Strategy," *Forbes*, August 16, pp. 98–99.
15. Davidson, William H. (1980) "The Location of Foreign Direct Investment Activity: Country Characteristics and Experience Effects," *Journal of International Business Studies*, 3, (Spring), pp. 35–50.
16. Johanson, Jan, and Finn Wiedersheim-Paul (1975) "The Internationalization of the Firm-Four Swedish Cases," *Journal of Management Studies*, (October), pp. 305–322.
17. Doyle, Peter, and Zeki Gidengil (1976) "A Strategic Approach for International Market Selection," *Proceedings European Academy for Advanced Research in Marketing*, Copenhagen, Denmark.
18. Davidson, William H. (1982) *Global Strategic Management*, New York: John Wiley and Sons.
19. Ayal, Igal, and Jehiel Zif (1979) "Market Expansion Strategies in

Multinational Marketing," *Journal of Marketing*, 43, (Spring), pp. 84–94.

20. Anderson, E., and H. Gatignon (1986) "Modes of Foreign Entry: A Transaction Cost Analysis and Propositions," *Journal of International Business Studies*, 17(Fall), pp. 1–26.

21. Root, Franklin J. (1994) *Entry Strategies for International Markets*, Revised and expanded edition. New York: Lexington Books.

22. Prahalad, C. K. and Yves Doz (1987) *The Multinational Mission*, New York: The Free Press.

23. Grimm, Matthew (1993) "Swatch Gets Into Shades," *Brandweek*, May 10, p. 9.

24. "A Spread to Match Tastes," (1990) *Financial Times*, June 4, p. 17.

25. Wind, Y., and S. Douglas (1981) "International Portfolio Analysis and Strategy: The Challenge of the 1980's," *Journal of International Business Studies*, (Fall), pp. 69–82.

26. Takeuchi, H., and Michael E. Porter (1986) "The Strategic Role of International Marketing: Managing the Nature and Extent of Worldwide Coordination" in M. E. Porter, (ed.) *Competition in Global Industries.* Cambridge, Mass: Harvard Business School.

27. Ghoshal, Sumantra (1987) "Global Strategy: An Organizing Framework," *Strategic Management Journal*, 8, pp. 425–440.

28. "Detroit South, Mexico's Auto Body," (1992) *Business Week*, March 16, pp. 98–103.

29. "The Trick to Selling Europe," (1993) *Fortune*, September 20, p. 82.

30. "Whirlpool Goes off on a World Tour," (1991) *Business Week*, June 3, pp. 98–100.

31. "Plugged into the Wireless World," (1993) *Business Week*, October 4, pp. 92–93.

32. Bartlett, Christopher, and Sumantra Ghoshal (1989) *Managing Across Borders: The Transnational Solution.* Boston: Harvard Business School Press.

33. Douglas, Susan P., and C. Samuel Craig (1986) "Global Marketing Myopia," *Journal of Marketing Management*, 2, (Winter), pp. 155–169.

CHAPTER 3

INFORMATION FOR GLOBAL MARKETING DECISIONS[1]

INTRODUCTION

Without adequate information about international markets, the firm cannot develop effective marketing strategies. Information is critical, whether a firm is just entering international markets, expanding its international operations, or attempting to rationalize its global activities. As the following examples illustrate,[2] many of the more glaring problems occur during initial market entry and market expansion. However, the firm must remain constantly vigilant to avoid major multinational mistakes.

Ignoring the need for research. A U.S. company learned that ketchup was not available in Japan. Anxious to capture "first mover" advantages, the company shipped a large quantity of its ketchup to Japan. The product was not purchased, as Japanese consumers prefer soy-based condiments rather than tomato-based condiments. A little market research before market entry would have avoided the mistake.

Insufficient research. Kentucky Fried Chicken entered the Brazilian market with hopes of eventually opening 100 stores. Initial sales of the operation in Sao Paulo were disappointing. In making the decision to enter the market, KFC had not adequately researched possible competition. Street corner vendors sold low-priced charcoal-broiled chicken virtually everywhere. Further, this chicken appealed to local tastes.

Misdirected market research. A U.S. soft drink company conducted research in Indonesia to determine market potential. Rather than conduct research throughout the entire country, it focused on the major urban areas. These results were projected to the entire population. Based on the research, the company established large bottling and distribution facilities. Unfortunately, there were major differences between rural and urban Indonesia. Sales were disappointing, as the product was purchased primarily by foreign visitors and tourists.

Failure to appreciate market differences. Cummins Engine Company encountered sluggish sales of its diesel engines in the European market. Unlike the U.S. market, the European market was highly integrated, with truck manufacturers making their own engines. This created a much more difficult competitive environment in which to do business. Research on the European market structure would have better prepared Cummins for the challenges it encountered.

Inadequate market research. When CPC International wanted to introduce its Knorr soups into the United States, it conducted test markets. This involved serving passersby a portion of warm soup made from a Knorr mix. Based on the taste tests, there was considerable interest in purchasing the product. However, sales were disappointing. Research should have been designed, not only to examine consumer reaction to the taste, but also to determine how receptive consumers were to preparing the soup from a dry mix. This would have uncovered the strong preference among U.S. consumers for canned soups.

Failure to appreciate cultural differences. Coffee and its preparation play an important role in the French household. Chase and Sanborn met considerable resistance when it attempted to enter the French market with its instant coffee. French consumers rejected the concept of an instant coffee that did not provide for the ritual of preparation that was so important to them. Marketing research would have helped Chase and Sanborn appreciate the ceremonial aspects of coffee preparation and how deeply ingrained it was in French culture.

GLOBAL INFORMATION NEEDS

As the preceding examples suggest, systematic collection of information is critical to successful strategy development in international markets. Although the costs and difficulties of collecting information from different countries throughout the world sometimes seem prohibitive, the consequences of not doing so can be disastrous. Information is needed to assess which countries or markets offer the more attractive opportunities, how to enter these markets, and whether to adapt marketing mix tactics to specific local market conditions, as well as how to assess the firm's performance.

Uses of Information

Information is needed to assess new and continuing opportunities and threats that emerge in markets throughout the world. Lack of familiarity with markets and the business environment in other countries, together with the myriad of opportunities and rapid rates of change in markets scattered across the globe, make it essential to conduct a thorough investigation of these opportunities in order to plan global market entry and expansion.

Monitoring trends with regard to market demand, competition, government policies, and other environmental factors provide input to adapt strategy to new threats and opportunities as well as changing conditions in the global market place. Again, the geographic scope of operations, coupled with the accelerating pace of change and uncertainty of future conditions, make systematic collection of this information and continued surveillance essential.

Managers also need to conduct market research into customer behavior in other countries to make decisions relating to market segmentation and marketing tactics in these countries. Customer reactions to ideas for new products and brands, advertising copy, or marketing ideas from other countries need to be tested. Price sensitivity, purchasing behavior, and preferences need also to be examined to develop effective competitive marketing tactics and coordinate strategy across national borders.

Management also needs to collect information to assess performance, both globally and in relation to specific countries or geographic areas, as well as in relation to specific business or marketing functions. Here, internal company data are needed to assess profitability and sales trends. Benchmarking against competitors and market trends is also helpful, to diagnose problems and identify areas where action is needed.

Types of Information

As in domestic research, two major types of information or data can be collected, secondary data and primary data. Information can also be obtained from external sources, outside the firm, or alternatively, internally, from company sources.

Secondary data are often an important source of information, particularly in market entry and expansion decisions. Various types of secondary data are available, ranging from government, economic, and social statistics to reports published by trade associations, industry reports, and other commercial publications. Computerized international data banks, such as PC Globe and TSM Global Economic Data Base are valuable sources of information. The ready availability and low cost of such data are a key advantage.

Primary data, on the other hand, are often expensive and difficult to collect, especially in developing countries where there is no well-developed research infrastructure. This is especially the case with large-scale surveys. Consequently, greater reliance is often placed on expert opinion, qualititative research, or small-scale studies, using convenience or judgement samples.

Information can also be collected from external or internal company sources. External sources provide information primarily with regard to environmental trends, demand patterns, competition, and the market infrastructure. Data relating to customer characteristics and response behavior are also typically obtained from external sources. Information on sales and costs to assess performance and profitability will most likely come from internal company records, through external syndicated sources may also be utilized. In some instances, internal resources can be utilized to collect primary data. For example, sales representatives and managers can often provide valuable information on customer needs and reactions. Attitudes and opinions of country or regional managers relating to market trends, competitor moves, or reactions can also be surveyed. Often these provide a valuable source of "expert opinion" relating to local markets.

Availability and Costs of Data Collection

Data availability and information costs differ from country to country. In many industrialized countries, an abundance of information is available, including data on population demographics, industrial production, company reports, consumer life-style studies, and store audit data. In developing countries, however, difficulties may be encountered in obtaining basic population or income data or even production statistics. In such countries, there is often no well-developed infrastructure for collection of economic or market-related information, and little experience in conducting market research. Consequently, substantial costs are entailed to develop basic information relating, for example, to sampling frames to conduct a survey, or alternatively, to train qualified interviewers and researchers to collect and analyze data. Yet potential market size may be considerably smaller than in industrialized nations and not warrant significant expenditures.

As a result, the economics of international market information decisions differ substantially from comparable domestic market decisions. In the first place, the lack of familiarity with foreign environments, and of operations within these environments, implies that information collection expenditures and research, especially in the initial entry stages, should be viewed as an investment rather than a current expense. This aids in avoiding costly entry mistakes and enables the development of more effective long-run international market expansion strategies.

The appropriate time horizon for evaluating these expenditures should be considerably longer. Often initial market size or potential may seem small or even nonexistent. However, long-run potential may be much greater. This is in part due to rapid rates of growth and change in many international markets, as for example, China or Eastern Europe. Furthermore, it is important to consider entry at an early stage of market development, to avoid allowing the market to be captured by competitors.

In addition, the nature of the information collection process, and notably the type of information required, vary with the phase of involvement and degree of experience in international markets. In the initial phase of entry, information relating to the external market environment is of key importance in order to identify opportunities and determine the appropriate mode of entry. Once initial entry decisions have been made, attention shifts to research relating to marketing mix decisions, as, for example, new product development and testing, advertising copy and media research, and price sensitivity. As experience in international markets develops and operations become more far-flung, greater emphasis is likely to be placed on building global information systems to improve resource allocation across markets and countries, and to take advantage of potential synergies through improved integration and coordination of international strategies.

PHASE 1: INFORMATION FOR INITIAL MARKET ENTRY

In the initial entry phase, information assessing opportunities and risks in different markets worldwide is required to select which markets to enter, the mode of operation, and what competitive strategy to adopt in these markets. It is particularly important to collect information *prior* to international market entry, to avoid costly mistakes that may occur due to lack of familiarity with local market conditions and structure or customer interests and desires. A Taiwanese manufacturer of jeans, for example, in entering the U.S. market, remembered to lengthen the leg-size of the jeans in order to fit the taller U.S. figure but forgot that with longer legs go bigger feet, and consequently made the ankle width too small for the American foot.

In collecting information for initial market entry decisions, management needs data at two different levels. In the first place, it needs information relating to the general business environment in a country or region, as, for example, the political situation, financial stability, the regulatory environment, and market size and growth, as well as the market infrastructure. This is information that is taken for granted in its domestic market, as management is typically aware of, and in touch with, the local business environment. In international market entry, however, it is of paramount importance in order to determine the most attractive market opportunities, and appropriate mode of entry or operation in the market. Secondly, management needs information relating to the specific product market or service industry the company plans to enter. This includes information on sales potential and rate of market growth, product market structure, and sources of direct and indirect competition, as well as the competitive situation.

The Business Environment/Climate

In examining the business environment or climate in a country, management needs to collect information to assess the favorability of the environment, as well as the risks associated with entering or operating in the country. This will require examining a range of aspects such as the political environment, the financial climate, and the legal and regulatory environment. These elements are often viewed as constituting risks, but can also provide incentives to market entry, for example, tax advantages for foreign investors, or less stringent product or environmental regulation than in the home country.

What information management should collect to assess the business climate, as also the relative importance attached to various aspects, depends on the industry, company size, and resources, as well as management objectives and attitudes. A large company in telecommunications, or oil refining, is likely to be more concerned with the political and financial stability of a country than a manufacturer of fashion accessories or T-shirts would be. Some examples of the type and sources of information used to assess the business climate are illustrated in Table 3-1.

POLITICAL ENVIRONMENT

Collection of information relating to the political climate, such as government stability, attitudes toward foreign investment, and the nature of the political regime, helps in assessing the favorability of the political climate to market growth and development as well as possible entry or investment issues faced by companies. A number of syndicated services and other sources such as Frost and

| TABLE 3-1 | SAMPLE INDICATORS FOR ASSESSING THE BUSINESS ENVIRONMENT |

TYPE OF INDICATORS	SAMPLE INDICATORS
Political	■ Government system: democratic, authoritarian, dictatorship ■ Frequency of government changes ■ Frequency of riots, insurrections, strikes ■ Military coups and influence ■ Attitudes to foreign business ■ Expert ratings of political stability
Financial	■ Rate of inflation ■ Foreign exchange risk ■ Restrictions on capital flows ■ Exchange controls ■ External debt ■ Exchange rate stability
Legal	■ Import-export restrictions (tariffs, quotas) ■ Restrictions on ownership ■ Product standards and regulations ■ Environmental standards ■ Regulation of competition, monopolies ■ Price controls and regulation ■ Patent and trademark legislation

Sullivan, the Economist Intelligence Unit, or BERI (Business Environment Risk Index) provide ratings of country or political risk. These range from single or multiple indicators of different types of risk to forecasts of risk for leading countries. In addition to using such sources, some companies undertake their own evaluation of the political climate based on expert opinion or assessment of indicators such as frequency of changes in the government, terrorist acts, frequency of riots, purges or military coups, frequency of strikes and social unrest, and strength of extremist parties such as fascists or radical socialists.

FINANCIAL AND FOREIGN EXCHANGE DATA

Examination of financial and foreign exchange risk factors such as the rate of inflation, currency depreciation, restrictions on capital flows, and repatriation of earnings is important, since they have a critical impact on overall levels of profitability and expected ROI. Such factors are particularly critical where foreign-based production is concerned, and where goods or services will move across national boundaries. A manufacturer of color TV sets planning the acquisition of a company or establishment of a plant in the United Kingdom to supply European markets will, for example, need to make a careful evaluation of the anticipated movement of the pound relative to other European currencies. Similarly, inflation and interest rates are an important factor for companies with high credit exposure, as for example, consumer credit card companies or retailers.

Again, a number of services specialize in assessing and predicting investment and foreign exchange risk for different countries. These include services provided by the major international banks, such as J.P. Morgan and Credit Suisse, or by economic forecasting organizations such as Wharton Econometrics. Companies can also make their own assessments. Relevant data can be found in sources such as *International Financial Statistics*. Some illustrative indicators are shown in Table 3-1.

LEGAL AND REGULATORY DATA

Management also needs to collect information on legal and regulatory factors, such as import-export regulations, restrictions on ownership, or modes of operation, tariff barriers, taxation, product regulation, and environmental standards. Regulation is often a major barrier to market entry and limits the mode of operation, as well as impacting the extent to which products or marketing strategies will need to be modified. Information on product standards and regulations is especially critical for industries such as pharmaceuticals, and food and agricultural products.

Management typically has to collect this information on a country-by-country basis from sources such as Dun and Bradstreet's *Exporters' Encyclopedia*, Price Waterhouse country guides or the Economist Intelligence Unit's *Investment Licensing and Trading Conditions Abroad* series. The general types of information needed are shown in Table 3.1.

Market Size and Growth Potential

In addition to assessing the business climate, management needs to consider market size and growth potential. This assessment should cover general country characteristics, such as population size and growth, or GNP per capita, which provide basic parameters for determining market size and potential, as well as characteristics that are specifically relevant for a particular product or service, as, for example, climate, religion, or level of engineering skills. Some illustrative examples of relevant variables are shown in Table 3-2.

Ratings, or composite indices evaluating business potential in a country, are published by various organizations. The Economist Intelligence Unit, for example, each year publishes three indexes: (1) market growth, (2) market intensity, and (3) market size, for countries in different regions of the world. A summary of these indexes for the twenty largest markets in the world is shown in Figure 3-1. *Market size* shows the relative importance of each national or regional market as a percentage of the world market based on indicators such as total population, private consumption expenditure, and steel consumption. *Market intensity* measures the richness of the market, or the degree of concentrated purchasing power it represents, based on indicators such as cars, telephones and TVs in use, steel consumption. *Market growth* is an average of cumulative growth on key indicators such as population, electricity production, ownership of cars, and trucks and buses in use.

DEMOGRAPHIC CHARACTERISTICS

Demographic characteristics such as population size are often important indicators of market size, since they provide an upper bound of market potential for products oriented to the mass population and also for certain industrial goods. Specific demographic characteristics, such as the number of working wives, the birth rate, and the number of young adults, may also be useful for products that are directed to specific demographic segments, such as baby foods or pop records.

GEOGRAPHIC FACTORS

The physical and topographical features of a country comprise a further set of characteristics that affect demand for specific product categories. Topographical characteristics are particularly critical for products associated with transportation and communication. Cellular phones, for example, have high potential in countries with mountainous terrain, where cable is difficult or expensive to lay. Climatic conditions also affect consumption patterns and production technology, and are important for clothing and sporting equipment such as skis and cowboy boots.

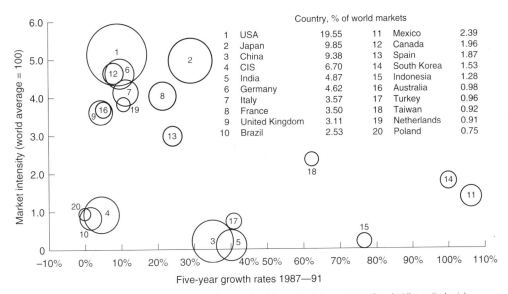

EIU Market Indexes: size, growth and intensity of 20 largest markets

Market intensity (world average = 100)

Five-year growth rates 1987—91

Country, % of world markets

1	USA	19.55		11	Mexico	2.39
2	Japan	9.85		12	Canada	1.96
3	China	9.38		13	Spain	1.87
4	CIS	6.70		14	South Korea	1.53
5	India	4.87		15	Indonesia	1.28
6	Germany	4.62		16	Australia	0.98
7	Italy	3.57		17	Turkey	0.96
8	France	3.50		18	Taiwan	0.92
9	United Kingdom	3.11		19	Netherlands	0.91
10	Brazil	2.53		20	Poland	0.75

Note: The position of the center of each circle shows the intensity of the market (when measured against the vertical axis) and is cumulative growth over the 1987—91 period (when measured against the horizontal axis). The size of the circles indicates the relative size of the markets as a percentage of the total world market. See text for definitions and methodology.

EIU Market Indexes, 1981, 1986, 1991

	Market size (% of World market)			Market intensity (World = 1.00)			Cumulative five-year market growth (%)
	1981	1986	1991	1981	1986	1991	1991
Major regions							
Asia	21.75	27.75	31.83	0.36	0.54	0.43	28.99
Western Europe	25.19	22.22	19.82	2.97	2.84	3.17	9.34
(EC)	19.01	18.87	19.32	3.35	3.06	3.82	13.44
(EFTA)	2.86	2.09	1.98	3.21	3.42	4.15	8.66
Eastern Europe	18.95	17.87	9.29	2.09	1.99	1.00	5.42
North America	22.99	20.01	21.52	4.34	3.98	5.08	8.67
Latin America	6.16	6.60	7.73	0.73	0.77	0.85	20.57
(LAIA)	5.64	6.02	7.05	0.78	0.81	0.91	22.26
Middle East	1.71	2.49	2.43	0.54	0.69	0.52	39.03
Africa	2.01	1.94	3.37	0.23	0.20	0.19	20.17
Oceania	1.25	1.13	1.16	3.33	3.02	3.63	3.10
World	100.00	100.00	100.00	1.00	1.00	1.00	
Major markets							
United States	20.96	18.08	19.55	4.40	3.99	5.13	8.99
Japan	9.07	8.10	9.85	3.42	3.29	4.98	29.13
China	6.64	11.56	9.38	0.26	0.61	0.23	34.81
CIS	13.16	12.17	6.70	2.03	1.97	0.96	4.12
India	1.53	2.44	4.87	0.09	0.17	0.13	39.72
Germany	4.93	3.95	4.62	3.91	3.47	4.65	9.83
Italy	4.06	3.69	3.57	3.35	3.38	4.15	11.30
France	3.77	3.39	3.50	3.38	3.22	4.05	21.76
United Kingdom	3.38	2.85	3.11	2.87	2.70	3.64	4.41
Brazil	2.21	2.58	2.53	0.78	0.88	0.85	1.16
Mexico	1.28	1.21	2.39	0.85	0.68	1.37	106.47
Canada	2.02	1.94	1.96	3.81	3.92	4.66	7.84

Source: *Crossborder Monitor*, August 4, 1993, "EIU Market Indexes," p. 12, The Economist Intelligence Unit. Reprinted with permission.

FIGURE 3-1

EIU Market Indexes.

| TABLE 3-2 | **SAMPLE INDICATORS OF MARKET POTENTIAL** |

DEMOGRAPHIC CHARACTERISTICS

- Population size (millions)
- Average annual population growth (percent)
- Urbanization (percent population in cities over one million)
- Percent population (aged 0–14 years)
- Population density
- Age structure of the population
- Life expectancy
- Infant mortality

GEOGRAPHIC FACTORS

- Size of a country (in square kilometers)
- Topographical characteristics
- Climatic conditions (average temperature)
- Annual rainfall and snowfall

ECONOMIC FACTORS

- GNP per capita
- Income distribution (percent of GNP in top 20 percent of households)
- Annual rate growth of GNP
- Growth rate of agricultural production
- Growth rate of manufacturing
- Growth rate of services
- Energy consumption
- Steel consumption

TECHNOLOGICAL AND EDUCATIONAL FACTORS

- Scientific/technological skills
- Existing production technology
- Existing consumption technology
- Adult illiteracy
- PC ownership per capita
- Number of Ph.D.s in science
- Percent of age group enrolled in tertiary education
- Percent of age group completing secondary education

SOCIOCULTURAL FACTORS

- Dominant values
- Life-style patterns
- Number of ethnic groups
- Number of languages
- Population per physician
- Dominant religion

ECONOMIC FACTORS

Economic data such as GDP, growth of GNP, consumer expenditure and buying power, and capital investment ratios, are also crucial in evaluating demand for both consumer and industrial goods and are the most commonly used indicators of aggregate market potential. Interest in products and willingness to buy must be backed by ability to pay. Examination of growth rates and growth forecasts also helps to assess future market potential.

TECHNOLOGICAL AND EDUCATIONAL FACTORS

The importance of evaluating technological and educational factors depends on the specific product category. Marketers of sophisticated manufacturing equipment are likely to be concerned with engineering skills, and of computer games with the level of education.

SOCIOCULTURAL FACTORS

Sociocultural characteristics such as dominant cultural and religious values, dominant ethnic groups, or life-style patterns are also important factors underlying demand for products such as food, clothing, and leisure goods. A marketer of exercise equipment should, for example, assess attitudes to health and exercise. Similarly, an Italian company selling grappa, a brandy, might be concerned with the number of Italian immigrants in a country.

The Economic and Market Infrastructure

A third category of macroenvironmental characteristics relates to the economic and market infrastructure, as for example, the telephone and communications network, distribution channel structure, availability and cost of energy, and management skills and training. These affect the costs and difficulty of doing business in a country and can be a barrier to market entry or impact the mode of entry or operation. If, for example, the telephone network is poorly developed, as in many Eastern European countries, communications will be difficult, adding substantially to operating costs.

In examining the economic and market infrastructure, management should collect information relating to resource costs and availability, as, for example, energy, labor, and capital costs or management skills. The development of the physical and communications infrastructure, the reach of various advertising and promotional media, and the relative concentration/fragmentation of retailing are also important factors to assess. Information on these can be obtained from a variety of sources, such as government statistical yearbooks, guides, and handbooks, such as the Economist Intelligence Unit Country Profiles as well as sources such as Euromonitor's *International Marketing Data* and *European Marketing Data*. Sample types of information are shown in Table 3-3.

TABLE 3-3	**SAMPLE INFRASTRUCTURE INDICATORS**

INTEGRATIVE NETWORKS

- Availability of communication networks
- Railroad network (kilometers)
- Road network (kilometers)
- Air freight (volume)
- Number of retail outlets per capita
- Concentration of retail ownership
- TV and radio ownership
- Magazine and newspaper circulation
- Number of telephones per capita
- Number of cars per capita

BASIC RESOURCES

- Gas consumption
- Energy consumption
- Electricity costs per kilowatt hour
- Monthly wage costs
- Work skills of labor
- Management skills
- Management training
- Capital availability
- Interest rates
- Rents

Product Market Data

In addition, wherever feasible, management should collect data relating to the specific product market. These should include information relating to sales and product usage, usage of complementary and substitute products, and competitive market structure (see Table 3-4). The relevant types of variables are essentially the same as those needed in relation to the domestic market. However, in international markets it is important to define the product market very broadly, to include all possible products and services that might be used as substitutes. For example, a manufacturer of washing machines and other household appliances might look at the cost and use of household help as well as commercial laundries.

PRODUCT SALES AND USAGE DATA

Here management needs information relating to levels of product ownership for consumer durables and equipment, or sales-purchase and repeat-purchase rates for nondurables, supplies and services, as well as rates of market growth. Availability of such data is likely to depend on the development of the product

| TABLE 3-4 | PRODUCT-SPECIFIC INDICATORS |

PRODUCT SALES AND USAGE

- Sales volume of product
- Ownership of product (percent households businesses)
- Annual growth in sales volume
- Unit sales of product
- Frequency of purchase
- Average purchase size

USE OF COMPLEMENTARY OR SUBSTITUTE PRODUCTS

- Sales volume and growth rates of complementary products
- Existence and size of user industries
- Sales and growth rates of substitute products
- Ownership of complementary products
- Size of second-hand market

COMPETITION

- Number of firms
- Presence of key competitors
- Growth rate of competing firms
- Market share of top three firms

market and the specific country. For consumer products, Nielsen data are available for most major industrialized countries. The Economist Intelligence Unit also publishes studies relating to different product markets such as soft drinks, babywear, cosmetics, and toiletries in various European countries. For industrial products and services, relevant data may be obtained from government sources such as statistical yearbooks or industry surveys and reports, or commercial sources such as Predicasts. Greater difficulty is likely to be encountered in obtaining such data for developing countries such as the African countries or Middle Eastern markets than for industrialized countries.

USE OF COMPLEMENTARY OR SUBSTITUTE PRODUCTS

Data relating to usage of complementary or substitute products should also be collected. A tire manufacturer will, for example, need to collect data relating to ownership and sales of trucks, automobiles, and other vehicles, as well as vehicle production, in order to assess the replacement market. Similarly, a marketer of new age beverages should collect data relating to sales of wine, beer, fruit juices, and carbonated beverages. Collecting information for substitute products and services is especially important where there is no existing product market in a country, in order to assess likely demand. Sources for such data will be the same as in relation to product usage.

COMPETITIVE MARKET STRUCTURE

Information on competition should also be collected. This might include, for example, the number and size of competitors in a country, their sales volume and rates of growth, relative market share, and so forth. For example, a company planning to export beer might obtain information on sales and market share of major international breweries such as Anheuser-Busch and Heineken, as well as local national and regional breweries. The feasibility of obtaining such data is likely to vary significantly with the specific product category. Industry surveys sometimes provide relevant information. Some data may be obtained from company reports or trade sources. Coverage is likely to vary by country and be scanty for small and developing countries.

Using Information to Make Market Entry Decisions

Once the information required to make market entry decisions has been determined, management needs to establish procedures to analyze this and assess country market attractiveness. Here, a wide variety of procedures can be adopted, depending on the volume of data, level of precision, and analytical sophistication required. Approaches range from qualitative evaluation and/or ranking of data, to the development of elaborate simulation models. The appropriate procedure depends to a large extent on the budget and time available for collecting and evaluating information, as also the role of management in the evaluation process.

Irrespective of the specific procedure adopted, systematic evaluation of potential opportunities on a worldwide basis is especially important. This helps to avoid haphazard market entry decisions based on familiarity with a particular country or market, or in response to a chance encounter or unsolicited order from a potential customer or distributor in a foreign country. A systematic evaluation of all countries and markets worldwide often helps to reveal new or unexpected opportunities and provides a key input into long-range planning for international market involvement, and determining priorities for international market entry.

One approach to dealing with the volume and diversity of data required to make a systematic evaluation of all countries worldwide is to adopt a sequential screening approach.[3,4] A number of sequential screens of relevant variables can be established, and countries or markets assessed successively on each screen. At each stage, those that do not pass certain minimal cut-off points or are ranked lowest on a given screen can be eliminated. A limited set of countries or markets for further in-depth investigation can thus be identified. This approach offers the advantage of limiting the data collection task, since countries or areas that are less attractive or have limited potential are eliminated early in the process. Only those with relatively good prospects are examined in greater depth, especially in relation to information, for example, on competition or product markets, which is less readily available and more expensive to collect.

A sequential screening approach can be implemented in a number of different ways, differing primarily in terms of analytical sophistication and management input.[1] A simple qualitative assessment can be made based on a number of indicators. Table 3-5 shows a simple screen for fashion boots. Minimum cut-off points are established at each stage to determine which countries pass to the next stage. Alternatively, indicators can be weighted based on management judgment and summated to develop an overall score for each country. Simple or complex simulation models can also be developed to assess countries based on selected indicators. These can, for example, incorporate a sensitivity analysis of the weights or value ranges for each indicator, as well assessing countries or markets relative to alternative modes of operation, entry proximity to other markets, or alternative future environmental scenarios.

Such evaluation procedures only provide one phase of input into manage-

| TABLE 3-5 | AN ILLUSTRATION OF AN INTERNATIONAL SCREENING PROCEDURE FOR A FASHION BOOT COMPANY |

PRELIMINARY SCREENING

1. Population:	10 million people and above
2. GNP Per capita:	$2,400 and above
3. Urbanization:	60% and above
	COUNTRIES REVIEWED: 123

GENERAL COUNTRY INDICATORS

1. Political stability:	Stable for at least 4 years
2. Economic stability:	Stable for at least 4 years
3. Predicted inflation:	10% and less (4-year period)
4. Economic growth:	Minimum 2%
5. Income distribution:	Top 20% of households less than 50% GNP
6. Climate:	Moderate or Cold
7. Export risk:	No lower than "B"
	COUNTRIES REVIEWED: 18

PRODUCT MARKET INDICATORS

1. Import restrictions:	No restrictions on footwear imports
2. Age distribution:	At least 50% age 15–64
3. Footwear expenditure:	Per capita footwear expenditure ($)
4. Market size:	Millions of pairs sold
5. Market growth:	Percent growth in footwear sales (1977–1990)
	COUNTRIES REVIEWED: 12

INFRASTRUCTURE

1. TV and radio ownership:	Percent of ownership of television and radios
2. Newspaper circulation:	Number of newspapers in circulation
3. Distribution:	Number of footwear outlets
4. Competition:	Presence of key competitors
	COUNTRIES REVIEWED: 6

ment decisions with regard to country entry. In addition, other factors enter into the decision, such as, for example, management goals and objectives with regard to international markets, the planned speed and timing of entry into international markets, management's long-run international expansion strategy, and the aggressiveness of the entry strategy. These elements, and the role of entry decisions in global competitive strategy, are discussed in more detail in Chapter 6.

PHASE 2: INFORMATION FOR LOCAL MARKET EXPANSION

In the initial phase of entry into international markets, heavy reliance is typically placed on secondary data. Once certain markets have been selected based on secondary data, the firm should engage in the collection of primary data to develop marketing strategies appropriate to the specific country. Here, an important research question is how far marketing tactics should be adapted to the local market. In addition, research is needed to identify new product opportunities. In both cases, an important issue is whether the same research design and procedures can be utilized across countries.

While in principle, similar types of information and similar research techniques apply as in domestic market research, in practice, a number of issues arise specific to international markets. Lack of familiarity with foreign markets may necessitate collection of preliminary information to aid in research design, and determine appropriate research questions and methods. Differences in the research infrastructure affect the organization of research and cost effectiveness of alternative research methods. Issues of data comparability and equivalence across countries and markets also impact research design, especially where results are to be compared across countries.

Preliminary Data Collection

Often limited management knowledge and experience in a foreign market, coupled with a paucity of secondary data sources or prior research relating to a market, mandate a preliminary phase of information collection. This is intended to aid in formulating research specifications and also in research design. This preliminary phase may include collection of background information, relating, for example, to the product market, complementary or substitute products, existing attitudinal and behavior studies, competitive analyses, etc. Information on the research infrastructure may also be collected, relating to questions such as availability of trained interviewees, reliability of mail services, levels of telephone or fax ownership, etc.

Qualitative research is also helpful in providing input for the design of a market survey. Such research enables identification of constructs, product class definitions, or relevant attitudes and behavior to be examined in subsequent phases of research. Qualitative data collection techniques are appropriate in these instances, as they are unstructured in character. Rather than imposing a specific response format on the respondent, they focus on probing how people think, feel, and react in response to specific situations or stimuli. They avoid the imposition of a cultural bias, since no conceptual model is prespecified by the researcher. Thus, the researcher gains insights into the problems to be studied and into differences as compared with the domestic market. Often this helps in revealing the impact of sociocultural factors on behavior and response patterns in the marketplace. They can, therefore, be used to pinpoint relevant aspects to be further examined and to identify appropriate concepts and constructs.

Lack of Market Research Infrastructure

In some countries, the research infrastructure is not as well developed as in markets within the Industrial Triad, where most marketing research is conducted. Research organizations qualified to conduct field research in other countries are often scarce. If qualified research organizations are not available, management may prefer to organize research in-house and to develop its own research capabilities. These may include, for example, development of in-house data bases, hiring of research personnel, and establishment of facilities to conduct concept or new product testing. Information can also be collected from sales personnel or distributors. Establishment of in-house research capabilities is, however, likely to entail significant costs and hence may only be feasible for a firm with substantial operations in a country. Consequently, in some countries management may have to make decisions based on relatively sketchy and less reliable information than is typically available in the domestic market.

Limited availability of secondary data and of government and trade sources of information also means that it is difficult to develop a sampling frame. In the case of consumer research, for example, telephone books and electoral or municipal lists, which are frequently used to develop sampling frames in industrialized countries, may not be available or not provide adequate coverage. In some cities, there are no street maps, as part of the population may live on boats or be itinerant, thus further complicating the research task. Similarly, directories and lists of companies or organizations may not be available. Consequently, sampling frames have to be developed from scratch.

Underdevelopment of the communications infrastructure can also significantly hamper information collection and survey administration. For example, the quality of the mail service may be poor, resulting in lengthy delays, or, in some cases, nondelivery of a significant proportion of mail. Telephone communications may be difficult, and telephone networks may not be well developed. While the spread of modern telecommunications, including, for example, satellite networks, cellular telephones, and fax machines, has considerably expanded the scope and facility of communication in many parts of the world, others still remain poorly served, hampering collection and transmission of market-information.

Data Equivalence and Comparability

Another issue is the equivalence and comparability of data collected. It is important that data have, as far as possible, the same meaning or interpretation, and the same level of accuracy, precision of measurement, and reliability, in all countries and cultures, insofar as global marketing strategy is concerned with decisions relative to several countries. Comparability in research design and data is especially crucial where research is conducted to determine how far to integrate strategies across different countries and product markets, as, for example, in whether to adopt a standardized advertising strategy. Even where research is only conducted in a single country, it is important to bear in mind that research relating to a similar product or service may subsequently be conducted in another country. Consequently, research designs should be developed so that findings from different markets can be compared.

The need for comparability gives rise to a number of issues in primary data collection. These include category equivalence of constructs, linguistic and metric equivalence of the measurement instruments, and equivalence of samples and data collection procedures. Procedures to reduce cultural bias in data interpretation are also crucial to limit nonequivalence arising from interpretation of the research findings.

CATEGORY EQUIVALENCE

First of all, the category in which objects or other stimuli are placed may vary from country to country. Relevant product class definitions may, for example, differ from one country to another. In the soft drink and beverage market, for example, forms of soft drinks, such as canned or bottled carbonated sodas and colas, fruit juices and drinks, iced teas and powdered and liquid concentrates, differ significantly from one culture to another. In many Asian countries, freshly squeezed fruit juices are widely available. Similarly, in the dessert market, items that are included will vary substantially, ranging from apple pie, jellies, and ice cream, to baklava, rice pudding, and zabaglione. This implies that what is included in the relevant competing product set will vary. Careful attention to such factors is an important consideration when developing product-related measures. In addition, the characteristics or attributes perceived by consumers as relevant in evaluating a product class may differ from one country to another. In France, for example, the hot–cold continuum is a key attribute in characterizing consumers' perceptions of fragrance. In the United States and the United Kingdom, however, this is not an attribute that is perceived as relevant by consumers.

CALIBRATION EQUIVALENCE

Equivalence has also to be established with regard to the calibration system used in measurement. This includes, not only equivalence with regard to monetary units and measures of weight, distance, and volume, but also other perceptual cues, such as color, shape, or form, which are used to interpret visual stimuli. While the need to establish equivalence with regard to monetary and physical measurement units is clearly apparent, other more subtle differences in instrument calibration are less obvious. Interpretation of the meaning attached to various colors varies from one culture or cultural context to another. White, for example, is a color of mourning in Japan, while in Chinese culture red is a symbol of happiness and plays a focal role in weddings—from invitations being printed in red and monetary gifts given in red envelopes, to the red dresses worn by the bride. Awareness of such nuances is an important consideration in instrument design and development, especially in relation to visual stimuli.

TRANSLATION EQUIVALENCE

Questionnaires or other stimuli have to be translated so that they are understood by respondents in different countries and have equivalent meaning in each research context. The importance of translating questionnaires and other verbal stimuli into different languages is readily apparent. Often this helps to pinpoint problems with regard to whether a concept can be measured by using the same or similar questions in each cultural context, and whether a question has the same meaning in different research contexts. The need to translate nonverbal stimuli to ensure that they evoke the desired image, and to avoid problems of miscommunication, is less widely recognized. Misunderstanding can arise, however, because the respondent is not familiar with a product or other stimulus, or because the associations evoked by the stimulus differ from one country or culture to another.

Translation of verbal and nonverbal stimuli thus plays a key role in establishing equivalence. Often translation provides a focal point both for uncovering and for making pragmatic decisions as to how to resolve equivalence issues.

SAMPLING EQUIVALENCE

The comparability of samples from one country to another has also to be considered, in terms both of relevant respondents and representativeness of the population of interest. Here, the question arises as to whether or not respondents should be the same in all countries. In the United States and other Western nations it is not uncommon for children to exercise substantial influence in the purchases of cereal, toys, desserts, and other items. In other countries, where families are less child oriented, children have less influence. Similarly, with the increasing proportion of working wives in many Western nations, husbands participate to an increased extent in grocery shopping activities, while in other countries, a single person, for example, the housewife or maid, may be primarily responsible. Differences in relevant participants in the buying process of organizations from one country to another also need to be determined, and can vary depending on propensity to delegate or centralize decision making.

Another issue to be considered in sampling is the extent to which samples are comparable and are also representative of the population of interest from one country to another. Here, a basic dilemma arises. Probability samples of the population of a country, although representative, are unlikely to be comparable with regard to their composition on characteristics such as income, education, or other sociocultural factors which may influence reactions as customers. If, on the other hand, samples are matched so as to ensure comparability on relevant characteristics, other confounding effects may be introduced, and representativeness is lost. For example, if, probability samples are drawn to investigate interest in a new product in different countries, mistaken inferences relative to the feasibility of standardization may be made due to differences in sample composition.

DATA COLLECTION EQUIVALENCE

Telephone, mail, and personal interviews differ from country to country in terms of their potential biases and reliability due to factors such as the communications infrastructure, the degree of literacy, and the limited availability and adequacy of sampling frames. Consequently, it is not clear that use of the same procedure is necessarily appropriate.

In the United States, telephone surveys enable coverage of a broadly distributed sample as well as facilitate control over interviewers. Telephone ownership is widespread, and hence telephone directories or listings provide reasonably accurate sampling frames. In other countries low levels of telephone ownership, and poor communications, limit the coverage provided by telephone surveys. In addition, telephone costs arc often high, and volume rates may not be available. Consequently, telephone surveys are most likely to be appropriate where relatively upscale or affluent socioeconomic segments are to be sampled.

Similarly, while in many industrial countries mail surveys provide a low-cost means of reaching a broad sample without necessitating a field staff, in other countries, especially developing or emerging nations, they may not be as effective. Mailing lists comparable to those available in industrial countries may not be available, or sources such as directories or electoral lists difficult to obtain. Consequently, as in the case of telephone surveys, mail surveys may only be appropriate in countries with high levels of literacy and where mailing lists are available.

Problems encountered with the use of both telephone and mail surveys imply that, in some countries, data may best be collected through personal interviews. This does, however, require the availability of trained interviewers who are fluent in the relevant language. Problems relating to the interviewer/interviewee interaction also need to be considered. In some countries, suspiciousness about the interviewer's motivations, and feelings that interviewing constitutes an invasion of privacy, as well as negative attitudes towards questioning by strangers, exist. This affects the willingness of respondents to participate or cooperate in both industrial and consumer surveys. Respondents may also tend to deliberately conceal information or give false answers.

As a result, use of similar procedures in different countries will not always generate comparable results and hence be appropriate. Accumulated experience from previous research is often helpful in providing indications of sources of bias. In addition, it can suggest which procedures are likely to be most effective and generate equivalent results in different countries and sociocultural contexts.

Data Interpretation and Cultural Bias

A final issue to be considered concerns cultural bias in data interpretation. In conducting research in foreign markets, there is a danger of cultural self-referent bias.[5] In other words, there is always a tendency for a researcher to perceive or interpret phenomena or behavior observed in other countries and cultures in terms of his or her own cultural self-referent. Cross-cultural bias can affect various stages of the research process. It can arise in research design, in communication between researcher and respondent, and in interpretation of the data.

Such bias is likely to be particularly acute where a researcher is investigating an unfamiliar sociocultural environment, or lacks experience with sociocultural patterns. As, however, the researcher builds up experience and familiarity with different markets, he or she is likely to develop increased sensitivity to sociocultural specificities. This experience may carry over to other similar markets. Study of the United Kingdom market may, for example, aid in understanding reactions in the Netherlands. Similarly, experience in the French market may prove valuable in investigating the Italian or Spanish markets.

Uses of Research for Local Market Expansion

Research is required to assess how far products and positioning strategies developed in relation to the domestic market need to be modified for foreign markets. Products may appeal to different customer segments, and desired customer benefits and preferences may differ in other countries. For example, in the automobile market, relative importance attached to gas mileage, road handling, and safety features varies from country to country. Similarly, tastes, preferences, and consumption scenarios for food products often vary. Research helps assess how product modification or changing positioning is likely to increase sales, either by broadening the customer base or by increasing market penetration.

Promotional themes, advertising copy, and packaging also need to be tested to assess their effectiveness in local markets. Again, differences in levels of literacy, cultural norms relating to sex and humor, aesthetic tastes, color associations, interpretation of symbols, and effective role models affect customer interpretation and response to different types of visual stimuli, emotional appeals, and promotional arguments.

Price sensitivity will also need to be examined, as this may vary from country to country depending on income levels, customer segments, competing and substitute products, price perception, etc. Research on purchasing behavior may also be required to determine appropriate distribution channels. Again, factors such as interest in service, delivery or convenience, customer brand and store loyalty, time available for purchasing, and preference for different modes of distribution vary from country to country and influence the effectiveness and reach of alternative distribution channels.

Research to identify opportunities for new products and services can also be conducted. This may range from monitoring environmental and technological trends and conducting life-style or customer satisfaction surveys, to in-depth interviews with customers, brainstorming, focus groups, etc. The new product or service concepts thus generated require testing, and those that are selected will go on to be market tested.

PHASE 3: INFORMATION FOR GLOBAL RATIONALIZATION

As the firm moves into the phase of global rationalization, it faces new information requirements as well as the need to make more effective use of data already collected. Secondary data that helped guide country entry decisions should now be used to monitor changes in the firm's operating environment. Countries that were stable politically, or welcomed foreign investment at one time, can become unstable and hostile to foreign investment. Economic growth can slow down or alternatively accelerate. Inflationary pressures may rise, and foreign exchange rates fluctuate. Similarly, information about consumer tastes and preferences gathered on a country-by-country basis needs to be consolidated, to identify commonalities across countries as well as emerging trends.

While emphasis on local market expansion generated a need for primary data to examine local market characteristics and to assess response to products and marketing stimuli, concern with improved coordination and integration of strategy and management systems across countries requires consolidation of data collected on a country-by-country basis. Information relating to performance for each product business and marketing function should be collected and coordinated across countries. The need to integrate data from various internal and external sources suggests the desirability of designing a global information system to monitor performance and determine how best to allocate resources on a global basis.

Designing a Global Information System

The sheer volume and complexity of information required to build a global information system poses a major challenge. Not only does information have to be collected from the far reaches of the globe, but, in addition, it has to be examined and analyzed relative to widely differing operating conditions in order to be of value in decision making. Advances in communications technology have substantially expanded capability to collect, transfer, and evaluate information on a global scale, thus facilitating control and coordination of operations worldwide; as a result, greater attention must be paid to the utility and value of information collected in order to avoid problems of information overload.

A global information system should be designed with three principal functions or uses in managerial decision making in mind. Information is needed to scan the global environment, to monitor and track market trends and customer demand, and to identify new market opportunities, and emerging competitive and other types of threats, as well as changes in technology and in the market environment. Information is also needed to evaluate performance of different business functions and of operations in different geographic regions, in order to determine whether and how to allocate resources worldwide. Finally, coordination and control of operations worldwide requires systematic collection of data, relating to the firm's activities, that are comparable from one country or organizational unit to another.

Environmental scanning requires collection of information similar to that used to identify and assess opportunities in initial international market entry. Here, however, greater emphasis should be paid to tracking trends and continually updating data sources to pinpoint new threats and opportunities. At the same time, a broad and long-term perspective should be adopted to monitor global, regional, and national political, economic, and social developments.

Evaluation of performance requires information relating to external market characteristics, such as market size and structure, strength of competition, product regulation, production and growth trends, as well as competitor performance to provide bench marks for company performance. Internal company data on performance should not only include financial measures such as ROI and cost/sales ratios relating to performance of different products, product lines, but also other measures such as market share growth, brand image, and customer satisfaction, to provide an overall evaluation and input for strategy development as well as short-term assessment. At the same time these measures should be comparable across countries in both real and monetary terms and measurement standards, in order to make comparisons and facilitate coordination of operations across countries.

Components of a Global Information System

The importance of adopting both long- and short-term perspectives suggests that three types of information are required. These include: (1) data relating to the macroeconomic environment of the country, as, for example, GNP and population size; (2) data relating to specific product and supply markets, their size, and their competitive structure; and (3) data on company sales and performance.

MACROENVIRONMENTAL DATA

The types of macroenvironmental data that are likely to be of use in scanning the global environment have already been discussed and do not require further elaboration here. It should, however, be noted that the specific variables to be considered depend on company objectives and the specific product markets.

Information systems should not be too heavily skewed toward the short term. General indicators of long-run global and national economic, financial, and social trends are also needed in order to monitor developments, such as trends in employment, growth of service industries, and number of building starts. A balance should thus be struck between general environmental indicators and those more directly related to specific corporate and marketing objectives.

PRODUCT MARKET DATA

The next level of information relates to specific product markets and competitive market structure. In the case of product markets, data relating to production, sales, or consumption of specific products and product types within the market will be needed. Where feasible, this might be obtained in units and dollar sales volume. Sales data should be obtained by specific product lines and variants. For example, personal toiletries might be broken down by shampoos, antiperspirants, and soaps, and then, within the shampoo market, by hair types and fragrance. For industrial products, breakdown by user industry and industry size might be included; and for consumer products, by sex, age, and income, or other relevant customer groupings.

Data with regard to the competitive market structure are also an important consideration in developing long-run marketing strategy and assessing performance. Information about the number of competitors, market share by company, product line, and brand provide baseline statistics in this regard. Where feasible, breakdowns by region and type of distributive outlets or customers should be obtained. Other information relating to competitive strategies and current trends in the relevant industry, trade margins, trends in investment in new product and plant facilities, hiring and dismissal of employees, and labor productivity are also helpful. However, such information is likely to be available only for industrialized nations and well-established product markets.

Scanner data and panel data are also increasingly available for consumer product markets in industrialized countries, from sources such as Nielsen and IRI. Attention to issues relating to comparability of product market definitions and data from one country to another is also growing, in order to meet the needs of multinational clients. In addition, computerization of information flows from retail point of sale or delivery point through the distribution system to the producer has considerably facilitated access to, and utilization of, this information by management.

COMPANY SALES AND PRODUCT MARKET PERFORMANCE

Internal company data are another important component of the global information system. The exact form that this takes will vary from company to company, depending on the nature and organization of existing operations. Information requirements of industrial, consumer goods, and service companies will differ due to differences in marketing strategy and organization. Irrespective of these differences, some data will be common to all companies.

These include, for example, ROI, market share as a percentage of total industry sales, market share relative to the top or leading three competitors' marketing expenditure relative to sales ratios, and growth in sales by product line.

Parallel to the product market data, and depending also on the size of the market and the degree of product line diversity, these data may be broken down to reflect territorial or regional measures of performance. For example, market share estimates and sales trends may be available by specific geographic regions. Sales and marketing expenses might be broken down by type of distribution channel—for example, direct or indirect—or different types of outlets. In industrial markets, sales and performance measures might also be evaluated relative to specific end-user markets, and for consumer goods relative to different consumer segments.

In addition to such general performance measures, more specific measures relating to individual marketing tools, such as sales force, advertising, sales promotion, and distribution efficiency might be included. These will, however, vary depending on the type of company. Industrial companies may, for example, collect more detailed information relating to performance by different types of sales persons, distribution channels, customer segments, and so on. Consumer companies, on the other hand, may be more concerned with media and sales promotion expenditures and volume by store type.

Information relating to company relations with external organizations will also be needed to evaluate and manage the flow of goods and services throughout the value-chain. This includes information relating to shipments from suppliers, including order frequency, inventory levels, price, delivery specifications, and quality standards. Outward distribution logistics have also to be monitored. This requires information relating to shipment of goods, inventory levels at various locations, such as factory to local market or point of entry depots, wholesalers or other distribution agents, and point of sale. This information has to be matched with the order amount and frequency by customer, expected delivery times, etc.

Information relating to customer satisfaction with product and service quality, delivery, and after-sales service should also be collected on a regular basis. Xerox, for example, measures customer satisfaction globally based on customer assessment of sales, service, and billing, as well as ratings of perceived product quality relative to competitors. Postinstallation customer surveys are conducted within 5 days of the installation of a new copier. These measures provide valuable input to determine how to improve product and customer satisfaction.[6]

Data Comparability and Analysis

As in relation to other types of data, issues of comparability arise in relation to internal company data. Incorporation of data from foreign operations into an international data bank system initially appears relatively straightforward. Data comparability from one country to another presents, however, a major obstacle. It is important to realize that the value of a number supplied by a subsidiary in one country is not necessarily identical to the supposedly comparable figure supplied by a subsidiary in another country. Sales volume measures, for example, may be expressed in real or monetary units. Real units, while accurately reflecting the number sold, can be misleading, in that the nature of the product can vary from country to country, corresponding to different market requirements. Automobiles and pharmaceutical products, for example, frequently require modification to conform to specific national product regulations, entailing different costs. Monetary units can thus reflect, not only design differences, but also differences in pricing policy, transfer pricing practices, and local taxation rules, as, for example, VAT. Monetary units also require conversion by an appropriate exchange rate. If exchange rates are floating, they can sometimes artificially reflect shifts in capital funds or temporary balance of payments. Procedures or mechanisms that adjust for such factors are thus required.

These difficulties are further compounded by variations in accounting procedures and standards in different countries.[7] Some movement is being made toward harmonizing accounting procedures across countries, but progress is slow. Costs are often not estimated in the same way or include different expense items. Rules for depreciation, or how the book value of assets is estimated, varies from one country to another. In addition, methods of compensation, such as fringe benefits, vary from country to country. Countries also have different rates of social security payments and methods for allocating them. Some adjustment has, therefore, to be made for such factors.

Even seemingly unambiguous measures of performance, such as market share, can be misleading. The definition of the relevant product market may vary from country to country, as, for example, in the case of soft drinks or pharmaceuticals, understating or overstating a firm's share of the market. In examining sales response to various marketing mix elements, differences in distribution channels and their efficiency, or in media availability and effectiveness, need to be taken into consideration. Distribution channels such as supermarkets or discount stores may not exist in some countries, thus impacting margins and distribution costs. Advertising to sales ratios are also affected by the availability of various media and their reach. In some countries, TV advertising may not be available. Media mixes thus vary considerably, rendering strict comparison of advertising to sales ratios of limited value.

Utilizing and Interpreting Data

The lack of comparability in data from different national contexts suggests that a number of difficulties are likely to be experienced in developing efficient procedures for data collection for a global information system. Rules for transforming data so that they are comparable from one context to another have to be devised, and methods for implementing these translation rules need to be established. This can give rise to considerable difficulties, especially across countries, where the market environment differs widely.

Another issue is how data are processed and integrated into the information system. Product market data pose problems, insofar as such data are not always readily available on an ongoing basis, particularly outside the industrialized nations. In the case of internal company data, a key issue is to ensure that procedures are established for obtaining information on a systematic basis without incurring significant time delays. This can be a problem if subsidiaries are required to engage in intensive recording for central headquarters, for purposes not perceived as directly related to their own operations.

The organizational complexity of assessing and comparing performance across multiple country and operating units suggests the desirability of building interactive computerized information systems. Data can be fed directly into the systems by computers or hand-held terminals by local operating units, for example, by sales representatives, delivery or warehouse personnel, or retail outlets, providing up-to-date information on performance for local, national, or regional headquarters. This can be used in tactical decisions and provides invaluable input to production, distribution scheduling, pricing, and promotional decisions, enabling rapid adjustment to changes in market demand and competition. Information can be transmitted to corporate headquarters to guide strategy decisions relating to product lines and market expansion or elimination, and in the design of global logistics.

SUMMARY

Information is an essential ingredient in the development of the firm's strategy for global markets. As a first step, the firm must identify its information needs. The types of information required to make decisions in the global environment will depend heavily on the phase of international involvement. In the first phase—initial market entry—information is needed to identify the most attractive market opportunities. In the second phase—local market expansion—the firm needs information to develop appropriate marketing strategies for each country market. The information needs in the third phase—global rationalization—focus on incorporating internal and external data to allow the firm to integrate and coordinate strategy across diverse markets.

Information requirements for initial entry can be met primarily through the use of secondary data sources. A variety of sources allow an assessment of the business environment in different countries. Information is also available to assess market potential and the cost of conducting marketing operations, as well as market size structure. Once these data have been collected, they can be incorporated into systematic procedures for country market screening and selection.

Information necessary for local market expansion is unlikely to be available from secondary sources and will require primary data collection. The difficulty or relative ease of this task will depend on the local marketing research infrastructure. Steps have also to be taken to ensure data equivalence and comparability across countries, and that data are interpreted correctly.

The final phase—global rationalization—focuses on the integration and linking of internal and external data. This allows the firm to plan, coordinate, and control diverse activities. At the heart of this, is a global information system that allows management to determine optimal allocation of resources worldwide.

REFERENCES

1. See Douglas, Susan P., and C. Samuel Craig (1983) *International Marketing Research*, Englewood Cliffs, NJ: Prentice Hall for a more comprehensive treatment of international research issues.
2. Ricks, David A. (1993) *Blunders in International Business*, Cambridge, MA: Blackwell Publishers.
3. Cavusgil, S. Tamer (1984) "Guidelines for Export Market Research," *Business Horizons*, 28, (November/December), pp. 27–33.
4. Douglas, Susan P., Patrick Le Maire, and Yoram Wind (1972) "Selection of Global Target Markets: A Decision-Theoretic Approach," *Proceedings of the XXIII Esomar Congress*, Cannes, France, pp. 237–51.
5. Lee, J. A. (1966) "Cultural Analysis in Overseas Operations," *Harvard Business Review*, Vol. XLIV, pp. 106–114.
6. Business International (1990) *Managing for Global Excellence*, New York: Business International Corporation.
7. Choi, Frederick D. S., and Gerhard G. Mueller (1992) *International Accounting* (2nd ed.), Englewood Cliffs, NJ: Prentice Hall.

PART II

INITIAL MARKET ENTRY STRATEGIES

CHAPTER 4

FIRST STEPS TO GLOBALIZATION

INTRODUCTION

To expand beyond its domestic market, the firm must modify its corporate mission to include an international component. The new corporate mission must clearly specify the importance of international markets in achieving the firm's long-run goals and objectives. How far, for example, are international markets prime targets for expansion and major sources of corporate growth? Does the firm aim to be a catalyst for cultural change by introducing innovation into foreign markets? Does it aim to be a global market leader, or among the top 10 firms in markets worldwide?

Successful market entry involves an assessment of market potential and developing the capability to make products that are competitive in world markets. Bajaj Auto, the world's second largest manufacturer of motor scooters, is keenly aware of the need to expand sales beyond the Indian market.[1] Even though they doubled exports of scooters in 1992, export sales still account for less than 3 percent of sales. Bajaj began manufacturing scooters through a collaboration with Piaggio (the Italian manufacturer of Vespa motor scooters) in 1960. When the relationship ended in 1971, Bajaj continued to manufacturer scooters that retained much of the original design. Competition between the former partners intensified and Bajaj's forays into Europe and North America were met by lawsuits claiming infringement on the original design. In 1981 Piaggio established LML Vespa in India to gain part of the growing Indian market.

Bajaj also faces competition in the domestic market from Kinetic Honda, a joint venture in which Honda has a 51 percent controlling interest. Kinetic Honda's scooters incorporate some innovative features, including a key start and an automatic transmission. While they have only 10 percent of the Indian market, compared to Bajaj's 70 percent, they export 30 percent of their production. Further, Kinetic Hondas are more popular among rapidly growing segments, the young and women.

Against this backdrop Rahul Bajaj, chairman of Bajaj Auto, indicates that "The vehicle industry is such that any substantial export by an Indian company is not possible without the active cooperation and support of a foreign company in the same field. . ." (p. 59).[1] Finding an international partner would provide Bajaj with access to technology and facilitate exports.

Part of the need to export is prompted by the changing dynamics of the Indian market. Ten years ago, there was a waiting list for Bajaj scooters. Now the company has to market them actively with a 300 person marketing department and by adding 140 dealers to the existing network of 330. Bajaj Auto hopes to produce one million vehicles by 1997. Entering foreign markets and expanding exports well beyond the current 3 percent are critical if it is to meet that goal.

Goals and objectives for international market entry have to be established in order to achieve the overall mission. These goals should determine the desired degree of involvement and level of risk management is willing to assume in international markets. Both are important parameters in determining resource allocation among markets and business functions. These also help guide the firm's investment strategy in international markets.

Another important step prior to international market entry is to define the nature of the firm's business in terms of specific customer benefits, target segments, technology used to provide benefits, and involvement in different stages in the value chain. The value chain consists of the activities in which the firm engages in order to bring goods and services to the market place, ranging from production and sourcing to marketing, distribution and service. Each of the components of the business definition needs to be clearly identified and understood. In addition, their applicability to international markets needs to be carefully assessed. This is a key input in developing a strategic plan to enter international markets and in determining the direction of the firm's strategic thrust in international markets.

Parallel to the definition and assessment of the business is the assessment of the firm's core competencies. First, the firm needs to define where these lie, whether in R & D, production, marketing, or other areas. The firm has to assess whether or not these skills and assets are readily transferable and can be effectively leveraged in international markets in light of potential differences in customer needs and interests, in the nature of competition and of the marketing environment. The firm can thus determine the nature of its competitive edge in international markets, and how far its competitive position may be enhanced through entering international markets, and realizing potential scale economies.

The business definition and the firm's core competencies, together with its goals and objectives, provide the basic parameters for determining the firm's strategic thrust in international markets. This establishes how the firm will compete within the boundaries of its business definition,[2] as well as its investment strategy and priorities relative to international markets. The strategic thrust is the driving force behind the firm's entry into international markets, underlying the choice of which countries to enter, how to enter or operate within these countries, and the timing and sequencing of entry decisions. These relationships are shown in Figure 4-1 and provide the framework for this chapter.

FIGURE 4-1

First steps to globalization.

THE CORPORATE MISSION STATEMENT

Once the firm decides to expand internationally, the corporate mission must assume an international character. The corporate mission statement should indicate the role of international markets in the firm's growth, profitability, and survival, as well as in relation to its strategic operating and human resources philosophy. Desired public image in global markets should also be stated in terms, for example, of perceived responsibilities to potential international customers, employees, governments and other relevant constituencies.

Many firms, especially small and medium-sized businesses, have no corporate mission statements. Even when they do, these often fail to incorporate a geographic or international dimension.[3] However, it is critical that the firm be able to articulate clearly its purpose in entering international markets and the role these markets are to play in its future development, as well as the overall philosophy guiding international operations. The corporate mission statement should provide overall direction and inspiration for the firm's operations.[4] It establishes corporate philosophy and self-image, and defines its responsibilities to relevant constituencies.

Once established, the corporate mission statement provides guidelines for strategic planning for international market expansion. More specifically, it lays out the corporate philosophy which provides direction and specifies the nature of the firm's activities in different countries, product businesses and management functions, and the degree of control exercised by corporate headquarters over these activities.[4] It also indicates the principles underlying relations with company personnel, with external organizations, as well as with other stakeholders in the firm's activities.

International Growth, Profitability, and Market Position

First of all, the mission statement should indicate the position the firm aims to occupy in international markets, and its role as a major source of growth and profitability. In the initial stages of international market entry, this role may be relatively modest, as international markets do not represent major areas of opportunity. Equally, the firm may not aim to become a global leader but be concerned only with a limited number of foreign markets. Blockway, for example, states, "our emphasis is on North American markets, although global opportunities will be explored." Similarly, F.W. Woolworth states that its mission is "to provide value to consumers in North America, Germany and Austria through distinctly individual but complementary retailing businesses."[5]

As the firm gains international experience and competition develops on a global scale, global market position may figure more prominently in the corporate mission statement. The centerpiece of GM's mission statement, for example, is its "commitment to being a global corporation, in every way, in planning, technology, sourcing and manufacturing processes, financing and marketing strategies, and in the products themselves."

Such commitment is more characteristic of a company with substantial experience in international markets than of a novice entering international markets for the first time. Yet with the growing integration of markets worldwide, even a novice may feel compelled to target a global market position to survive in an increasingly competitive global environment. Current advances in communications technology and logistics management, facilitating rapid international expansion, reinforce such ambitions. The new mininationals, such as Loctite, Pall, and Cisco, rely heavily on sophisticated information systems to keep in touch with customer needs and the latest technological trends, as well as to link their operations worldwide.[6]

Corporate Philosophy

Another aspect of the mission statement concerns the company's strategic and operating philosophy, its basic beliefs, and its values: from service to customers, friendliness, and corporate attitudes, to concern with environmental issues, and human and animal rights. Certain industries such as automobiles, packaging, detergents, and chemicals emphasize environmental issues. GM, for example, emphasizes that "it is committed to a cleaner environment throughout the world, and is diligently working to ensure that its plants and products contribute to a better environment everywhere." U.S. emissions standards have been introduced for new models marketed in countries such as Austria, Sweden, Switzerland, Norway, and Finland, where emission standards are less stringent. Similarly, P & G has begun to introduce into the United States phosphate-free detergents and environmentally friendly packaging such as sachet refills for plastic detergent containers, developed in response to environmental pressure in Europe.

In other industries, concern with animal and human rights may be an important aspect of corporate philosophy. For example, a distinctive element of Body Shop's strategy, heavily emphasized in its promotions, is the development of cosmetics products without animal testing. Its packaging also reflects concern about the environment.

A company should apply its corporate philosophy to its operations worldwide, and try to promote those beliefs in countries where there is no, or limited, concern with such issues. In such cases, this often implies application of higher standards than are currently prevalent or required in a given country. For example, Volvo began offering fluorocarbon-free air conditioning in cars it sold in the United States, before it was required to do so by law.

Public Image and Responsibility

Closely linked to the corporate philosophy is concern with public image and perceived responsibilities to customers, employees, governments, and other constituencies in international markets. The specific constituencies emphasized may depend to a large extent on the industry. For example, in the pharmaceutical industry, responsibilities relative to the medical community and potential customers are often of primary concern. Johnson and Johnson emphasizes "our first responsibility is to the doctors, nurses and patients, to mothers and all others, who use our products and services. In meeting their needs, everything we do must be of high quality."

Again, to the extent that the firm's operations are international in scope, such principles are applied throughout all the countries and markets in which the firm is involved. In some cases operation in certain types of international markets may pose specific ethical issues. For example, in marketing to developing nations, problems associated with marketing to poor or illiterate consumers may arise. For example, European, U. S., and Japanese drug companies have long been accused of dubious marketing practices in developing countries. These include selling drugs that have not been approved in industrialized nations, excessive pricing, and convincing developing countries to spend too much on unnecessary or unsuitable drugs rather than clean water and basic sanitation.[7] Coping with these negative perceptions is a major preoccupation for many multinationals. Warner Lambert, for example, has established Tropicare, a health care program in Africa, emphasizing preventive self-help, local management participation, training of local health-care providers and community leaders and conformity to international standards. The program has been highly successful in helping to raise health care standards in several African nations, enhancing the company's image, as well as that of the industry.

Corporations may also be concerned with generating a favorable image with host governments as solid and reliable corporate citizens. They may express their social responsibility and commitment by avoiding accusations of tax evasion through use of transfer pricing mechanisms, investing in local projects rather than repatriating profits, and developing educational and training programs for local employees and other members of the community.

The corporate mission should thus state in broad general principles the philosophy that determines the desired long-run position in international markets and guides the development of strategy to achieve those goals. These principles should be sufficiently flexible to enable the firm to respond to changes in environmental conditions, such as increased ecological concerns, or technological change, while at the same time providing direction for the firm's global strategic thrust.

ESTABLISHING GOALS AND OBJECTIVES

The corporate mission statement lays out a vision of the firm and charts its future course. It outlines the company's overarching philosophy and provides a broad set of general principles to guide the development of strategy. Within this context, specific goals and objectives relative to international market entry need to be established, to provide guidelines for strategic planning and determine the required allocation of resources to international operations.

Establishing goals and objectives prior to international market entry provides direction and focus for the firm's thrust into international markets. Without such goals, choice of countries may be haphazard, based on familiarity with the country, a chance encounter with a potential distributor, or unsolicited orders from overseas. Equally, a creeping commitment to international markets may develop, with lopsided emphasis on certain countries or product markets. Goals should be straightforward and stated in measurable terms so that success or failure can be assessed. They should specify the desired level of involvement, the level of performance to be achieved, and over what time period. Typically, there should be annual objectives and a longer term plan, e.g., 5 years. At the end of each year, goals are reassessed and modified depending on actual performance.

Explicit determination of international markets' role in long-run growth and profit objectives also sets benchmarks for assessing the appropriate allocation of resources and the development of an investment strategy for international operations. Commitment of resources such as capital, and management time and effort to international operations, should be commensurate with their projected role in achieving long-run objectives. Equally, resources need to be devoted to investigating and assessing international opportunities, as well as setting up international operations and investment strategy and developing strategic plans for international markets so as to achieve targeted objectives.

In establishing goals and objectives for initial entry into international markets, two aspects are of particular importance: (1) the desired degree of involvement in international markets, and (2) the level of risk management is willing to assume. The degree of involvement depends on the role of international markets in the firm's long run growth and expansion. The level of risk, on the other hand, influences investment strategies and priorities for resource allocation, such as choice of target countries, the mode of entry or operation, and the timing of market entry.

Degree of Involvement in International Markets

A key parameter in developing plans for international market entry is the desired degree of involvement in, and commitment to, international markets. Of particular significance are the extent to which the firm views international markets as a prime source of future growth and profits, and the rate and aggressiveness with which the company plans to enter international markets.

As noted earlier, interest and commitment to international markets may vary from one company to another. Some companies have limited commitment to international markets, viewing them primarily as a means to dispose of surplus production, or to counterbalance fluctuations in the domestic market. Others view international markets as the key to success, and to securing a strong competitive position. Consequently, commitment to international markets is an important driver of the firm's strategy.

The position of a firm on this spectrum can vary within the same industry. Chrysler, one-fifth the size of GM, for example, has limited its involvement in overseas markets and focused on the North American market.[8] It sold its foreign operations in the 1970s to ease a cash crisis. Fast-growing foreign markets are supplied primarily from North America, either with complete cars or knocked-down kits. GM and Ford, on the other hand, are heavily involved in international markets and compete on a global scale. How involved a company becomes in international markets depends on a number of factors, including individual firm characteristics such as company size and availability of resources to develop international markets, management attitudes and entrepreneurship, and industry characteristics such as the structure of competition and relative attractiveness of domestic vs. foreign market conditions (see Figure 4-2).

LACK OF FAMILIARITY WITH INTERNATIONAL MARKETS

Especially in the initial stages of market entry, a company may prefer to limit international involvement. Often managers perceive foreign markets as entailing greater risk and uncertainty due to lack of familiarity with customer demand

FIGURE 4-2

Factors determining involvement in international markets.

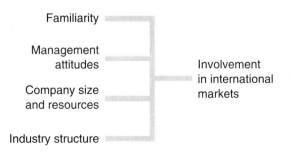

and characteristics, the organizational environment, trade regulation, tariffs, and quotas, as well as cultural and communication differences in foreign markets. Control and coordination problems may also arise due to the physical and psychic distances involved.

MANAGEMENT ATTITUDES

Management attitudes are key factors underlying commitment to international markets.[9] Where management is relatively conservative and concerned with stability, international objectives are often modest. On the other hand, where management is dynamic and aggressive about entering international markets, company objectives will be considerably more ambitious. Such attitudes are in turn conditioned by factors such as the international orientation and interests of top management, its confidence in the firm's competitive advantage in international markets, and the perceived attractiveness of international market opportunities.[9,10]

COMPANY SIZE AND RESOURCES

Company size and available resources such as capital and management skills may also influence objectives relative to international market entry. Company size determines to a large extent the ability to raise capital to expand internationally and to set up operations in other countries. Similarly, acquisition of management skills, and expertise in international operations, may be more readily accessible by large corporations. Advances in information technology and logistics management, as well as the development of an infrastructure of agencies and services specialized in international operations, have, as noted earlier, considerably facilitated international expansion even by small and medium sized companies.

INDUSTRY STRUCTURE

Industry characteristics and conditions also help mold international market objectives. In situations where the domestic market has matured, aggressive international expansion may provide the only route to enhanced growth and profitability. Competitive structure, and the degree of market integration, also play an important role in conditioning involvement in international markets. Where an industry is characterized by a small number of global competitors and markets are integrated worldwide, a firm may have little choice but to expand aggressively in international markets if it is to survive. On the other hand, where markets are fragmented and vary considerably from one country to another, the firm has greater flexibility in choosing the degree of involvement. For example, it might decide to enter a limited number of countries or geographic areas, or gradually roll out into international markets.

Resource Allocation

Determining the degree of involvement and commitment to international markets provides guidelines for establishing the amount of management time and effort and other resources, that should be devoted to developing international operations. Where a proactive orientation to international markets is adopted, top management must be involved in strategic planning for international markets to ensure commitment to this expansion. Otherwise, the domestic market may remain the key priority and focus of attention. Management expertise in handling international market operations and knowledge of specific regions or country markets is essential if mistakes are to be avoided. Where commitment is limited, external services such as export management firms or international trading companies provide an alternative means of managing international market entry.

Commitment of financial resources to planning international market entry and establishing operations in foreign markets is also necessary. Prior to entry into international markets, resources need to be allocated to investigate international marketing opportunities, to select which countries to enter and to determine how to enter these markets. It is important to adopt a long-run perspective, and to view expenditure for information on international markets as an investment, rather than expecting an immediate payoff. Entering into international markets without collecting adequate information to assess market potential or develop appropriate marketing strategies can result in errors that can be extremely costly to rectify.

A major U.S. manufacturer of sun lotion entered the Brazilian market without conducting any prior research into consumer shopping behavior and preferences. Following the same strategy used in the U.S. market, the product was distributed through supermarkets. However, Brazilians lacked confidence that a toiletry product marketed through such a channel would be of good quality, and preferred the reassurance provided by a competing brand sold through local pharmacies. As a result, the U.S. company suffered a major setback and had to withdraw its brand from the market, losing the opportunity to exploit the growing demand potential in Brazil.

Resources may also be needed to establish production facilities, or a marketing and sales organization specifically geared to international markets. In some instances, surplus production or management capacity provides the motivation for entering international markets. Supplying foreign markets can help to counterbalance seasonal or other types of demand fluctuations. For example, sales of agricultural machinery in Australia complement those in the United States, since the two countries' growing seasons differ. In other cases, expansion of domestic facilities, or establishment of a foreign production base, sales office, or marketing organization, may be needed. Such expansion requires a major commitment of resources and a long-term perspective. While establishing marketing operations in other countries may initially seem costly, it helps ensure more effective control of those activities and improved promotional effort as compared with the use of import/export agents or distributors. It is thus important to view this as a necessary investment to build an effective international marketing organization, rather than as simply a short-run expense.

Level of Risk

Closely linked to the degree of involvement or commitment to international markets is the level of risk the firm is willing to assume. Risk is a factor in the choice of country or geographic area to enter, as well as a determinant of the mode of entry or operation in foreign markets. The firm contemplating entry into international markets faces many different types of risks. For the sake of simplicity, the four major categories of risk identified by Ghoshal[11] are considered here; namely, macroenvironmental risks, government policy risks, competitive risks, and operational risks. *Macroenvironmental* risks arise from cataclysmic events such as war, as well as unstable political or economic conditions, over which the firm has no control. *Policy* risks arise from decisions by governments, such as tariffs, product regulation, and restrictions on foreign investment which the firm can control or influence to some extent. *Competitive risks* arise from the actions of competitors in domestic and international markets, such as entering a market, launching new products, attacking, or defending a position. *Operational risks* are those associated with actions taken by the firm in international markets, such as introducing products or services into countries where there is no established market, or they appear to run counter to existing behavioral life-style patterns.

These various types of risk impact on the decision whether and how to enter a given country or market (as shown in Figure 4-3). Once the firm has determined how much risk it is willing to accept, and how to manage different levels and types of risk, it is ready to proceed.

MACROENVIRONMENTAL RISKS

The first type of risk relates to the impact of macroenvironmental conditions on the conduct of business in a country or region. These risks range from specific

FIGURE 4-3

Components of risk.

events such as war, insurrection, and earthquakes, which interrupt the conduct of business and threaten life, physical plant, and equipment, to unstable economic and financial conditions, which have a negative impact on business and profitability.

Cataclysmic events can wipe out assets or halt the conduct of business. The 1991 Gulf War, for example, halted business in Iraq and Kuwait, at a cost to U.S. firms estimated to be in the millions of dollars. Business has no control, and frequently cannot predict cataclysmic events. Failure to have adequate contingency plans can, however, cost the firm dearly in terms of lost production, sabotage, canceled contracts, nationalized assets, defaulted loans, and civil litigation.

Political instability is another source of risk; for example, the breakup of the former Soviet Union and the resulting political turmoil drastically changed the favorableness of the business climate and resulted in the abandonment of the American Trade Consortium, a project set up by five U.S. companies to invest between $5 and $10 billion in the U.S.S.R.[12] Despite the risks, a number of companies large and small are investing in Russia and making record profits.[13] Hewlett-Packard increased sales 400% in 1993. Motorola is selling cellular phones, while Hyundai has acquired timber rights in Eastern Russia and Estee Lauder is setting up cosmetic sales rooms from Moscow to Siberia.

Unstable economic and financial conditions constitute another potential source of risk. Instability may stem from factors such as the absence of a well-developed and diversified industrial base or dependence on a single industry. In countries such as India and Egypt, lack of a well-developed industrial base, coupled with turbulent social conditions, generates an uncertain and unstable economic environment. In other nations, such as Colombia and Venezuela, the economy is heavily dependent on a single commodity, such as coffee or oil. When prices of the commodity are depressed in world markets, severe economic problems arise, including lack of foreign exchange. A sizeable external debt, and high rates of inflation, also generate adverse economic and financial conditions. In many Latin-American countries, such as Bolivia and Brazil, high rates of inflation have created highly unstable and volatile business conditions influencing prices, wage rates, and interest rates.

While unstable market conditions are beyond the control of the firm, they are typically more readily predictable than cataclysmic events. Consequently, assessment of such risks should play a key role in the firm's strategic planning, influencing decisions such as whether to enter a country, where to locate production or other facilities, and how to manage contracts or other relations with companies in other countries.

POLICY RISKS

A second type of risk concerns policy decisions by governments, whether domestic or foreign, relating to international trade and business operations. These decisions include restrictions on trade with specific countries or certain types of products and services, as well as restrictions placed by host governments on foreign direct investment, entry of foreign goods, or repatriation of profits.

Dramatic changes in government have a negative impact on the business environment. Depending on their political philosophy and campaign platforms, governments can adopt differing policies with regard to issues such as privatization of state-owned enterprise, regulation of industry, taxation, and fiscal policy. Such policies dramatically affect the conditions for doing business and the ease of raising capital.

For political or other reasons, domestic governments can place restrictions on trade and investment in certain countries. For example, restrictions on trade by U.S. companies with Vietnam and sanctions on trade with South Africa have only recently been lifted. A number of U.S. companies including Pepsi had, however, already developed mechanisms for selling in the Vietnamese market.[14]

Fear of domination by foreign interests, nationalist sentiments, or desire to retain control over economic growth can result in restrictions on foreign direct investment and ownership. For example, India has only recently permitted majority investment by foreign companies, while China also favors joint ventures rather than wholly owned foreign direct investment. Xerox, for example, has set up a joint venture in Shanghai to sell desk top copiers, while Wing Merrill a U.S. energy company, has set up a consortium to build a giant power plant in Henan in Northern China, and Compaq has a joint venture with Beijing Stone, a leading Chinese competitor.[15] Restrictions placed on repatriation of profits, the employment of expatriates, and requirements to train local nationals also limit a firm's ability to leverage resources and control operations. Concern to protect domestic industry and to develop or protect a favorable trade balance may result in the erection of trade barriers such as tariffs and quotas, as well as differential rates or requirements as to local content.

Such factors may significantly impact a firm's ability to compete in a given market, as well as artificially distorting global logistics. Assessment of such risks, and in particular the likelihood of their change, is thus an important element in developing an investment strategy for international markets.

COMPETITIVE RISKS

A third type of risk arises from the actions of competitors in international markets, both those in response to the firm's own actions and those of a proactive nature. These may range from maintaining the status quo to preemptive moves into undeveloped markets, launching aggressive price wars or promotional campaigns. For example, Kelloggs responded aggressively to the entry of Cereal Partners (a joint venture of General Mills and Nestlé) into the international cereals market, by launching new brands directly positioned to counter those of Cereal Partners.

Foreign markets that appear to one firm to offer attractive opportunities are likely to be perceived as attractive by other domestic and foreign competitors. While such risks also occur in domestic markets, they are further heightened in international markets by the high costs associated with market entry, and increased difficulties of monitoring and anticipating likely actions by foreign competitors.

Competitors may make preemptive moves and steal a march on other firms by entering a foreign market early, building up customer franchise and loyalty, and tying up distribution channels. The firm may thus experience considerable difficulty in entering the market, and have to rely on second-tier distributors with less extensive or effective distribution networks and capabilities. Preemptive strategies are, however, vulnerable to subsequent entry by competitors who take advantage of the first mover's market development efforts, significantly reducing its profits. Such risks may be especially high for technologically sophisticated products, where competitors may be able to leapfrog to the next generation of technology.

Threat of entry by foreign competition into a firm's domestic market poses yet another type of risk. Foreign competition may have superior products or technology, or be able to realize significant economies of scale through geographic market expansion. As a result of these combined advantages they are able to put pressure on prices and pose a significant competitive threat.

In entering a foreign market, a firm may be faced with a variety of competitors, who pose different threats. Local competitors may benefit from lower overhead costs and operational costs as well as greater production and operational flexibility. Hence they may provide aggressive price competition or cherrypick profitable market segments. Multinational competitors, on the other hand, may benefit from flexibility in shifting resources and their competitive thrust from one market to another. Consequently, they may be able to shift production and sourcing from one location to another, to take advantage of changing factor costs and exchange rates. Further, they may use profits in protected markets to mount aggressive attacks against competitors in other markets.

OPERATIONAL RISKS

Another type of risk to be considered, specific to international markets, is that associated with operating in a new and different sociocultural environment. In many instances, the most attractive payoffs in international markets arise from introducing products and ideas new to a country or culture. In cases where these products represent radical departures from existing life-styles, it involves introducing cultural change. For example, Kelloggs has dramatically changed breakfast habits around the world by introducing consumption of cereal for breakfast in numerous countries. Similarly, De Beers has successfully introduced the practice of giving diamonds as an engagement ring in countries such as Japan and Thailand.

Such strategies, nonetheless, entail a number of risks insofar as heavy marketing and promotional expenditures are necessary to launch such products and services, and to inform potential customers of their availability, their benefits, and how and when to use them. A new distribution infrastructure often has to be established, as in introducing contraceptives or baby formula in developing countries. Substantial promotional efforts will also be needed to convince distributors of the product's viability, and ultimately to stock it.

However, customers may be reluctant to change existing behavior patterns, especially if those patterns are deeply ingrained or part of established cultural modes. Distributors may also be reluctant to take on products whose success is unproven. In Japan, for example, foreign companies frequently need to undertake heavy advertising campaigns well in advance of a new product launch in order to convince distributors to stock the product, rather than to develop customer awareness.

In addition to the risk of market failure, international market entry also entails risks associated with inadequate resources to achieve desired objectives. In particular, lack of management skilled in handling international operations, or with knowledge of specific markets or countries, can pose a problem, just as lack of adequate financial resources can.

RISK MANAGEMENT AND ASSESSMENT

In assessing the various types of risks, their interaction and impact on strategy and in particular, entry decisions need to be considered. The impact of various types of risks is not necessarily cumulative. In some instances, the different types of risk may be compensatory. Competitive risks, for example, may be lower in countries where macroenvironmental risks are higher. Furthermore, risks change over time though at varying rates. Changes in exchange rates or wage rates can, for example, erode the competitiveness of a given production location or sourcing strategy, or affect the internationalization strategy of a competitor.

The extent to which a firm can control or manage the various types of risk varies. As noted earlier, macroenvironmental and policy risks are largely beyond the control of the firm.[11] Consequently, a firm has to determine an acceptable level of risk and how far such risks may be compensated for by attractive market opportunities. A firm can to some degree manage competitive and operational risks through its own strategies. But management still has to determine the extent to which it is willing to pursue an aggressive, proactive, and hence high-risk, strategy in the hope of increased gains. Determination of attitudes toward risk is thus an important element conditioning, not only country choice and mode of entry decisions, but also allocation of resources to international markets and strategy formulation.

DEFINING THE BUSINESS

The third step in establishing the basic parameters to guide the development of international marketing strategy is to establish the business definition. Management entering international markets for the first time is typically concerned with finding additional markets in other countries for the firm's current range of products and services. This minimizes the costs of product adaptation as well as the need for extensive changes in marketing strategy. It is, however, important to assess whether and how far the existing business definition is appropriate to other countries. In some instances, existing products and services may only find a relatively limited audience in other countries. Consequently, management needs to consider changes if it wishes to broaden the potential market base. In other markets, the business definition may not be well adapted to the market environment, and may require modification in response to different factor conditions, technology, or competition.

Following the marketing concept, rather than defining a business in terms of a product category such as an SIC code, a business should be defined in terms of customer needs and benefits. Such a definition provides a broader perspective of the business, its functions, and market context, as well as identification of potential competing and substitute products. Application of a strategic approach further extends this concept to include, not only customer benefits and target segments, but also the technology used to provide desired benefits, and participation in different stages in the value chain.[2]

The customer *functions* comprise the benefits to be provided. Following the marketing concept, customers are viewed as seeking benefits that are supplied by products and services rather than the products themselves. For example, the benefits provided by a fast food outlet include speed of service, reliable quality standards, nutrition, and refreshment.

The customer *segment* dimension determines the specific customer segment targeted. Makita and Ryobi, for example, target small hand-powered tools to the "do it yourself" amateur segment, as well as a "professional" segment consisting of small mechanical and repair businesses such as plumbers, carpenters, electricians, and locksmiths. Identification of desired customer benefits and target segments determines the positioning of products and services and thus provides key parameters for establishing the marketing plan and the marketing mix.

Technologies consist of alternative ways in which customer benefits and functions are satisfied. Several technologies may provide the same function or fulfill the same need. Thus, for example, X-ray machines may be computerized and use cathode rays or conventional technology. The stages in the value chain relate to a firm's choice with regard to participation in different stages from raw material extraction to service and delivery. Thus, while customer benefits and segments relate to demand aspects, technology and the value chain relate to how the firm meets demand. In particular, they establish sourcing requirements, as well as base lines for the organization of other business functions such as production, financing, management, and external relations with other organizations.

Traditional approaches to business definition often view international markets as an aspect of market segmentation.[16] A given country or geographic area is viewed as a specific or distinct target. A company can limit its activities to specific geographic areas, regions, or national markets due to constraints such as freight costs and tariff barriers. The implicit assumption is that relevant aspects of other dimensions, i.e., functions, technologies, and participation in the value-added system (though not necessarily the firm's choice among these alternatives), will be consistent across geographic segments.

Management should question this assumption when extending the scope of the business internationally. Extension of the scope of the business across national boundaries does require reassessment of the business definition. The diversity of conditions in different countries implies that customer functions, relevant segments, and alternative technologies, as well as the parameters influencing participation in the value-added system, can vary substantially from one part of the world to another (see Figure 4-4).

Customer Benefits

Customers in foreign markets may seek different product benefits due to differences in income, consumption patterns and preferences, value systems, or other factors. For example, short-distance transportation needs may be met in countries such as China or Holland by bicycles, in Thailand and the Philippines by motorbikes, and in Taiwan by small, fuel-efficient automobiles. Consequently, in such countries the functional and performance characteristics of bikes and motorbikes are emphasized. In the United States and many industrialized western countries, bicycles and motorbikes are predominantly used for sports and recreational activities. Hence, characteristics such as appearance, speed, and accessories are more crucial. Similarly, in the case of household cleansing products, German housewives prefer chlorine- and ammonia-based products with no fragrance. In other markets, pine or lemon fragrances are perceived to add freshness to cleansing properties. Attention to such factors is important both in country and market selection decisions, as well as in assessing how far products or positioning needs to be adapted to local markets.

FIGURE 4-4

Degree to which home market definition can be used in other markets.

Home market business definition	Country market business definition				
	Country 1	Country 2	Country 3	Country 4	Country N
Customer benefits	S[a]	D	D	D	
Segment	S	S	S	D	
Technology	S	S	S	D	
Value chain	S	S	S	D	

a

S indicates that the component of business definition is the same
D indicates that the component of business definition must be modified

Note: In country 1, the components of the value chain are the same suggesting that a similar strategy could be pursued. In country 4, all components are different suggesting the need for adaptation in entering this market.

Customer Segments

The business definition also encompasses the customer segments targeted. For example, a personal computer business might target the educational segment, the business segment, or the home segment. Similarly, a cosmetic business might target male consumers, female consumers, teenagers with acne problems, older women with aging-skin problems, contact lens wearers, or any combination of these segments.

In international markets, the firm must consider whether similar segments defined in terms of demographic or economic characteristics, or similar interests, can be identified. In some cases, similar segments with similar needs and interests can be identified in different countries or geographic areas, though the size or relative significance of the segment varies from one country to another. For example, in the cosmetics market, a segment of affluent women aged 40 or over, interested in antiwrinkle or skin-rejuvenating products, may be identified in many countries throughout the world. Similarly, a segment of young consumers interested in hard rock videos, CDs, and tapes may be found in countries, and notably in major cities, throughout the world.

In other instances, segmentation may differ from country to country. In some countries, customer needs and interests are relatively homogenous, and markets may not be sufficiently large to make segmentation economic. For example, in hair coloring, the same product line may be targeted to women of all ages, and a distinct male segment may not be identifiable. In other cases, certain segments, such as eye makeup targeted to contact lens wearers, may exist only in a limited number of countries.

Sometimes, customer demand, taste preference, and other characteristics differ significantly from country to country or one geographic area to another, resulting in segments defined primarily on a geographic basis. In the case of food, for example, taste preferences differ markedly from one country and region to another. Consequently, the market for products such as frozen main dishes or microwaveable soups is often segmented on a country-by-country or regional basis. Similarly, the market for kitchen appliances such as stoves or refrigerators might be segmented on a country basis, since consumer habits vary from one region to another in terms of stove top vs. oven cooking or use of electricity vs. gas.

Technology

The third component of the business definition concerns the technology used to deliver customer benefits. Different technologies may be used to satisfy customer needs or generate products or services. For example, next day delivery may be achieved through use of facsimile machines or overnight air delivery. Detergents come in various forms, including powder, liquid, ultraconcentrates, and time-release capsules.

In international markets, differences in factor conditions, the technological infrastructure, and also the technological sophistication of end-users from one country to another, often necessitate use of different technologies and impact the economics of alternative technologies. In countries where labor costs are low, labor-intensive technologies are likely to be preferred over capital-intensive technologies. For example, in developing countries, crops are picked by hand rather than by using machinery. Similarly, lack of electrical current or a well-developed computer infrastructure may result in the use of hand-cranked sales registers and stock taking by sales personnel rather than use of scanner, electronic registers, and computerized inventory systems in wholesale and retail outlets. Low levels of literacy, education, and technological sophistication may also hamper utilization of technologically complex machinery and equipment. Consequently, relatively simple, "user friendly" equipment requiring little maintenance will be required.

The technology used will also need to be compatible with the existing infrastructure. For example, differences in the telecommunications infrastructure in various countries require the use of equipment and technology compatible with that infrastructure. For example, switching technology and the development of cellular communications infrastructure varies from one country to another, requiring product and systems adaptation.

Value Chain

The fourth and final component of the business definition consists of participation at different stages in the value chain. Following Porter,[17] a number of stages can be identified in the sequence of activities performed in bringing a product or service from its inception to distribution in the marketplace. The process starts with R&D activities involved in the design of a product or service. Once the product or service is brought into full-scale production, sourcing operations or "inbound" logistics are required to bring supplies and components to the production site, where production operations take place. These stages are considered "upstream activities." "Downstream activities" occur subsequent to production, and include physical distribution of goods and services to the market, marketing and sales promotion activities, and point of sale or postservice activities. This sequence is shown schematically in Figure 4-5.

An important aspect of the business definition is to determine the level of participation in each of the stages of the value chain. Depending on the industry, each stage will entail commitment of resources and specific skills. For example, R&D costs in the pharmaceutical industry are astronomical. Merck estimates that, on average, it costs $359 million over 10 years to bring a new drug to market.[18] Similarly, distribution of consumer packaged goods often entails extensive distribution, advertising, and sales promotion costs. Different stages also require different types of expertise and management skills and other resources. Upstream activities require tight cost controls, logistical coordination, and effective operations management. Downstream activities, and especially marketing and promotional activities, rely more heavily on interpersonal

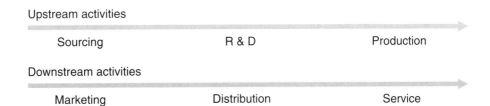

FIGURE 4-5

Value chain.

and creative skills. Decisions relating to participation in the value chain determine the level of investment required, the type of resources, and their allocation among different stages. Such decisions are conditioned by the firm's size and its current assets and other resources, as well as its core competence or distinctive competitive advantage.

Firms in a given industry differ in the extent to which they choose to be involved in different stages in the value chain. Braun, for example, contracts out production of its appliances to other firms. Its expertise lies primarily in the design of distinctively styled small household appliances, and it also prefers to retain control of the marketing and distribution of products marketed under its brand name. Conversely, companies producing for private label often focus on production efficiency, while marketing and promotion are handled by the retailer. The South Korean automobile and consumer electronics companies, such as Hyundai, Kia, Samsung, and Lucky Goldstar, have typically followed this type of strategy in trying to break into U.S., European, and Japanese markets. Initially, they produced components for large U.S. manufacturers or for private label. More recently, however, they have shifted to developing their own brands, and trying to establish a strong quality image in international markets.

Decisions with regard to participation in the value chain are especially crucial, where they affect the level of investment and risk entailed in entering international markets. Establishment of production, warehousing or distribution facilities, or sales offices in other countries is likely to entail significant outlays in plant and equipment and increases risk. Hiring and management of staff to run foreign sales operations also entail substantial costs. Licensing, and contracting out of production, or distribution through export or import agents, significantly reduces overhead but at the same time limits the ability to control distribution of the product and service, as well as information and contact with markets in other countries.

In some instances, market potential in other countries is not sufficiently large to warrant the establishment of production facilities or a marketing organization. Consequently, if a firm possesses a patented technology, trademark, or brand name, it can license production and distribution rights to another firm for a specific foreign market. Alternatively, while retaining control over production, the firm can use export management companies or export agents, or piggyback on the distribution system of another firm in order to obtain access to international markets. Whirlpool, for example, successfully piggybacked its products on Sony's distribution system to gain access to the Japanese market.

In some cases, companies contract out production or source products from local companies in foreign markets while retaining control over distribution. This enables them to avoid production overhead and labor problems, while at the same time leveraging brand image and marketing expertise internationally. For example, P&G initially subcontracted production of detergent products to local manufacturers in Italy in order to avoid potential labor problems, given the existence of strong labor unions with hostile attitudes toward U.S. management.

Similarly, some companies may prefer to perform service operations themselves to ensure that service standards are maintained. International Harvester, for example, had to set up training programs for mechanics in Turkey to ensure that their tractors and other farm equipment were properly serviced. Sometimes, companies decide to perform in-house functions such as service and maintenance, which are normally left to external organizations. Either appropriate organizations are not available, or quality standards are inadequate. Others find that contracting local service companies or distributors to perform maintenance and service activities is more efficient. IBM, for example, found that, in Southeast Asia, local distributors were able to service computers more efficiently than their own subsidiaries.

In brief, management should assess the relevance and appropriateness of the domestic market business definition to international markets. In some instances, it is feasible to extend the domestic definition directly to international markets, thus expanding the geographic scope of operations. In other cases, it is preferable to change or adapt the definition to differences in market conditions in international markets. A firm may thus decide to broaden or narrow the scope of its activities, given these conditions and the desired degree of involvement, as well as the nature of the competition in international markets.

CORE COMPETENCE

The second important parameter in determining the firm's strategic thrust in international markets is its core competence: the specific skills and assets that underlie the firm's distinctive competitive advantage relative to other firms, and that provide the motor for strategy development. The firm's core competence should provide the basis for defining the strategic architecture of the firm, as management determines how to apply core competencies and skills to different products and functional areas.

A well-defined core competence should possess three key characteristics: (1) it should provide access to a variety of markets (2) it should provide a contribution to perceived customer benefits and (3) it should be difficult to imitate. Core competencies that have application in a variety of areas are preferable, since they provide a broad base for expansion and can be widely leveraged. Cargill, a leading international merchandiser of commodities, for example, leverages its core competencies in handling bulk commodities, transportation, food processing, and financial risk management across a wide range of commodities—producing fertilizer, flour, corn syrup, and salt; processing steel; fabricating wire products; importing shrimp; and providing financial, trading, and brokerage services.[19] Competence in display systems enables a company to participate in such diverse businesses as calculators, miniature T.V. sets, and monitors for laptop computers.[20] Competencies in mass-merchandising techniques and other downstream activities can also be applied across a broad range of products.

Core competencies should also add to customer benefits. Thus, for example, Sony's competence in miniaturization enabled it to pioneer highly successful consumer products such as the Walkman, the Watchman, and the Discman. Similarly, Casio's competence in display screens and precision casing has generated wafer-thin card calculators, miniature T.V. sets, and watches to suit consumer desire for small, clearly visible portable products.

A core competence should also be difficult to imitate, so that it will provide the company with a sustainable competitive advantage. This is probably the most difficult criterion to satisfy but is especially crucial in international markets. If a core competence is easily imitable by a local competitor, who benefits from preferential treatment by government bodies, local customers, and other organizations, as well as lower overheads and operating costs, it may be difficult for a firm to sustain its advantage in international markets. For example, after launching a computerized x-ray machine in the hospital equipment market, GE was rapidly undercut by Toshiba with a similar machine equipped with additional features.

Building strategy based on the firm's core competencies provides a solid foundation and a long-run vision for future growth. While a competitive lineup of products may provide short-run profits, their success may be short-lived, as customer tastes evolve or competition enters the market. Emphasis on core competencies, on the other hand, allows for continuous generation of new ideas and strategic options designed to outmaneuver competitor initiatives. Core competencies are grounded in the specific skills or expertise possessed by a firm in a given area or stage of the value chain. Here, an important consideration is the extent to which assets are readily transferable to foreign markets or leveragable internationally (see Figure 4-6).

Skills in upstream areas such as product R & D, process technology, or pro-

FIGURE 4-6

Opportunities to leverage core competencies.

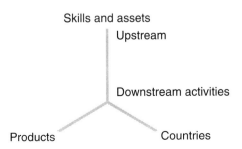

duction are often more readily leveragable than skills in downstream activities such as marketing, distribution, or service. For example, P & G leverages the expertise of its Japanese R & D unit in surfactant technology to develop detergent products for other parts of the world. Similarly, Japanese automobile manufacturers such as Toyota and Mazda have been able to transfer their production management skills to other countries such as the United States and the U.K.

Marketing and distribution skills are typically less readily transferable and may require some degree of adaptation to differences in local environmental conditions, customer tastes, and preferences. P&G, however, has effectively been able to transfer their mass merchandising and brand management skills throughout the world. Similarly, Avon utilizes door-to-door marketing by salesladies in countries as diverse as Germany, Japan, and Thailand.

In some instances, however, differences in the nature of the marketing environment and resource conditions may make it difficult to transfer a firm's skills or core competence to foreign markets. For example, while P&G and Avon have been able to transfer their merchandising skills effectively to other countries, Radio Shack was unsuccessful in attempting to transfer its concept of stores selling private label merchandise to Europe. European customers relied heavily on salesperson's advice in making their decisions and preferred to purchase national brands.

Similarly, firms may find that the customer benefits generated by their core competence do not match specific customer requirements in other countries. For example, where a core competence is grounded in highly sophisticated technology, it may not be transferable to markets in developing countries. Thus, for example technically complex, labor-saving agricultural machinery may not find a market in developing countries, where labor costs are low and agricultural laborers do not have the necessary skills to operate and maintain it effectively. Similarly, UPS's efficiency in distribution system management is unlikely to be profitable in countries where there is little or no interest in rapid delivery.

Equally, a firm's core competence may not provide a competitive advantage in foreign markets due to differences in the nature of competition and their competitive offerings. For example, in countries where the postal system is highly efficient, such as Japan, UPS may not find its core competence able to generate a significant competitive advantage. Similarly, a local competitor with a similar core competence may already have established a strong position in the local market, which may be difficult to challenge. For example, McDonalds in Bombay, India, will meet competition from local businesses that deliver individual home-cooked meals to offices by bicycle, as well as local restaurants selling veggie burgers.

In essence, in entering international markets, a firm needs to assess whether and how its core competence in its domestic market can be effectively transferred to other countries, and if so, to which countries? In some instances, this is directly transferable, as, for example, where product offerings find a market in other countries or where skills in a particular area such as production or R&D can be utilized to develop products adapted to local customer preferences and market conditions. In other cases, some adaptation may be required, as in the case of marketing and distribution skills. For example, in Japan, foreign firms have to learn how to establish relations with distributors at both the wholesale and retail level, and furthermore, how to gain their trust and confidence.

Some skills and assets generate additional value or benefit from being utilized across international boundaries. For example, a corporate or brand image could be enhanced through increased visibility in international markets. Brand names, such as Coke, Pepsi, and Levi, have gained significantly in value from their international exposure. Similarly, a company may be able to achieve greater economies of scale through international expansion.

The core competence reflects the firm's ability to perform certain activities better than its competitors and gain a competitive advantage. The core competence(s), along with the firm's goals for international expansion, form its strategic thrust. It may be useful to think of the core competence as the "ability" component of the strategic thrust, while the firm's goals are the "resolve" to compete in international markets.

STRATEGIC THRUST

The firm's strategic thrust provides focus and direction to the firm's efforts. It indicates how to orchestrate its core competence into actions and channel its efforts along paths that move the firm in the desired direction. It defines the arena or terrain in which the firm seeks to compete, and hence the foes it hopes to conquer. It establishes strategic priorities and determines the investment in financial, physical, and management resources required to achieve desired goals and objectives.

The strategic thrust also determines the aggressiveness of the firm's expansion into international markets and thus the level of investment required to achieve desired objectives and the commitment of resources to international markets. At the same time, it establishes priorities for the allocation of those resources across functions, geographic areas, and product businesses.

It also defines the nature of the firm's competitive posture in international markets. A firm may either adopt a proactive stance relative to international markets, entering markets ahead of other competitors, or alternatively wait until markets have been developed by market leaders and then enter. Equally, a firm may adopt an aggressive posture, directly confronting major competitors in key international markets, or alternatively seek to avoid competition by entering neutral markets.

Competitive posture not only influences the specific decisions with regard to country selection or market choice, but also interacts with investment strategy. A proactive stance will, for example, require substantial investment in developing awareness and promoting demand, and also establishing distribution channels. Furthermore, a lengthy time horizon for planning will be required before this investment pays off. Similarly, confrontational strategies require substantial resources to mount an effective attack and to sustain that position against retaliatory moves by competition.

Geographic expansion goals, together with the investment strategy and competitive posture defined by the firm's strategic thrust, provide the parameters for developing strategy for initial international market entry. Here, the key decisions center on the choice of countries to enter, the mode of operation or entry into these countries, and the timing and sequencing of entry. While these are often viewed as distinct and separate decisions, they are, nonetheless, highly interrelated. Decisions with regard to the number and size of countries to enter, will, for example, be affected by decisions relating to the selected mode of operation as also the timing of entry. In entering small markets, a firm may, for example, decide to adopt entry modes that entail limited involvement, such as licensing. This will enable rapid entry of a larger number of markets. Similarly, risks of entry into politically hostile or economically volatile markets may be shared through joint ventures or other forms of collaborative agreements. Rapid entry into a larger number of markets to establish a strong competitive position may also be reinforced through the development of strategic alliances.

SUMMARY

The most important step in entering global markets is the first. Well-planned and well-executed forays into international markets provide the basis for continued expansion. Conversely, haphazard and ill-conceived market entry is not only doomed to failure but deters the firm from venturing into international markets again. Success in international markets must be based on a thorough understanding of the markets being entered and a clear vision of how the international dimension fits into the firm's overall corporate mission. Once the commitment to international markets has been made and incorporated into the firm's corporate mission, the firm must follow a step-by-step process, beginning with the establishment of goals and objectives.

First, the firm must decide on the degree of involvement in international markets and the resources it is willing to commit to the international arena. Both these decisions are tempered by the level of risk the firm is willing to accept. Perhaps the most critical component of the firm's decision to enter international markets is its business definition. The firm must first fully understand its current domestic business in terms of customer benefits, customer segments, the technology employed, and participation in various stages in the value chain. This understanding can then be translated into business definitions appropriate to the different markets the firm is planning to enter. Sometimes, the business will be identical. However, often the firm enters what amounts to a different business in terms of customer benefits, segments, technology, or stages of the value chain.

Once these steps have been taken, the firm needs to examine how its core competence can be leveraged effectively in international markets. The core competence forms the basis for determining its strategic thrust and its blueprint for success in international markets. While following these steps will not guarantee success in international markets, failure to do so presages disaster.

REFERENCES

1. "Hamara Baja," (1993) *Business India* , October 11–24, pp. 58–64.
2. Day, George S. (1990) *Marketing Driven Strategy*, New York: The Free Press.
3. Pearce, John A., and Fred David, (1987) "Corporate Mission Statements: The Bottom Line," *Academy of Management Executive*, 1, (2) pp. 109–116.
4. Ackoff, Russell L. (1986) *Management in Small Doses*, New York: John Wiley and Sons.
5. David, Fred R. (1989) "How Companies Define Their Mission," *Long-Range Planning*, 22, (1) pp. 90–97.
6. "Mini-Nationals Are Making Maximum Impact," (1993) *Business Week*, September 6, pp. 66–69.
7. Business International. (1991) *Building A Global Image*. New York: Business International Corp.
8. Taylor, Alex, (1994) "Will Success Spoil Chrysler," *Fortune*, January 4, pp. 88–92.
9. Bilkey, Warren J. (1978) "An Attempted Integration of the Literature on the Export Behavior of Firms," *Journal of International Business Studies*, 9, (Spring-Summer), pp. 33–36.
10. Cavusgil, S. Tamer (1980) "On the Internationalization Process of Firms," *European Research*, (November), pp. 273–80.
11. Ghoshal, Sumantra (1987) "Global Strategy: An Organizing Framework," *Strategic Management Journal*, 8, pp. 425–440.
12. Kraar, Louis (1989) "Top U.S. Companies Move Into Russia," *Fortune*, July 31, pp. 165–170.
13. Hofheinz, Paul (1994) "Rising in Russia," *Fortune*, January 24, pp. 92–96.
14. "Destination Vietnam," (1994) *Business Week*, February 14, pp. 26–27.
15. "China Fever Strikes Again," (1993) *Business Week*, March 29, pp. 46–47.
16. Day, George S. (1984) *Strategic Market Planning*, St. Paul: West Publishing Company.
17. Porter, Michael, (1985) *Competitive Advantage: Creating and Sustaining Superior Performance*, New York: The Free Press.
18. Nichols, Nancy A. (1994) "Scientific Management at Merck: An Interview with CFO Judy Lewent," *Harvard Business Review*, (January-February), pp. 88–99.
19. "How a Commodities Giant Leverages Core Competencies," (1992) *Business International*, January 20, p. 13.
20. Prahalad, C. K., and Gary Hamel, (1990) "The Core Competence of the Corporation," *Harvard Business Review*, May-June, pp. 79–91.

CHAPTER 5

DEFINING GLOBAL COMPETITIVE ADVANTAGE

ESTABLISHING GLOBAL COMPETITIVE ADVANTAGE

The firm's direction in global markets derives from its strategic thrust. However, its success in global markets is determined by whether it is able to establish a sustainable competitive advantage. This provides the basis for crafting the distinctive features of a strategy that enables the firm to triumph over its competition. It establishes strategic priorities and determines the level of investment required and allocation of resources among different functions in order to achieve desired objectives. It provides focus and direction to the firm's efforts in entering international markets, and in relation to decisions as to how and which markets to enter. (see Figure 5-1)

Defining the firm's competitive advantage in international markets involves examination of the underlying core competence. Just because the firm has the "ability" to do something does not necessarily mean that this provides a competitive advantage in global markets. The firm needs to examine whether the competitive advantage it has developed in its domestic market will extend into foreign markets. Conditions in the domestic market may generate an advantage in competing internationally. On the other hand, the nature of competition and type of competitors in foreign markets differ and may impact on the relevance of its competitive advantage.

Bases of competitive advantage vary in the ease with which they can be leveraged internationally and in different markets. The firm needs to examine its ability to leverage its competitive advantage internationally, together with the investment required to acquire or develop assets or resources, to implement its strategic thrust.

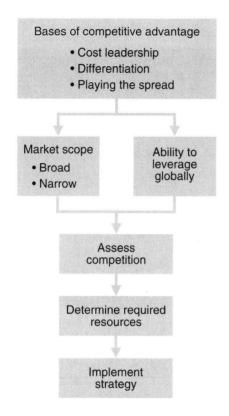

FIGURE 5-1

Establishing a global competitive advantage.

THE COMPETITIVE ADVANTAGE OF NATIONS

The competitive advantage developed in the firm's home market is molded to a substantial degree by national environmental conditions. The national context plays a key role in furnishing key ingredients for success in international markets, such as access to resources and skills needed to develop a competitive advantage in an industry, information shaping perceived opportunities and corporate goals, and competitive pressures to invest and innovate.

Following the theory developed by Porter[1] in *The Competitive Advantage of Nations*, four sets of factors, characteristic of the national environment, influence the firm's ability to establish and sustain competitive advantage in international markets. These are: factor conditions; demand conditions; related and supporting industries; and firm strategy, structure, and rivalry. All of these factors interact to form the "national diamond"—"the playing field that each nation establishes and operates for its industries," and the context in which firms grow and learn how to compete. (see Figure 5-2)

FIGURE 5-2

The determinants of national advantage. *Reprinted with the permission of The Free Press, Macmillan Publishing Company, a Member of Paramount Communications from The Competitive Advantage of Nations by Michael E. Porter, Copyright © 1990 by Michael E. Porter.*

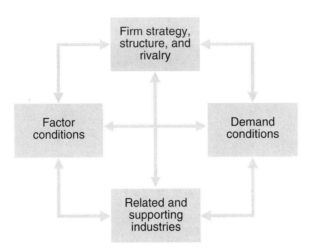

Factor Conditions

Availability of resources such as capital, land, natural resources, climate, and skilled labor is at the heart of traditional international trade theory. According to this theory, a nation will have a comparative advantage in producing and exporting goods that make use of the factors or resources with which it is well endowed. Thus, for example, Canadian and U.S. farmers have an advantage in producing wheat, due to the availability of large fertile plains as well as low-cost capital to purchase agricultural equipment and develop advanced production and harvesting techniques.

Two types of factors or resources are important; *basic* resources, such as natural resources, climate, size, demographics, and *advanced* factors such as communications, market infrastructure, technology, and specialized skills. While basic resources provide a natural advantage on which firms can build, advanced resources are often more crucial in developing a competitive advantage in international markets.

Basic resources, such as a large low-cost labor pool or local raw materials, can provide a firm with an initial competitive advantage. But this advantage needs to be upgraded and reinforced through the development of more sophisticated resources, such as research or specialized skills, to build a sustainable advantage in global markets. In an era of global competition, improvements in international communications and distribution logistics mean a company can easily gain access to such factors as labor or new materials worldwide and meet competition through developing a global sourcing strategy, or alternatively circumvent competition through use of alternative technologies. Silk manufacturers in Como, Italy, for example, have lost their dominant position in the silk industry due to low-priced competition from Korean firms.[2] While the Koreans have not yet developed the design expertise of Como's artisans, they buy the patterns and reproduce them with a high degree of accuracy at 30–50 percent less than the price in Italy.

Disadvantages or a lack of basic resources can stimulate a company to invest in advanced factors and to innovate. Where companies face high land or labor costs or lack of local raw materials, they may invest in technology-intensive or automated methods, or devise creative methods to overcome these disadvantages. Japanese companies, for example, developed just-in-time production methods to combat prohibitively high land costs. Similarly, Italian steel producers pioneered minimill technology, which requires little capital, is efficient on a small scale, and utilizes scrap metal, in order to overcome high capital costs, high energy costs, and no local raw materials.

Advanced factors such as specialized skills, new technologies, research facilities, and communications infrastructure provide a more enduring basis for global competitive advantage than basic resources, and are more difficult for foreign competitors to imitate. Invariably, they are specialized and tailored to a specific industry's needs, rather than generalizable, and require sustained investment and upgrading to meet these evolving needs. Holland, for example, has developed major research institutes that focus on growing, packaging, and shipping flowers and horticultural products. As a result, it maintains a leadership position in exporting flowers worldwide.

Demand Conditions

Demand conditions in the home market provide an important impetus for developing and improving the base of a firm's competitive advantage. Firms are often most sensitive and responsive to the needs and interests of domestic customers. Consequently, the nature of these needs, and the specific benefits desired by domestic customers, play an important role in shaping product attributes and in creating pressures for innovation and improvements in product quality.

Highly sophisticated and demanding buyers in the home market stimulate firms to innovate and improve products, thus providing them with an advantage in world markets. The importance German automobile buyers attach to high performance and technical excellence, for example, has been a major factor in the growth and strong position of German automobiles in the world luxury car market.

The character of demand and buyer needs in the home market also influences how companies perceive emerging needs and respond to specific market segments. For example, in Japan, homes are small, summers are hot and humid, and energy costs are high. Japanese companies have responded to these conditions by developing compact, quiet, energy-saving household appliances such as tumble dryers and air conditioners. Similarly, concern in Sweden with handicapped people has resulted in the development of a highly competitive industry focusing on their needs.

Related and Supporting Industries

The third element of competitive advantage is the presence of related and supporting industries that are internationally competitive. These industries create advantages both downstream and upstream by delivering inputs or providing services rapidly and efficiently, with preferential treatment to domestic customers. Technological leadership by U.S. firms in the semiconductor industry, for example, paved the way for the success of U.S. companies in computer and other technically advanced industries. These relationships can also be bilateral, in that success of U.S. companies in computers also fostered development of the semiconductor industry.

In addition to providing rapid access to components and services, the existence of related industries allows firms to develop close working relationships and exchange information with each other. Companies can thus encourage suppliers or service organizations to innovate, improve product and service quality, and provide information and feedback on their activities. These networks are, however, not closed. Suppliers and service organizations also compete in the global arena and derive part of their impetus from this interaction.

As a result of these benefits successful industries are often found in "clusters" in a country. For example, one cluster in Germany centers around textiles and apparel, including cotton, wool and synthetic fabrics, dyes, women's shirts, sewing machine needles, and other textile machinery.

Firm Strategy, Structure, and Rivalry

The national environment also has an impact on how companies are organized and managed, as well as the nature of domestic rivalry. These elements in turn play a key role in determining the specific type of competitive advantage they have in international markets. In Italy, for example, traditional family values have fostered the development of small family-owned businesses. These are often successful in design-oriented industries such as footwear, woollens, lighting, etc., where response to rapid changes in fashion, and entrepreneurial ingenuity, are key success factors. In Germany, on the other hand, emphasis on hierarchical management systems and technical expertise breeds success in engineering industries such as optics and chemicals, where precision manufacturing and methodical quality improvements are important.

Corporate goals and attitudes towards risk also vary from one country to another. In the United States, the availability of venture capital and willingness to assume risk and innovate have fuelled success in new industries such as biotechnology and software.

The factor identified by Porter as crucial to the creation of a sustainable competitive advantage is the existence of strong domestic rivalry. This pressures firms to cut costs, to improve quality and service, and to innovate. Since domestic firms operate within the same national context, they compete for the same resources and customer markets. As a result, their rivalry is often more intense and personal than that with foreign competitors. Intracountry rivalry is often further intensified by the geographic concentration of industry "clusters." Thus, for example, the major Swiss pharmaceutical companies are concentrated in Basel, the U.S. auto industry in Detroit, and Italian jewelry companies in Arezzo and Valenza Po.

Domestic rivalry thus creates pressures for constant and continued upgrading of the bases of competitive advantage. Domestic competitors compete on the same terms, and have no natural competitive advantage or barriers such as government protection or low wage costs. Consequently, they must focus on improving internal operations such as production or process efficiency, or developing new products and ideas. Ironically, such competition often also spurs them to enter the global market to seek new opportunities, or to gain advantages from greater economies of scale. Thus, fierce domestic competition both motivates and develops the response mechanisms to enable them to succeed in global markets.

The Dynamics of the Diamond

These four sets of factors interact to develop the basis of national competitive advantage (see Figure 5-2). For example, product quality or process improvements based on technology or specialized skills will only occur where they are stimulated by fierce domestic rivalry and corporate goals. Hence, the four sets of factors constitute a reinforcing system that contributes to international success. The strength of this interaction depends on two factors: the geographical concentration of an industry, which accelerates diffusion of innovation, development of specialized resources, and of supporting industries; and the development of industry clusters, which facilitate the creation of "advanced" factors such as specialized technology and skills, while the success of downstream industries stimulates growth in supplier industries, and vice versa.

This pattern of interaction thus provides the national platform on which the firm competes, and provides the basis for the development of its competitive advantage in international markets. In turn, as firms or industries become successful in international markets, they need to "upgrade" their competitive advantage—by innovation and by investment in "advanced" factors such as technology or infrastructure, thus further reinforcing and sustaining the base of their national competitive advantage. The process thus becomes a mutually reinforcing system for continual progress and upgrading.

BASES OF COMPETITIVE ADVANTAGE

The competitive advantage of the country in which a firm is based provides the platform on which it develops its own competitive strategy for international markets. Within this national context, and the specific resources, market, and competitive environment that it provides, the firm must assess the nature of its sustainable competitive advantage in its domestic market. The firm must also determine how far and how readily its competitive advantage can be leveraged in international markets, and if so, to which countries.

As discussed earlier, this sustainable competitive advantage is grounded in the firm's core competence, or the specific skills and assets that drive its strategy. These may lie, for example, in efficient production and process management, as in the case of the Japanese automobile manufacturers. Alternatively, they may lie in the firm's ability to manage mass distribution channels, as, for example, with P&G.

While several frameworks for classifying alternative competitive strategies have been proposed, one of the better known is that developed by Porter.[3] This identifies three principal competitive strategy types: cost leadership, differentiation, and focus. As observed by Wind and Robertson,[4] implicit in this framework are two underlying dimensions, strategic target (industrywide vs. a particular niche) and strategic advantage, i.e., cost vs. perceived uniqueness. Both cost leadership and differentiation are broad-line strategies, though they differ in the nature of their strategic advantage. A focused strategy, on the other hand, is directed towards a limited segment of the market. Although the distinction is only briefly mentioned by Porter and seldom discussed in depth elsewhere, a focused strategy may emphasize either cost advantage or differentiation.

This framework has been further refined by Day,[1] who argues that the choice between differentiation and lowest delivered cost is not necessarily mutually exclusive. Some firms, for example Kelloggs, may be able to combine both strategies effectively. In some instances, improved product quality and customer value may indirectly lead to lower costs: higher quality leads to higher market share, which in turn leads to lower unit costs due to scale economies. This strategy is termed *playing the spread.*

Overall, the refined framework as shown in Figure 5-3 consists of three dimensions: emphasis on customer value, emphasis on costs, and scope of market coverage. This yields a broad array of possible strategies based on core competence and selected market. Some combinations are, however, clearly more likely and more feasible than others. For example, if a firm offers moderate prices, but does not clearly differentiate its products, it risks being outpositioned by competitors superior on the cost, or differentiation, dimension.

While this framework was initially developed in relation to domestic markets, it can also be applied to international markets. The various alternatives do, however, differ in the ease and the extent to which they can effectively be leveraged in international markets, as also the implications for country entry and timing decisions.

Emphasis on Cost Superiority or Leadership Strategies

Emphasis on cost superiority typically implies a strict "no-frills" offering, as, for example, in discount airlines or discount retailing. Alternatively, the firm may

FIGURE 5-3

Generic competitive strategy. *Reprinted with the permission of The Free Press, Macmillan Publishing Company, a Member of Paramount Communications from Market Driven Strategy: Processes for Creating Value by George S. Day. Copyright © 1990 by George S. Day.*

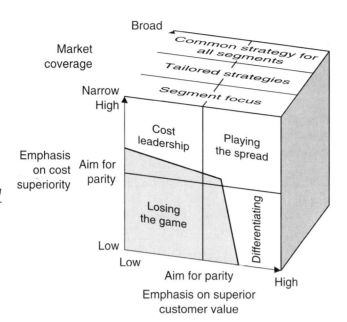

offer a standard and limited range of acceptable products, as does, for example, the Swedish retailer, Ikea. Such strategies are likely to be most effective in markets where customers are highly price-sensitive, or alternatively in targeting a price-sensitive segment.

The Swedish furniture retailer, Ikea, focuses on designing and selling low-cost, high-quality furniture to customers willing to load purchases into their cars themselves and assemble items at home. Ikea is able to cut costs by designing products, buying from outside suppliers, and selling direct to customers, thus creating a direct designer-to-user link, rather than selling through dealers.[5] Ikea has been able to leverage this strategy in Europe and parts of North America, tapping a price-sensitive segment in the market for modern furniture.

Pursuit of cost leadership to the exclusion of other strategic dimensions is unlikely to have "broad" appeal in most markets in industrialized nations, especially where it results in products that are of markedly inferior quality relative to competition. This may, however, vary from country to country. Markets in some countries may be considerably more price-sensitive than in others. In developing countries in particular, markets are likely to be highly price sensitive for a wide range of goods and services, and segments oriented toward quality or service may be very small. Yet, even when targeting quality or service segments, the firm must pay attention to costs in order to remain competitive with products or services of comparable quality.

A cost leadership strategy is predicated on the development of a superior delivered cost position. Often this position is associated with the scale or scope of the operation, coupled with tight cost control, and entails emphasis on efficient production management. It typically requires capital to invest in large scale operations and efficient technology, as well as unrelenting attention to cost control, close labor supervision to achieve high levels of productivity, and low cost distribution. A cost advantage is production driven and implies emphasis on manufacturing and distribution functions rather than marketing, although there are opportunities for cost efficiency in marketing activities as well.

Such strategies are thus most likely to be effective in industries where there are few opportunities for product differentiation but significant opportunities for economies of scale. Hence, production costs form a major component of the value-chain. These are often mass markets for standardized functional items such as watches, household appliances, light bulbs or commodity chemicals.

Given the characteristics of these industries, they are often located in countries that benefit from low-cost labor, strong engineering skills, and a highly disciplined work ethic. Firms located in these countries are able to benefit from those resources and develop commanding positions in world markets.

In Japan, for example, traditional values of loyalty and conformity have generated a well-disciplined work force and the development of efficient production management techniques. This latter factor has been the major strength of Japanese firms in international markets. As one writer has observed,[6] "The secret of the effectiveness of Japanese managerial methods is that they make it economically feasible to train and retain the type of worker necessary for high value-added manufacturing and advanced services." Japanese production management is thus renowned for its production efficiency and its ability to achieve high levels of labor productivity.

Japanese firms have thus predominantly been a major source of competition in industries where there are significant economies of scale, as, for example, in the automobile or construction equipment industries, and where there is a high level of customer price sensitivity, as, for example, in consumer electronics, cameras, and watches. In such industries, Japanese firms have been able to leverage their cost-efficient production techniques and management capabilities in international markets to achieve strong market positions worldwide.

Sony, for example, while second runner in the Japanese domestic market to companies such as Hitachi, Matsushita, and Toshiba, has nonetheless been able to achieve a dominant position worldwide in consumer electronics and particularly in color TVs, stereos, and radios. Similarly, Honda has been able to achieve a significant position worldwide in the automobile and motorcycle industries by leveraging its capabilities in production.

LEVERAGING COST LEADERSHIP

Cost leadership strategies can be leveraged readily in international markets insofar as they rely on economies of scale. The economies are enhanced by extending the geographic scope of markets, which allows the firm to benefit from additional experience effects, and reducing costs further. The firm's cost leadership position is further strengthened, creating a barrier to new entrants and enabling the firm to dominate its competition. In a number of industries such as electronics, Japanese firms aggressively slashed costs in order to increase market share worldwide. This fueled what Abegglen and Stalk[7] termed a *winner's competitive cycle*. The cycle feeds on itself, with increased volume leading to decreased costs, which in turn lead to increased profits, enabling the firm to make investments in additional growth. However, in world markets, cost leadership strategies can be effectively leveraged only in industries in which customer preferences are highly similar from one country to another, and in which there is a high degree of price sensitivity. In other words, customers are willing to trade off additional product features, functions, or customization for lower prices. A price advantage is readily discernible by potential customers and less susceptible to environmental factors other than tariff barriers or trade margins.

On the other hand, cost leadership strategies are highly vulnerable to the emergence of new process technologies, which reduce costs further, fluctuations in foreign exchange rates; protectionist measures; and the entry of competition from low-cost factor locations. In many consumer electronics industries, such as microwave ovens and VCRs, Korean manufacturers have largely been able to undercut Japanese manufacturers and gain major market share in key world markets (see Figure 5-4).

Differentiation Strategies/ Enhancing Customer Value

In contrast to cost leadership strategies, differentiation strategies emphasize the creation or enhancement of customer value. These strategies include techniques such as offering superior products and service, developing a strong brand or

FIGURE 5-4

Strengths and weakness of strategic alternatives.

Strategies	Ability to leverage globally	Vulnerability
Cost leadership	• Relatively direct • Extends economics of scale and scope	Basis for cost leadership erodes due to changes in: • Technology • Factor inputs
Playing the spread	Depends on similarity of market structure	Same as cost leadership and differentiation
Differentiation	• More difficult and complex • Tastes and preferences differ • Requires sensitivity to local conditions	Markets evolve • Changes in taste • Better competitor's products and services

corporate image, being more responsive to customer requirements than competitors, developing innovative new products or product features, and designing unique methods of distribution. In essence, therefore, differentiation strategies focus on developing a competitive advantage by providing a unique product or service that possesses certain distinctive attributes desired by target customers, for which they are willing to pay a premium.

Offering superior product quality and service is widely recognized as a prime means of enhancing customer value, especially in many industrial markets. Findings from the PIMS project (Profit Impact of Market Strategy) and other studies also suggest that product quality is strongly linked to long-run performance.[8] While improved quality has an impact on relative price, it also generates market share and has little effect on costs. In effect, industrial customers are often willing to pay a premium for superior quality and service, since they generate cost savings for them by providing consistent and reliable product input, thus enhancing their performance.

Improved quality is achieved, not only via conformance to strict standards and quality control, but also through efficient product design, and by matching the product and delivery system to the needs of the customer. The firm must emphasize total quality management focusing first on features or attributes of importance to customers, designing products according to these needs, and production and delivery to meet customer requirements. The establishment of the Baldridge Award for Quality Management, and the ISO 9000 standards in the EU, is indicative of the growing importance attached to quality improvement in many industrial markets.

The firm can also enhance customer value by responding more rapidly than competitors to emerging or changing customer needs—developing new products, product features, or services to meet these requirements. As the pace of competition becomes increasingly fierce, and time an increasingly valuable commodity, rapid response can provide an important competitive advantage. Not only can firms target customers who are especially sensitive to rapid response, but they may also be able to preempt competition in entering new markets or introducing innovative new products and services. They can thus develop customer loyalty and awareness, and lay claim to prime distribution channels and outlets, creating barriers to entry of competition.

Rapid response and innovation strategies are especially effective in certain types of markets, such as service industries and fashion-oriented industries. In service industries, rapid response or timeliness is often crucial to satisfying customers and, in some sectors, such as fast foods or courier services, central to the service offering. In industries characterized by rapid technological change or changes in fashion, rapid response and innovativeness may also be important. To respond quickly, the firm will have to monitor changes in customer requirements, fashion trends, and technology, together with flexible manufacturing procedures and efficient order and delivery systems.

Differentiation can also be achieved by developing unique distribution or delivery systems, or a strong brand or corporate image. For example, management may be able to tap a specific market or provide improved accessibility through a distinctive mode of distribution. Avon Cosmetics has, for example, derived its competitive advantage from using housewives as salespeople. A strong brand image can also provide an important competitive advantage especially for products where there are few readily discernible differences in product quality, as for example, colas, or alternatively in industries where image is a key factor in purchase decisions, as for example, in cosmetics, fragrances, and designer clothing.

A differentiation strategy is founded primarily on strong marketing skills. It requires constant attention to changes in customer needs and interests, and the capability to develop creative ways of responding to those needs, incorporating them rapidly into production and delivery systems. This strategy therefore requires effective coordination among the various functional areas, such as R&D, product development, and marketing, and the development of feedback mechanisms to guide and monitor changes.

Collaboration and feedback from distribution channels, the sales force, and other external agents are also important elements of an integrated delivery system. Ability to attract and retain highly skilled and creative workers, and a corporate culture that encourages individual initiative and the generation of new ideas, are also needed to fuel market-driven strategies.

Differentiation strategies are typically most successful in industries where marketing costs are a significant component of the value-chain, and where there are substantial opportunities for differentiating products. Customer sensitivity to, or interest in, additional features is crucial. Many consumer goods offer such opportunities, especially where fashion, design, or style are important factors in the purchase decision, particularly when items are viewed as symbols of personal expression.

Increasingly, many industrial markets in westernized nations are characterized by greater concern with product quality and service improvements rather than short-run cost savings. In countries outside the Industrial Triad, however, concern with product quality and service, innovative features, and rapid response may be less widespread, especially if they entail higher costs. Differentiation strategies may, therefore, tap a somewhat restricted market base, consisting only of more affluent consumers or more sophisticated multinational firms.

Differentiation strategies are more likely to be pursued by firms with comparative advantage in mass merchandising, creative skills, or facility with personal relations. U.S. and West European companies have thus been prone to pursue differentiated strategies in international markets. While this has been in part stimulated by their relative disadvantages in wages and other factor costs compared with many Asian competitors, it has been further reinforced by the availability of creative talent and well-developed and highly sophisticated marketing skills.

In some cases, companies have leveraged well-known brand names such as Kelloggs, Coca-Cola, Pampers, or Bic worldwide, or have developed international reputations for product quality, reliability, and service as, for example, has IBM.

LEVERAGING DIFFERENTIATION STRATEGIES

Differentiation strategies are typically somewhat more difficult to leverage in international markets than cost leadership strategies. Since they depend on superior quality and service, innovative features, or more rapid response to customer needs, some tailoring to country-specific characteristics or the marketing environment will be required. This tailoring in turn necessitates close monitoring of customer needs and interests, and the development of experience and understanding of country and market-specific factors.

On the other hand, once a differentiation strategy has been adapted to world markets, it is often less vulnerable than a cost leadership strategy, at least in the short run. Direct comparisons on quality, image, or service are more difficult than those based on price. Furthermore, firms pursuing successful differentiation strategies typically develop close ties with customers and distributors, or have strong brand or corporate images and reputation that make it difficult for competitors to break into the market. Apple Computer provides an interesting example of how a company can leverage a differentiated brand image to compete effectively in world markets. Apple, a pioneer in the personal computer business, entered the market with a human-centered image of "a computer for the rest of us," to differentiate itself from the giant monolith, IBM. This image is embodied in the Apple name and its simple, colorful logo of an apple with a bite out of it. This logo was leveraged in international markets, without translating the name, by placing logo and name close together, so that the connection between the two could be made. The simplicity and clarity of the logo helped to convey the image of high-quality, easy-to-use innovative products, and creative managerial techniques.[9]

Playing the Spread

While, traditionally, cost leadership and product differentiation have been viewed as mutually exclusive alternatives, some firms may effectively combine both and play the spread.[10] Improved product quality and service, and development of more sophisticated features and systems to enhance quality, may in the short run raise costs. However, they will expand share in the long run, thus reducing total costs through scale and scope economies and experience effects.

Some companies, notably in consumer packaged goods, have been successful in enhancing customer value and at the same time reducing costs. Kelloggs, for example, has been highly successful in developing innovative health-oriented product line extensions while at the same time investing in sophisticated plant and equipment in order to reduce manufacturing costs. Heinz has spent heavily on advertising in order to develop a strong brand name while, at the same time, managing costs by purchasing low-cost materials and investing in plant automation and processing.

Strategies that balance cost savings with improved customer value are most likely to be effective in markets where customers are interested in quality and service improvements but are at the same time cost conscious. These are also likely to be markets where customers are less interested in expensive product features, which means a company playing the spread will not find itself threatened by companies 'cherry-picking' profitable segments with specialized interests.

Timex, for long the leader in the low-cost functional segment of the watch industry, has now expanded its product line, acquiring the Guess, Monet, and Nautica names to give it a position in the upscale fashion end of the market. In addition, new low-priced fashion lines have been added, such as the Indiglo Luminescent Line, and the Disney line for children. Timex thus aims to keep up with the evolution of the watch from a functional item to a fashion accessory, catering to new fashion trends at prices ranging from $20 to $300.[11]

Ability to leverage a playing-the-spread strategy across countries is likely to depend on similarity of market structure. Where customer demand is equally broad based, with similar concerns with regard to product quality and price, playing-the-spread strategies may be effectively leveraged. If, however, demand is considerably more heterogeneous, with pockets of specialized interests or customers more price-sensitive, a firm may encounter difficulty and need to adapt to specific market segments.

MARKET SCOPE

The second dimension of competitive strategy concerns the scope of market coverage. As noted earlier, a firm can either have a *broad market scope*, targeting all potential customers with a common strategy, or alternatively, adopt a *focused* strategy, targeting a specific market segment.

While, conceptually, any of the three bases of competitive advantage can be developed relative to these two options, in practice certain combinations are more likely to be successful. Emphasis on cost can be effective for firms with a broad market scope, or for firms focusing on a specific market segment. Differentiation strategies, on the other hand, may be less vulnerable when targeted to specific segments, while playing the spread is most likely to be effective relative to a broad market scope.

Broad Market Scope

Targeting a broad market base with a common strategy is most likely to be appropriate in cases where there is broad-based demand for the product and relatively few differences among customers in terms of desired benefits or usage scenarios. Markets for products such as consumer electronics and consumer packaged goods typically fall into this category in most industrialized countries. A firm pursuing a cost leadership strategy may also prefer to target a broad market base. This enables it to take advantage of potential economies of scale and experience effects, further enhancing its cost advantage.

Adoption of a broad-based market penetration strategy is also desirable where there is substantial potential for market growth. By targeting a broad market base, the firm can establish a dominant market position early, building brand or corporate image and developing good relations with distributors. If the firm makes a major promotional effort, it can also play a key role in stimulating market growth. Bic, for example, adopted a strategy of targeting a broad market base when introducing its disposable products—lighters, pens, and razors—in international markets. It was able to build market share rapidly and broaden its distribution, thus further developing its market base.

On the other hand, targeting a broad market base is likely to require substantial resources in order to establish and maintain distribution networks, and to mount major promotional campaigns to support the product and maintain interest among potential customers and distributors. Consequently, such strategies are most appropriate for large firms with strong market positions to defend, and the resources to commit to market growth and development.

Focused Segment

Targeting a focused segment, on the other hand, is likely to be appropriate in markets where there is a highly distinctive segment with very specialized and clearly defined needs, which can effectively be reached through a focused positioning and marketing program. Rolls-Royce, for example, has targeted the prestige segment in the luxury automobile market worldwide, just as Ferrari targets the luxury sports car segment, and Cray Computers targets the supercomputer segment of the computer market.

Focusing on a specific customer segment is likely to be appropriate for a firm that lacks the resources to compete on a broad-line basis, or whose core competence and distinctive skills are only relevant to a specific market segment. Targeting a focused segment may, therefore, enable a firm to concentrate on specific items in the product line that require highly specialized skills or technology, or on an especially lucrative market segment.

Where a firm can identify a segment with similar needs and interests in international markets, it may be able to target that segment worldwide, thus effectively leveraging specific skills or a specific positioning worldwide. Body-Shop, for example has been highly successful in targeting environmentally conscious consumers worldwide with its line of shampoos and cosmetics. These products are made of natural ingredients and are not tested on animals. In industrial markets, corporations with worldwide operations may coordinate or centralize sourcing for their various international subsidiaries. Insofar as such corporations have needs distinct from those of nationally oriented corporations, they can be effectively targeted through a global focused strategy.

Focused strategies may also be appropriate where a firm faces entrenched competition from local firms, or if large, powerful firms dominate media and distribution channels. In this case, obtaining broad market penetration is likely to be expensive. Equally, if the market infrastructure is not well developed, a focused market segment may be more readily accessible, avoiding the costs of investing in developing the market infrastructure.

Hybrid Strategies

In some instances, firms pursue hybrid strategies, targeting a broad base in their domestic market and a specific segment in international markets, or vice versa. Corona, the Mexican beer, is targeted to a broad base in its domestic market, but positioned as a chic upscale imported beer in the rest of North America and Europe.

This strategy is likely to be effective if demand in international markets is more heterogeneous, or differs in terms of desired features, or price-sensitivity, or is characterized by greater competitor activity than the domestic market. In this case management can target a specific segment with interests and characteristics similar to those of the domestic market or one with high demand potential. This may be especially desirable if the market infrastructure, particularly in terms of distribution and communications, is not well developed, and would require substantial investment.

Once an initial bridgehead has been established, and demand begins to develop, the firm can then begin to target a broader market base, expanding the distribution network and increasing its promotional efforts accordingly. A firm then runs the risk that a competitor will invest in developing a broader market base early on, and hence preempt the firm's growth strategy. Hybrid strategies that involve tailoring products and programs to national markets are likely to be pursued by firms that are playing the spread, since they avoid direct competition with firms pursuing cost leadership strategies. At the same time, they can maintain a superior cost position relative to firms pursuing pure differentiation or focused strategies, by exploiting potential economies of scope.

It is important to note, however, that tailoring products and programs to specific national preferences is likely to increase costs. Consequently, tailored strategies are only likely to be appropriate where the costs of tailoring are outweighed by the potential for increased market penetration and growth. Such a strategy is thus more likely to be pursued by a firm seeking to develop local market penetration and to take advantage of economies of scope than by a firm focused on short-run profits in initial entry into international markets.

ASSESSING COMPETITIVE POSITION

Once the firm has determined the basis for its competitive advantage and how it can be leveraged in international markets, the next step is to assess how far this provides a sustainable competitive advantage in the international arena. The firm must compare its competitive position with that of competitors in other countries, to assess its relative strength and potential weaknesses. Then it must determine the financial investment and resources required to establish and sustain the targeted position.

This assessment in turn impacts the choice of countries to enter, based on the strength of competition in a given country, and how that country fits into the firm's overall competitive design. The mode of entry decision is also influenced by this assessment. For example, where the firm lacks adequate resources to sustain a given competitive position alone, it could enter into a collaborative agreement or alliance with other firms in order to achieve its goals.

Assessing Competition

Two major types of competitors can be distinguished in international markets: multinational competitors, and local competitors. These two types differ, not only in terms of the bases of their competitive advantage and resources, but also in their ability to leverage their advantage, as well as other resources, across international markets. They may also differ in the extent to which they target specific segments and possess specific competencies and advantages relative to various markets. Consequently, the nature of the competitive threats they pose differs.

MULTINATIONAL COMPETITORS

Some industries such as automobiles, tires, detergents, and razor blades are dominated worldwide by a few large multinational companies. These companies compete broad-line, with complete product lines covering all segments. For example, Bridgestone and Goodyear compete worldwide in the tire market, while Unilever, P&G, and Colgate dominate the detergents industry throughout the world, challenged only by a few regional and national competitors in countries such as Japan, Germany, and India.

Such large multinationals possess a number of strengths in competing in world markets. In the first place, they have the advantage of size and can readily exploit potential economies of scale and volume. These may not only exist in production and advertising development, but are also particularly significant in R&D in certain industries, such as pharmaceuticals and aerospace.

In addition, large multinationals often benefit from superior access to certain types of resources. These may include new low-cost materials and resources in other countries to which a large multinational can gain access through a global sourcing network. Its size may also enable employment of specialized skills and expertise, for example, research, management, or technological skills, or specialized systems and equipment, which are uneconomic for a national company.

Second, the large multinational can serve the needs of its customers worldwide. This may be especially important for companies such as international banks that have operations or branches in other countries and need compatible or interlinked operating systems. Alternatively, consistent product quality in purchases of raw materials and components for operations worldwide may be an important criterion. Operation in world markets also enables a firm to develop an international reputation and corporate image. IBM, Shell, and Sony, for example, all benefit from their global corporate reputation.

Perhaps most importantly, the multinational is able to benefit from the transfer of experience and know-how from one country to another, and has the flexibility to shift resources and skills from one part of the world to another. Ideas for new products, advertising campaigns, or experience developed in operating in one country environment can be transferred to another. Similarly, capital or managerial skills can be shifted from one market to another in response to new competitive threats. Further, production or sourcing can be moved to another location if foreign exchange rates fluctuate or labor costs increase. Thus, the multinational benefits from an international network of resources and operations that can be utilized to combat competitor moves and respond to changing environmental conditions.

On the other hand, multinationals, especially those that are high profile or operate in strategic industries, often encounter hostile attitudes from host governments that are concerned with protecting or developing national industries and fear loss of sovereignty due to the economic power of multinationals. This fear can result in measures to restrict the power of multinationals, such as restrictions on ownership, repatriation of profits, taxation, or requirements "to buy local."

Also, the sheer size and scope of multinational operations can generate inefficiencies and render management cumbersome and unwieldy. The additional layer of management required to coordinate and control operations across national boundaries adds to administrative costs and complexity. Longer lines of communication and responsibility can also hamper a firm's flexibility and ability to react quickly to competitor moves or changing environmental conditions.

Large multinationals may also find it uneconomic to service small niche markets, especially where there are limited opportunities to take advantage of economies of scope or identify similar niche segments in other countries. Multinationals are thus likely to be most effective in targeting markets where there are potential synergies arising from cross-border operations.

LOCAL COMPETITORS

Another type of competitor consists of companies that have strategies that are purely domestic in scope (that is, they have no or very limited activities outside their domestic market). For example, various major Japanese detergent and food companies, such as Lion and International House, have focused their efforts primarily on the Japanese market, with very limited efforts to expand internationally.

Competitors whose operations are national in scope frequently benefit from a number of advantages relative to large multinationals. In the first place, just as multinationals are sometimes regarded unfavorably by host governments, national companies may benefit from protectionist measures. This is particularly likely in industries that are important sources of employment, such as automobiles or textiles, or are of strategic importance, such as steel or computers, or where government procurement is significant, for example, mass transit and telecommunications. State-owned companies also often benefit from government subsidies, interest-free loans, and support as well as protectionist measures. In addition, in many countries, public transportation, utilities, and telephone services are all state run.

Secondly, national companies, especially those owned domestically, often benefit from local consumers preferences to "buy national." This preference may be motivated by patriotic or chauvinistic attitudes as well as beliefs that local companies will be more reliable, provide better service, have shorter delivery times, and be able to respond more effectively to urgent requests or customized orders than multinational suppliers.

Country-centered competitors may also be able to establish better links with local distributors and tailor strategies more effectively to local customer needs. Whether this constitutes a competitive advantage depends on how effectively a multinational responds to local market characteristics, and on the priority it accords to servicing global rather than local customers.

Small national companies can also be considerably more flexible and better able to respond rapidly to niche markets or emerging trends. They lack the burdensome overhead and administrative costs incurred by large multinationals, as well as the lengthy reporting channels, and lines of responsibility and international accountability, characteristic of a multinational. Equally, they can service specific national segments with unique needs that a multinational often cannot meet economically.

The disadvantages and areas of vulnerability of the national competitor are to a large extent the converse of the strengths of the large multinational. National firms lack the advantages associated with size and a worldwide network of operations, namely, extensive financial and managerial resources, and the ability to shift resources from one market or location to another in response to changing competitive or environmental conditions.

While these two distinct types of competitors can be identified and are likely to predominate in international markets, some competitors have operations that are primarily regional or of limited international scope. For example, Henkel, the German detergent and personal products manufacturer, focuses primarily on the German market, as well as on other European markets such as France and Italy. Similarly, Kao, the Japanese detergent manufacturer, operates primarily in Japan, with limited activities in some proximate Southeast Asian markets.

In essence, therefore, two types of competition can be identified—competition that is played out primarily on an international or global scale between large multinationals, and competition that takes place primarily on a domestic scale. In the first case, competition focuses on the battle for global market share. Competitors have to monitor closely competitor moves in markets worldwide, entry into new markets or businesses, expansion or retraction of the product line, price cutting or alignment, and negotiation of new strategic alliances or distribution agreements. These may signal future competitive position in world markets. Firms have to respond to these actions, bringing the full force of their global resource networks to bear against competition. Domestic competition, on the other hand, focuses on position relative to a single market and is likely to center on tactical moves such as pricing, promotion, and new product or brand launches.

These two battle arenas are not independent. A domestic competitor can, for example, cherry-pick a multinational's market position, or a multinational can decide to drive a domestic competitor out of business. Nonetheless, the scope and impact of competitor moves is likely to vary significantly.

Determining Required Resources

Having assessed the nature of competition, and competitor strengths and weaknesses, the firm next has to determine the resources required to sustain the targeted competitive position. In particular, the firm needs to assess the financial and management resources needed to build and defend its position in international markets. This influences decisions with regard to which countries to enter and when, as well as how to enter these markets in order to build the targeted position.

The resources required will depend to a substantial extent on the bases of the firm's competitive advantage and on the chosen market scope. As noted earlier, cost leadership strategies will require continued surveillance of costs and administrative controls, as well as sustained investment in production design, plant, and equipment to continually improve and update design and manufacturing processes. However, to the extent that increased sales allow the firm to take advantage of economies of scale and experience effects, unit costs may decline.

Differentiation strategies, on the other hand, are grounded in strong marketing and creative skills, and often require adaptation to foreign markets. Consequently, experience and understanding of foreign market characteristics, as well as the ability to adapt creatively to that environment without the firm losing its competitive edge, are likely to be crucial. The firm will need to devote effort, not only to adapting strategy, but also to implementing it effectively, developing relationships with distributors, building customer loyalty, etc. Expenditure on advertising and other promotional activities is also likely to be required in order to generate awareness of, and interest in, the firm and its products, as well as to build a strong image and reputation for quality and service.

The chosen breadth of market scope will also play a key role in determining the nature and level of resources required to enter foreign markets. Where the firm targets broad markets internationally, more resources will be required per country, in order to develop and market the range of product models and variants required to cover the entire market. The firm will also need to devote substantial resources to developing distribution networks and logistical systems to reach all potential customers.

Targeting global segments, on the other hand, may entail less commitment of resources, especially where operations are centered on densely populated urban areas. Such customers can be reached more efficiently, although links between marketing operations in each area will need to be established.

If a firm determines that it lacks the resources needed to implement its proposed strategy, management may need to consider entering into collaborative agreements with other companies. Where the firm lacks the capital to establish production and plants in other countries, for example, management may consider negotiating a joint venture or licensing technology to a foreign company. Similarly, where management lacks experience in international markets and regards the costs of developing direct contracts with distributors as prohibitive, a joint venture with a local company in the foreign market may provide access to local market know-how and distribution networks.

The strength and position of competitors in international markets also have an impact on required resources, and in turn on strategies with regard to which countries to enter and when. Where competition is already well established in a foreign market, substantial resources will be required in order to challenge that position. Where direct competition is absent, resources will be required to develop awareness and interest among customers, as well as distribution systems.

SUMMARY

Success in international markets hinges on doing something better than one's competitors. This "something" translates into a competitive advantage that is sustainable in a number of countries. The challenge unique to international marketing is that a competitive advantage in one country or set of circumstances may not translate into a competitive advantage in another. According to Porter, certain aspects of competitive advantage are specific to the country or geographic location of the firm. This national competitive advantage is made up of four components: (1) factor conditions, (2) demand conditions, (3) related and supporting industries, and (4) firm strategy, structure, and rivalry. These components interact to provide a platform on which to compete in international markets. The most visible manifestations of the role of national competitive advantage are the grouping of particular industries in certain countries, and the dominance of certain countries in particular industries.

Regardless of where a particular firm is located, firm-specific competitive advantage resides in being the cost leader, or successfully differentiating one's product from competitive offerings, or playing the spread. Cost leadership emphasizes the price component of the marketing mix in competitive strategy rather than product, promotion, and distribution. Pursuit of this strategy requires development of a superior delivered cost position. This is typically based on achieving economies of scale and scope, coupled with tight cost control and efficient production management. Differentiation, on the other hand, focuses the marketing effort on the product and promotional components of the marketing mix, with some attention to distribution. Differentiation is achieved by offering superior products, developing a strong brand image, being more responsive than competitors to customer requirements, constantly innovating, or designing unique methods of distribution. Increasingly, however, it is recognized that competitive advantage does not have to be an either/or proposition. Firms may be able to play the spread and combine both strategies.

The market scope of the firm's activities, and more particularly, whether the firm adopts a broad-based strategy (targeting the entire market) or focuses on a specific segment, has implications, not only for how easily its competitive advantage can be leveraged, but for the type of competition it will face. Broad-based strategies are likely to encounter both local and multinational competitors in many if not all markets and often require adaptation to local market conditions and competitive strategies. Focused strategies on the other hand, are more readily leveraged as they target the same or similar segments worldwide.

REFERENCES

1. Porter, Michael E. (1990) *The Competitive Advantage of Nations*, Cambridge, Mass.: Harvard University Press.
2. Levine, Joshua (1992) "Trouble in Paradiso," *Forbes*, October 12, pp. 100–106.
3. Porter, Michael E. (1980) *Competitive Strategy*, New York: The Free Press.
4. Wind, Yoram, and Thomas S. Robertson (1983) "Marketing Strategy: New Directions for Theory and Research," *Journal of Marketing*, 47, (Spring), pp. 12–25.
5. "Ikea's No-Frills Strategy Extends to Management Style," (1992) *Business International*, May 18, pp. 149–150.
6. Johnson, Chalmers (1988) "Japanese Style Management in America," *California Management Review*, (Summer), pp. 34–35.
7. Abegglen, James, and George Stalk, Jr. (1986) "The Japanese Corporation as Competition," *California Management Review*, 28, (Spring), pp. 9–27.
8. Buzzell, Robert D., and Bradley T. Gale (1987) *The PIMS Principles: Linking Strategy to Performance*, New York: The Free Press.
9. Business International, (1991) *Building a Global Image*, New York: Business International Corporation.
10. Day, George S. (1990) *Market-Driven Strategy*, New York: The Free Press.
11. "At Timex, They're Positively Glowing," (1993) *Business Week*, July 12, p. 41.

CHAPTER 6

MARKET SELECTION DECISIONS
Timing and Sequencing of Entry

INTRODUCTION

Market choice decisions are among the most critical decisions made by a firm seeking to establish a global strategy. The choice of which markets to enter commits a firm to operating on a given terrain and sets the pattern for future development. It signals the firm's intent to its competitors and determines the basis for future battles. Hence, as in a chess game, a wrong move early on will presage future disaster. Once operations in a given market have been established, local management hired, and relations with local distributors and other firms developed, substantial penalties are incurred by withdrawing from the market. Ill-conceived, ill-timed, or poorly executed entry decisions can thus seal the firm's fate in its quest to establish a successful global strategy.

Historically, market choice has been equated with country choice; firms focused on selecting the most appropriate country or countries in which to do business. While this perspective was appropriate when market boundaries closely followed political boundaries, this is no longer the case. Markets are both becoming more segmented within country boundaries and at the same time interlinked across country boundaries. The growing integration of markets worldwide in industries ranging from financial services to automobiles, chemicals and household appliances and food, together with the emergence of competition on a global scale, suggests that market choice decisions are considerably more complex than the traditional "country" perspective would suggest.

As more and more firms already have operations in international markets, they need to consider such decisions in the context of the network of existing operations, and hence the dynamics of international market expansion. The growing interdependence among countries and potential for leveraging strategy, systems, and resources across national boundaries further compounds the complexity of these decisions. In addition, as global competition becomes an increasingly potent force, assessment of likely reactions of key competitors to market choice decisions, as well as their own entry decisions and expansion strategies, becomes critical. Consequently, greater attention needs to be paid to the strategic aspects of market choice decisions, and in particular, their impact on the firm's competitive position in international markets.

As noted in Chapter 1, many large companies have already entered international markets. Few, except for those from developing countries, or small and medium-sized manufacturers, are thinking of entering international markets for the first time. Yet, many are entering new countries, as markets open up and competition becomes more global. In deciding whether and which new countries to enter, management needs to consider the same factors as in initial entry, and, particularly, the role such choices will play in the firm's global competitive strategy. Consequently, the following discussion applies to firms entering into additional international markets, as well as first time entrants.

PARAMETERS FOR MARKET CHOICE DECISIONS

Adoption of a strategic perspective on market choice decisions implies that the firm views them as key building blocks in designing an effective global strategy. This establishes the terrain on which the firm competes, with whom it competes, and the level of investment or resources required to compete on the selected terrain. This perspective on market entry decisions requires consideration, not only of market and country characteristics, but, as indicated in Chapter 4, the firm's goals and objectives with regard to international markets, as well as the firm's strengths and weaknesses relative to its competitors (and hence its competitive advantage in world markets). These in turn determine the level of investment and required commitment of resources for successful international expansion.

The firm's strategic thrust in international markets, coupled with market characteristics such as size, rate of growth, and interlinkages, determine the attractiveness of a given market to management as well as the perceived risks associated with entry. Managers should, however, also consider the global competitive environment and the strategic positions of their competitors in selecting markets, and view market choice as a key element of the firm's competitive strategy in international markets (see Figure 6.1).

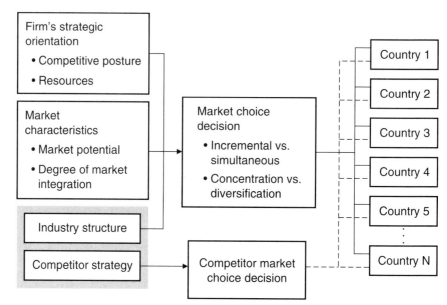

FIGURE 6-1

Developing a market entry strategy.

Firm's Strategic Orientation

The aggressiveness of the strategic thrust, and the desire for international expansion, influence market selection decisions.[1,2] In particular, management attitudes and willingness to assume risk[2,3] determine the resources they are willing to commit to aggressive international expansion, as well as their willingness to take a proactive stance relative to competition.

COMPETITIVE POSTURE

Some firms are relatively conservative and are reluctant to commit resources to international markets. As noted earlier, particularly in the initial stages of entry, some firms prefer to enter international markets cautiously, focusing on neighboring countries or ones that are perceived as similar in terms of language, culture, and business practices and more likely to provide a favorable climate for investment.[4]

Managerial attitudes towards environmental risk also influence choice of markets to enter. Risk-averse firms tend to avoid country markets with high perceived levels of political, financial or economic risk, as, for example, countries characterized by political instability, high rates of inflation, or economic depression. Similarly, such firms tend to adapt less aggressive competitive strategies. They are less likely to confront major competitors in their home markets, or take the initiative by entering country markets in an early stage of their development.

Other firms are considerably more aggressive and willing to commit substantial resources to international expansion. In product markets where there are potential economies of scale, opportunities to leverage strategy and resources, or strong international competition, obtaining market share worldwide is essential for success. Coca-Cola has been particularly aggressive in battling Pepsi for market share worldwide. In reentering the Indian market in 1993, after a 16-year absence, Coke teamed up with Parle Group, the largest Indian soft drink company. This provided Coke with immediate access to a network of over 60 bottlers compared to Pepsi's 22. In addition to establishing a major presence immediately in the Indian market, Coke also began marketing Parle's highly successful mango drink, Frooti, outside India.[5,6]

RESOURCE COMMITMENT

Market entry decisions require commitment of various types of resources. Financial resources are required to conduct the initial investigation of international markets, and to establish operations in other countries, to develop promotional activities and distributor relations, to finance inventory, and to adapt products. Management time and effort are also required to make decisions with regard to international markets and to develop competitive strategy, as well as to manage foreign operations and build up familiarity with the local market environment.

Willingness to commit resources to international markets is often conditioned by risk perceptions. Foreign markets are often associated with high perceived risk, resulting in caution in allocating resources to these markets. In some instances this is due to lack of familiarity with such markets. Hence, as international experience increases, perceived risk declines and willingness to allocate resources to international markets increases.

3M provides an example of a firm that has prospered in international markets by pursuing a cautious entry strategy. Management has ignored traditional concerns about market size and critical mass. One of its guiding principles has been "Make a little, sell a little." This has involved entering a market with a modest investment and one basic product. As it gains experience in a foreign market, it adds new products one at a time, stretching existing company resources to the limit rather than making a major investment in an aggressive export drive. As one top executive said, "We never rush in, we ease in." Following this strategy, 3M has successfully expanded international operations to the point where half of its sales come from international markets.[7]

Management willingness to commit resources to international markets also impacts entry strategy. Simultaneous entry into multiple markets requires significantly greater commitment of financial and managerial resources than an incremental entry strategy (entering a single contiguous country prior to subsequent further expansion).[8] Similarly, entry into markets that are markedly different from the domestic market requires acquisition of knowledge relating to market conditions and the market infrastructure. Management has also to determine the firm's capability to operate in that environment and to adapt products and strategies to specific market characteristics.

Aggressive competitive strategies, such as entering into the domestic market of key foreign competitors, also require substantial resources, not only for the initial move, but also to respond to competitive retaliation. A competitor attacked in a domestic market, for example, may respond by entering the challenger's domestic market. Preemptive entry moves, such as entering a market ahead of competition, also require investment in market and infrastructure development and may be exploited by other competitors.

Market Characteristics

Evaluation of market characteristics is a crucial input into market choice decisions. A firm adopting a strategic perspective must go beyond reliance on aggregate macroindicators such as level of GNP, or population size, and consider the interdependence, interrelatedness, or similarity of markets. This impacts target market scope as well as the extent to which strategies have to be tailored to specific market infrastructure characteristics, or can be leveraged across different markets.

MARKET POTENTIAL

Just as with domestic product markets, market size and rate of market growth are key indicators of international market attractiveness. The underlying rationale is that obtaining market share is easier in high-growth markets. At the same time, large markets and those with high rates of growth require a higher level of resource commitment and, consequently, entail higher risks. Market size and growth are not necessarily correlated. While major industrialized countries constitute large markets for established products and service, rates of growth are often low. For example, rates of GDP growth in the United States and Canada, and in Western Europe, have hovered around 2–3 percent since 1986.[9] In the newly industrialized and developing countries, on the other hand, market size, especially for consumer goods and services, is often small, but rates of growth and market potential are high. In South Korea, Taiwan, Singapore, and Indonesia, annual rates of growth have remained well above 6 percent. India and China are also becoming important world markets, with their large populations of 900 and 1200 million, respectively. These markets offer considerable future potential for many products and services. Many companies eyeing this potential are getting on the bandwagon early, establishing a foothold in the market. Investment in China by U.S. companies alone was over $5 billion in 1993,[10] and exports are also growing rapidly. AT&T, for example, has established a joint venture to manufacture fiber-optic cable, while United Technologies's Pratt and Whitney and Otis Elevator divisions are also planning major investments. Merck is opening up a new hepatitis-B vaccine factory in Beijing, and Baskin-Robbins is opening China's first ice-cream parlor.

As discussed in Chapter 3, the firm needs to consider other factors, depending on the specific product market or company objectives. A company marketing biodegradable diapers, for example, might wish to consider birth rates and trends in infant mortality, as well as the strength of environmental concerns. A company marketing designer fur coats would need to look at climate, luxury taxes, the strength of animal protection movements, and attitudes towards wearing fur.

DEGREE OF MARKET INTEGRATION

In addition to market size and growth, the firm needs to consider the interrelatedness of country markets. This includes both the similarity and the degree of market integration between countries, as well as infrastructure and communication linkages between countries. The similarity of demand characteristics and the market infrastructure from one country to another affects the extent to which similar strategies can be used in different countries. For example, customer interests and purchasing characteristics across a number of contiguous markets such as the Benelux and Scandinavian markets may be sufficiently similar to target these countries as a group. This group might provide the same potential as a single large country market. The firm also needs to examine differences and similarities in the marketing infrastructure, such as the media network, the distribution system, and product and advertising regulation. These facilitate or hamper the extent to which similar strategies can be utilized in different countries, and hence the feasibility and costs of marketing to a group of countries as opposed to targeting a single country.

In addition, markets in many industries are becoming increasingly integrated worldwide. As more and more companies operate across national boundaries, increasingly they have begun to centralize and coordinate operations such as purchasing across national boundaries. In industries such as petrochemicals and automobiles, companies purchase for their operations worldwide, or at least on a regional basis. Consequently, rather than targeting national firms in a single country, companies in such industries need to target firms on a regional or a global scale, and match their supply and service capabilities with those of their clients.

Advances in telecommunications are making transnational media an increasingly potent force in creating linkages between markets. Various newspapers and magazines, such as the *Wall Street Journal* and *Newsweek*, have developed regional editions. Others, such as *Fortune, Business Week*, the *Financial Times*, and the *Economist*, have increased their international subscription base. TV and cable networks, such as Star TV in Asia and MTV, are also developing as regional media linked into global networks.[11] Similarly, retailers such as Carrefours, K-mart, Toys 'R' Us, and Marks and Spencer are beginning to expand across national boundaries. The media and retail infrastructure linkages provide improved and more efficient vehicles for targeting across national boundaries.

The Competitive Environment

The nature of the competitive environment is yet another key factor impacting market choice decisions and their role in global strategy. Traditionally, firms have examined competition on a country-by-country basis and viewed it primarily as a barrier to entry. Taking a more strategic perspective necessitates examining competition on a worldwide rather than country-by-country basis. In addition, rather than taking a static approach to competitive analysis, the dynamics of competitor strategy, and their implications for country choice decisions, should be considered. The firm needs to examine both industry structure and the entry and expansion strategies of competitors worldwide.

INDUSTRY STRUCTURE

Industry structure is a key determinant of competitive behavior. In the context of market entry decisions, the degree of concentration or fragmentation is key in determining the extent to which a firm's market entry decisions are conditioned by those of its competitors.[12,13] If, on the one hand, industry structure is highly fragmented and characterized in all countries by a large number of medium-sized or small firms, such as in the textile or the machine tool industry, a firm may have considerably greater latitude with regard to country choice, and competitor decisions may not exert major influence. On the other hand, if the industry is dominated worldwide by a relatively limited number of firms, whether of similar or different national origins, each firm needs to take into consideration prior and planned moves of competitors, as well as their likely reaction, in deciding which countries to enter.

For example, in entering the Russian market, Procter & Gamble has been able to use its marketing skills to launch new products. However, despite an aggressive marketing effort, profits remain elusive. In addition to the high costs of operating in Russia, P&G faces competition from its traditional rivals in European markets, Unilever and Henkel. Unilever is selling its Omo detergent, Lux soap, and Signal toothpaste, and Henkel has entered into a joint venture to make upgraded versions of local detergents that sell for significantly less than P&G's.[14]

The degree of concentration or fragmentation may vary, depending on the particular region of the world or country, or the strategic group within an industry. In some industries, competition is concentrated in some regions and fragmented in others. For example, in the United States and Western Europe the packaged foods industry is becoming increasingly concentrated, with the growing number of mergers and acquisitions, but remains fragmented in other parts of the world, such as South America and Southeast Asia.

In a fragmented industry, where markets in all countries are characterized by a number of small firms, market attractiveness, coupled with a firm's level of commitment to international expansion and attitudes toward risk, are likely to be the key factors in market choice. Such industries are, however, typically characterized by limited potential for economies of scale, and by heterogeneous and fragmented demand. Customized niche strategies, focusing on specific customer needs or segments, are common.

Where a relatively limited number of firms dominate an industry worldwide, on the other hand, competitor entry strategies and likely reactions are key inputs into market choice decisions. A firm may prefer to avoid competition by entering neutral markets where no major competitors are present. In the agricultural equipment industry, for example, John Deere and International Harvester systematically entered different foreign markets to avoid direct confrontation.[12] In other instances, a firm may opt to follow or confront major competitors in all markets in which they are established. This is designed to contain their international expansion and hinder their ability to take advantage of economies of scale, or leverage a position to build world market share. In the U.S. tire industry, Goodyear was the leader in expanding into international markets. Other tire companies such as Firestone and Goodrich tended to follow Goodyear rapidly into the same foreign market. If another company entered a market first, Goodyear responded by entering into the same market.[12]

Increasingly, as markets open up and competition begins to take place on a global scale in more and more industries, avoidance strategies become less and less feasible and are fraught with hazards. Coca-Cola and Pepsi-Cola, for example, bitter rivals in the soft drink market in the United States, have in the past tended to focus on entering different foreign markets. They have shown this tendency particularly where market potential appeared limited, and substantial difficulties were encountered in market entry. Pepsi-Cola, for example, focused on developing barter agreements in the former Soviet Union and other Eastern European countries. Coca-Cola, on the other hand, entered China and developed the Japanese market. Today, however, Coke and Pepsi are battling it out in the same markets worldwide. Coke has announced plans to make a major investment in the Indian market, which Pepsi entered in 1990, and is also investing in operations in Romania and Hungary. Pepsi, on the other hand, is increasing investment in Japan.[15] Pepsi also plans to invest $750 million in the Mexican market, dominated by Coca-Cola with a two-thirds market share. It has already spent over $115 million in Mexico buying an equity stake in a number of its bottling operations in Guadalajara and Monterey, as well as in suburbs of Mexico City, in order to expand rapidly throughout Mexico. Coke is countering by buying a minority stake in its bottler, Formento Economico Mexicano, in order to defend its market position.

COMPETITOR STRATEGY

The dynamics of market choice decisions suggest the critical importance of examining the expansion strategies of major competitors, as well as their likely response to the firm's entry decisions. This implies monitoring the pattern of competitors' entry decisions and their potential impact on the firm's competitive position worldwide. Rapid expansion into multiple markets may enhance a competitor's advantage whether production or marketing driven. Competitor entry into key markets can also block subsequent entry by other competitors or render such markets less attractive, and restrict the choice of countries open to a firm.

Potential competitor reactions to the firm's entry or country choice decisions also have to be assessed. These reactions depend in part on the strategic intent of the entry decision, as well as the competitive posture of key competitors. For example, entry into a neutral or minor market may provoke limited response from competition as compared with aggressive entry into a competitor's home market or other key world markets. Firms from newly industrializing and developing countries entering international markets often face competition from well-established multinationals. Consequently, they need to assess carefully how such multinationals are likely to react to their challenge. For example, in 1989–1990, Acer, the Taiwanese computer firm, entered the rapidly growing personal computer market in Europe with its low-end product line.[16] In retaliation, IBM and Compaq launched an attack on the "clone" industry in 1992, introducing new product lines at dramatically lower prices.

Other firms from developing countries have preferred to avoid confronting established competition in entering international markets. TVS-Suzuki, an Indian motorcycle company, has, for example, decided to focus on growing markets in East European markets rather than entering the highly competitive U.S. and European markets. Another Indian motorcycle company, Hero, follows a similar strategy, exporting primarily to Latin America, Asia, and Africa.[17] In making entry decisions, a firm has thus to consider, not only the extent to which such decisions will enhance its competitive position in world markets, but also whether its resources are adequate to sustain that position in the light of anticipated competitor moves.

MARKET CHOICE DECISIONS

In addition to considering these various elements, the firm needs to integrate them into the overall design of its blueprint for international expansion. The interdependence of markets and entry choice thus become part of a carefully planned strategy to beat competition in world markets. In designing this strategy, firms have to answer two underlying questions: whether they will enter markets incrementally or simultaneously; and whether entry will be concentrated or diversified across international markets.

Incremental versus Simultaneous Entry

A firm may decide to enter international markets on an incremental or experimental basis, entering first a single key market (or, alternatively, a smaller neutral market) in order to build up experience in international operations, and then subsequently entering other markets one after the other. Alternatively, a firm may decide to enter a number of markets simultaneously in order to leverage its core competence and resources rapidly across a broader market base.[18]

As noted previously, entry on an incremental basis, especially into small markets, may be preferred where a firm lacks experience in foreign markets and wishes to edge gradually into international operations. Information about, and familiarity with operating in, foreign markets are thus acquired step by step. This strategy may be preferable if a company is entering international markets late and faces entrenched local competition. Equally, if a firm is small and has limited resources, or is highly risk-averse, it may prefer to enter a single or limited number of markets and gradually expand in a series of incremental moves rather than making a major commitment to international expansion immediately. Nokia Data, the Finnish information systems company, first entered other Nordic countries, including Sweden, Norway, and Denmark, before entering into highly competitive markets in the rest of Europe.[19]

Some companies prefer a rapid entry into world markets in order to seize an emerging opportunity or forestall competition. Rapid entry facilitates early market penetration across a number of markets and enables the firm to build up experience rapidly. It also enables a firm to achieve economies of scale in production and marketing by integrating and consolidating operations across these markets. This may be especially desirable if the product or service involved is innovative or represents a significant technological advance, in order to forestall preemption or imitation by other competitors.[8] While increasingly feasible due to developments in global information technology, simultaneous entry into multiple markets typically requires substantial financial and management resources and entails higher operating risk.

Concentration versus Diversification

The firm also must decide whether to concentrate resources in a limited number of similar markets, or alternatively to diversify across a number of different markets.[18] A company can concentrate its efforts by entering countries that are highly similar in terms of market characteristics and infrastructure to the domestic market. Management could also focus on a group of proximate countries, such as the Scandinavian countries or the Gulf States, that can be served from a common base in order to reduce operating costs.

Alternatively, a company may prefer to diversify risk by entering countries that differ in terms of environmental or market characteristics.[20] An economic recession in one country could be counterbalanced by growth in another market. The strength of competition also often varies from one market to another, and profits in a relatively protected or less competitive markets may be funneled into more fiercely competitive markets. Spreading out operations over a broader geographic base, and investing in different regions throughout the world, may also diversify risk, since in some industries, markets in different regions are not interdependent; i.e., trends in one region will not spill over to another.

Whether a firm chooses to concentrate or diversify its international operations is likely to depend on the firm's attitude toward risk and on its resources and degree of experience in international markets, as well as on the degree of market integration. Firms with limited resources and commitment to international expansion may prefer similar interlinked markets. Firms willing to commit a substantial level of resources to the development of international operations, on the other hand, may select more diverse and dispersed markets so as to diversify risk. Figures 6.2 and 6.3 illustrate dispersed versus concentrated options.

THE COMPETITIVE DYNAMICS OF MARKET ENTRY

In industries where competition is fragmented, country choice decisions are largely determined by the firm's goals relative to international markets. However, in industries where world markets are dominated by a limited number of large, multinational firms, competitive factors become a key consideration. Well-conceived and -timed market entry decisions are crucial for the firm to compete effectively in world markets.

For a firm wishing to take an active stance in establishing its position as a key player in international markets, three principal types of entry strategies are available: preemption, confrontation, and build-up. A *preemption* strategy entails entering the market ahead of competition in order to capture first-entrant

FIGURE 6-2

A geographically dispersed strategy.

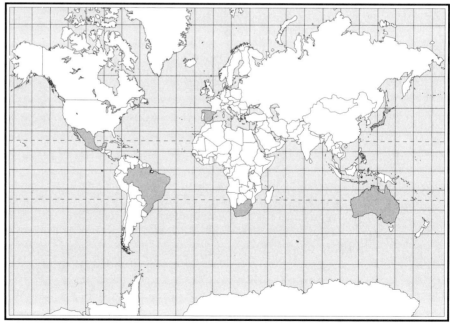

- Japan   • South Africa   • Mexico
- Autralia   • Spain   • Brazil

- Belgium
- Italy
- France
- Netherlands
- Germany
- United Kingdom

FIGURE 6-3
A geographically concentrated strategy.

advantages. Early entry enables a firm to build up a dominant or entrenched market position, which may be relatively impregnable to attack by competition and impede successful entry by others. A *confrontation* strategy, on the other hand, entails entering a market in which a key competitor is already established in order to challenge or contain its competitive position. Confrontation may work in industries where there are significant economies of scale or leverage potential. A competitor left unchallenged in a major market may be able to leverage its position to build world market share and ultimately decimate competition. With a *build-up* strategy, a company enters neutral markets with limited or no competition, either to accumulate experience prior to challenging major competitors in world markets or simply to build global market share, while avoiding key competitors. While these three are not the only possible entry strategies open to a firm—as discussed earlier, a firm might, for example, follow the entry strategies adopted by market leaders or attempt to avoid competition altogether—they represent the principal proactive strategies aimed at capturing a leading position in world markets.

Preemption

A preemption strategy implies being the first to enter world markets or a key country market so as to reap 'first-mover' advantages and steal a march on competitors. This has been a guiding principle for 3M in entering international markets. Its strategy is termed *FIDO* for "First In (to new markets) Dominates Others." However, as indicated earlier, it enters cautiously with a single new product, often initially exporting, and then gradually adding other new products one at a time.[7]

A preemptive strategy enables a firm to establish a position in the market, building up customer and distributor franchises and dominating distribution channels so as to hamper entry by other multinationals or to forestall the emergence of local competition. In some cases, this strategy requires the firm to enter a market early, before there is sufficient demand for the move to be economically viable. In this situation, substantial investment may be required in the short run to develop demand and establish a position, with the expectation of future payoffs. For example, AST Research, Inc., entered the Chinese PC market early, before IBM, Compaq, and Apple. It established a market presence by advertising in Chinese computer magazines, and shuttled managers to China to demonstrate its products.[21] This paid off and allowed it to capture over 25% of the market in China. While it faces increasing competition from IBM, Compaq, and Apple, its early entry places it in a good competitive position in the Chinese PC market. Furthermore, AST is planning a $16 million joint venture to produce 100,000 PCs locally to meet growing demand, forecast to grow at over 22 percent a year for the decade.

As in the case of a pioneer in a new dynamic market, the first entrant into an international market may benefit from a number of advantages. The firm may, for example, be able to develop customer awareness and build up customer franchise and loyalty. First entrants may also be able to tie up distribution channels by selecting the most efficient distributors, establishing good relations with them, and building a strong and highly effective distribution network. Subsequent entrants may have difficulty in persuading these distributors to take on their products, especially if this entails switching, and so are left with less efficient distributors. Consequently, they may have difficulty in obtaining widespread distribution and developing an effective distribution network.

Kelloggs, for example, entered the cereal market in a number of European countries at an early stage and devoted substantial effort to developing demand for breakfast cereal, building a high degree of customer and distributor loyalty.

Quaker and General Mills thus experienced considerable difficulty in attempting to penetrate these markets later. As a result, General Mills set up Cereal Partners International in collaboration with Nestlé to take advantage of Nestlé's distribution strength to market cereal brands internationally.[22]

Preemptive strategies are particularly effective where penetration of distribution channels is the key to successful market development, as is the case in mass distribution consumer packaged goods. Being first to enter distribution channels may be especially critical in industries that are dominated by a few major players, as for example, in cereals and detergents, and where marketing and distribution costs are a significant component of the value chain.

Preemptive strategies are also desirable where a product or service is highly innovative and well differentiated from competition. In this case, a firm may decide to enter key markets worldwide simultaneously in order to forestall imitation or introduction by competition of a similar type of product or service. Getting a jump on competition may be especially critical where an innovation is not adequately covered by patent or trademark rights. This avoids the risk that an innovative product or marketing strategy will be copied and introduced by competitors in other country markets.

The "Pringles" concept—potato chips made from dehydrated potatoes and packaged in a tall canister, was developed by P&G and marketed solely in the United States. Nabisco copied the idea highly successfully in Japan, introducing Chipstar, a comparable product in natural and spinach flavors. P&G exported the product to Cadbury-Schweppes, which marketed it in the U.K. under the brand name "Stackers." When Cadbury divested its food products division, the brand name was sold to Bahlsen, a German food products manufacturer, which now markets the brand throughout Europe. As a result, P&G faces substantial competition in marketing Pringles in Europe.

Preemption also enables the firm to recoup its R&D and other development costs over a broader market base and to sustain a skimming pricing strategy. Neither strategy might be feasible if certain countries or markets were left open to be exploited by competitors. In industries where global competition is already well established and markets are integrated worldwide, such as commercial airframes and jet engines, heavy construction equipment, automobiles, and computers, opportunities for preemptive strategies are typically limited. Major competitors are present in most markets worldwide. The only remaining opportunities are in markets currently opening up, such as India, China, or the former Soviet Union, or in developing countries in Africa and Asia.

Confrontation

Confrontation strategies also entail an aggressive competitive posture. However, rather than focusing on early market entry in order to forestall competition, a company challenges a major competitor in its domestic market or another key world market. Nike, for example, decided to confront Adidas and Puma in their home market, Germany, in order to build a strong position in Europe. Alternatively, a firm might launch a frontal assault on a major competitor by introducing an innovative product or service worldwide. For example, Bic launched an all-out attack on Gillette in introducing its new disposable razor worldwide.

In general, a confrontation posture entails a challenge to a market leader or a major competitor(s). The objective of the confrontation may be either to take over market leadership and strengthen the challenger's own position in world markets, or alternatively to prevent the market leader from dominating the market and hence be in a position to dictate how the market develops.

Confrontation strategies are likely to be effective in situations where a major competitor is firmly entrenched in a key market and has a lopsided emphasis on its domestic or other major market. If the firm derives a large share of its profits from this market and has limited or no involvement in other foreign markets, it will be particularly vulnerable to attack. An aggressive foreign competitor can enter the market, undercutting prices. This will have a major impact on the domestic competitor's profit margins and overall profitability. It will, however, have considerably less impact on the foreign entrant, for whom this market represents a very small proportion of total sales.

Michelin pursued this strategy in entering the U.S. radial tire market. In order to forestall the possible entry by Goodyear into the European market, Michelin entered the U.S. market with an aggressive pricing strategy, thus cutting at Goodyear's profit base.[23] This example also demonstrates some of the dangers of this strategy. Goodyear retaliated by cutting prices in the European market, thus undercutting Michelin's profit base.

Confrontation strategies are most likely to be successful where there is limited likelihood of retaliation, especially with regard to third-country markets or the aggressor's home market. The latter may be especially problematic, as the Michelin/Goodyear example demonstrates, in that the counterattack is directed at the competitor's power base.

Confrontation strategies are also effective where there are potential economies of scale associated with marketing on a global basis, or where corporate identity, brand image, or an innovative product or strategy can be leveraged internationally. In such cases, advantages may accrue from obtaining global market share. Consequently, firms may find it desirable to invest in an aggressive strategy in order to become a market leader.

Build-up

The third type of strategy involves entering somewhat smaller and individually less attractive markets that have not been entered by major competitors. An individual firm decides to avoid direct competition with major competitors in the short run. This strategy may be adopted where a firm feels the need to build up experience in international markets, prior to challenging major competitors in key international markets.

A firm may enter a number of small neutral markets, which may be too small to warrant the attention of the market leader. It can then build up market share and accumulate experience so as to achieve economies of scale and reduce unit costs. Ericsson, for example, faced by entrenched competition from national telecommunications companies in key European-markets, focussed on developing modular PBX systems for small and medium-sized businesses in peripheral European and African markets.[24] Once these markets were developed and Ericsson had accumulated experience in marketing to small and medium-sized businesses, the company targeted similar segments within the major European markets. It was thus able to leverage experience in neutral markets to penetrate competitor dominated terrain with considerable success.

Build-up strategies are likely to be most appropriate where potential economies of scale are limited and significant adaptation to specific market characteristics is required. Hence, a firm cannot obtain a significant cost advantage by expanding on a global scale (as is feasible in the watch industry or consumer electronics). Build-up strategies are also cffcctive where country markets are fragmented or isolated. Some country markets may be too small or less desirable than others and hence not be considered viable by market leaders. These provide an appropriate target for a build-up strategy. Similarly, if markets are not isolated, significant costs may be incurred in entering each country market, and ability to transfer products, ideas, or experience from one country market to another may be limited. Consequently, they are not attractive targets for market leaders. Conversely, in markets that are integrated, where customers and competitors operate or move across national boundaries, opportunities for build-up strategies may be more limited.

SUMMARY

The increasing interdependence of markets, and the growth of competition on an international scale, require adoption of a strategic approach to international entry decisions. Country entry decisions can no longer be viewed as discrete and independent, based predominantly on assessment of market attractiveness. A dynamic perspective is needed that views entry decisions as a key element of competitive strategy. The framework presented in Chapter 6 provides such a perspective and suggests the various elements that need to be considered in designing a strategy to build a strong competitive position in world markets. In the absence of strong competitors, the firm's goals and objectives, and its willingness to commit resources to international markets, assume key importance in fashioning this strategy. Where, however, the firm is faced by a number of major competitors, entry moves play an important role in the competitive game.

Depending on the position and relative strength of key competitors, various alternative strategies may be adopted. Preemptive moves early in the game may help the firm to outdistance competition and build a strong position against future attack. Confrontational strategies, on the other hand, should only be undertaken from a position of relative strength with the intent of attacking a competitor where it is vulnerable. A build-up strategy is best suited to a smaller competitor or a late entrant who needs time to build up strength either as a prelude to launching a major attack on established competitors or simply as a way to expand global market share.

A strategic perspective on country choice decisions helps the firm make entry decisions part of its overall strategic plan. In particular, it underscores the importance of viewing these as interrelated and as a key component of competitive strategy in international markets. An important aspect is monitoring competitor moves and formulating strategy relative to their current and anticipated future position. Proactive market entry strategies are thus critical to successful expansion in world markets.

REFERENCES

1. Bilkey, Warren J. (1978) "An Attempted Integration of the Literature on the Export Behavior of Firms," *Journal of International Business Studies*, 9, (Spring-Summer), pp. 33–46.
2. Cavusgil, S. Tamer (1980) "On the Internationalization Process of Firms," *European Research*, (November), pp. 273–80.
3. Dichtl, Ernst, Hans-Georg Koeglmayr, and Stefan Mueller (1990) "International Orientation as a Precondition for Export Success," *Journal of International Business Studies*, 21, (First Quarter), pp. 23–40.
4. Johanson, Jan, and Finn, Wiedersheim-Paul (1975) "The Internationalization of the Firm-Four Swedish Cases," *Journal of Management Studies*, 12, pp. 305–322.
5. Skaria, George (1993) "The Coke Challenge," *Business Today*, November 7–21, pp. 50–61.
6. Prasad, Jeanne (1993) "Watch the Thunder," *Business India*, July 19–August 1, pp. 53–60.
7. Rose, Robert (1991) "How 3M, by Tiptoeing into Foreign Markets, Became a Big Exporter," *Wall Street Journal*, March 29, pp. 1–ff.
8. Ayal, Igal, and Jehiel Zif (1979) "Market Expansion Strategies in Multinational Marketing," *Journal of Marketing*, 43, (Spring), pp. 84–94.
9. "The World Economy in Charts," (1993), *Fortune*, July 26, pp. 94–96.
10. "Behind the Great Wall," (1993) *Business Week*, October 25, pp. 42–43.
11. Kraar, Louis (1994), "TV Is Exploding All Over Asia," *Fortune*, January 24, pp. 98–101.
12. Davidson, William H. (1982) *Global Strategic Management*, New York: John Wiley and Sons.
13. Knickerbocker, F.T. (1973) *Oligopolistic Reaction and Multinational Enterprise*, Business School, Boston.
14. Reitman, Valerie (1993) "P&G Uses Skills It Has Honed at Home to Introduce Its Brands to the Russians," *Wall Street Journal*, April 14, pp. B1–ff.

15. "Pepsi Co. to Invest About $750 Million in Mexican Market," (1993) *Wall Street Journal*, March 5.
16. Acer in Europe (1992), INSEAD Case.
17. "Hero Motors," (1993) *Business India*, September 13–26, pp. 78–80.
18. Doyle, Peter, and Z.B. Gidengil (1977) "A Strategic Approach to International Market Selection," *Proceedings of the American Association*, AMA, Chicago, IL, pp. 359–377.
19. Nokia Data, (1989) IMO Case.
20. Keegan, Warren (1977) "Strategic Marketing: International Diversification Versus National Concentration," *Columbia Journal of World Business*, (Winter), pp. 119–129.
21. "What Country Has a Computer for Every 6,000 People," (1993) *Business Week*, September 13, p. 50.
22. Knowlton, Christopher (1991) "Europe Cooks Up a Cereal Brawl," *Fortune*, June 3, pp. 75–77.
23. Hamel, Gary, and C.K. Prahalad (1985) "Do You Really Have a Global Strategy?" *Harvard Business Review*, (July-August), pp. 139–44.
24. Hout, T., M.E. Porter, and E. Rudden (1982), "How Global Companies Win Out," *Harvard Business Review*, (September-October), pp. 98–108.

CHAPTER 7

MODES OF ENTRY INTO GLOBAL MARKETS

INTRODUCTION

Closely linked to decisions regarding country choice are decisions about how to conduct operations in international markets, that is, whether to export, negotiate a licensing or franchise agreement, establish a joint venture, or set up a wholly owned subsidiary.[1] While, in principle, market choice and mode of entry are separate decisions, specific country characteristics, as well as international market entry and expansion strategies, impact mode-of-entry choice.

Country characteristics such as market size, growth rate, political stability, environmental risk, operating conditions, and infrastructure impact management's willingness to commit resources to a given country or market and mode of entry. Small markets are often best served through exporting or licensing, for example. Equally, management may prefer to limit resource commitment to countries with high levels of risk or poor infrastructures, through licensing agreements or joint ventures with local partners. Similarly, if management wishes to enter a number of countries rapidly, the resources and time required to establish wholly owned subsidiaries may be prohibitive, leading it to use licensing or joint ventures.

Product characteristics, the nature of demand, and trade barriers, as well as management goals and expansion objectives, also influence mode-of-entry decisions. Bulky, low-value products, for example, require production close to the market, due to freight costs, though these costs may be offset by production economies of scale. Tariffs or other trade barriers encourage modes entailing production or assembly within the foreign market. Similarly, management goals and expansion objectives affect commitment of resources to international markets and interest in entering into contractual obligations with other foreign organizations.

FACTORS IMPACTING THE CHOICE OF MODE OF ENTRY

Following the framework in Figure 7-1, five sets of factors should be considered in determining the mode of entry. Three of these, *country characteristics, trade barriers*, and *product market characteristics*, are external environmental characteristics that are givens in the firm's entry decision. Two of them, *firm objectives*, and *country selection strategies*, are internal, firm-specific characteristics, whose central role in the firm's international strategy was discussed in Chapters 4, 5 and 6. How each of these five sets of factors impacts mode of entry is examined in more detail next.

FIGURE 7-1
Factors impacting the choice of mode of entry.

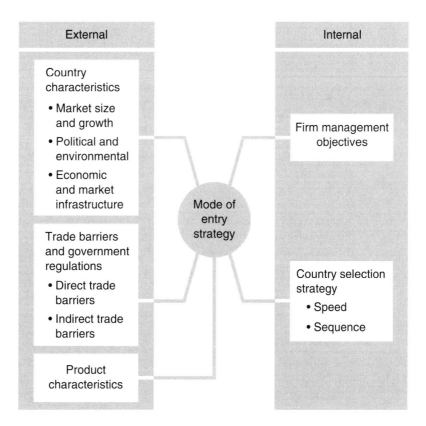

Country Characteristics

Three broad categories of country characteristics must be considered: country size and growth, political and environmental risk, and the economic and market infrastructure. While numerous other country characteristics may also be considered in entry decisions, the importance and specific nature of these depend on the individual firm and product or service.

MARKET SIZE AND GROWTH

Country size and rate of market growth are key parameters in determining mode of entry. The larger the country and the size of its market, and the higher the growth rate, the more likely management will be to commit resources to its development, and to consider establishing a wholly owned subsidiary or sales organization, or to participate in a majority-owned joint venture. Retaining control over operations provides management with direct contact and allows it to plan and direct market development more effectively.

Small markets, on the other hand, especially if they are geographically isolated and cannot be efficiently serviced from a neighboring country, may not warrant significant attention or resources. Consequently, they may best be supplied via exporting or a licensing agreement. While unlikely to stimulate market development or maximize market penetration, this approach enables the firm to enter the market with minimal resource commitment and frees up resources for potentially more lucrative markets.

POLITICAL AND ENVIRONMENTAL RISK

Management is often reluctant to commit resources to countries with high levels of political and environmental risk and may avoid modes of entry that entail establishment of production or warehousing facilities or a substantial sales organization. Management is likely to be particularly cautious where a substantial investment in plant and equipment is entailed, and where a particular activity constitutes a crucial component of the value chain. Companies have, for example, been especially wary of countries with histories of expropriation, such as Argentina, Chile, and Peru, or where there is substantial risk of political insurrection or instability, such as the Philippines, Cambodia, or Nigeria.

Sometimes governments can be volatile, suddenly reversing previous decisions. Seagrams, for example, entered a joint venture in the Ukraine to produce vodka, initially with the intention of exporting it to Russia as well as the west.[2] The Ukraine government granted tax holidays and other exemptions to attract foreign investors and guaranteed that conditions would not change for 5 years. However, the deteriorating economic situation led the government to increase excise taxes substantially, tripling the price of vodka. This resulted in a flood of smuggled liquor. In addition, the government declared spirits exporting a state monopoly and refused to give permission for export production. As a result, Seagrams is producing a small amount of vodka for the Ukrainian market, and importing its well-known labels such as Chivas Regal, Passport Scotch, Martell

Cognac, and Mumms Champagne. These end up being sold primarily to black marketeers, who have hard currency to purchase luxury items.

ECONOMIC AND MARKET INFRASTRUCTURE

The economic and market infrastructure comprises a third set of country characteristics that have an impact on decisions relating to the mode of entry or operation. When the physical infrastructure (transportation system, communications networks, or energy supply) is poorly developed, management is likely to encounter substantial difficulties and development costs in establishing its own production, distribution, or sales facilities. For example, Guardian Industries, one of the world's largest glassmakers, established a joint venture in 1988 to build a glass manufacturing plant in Hungary. The roads leading to the plant were in poor condition, and Guardian had to work with the government to repair them. In addition, equipment that Guardian had initially planned to buy in Eastern Europe had to be imported from the United States and Western Europe.[3] Poor infrastructure, particularly in telecommunications, has been a major problem confronting foreign investors in Eastern Europe, particularly in Poland and the Czech Republic, and one which has often been underestimated. While Western Europe has an average of 43 telephones lines per 100, most countries in Eastern Europe, except for the Baltic States, have between 10 and 15. Poland has the lowest number at 9.5, and improvements are hampered by strict government controls on foreign investment, and requirements that over half the equipment has to be produced in Poland.[4]

Trade Barriers and Government Regulations

In some cases, government regulations restrict mode-of-entry options open to foreign companies, especially in strategic industries such as telecommunications, transportation, and computers. As markets worldwide become more interdependent and integrated, many governments have removed or reduced ownership restrictions. For example, the Indian government, which previously used ownership restrictions extensively to limit the entry and influence of foreign enterprise, has lifted these restrictions. As a result, Coca-Cola, which withdrew from India in 1977, when majority foreign ownership was not permitted, has reentered the market.

Regulation of contracts with distributors and other organizations, especially relating to exclusive agreements or termination of contracts, also have to be considered. Often substantial notice has to be given prior to termination of a contract. Costs of terminating management and labor contracts also need to be considered. For example, in Italy a manager has to be given a "notice" period payment plus severance payment based on salary and years of service.[5]

Trade barriers, such as tariffs, quotas, customs, or product regulation, also influence mode of entry decisions. Direct trade barriers restricting the import of foreign goods, such as tariffs and quotas, impact decisions relating to local production or assembly. Indirect trade barriers, such as product regulation, preference for local suppliers, customs, and certification formalities, encourage establishment of contractual agreements with local partners.

DIRECT TRADE BARRIERS

Tariffs or quotas on the import of foreign goods and components favor establishment of local production or assembly operations. A number of countries such as Malaysia and Brazil have preferential tariffs for unassembled components to encourage labor-intensive local assembly. Ford and GM both have assembly operations in Brazil, where 70 percent of parts are produced locally.[6] The potential threat of such barriers will encourage companies to shift from exporting to local production or assembly, especially in industries where this would have a significant impact on the balance of trade.

Japanese automobile manufacturers have invested heavily in establishing production plants in Europe in order to bypass quota restrictions on imports. Prior to the establishment of the European Union, Italy had an annual quota of 3,500 Japanese-produced cars, and 10,500 for cars from other parts of the Community. France, on the other hand, limited Japanese imports to 3 percent of the market, and the U.K. to 11 percent. Harmonization of these restrictions within the EU has resulted in voluntary restrictions on Japanese imports to 1.2 million vehicles (11.7 percent of the market in 1992.)[7] Nissan, Toyota, and Honda have all established assembly plants in Britain, while Mitsubishi is negotiating a joint venture with Volvo.[8] Sony has also set up plants in Wales, France, Germany, and Italy, which supply over 50 percent of Sony products sold in Europe to circumvent tariffs and quotas on consumer electronics items.[9]

INDIRECT TRADE BARRIERS

Product or trade regulations and standards, as well as preferences for local suppliers, also have an impact on mode of entry and operation decisions. Preferences for local suppliers, or tendencies to "buy national," often encourage a company to consider a joint venture or other contractual arrangements with a local company. The local partner helps in developing local contacts, negotiating sales, and establishing distribution channels, as well as to diffuse the foreign image. In entering the Japanese market, foreign companies such as Caterpillar, Hewlett Packard, and NCR have found this an effective means to penetrate the close ties among suppliers and manufacturers characteristic of the Japanese industrial system.[10]

Product and trade regulations and customs formalities similarly encourage modes involving local companies who can provide information about and contacts in local markets, and can ease access. In some instances where product regulations and standards necessitate significant adaptation and modification, the firm may establish local production, assembly, or finishing facilities.

The net impact of both direct and indirect trade barriers is thus likely to be a shift toward performing various functions such as sourcing, production and developing marketing tactics in the local market.

Product Characteristics

The physical characteristics of the product or service, such as its weight/value ratio, perishability, and composition are important in determining where production is located. Products with low weight/value ratios such as expensive watches, are particularly susceptible to direct exporting, especially where there are significant production economies of scale, or if management wishes to retain control over production. Conversely, in the soft drink and beer industry, companies typically establish licensing agreements, or invest in local bottling or production facilities, as shipment costs, particularly to distant markets, are prohibitive. Heineken, for example, has been establishing joint ventures to build breweries in India, Thailand, Vietnam, and China.[11] In some cases, as, for example, a proprietary brand of spring water, exporting is the only option.

Where the product or service incorporates proprietary assets such as technology, brand name, or image, management is often reluctant to participate in joint ventures, especially where this entails potential loss of control over production quality or distribution, or sharing proprietary information or technology. IBM has traditionally avoided joint ventures for this reason, and withdrew from India, when the government would not permit majority-owned joint ventures. Sometimes licensing and franchising or other contractual agreements are best established where the right of the licensee, franchisee, or local partner to utilize the proprietary asset (i.e., technology, trademark, or corporate name) is clearly established, and provision for quality control and monitoring of operations is provided.

Firm/Management Objectives

Companies with limited objectives for their international operations tend to favor modes of entry entailing minimal commitment. Such firms often prefer to rely on export management companies or agents, or to establish licensing agreements. These modes of entry require few financial resources and only limited management attention, as responsibility for international markets is handled by another organization.

A firm with a proactive, aggressive approach to international market growth is more likely to favor establishing an export sales organization and to move rapidly towards modes of operation such as joint ventures or wholly owned operations, which provide substantial control over production and marketing in foreign markets. Molex, a mid-sized U.S. manufacturer of electronic connectors for computer circuit boards and automobiles, entered rapidly into international markets in the early 1970s, as its customers began to source from cheaper foreign suppliers. Molex quickly established foreign plants to take advantage of low-cost labor and built up sales to local manufacturers as well as U.S. multinationals.[12]

Country Selection Strategies

Where a company desires to enter a country rapidly to take advantage of emerging market opportunities, options such as licensing, franchising, or acquiring existing companies may be appropriate, since they take advantage of established production facilities and distribution networks, as well as market knowledge and local contacts. Burger King, for example, opted to enter the Brazilian market via the acquisition of Bob's, Brazil's second largest fast food chain, with 84 outlets. They plan to keep the Bob's name in Rio, where the chain was founded, and change the name to Burger King in all the others.[13]

Conversely, when a company decides to adopt a more cautious strategy to entry into international markets, management may prefer initially to export, gradually shifting to establishment of a local sales force and, finally, establishment of production in foreign markets. This incremental process has been typical of many Scandinavian small and medium-sized firms.[14] For example, Pharmacia, a large Swedish pharmaceutical company, initially entered foreign markets because of orders received from buyers in other countries. After some time, they appointed an agent, or sold licenses for some parts of their product line in these countries. After a few more years, they established sales subsidiaries in these countries. Finally, they started manufacturing activities, starting with the least-complicated activities and successfully adding more complex ones.[15]

Simultaneous entry into a number of markets may also strain the resources of the firm, prompting entry into collaborative agreements and joint ventures. Such arrangements are particularly likely in industries characterized by high rates of technological change. While rapid entry into multiple markets is desirable in order to preempt competition, a company may lack resources to establish wholly owned subsidiaries and prefer to focus on R&D and technological improvements rather than marketing. Joint ventures, or in some cases licensing, may be the preferred mode of entry. Apple Computer, for example, facing rapid technological evolution and growth in the newly emerging U.S. personal computer market, was reluctant to devote resources to international marketing. The threat of clone products from Southeast Asia swamping the market led them to adopt a compromise solution, developing a series of licensing arrangements and joint ventures, especially in Central and Latin American Markets.

Factors Influencing Modes of Entry

While cost effectiveness is clearly a key factor in assessing alternative modes of entry, it is often difficult to estimate costs precisely, given uncertainties with regard to sales potential and growth. Four other factors are helpful in evaluating modes of entry: the *location of production, commitment of financial and managerial resources, degree of control,* and *flexibility* (see Figure 7-2 for an overview).

LOCATION OF PRODUCTION

In exporting, production is located in the domestic market, while all other modes entail production in other countries. In practice, the choice of exporting

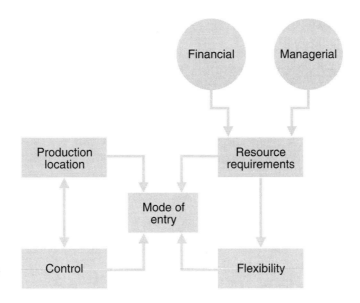

FIGURE 7-2

Dynamics of market entry.

vs. local production is likely to be determined by cost factors. In some cases, sales volume in foreign markets is not adequate to support the minimum economic scale of production. Equally, the existence of potential economies of scale may outweigh freight and shipping costs. In addition to cost considerations, local production offers certain advantages arising from proximity to the market—for example, improved feedback with regard to product design and modification, better and speedier service, and information relating to market trends. For example, Hyundai's Information System Division, in entering the U.S. personal computer market, decided to design and assemble PCs at its California base in order to respond quickly to the rapidly changing market.[16]

RESOURCE COMMITMENT

Indirect exporting and licensing typically entail low levels of financial and managerial resource commitment. Joint ventures provide a way of sharing risk, financial exposure, and the cost of establishing local distribution networks and hiring local personnel. But negotiating and managing joint ventures often absorbs considerable management time and effort. However, modes of entry that entail minimal levels of resource commitment are unlikely to foster development of international operations and may result in significant opportunity loss.

CONTROL

Mode-of-entry decisions also need to consider the degree of control management requires over operations in international markets. Often control is closely linked to the level of resource commitment. Modes of entry with minimal resource commitment, such as indirect exporting, provide little or no control over international market development, nor over the conditions under which the product or service is marketed abroad. Consequently, the product may be under- or overpriced, resulting in loss of sales or potential profits. It may also be poorly stored, resulting in physical deterioration. In the case of licensing and contract manufacturing, management needs to ensure that production meets its quality standards. Joint ventures also limit the degree of management control over international operations and can be a source of considerable conflict where the goals and objectives of partners diverge. Wholly owned subsidiaries provide the most control but entail substantial commitment of resources.

FLEXIBILITY

Management must also weigh the flexibility associated with a given mode of entry. Modes that entail contractual arrangements with other firms or substantial equity investment in production, warehousing, or sales facilities in foreign markets are typically the least flexible and most difficult to change in the short run. Licensing and other contractual agreements limit the firm's ability to adapt or change strategy during their duration and need to be evaluated carefully, especially where market conditions are changing rapidly. Similarly, wholly owned production or distribution networks in international markets may be costly and difficult to divest. (See Figure 7-3 for an overview of different modes of operation.)

FIGURE 7-3
Modes of operation.

EXPORTING

Export is the most common mode for initial entry into international markets. Sometimes, an unsolicited order is received from a buyer in a foreign country, or a domestic customer expands internationally and places an order for its international operations. This prompts the firm to consider international markets and to investigate their growth potential, as the case of Pharmacia discussed earlier illustrates. In some cases, however, a firm moves aggressively into exporting. Loctite, the U.S. manufacturer of adhesives and sealants, pushed hard into international markets immediately after its founding in 1953, and by 1960 generated 60 percent of its sales abroad. It has subsequently moved gradually into establishing joint ventures with local distributors and setting up overseas plants in a number of countries such as Iceland, Brazil, and China. Over 60 percent of its sales now come from international markets.[17]

Exporting is thus typically used in initial entry and gradually evolves towards foreign-based operations. In some cases where there are substantial scale economies or a limited number of buyers in the market worldwide (for example, aerospace), production may be concentrated in a single or limited number of locations, and then exported to other markets. Boeing, for example, the largest U.S. exporter, concentrates production at its home base in Seattle, Washington.

Exporting can be organized in a variety of ways, depending on the number and type of intermediaries. As in the case of wholesaling, export and import agents vary considerably in the range of functions performed. Some, such as the export management companies, are the equivalent of full-service wholesalers and perform all functions relating to export. Others are highly specialized and only handle freight forwarding, billing, or clearing goods through customs.

In establishing export channels, a firm has to decide which functions will be the responsibility of external agents, and which will be handled by the firm itself. While export channels may take many different forms, for the purposes of simplicity, three major types may be identified: *indirect, cooperative*, and *direct*.[18] Indirect channels involve the use of export agents, often export management companies. Cooperative channels involve collaborative agreements with other firms concerning the performance of exporting functions. In direct exporting, the firm handles the export function internally, through a sales organization located in either the domestic or the foreign market (see Figure 7-4 for a summary of the advantages and limitations of different types of exporting).

Indirect Exporting

One approach to exporting is to use export agents, or trading companies, or to sell to the sales offices of foreign organizations located in the firm's domestic

	Indirect	Direct
Advantages	• Limited commitment • Minimal risk • Flexibility	• Better contact • More control • Better sales effort
Limitations	• Potential opportunity loss • Lack of control • Lack of contact with market	• Investment in sales organization • Commitment to foreign market

FIGURE 7-4
Advantages and limitations of exporting.

market. Responsibility for the exporting function, such as identifying potential buyers and distributors in other countries; organizing shipment of goods, insurance, and financing; or providing documentation to satisfy customs formalities, is thus transferred to another organization. Especially in cases where the exporting organization takes title to goods, the firm assumes no risk with regard to export sales, and minimal effort is entailed. Such sales are comparable to those made to domestic customers.

Such an approach to exporting is most likely to be appropriate for a firm with limited international expansion objectives. If international sales are viewed primarily as a means of disposing of surplus production, or as marginal, use of agents may be appropriate. It may also be adopted by a firm with minimal resources to devote to international expansion, which wants to enter international markets gradually, testing out markets before committing major resources and effort to developing an export organization.

It is important for a firm to recognize, however, that use of agents or export management companies carries a number of risks. In the first place, the firm has little or no control over the way the product or service is marketed in other countries. Products may be sold through inappropriate channels, with poor servicing or sales support and inadequate promotion, or be under- or overpriced. This can damage the reputation or image of the product or service in foreign markets. Limited effort may be devoted to developing the market, resulting in potential lost opportunities.

Particularly significant for the firm interested in gradually edging into international markets is that, with indirect exporting, the firm establishes little or no contact with markets abroad. Consequently, the firm has limited information about foreign market potential, and little input to develop a plan for international expansion. The firm will have no means to identify potential sales agents or distributors for its products and facilitate transition towards the establishment of its own export distribution channels. Apple Computer, for example, shifted from supplying China through Hong Kong-based distributors and established an office in Beijing to provide strong promotional effort and service support to computer developers and consumers in China.[19] An agreement was signed with a Chinese computer company, the Legend group, to market and service Apple computers through its nationwide distributor network. A training center for software developers, resellers, and students was also set up at Tsinghuan University in Beijing.

Consequently, use of indirect export channels is unlikely to provide an effective first step towards international market expansion. While appropriate in some cases, indirect exporting should be used with extreme caution by a firm with plans to develop and grow in international markets.

Cooperative Exporting

For a firm that wishes to exercise some degree of control over international sales but lacks the resources or sales volume to establish its own export sales organization, cooperative exporting is an alternative. Here, a firm enters into a collaborative agreement with another firm to cooperate on research, promotion, shipping, distribution, or other activities relating to export markets.

Commodities, such as rice, woodchips, dried fruit, or oranges, are particularly susceptible to such cooperative agreements. Organizations such as the California Dried Fruit Export Association or the American Cotton Exporters undertake research to identify potential international markets, organize shipping and freight, and develop advertising and promotional campaigns for international markets. In the United States, the Webb-Pomerene act and subsequent legislation exempt such associations from prosecution under antitrust legislation.

Another type of cooperative agreement common in export marketing is piggybacking, in which one company markets its products or services through the distribution organization of another company in a foreign market. In general, the products sold by both companies need to be compatible rather than competing, so that the products of the piggybacking company complement or fill out the product line of the distributing company. Often, this type of arrangement is mutually beneficial. Minolta, for example, originally sold its low-priced photocopying machines in the United States through the IBM office equipment sales organization. This arrangement provided Minolta with much broader distribution coverage and more effective servicing capabilities than they might otherwise have been able to obtain. At the same time, the low-end copying machines filled out the IBM line of high-priced copiers.

Cooperative export ventures can be established in a variety of ways. Depending on the precise terms of the agreement, they may have the advantages and limitations of either direct or indirect exporting shown in Figure 7-4. In any case, they involve lower investment costs and improved sales effort as compared with indirect exporting. However, the degree of control may vary.

Direct Exporting

Where sales volume is sufficient and the firm wishes to devote major effort to developing international markets, establishing its own export sales organization is often desirable. This organization may be located either in the domestic market or in foreign markets. In this case, the export organization takes over responsibility for all exporting functions, from identifying potential markets and target segments, arranging export documentation and shipment, to developing a marketing plan, including pricing, promotion, and distribution for international markets.

While direct exporting entails higher costs and greater commitment to export market development, it is likely to result in a more effective promotional and sales effort, and also enables the firm to maintain greater control over the conditions under which its products are sold in international markets. It also provides improved contact, and feedback to identify new opportunities and market trends, to monitor performance and competitor moves, and to adjust plans and strategy accordingly.

While, for some companies, exporting is a first or intermediate step on the path to international market expansion, for others it remains the dominant mode of operation in international markets. Small and medium-sized companies targeting specialized niche segments in global markets sometimes remain exporters. The companies of the German "Mittelstand" (literally, "mid-ranking"), for example, constitute the core of Germany's export machine.[20] Supported by a global infrastructure of German government agencies, trade associations, and banks, these companies export quality products to specialized niche markets worldwide. The Gasbau Hahn factory outside Frankfurt, sells high-quality custom-built glass showcases equipped with fiber-optic lighting, precision climatic control, and sophisticated protection equipment to top-flight museums, such as the Metropolitan Museum of Art in New York and the British Museum in London. Often, these companies are family-owned businesses that rely on advanced technology, continued innovation and R&D, and maintain close contact with potential customers to adapt their products to changing customer needs and market trends.

FOREIGN MANUFACTURING: CONTRACTUAL AND LICENSING ARRANGEMENTS

Where market size, shipping costs, tariff barriers, and other factors suggest the desirability of establishing production close to foreign customers, but the firm is reluctant to engage in such operations, it has a number of alternatives. Contract manufacturing, for example, enables the firm to develop and control the marketing, distribution, and servicing of its products in international markets, while handing over responsibility for production to a local firm. Licensing, on the other hand, enables a firm to reap the benefits of technological innovation, a brand, a corporate name, or other proprietary assets in international markets, without itself engaging in either foreign production or marketing operations. Similarly, in service industries, establishment of franchising agreements with local entrepreneurs enables the franchisor to expand internationally through tapping local sources of capital and entrepreneurial talent. Another alternative is to establish a joint venture with another firm or organization for international manufacturing or marketing activities. (See Figure 7-5 for a summary of the advantages and limitations of the various forms of contractual modes of entry.)

Contract Manufacturing

In the case of contract manufacturing, the firm contracts out production to a local manufacturer but retains control of marketing. This strategy may be appropriate in countries where market size is not sufficient to warrant establishing a manufacturing facility and where there are high tariff barriers. For example, P&G contracted out manufacturing of its Ariel detergent in Russia to lower manufacturing costs and bypass tariffs on imported goods.[21] Alternatively, management may lack resources or be unwilling to invest equity in such a facility. In essence, management rents the production capacity of a local manufacturer.

Contract manufacturing also offers substantial flexibility. Depending on the duration of contract, if the firm is dissatisfied with product quality or reliability of delivery, it can shift to another manufacturer. In addition, if management decides to exit the market, it does not have to sustain possible losses from divesting production facilities. On the other hand, it is necessary to control product quality to meet company standards. The firm may encounter problems with delivery, product warranties, or filling additional orders. The manufacturer may also not be as cost efficient as the contracting firm, or reach production capacity, or attempt to exploit the agreement.

The dangers of inadequately protecting technology are well illustrated by the case of Schwinn, the U.S. bicycle manufacturer. Faced by gradual erosion of market share in the United States, and cheaper foreign competition, Schwinn decid-

FIGURE 7-5

Advantages and limitations of contractual modes of operations.

	Contract manufacturing	Franchising	Licensing
Advantages	• No investment required • Avoids tariff barriers • Quick mode of entry • Flexible • Lower manufacturing costs	• Limited financial investment • Taps local managerial talent (services) • Improved managerial motivation	• No investment • Minimal risk • Exploit small markets • Quick way to obtain entry
Limitations	• Need for quality control • Supply limitations	• Often requires training program for managers • Need for financial and product quality control	• Limited returns • Builds up potential competition • Restricts future market development • Requires quality and financial control

ed to source bikes first from Japan and then from Giant, a Taiwanese manufacturer. It closed its U.S. factory and set up a partnership with Giant, providing its partner with technology and engineering expertise.[22] Giant refused to sell any equity to Schwinn, which lost control over strategy. Giant gained valuable knowledge about the U.S. market, including distribution channels, and decided to launch its own brand name in the United States and in Europe, undercutting Schwinn on price. To compete, Schwinn forged a new alliance with China Bicycles, a low-cost manufacturer in Shenzhen, China. Again, Schwinn transferred technology to China and improved its quality standards. China Bicycles then bought the Diamond Back name and entered the U.S. market in competition with Schwinn. With both Giant and China Bicycles cutting into its market share, Schwinn was forced to file for bankruptcy and was bought by Scott, a ski accessory manufacturer with plans to focus operations on mountain bikes.[23]

Thus, while contract manufacturing offers a number of advantages, especially to a firm whose strength lies in marketing and distribution, care needs to be exercised in negotiating the contract. Where the firm loses direct control over the manufacturing function, mechanisms to ensure that the contract manufacturer meets the firm's quality and delivery standards need to be developed.

Licensing

Licensing is an appropriate mode of entry if the firm has some type of proprietary asset, such as a patented product or process technology, trade mark, or brand name, from which it wishes to benefit on an international scale without committing resources to international operations. In a licensing agreement, a firm gives a licensee the right to utilize the patented technology, trademark, or brand name in return for payment of royalty fees. Typically, these fees are a percentage of sales covered by the agreement.

Licensing agreements thus enable a firm to benefit from international sales utilizing its proprietary assets, with minimal commitment of resources and risk. However, such agreements only provide limited returns. In addition, market development may be limited if the licensee does not devote adequate attention or have the resources to develop markets fully.

The risks of licensing are well illustrated by the experiences of PepsiCo and Xerox. PepsiCo licensed Perrier, the French mineral water company, to bottle and distribute its brands in France. However, Perrier was less well placed than its competitors, Badoit and Evian, in hyper- and supermarkets. As these channels became dominant forces in grocery distribution, Pepsi lost market share and eventually terminated its agreement with Perrier.[24] Xerox made a similar but graver error by granting the Rank organization in the U.K. the exclusive rights to market all products covered by Xerox patents in markets outside the United States in perpetuity. The Rank–Xerox venture failed to take advantage of this opportunity and barely developed markets in Europe, let alone the rest of the world. As a result, Xerox had to buy back the licensing rights—a process that extended over a number of years and is estimated to have cost Xerox millions of dollars.

Licensing can also hamper subsequent international market entry by the licensor. Even if a firm limits the duration of the licensing agreement, it may be difficult to enter the market at the expiration of the contract. The former licensee may constitute a potential competitor, and furthermore, the firm will have to start afresh in collecting information about the market, establishing contacts and distribution channels. In addition, in some cases the licensee stops royalty payments, and the firm may have difficulty tracking sales on which royalty payments are due.

In recent years, there has been substantial growth in international licensing of trademarks from designer names such as Pierre Cardin and Laura Ashley, and cartoon characters such as the Disney characters or the Flintstones, to sports teams such as the New York Knicks and the Chicago Bulls. Disney alone derives millions of dollars from licensing its characters for use on children's games, clothing, and other novelties.

In this case, there is a further danger that the licensee will use the trademark on products that do not meet approved standards of quality or reliability, or will market them inappropriately. This may damage the reputation and value of the trademark. The value of the Coty designer name, for example, declined dramatically after perfume sold under the name was sold through mass distribution channels, including drug stores and discount outlets.

Consequently, as in the case of contract manufacturing, it is important to monitor the activities of the licensee and establish strict quality and financial controls, to ensure that the licensee meets agreed standards. Establishing a licensing agreement does not mean a firm abrogates all rights to international market development. Rather the licensing agreement should be established in the context of the firm's overall strategy with regard to long-run market development. Even for a firm that plans to develop aggressively in international markets, a licensing agreement may be an appropriate means to enter a small market quickly, thus allowing the firm to focus on the development of other, larger markets.

Franchising

Closely related to licensing agreements are franchising agreements—a form of licensing in service industries such as fast-food, retailing, car hire, hotels, employment agencies, or car dealerships. The franchisor gives the franchisee the right to do business in a specified manner under the franchisor's name in return for a royalty payment, typically a fee or percentage of sales. McDonald's, Domino's Pizza, Hilton Hotels, Hertz, Body Shop, and Manpower are all examples of businesses that have expanded internationally primarily through franchising.

As in the case of licensing, franchising agreements enable the firm to expand internationally without making the substantial capital investment that would otherwise be required. This is especially significant in service industries, where the cost of purchasing or renting sites to operate worldwide would be prohibitive. McDonald's, for example, which has over 14,000 restaurants in over 70 countries, estimates that the initial establishment of a McDonald's in the United States costs approximately $1.1 million.

Establishment of franchising agreements is also advantageous where contact with customers and efficient day-to-day running of the business is a key component of success. The franchisor can thus tap a pool of local entrepreneurial talent with skills in handling local personnel, dealing with local customers, and managing the idiosyncrasies of the local operating environment. In addition, the franchisee is likely to be highly motivated, since he or she is an owner in charge of running the business on a day-to-day basis, participates directly in the profits, and has a substantial degree of management autonomy.

On the other hand, as in the case of licensing, it is important for the franchisor to monitor how franchises are run in different parts of the world, and to establish strict performance standards in order to ensure uniformity of service and product offering worldwide. Otherwise the value of the franchise and its name is lost. Enforcing standards is even more crucial and difficult for franchisors than for licensors, since a franchise sells an "intangible" way of doing business, rather than a physical product.

McDonald's provides an interesting illustration of how to establish an effective system to maintain uniform performance standards throughout operations worldwide. In the first place, McDonald's establishes and enforces strict standards for the quality and amount of meat in the Big Mac, as well as for the hamburger bun. French fries must also meet exacting standards for length and texture. Often this has meant that McDonald's has had to search for local supplies of the right quality and in some cases to establish its own facilities. For its Moscow operation, for example, McDonald's of Canada built a $40-million plant outside Moscow to process its meat, dairy, bakery, and potato products. Russet Burbank seed potatoes and cucumber seeds were imported from the Netherlands, and local farmers trained to grow and harvest them to meet McDonald's standards.[25,26]

In addition to food quality standards, McDonald's also has developed standards for cleanliness, maintenance of the outlets, and service. Rapid, friendly service, and attention to customers, are hallmarks of the McDonald's operation. The company has set up a training program for restaurant managers in Illinois, at the end of which participants receive a diploma in hamburgerology. For the Moscow operation, restaurant managers were trained in Europe and Toronto, and new employees instructed to serve with a smile—a custom new to Russia. A team of inspectors also travel to outlets worldwide to ensure that food quality, outlet maintenance, and service standards are met.

As the example of McDonald's illustrates, although limited equity is at stake, running a worldwide franchise successfully entails a significant amount of effort. In particular, establishment of performance standards and of mechanisms to monitor and control them is essential to the continued success of the franchise.

JOINT VENTURES

Another means of limiting equity exposure in international markets is to establish a joint venture, typically with a local partner. Joint ventures can also provide an effective means for U.S. and European companies to enter countries with substantially different economic systems or market environments, such as Japan, China, the CIS republics, or developing countries. Joint ventures can take a variety of different forms depending on the firm's objectives, capital requirements of the venture, and government regulations with regard to foreign ownership (see Figure 7-6).

Where the objective of the joint venture is to undertake a major infrastructure or agricultural development project, such as a dam, an irrigation project, or an iron ore mining project, multiple foreign partners are often involved and a consortium established. Banks or other financial institutions provide the financing for the project, while others provide the technological expertise. Often such projects are undertaken in developing countries and entail participation by government agencies to provide control and ensure establishment of locally based management once the project is completed.

More common forms of joint venture are those between two private companies. For example, a firm may establish a joint venture with a local company in a foreign market. Often the foreign company brings to the venture technological and production expertise, and sometimes a brand name and corporate reputation, while the local partner provides access to the distribution network, as well as knowledge and familiarity with the local market environment.

Black and Decker, for example, entered into an alliance with Bajaj Electronics, Ltd., in India to distribute its power tools. Bajaj has a 50,000-strong retail network throughout India and already sells a wide range of consumer appliances. Given its turnover, Bajaj is capable of providing Black and Decker with financial and marketing muscle and is ideally suited to mass-market the Black and Decker range of products.[27]

A joint venture offers a number of advantages as a mode of entering a foreign market. While it entails some commitment of resources to the foreign market, it

FIGURE 7-6

Advantages and limitations of joint ventures.

	Joint venture
Advantages	• Reduces capital and other resources required • Spreads risk • Access to expertise and contacts in local markets
Limitations	• Potential problems and conflict between partners • Communications and management problems • Partial control

provides potentially greater returns and control over the management of production and marketing operations in this market. Equity risks are shared with the local partner. In addition, and perhaps most significantly, the local partner provides familiarity with and understanding of local market conditions, and also often has contacts with local distributors and other key agencies in the marketplace. The company gains knowledge and feedback on market conditions, customer requirements and response, key competitors, and their likely reactions, and gradually acquires experience in operating in this market.

A firm may find it particularly advantageous to establish a joint venture in entering foreign markets with which it has little familiarity, and which are perceived as significantly different (or culturally distant) from its domestic market. Japan, for example, is a market where foreign companies often find local partners helpful to obtain local market contacts and develop understanding of the complex distribution system.

Nabisco, for example, established a joint venture with the Yamazaki bakery company to enter the Japanese market. Nabisco provided capital, production skills, and its famous brand names, such as Ritz crackers, while Yamazaki provided access to its chain of bakeries, as well as to other distribution outlets where its products were sold.[28] Similarly, Wella, the German hair product company, initially entered Japan through a joint venture with a company selling chairs to beauty salons. The joint venture provided Wella with access to beauty salons, where it was able to gain an initial foothold in the market. After obtaining the endorsement of beauty salon operators, Wella was able to develop more widespread distribution in pharmacies and other outlets. Subsequently, as distribution became more widespread, Wella bought out its beauty salon chair partner.

Joint ventures may also be established in entering countries with substantially different economic systems, such as China and the republics of the former Soviet Union. In China, for example, the government encourages, though does not require, joint ventures, in order to foster growth and transfer of technology and management expertise to local companies.[29] GM has set up a $100-million joint venture with Gold Cup, a Chinese vehicle manufacturer, to assemble pickups. GM has a 30 percent equity stake and provides mainly capital, while the Gold Cup Automobile Company provides the production plant and about 5,000 workers.[30] The plant will assemble partial knockdown kits imported from the United States and paid for in hard currency.

Such joint ventures have not always been immediately successful, however. In 1983, American Motors negotiated a joint venture with the Beijing Automobile Works to produce and sell jeeps in China.[31] The initial agreement was for AMC to own a 31 percent stake, contributing $8 million in cash and another $8 million in technology, while the Chinese agreed to put up $31 million in assets. The joint venture was to modernize an old Chinese jeep, the BJ 212, and to develop a new generation vehicle for sale in China and other neighboring markets. The joint venture rapidly ran into difficulties. AMC planned to assemble jeeps from kits of Cherokee parts imported from the United States. However, the imposition of foreign exchange restrictions by China due to a shortage of hard currency meant that the joint venture could no longer import Cherokee kits. In addition, the firm did not receive payment for jeeps already assembled. Such problems continued, with minor concessions by the Chinese to permit import of a limited number of kits. Chrysler then took over AMC in 1987 and continued operations. By 1994 the plant in Beijing was producing nearly 20,000 Jeep Cherokees, and Chrysler has plans to expand the operation.[32]

A number of the joint ventures planned in the former Soviet Union during *perestroika* ran into difficulties when the USSR dissolved. The American Trade Consortium, whose members included six major U.S. companies, such as Chevron, Archer Daniels-Midlands, and Johnson & Johnson, suspended its activities.[33] The consortium had originally planned up to two dozen joint ventures involving $10 billion. Chevron is, however, still pursuing its negotiations with the government of Kazakhstan to develop the Tenghiz oil field.

Other projects such as British Airways' project to develop a new airline, Air Russia, with Aeroflot have become bogged down. Yet others are continuing. Fiat has taken a 30 percent stake in the Russian automaker VAZ, while Philip Morris, RJR Nabisco, Bristol Myers Squibb, Pratt & Whitney, Gillette, and ABB have all found ways to manufacture in Russia forming joint ventures and reopening plants with Western machinery.[34]

While, in the phase of initial entry into an unfamiliar market, a joint venture with a local partner can provide information, contacts, and local marketing expertise, problems often arise in the long run. These are well documented.[35,36] In fact, it has been estimated that between 50 and 70 percent of joint ventures eventually break up.

In the first place, communication difficulties can arise between the two parties, as the Beijing-Jeep venture illustrates. Even where the partners are both from the Industrial Triad, communication difficulties can arise. Companies are often characterized by different corporate cultures or management styles, which can give rise to problems. The joint venture between Dunlop of the U.K. and Pirelli of Italy, for example, floundered due to inability to build an Anglo-Italian corporate culture.[37]

Conflicts can also arise with regard to issues such as repatriation of profits, where the local partner desires to reinvest them in the joint venture while the other partner wishes to repatriate or invest them in other operations. Furthermore, as the joint venture progresses, the goals of the two partners may diverge. As the case of Wella and the beauty salon chair manufacturer illustrates, once a company has acquired experience within a market and developed contacts through the joint venture, it may no longer feel the need for the local partner. In addition, the joint venture may not fit into plans for global rationalization and improved coordination and integration of strategy across national boundaries.

As a result, many joint ventures have a limited life-span and generate considerable dissatisfaction on the part of participants. Only where both partners successfully develop a corporate mission and agree on a common strategy and mode of governance for the joint venture is it likely to succeed. Organizational and management mechanisms need to be built to foster mutual trust and commitment to the joint venture.[37]

As more companies became involved in international markets, traditional joint ventures, involving a foreign entrant and a local partner, are giving way to more complex strategic alliances. These alliances often involve multiple partners and sometimes focus on a single stage in the value-chain, such as R&D, production, or distribution. Since such alliances are rarely established in the initial entry phase and are more likely to develop as the firm attempts to expand globally, they are covered in detail in Chapter 15.

WHOLLY OWNED SUBSIDIARIES

The difficulties encountered with managing joint ventures and other types of contractual agreements can lead companies to prefer establishing wholly owned subsidiaries, where permitted and when the firms have the resources to do so. Subsidiary operations provide complete control over production and marketing and eliminate potential conflicts of interest and management problems that may arise in contract manufacturing, licensing, or joint ventures. All the profits of a wholly owned subsidiary accrue to the firm. In addition, the firm can devote maximum effort to developing the market in the desired direction, promoting international brands, or developing new products that draw on the firm's skills or resources in other parts of the world. In deciding to establish wholly owned operations in a country, a company can either acquire an existing company or build its own operations from scratch—a greenfield plant. (See Figure 7-7 for a summary of the advantages and limitations.)

FIGURE 7-7

Advantages and limitations of wholly owned subsidiaries.

	Acquisition	Greenfield
Advantages	• Rapid entry • Access to distribution channels • Existing management experience • Established brand names, reputation • Reduces competition	• State of the art technology • Integrated production • Operational efficiency
Limitations	• Integration with existing operation • Communication and coordination problems • Fit with existing business	• Investment cost • Need to build business • Time delays

Acquisition

Acquiring an existing operation offers a number of advantages, in that it enables rapid entry and often provides access to distribution channels, an existing customer base, and in some cases established brand names or corporate reputations. Danone, the French food company, for example, acquired the HP sauce brand in order to gain access to distribution channels in the U.K. market. In some cases, existing management remains, providing a bridge to entry into the market and allowing the firm to acquire experience in dealing with the local market environment. This may be particularly advantageous for a firm with limited international management expertise, or little familiarity with the local market.

Acquisition is also desirable if the industry is already highly competitive and there is little room for a new entrant, or there are substantial entry barriers. Electrolux, for example, entered the U.S. market by acquiring a U.S. vacuum cleaner company and subsequently White-Westinghouse, with brand names such as Frigidaire and Kelvinator. It thus acquired immediate access to the U.S. market, together with a network of dealers.[38] Similarly, in 1990, Renown, the largest Japanese clothing maker, acquired Aquascutum, the upscale British clothing firm.[9] This provided Renown with a base to expand in Europe and the United States, as well as an entry into the prestigious clothing market in Japan.

The sell-off of state-owned companies in many Eastern European countries has provided unique opportunities to enter these markets through acquisitions. Many of the major acquisitions have been in the Czech Republic and Hungary. For example, Volkswagen of Germany paid $6.6 million for Skoda, the Czech auto manufacturer, while Suzuki of Japan bought Autokonzern of Hungary. The acquisitions have spanned a range of industries from autos and glass to hotels and food processing. Sarah Lee bought Compack, a Hungarian food-processing company, while Electrolux of Sweden acquired Lehel, a Hungarian appliance manufacturer. Kraft Jacobs Suchard, which belongs to the Philip Morris group, has also acquired a number of companies in Central and Eastern Europe as part of its strategy to expand in these markets. It purchased 82 percent of Poiana-Produse Zaharoase, Romania's largest chocolate producer.[39] Suchard plans to develop sales of Poiana's existing brands and to focus on the domestic market rather than on exports.

Some of these acquisitions have, however, run into difficulties. GE, for example, paid $150 million to acquire the Hungarian light bulb manufacturer Tungsram, hoping to use it as the cornerstone of its expansion into the European light bulb market.[40] However, GE rapidly discovered Tungsram's plant and equipment were outdated, and that the company had been cash-starved by the Communist government for years. In addition, Tungsram's 30 percent wage advantage over its European competitors, Philips and Osram, rapidly evaporated with rising inflation.[41] GE also cut the work force in half and restructured management to improve efficiency, thus angering workers.

Other acquiring companies in Eastern Europe have encountered significant problems with modernizing outdated plant, equipment, and energy supplies, as well as labor attitudes. Workers accustomed to operating under state-managed ownership have little concept of productivity. Plants often suffer high levels of absenteeism, lack of quality control, and poor labor attitudes. For example, Curtis International, a multinational conglomerate, purchased Wojewodzki Water Services Enterprise in Poland. Workers immediately went on strike because they feared layoffs.[42] Extensive negotiations followed, with assurances that there would be no job cuts. The issue was finally resolved by installing new Japanese production equipment and converting the plant to TV production.

Greenfield Operations

The difficulties encountered with acquisitions may lead firms to prefer to establish operations from the ground up, especially where production logistics is a key industry success factor, and no appropriate acquisition targets are available, or they are too costly. Japanese automobile companies have, for example, entered the European market by establishing greenfield plants, primarily in the U.K.[9] Nearly $3 billion was spent by the three leading Japanese automakers in building new assembly plants there—enabling them to utilize the latest production technology while at the same time selecting the most advantageous location from the standpoint of labor costs, land cost, taxes, and transportation.

Establishing new plants also facilitates development of a globally integrated system of production and logistics. Engines can thus be produced in one plant, chassis in another, and then both can be shipped for assembly close to the final market. The ability to integrate operations across countries, and to determine the direction of future international expansion is often a key motivation to establish wholly owned operations, even though it takes longer to build plants than to acquire them.

Establishing wholly owned operations, whether by acquisition or greenfield operations, entails total commitment and involvement in international expansion. Management has no local partner to rely on and will have to develop familiarity and expertise in dealing with the local market environment independently. This may be easier if local management can be retained, but then difficulties of managing and integrating operations with those of the firm elsewhere may arise.

Inevitably, both acquisition and greenfield wholly owned operations are costly in terms of capital and management resources. The commitment of equity to international operations provides control but at the same time exposes the firm to greater risk from the various sources discussed earlier. Wholly owned operations are thus likely to be most appropriate where the firm has total commitment to development on a global scale.

SUMMARY

Selecting the appropriate international markets to enter is more than a choice of geographic terrain. It also involves decisions concerning how the potential of a particular market can be tapped best. This involves a careful assessment of the opportunities as well as the risks associated with conducting business in a particular country. Many of the factors that influenced selection of the country market initially also influence mode of entry: country characteristics, the political and environmental risks associated with presence in a country; the level of market development, in terms of infrastructure and customer sophistication; trade barriers and government regulation; product characteristics; and the firm's objectives for international markets.

All these different factors have to be assessed simultaneously to arrive at the best way to enter a particular country. Further, there are a number of implicit and explicit trade-offs between country selection and mode of entry. More attractive countries tend to be entered via modes that entail substantial commitment, while less attractive countries entail modes of entry with less commitment. Ultimately these decisions involve the evaluation of alternative modes of entry relative to: (1) production location, (2) resource commitment, (3) degree of control, and (4) flexibility.

Exporting is the most common mode of initial entry into international markets and involves the least amount of risk and often the most modest gain. Indirect exporting involves the use of export agents or trading companies. Cooperative exporting allows the firm slightly more control through a collaborative agreement with another firm. Finally, direct exporting involves establishing an export organization to perform all the functions and activities involved in selling to international markets.

When such factors such as market size, shipping costs, and tariff barriers recommend a greater presence in international markets, firms often engage in contractual and licensing agreements. Contract manufacturing allows the firm to establish a greater presence in a market while it controls the marketing, distribution, and servicing of its products. If the firm has a proprietary asset, it can enter into a licensing agreement. Typically these cover a specific time period and territory and provide a royalty payment. A related form of market entry is franchising, which is a form of licensing in service industries.

Joint ventures provide a major presence in a particular international market, while at the same time limiting exposure. These work best where each party brings value to the venture. While joint ventures provide access to markets on a variety of levels, they can be difficult to manage and somewhat unstable. An alternative providing greater control is to establish a foreign subsidiary, either by acquiring an existing company or by building greenfield operations. This is costly and requires a substantial commitment to international markets.

REFERENCES

1. Root, Franklin D. (1994) *Entry Strategies for International Markets*, New York: Lexington, revised and expanded edition, for an in-depth treatment of entry strategies.

2. "A Mean Political Hangover for Seagrams in Ukraine," (1994) *The New York Times*, January 27, pp. D1 ff.

3. Feinburg, Andrew (1991) "The New Europe," *World* KPMG Peat Marwick no. 1, pp. 14–19.

4. "The West Rings the Changes in Eastern Europe," (1993) *Financial Times*, October 1.

5. "Goodbyes Can Cost Plenty in Europe," (1992) *Fortune*, April 6, p. 16.

6. "Imports Take on Brazil's Car Makers," (1991) *Financial Times*, January 10.

7. Melcher, Richard A., and Stewart Toy (1992) "On Guard, Europe" *Business Week*, December 14, pp. 54–55.

8. "Protectionism is King of the Road," (1991) *Business Week*, May 13, pp. 57–58.

9. Kirkland, Richard (1990) "The Big Japanese Push Into Europe," *Fortune*, July 2, pp. 94–98.

10. U.S. Japan Trade Group (1985) "Japan: Opportunities and Obstacles," New York: John Wiley and Sons.

11. "Heineken in Indian Venture," (1994) *Financial Times* February 3.

12. "You Don't Have To Be A Giant To Score Big Overseas," (1987) *Business Week*, April 13, pp. 62–63.

13. Penteado, J.R. Whitaker (1993) "Fast-Food Franchises Fight for Brazilian Aficionados," *Brandweek*, June 7, pp. 20–24.

14. Johanson, Jon, and Jan-Eric Valhne (1990) "The Mechanism of Internationalization," *International Marketing Review* 7(4), pp. 11–24.

15. Johanson, Jon, and Jan-Eric Valhne (1977) "The Internationalization Process of the Firm—A Model of Knowledge Development and Increasing Foreign Market Development," *Journal of International Business Studies*, Spring/Summer, pp. 23–32.

16. "Made in the U.S.A. . . . by Hyundai," (1992), *Business Week*, October 26, p. 96.

17. "Reinventing America," (1992) *Business Week*, special edition, January.

18. Terpstra, Vern, and Ravi Sarathy (1994) *International Marketing*, 6th ed. Chicago: The Dryden Press.

19. "Apple Computer Inc., Expands in China, Opens Beijing Office," (1993) *Wall Street Journal*, September 16, p. A17.

20. "Think Small: The Export Lessons To Be Learned From Germany's Mid Size Companies," (1991) *Business Week*, November 4, pp. 58–65.

21. "P&G Uses Skills It Has Honed at Home to Introduce Its Brands to the Russians," (1993) *Wall Street Journal*, April 14.

22. Tanzer, Andrew (1992) "Bury Thy Teacher," *Forbes*, December 21, pp. 90–95.

23. "Pump, Pump, Pump at Schwinn," (1993) *Business Week*, August 23, p. 79.

24. "C'est la Guerre for Coke and Pepsi," (1991) *Financial Times*, February 18, p.15.

25. Blackman, Ann (1990) "Moscow's Big Mac Attack," *Time*, February 5.

26. "Russia's Economy Shows an Appetite for Fast Food," (1993) *Wall Street Journal*, February 26.

27. Raman, A.T., and N.C. Mohan (1993) "Strategic Tie-Up," *Business India*, February 15–28, p. 9.

28. Douglas, Susan P., and C. Samuel Craig (1990) "Achieving Success in Japanese Consumer Markets," *Japan and The World Economy*, 2, pp. 1–21.

29. Vanhonacker, Wilfried, and Yigang Pan (1993) "The Impact of National Culture, Business Scope and Geographic Location on Joint Venture Operations in China," INSEAD Euro-Asia Centre Working Paper.

30. "GM Sets Venture in China to Assemble Pick-up Trucks," (1992) *New York Times*, January 16, p. D4.

31. "One Company's China Debacle," (1989) *Fortune*, November 6, pp. 147–152.

32. "New Worlds to Conquer," (1994) *Business Week*, February 28, pp. 50–51.

33. "Let's Make a Deal—But a Smaller One," (1992), *Business Week*, January 20, pp. 44–45.

34. Hofheinz, Paul (1994) "Rising in Russia," *Fortune*, January 24, pp. 92–97.

35. Gomes-Casseres, Benjamin (1989) "Joint Ventures in the Face of Global Competition," *Sloan Management Review*, Spring, p. 17–26.

36. Main, Jeremy (1990) "Making Global Alliances Work," *Fortune*, December 17, pp. 121–126.

37. Perlmutter, Howard, and David Heenan (1986) "Cooperate to Compete Globally," *Harvard Business Review*, March–April, pp. 136–152.

38. Steward, Thomas A. (1990) "A Heartland Industry Takes on the World," *Fortune*, March 12, p. 110.

39. "Suchard Buys Romanian Group," (1994) *Financial Times*, February 11.

40. Perlez, Jane (1994) "G.E. Finds Tough Going in Hungary," *New York Times*, July 25, pp. D1 ff.

41. Bruner, Richard (1992) "Tungsram's Leading Light," *International Management*, December, pp. 42–45.

42. Hofheinz, Paul (1991) "New Light in Eastern Europe," *Fortune*, July 29, pp. 145–152.

PART III

MARKET EXPANSION STRATEGIES

CHAPTER 8

ESTABLISHING DIRECTION FOR LOCAL MARKET EXPANSION

INTRODUCTION

In the second phase of internationalization, attention shifts from identifying international marketing opportunities and market entry decisions to concern with local market development. Firms operating in international markets begin to accumulate experience in coordinating and controlling distant operations. They have already made investments in gaining knowledge, collecting information, understanding local markets, and developing marketing organizations in these countries. As a result, management now becomes concerned with consolidating local market position and exploiting newly acquired assets, such as management skills and know-how, physical facilities, sales organization, and distribution networks.

This phase of global market development is well illustrated by the strategy the Campbell Soup Company is employing as it attempts to expand its presence in international markets. Currently, Campbell's derives 88 percent of its sales from the relatively mature U.S. food industry.[1] By the year 2000, Campbell's hopes to generate half its revenue from outside the United States.[2] Gaining global share is not going to be easy, as its competitors, CPC International and H. J. Heinz, are well entrenched and generate a significant portion of their sales outside the U.S. market.

A key component of Campbell's strategy is to develop products suited to local tastes. In Poland, where soup consumption is three times higher than in the United States, it has developed varieties of condensed *zupa*, including chicken noodle and *flaki*, a peppery tripe soup. For China, Campbell kitchens in the United States and Hong Kong have developed an extensive array of exotic soups, including duck gizzard, watercress, scallop broth, radish-and-carrot, pork, fig, and date soup. However, their biggest selling soups in Asia are U.S. soups such as cream of mushroom and cream of chicken. In Mexico they have developed *Crema de Chile Poblano* and in the Argentine market; split pea with ham has proven popular.

Developing varieties that suit local tastes is not the only challenge that Campbell faces. For example, in Argentina there is a strong preference for powdered soups, and CPC's Knorr brand controls 80 percent of the market. Campbell has enjoyed some success by stressing the fresh ingredients in *Sopa de Campbell*. In Poland, where 98 percent of the soup is homemade, Campbell has targeted working mothers and stressed convenience. Again they face competition from CPC, which has bought a Polish soupmaker, Amino.

In addition to soup, Campbell is beginning to develop a global capability in baking to expand its Pepperidge Farm business. This includes the acquisition of Freshbake Foods Group PLC (U.K.) in 1988 and Arnott Ltd. (Australia) in 1985. Arnott's provides a low-cost manufacturing base to supply the Asian market. However, both acquisitions provide their own difficulties. Freshbake's products have not been well received by the British market, and there was strong local opposition to the acquisition of Arnott by a non-Australian firm.

Changes in strategy designed to achieve greater market penetration may also necessitate redefining the nature of the business. Different customer benefits may be stressed and new segments targeted, technology may be adapted to specific local market conditions, and changes made in the firm's involvement in the various stages in the value chain. Similarly, acquiring new skills and assets may require reassessing core competencies and how these may be most effectively used to further local market development. Emphasis on economies of scale may be replaced by concern with economies of scope and sharing assets across broader product lines.

As a result, the firm often needs to redefine its competitive posture and generate a new strategic thrust that emphasizes local market development. Planning and strategy development become organized on a national market basis, resulting in an assortment of multidomestic businesses. (See Figure 8-1 for an overview.)

REDEFINING THE BUSINESS

When firms initially enter foreign markets, they often define the business in the same way they did for the domestic market. As local markets begin to grow and the firm modifies its strategies to meet local market conditions, it develops new products and product variants, acquires new brands, products, or product businesses, and begins to expand the boundaries of operations. Hence, management must redefine the business as customer benefits change, new or different customer segments are targeted, and new technologies are adopted. Involvement in the stages of the value chain will also need to be reevaluated (See Figure 8-2).

Customer Benefits

As a firm expands in foreign markets, the type or range of customer benefits it targets may change. In some instances, a given product or service may satisfy

FIGURE 8-1
Market expansion
strategy.

FIGURE 8-2
Redefining the
business.

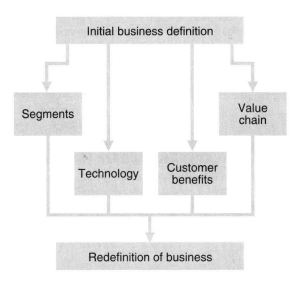

different customer benefits in international markets. For example, McDonald's hamburgers in Japan not only satisfy needs for quick, nutritious meals, but are also "special, different" meal treats. Similarly, in introducing Nescafé instant coffee into the Japanese market, Nestlé positioned it as a "sophisticated, foreign" drink. Since green tea was the traditional, everyday beverage, coffee was perceived as an expensive special occasion beverage for honored guests. When Nestlé subsequently introduced Nescafé Gold, a freeze-dried coffee, it was priced at a 35 percent premium. President, the most prestigious brand, was priced at a 20 percent premium over Gold, further enhancing the sophisticated, luxury positioning of instant coffee.[3]

Adding new products or product businesses also expands the range of customer benefits targeted by the firm. For example, in Mexico, PepsiCo added gum and candy to its basic line of soft drinks, potato chips, and other savory snacks, targeting preferences for candy as well as sweet and savory snacks. Its Sonrics candy business is now the second largest in Mexico, with a 21 percent market share. The sweet snack line was further extended with the acquisition of Empresas Gamesa, Mexico's largest cookie company, in 1991.[4] The emphasis on large kilo boxes sold through supermarkets and Mom-and-Pop stores was shifted to smaller package sizes of 300 grams and single-size servings. As a result, PepsiCo has substantially expanded its snack business to satisfy both sweet and savory tastes, and is now the largest consumer products company in Mexico.

New product development and product line extensions may also be geared to satisfy new or different customer benefits. In some instances, these may be unique to international markets. GM, for example, developed the BTV (basic transportation vehicle) to meet the needs of small businesses in developing countries, such as Malaysia, for a low-cost commercial vehicle.[5] A business could buy the basic frame and then add the body pieces suited to its specific needs, such as wooden slats, canopy roof, sliding door, solid panels, and interior seats. Thus, needs for a variety of vehicles could be met at relatively low cost.

Customer Segments

Local market expansion may also result in targeting new customer segments. In some instances, the same product or service may be targeted to different customer segments. For example, in Europe and the United States, nonalcoholic beers such as Kaliber, Buckler, and Moussy, are targeted to consumers who want to drink a beer, but without alcohol. Pregnant women, diabetics, or those concerned about drinking and driving fall into this category. In Saudi Arabia, and other countries where alcohol consumption is prohibited, the target market is broader, consisting of all adult males. Expansion of the product line may also lead to targeting new customer segments. For example, Coca-Cola added Real Gold, an iron tonic drink, to its line of soft drinks in Japan, adding a new target segment—older customers interested in mineral and tonic drinks—to its traditional market base of young adults.

Technology

Different technology may also be utilized in other countries due to differences in user education, in usage conditions and equipment, or in resource availability and cost. In India, for example, where few consumers own washing machines, a substantial part of the laundry detergent market consists of bar soap rather than the ultraconcentrate and liquid detergents common in the Industrial Triad. In many Western European countries, the prevalence of front loading machines has stimulated development of dispenser balls for liquid detergents, as well as capsule release detergents and softener.

Similarly, in developing countries, agricultural or industrial equipment may need to employ simple technology due to lack of an adequate maintenance infrastructure or user sophistication. For example, an African government purchased mechanical dusters to distribute pesticides and loaned them to farmers. The dusters were finely machined and required regular oiling and care. The farmers left them out in the fields and did not lubricate them. As a result the dusters rapidly seized up and became rusty. Consequently, the government went back to a French hand-operated duster, which was heavier to operate and less effective but requires less care and lubrication.[6]

Product line expansion and broadening the market base may also require changes in technology. For example, in low-labor-cost countries, labor-intensive methods may be substituted for capital-intensive technology, in order to reduce costs, lower prices, and target a broader market base.

Value Chain

Availability of suppliers or needed resources, such as firms with required production skills to provide necessary components, or service organizations to provide after-sales service and maintenance may also affect a firm's participation at different stages in the value chain in foreign markets. In some cases, the absence of firms with appropriate skills may result in a need to integrate backwards or forwards in the value chain. In other cases, availability of competent local firms with requisite skills may enable the firm to purchase supplies, components, and other services in the market, rather then producing or supplying them internally.

In some instances, local distributors may have competent trained sales personnel and be able to promote and provide after-sales service more effectively than the manufacturer itself. For example, in France, Rank Xerox initially sold its copiers directly to potential customers through the company's own sales force. As sales expanded, it withdrew its sales force and sold through independent distributors with exclusive territory rights in order to obtain broader coverage.[7]

Differences in the market infrastructure and in the growth of local market operations from one country to another often leads to a redefinition of the business in each country adapted to local market circumstances. Insofar as operations in each market are allowed to develop independently, they tend to become distinct and separate, resulting in the emergence of multidomestic businesses. Each business develops along its own path in response to local demand conditions and market dynamics, developing its own specific skills and competencies. For example, Phillips has set up a plant in India to manufacture components for black-and-white TV sets and for the lighting equipment it assembles in the Indian market. India provides a low-cost production location and manufacturing close to the assembly location avoids shipment and customs clearance delays.[8]

LEVERAGING CAPABILITIES—ACHIEVING ECONOMIES OF SCOPE

As local market operations grow and develop in new directions, the firm begins to acquire new skills and assets. These include both intangible skills and assets (knowledge of and familiarity with the local environment; contacts with local distributors, government officials, or financial institutions), tangible assets (local production facilities, a local sales force or marketing organization, or warehousing and distribution facilities). Acquiring these assets may thus suggest a need to reassess and refine the firm's core competence and to look for additional ways to leverage its core competence.

In the initial stage of entry into international markets, the firm's core competence typically centers on production skills, such as a quality or innovative product; marketing assets, such as a corporate or brand image; or management skills, such as mass merchandising techniques. These competencies have been developed in relation to the domestic market and are leveraged internationally. As local markets develop, attention shifts to leveraging competencies across products and product lines within countries.

In some instances, the firm may leverage its image or brand name by expanding into new product lines or product business. For example, Playboy, in addition to licensing foreign editions of its flagship magazine in Eastern Europe and Asia, and supplying TV programming to Europe and Latin America, has licensed use of its name and logo on casual clothing, jogging suits, jeans, sunglasses, and even pinstripe suits and attache cases in China. The line will be sold in boutiques in government-run stores, as well as other stores and kiosks.[9] Playboy also has plans to introduce branded condoms in Asia, in collaboration with a local partner, the MBG Group, a Malaysian conglomerate,[10]

Addition of new products and product lines is typically most effective where these take advantage of potential economies of scope. These arise from shared R&D, management, marketing, production, and other assets across product lines and businesses, thus spreading overhead across a higher sales volume and reducing unit operating costs.[11] In essence, three different types of overhead expenses may be shared, relating to physical assets, external relations with suppliers and distributors, and information including technological know-how and marketing experience.[12] (See Figure 8-3.)

Shared Physical Assets

As foreign sales grow the volume generated may warrant establishing local production as well as warehousing and distribution facilities. Import agents or distributors may be replaced by a wholly owned marketing subsidiary and a more extensive sales network. Concern for using these facilities more effectively, especially where there is some surplus capacity, encourages or reinforces interest in developing new products or product variants to fill out the existing product line. For example, in the U.K., Heinz added a line of frozen Chinese dinners to its major product lines—ketchup, baked beans, and soup. The line was created in collaboration with a popular U.K. restauranteur and marketed under the label Memories of China from Ken-Lo. In Spain and Portugal, Heinz added *tomate frito* cooking sauce to its line of ketchups and sauces, while in Italy its confectionery businesses Sperlari, and Scaramellini, explored new tastes, adding sugared gums, soft candies, light soft nougats, and gift chocolates to their hard candy product line.[13]

New products and product variants, which can be marketed through the existing sales organization and utilize the same distribution infrastructure, make more efficient use of their network and spread costs over a higher sales volume. Kelloggs, for example, has added various types of grocery products in several countries, which can be marketed through the same organization and distribution channels as its flagship line of cereals. For example, in the U.K., it markets Boil in the Bag rice, a powdered breakfast drink called Rise and Shine, and has even experimented with powdered milk shakes. In Mexico, Kelloggs markets

FIGURE 8-3
Achieving economies of scope.

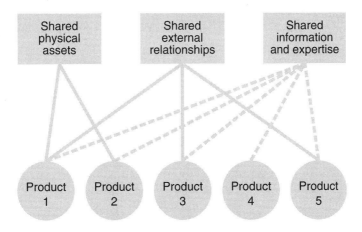

powdered cornflakes as a breaded coating or an ingredient for making pie crusts.

As noted in Chapter 2, Coca-Cola has successfully added a cold coffee drink in a can to its product line in Japan.[14,15] The drink, marketed under the brand name Georgia, built on Coca-Cola's lengthy experience in the soft drinks market in Japan as well as utilizing the distribution network established to market its flagship Coca-Cola brand. In particular, Georgia made effective use of Coca-Cola's experience in vending machine distribution in Japan. Vending machines, which are often placed on sidewalks outside grocery and liquor stores and in railway stations, account for a significant proportion of soft drink sales in Japan. In addition, vending machine technology in Japan is highly sophisticated; machines can be used, not only to refrigerate drinks, but also to heat cans. Hence, Georgia was sold with a dual positioning, as a cold soft drink and as a hot breakfast drink for the busy commuter, available in vending machines at railway stations and other high traffic locations.

Shared External Relations

Developing marketing operations in a country also requires establishing relations with other types of organizations. Once local production facilities are constructed, contacts with local suppliers need to be established. Equally, if the firm establishes its own marketing or sales organization, contacts need to be made with local distributors, wholesalers and retailers, as well as local advertising agencies, marketing research firms, financial institutions, and other types of service organizations. Again, these contacts, and the effort put into developing good relations with such organizations, can benefit a range of products and product businesses.

Contacts with suppliers may be exploited for multiple product businesses. For example, consumer electronics manufacturers such as Matsushita, may use the same suppliers for components such as chips, electronic circuit boards, and connectors, which go into different products, such as TV sets, VCRs, and telephones. In the same way, contacts established with advertising agencies or market research companies can be utilized for different products and brands.

Shared Information and Experience

Intangible assets, such as information and experience, can also be leveraged across different product lines and businessess. These assets include technological know-how, knowledge about a particular market or country environment, or experience in marketing in that environment.

R&D know-how, and in particular basic research, may be applied to develop new products geared to specific local needs. In some cases, these may be variants or extensions of the existing product line, in other cases, new and different products. Basic research may also be applied to develop radically different product businesses. Japanese beer companies such as Kirin and Suntory, for example, have applied fermentation expertise to develop biotechnological businesses. Similarly, Kao has utilized its expertise in coating technology to expand from detergents to floppy disks.

Knowledge acquired for initial market entry about a country and its marketing infrastructure may also help the firm to broaden its product offering, and provide an invaluable input in developing marketing strategy for new products and services. Knowledge about customer preferences and interests and about specific customer segments, may help the firm in developing new products or tailoring product positioning and marketing strategies to these specific interests and market segments. Findus, the frozen foods division of Nestlé, for example, develops variants of its frozen main dishes line adapted to local market preferences. In France the line includes *coq au vin* and *beef bourgignon*; in Italy, *lasagna* and *vitello con funghi*; in the U.K., ocean pie and steak and kidney pie; and in Singapore, *dim sum* dumplings.

Exploiting country market knowledge and experience through adding new products and broadening the product line is likely to be especially rewarding where a substantial investment has been made in gaining information and understanding a country market and the nature of its marketing infrastructure. Japan, for example, is frequently viewed by western firms as being difficult to penetrate and very different from other countries in the Industrial Triad, due to its highly distinctive sociocultural characteristics and its idiosyncratic distribution structure.[16] Firms must often devote substantial time and effort to understanding the Japanese market environment in order to be successful. This investment can then be amortized through marketing products and services adapted to the unique characteristics of the Japanese market. In addition to Georgia and Real Gold, Coca-Cola also developed an energy health drink called Aquarius, targeted to the sports drink segment in Japan. Nabisco has also developed a line of miniature chocolate parfait cupcakes and rice-based snacks specifically for the Japanese market.

Acquiring new skills and assets related to the local market environment leads to the development of new products and the addition of products to the firm's initial product offering, based on its domestic product line. In some instances, this may result in the development of new products or product variants geared to specific local customer tastes and interests. In other instances, addition of products and brands may be designed primarily to make more effective use of existing production capacity, distribution facilities, marketing organization, or sales force. In both cases, however, broadening the product base is likely to stimulate reformulation of the firm's competitive posture in the local market, as well as its strategic thrust and objectives in penetrating local markets.

REFORMULATING COMPETITIVE POSTURE

Redefining the business, and acquiring new skills and assets as a result of local market expansion, suggest the need for the firm to reassess and reformulate its competitive posture in international markets. The scope of the firm's offerings in the market place may need to be reevaluated and redefined as the firm seeks to establish a broader market base. Greater attention to local competitors is necessary to meet or match their actions in the marketplace. In addition, firms need to consider adopting a proactive stance when introducing innovative products and ideas into the marketplace and responding to potential competitive threats, if they are to gain and sustain a market leadership position.

Breadth of Market Scope

In the initial phase of entry into international markets, the firm tends to adopt a focused approach, marketing a limited product range, often emphasizing its flagship domestic brands or star products and targeting market segments that appear more interested in, and likely to adopt, these products and services. As operations in the local market develop and the firm begins to expand the range of its offerings, rather than competing in a limited or focused segment of the market, it is likely to shift to competing broad-line in all market segments or sectors. It may also begin to extend its operations to related product lines and product businesses, either through acquisition or internal development, in order to exploit potential economies of scope.

Honda, for example, initially entered the motorcycle market in the United States with a range of small, high-quality bikes between 50cc and 450cc. These models had been highly successful in the Japanese market. This move dramatically expanded sales of small bikes and changed the character of the motor bike market in the United States. Previously, the market had focused on large bikes and was dominated by manufacturers such as Harley Davidson. As the small bike market matured and other Japanese manufacturers such as Yamaha, Kawasaki, and Suzuki entered the United States, Honda began to expand the range of its product offerings to include larger bikes, to cover the entire market spectrum.

Similarly, Perrier initially entered the U.S. market with a niche positioning for its mineral water. Only the small 1/3 liter bottles were marketed in the United States, positioned as a mixer, or sophisticated nonalcoholic drink, in contrast to the large liter bottles common in the European market. With the decline in alcohol consumption in the '70s, Perrier decided to reposition its mineral water as a soft drink, introducing liter-size bottles and placing them in the soft drinks section of grocery and supermarket shelves. Thus, Perrier shifted from an initial market niche positioning as a specialty item to competing head on with a mass market positioning in the broader spectrum of the soft drink market.

Attention to Local Competition

Broadening market scope leads logically to greater attention to local competitors and their actions. While, with a niche or specialty positioning, a firm can afford to compete selectively and to emphasize product and service differentiation, a broader-based market position requires greater concern with competitors' offering and market strategies.

Introducing and positioning new products and product line extensions requires consideration of the range of offerings of both local and multinational competitors, and their positioning. Product variants, or new products adapted to local market conditions and characteristics, may challenge the offerings of local competition or be designed to compete more directly with local products. For example, EFFEM (Mars) recently introduced an almond-flavored version of its Snickers bar as well as almond-flavored M&Ms in Japan, thus competing directly with the flavors offered by local Japanese chocolate manufacturers such as Pokka.

Where a broad market base is targeted, competition with local firms may also result in greater attention to price and price-sensitivity. In the Indian pharmaceutical market, for example, multinational drug companies face competition from Indian companies such as Randaxy, Cipla, Dr. Reddy, and Nicholas Piramal, who have lower overheads and minimal R&D costs. In addition, ingredients for certain drugs are subject to price control. As a result, Pfizer has been reformulating drugs with ingredients outside price controls, in order to remain price competitive, and has taken up manufacturing animal health products.[17] Similarly, in detergent markets, major players all pay close attention to competitors' promotional activity, deals, trade-ins, markdowns, and cents-off offers.

Proactive Posture

Concern with local market development and with broadening the market base is also likely to encourage adoption of a proactive stance. In some instances the firm will pursue aggressive introduction of new products and product line extensions in order to maintain a market leader position. In entering foreign markets, a firm often introduces a product that is new to the market that, in some cases, embodies a substantially different life-style pattern or culture. For example, Levi's and Wrangler spearheaded the adoption of jeans by younger consumers and for casual wear in many countries throughout the world. Once the innovation has been adopted and begins to spread more widely throughout the country, local competitors may begin to emerge, developing me-too brands, or aggressively undercutting prices. In order to keep ahead of the market or to maintain its leadership position the firm will often introduce new product variants.

For example, in Japan, Levi Strauss encountered substantial competition from local manufacturers with low-priced, me-too brands. It countered with an aggressive advertising campaign with film clips featuring famous U.S. film stars such as John Wayne and Marilyn Monroe wearing Levis jeans. The campaign, called "Heroes Wear Levis," was intended to reinforce Levi's image and to reinstate Levis as the traditional and authentic jean.[14]

Thus, as the firm adapts to local market conditions and actively pursues local market development, it should adopt an aggressive competitive posture. This should aim to leverage its global image and management and marketing skills, in order to compete in local markets. This new competitive posture leads in turn to the development of a new strategic thrust centering on local market development.

DETERMINING THE STRATEGIC THRUST

As local market penetration is emphasized responsibility for strategy development, often shifts from corporate headquarters to local management, on the grounds that they are closest and best qualified to understand the local market environment and hence to engineer the new strategic thrust. Attention shifts from exporting products and strategy from the domestic market to making product and strategy modifications tailored to local market characteristics in order to broaden the market base and tap new segments. The firm will favor product line extensions, together with development and acquisition of new products and brands tailored to specific local preferences.

The firm also needs to consider adapting marketing mix elements such as promotional copy, pricing, and distribution channels to local market conditions. In the initial stages of market entry, minimal adaptation is emphasized in order to maintain a consistent image across markets and to minimize entry costs. In the local market development phase adaptation of advertising copy and development of new themes should be undertaken whenever the costs are outweighed by potential increases in sales. Similarly, pricing decisions should be geared to stimulate local market penetration. The firm may therefore need to pay greater attention to price elasticities and competitor prices in local markets, rather than pricing on a cost-plus basis.

Mechanisms to ensure marketing strategies are effectively implemented will also need to be established. Moreover, considerable autonomy will need to be given to country management to develop and manage programs so as to ensure responsiveness to local market characteristics and speedier reaction to competitor moves and emerging market trends. Yet at the same time, corporate headquarters will need to monitor and control operations to ensure long-run corporate objectives are attained.

SUMMARY

Moving into the second phase of internationalization, attention shifts to developing local market potential, building on the base established during initial market entry. Often this leads to product line extension, adding new product variants or brands, or developing new products tailored to local market demand. Management can thus take advantage of economies of scope; sharing R&D, production plants or warehousing facilities, external relations with suppliers and distributors, and information and marketing expertise across product lines and businesses.

As a result, the firm's business definition will need to be reassessed as the scope of market boundaries expands. This will include changes in customer benefits or segments targeted as well as technology adopted and involvement in different stages in the value chain. The change in direction may also trigger a redefinition of the firm's competitive posture in any given international market in terms of breadth of market scope, differentiation relative to local competition, and adoption of a proactive or reactive posture. The redefinition generates a new strategic thrust that provides the basis for planning and implementing marketing tactics to achieve local market expansion objectives.

REFERENCES

1. Berman, Phyllis, and Alexandra Alger (1994) "Reclaiming the Patrimony," *Forbes*, March 14, pp. 50 ff.
2. "Campbell: Now It's M-M Global," (1993) *Business Week*, March 15, pp. 52–54.
3. Aizawa, Kiyokazu (1989) "Our Struggle to Penetrate the Japanese Market, and How We Attained Success," ESOMAR Seminar Barcelona.
4. Poole, Claire (1991) "Pepsi's Newest Generation," *Forbes*, February 18, pp. 88–92.
5. General Motors Malaysia Snd. Bhd. (1974) Harvard Business School Case.
6. Robinson, Richard D. (1961) "The Challenge of the Underdeveloped National Market," *Journal of Marketing*, October, pp. 24–25.
7. "Rank-Xerox Reorganizes Distribution to Succeed in Europe," (1988) *Business International*, February 15, pp. 2–5.
8. Pania, T. (1993) "Preparing for Battle," *Business India*, October 12–15, pp. 66–71.
9. Levine, Joshua (1992) "The Rabbit Grows Up," *Forbes*, February 17, pp. 122–127.
10. "Playboy Looks Overseas as U.S. Climate Grows Hostile," (1993) *Wall Street Journal*, September 29.
11. Teece, David J. (1980) "Economies of Scope and the Scope of the Enterprise," *Journal of Economies Behavior and Organization*, I, pp. 233–247.
12. Lorange, Peter, M. S. Scott Morton, and Sumantra Ghoshal (1986) *Strategic Control*, St. Paul, MN: West Publishing Company.
13. Heinz, *Annual Report 1991.*
14. Douglas, Susan P., and C. Samuel Craig (1990) "Achieving Success in Japanese Consumer Markets, *Japan and the World Economy* 2, pp. 1–21.
15. Rapoport, Carla (1990) "You Can Make Money in Japan," *Fortune*, February 12, pp. 85–92.
16. Czinkota, Michael R., and Jon Woronoff (1991) *Unlocking Japan's Market.* Chicago: Probus Publishers.
17. "Wait and Then What?" (1994) *Business Asia*, January 3, pp. 6–7.

CHAPTER 9

POSITIONING AND SEGMENTATION

INTRODUCTION

Once a firm has determined which markets to enter, the mode of entry, and its goals and objectives relative to international expansion, it next has to draw up operational plans for marketing the product or service in international markets. These plans will be guided by the firm's competitive posture in international markets and the nature of its strategic thrust.

Central to developing operational plans are decisions about how to position the product or service, and which customers or market segments to target. The choice of markets to enter determines the geographic terrain on which the firm will compete and signals its territorial objectives to its competitors. Positioning decisions determine the place the product or service occupies within a given product market and the products or services with which it will compete, both directly and indirectly. They determine which customers are targeted and how the product or service is perceived by customers, distributors, and other marketing agents.

Positioning decisions provide guidelines for marketing mix decisions. Positioning decisions help to determine whether a product should be upgraded or simplified, or new products or product variants developed to meet competition, or differences in customer requirements in international markets. Positioning decisions also suggest which attributes or customer benefits should be emphasized in advertising or promotional platforms, what type of role models or usage occasions should be featured, and the nature of the product or brand image. Media allocation decisions need to be geared to the exposure patterns of target customers, and other promotional activity to their purchasing patterns and interests.

Similarly, positioning is a fundamental consideration in pricing decisions, which in turn are often important perceptual cues to customers and competitors alike. Positioning as an "up-market" quality item justifies a higher price point, and equally higher margins for distributors to provide additional customer service. Conversely, a "down-market" positioning requires competitive pricing and close attention to distribution costs and margins. In the same way, distribution decisions are guided by positioning and the type of outlets or distribution channels favored by target customers. In consumer markets, positioning decisions determine whether or not distribution should be selective or intensive, and whether nonstore channels are used. In industrial markets, positioning has an important impact on whether direct or indirect channels are used, as well as on the importance attached to developing "key" accounts and long-term contractual relationships with customers.

Haagen-Daz's international market entry strategy demonstrates the importance of positioning strategy. In the United States, Haagen-Daz competes with a range of other premium ice creams including Ben & Jerry's and Steve's. In international markets, ice cream is often consumed as a snack or dessert but is typically viewed as an everyday item. So Haagen-Daz had to establish a position for its ice cream as a high-end item. Part of the positioning problem has been to define what a premium ice cream is in markets where none existed. In addition, Haagen-Daz has extended the idea of a premium ice cream as being indulgent, to include sensuality. In the U.K., for example, their ads show seminude couples feeding ice cream to each other. An equally controversial approach was used in Japan. To enter international markets Haagen-Daz crafted a carefully orchestrated three-step process. First, the brand is introduced at a few high-end retailers. After initial acceptance is gained, the company builds company-owned stores. The third step is mass market distribution in supermarkets and convenience stores.[1]

Positioning and target segment decisions are thus at the heart of the firm's thrust into international markets. They reflect its choice of which product markets to enter and with whom to compete in those markets, as well as the aggressiveness of its entry and competitive strategy, and the extent to which it seeks to innovate and change, rather than adapting to existing behavior patterns. (See Figure 9.1.)

POSITIONING AND SEGMENTATION

In domestic markets, the firm must determine the place its products occupy within a given market, what benefits it will stress, and what customers or market segments it will target. In international markets, these positioning decisions are broader in scope, and in some respects more crucial. They need to be based on a clear understanding of the structure of the product market and of differences and similarities in the relevant set of competing products and market segments from one country or region to another. This is especially critical insofar as product usage patterns and occasions, as well as competing and substitute products and services, vary substantially from one country to another. Products positioned

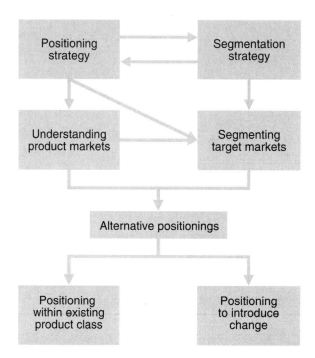

FIGURE 9-1
Framework for
segmenting and
positioning.

for one usage or target segment, or stressing certain benefits in one country, may best be positioned differently in another country or region.

In some cases, domestic positioning strategies need to be adapted to international markets. For example, Jägermeister, a German cordial with medicinal properties, is popular among older consumers in Europe. In the United States it is targeted to college students and positioned as the "in" drink.[2] Jägerettes, coeds in black body suits, are hired to promote the cordial at parties and bars that are popular with singles and college students. Promotions include handing out Jägermeister T-shirts, cowboy hats, and Frisbees. The strategy has been highly successful, propelling Jägermeister to the number four imported cordial in the United States behind Kahlua, Bailey's Irish Cream, and Grand Marnier.

In some instances, management may desire to introduce a dramatically new product or service into a foreign market. In this case, there will be no established or clearly defined product market structure, and management will have to determine how to create a new product class. This entails identifying alternative functions or roles that the product can fulfill, as well as possible substitute products or services, and examining the match of a position with trends in current customer interests and behavior patterns.

In essence, positioning decisions in international markets entail: (1) understanding the nature of product market structure in other countries; (2) examining target markets, the degree of segmentation, and the similarity of customer needs, interests, and segments across countries; and (3) determining what benefits to stress and what customers to target in different countries worldwide.

UNDERSTANDING PRODUCT MARKET STRUCTURE

A clear understanding of product market structure is crucial to effective positioning decisions. Examining the existing product set provides insights into the nature of the competitive arena, as well as which products or brands are likely to compete directly or indirectly, and where potential gaps or opportunities may lie. Where there is no existing market for the product or service in another country, and management is concerned with introducing an innovation into the market, understanding customer behavior patterns and interests relative to the intended usage situation becomes crucial. In particular, understanding the environmental forces underlying these patterns helps to guide positioning decisions.

Identifying the Product Market Boundaries

In examining product market structure, the firm must first establish the relevant set of competing products, and identify relevant product market boundaries. The firm must adopt a broad perspective in defining product market boundaries insofar as products may be perceived as appropriate for different usage situations, or satisfy different functions in different countries. In addition, the specific types of products or product variants within the relevant product set often vary from one country or culture to another.

For example, the definition of a soft drink, and how soft drinks are perceived, varies from one country to another. In some countries, items such as beer and milk are viewed as soft drinks; in other countries, beer is perceived as an alcoholic drink, and milk as a beverage for children. Similarly, the items included in the product set often vary. In the United States, soft drinks consist predominantly of canned sodas, and notably colas; in Southeast Asia, the category includes freshly squeezed fruit juices, and in Europe it includes fruit concentrates and cordials diluted with water. (See Figure 9.2.)

Management should adopt a broad perspective in defining the nature of product market boundaries, centering on the usage situation or function, rather than the product form, in order to identify competing and substitute products and to determine an appropriate positioning strategy.

Assessing Product Differentiation and Branding

Once product market boundaries have been defined, management has to determine the specific product forms to include in the competitive set. Again, these may vary from one country or culture to another, not only in product types, but also in the range of specific product variants available. For example, in countries

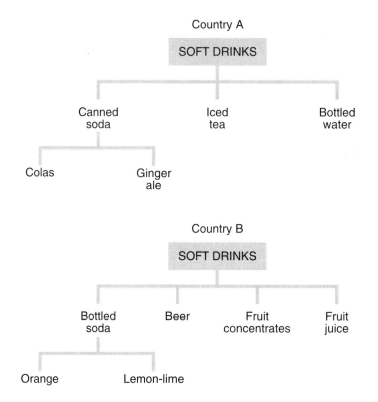

FIGURE 9-2
Understanding product market structure.

where hand washing of clothes predominates, the dominant product form of detergent, if any is used, is bar soap. Introduction of washing machines is often accompanied by use of synthetic detergents. In more developed detergent markets, a broad range of product variants is typically available, including powder, flakes, liquid, and ultraconcentrate forms, with formulations for heavy duty or delicate washes, for presoak, cold or hot water, low or high-sudsing versions, and with or without fabric softener or bleach.

Similarly, coffee is available in different product forms around the world. In some countries, coffee beans are the dominant form, while in other countries, instant coffee (spray dried or freeze dried) predominates, and in others, ground coffee in cans or vacuum packs. Within a given form, a range of variants is available: including the type of roast (French or Italian), caffeinated vs. decaffeinated varieties, and different flavors (such as Amaretto and Hazelnut). While in some countries, such as the United States, a wide range of variants is available, in other countries the range may be limited to two or three types of beans, or instant coffee.

The significance and strength of branding also varies from one product market to another. In countries such as India, China, and several African countries, where mass media have limited reach and distribution channels are fragmented, branding is not well developed. For example, sales of processed foods such as canned and frozen vegetables are limited, and grocery items such as flour, rice, pasta, and cooking oil are sold as commodities. Competition is based predominantly on price and distribution efficiencies. Opportunities may exist for differentiation through branding, but doing so is likely to entail substantial marketing expenditures.

The importance of developing strong brands also depends on the specific product market and is typically more critical in consumer than industrial markets. Brand strength is especially crucial in markets where image or other subjective attributes play an important role in customer purchase decisions. In Japan, for example, affluent consumers, including Japanese Yuppies, the youth market, are attracted by foreign designer brands such as Ralph Lauren, Armani, Hermes, and Celine.[3] Often they prefer to pay high prices for a few such status items rather than buying a wider range of less-expensive brands.

Strong brands in fast-moving consumer goods categories, sold through supermarkets, hypermarkets, or other mass distribution outlets, provide a means for manufacturers to counterbalance increasing retailer power and obtain widespread distribution. This is especially critical in Europe, as retail distribution has become more concentrated, dominated by a small number of large-scale retailers that are expanding across national boundaries.[4] At the same time, the growth of deep-discount chains in Britain, France, and Germany, and the spread of private label goods offering better value for money, has caused a marked erosion in loyalty to manufacturer brands. In Britain, for example, private label items now account for over 30 percent of supermarket sales volume.[5]

In addition to examining the strength of branding, the firm also has to consider the degree of brand concentration or fragmentation. Markets such as tractors, razor blades, and agricultural equipment are dominated worldwide by a few powerful brands, while in other markets, brands are considerably more fragmented. The firm also has to determine the importance of international (as opposed to national, local, or regional) brands. In many detergent markets throughout the world, for example, the brands of the three major international detergent manufacturers, P&G, Unilever, and Colgate, tend to dominate. Brands of Henkel, the German manufacturer, occupy a significant market share in some countries, but not others. In Japan Japanese manufacturers such as Kao are a major force and also have a presence in other Asian markets such as Taiwan, Singapore, and Hong Kong.

Examining product market boundaries, the hierarchy of product forms and variants, and the strength of branding, lays out the nature and dimensions of the competitive terrain on which the product is to be positioned. It defines the specific types of products or variants with which the firm will compete, where competitive gaps exist, and the strength of competition in the various parts of the competitive terrain. Management has to assess these dynamics relative to the nature and distinctive competitive advantage of its own product offering in order to determine an appropriate positioning.

Dimensioning the Product Market

Next, management has to assess the dimensions of the product market in different countries. Here, management should consider the size, intensity, and growth rate of demand in different countries. These factors impact, not only the profit potential of a given market, but also the costs associated with market development. Initial entry costs into new markets are often high, limiting the attractiveness of small markets unless they have high growth potential. Equally, marketing costs will be higher if markets are highly fragmented and demand dispersed, than if demand is intense and concentrated.

As indicated in Chapter 3, product market size, intensity, and rate of growth are indicators commonly used to assess market potential in domestic markets. There often is a wide variation in market size and the state of market development in different countries throughout the world. In many cases, there is a trade-off between market size and rate of growth. For example, while markets for many products such as washing machines and automobiles are large in industrialized nations, in North America, Japan, and Western Europe, growth potential is often low and is primarily a function of the need to replace existing machines. On the other hand, current market size for such consumer durables in developing nations such as China, Indonesia, or Brazil is small, but growth potential is high. In particular, the size of the population and high rates of economic growth in those countries promise considerable future potential.

In evaluating countries, both population size and age distribution are important considerations. In countries in the Industrial Triad the population tends to be older with many consumers in their 70s and 80s. In developing countries, particularly Asia, the majority of the inhabitants may be under 30. For example, by the year 2005 68 percent of Pakistan's population will be under 30. This is followed closely by Bangladesh (64%), Vietnam (61.4%), and the Philippines (60.7%). In fact, nine of the world's 15 most populous countries are in Asia, as well as four of the five countries with the largest populations under 30. The only exception is the United States which ranks fourth in the number of inhabitants under 30.[6]

Market intensity or concentration also has to be considered, since it has an impact on marketing costs. The firm needs to assess frequency and size of a purchase as well as the spatial concentration or fragmentation of buyers. Again, while important in domestic markets, variation in patterns of market intensity and concentration is often more marked in international markets. In developing countries, for example, buyers purchase more frequently and in smaller quantities, due to lack of storage space and financial resources, than do buyers in other parts of the world. In India, cigarettes and razor blades are sold as singles, especially in rural areas, while shampoo is commonly sold in small 50 ml bottles, a size positioned for travel or trial in Western markets. This often adds to packaging and transaction costs.

In industrial markets, adoption of just-in-time policies, as well as average purchase size, vary from country to country. Where markets are highly fragmented and dominated by small businesses, as, for example, in the retail and other sectors in Japan, purchases are often relatively small and purchase frequency high, due to lack of storage space and capital to finance inventory. Again, this adds to transaction and shipment costs and can lead to lengthy channels of distribution with multiple intermediaries.

Management also has to consider the degree of spatial market concentration. In consumer markets this is often closely linked to the degree of urbanization, and in industrial markets to the strength and significance of small family businesses. Particularly in developing and newly emerging countries there is often a sharp division between urban and rural markets. In Thailand, for example, average income in Bangkok is four times that in rural areas. As a result, demand for many consumer goods, especially those from industrialized nations, is often concentrated among wealthy consumers in major urban centers. In cities, the distribution and media infrastructure is often relatively well developed, making such consumers readily accessible. Even where potential demand for certain goods exists in rural areas, poor physical distribution infrastructure often restricts the firm's ability to reach such markets.

Yet another aspect to consider is the degree of market development. In some instances, the firm targets a market in which demand is relatively well developed and products similar to the firm's are already available. In other cases, the firm aims to introduce to the market a product or service that may entail a substantial change in existing consumption and behavior patterns. U.S. cola companies, for example, not only had to gain acceptance of the cola taste in other countries but also had to convince consumers to drink carbonated soft drinks. Conversely, in entering the U.S. market, Perrier had to persuade consumers to drink bottled spring water, rather than tap water.

Management should therefore assess whether or not there is an existing market for the product or service, and if so, how well developed or mature this market already is. This entails identifying the stage in the product life cycle in terms of the length of time such products have been available, the pattern of growth in market sales volume, and the number of product variants. Where the market is already mature or in the late growth stage, the firm will need to differentiate its product offering relative to those of its competitors, and develop an innovative positioning.

If, on the other hand, there is no existing market for the product, management will need to undertake a broad survey of consumer attitudes and behavior towards products and services that might be possible substitutes, and of possible indicators of latent demand. In the case of fast food, examining existing food consumption patterns and preferences and how they are changing, as well as time pressures, attitudes, and perceptions of different types of fast foods, will provide some insights into latent demand and the need for product or positioning changes. For example, in India fast food is likely to appeal to young adults. Hindu dietary restrictions prohibit sale of beef-based products and will require substitution of mutton hamburgers or veggieburgers.

SEGMENTING INTERNATIONAL MARKETS

Next, management has to determine how to segment markets. This hinges to a substantial degree on the similarity in customer needs, interests, behavior, and response patterns across countries and geographic areas, as well as on the breadth of market scope. Where management targets a broad-based target market, and customer needs and interests are similar across countries in a region or area, management may be able to identify similar groupings of countries, and segment by groups of countries or regions. If, on the other hand, behavior is substantially different from one country to another, markets may best be segmented on a country-by-country basis. Where, on the other hand, management targets a focused segment, it needs to assess whether or not global or regional segments with similar needs and interests may be identified and targeted. In other instances, a specific market segment in one country may have interests similar to those of a broad-based target segment in another country. For example, affluent urban consumers in developing countries may provide an appropriate target segment for products and services with broad appeal in industrialized countries. Segmentation decisions are closely linked to decisions relating to market scope, and impact how far product and positioning strategies need to be tailored to specific country markets.

Similarity in Customer Needs and Interests

For some product markets, customer needs and interests are highly similar worldwide, while for others there are substantial differences from one country to another. The degree of similarity also varies by geographic region; often there are marked differences between customers in the Industrial Triad and those in the emerging Third World.

In some product markets there is substantial similarity in behavior among groupings of countries within a region. For example, consumer markets in the Scandinavian countries often exhibit substantial similarity, as do markets in Southeast Asian countries. These similarities offer opportunities for segmentation by country groupings. Alka Seltzer, for example, identified three groups of countries within Europe, based on willingness to admit to a hangover and upset stomach. In the Scandinavian countries, people took pride in admitting to a hangover, and Alka Seltzer was positioned for "the morning after the night before." In the Benelux countries and the U.K. it was socially acceptable to admit to the occasional hangover, so Alka Seltzer was positioned "for headaches and upset stomachs." In Latin countries, on the other hand, hangovers "simply do not occur," so Alka Seltzer was positioned as suitable for "upset stomachs."

Customer needs and interests are most likely to be the same worldwide in industrial markets, especially where there is a high degree of concentration and a relatively limited number of buyers. For example, in markets such as aerospace, aircraft, turbine engines, bulk chemicals for drugs, quartz watch movements, TV tubes, and computer disk drives, customer demand is relatively homogeneous worldwide.

In other markets, customers are interested in the same basic product worldwide but require some minor modifications for specific markets. For example, small electrical appliances such as hairdryers, irons, and power tools can be marketed worldwide with minor modification in color and design. Product design can incorporate similar components, while modifications are made in voltage, cabinets TV system (PAL, SECAM, or NTSC), or other essential features to meet specific local needs.

In yet other markets, such as many food products, customer demand is substantially different from one market to another, requiring the design or development of products specific to local needs. For example, prepared or prepackaged main dishes need to be adapted to food preparation and storage habits as well as culinary tastes. In the United States, for example, prepared main dishes are predominantly frozen, and range from standard TV turkey dinners (low-calorie or low-sodium lines) to premium gourmet dinners and ethnic (Chinese, Spanish, Indian) dishes. In Europe, prepared main dishes often include dehydrated as well as frozen lines, and typically include favorite national dishes such as *coq au vin, boeuf bourguignon* in France, *lasagna* and *canneloni* in Italy, and chicken, meat pies, and fish dishes in the U. K.

Even in some industrial markets there are substantial differences in customer preferences from one country or geographic area to another. For example, tractor design for the U.S. market differs substantially from that for developing countries, such as in Africa. While in the United States tractors are designed to plough vast acreages and have large fuel tanks, farmers in African countries need much smaller models capable of ploughing small tracts.

The degree of similarity in customer needs and preferences across countries and geographic regions is thus an important input in segmenting markets internationally and determining how far products need to be modified or designed specifically for individual markets. Where there are differences by or within geographic areas, management needs to determine how best to segment markets—depending on the degree of similarity and the magnitude of differences between countries and regions.

Similarity of Segmentation

In addition to considering the similarity of customer needs and interests at the aggregate product market level, the firm also needs to consider similarity of market segments across countries and geographic areas. Here, management needs to consider the degree of market segmentation as well as whether similar segments can be identified worldwide or within a region, or are specific to a particular country or region.

THE DEGREE OF MARKET SEGMENTATION

The degree of market segmentation often varies from one country or geographic area to another and is often closely linked to the stage of market development. Markets in industrialized countries such as the United States or Western Europe are often highly segmented, while those in developing or emerging countries are more likely to be unsegmented. For example, the cigarette market in the United States is highly segmented by length of cigarettes, filter vs. nonfilter, low tar vs. regular, and menthol vs. nonmenthol, and various combinations of these. In developing countries, on the other hand, there are typically at best two segments, premium (often U.S. brands such as Marlboro and Winston) and cheaper local brands.

Similarly, organizational markets are often segmented on the basis of firm size, industry, and degree of technological sophistication in industrialized countries. In other countries market demand is relatively modest, and potential segments are not large enough, or sufficiently identifiable or accessible, to warrant products or marketing strategies tailored to specific customer needs.

IDENTIFYING GLOBAL AND REGIONAL SEGMENTS

Another issue is whether target segments with similar interest and response patterns can be identified across countries and regions or worldwide. Certain customer segments are more likely to exhibit similar behavior worldwide than others. For example, businessmen and women from different countries often exhibit similar preferences with regard to expensive pens, watches, and other personal items, and are prime targets for international business media such as *Fortune* and *Business Week.* The same cartoon characters from Disney, films such as *The Lion King, Batman,* and *Aladdin,* and toys such as Barbie dolls attract children worldwide.

Equally, ethnic groups often maintain traditional food-eating patterns, sports, and entertainment interests after immigrating to other countries, and thus make up global segments with similar tastes and interests for specific ethnic products. For example, Hispanic immigrants in the United States from various Central and Latin American countries often remain heavy consumers of traditional Latin food products such as pinto and black beans, chili peppers, tacos, and tamales. Similarly, Indian and Pakistani immigrants to the U.K. have retained traditional food consumption patterns and are prime targets for Indian spices and pulses. This has prompted a range of firms to develop products suited to these new tastes. For example, in the United States Knott's Berry Farm has added Peggy Jane's Oriental Chicken Salad Dressing, and Hormel has purchased the House of Tsang. Other firms are offering condiments suitable for Caribbean, Indian, Thai, and Mexican tastes.[7]

In some instances, regional segments with similar tastes and interests can be identified. For example, with the integration of European markets, different Euro-lifestyle segments have been identified.[8] These are consumers in different European countries who have similar life-style patterns and purchasing habits. For example, one major life-style segment consists of the "Euro-Vigilantes" who are highly price-conscious, always seeking bargains. Another is the "Euro-Dandies," who are fashion conscious and trendy, spend a substantial amount on clothing and other personal items, and susceptible to new fashion ideas and trends.

Yet other segments are country-specific, and hence their size and economic feasibility need to be carefully investigated. Unless such segments are substantial, or are potential targets for several product lines, thus allowing the firm to benefit from potential economies of scope, they may not be economically feasible. In some cases, however, there may be spillover effects from increased visibility of the company name or brand image.

Market Linkages

The growth of market linkages has fostered the spread of global and regional market segmentation. In some instances, these links facilitate accessibility to such segments. Three types of market linkages are instrumental in this regard: communication linkages, such as media, satellite networks, and integrated computer systems; travel linkages, through the movement of customers from one geographic location to another; and organizational linkages, such as professional and social associations, and links between subsidiaries or branch offices of a company in different countries.

Communication linkages stimulate the transfer of ideas and information from a customer segment in one country to a similar segment elsewhere. This transfer spreads new trends and fosters the emergence of similar desires and interests among a segment worldwide. A segment that seems to transcend geographic and cultural boundaries is the teenager. A U.S. advertising agency video-taped teenagers' bedrooms from Jakarta to Los Angeles. They found remarkable similarities, ranging from Levi's jeans and Nike footwear to Sega videogames.[9] However, just because the products they purchase are the same doesn't mean that the same approach or appeal can be used. Levi Strauss found that the urban realism portrayed in its U.S. ads made European teens uncomfortable. Instead Levi's used ads that evoked images of a mythical America, including one that relied, not surprisingly, on the Old West. It showed two girls in a covered wagon stopping to watch a young man bathing in a creek, wearing only Levi's.[10] Young Russian or Chinese teenagers watch western heavy metal bands or rap music and yearn to belong to these cults and to possess, not only the recordings, but also the shirts, shades, earrings, leather jackets, and other accoutrements that identify them as members of the New Wave.

Travel and direct exposure to ideas, life-styles, production methods, and ways of doing business in other countries has a similar and sometimes more direct impact on interests and behavior patterns. For example, businessmen and women who travel extensively become exposed to trends in other countries, and to the latest in notebook computers, fax machines, cellular phones, and other types of office and communications equipment owned by their counterparts in other countries. Equally, they may observe more sophisticated production technology and more efficient machinery in other countries and decide to adopt these in their own operations.

International organizations provide yet another mechanism for transmitting ideas and information across countries. In consumer markets, social groups, religious organizations, international sports organizations, and literary associations provide vehicles for exchanging information on specific interests and act as integrating forces for specific interest groups.

Organizational linkages form an important cohesive force in industrial markets. Internal linkages, such as those between subsidiaries or branches of a firm in different countries, are especially critical and often lead to the creation of global customers (firms that establish companywide purchase specifications for supplies and components throughout the world). Other types of vertical and horizontal linkages such as trade associations and distributor associations also facilitate the exchange of information and foster market integration.

As such linkages become stronger and are further reinforced by linkages in market infrastructure and improved communications, they constitute an important force towards market integration. In some product markets similar segments can increasingly be identified in countries throughout the world. In others, differences in demand between countries are shrinking rapidly, reducing the need for radical modification of products and marketing strategies for individual country markets.

ALTERNATIVE POSITIONING STRATEGIES

Once management has decided how to segment markets, the product or service has to be positioned in international markets. In reality, these two decisions are often closely linked, insofar as segmentation positions define target market scope. In some cases, management may be concerned with satisfying existing needs and interests, or positioning the product or service within an established or emerging product market—for example, introducing diet colas into the soft drinks market. In others, the product or service is new and different. In this case, management is introducing change into existing behavior patterns and aims to create a new product market or product class. In practice the degree of innovation is a continuum, and almost all cases of international market entry entail some degree of innovation.

Positioning Within an Existing Product Class

Following the direction of the firm's competitive strategy in global markets (as discussed in Chapter 5), together with an examination of perceived differences among customers in international markets, management has first to decide whether to pursue a narrowly defined target market, focusing on a specific customer segment, or to target a broad market base. In addition, the firm has to determine whether the product or service is targeted to the same or similar customers and segments as in the domestic market, and whether it will stress the same positioning or benefits.

Figure 9.3 shows hypothetical positioning of four different brands in a product category in two countries. In country 1 there are three brands, w, x, y, that appeal to individuals in the three major segments, A, B, and C. In country 2, segment C does not exist and brand x must also compete with brand z. The situation is even more complex than Figure 9.3 suggests. To begin with, brands may not map into a product space in the same manner in different countries. There are different competing brands as well as different evaluations of what constitutes high efficacy and a high price. Further, the product category may be defined differently, and even if the category is the same, there may be different dimensions used to evaluate brands. Also, a segment that exists in one country may not exist in others.

When the firm decides to focus its efforts on a specific segment in international markets the characteristics and specific preferences of the target segment

FIGURE 9-3
Perceptual maps showing products and segments in two countries.

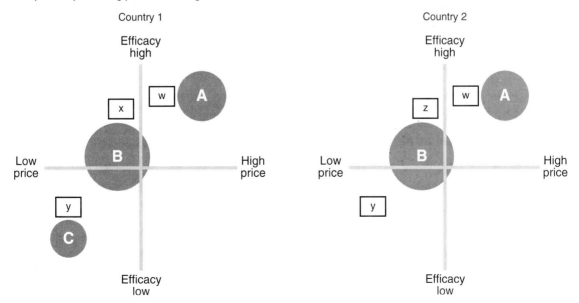

need to be clearly defined. This segment may be environmentally conscious consumers within the cosmetics market, or upscale consumers in the watch or designer clothing market, or teenagers in the record market.[11] The specific interests of the target segment enable management to develop a focused positioning, emphasizing these preferences, and tailoring promotion, pricing, and distribution to their characteristics, media habits, and purchase behavior.

Targeting a broader market base, on the other hand, implies the firm will need a broader positioning (and hence appeal). At the same time, management should gear promotional and pricing tactics to tap a wide range of customers, and develop media coverage and distribution aimed at the entire market. Management also has to consider whether it should stress the same positioning strategy and product benefits in all markets worldwide. In some instances, this may also involve shifting from a broad-based to a focused position, or vice versa. (See Figure 9.4)

FOCUSED-SEGMENT POSITIONING STRATEGY

Focusing on a specific customer segment is likely to be appropriate when management desires to leverage a distinctive image or style successful in the domestic market internationally. In some instances, management pursues a focused positioning strategy in the domestic market and is able to identify a similar segment with similar interests and response patterns in international markets. Body Shop, for example, has been highly effective in developing a distinctive image and tapping environmentally conscious consumers in the cosmetics market in a number of countries worldwide.

In other situations, management may find that only a small number of individuals in international markets, for example, more affluent customers or those more open or interested in foreign products, are likely to be potential customers. Likelihood of more widespread adoption may appear limited, at least in the short-run. In India, for example, only the 20 million upper middle-class households with annual incomes of over $14,000 may be potential customers for

FIGURE 9-4
Positioning within an existing product class.

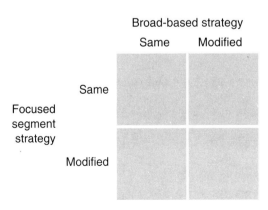

products such as Ray-Ban classic metal aviator sunglasses, soft contact lenses, or cars.[12]

Equally, if the firm has limited resources or is willing to commit only limited effort to international markets, focusing on a specific customer segment may be an appropriate strategy. When facing entrenched competition from local firms, or when large, powerful firms dominate media and distribution channels, substantial difficulties and high costs are likely to be incurred in attempting to obtain broader market penetration. A specific market segment may be more accessible than a broad target market, and pursuing it will avoid the costs of developing broad-based distribution. When the characteristics of the segment selected are the same, and they share similar interests and response patterns in different countries worldwide, management can adopt a uniform positioning strategy.

Same Focused Position. Adopting the same positioning strategy may be particularly desirable when management aims to target the same global segment worldwide, as in the case of Body Shop and Benetton. A uniform strategy enables the company to leverage corporate or brand image in international markets. Benetton, for example, has been able to develop a global identity for its line of casual clothing with its green logo, its uniform store decor and presentation, and its slogan, "The United Colors of Benetton." Benetton has also used shock tactics in developing its image as a socially responsible company in world markets with its media campaigns.[13]

Similarly, products or services targeted to upscale consumers worldwide, such as premium liquor brands, expensive watches, and pens, often adopt the same positioning strategy worldwide. Such items are often positioned as status symbols for the target group. Advertising for Rolex watches, for example, underscores the prestige associated with ownership. Premium liquor brands such as Smirnoff vodka, Chivas Regal scotch, and Martell and Courvosier cognac focus on developing global images, tightly controlling pricing and distribution of their products to ensure consistency of image in both industrialized and developing markets.[14]

Rolls Royce PLC also targets the upper end of the luxury car market with its Bentley and Rolls Royce lines, which range in price from $138,500 to $319,300. Traditionally, their major markets have been the United States and British diplomats around the world. Sales, however, have plummeted in both segments, with the shift away from conspicuous consumption and emphasis on fuel economy in the United States as well as concern about diplomatic expenses. As a result, Rolls Royce has had to target other markets, including opening a showroom in Moscow, currently one of the fast-growing markets in the world for luxury cars.[15] The key buyers are Russia's newly rich *biznezmen*, entrepreneurs operating in dollar import and export of metals, oil, and chemicals.

Playboy Enterprises is also able to target its traditional segment of 30- and 40-year-old males in formerly repressed societies, such as Eastern Europe and

China, as well as Latin America, with foreign editions of its magazines and licensed products.[16] In these societies, its traditional hedonist appeal and racy sexist approach are highly effective. In the U.S. market, on the other hand, Playboy's image is maturing and is shifting to focus more on couples.[17]

Adopting the same positioning enables management to develop a consistent global and uniform image of the product, service, or company, and to leverage this worldwide, taking advantage of emerging global media.

Modified Focused Position. In some instances, even when the same customer segment is targeted in international markets, differences in desired benefits, usage conditions, and competitive market structure suggest the desirability of adopting a different positioning, emphasizing different product benefits in different countries.

For example, in the U.K., Range Rover targets the market for utilitarian four-wheeled farm or estate vehicles based on its rugged image as a safari or cross-country vehicle. In the United States and other international markets, the company presents a more sophisticated image as a four-wheel-drive off-road vehicle, emphasizing its use by the Queen and other members of the British Royal Family.

In general, a focused domestic positioning is seldom substantially modified for international markets, since market size is by definition restricted, and modification can entail substantial costs. Synergies are more likely to be obtained from leveraging the same image and positioning internationally. If, on the other hand, the firm targets a broad market base in its domestic market, but a focused segment in all or some international markets, it is likely to modify its positioning and the benefits it stresses. For example, Mercedes is positioned as a family car in Germany and is often used as a taxi there and in some other countries, but it is positioned as a status and prestige luxury car in the U.S., Japan, Russia, and many other countries, with commensurately higher prices.[18]

Similarly, Orangina, a popular orange soft drink in France, is targeted to career women aged 24–44 in the United States. In adopting this target, Orangina had to contend with the dominance of colas in the U.S. soft drinks market and the perception that orange is not an adult drink. Further, Orangina's tart taste did not appeal to children. Consequently the company decided to target women through an extensive sampling program to women's business groups.[19] Such strategies are often designed to introduce a product or brand to a broader-based market gradually.

BROAD-BASED POSITIONING STRATEGY

Targeting a broad market base may be desirable for mass market items when there are potential economies of scale, relatively few differences among customers in terms of desired benefits or usage scenarios, and limited potential for market segmentation. Markets for consumer electronics, household equipment, detergents, and standard consumer packaged goods typically fall into this category in most industrialized countries.

Adoption of a broad-based market penetration strategy is also desirable where there is substantial potential for market growth and access to distribution is key. By establishing a broad market base, the firm is well placed to develop a dominant market position and block the entry of new competitors into the market, as well as to play an important role in stimulating market growth.

On the other hand, targeting a broad market base is likely to require substantial resources to establish or penetrate distribution networks, and to mount major promotional campaigns to develop awareness and interest in the product or service among potential customers and distributors. Consequently, such strategies are likely to be most appropriate for large or leading competitors who have major commitments to growth and development in international markets. Coca-Cola, for example, spent more than $400 million, approximately $25 for each person in East Germany, to develop an infrastructure of bottling plants and distribution centers in order to establish its brand and gain a strong positioning in the country.[20]

Same Broad-Based Position. As in the case of a focused positioning, management may decide to utilize the same positioning in different countries or parts of the world where desired benefits and usage conditions are the same and management aims to leverage an image worldwide. Kodak, for example, emphasizes quality in marketing its film worldwide. The company stresses the need for quality film to ensure good results, and the disastrous effects of using poor film. The launching of the Kodak Gold line in world markets was intended to reinforce this quality image.[21] Similarly, Polaroid focuses worldwide on the use of instant photography for family occasions—showing photos of families, babies, or young children in advertising campaigns in different countries.

Nike also is focusing on building its name into a global megabrand, using famous U.S. athletes such as Andre Agassi, Charles Barkley, and Michael Jordan to develop a creative life-style image appealing to consumers worldwide.[22] While campaigns and the stars are typically targeted to youth, the image of pursuing fitness in everyday life is intended to reach a much broader base of consumers.

PepsiCo also targets its restaurants (Pizza Hut, KFC, and Taco Bell) at a broad-based market worldwide. The potential market for affordable American food outside the United States is viewed as vast. Maintaining its position may entail modifications in operations in different countries. For example, in Poland, a Pizza Hut restaurant adjoins a food court featuring Pizza Hut, KFC, and Taco Bell. Customers can pay either $4–6 in the restaurant, or $3 in the food court.

Modified Broad-Based Position. In some cases, adopting a broad-based positioning will require modification due to differences in customer tastes and interests, the nature of competition, the maturity of the product market, or simply customer purchasing power. For example, when Rowntrees planned to introduce After Eight, the thin chocolate after-dinner mint, into the French market, they found substantial differences in chocolate preferences. While in the U.K.

the combination of chocolate and peppermint was widely accepted, in France the concept was almost sacrilegious.[23] Blind taste tests showed, however, that the French enjoyed the taste. Consequently, the same name, pack, and presentation were used in France, while the advertising featured a dinner party in an English country house setting, complete with butlers, Rolls-Royce, and chauffeurs, providing a sophisticated British image, but no mention of the mint–chocolate combination.

Similarly, when the Renault 5 was launched throughout Europe, the positioning and benefits stressed had to be adapted to different European countries.[24] When the Renault 5 was initially launched in France, it was positioned as suitable for both town and country driving, and was the first of its kind in the 1200 cc class. The highly successful advertising campaign that accompanied the launch took the form of an amusing cartoon strip showing the Renault bouncing down the road, announcing itself as the "Super Car" with a smile on its front bumper and eyes in the place of headlights.

When Renault decided to launch the 5 in other European markets, the only other country in which it proved feasible to use the same positioning was Belgium. In other countries, the positioning had to be adapted due to differences in features customers sought in cars, and in competition from one market to another. In Italy, the principal competitor was Fiat. Road handling, performance, and comfort were the characteristics considered the most important by automobile drivers, and Renault felt that, if it used an amusing positioning, Italian drivers would not take the car seriously. Consequently, the positioning emphasized these features and heralded the Renault 5 as the "citizen" of the world.

For the same reasons, competition from VW suggested that a lighthearted positioning was unlikely to be effective in Germany. In addition, Germans were highly concerned with engineering, road performance, and other technical aspects of the automobile. For them, purchasing an automobile was a serious matter and should be treated as such. Consequently, the campaign placed emphasis on technical and performance characteristics, such as the various features of the new engine, as well as its fuel performance, seating, and luggage capacity. In Sweden, the primary competitor was Volvo, again suggesting the difficulty of an amusing positioning. Swedes were particularly concerned with car safety features. The Renault positioning in Sweden thus emphasized safety, highlighting the braking capacity, shatterproof windshield and mirrors, and the efficiency of the seat belt system of the new car.

Some 20 years later, when Renault was introducing the new Renaults, they decided to adopt the same positioning, in different countries emphasizing its convivial and energetic personality.[25] Copy execution was, however, different for each major market. In France, the R5 was portrayed as part of the family, taking on the role of a cherished family pet. The British campaign "What's Yours Called," asked people to give the R5 a name. In one spot, a man wakes up from a nightmare, in which his R5 has been crushed, calling "Sarah, Sarah," much to his wife's surprise. The Italian ad emphasized the R5's friendliness to female drivers. Only in Spain, did execution differ from the norm. There, the R5 was shown racing down a highway giving a virile impression of speed and power.

Sometimes, companies modify positioning in targeting customers in Third World countries, either positioning products for different uses or changing emphasis from premium to "no frills." For example, one company successfully positioned its line of powered garden tools and equipment as agricultural implements in developing countries.[26] Other companies focus on stripped-down models of tractors and other types of equipment. Aircraft sold to airlines from Third World countries and intended for domestic routes tend to have interior equipment limited to the bare essentials, rather than the customized and well-upholstered interiors supplied to U.S. and other major airlines.

Positioning to Introduce Change

In some instances management is able to position a product or service within an existing product market, and focus on developing a differential competitive advantage. In other cases, entry into international markets involves developing interest and demand for a new product class or service. In some instances doing this may run counter to existing attitudes and behavior patterns. Depending on the nature of the innovation, a firm can adopt different positioning and segmentation strategies. As in the case of positioning within an existing product class, management can either target a focused segment or, a broader market base.

TARGETING A SPEARHEAD SEGMENT

In some instances, management may be able to identify a target segment that will act as a spearhead to the introduction of the product or service into the country. This segment might comprise individuals or organizations that are especially open to change, such as those who have travelled extensively or are frequently exposed to international media. Younger consumers are also often more open to change. Another strategy is to target those who have roots in or come from the country or culture of origin of the product or service.

Management may initially target expatriates and immigrants in international markets, hoping that there will be a spillover effect leading to more widespread adoption. Although not part of a deliberate marketing strategy, U.S. army commissaries abroad have provided the spearhead for the introduction of U.S. products such as cola drinks, cigarettes, and even Nescafé instant coffee into the countries where they were based. Similarly, El Paso, the Puerto Rican food manufacturer, has targeted Hispanic immigrants in the United States with its brands of Hispanic products such as chili and hot pepper sauces. The availability of such items in many supermarkets has led to their adoption by a broader consumer base. Mild Seven, a Japanese brand of cigarettes has also been introduced into a number of countries by initially targeting Japanese expatriates.[27] Brooke Bond, of the Unilever group, targeted Indian immigrants to the U.K. in introducing their Taj Mahal brand of tea, a highly popular brand in India. Similarly, Indian workers in the Gulf States are prime targets for Brooke Bond Yellow label tea, and for their new instant coffee brands.

Both Coca-Cola and Pepsi-Cola have adopted a similar strategy in introducing their colas into international markets.[28] The youth market is targeted, often with an all-American image featuring pop singers such as Madonna and Michael Jackson. Yet the companies expect these images will have a broader-based appeal. In addition, as members of the youth market age, they will continue drinking the colas they became hooked on in their youth, and which are a symbol of the youth culture.

In industrial markets, companies that are more dynamic and innovative, and have a history of adopting new products and technology, are more likely to be prime targets for innovative technologically sophisticated products. Equally, large companies or organizations with substantial resources are often attractive prospects for major capital equipment. For example, large teaching and research hospitals are often the best prospects for new medical equipment.

POSITIONING RELATIVE TO VALUE TRENDS

Another alternative is to gain acceptance by positioning the product or service relative to key or emerging value trends or life-style patterns. A firm can stress product benefits or attributes consistent with a dominant trend, or how the product or service fits current trends, and aids in achieving the desired image or life-style indicated. For this positioning to succeed, it is important for management to identify value trends or life-styles which are on the rise and viewed as cutting-edge.

Perrier employed this strategy successfully in introducing bottled water into the United States. Perrier water was initially introduced into the United States as a mixer for alcoholic drinks or a "chic" alternative to alcohol, and sold in small bottles in the gourmet section of supermarkets. As sales of alcohol declined, Perrier decided to reposition its bottled water as a soft drink. Perrier introduced a large liter bottle placed in the soft drink section, and emphasized the health benefit of drinking bottled water as opposed to soft drinks that contained sugar and caffeine. The upscale image was retained as an "in" drink for the nondrinker or trendy jogger. The company sponsored a number of events such as the Boston and the New York marathons to reinforce the healthy image of Perrier. As a result it was successfully positioned as a healthy and trendy alternative to colas and other soft drinks.[29]

Kelloggs was the driving force behind the introduction of breakfast cereals in many countries throughout the world. Kelloggs spent heavily on advertising emphasizing the nutritious value of the cereal, its convenience, and how it provides energy and a good start for the day.[30] Especially in markets where an increasing number of women are employed and have less time to prepare traditional, nutritious breakfasts for their families, this positioning has proved highly effective.

The choice of product positioning and target market provide the basic parameters for developing plans translating the marketing mix into action. At the same time, positioning decisions are closely linked to management evaluation of market and company sales potential, as well as market share goals, and the marketing resources allocated to achieve that share.

ASSESSING LEVERAGING POTENTIAL

The firm needs to consider potential opportunities for leveraging assets or core competencies developed in the domestic market. Positioning decisions have an impact on the extent to which tangible assets such as production facilities, R&D, and distribution facilities can be utilized or leveraged in entering overseas markets. A positioning that involves substantial product modification can result in loss of potential economies of scale in production. Existence of potential scale economies can lead management to adopt the same positioning strategy in international markets. This has, however, to be weighed against the size of the potential market if the same position is utilized.

Similarly, in the case of promotional materials, adoption of the same positioning strategy, emphasizing the same product attributes in international markets, allows the firm to use the same promotion materials. Substantial economies can thus be achieved in creating advertising copy and in the production costs of TV and print commercials. Even if some modification is required, for example, dubbing commercials in the appropriate language, or adapting scenarios, economies can be achieved in the development of advertising strategy.

American Express is leveraging its successful testimonial campaign to nearly 30 countries, including Hong Kong, Singapore, Spain, and Brazil. The basic format of the commercials is unchanged, successful merchants expounding on their business philosophy and extolling the virtues of the American Express card. A pool of 60 ads has been produced locally in different countries, but they are carefully orchestrated by a team that includes the Executive Creative Director of American Express's advertising agency, Ogilvy & Mather. This insures that the same look and production values are achieved worldwide. In the U.K., the testimonials include designer and retailer Sir Terence Conran; in Italy, fashion designer Ottavio Missoni; in Germany, hotelier Karl Nuser; and in Japan, innkeepers Koin and Emiko Horibe.[31] Some of the commercials, such as Club Med, travel well and can be used in multiple countries.

The desire to leverage intangible assets such as product or brand image, reputation for quality and service, or creative ideas also influences positioning decisions. Concern to develop a uniform product or brand image across countries will lead management to prefer the same or similar positioning in international markets, stressing the same product benefits and attributes. Developing a uniform image is especially desirable to firms targeting organizations with operations in multiple foreign markets, or customers who travel internationally, such as international businessmen and -women.

Products or services that are highly visible, such as personal items (clothing, cigarettes, watches), also benefit from a uniform image, since that image is often an important element in the purchase decision. The power of an image will be reinforced, if it is projected internationally, as the examples of Coca-Cola, American Express, Sony, and Nike illustrate. Conversely, confusion can arise in the minds of customers, and the brand's identity can be weakened, if the firm projects a different positioning or brand image in each national market. As markets become increasingly integrated worldwide, and international media expand in importance, such factors become even more crucial in positioning decisions.

SUMMARY

One of the more critical decisions a firm faces is how to position its product or service across different geographic markets and segments within the markets. The positioning decision has profound implications, not only for potential customers, but also for probable competitors. Further, the positioning decision guides decisions relating to the firm's marketing mix. Product positioning in international markets is considerably broader than it is in the domestic market. Even if the positioning is the same from market to market, the nature and size of the target market may vary considerably.

The selection of an appropriate position begins with a clear understanding of the relevant product market structures in each country. This understanding provides insights into the appropriate market boundaries and the set of competing products. Management can then define target segments within each market and assess the degree of similarity that exists across markets. The degree of similarity in turn has direct implications for not only the size and growth potential of the target market but also the costs of adopting a particular positioning, as well as its eventual profitability.

The analysis and assessment stage provides the basis for developing an appropriate positioning strategy. Here, the firm has two broad options: (1) positioning within an existing product category, and (2) positioning to introduce change. If the most appropriate positioning strategy is within an existing product category, the firm must still decide whether to have a focused or broad-based positioning strategy and must determine the degree of modification necessary to ensure the strategy's success. Positioning to introduce change often involves more risk and is more difficult to pursue but also holds greater potential rewards.

Underlying the entire positioning decision is an assessment of how readily key assets and core competencies can be leveraged. Here, the firm has to consider tangible assets, such as production facilities and R&D, and intangible assets such as brand image or reputation. Leveraging core competencies from the domestic market may also allow the firm to realize economies of scale or scope and certain synergies that have far-reaching benefits, and may help make the firm more competitive.

REFERENCES

1. Maremont, Mark (1991) "They're All Screaming for Haagen-Daz," *Business Week,* October 14, p. 121.
2. Palmeri, Christopher (1993) "Meet the Jägerettes," *Forbes,* February 15, pp. 108–ff.
3. Trucco, Terry (1990) "Imports, Badges of the Good Life," *Intersect,* February, pp. 16–21.
4. Nielsen AC (1990) *The Nielsen European Passport.*
5. "The Eurosian of Brand Loyalty" (1993) *Business Week,* July 19, p. 22.
6. "Asia by Numbers" (1994) *Business Asia,* February 14, p. 12.
7. McMath, Robert (1993) "Third World Immigrants Add Spice to American Cuisine," *Brandweek,* March 1, p. 29.
8. GFK, Euro-life Style Report, Germany, no date.
9. Tully, Shawn (1994) "The Universal Teenager," *Fortune,* April 4, pp. 14–16.
10. Dwyer, Paula, and Russ Mitchell (1994) "The Euroteens (and How to Sell to Them)," *Business Week,* April 11, p. 84.
11. Hassan, Salah, and Roger Blackwell (1994) "Competitive Global Market Segmentation," In: Hassan, Salah, and Roger Blackwell, eds. *Global Marketing: Perspectives and Cases.* Orlando, Florida: Harcourt Brace, The Dryden Press.
12. Jacob, Rahul (1992) "India Is Opening for Business," *Fortune,* November 16, pp. 128–130.
13. "Benetton Profits from Shock Tactics" (1992) *International Management,* July/August p. 20.
14. Saporito, Bill (1991) "Liquor Profits," *Fortune,* November 4, pp. 172–184.
15. "BMW, Mercedes, Rolls-Royce—Could This Be Russia?" (1993) *Business Week,* August 2, p. 40.
16. "Playboy Looks Overseas as U.S. Climate Grows Hostile" (1993) *Wall Street Journal,* September 29.
17. "The Rabbit Grows Profits," (1992) *Forbes,* February 17, pp. 122–127.
18. Taylor III, Alex (1991) "BMW and Mercedes," *Fortune,* August 12, pp. 56–63.
19. Underwood, Elaine (1992) "Orangina Gives Its Self Away," *Adweek's Marketing Week,* May 18, p. 16.
20. "We Got the Achtung Baby" (1993) *Brandweek,* January 18, pp. 23–24.
21. "Global Campaign for Kodak," (1992) *Adweek,* June 1, p. 1–3.
22. Grimm, Matthew (1993) "Nike Vision," *Brandweek,* March 29, pp. 19–25.
23. Rijkens, Rein (1992) *European Advertising Strategies.* London: Cassell, pp. 1–14.
24. Douglas, Susan, and Bernard Dubois (1977) "Culture et Comportement

du Consommateur," in *Techniques Commerciales,* Encyclopedia du Management, Paris.

25. "Visions of the Euroconsumer," (1989) *International Management,* September, p. 36.

26. Keegan, Warren J. (1969) "Multinational Product Planning: Strategic Alternatives" *Journal of Marketing,* vol 33, pp. 58–62.

27. Koeppel, Dan (1990) "Japan's Mild 7 Cigarette Targets Asians in the U.S.," *Adweek's Marketing Week,* August 13, pp. 4–5.

28. Sellers, Patricia (1994) "Pepsi Opens a Second Front," *Fortune,* August 8, pp. 70–76.

29. "Perrier Pours into U.S. Market, Spurs Water Bottler Battle" (1979) *Marketing News,* September 7, pp. 1–9.

30. "The Continental Breakfast Gets More Snap, Crackle and Pop" (1988) *Financial Times,* March 6, p. 10.

31. Barry, Jon (1994) "Don't Leave Home Without It, Wherever You Live," *Business Week,* February 21, pp. 76–77.

CHAPTER 10

TAILORING PROGRAMS TO LOCAL MARKETS

INTRODUCTION

In general, the firm would prefer to standardize as much of the marketing mix as possible across countries. Standardization has a number of benefits, including economies of scale in production and promotional costs, presentation of a unified image across countries, and easier transfer of ideas and experience, as well as coordination and control of international operations. (See Table 10.1.) Yet, total standardization is rarely feasible or desirable. There are numerous barriers to standardization, ranging from regulation to differing consumer preferences. (See Table 10.2.) Consequently, some tailoring of programs to the local market is often needed.

In some instances, government or trade regulations relating to product content and labelling, necessitate modification of programs. In other cases, a competitor may have preempted a copy platform, or certain distribution channels, requiring changes in the firm's marketing programs. Alternatively, certain types of media or distribution channels may not be available or have the same reach in other countries, so marketing tactics have to be adapted to reach the target market.

Differences in customer response patterns, purchasing behavior, media exposure, life-style patterns, organizational structure, and the heterogeneity of customer behavior from one country to another also help determine the need to modify marketing programs. Typically, the broader the range of customers the firm aims to reach, the more likely some adaptation of marketing programs will be required. Focused strategies on the other hand often target customers with similar behavior and response patterns across countries and require little modification, other than that necessitated by differences in regulation or the marketing infrastructure.

A major dilemma in deciding whether or how far to tailor marketing tactics to the local market is the effect this will have on global image. For example, when Pizza Hut's partner in Japan, Asahi Breweries, wanted to add hamburgers, chowders, and chips to the menu, and to change the Pizza Hut spice and dough formulations to Japanese tastes, Pizza Hut refused. Pizza Hut management felt this

TABLE 10-1	**BENEFITS OF STANDARDIZATION**

COST SAVINGS

■ Economies of scale in production/marketing
■ Minimizes product/advertising development costs

UTILIZATION AND TRANSFER OF KNOW-HOW

■ Experience transfer
■ Idea transfer

UNIFORM IMAGE OF QUALITY AND SERVICE

■ Global customers
■ International communication

EASIER COORDINATION AND CONTROL

■ Uniform standards

move would dilute the Pizza Hut image and unique selling concept based on pizzas, salads, and pasta, and give the venture a coffee-shop image. As a result, the joint venture broke up, with each partner taking half of the jointly owned stores.[1]

Kentucky Fried Chicken (Japan), on the other hand, provides an interesting example of how to adapt to local marketing conditions while still leveraging a global image. KFC entered Japan through a joint venture with Mitsubishi, which had just acquired a poultry operation and wanted to develop the market for chicken in Japan. Initial results of the joint venture were disappointing. KFC followed the same locational strategy as in the United States, setting up free-standing outlets in suburban locations. This policy was ill-adapted to the Japanese environment—the high population density, crowded streets, and relatively small number of women drivers. Consequently, KFC adopted a new approach. Smaller outlets were established in crowded locations. Equipment had to be shrunk to fit the smaller space, and a wax model of Colonel Sanders was placed on the sidewalk to mark out the location. While fried chicken was still the focal point of its menu, other items such as smoked chicken and fish were added. An advertising campaign developed by Dentsu showed Colonel Sanders as a boy baking bread. This helped to establish a friendly, homely image, as well as the traditional and authentic nature of their chicken recipe, rather than stressing specific product benefits, as in the United States. In addition to serving customers quickly, employees were trained to be extremely courteous, bowing politely on handing over an order in accordance with Japanese etiquette.

The degree to which marketing tactics are tailored to local markets can also

TABLE 10-2	**BARRIERS TO STANDARDIZATION**

DIFFERENCES IN CUSTOMER CHARACTERISTICS AND RESPONSE PATTERNS

- Sociocultural values & life-styles
- Perceptions and associations

GOVERNMENT REGULATION AND RESTRICTIONS

- Product/Advertising regulation
- Tariffs, buy local

DIFFERENCES IN MARKETING INFRASTRUCTURE

- Media
- Distribution

LOCAL COMPETITION

- Type of competitors
- Competitive behavior

vary. In some instances, advertising copy or product labelling may simply be translated into the local language. Other cases may require a different execution of the copy theme, changing the scenario or the endorser or even adopting a different copy theme altogether. Similarly, the need for product adaptation may range from minor modifications to radical redesign.

The need for modification is also likely to vary from one element of the marketing mix to another. Positioning and product design may, for example, remain substantially the same, with only minor modifications, while advertising copy, pricing, and distribution have to be adapted. Alternatively, distribution might be the same, but product and promotional tactics have to be adapted. This is shown in Figure 10.1 for two different companies. Similarly, the need for modification may vary from one country to another. Products, services, and programs designed for markets in industrialized nations are more likely to require major modifications for developing nations, but only minor changes in other industrialized nations.

PRODUCT MODIFICATION

A first decision to be made in drawing up plans for international markets is whether, and how far, to design and adapt products to different usage and environmental conditions in other countries.

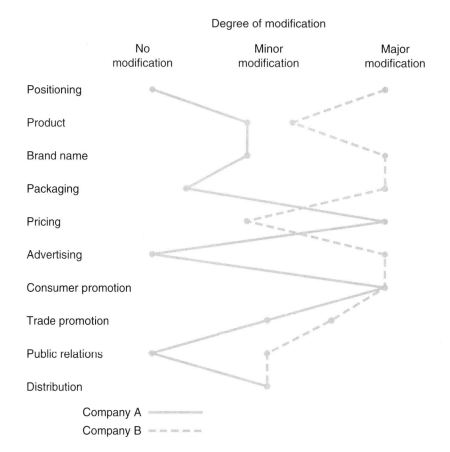

FIGURE 10-1

Dimensions of global marketing strategy.

Failure to modify products to market conditions can, in some cases, result in market disasters, as in the ill-fated launch of Betty Crocker cake mixes by General Mills in the U.K. illustrates.[2] When General Mills tried unsuccessfully to market cake mixes such as angel's food cake, and devil's food cake in the U.K., British housewives simply did not believe that they would be able to produce the exotic cake pictured on the package from a mix. Furthermore, the cakes were not well adapted to the English habit of eating cake for tea, often with their fingers, rather than as a dessert. Green's, a local competitor, ran a "Bake Your Favourite Cake" competition. They then developed a line of highly successful mixes based on the most frequent entries. This included the plain cakes favored by the English, such as the Victoria sandwich, orange spongecake, scones, and rock cakes.

Modifying products to different market environment and usage conditions can entail, however, substantial costs, as well as incurring delays in market entry and penetration. It eliminates or reduces the potential for spreading product R&D and design costs and overheads over multiple country markets. The costs of adapting or modifying products, therefore, have to be weighed against the likelihood of greater market penetration as a result of product adaptation.

In some instances, products are deliberately *not* adapted, as the lack of adaptation generates a prestigious image. For example, large luxury U.S. automobiles with high fuel consumption, such as Cadillac, although ill-adapted to narrower European streets, have a prestige value in Europe by virtue of their lack of adaptation and the implied costs of maintaining and using such automobiles, given higher fuel costs in Europe. However, the number of consumers who can afford such costs and place value on a U.S.-built luxury car is limited. Similarly, in Japan, it is prestigious to own a car with the steering wheel on the left, as the car has obviously been imported.

In some instances, product modifications are mandatory in order to meet product standards or other regulations. Adaptation to different measurement or calibration systems is also often necessary or highly desirable. Language and other cognitive factors may necessitate adaptation in packaging or instructions. Usage conditions such as climate or technological infrastructure may also require changes for the product to function or be used effectively in a given national or environmental context. Management, therefore, has to determine the cost of making such modifications and what impact this will have on other elements of the mix, such as price or distribution.

Product Standards and Regulations

In some cases, products have to be modified to conform to national product regulations and quality standards. Such regulations are most common in relation to products such as pharmaceuticals, food, electrical appliances, and automobiles. The standards set by the U.S. Food and Drug Administration and the Pennsylvania Department of Agriculture for food products and drugs are among the strictest in the world and have been used as a model by the European Union in setting product standards. The International Organization of Standards has also developed a set of quality management standards, ISO 9000, which are required of suppliers by a growing number of firms such as DuPont, General Electric, British Telecom, and Philips Electronics.[3] Products that involve potential safety hazards, like electrical appliances or clothing, also often have to meet safety regulations.

In some instances, product regulation may prevent a product from entering a specific national market. The antipollution requirements for automobiles in the United States, for example, have blocked such European sports cars as the Morgan or the Lotus from competing in the U.S. market. Similarly, the introduction of tighter European standards for pharmaceuticals has blocked the expansion of Indian drug manufacturers in these markets.

Measurement and Calibration Systems

Another type of modification relates to measurement and calibration systems. Packaged grocery products, such as cereals or detergents, which are sold in pound or half-pound packages in countries on the imperial measurement system, may need to be sold in kilo or 250-gram packages in countries on the metric system. Similarly, automobile speedometers and maps need to be adapted from miles to kilometers, or vice versa, and bottles and cans from gallons, quarts, and pints to liters. Electrical appliances such as typewriters, sewing machines, hairdryers, and phonographs need to be adapted to different voltage and cycles. Even a product such as Apple's Newton personal digital assistant had to be adapted to recognize different handwriting styles in each country in Europe.[4]

Increasingly, however, products marketed across different market boundaries with different calibration systems are being designed for multicountry use. Speedometers show both miles and kilometers, and hairdryers, coffee grinders, electric shavers, and other electrical appliances are dual voltage. S.C.M.'s Procter-Silex group has even invented a toaster that adjusts for almost any sized bread in the world and can be used to toast pastry rolls and bagels as well.

Climatic and Usage Conditions

Products also often need to be modified in order to operate effectively under different environmental or climatic conditions. Construction materials such as bricks and cement have to be reformulated for the Middle East to prevent drying out and cracking. P&G also had to reformulate the gel used in its diapers in Japan, due to the high levels of humidity that frequently resulted in chafing.[5]

Trucks, automobiles, machinery, and other types of equipment may also need modification to deal with differences in the physical infrastructure, such as unpaved roads, power fluctuations, and shortages. Trucks and automobiles may need structural reinforcement to cope with poor road conditions in countries such as India or Eastern Europe. Similarly, electrically powered machinery and equipment needs to be designed to withstand sharp fluctuations in voltage in these countries.

Products may also need modification for usage conditions in different countries. For example, modifications in size may be necessary due to differences in space available in homes, or retail store outlets, or in purchasing frequency and purchasing power. In many Asian countries small compact package sizes in items such as detergents, soap, and shampoo are popular. Unilever, for example, sells a 50-ml size bottle of its Sunsilk shampoo and 75-gram bars of Lifebuoy and Lux soap in India, as higher priced brands are used less frequently and saved for "special" occasions. In Japan, P&G had to make its Pampers diapers thinner. Japanese mothers change babies' diapers about 14 times a day—more than twice as often as most U.S. mothers. Consequently, they wanted a less bulky diaper that could be stored more easily in the limited storage space available in the average Japanese home.[5]

Household appliances such as washing machines, dishwashers, refrigerators, and freezers may also require modifications in model design. In countries where running hot water is not widely available, heating units need to be added. In the U.K. and some other European countries, smaller-stacked units that fit readily into limited kitchen space are preferred. Refrigerators are also typically smaller in Europe than in the U.S. In Japan, they have three separate compartments, each at different temperatures, one for frozen food, one for chilled food, and one to keep items cold. In addition, there are numerous inner compartments and drawers for different items.

In marketing to developing countries, adaptation of tools and machinery to facilitate operation and maintenance may be necessary. Simple, easy-to-maintain agricultural tools and equipment are often more effective. Small tractors with smaller fuel tanks than the large-scale equipment sold in the United States and Canada may be better adapted to small farms in developing countries. Japanese manufacturers of agricultural equipment, such as Komatsu, have been highly successful in marketing simplified versions of their product lines in developing countries.

Language and Symbolism

Typically, package labelling and assembly or usage instructions need to be translated into the local languages, especially where there are dosage or usage instructions. Where sales volume is low, a firm may adapt such simple solutions as pasting on a label with appropriate instructions, or including a translation with the standard labeling. Visual directions have also been utilized. Ikea, for example, provides visual directions for the assembly of its furniture.

In addition, a firm must pay attention to the symbolism associated with packaging and language. In some instances, use of a foreign language carries a prestige or quality connotation, such as French or Italian for perfume, clothing, or accessories. Use of English on labels in Eastern European countries, Russia, or developing countries can impart a certain cachet. In Poland, for example, P&G found that detergent labels written in imperfect Polish were more effective than those accurately translated. They indicated that foreign companies were trying to fit in, but weren't quick enough to be fluent.[6]

Color associations also may trigger a need for modification. Green, for example, has negative connotations in a number of Southeast Asian countries; it symbolizes danger in Malaysia. Consequently, it is rarely an appropriate color for packaging. Similarly, yellow may arouse superstitions and needs to be avoided in certain markets.

Increasingly, as in the case of calibration systems, products destined for multicountry markets are being packaged in multilingual packaging. Many products sold in several European countries, such as shampoos, cookies, and packaged soups, are labelled in at least four of the major European languages. The European packaging for P&G's Head and Shoulders shampoo, for example, is in eight languages.

Style, Design, and Taste Preferences

Product modifications to match customer preferences in terms of style or design may also be required. For example, Avon modified the packaging of its cosmetics in Japan to satisfy customer preferences. The plastic tubes and packaging used in many Western markets were perceived by Japanese women as cheap and of inferior quality. Consequently, Avon switched to the opaque glass containers used by Japanese cosmetics manufacturers for middle or bottom-of-the-line, as well as expensive, products.

Products may also need to be reformulated to match customer taste preferences. Often there are differences in preferences on the sweet/bitter dimension among countries. Thus, for example Campbell's had to reduce the amount of sugar in its tomato soup in the U.K. In Japan, Nabisco reduces the sugar content in its cookie lines, and the salt content in its snacks.[7] Even Coca-Cola modifies the sugar content of Classic Coke, adding more sugar in Latin American markets.

In some cases, new product variants are added in response to local tastes. In Japan, McDonald's has added the Teriyaki McBurger: a bun containing a disc of chicken covered with a sweet-and-sticky soy sauce and topped off, like a Big Mac, with lettuce and mayonnaise.[8] McDonald's (Japan) also offers monthly specials. A Moon-Viewing Burger, a hamburger topped with a fried egg, to resemble the full moon, was offered during the autumn season of moon viewing.[9]

Although modifying products entails increased costs, management often makes such adaptations in order to penetrate a broader customer base. In some cases, modifications are necessary in order to enter the market, such as to meet regulations on product standards or content. In yet other cases, product modifications may be designed to tap a broader market base, to adjust to differences in customer preferences and tastes, or in positioning relative to competing products and brands.

TAILORING COMMUNICATIONS STRATEGY

Communications strategy, and promotional tactics, often need to be tailored to specific foreign markets or countries. The copy or sales platform, or its execution, may be adapted to differences in customers' perceptions and response patterns. Choice of media may be changed to reach the desired target market as a result of differences in the availability and reach of various media. In-store promotions may be adapted to differences in government regulation and the nature of the distribution structure. The relative importance of different promotional tools in the overall mix may also need to be adapted to the specific market content, and the relative effectiveness or availability of different tools.

For example, in relaunching Coke in India in 1993, Coca-Cola used a dramatically different type of campaign from its usual heavy TV advertising approach, since TV ownership is relatively low in India. Instead, heavy emphasis was placed on signage and outdoor display.[10] The launch took place in Agra, the site of the Taj Mahal and a Pepsi stronghold. On the first day of the launch, a cavalcade of trucks, specially designed three-wheeler vans, tricycles, and handcarts flooded the streets of Agra, with horns blaring to announce the second coming of Coke. The trucks had dynamic digital displays on each side, alternatively showing the Taj Mahal and the Coca-Cola logo, while the tricycles had huge red Coca-Cola umbrellas. At the same time, messengers on motorbikes sped to bazaars in various parts of the city, releasing red balloons to announce that the Coke bottles would shortly be arriving. Retailers were provided with special display racks for Coke bottles, as well as specially designed iceboxes to keep Coke bottles cold. Red kiosks selling Coke were also set up throughout the city.

In other cities in India, Coke made extensive use of outdoor advertising and signage. In Bombay, it developed 3-D neon hoardings for the metro, as well as digital hoardings for its trucks and dynamic display boards for small retail outlets. This was backed by the TV launch commercial, "Share my Dream, Share my Coca-Cola," based on a 1971 commercial first used in Spain but adapted to the Indian launch, using Indian models.

Yet even where the positioning is the same across countries, differences in environmental and market characteristics may force the company to adapt its execution of the communications and copy platform. For example, in advertising Virginia Slims in Japan, Philip Morris was able to use the same emancipated woman image but had to change the slogan "You've Come A Long Way, Baby," to "Oh So Slim, So Sexy," to reflect more accurately the status of women in Japanese society.[11]

In adapting promotional tactics, three major types of factors need to be considered: government regulation of advertising and promotion, customer perceptions and interpretation of stimuli, and availability and reach of media and the structure of distribution.

Government Regulation of Advertising and Promotion

Government attitudes toward, and regulation of, advertising and promotion vary considerably from one country to another. Some countries, notably in Europe, strictly regulate advertising content and media availability, particularly in relation to television advertising. This often reflects an underlying belief that television is an important educational medium, which should be carefully monitored. Other promotional activities, especially in-store and direct promotions, are also often regulated, largely to protect consumers and to ensure fair competition. Other countries (notably developing countries) have little regulation of promotional activities, as mass media are not well developed and consumer protection is not viewed as an important issue.

MEDIA ACCESS

One means of regulating promotional activity is to restrict access to media. In the past a number of governments have restricted the amount of advertising time on television, especially on government-controlled channels. Norway, Sweden, and Switzerland have had a total ban on advertising on television. Other countries have limited the amount of time available and when commercials can be aired.

In Germany, for example, the three government TV stations each had 20 minutes of advertising per day in two time blocks between 6 and 8 p.m. However, with the liberalization of the airwaves and the growth of cable television and direct satellite broadcasting, a number of private channels have been established, such as Canal Plus in France and Odeon in Italy. More TV advertising time has become available, and restrictions on advertising time have been relaxed.[12] The EU has, however, enacted restrictions on advertising time.

Restrictions on media availability result in considerable pressure and competition for available advertising time. Consequently, firms often need to adapt promotional strategy to place greater emphasis on other media or promotional tools. In particular, a firm may encounter difficulties in attempting to launch a new product with a heavy advertising campaign, as is common in TV cultures such as the United States or the U.K. Firms may need to reallocate advertising time among other products in order to have sufficient time to launch a new product.

ADVERTISING CONTENT

Significant restrictions on advertising copy content also exist in a number of countries. In some instances, these are motivated by concern with maintaining standards of morality and decency. Moslem countries such as Malaysia and Indonesia, as well as the Gulf States, for example, regulate ads depicting women. In other instances, regulation is designed to maintain fair competition. Germany, for example, restricts the use of comparative advertising, as well as superlatives. The EU has, however, proposed to allow comparative advertising.

Advertising of certain product categories such as tobacco, alcohol, and pharmaceuticals on radio and on TV is also restricted in some countries. In Europe such restrictions will become more widespread as greater harmonization of regulation within the EU takes place. Advertising of many additional products may also be restricted if much of the proposed regulation being considered is adopted. These relate both to specific industries such as food, toys, financial services, and cosmetics, as well as to types of claims, such as nutritional and health claims, or promises of social success.[13]

Governments also regulate advertising to children. Canada, for example, requires that all story boards be submitted to a regulatory body for approval. Others restrict the products that can be advertised to children, or the content of the commercial. In Italy, for example, children cannot be shown eating snacks in a commercial, and in the Netherlands, candy commercials targeted to children must show the child brushing his or her teeth. In France, children are not allowed to endorse products.[14] The European Union has also placed restrictions on TV advertising aimed at children.[15]

Such restrictions imply that firms may have to make adaptations in their advertising copy and in some instances develop a new platform, even though they want to keep the same positioning. Kelloggs, for example, has not been able to use a commercial developed in the U.K. to promote its brand of corn flakes in other European countries. In the Netherlands, the reference to iron and vitamin content was not permitted. In France, a child could not be shown endorsing a product, while in Germany it was not allowed to make comparative claims.

SALES PROMOTION

Use of other sales promotion tools, such as coupons, gifts, and games, is restricted in a number of countries in order to ensure fair competition and protect consumers.[15] For example, while in the United States coupons are a major form of sales promotion for consumer goods, they are banned in Austria, Germany, and Greece. Premiums and gifts are also limited in a number of countries. In France and Greece, for example, they must be limited to 5 percent of product value, and in Italy to 8 percent. Sweepstakes and games of chances are also restricted or regulated in a number of countries such as Britain, Japan, Argentina, South Africa, Portugal, France, and Belgium. As in other areas, the European Union is moving towards harmonization of sales promotion regulation, though priority has been given to advertising regulation.

Again, such restrictions imply that sales promotion tactics need to be tailored to specific countries, and that opportunities to standardize sales promotion techniques across markets are limited. In-store price reductions are often heavily used, as well as trade discounts. Consequently, responsibility for sales promotion is typically given to local management.

Media Infrastructure

Communications programs also need to be tailored to the media infrastructure in a given country market or region. In particular, differences exist across countries and regions with regard to the availability, reach, and cost of various media and promotional tools. As a result, different media may be more cost effective in reaching a given target market or in delivering a given message.

In launching the Mondeo in Europe, Ford made heavy use of direct marketing.[16] Promotional packets were mailed out to target customers, including both Ford and non-Ford owners. The contents of the packets varied from country to country, but all had the address of the closest Ford dealer. Since direct marketing is relatively undeveloped in Europe—the average Frenchman, for example, receives 55 pieces of direct mail per year—this provided a novel approach. The campaign was coordinated with the commercial featuring the Mondeo as a car that has "Beauty with Inner Strength."

While the basic packet and templates were the same, each market undertook its own mailings and adapted the promotion packet to the local market. In Spain, Belgium, and Scandinavia, the packets included "swipe" cards that could be taken to local dealers and redeemed against a lottery ticket for a Mondeo. In the U.K., classical music tapes were included, and in Germany leather wallets, in keeping with the upscale aspirations of consumers. Germany was the only country not to use the "Beauty with Inner Strength" line. Instead, the proposition centered on the Mondeo as the "new driving experience" and emphasized the Mondeo's safety and environmental friendliness.

MEDIA AVAILABILITY AND REACH

Media availability and reach vary significantly from country to country, depending largely on the level of economic development, literacy, and levels of education, as well as on government regulation. The degree of media spillover, and the reach of international or regional media, also vary from one area of the world to another.

Ownership of TV sets and radios varies considerably from one geographical region to another. While in industrialized countries almost all households own TVs and radios, ownership is often low in many developing countries, such as India, China, and Nigeria. This does, however, underestimate media reach in these countries, as family members, friends, and neighbors will often gather together to watch TV and listen to the radio. Yet reach is often biased toward more affluent consumers. As a result, its use has to be matched to the desired target market.

The effectiveness of print media is impacted by levels of literacy and education as well as circulation. Again this varies considerably from country to country. In Germany, the U.K., and Japan, magazine and newspaper circulation are high compared with countries such as Italy or Spain, where radio and visual media are more effective. Equally, print media are of limited value in developing countries with high levels of illiteracy. Consequently, marketers may need to rely on other types of media, such as billboards and transit advertising.

Outdoor and transit advertising have been used effectively in Eastern Europe, Russia, and China. Colgate Palmolive was the first company to place ads on buses in Moscow and Kiev, to develop awareness of its products among Soviet consumers and dentists.[17] IBM used billboards to announce its arrival in Czechoslovakia.[18] Unique types of outdoor media available in some countries, such as the *abribus* (public transportation boardings) in France and the *kinekon* (illuminated signs) in Japan, are also particularly effective in these environments and provide a high degree of exposure.

The degree of spillover and reach of international media also varies considerably from one area to another. In Europe, for example, there is considerable spillover of German and French TV channels into neighboring countries—Austria, Switzerland, and Belgium. International media are also growing in importance in many parts of the world, spurred largely by the spread of satellite television channels such as the Sky Channel, Super Channel, and MTV in Europe, and Star TV and a consortium called the Gang of Five in Asia.[19] Language barriers, programming costs, and customer preferences for local programs limit the volume of global advertising on such channels, as the majority are produced in English. In addition, relatively few marketers have pan-regional or global brands or can use global advertising appeals effectively. However, such channels are likely to be a potent force in marketing in the future.

In 1993, for example, Nike planned a $15-million campaign across Europe using pan-European TV such as MTV-Europe and Eurosport. The campaign focused on the "Just Do It" slogan, which had been highly successful in the United States.[20] Gillette utilized Murdoch's Sky Channel in Europe and Network

Ten in Australia to launch a global advertising campaign for its highly successful Sensor razor. Equally, the Mandarin hotel chain uses Star TV, which spans India, Hong Kong, China, and the Gulf States, to promote its hotels in Asia.

International print media have also expanded their reach in response to the globalization of business. A number of English-language newspapers and magazines, such as the *Economist,* the *Financial Times, Business Week, Fortune,* and *Newsweek,* have made substantial efforts to increase their international circulation, in some cases publishing special international or foreign language editions. These media provide appropriate vehicles for reaching global segments such as businessmen or international travelers. A number of magazines such as *Elle, Vogue,* and *Cosmopolitan* have also focused on increasing their international circulation, though primarily through the development of separate language editions.

MEDIA COSTS AND EFFECTIVENESS

In addition to differences in availability and reach, media and other promotional tools also vary in terms of relative cost and effectiveness from one country to another. Variability in media costs is not necessarily related to reach in terms of cost per 1000. Rates for TV time, print, and magazines vary considerably throughout Europe.[21] For example, rates in Germany are high relative to those in France and the U.K. Restrictions on availability of TV advertising time in a number of countries, discussed earlier, also tend to create upward pressures on rates and result in greater use of other types of media or promotional techniques such as outdoor media, in-store promotion, and direct mail campaigns.

Differences in the distribution infrastructure from one country to another also influences the use and effectiveness of promotional tools such as couponing, games, in-store displays, and price rebates. In countries where the distribution structure is highly fragmented and characterized by small, family-owned stores, negative distributor reactions and high administrative costs impede use of promotions such as premiums, games, and couponing, where these are permitted. In addition, use of in-store displays and multiple packs may be precluded by limited store space. Consequently, greater reliance may need to be placed on personal selling to distributors and push strategies rather than consumer-oriented appeals.

Use of Western promotional techniques, such as sampling, can also run into difficulties, as P&G discovered in Poland.[5] P&G launched its Vidal Sassoon Wash & Go shampoos in Poland with a massive advertising campaign, and distributed samples to households. At first, Polish consumers were surprised and happy to receive something free without waiting in line. However, the campaign backfired as Poles raided neighbors' mailboxes to filch the samples and sell them.

In essence, differences among countries in the availability, reach, and cost effectiveness of various media vehicles often suggest the desirability of tailoring media selection and use of other promotional tools to specific market environments. In some instances, adaptation only entails changes in relative emphasis placed on different media vehicles, such as using print or outdoor advertising as opposed to TV advertising. In other instances, this tailoring may require the firm to develop a radically different communication strategy, for example, emphasizing a push strategy and promotion to the trade, rather than a "pull" strategy targeted at the end customer.

Customer Response

Customer response can also hamper use of a uniform communications strategy across different countries and can require the firm to tailor its copy theme or its execution to individual markets. The firm clearly needs to consider issues such as language and literacy in developing copy and other promotional materials for international markets. Yet more subtle factors include perceptions, associations, interpretations of symbols, and culturally embedded reactions towards certain types of appeals, such as "hard sell," sex, and humor. Often these are important barriers hampering the effectiveness of standardized advertising campaigns. As a result, promotional copy often needs to be modified from country to country in order to avoid miscommunication and misinterpretation of the message. Modifications may also be needed to arouse interest and to ensure the appeal is effective in different markets.

LANGUAGE AND LITERACY

Language and literacy are clearly important factors in developing promotional materials for international markets, especially where the message has a substantial informational component. Print media require particular attention in this regard. The firm needs to exercise care in translation, to ensure the appropriate meaning or message is conveyed effectively. Often, a literal translation of a slogan or theme will run into difficulties. In Poland, for example, translations of ads for Milky Way candy bars and Persil were said to be so literal they did not make sense.[18] In the case of TV and cinema, language poses less of an issue, since sound-tracks can be dubbed or, in some instances, multiple sound tracks utilized.

In some instances, notably ads with limited informational content, copy may deliberately *not* be translated into the local language, as in the case of packaging, in order to convey an aura, a mystique, or a prestige image. For example, copy for French perfume ads is often not translated, to emphasize its sophisticated, chic image. Similarly, in Japan and some other Asian countries, some advertisements for upscale products including cosmetics and cars are in English, as this conveys a prestigious image.

The firm also has to consider the extent to which it can rely on visual imagery and graphics rather than verbal communication to convey a message. Polaroid has, for example, effectively used the mime Marcel Marceau in commercials for its instant cameras. The benefits of instant photography can easily be demonstrated visually and have universal appeal. Use of visual imagery can be effective for products such as clothing or personal items, where more importance is attached to symbolic connotations of the product than to its physical characteristics, and there is little or no informational content in the message. It is, however, important to note that visual images are also open to misperception or misinterpretation.

PERCEPTION AND INTERPRETATION OF VISUAL STIMULI

Perceptions and interpretation of visual stimuli, as well as the associations they evoke, vary from one country or culture to another. For example, in India, use of an elephant as a logo for batteries to symbolize their long life was considered inappropriate, as elephants are viewed as a symbol of majesty. An American company blundered by using a green hat in a commercial in Hong Kong, where a green hat symbolizes a wife's infidelity.[2]

Use of celebrity endorsement or role models may require changes. In some cases, for example, in promoting detergents, household cleansers, and food products, local celebrities or models are effective, as they are readily identified. In other instances, use of foreign celebrities and role models is highly effective. Pepsi-Cola, for example, has used Michael Jackson and M.C. Hammer extensively in its global advertising campaigns. Sports celebrities such as Charles Barkley, Michael Jordan, and Andre Agassi have also been used successfully for a variety of products such as cameras, running shoes, soft drinks, and fast food. In Japan, use of U.S. deceased film stars such as Marilyn Monroe and James Dean, as well as Western models, is popular in advertising cosmetics and other personal products.

Use of animation and cartoon characters can also be an effective means of bypassing problems of visual perception and interpretation. Cartoon characters such as Tiny Toons and Barney the Dinosaur are widely accepted and popular with young consumers worldwide. Kelloggs has effectively used Tony the Tiger to promote its Frosted Flakes brand worldwide.[22] The commercials for Frosted Flakes are almost identical worldwide but make some adjustments for local markets. The ads feature Tony the Tiger and his teammate playing tennis, since the game has worldwide appeal. However, in Europe, Tony and his partner do not leap the net when they win the match, as this is not customary in Europe.

APPEALS AND EXPRESSIONS OF TASTE

Response to different types of appeals also varies from one cultural context to another. While aggressive or hard-sell appeals are effective in some environments, they are regarded as offensive in others. In the United States use of hard-sell techniques is common. Some overselling, or vaunting of claims regarding products and service, is accepted and even expected by customers. In other countries such as the U.K., aggressive selling is regarded as brash and distasteful, and in Japan it tends to arouse negative reactions.[23]

In Eastern Europe and Russia, heavy advertising often evokes negative reactions, as it smacks of Communist-style propaganda. In Japan, advertising rarely stresses specific product or service attributes and is more commonly geared to developing a favorable corporate or brand image, stressing reliability and quality.[24] In particular, comparative advertising is extremely distasteful to the Japanese, who prefer harmony and courtesy in personal relations. An aggressive commercial aired by Pepsi in Japan showing M.C. Hammer mistakenly drinking Coca-Cola instead of his favorite Pepsi, with disastrous results for his performance, attracted considerable attention but was extremely controversial and subsequently withdrawn.[25]

Appeals to humor and concepts of humor also vary from one cultural context to another. Humor appeals are widely used in the U.K., where humor tends to be dry and cynical. In Asian countries, such appeals are less effective due to concern with loss of face. Acceptability of sex appeals, and concepts of appropriate moral or social conduct also vary from one culture to another. For example, use of female nudity in commercials is widely accepted in Sweden and France. In India, on the other hand, even suggestions of female nudity are considered indecent, and in many Muslim cultures use of women in commercials at all is not permitted.[2]

Such differences in cultural norms and attitudes mean that promotional appeals need to be adapted to the cultural norms of the target market. Failure to do so is likely to generate negative response and even hostile attitudes, and is often a recipe for disaster.

TAILORING PRICING STRATEGIES

Differences in price sensitivity, customer's ability to pay, and competition from one market or geographic area to another suggest that market penetration and profits will be maximized by adjusting prices to local demand conditions. The price of McDonald's Big Mac, for example, varies considerably from one country to another. In 1994, the price ranged from $1.03 in China to $3.96 in Switzerland.[26] (See Table 10.3.) McDonald's aims to target a broad-based market in all countries and works to hold down costs to ensure that the Big Mac is within the reach of the average local consumer.[27] In 1992, when the Russian government imposed a sales tax, McDonald's (Moscow) reduced prices by 28 percent to maintain its position as a popular-priced restaurant. In addition, McDonald's now buys supplies such as foil bags and cardboard containers for apple pie from local suppliers for rubles rather than importing them.

Differential pricing (establishing different pricing schedules from one market to another) may, however, give rise to the emergence of gray markets. These occur when resellers buy from company subsidiaries or distributors in other countries who offer the product or brand at a lower price than do authorized distributors in their own country. Differences in local product costs, shipping and freight, and distributor margins, as well as government regulation of pricing from one market to another, further complicate establishing a uniform pricing strategy. Furthermore, pricing decisions often play a key role in the firm's competitive strategy and depend on the relative emphasis placed on cost leadership as opposed to differentiation in each market.

TABLE 10-3	THE HAMBURGER STANDARD

THE HAMBURGER STANDARD

	BIG MAC PRICES	
	PRICES IN LOCAL CURRENCY*	PRICES IN DOLLARS
UNITED STATES	$2.30**	$2.30
Argentina	Peso3.60	3.60
Australia	A$2.45	1.72
Austria	Sch34.00	2.84
Belgium	BFr109	3.10
Brazil	Cr1,500	1.58
Britain	£1.81	2.65
Canada	C$2.86	2.06
Chile	Peso948	2.28
China	Yuan9.00	1.03
Czech Rep	CKr50	1.71
Denmark	DKr25.75	3.85
France	FFr18.5	3.17
Germany	DM4.60	2.69
Greece	Dr620	2.47
Holland	F15.45	2.85
Hong Kong	HK$9.20	1.19
Hungary	Forint169	1.66
Italy	Lire4,550	2.77
Japan	Y391	3.77
Malaysia	M$3.77	1.40
Mexico	Peso8.10	2.41
Poland	Zloty31,000	1.40
Portugal	Esc440	2.53
Russia	Ruble2,900	1.66
Singapore	$2.98	1.90
S. Korea	Won2,300	2.84
Spain	Ptas345	2.50
Sweden	Skr25.5	3.20
Switzerland	SFr5.70	3.96
Taiwan	NT$62	2.35
Thailand	Baht48	1.90

*Prices may vary locally
**Average of New York, Chicago, San Francisco and Atlanta.
Source: From *The Economist,* April 17, 1993. © 1993 The Economist Newspaper
Ltd. Reprinted with permission.

Demand Conditions and Price Sensitivity

Price sensitivity in a given product market often varies considerably among different market segments and from one country or region to another. In some instances, greater price sensitivity is a function of income and ability to pay; in others, it may reflect differences in perceived price/quality ratios or desired product benefits. For example, in the market for film, customers in some countries such as the U.K., perceive little difference in quality between brands and are highly price-sensitive, while in others they are brand loyal.

Income levels vary from one region of the world to another and impact consumers' ability to pay. In particular in developing countries, low income levels may limit the potential market for consumer durables to a relatively small number of upper-income customers. For example, In India, the market for many products such as washing machines, color TVs, radios, and toilet soap and laundry detergents is limited to 300 million middle-class consumers. Nestlé estimates that the market for rice noodles, ketchup, and instant coffee brands is 100 million, and Bausch and Lomb believes that 30 to 50 million Indians can afford soft contact lenses.[28]

Price sensitivity is also influenced by psychological factors such as the image of a product. In some instances, products or services are able to command a premium price in international markets due to prestige associations with the country of origin. For example, furniture from Scandinavia, perfume from France, and woollen goods from Italy are all able to command premium prices due to their national origin.

In some cases, low income levels mean that adoption of a premium pricing strategy will change the positioning of a product or brand. For example, the prices of P&G's Camay soap, Pert Plus shampoo, and Oil of Olay night cream in Russia position them as luxury items, suitable for gifts. As a result, Russians give bars of Camay soap (eight times the price of Russian soap) as gifts on occasions such as New Year's Eve or Women's Day.[29] Similarly, in some Asian countries, American brands can command premium prices, as they are perceived as superior in quality to local competitor's products and the embodiment of the American Dream. In China, for example, P&G sells its Whisper sanitary napkins for 10 times the price of local products, while Johnson and Johnson's baby shampoo and Band-Aids command a 500 percent premium. In India, Gillette launched a disposable razor for two times that of competing products.[28]

Demand factors, and, in particular, sensitivity to price, play an important role in determining the degree of market penetration, as well as impacting product positioning. Yet while demand is a key input into pricing decisions, other factors such as prices of competing and substitute factors, distributor margins, production and shipment costs, and price regulation also have to be considered in making pricing decisions.

Competing and Substitute Products and Services

Another important element in pricing decisions is the price of competing and substitute products. Pricing should reflect the perceived value of the product or service relative to close competitors or alternative means of performing the same function or satisfying the same need. This is especially crucial where the firm's competitive strategy emphasizes cost superiority rather than differentiation on product features or service.

In addition to examining prices of products and services in direct competition, prices of substitute products and services (i.e., which satisfy the same need) should also be considered. This is particularly important when introducing a new product or service into a country where there is no existing market for the product. For example, in introducing labor-substitution machinery, such as washing machines or dishwashers, management needs to consider the relative cost and availability of domestic help. Similarly, a firm introducing frozen pre-pared main dishes needs to consider the cost and availability of take-out meals from restaurants, and sale of prepared dishes by specialty food stores. For exam-ple, McDonald's in India has to take into consideration the cost of local services that deliver home-cooked meals to office workers, as well as other local fast food and veggieburger restaurants.

In addition to adapting to the current price structure of the product market targeted, management has also to consider the likely reaction of competing firms to a given pricing strategy, and the possible entry of competitors into the market. For example, in the European PC market, IBM, Compaq, and Apple face competition, not only from Acer, the Taiwanese manufacturer of IBM clones, but two German discounters, Vobis and Escom. Entering the market in 1991, both construct PCs from Asian subassemblies and sell them through their own stores at discount prices of 15 to 30 percent below IBM or Compaq.[30] Both have grown rapidly, and by 1993, Vobis had gained 19 percent of the German market, and 5 percent of the European market. IBM and Compaq retaliated by slashing prices by 40 to 60 percent, cutting deeply into their own margins.

In adopting an aggressive pricing strategy, management, therefore, needs to consider whether its underlying cost structure will enable it to sustain aggressive retaliatory pricing over the long run, and the impact this will have on its own profit margins and market share. Especially where aggressive pricing in interna-tional markets is below domestic market prices, firms are likely to be accused of dumping. Governments may also take retaliatory measures such as imposition of quotas or tariffs. For example, aggressive pricing of VCRs by Korean consumer electronics manufacturers in entering several European countries resulted in the EU imposing dumping duties.[31]

On the other hand, a price-skimming strategy, even where the product is not currently available in a foreign market, is vulnerable to the entry of competition. This is especially the case with technologically advanced products where a firm attempts to recoup R&D costs in its initial pricing strategy. The technology may be copied or even leapfrogged by a foreign competitor with lower labor and pro-duction costs. For example, when GE introduced a computerized catscanner into foreign markets, it was undercut by Toshiba by 40 percent within 3 months with a machine that also incorporated a three-dimensional X-ray.

Cost Factors

Management also has to consider cost factors in making pricing decisions, since in the long run prices have to cover production, distribution, and promotional expenses. The nature of these costs will vary, depending on where production is located—in the domestic market or in the foreign market.

Where production is located in the domestic market and the product or service is exported, the costs of shipping, packaging, insurance, and processing documentation for foreign markets have to be assessed. The firm must evaluate tariffs, customs and other import duties, and local inventory management and storage costs. Often these items add substantially to costs of supplying foreign markets, resulting in price escalation. It is, for example, not uncommon for the price of an exported good to be double its domestic market price.

Lengthy channels of distribution and high distributor margins add further to price escalation. In Japan, for example, long channels of distribution, often including several tiers of wholesalers, entail high distribution costs. In addition, such channel practices as granting wholesale and retail rebate and discounts, return policies, and credit terms add significantly to margins. Value-added taxation (VAT) systems add even further to distribution costs. VAT is levied at each stage of the distribution system, or each time title to goods changes hands. Thus, the greater the number of intermediaries, the more distribution costs increase.

Price Regulation

Pricing decisions also have to take into consideration local price controls and regulation. Governments and other regulatory agencies may control prices in order to fight inflation, set ceilings on prices in selected industries, or limit distribution margins to keep prices down, or otherwise act to regulate prices. In countries with high rates of inflation, government may intervene in order to prevent spiralling inflation. For example, in 1988 both the Argentine and Brazilian governments froze prices temporarily in order to contain inflation.

In other cases, governments regulate pricing in certain industries. Prices of basic foodstuffs such as bread, milk, and rice are fixed in some countries in order to contain food costs. Prices are also regulated in monopolistic or oligopolistic industries, in order to limit competition or prevent excessive pricing. Airfares, energy prices, and postal and telephone changes are all regulated in a number of countries.

Regulations of pharmaceutical prices is especially likely to occur in countries with a system of socialized medicine. For example, most European countries regulate drug prices in order to contain health costs. Such regulations severely limit the freedom of pharmaceutical companies to set prices. In France, for example, there is a strict system of price controls for drugs, while the British National Health Service limits prices of drugs that qualify for reimbursement. In Japan, the government determines the prices at which consumers are reimbursed for the drugs that physicians dispense.

While differences in demand, price sensitivity, prices of competing products, cost factors, and price regulation, necessitate tailoring prices to specific market conditions, it is important to recognize that gray markets may emerge, resulting in a flow of products from low- to high-priced market. This is particularly likely to occur where there are significant differences in ex-factory prices or, alternatively, distributor margins from one market to another. For example, differences in the ex-factory price of Duracell batteries in the United States and Belgium resulted in U.S. distributors buying from Duracell's factory in Europe. Poor storage conditions and shipment delays meant that the batteries were often defective, thus damaging Duracell's reputation.

Although, in some cases, gray markets may increase the manufacturer's overall sales, they cause dislocation in international pricing and distribution strategy. Especially where the firm has a system of authorized dealers responsible for servicing and warranty repair, as, for example, cameras and other equipment, negative consequences are likely to arise. Authorized dealers will object to undercutting by unauthorized gray market dealers, while customers may be confused and complain about lack of service from unauthorized distributors. Consequently, it is generally desirable to take measures to limit the development of gray markets. In addition to standardizing prices, manufacturers can, for example, differentiate models or warranties in each market, try to control or cut off supplies to gray marketers, or promote awareness of gray market products.

TAILORING DISTRIBUTION STRATEGY

Differences around the world in distribution structure and in the availability and coverage of different types of distribution channels frequently make adapting distribution strategies to local market conditions essential. Identifying and motivating efficient distribution and channel members is often of crucial importance, especially in markets in developing nations. A key to Carrier Aircon's successful development of the market for air conditioners in India has been the establishment of its own dealer network.[32] Carrier initially set up operations in the Indian market in 1987, primarily targeting private and government institutions. With the reduction of excise duties on white goods, Carrier decided to target the more lucrative individual consumer market, focusing on professionals such as doctors and lawyers, as well as merchants. It has set up a strong network of 150 dealers concentrated primarily in the north. Carrier focused on wholesale activities, leaving dealers to handle sales both to individuals and for huge air conditioning projects for companies and institutions. The number of dealers in each area is limited, to avoid creating competition among dealers. Dealers have been recruited primarily from "service-class" people who previously worked for other companies, rather than from traders. As a result, they are more motivated to succeed and provide a high level of service.

Differences in customer purchasing patterns and desired services, competitor control of certain channels, and government regulation or intervention in the distribution system, also need to be considered in designing distribution channels in international markets.

Distribution Structure

Distribution structures differ significantly from one country to another in terms of the importance or role of mass distribution organizations, the locus of power in the distribution channel, and the technological sophistication of channel members. These are in part a function of differences in the historical evolution of the distribution sector, as well as government support of small retail businesses, customer shopping patterns and preferences, population density, and the topographical characteristics of a country.

In a number of countries, particularly in the food sector, small independent family businesses predominate, and the organized sector of large-scale distributors is very small. In developing countries, small businesses and open air markets often account for 90 percent of retail sales. Large-scale modern forms of distribution such as supermarkets, hypermarkets, and discount and department stores are to be found only in large cities, if at all, and account for a small percentage of sales. Even in some industrialized countries, such as Italy and Japan, the role of organized mass distribution outlets such as supermarket or department store chains is limited, and small family businesses still account for over 60 percent of retail sales. In Italy, more than 40 percent of fast-moving goods, food and groceries, tobacco, soft drinks, and OTC medicines is sold through nontraditional forces of distribution such as market stalls, kiosks, and peddlers.[33]

The fragmentation of distribution has major implications for distribution strategy. Especially where small businesses do not belong to central buying organizations, as for example, voluntary chains or retail buying groups with a central buying organization, and where channels of distribution are long, manufacturers often have to sell through wholesalers. This limits their ability to establish direct contact with retailers.

In Japan, for example, in many markets there are no national wholesalers. Consequently, a firm has to sell through regional wholesalers, who supply local wholesalers, who in turn sell to retailers.[34] This structure increases the amount of effort and number of contacts required, in some cases even to gain access to distributors. For example, the manager of Smith, Klein and French in Japan had to make contact with wholesalers through the chairman of the drug wholesale association. He subsequently made personal visits to distributors throughout Japan in order to establish good relations and trust.[7]

As this example illustrates, distribution through small retail businesses often limits the feasibility of pursuing a pull strategy. Especially if store space is limited and stores are not self-service, it is difficult to pull products through the channel based on heavy promotion to the end consumer through advertising and in-store promotion. Often retailer salespersons play a key role in determining which product or brand is selected by customers. Consequently, greater emphasis will need to be placed on promotion to various channel members, and on pushing the product through the channel.

In some instances, an unsophisticated distribution system and poor infrastructure hamper development of an effective distribution strategy. For example, when Unilever bought an ice-cream company in the former Czechoslovakia in 1991, it found there was no reliable distribution system to get its products to stores. Forced to rely on the state-run system of trucking and storage, Unilever's ice cream often arrived at stores half-melted. As a result, Unilever had to devote substantial time and effort to set up an effective system of wholesalers and transportation in Eastern Europe.[35]

Similarly, the distribution system for packaged goods in China is unsophisticated and highly fragmented.[36] There are few self-service outlets, though the department- and government-run stores operate mini supermarkets. These are, however, concentrated in urban centers and are mostly patronized by more affluent consumers. Traditional small retailers are frequented by many people, but not all can afford packaged foods. Turnover is often low and products are poorly stored and can deteriorate, as well as be inaccurately priced. This constitutes a major barrier to the growth of food companies such as Nestlé, Kraft, and President of Taiwan in China.

The technological sophistication of distributors—their use of scanner systems, or computerized inventory and ordering systems—also varies from one market to another. Use of this technology enhances ability to manage distribution logistics to track new products and slow-moving items, and to monitor the impact of promotions. This capability substantially enhances bargaining power with manufacturers and impacts willingness to give shelf space to slow-moving or new items.[33] As a result, manufacturers have to advertise heavily and establish a strong brand or product image in order to develop countervailing power and persuade retailers to stock new products as well as their existing brands. In Europe, for example, the spread of scanner technology, and the concentration of food retailing, together with cross-border expansion, have substantially increased retailers' power in negotiations with food manufacturers.[37] Consequently, manufacturers have to develop brand strength and broaden geographic coverage in order to obtain distribution.

Customer Shopping Patterns

Customer shopping patterns and preferences also vary considerably from one market to another, and are key factors in designing distribution channels. In particular, population density, customer mobility and desire for service are important factors in fashioning the nature and spatial structure of retail distribution.

The spread of U.S.-style warehouse clubs such as Costco in Europe increases pressure on margins and prices, as well as accelerating the shift towards volume-based purchasing patterns.[38] In some countries, such as the United States, most consumers have access to a car for shopping and can travel some distance to shop. Availability of parking is often more crucial in determining store choice than proximity or home delivery service. Mobile consumers are likely to shop less frequently, travelling further and purchasing in larger quantities than less mobile consumers. Consequently, in these countries, manufacturers can reach a broad-based target market through large scale distribution outlets.

In other countries, consumers shop on foot or use public transport. They often shop more frequently—daily or several times a week for food—and purchase in smaller quantities. This behavior may be further encouraged by lack of space in which to store items, absence of refrigerators in the home, and a preference for fresh items rather than packaged products. For example, in Japan, a typical diet is composed of fresh or lightly cooked items, such as raw fish and vegetables. Many Japanese housewives shop for food daily, in some cases twice a day. This shopping pattern reinforces the fragmented distribution structure and role of small, Mom-and-Pop-type stores. As a result, food and beverage manufacturers have to adapt strategies accordingly, utilizing indirect channels or providing support and rapid delivery to retailers. Coca-Cola, for example, established a highly effective system of direct distribution, bypassing the cumbersome wholesaler soft-drink network, setting up its own fleet of 9,000 delivery trucks. Deliveries are made weekly to retailers, ensuring rapid and efficient distribution as well as providing an effective mechanism for stocking street vending machines, which are a major source of distribution for soft drinks in Japan.[7]

The distribution system in Japan is beginning to change, however, with the growth of suburban discount stores, supermarket chains, and shopping malls. The rate of change varies depending on the retail sector. Discounting in particular appears to have the greatest impact in clothing, furniture, and electronic goods.[39] In the traditional sector, considerable importance is attached to service, and time is devoted to interchange with the storekeeper. In department stores, personnel greet customers on entry, and considerable attention is devoted to assisting the customer with a purchase, including elaborate packaging of items. Again, manufacturers may need to adapt channel strategy to provide the requisite level of service. Max Factor, for example, set up franchised counters in department stores and specialty cosmetic outlets, supported by heavy advertising and promotion, in order to provide the desired level of customer service.

Competitor's Distribution Strategy

Management also needs to consider competitor's distribution in designing distribution channels. For example, where the modern, organized sector is relatively small, and a competitor has preempted this channel, a firm may have to utilize second-level, less efficient distributors, adding to distribution costs. Furthermore, such distributors may not provide the desired level of promotion and service backing for the product, requiring supplementary efforts or development of a more creative strategy to reach potential customers.

Preemptive moves by competitors are especially likely to hamper subsequent efforts to enter a market by other firms, and to block access to distribution channels. For example, Kelloggs pioneered introducing breakfast cereal, and notably its flagship Corn Flakes brand, into foreign markets. As a result, Quaker Oats and General Mills experienced considerable difficulty in getting distributors to stock their cereal products. General Mills formulated a joint venture with Nestlé—United Cereal Partners—to market its cereal brands worldwide. Nestlé's strength in distribution gained the joint venture access to broad-based distribution channels in international markets.[40] In some instances, adoption of a distinctive distribution strategy can provide a competitive edge. For example, in entering the European market in 1987, Dell sold its PCs through mail order—

the same strategy that had proved effective in the United States. Backed by an intensive educational campaign and promise of superior service, the tactic proved highly effective.[41] Compaq, on the other hand, ruled out direct selling and focused on building a strong dealer network, offering exclusive arrangements to motivate them.[42]

Government Regulation

Government regulation of distribution often has an impact on channel design and may necessitate adaptation of distribution policy. In a number of countries, government regulation of distribution has been designed to protect small retail businesses. They are an important political force, and this protection has been an important factor underlying their survival. Protective regulation has taken a number of forms, including regulation of store location, store opening hours, and the opening of large-scale stores. Governments may also directly intervene in distribution by establishing government-controlled monopolies.

Government regulation of store location is widespread in Japan and many European countries but varies in nature and intent. In some densely populated countries, such as the U.K. and the Netherlands, it has primarily been designed to prevent strip development and establishment of free-standing stores on major highways outside towns, and to maintain the vitality of the city center as a shopping area. In other countries, regulating location is intended to protect small retailers. For example, in France, hypermarkets developing out-of-town sites can only do so by establishing a shopping center, allocating an equal amount of floor space to small independents and to large-scale distributors. Often they also have to provide or contribute to infrastructure and access costs to such sites. Such regulation limits the attractiveness of suburban store sites. As a result, many fast food chains and large retailers have shifted from a policy of free-standing locations in suburban locations to center city sites in many countries.

Governments also establish distribution monopolies for products such as tobacco, alcohol, and salt. For example, in Japan, a tobacco monopoly (JTS) controlled distribution until 1981. After the market was opened up, both Philip Morris and R.J. Reynolds distributed their brands through the JTS system in order to obtain broad-based distribution and achieve widespread availability in the numerous kiosks and vending machines through which cigarettes are distributed in Japan.

SUMMARY

As the firm focuses attention on developing its position in local national markets and broadening its market base, programs will need to be tailored to local market conditions—demand, government or industry regulations, or competition. The firm has to strike a balance between adapting to local markets to achieve deeper penetration, and realizing economies of scales or efficiencies through standardization, leveraging its competencies, image, and market position across national boundaries.

Products may need to be adapted to different usage conditions, products, standards, and requirements, and customer preferences. Advertising platforms and promotion themes need to be modified in the light of government regulation, availability and reach of media, and customer response patterns. Similarly, pricing needs to take into consideration differences in demand conditions and price sensitivity, competing and substitute products and services, and regulation from one market to another, while at the same time covering costs. Finally, distribution tactics will need to be tailored to local customer shopping patterns, the structure of distribution, competitor control of outlets, and government regulation. (See Figure 10.2.)

FIGURE 10-2

Tailoring the marketing mix.

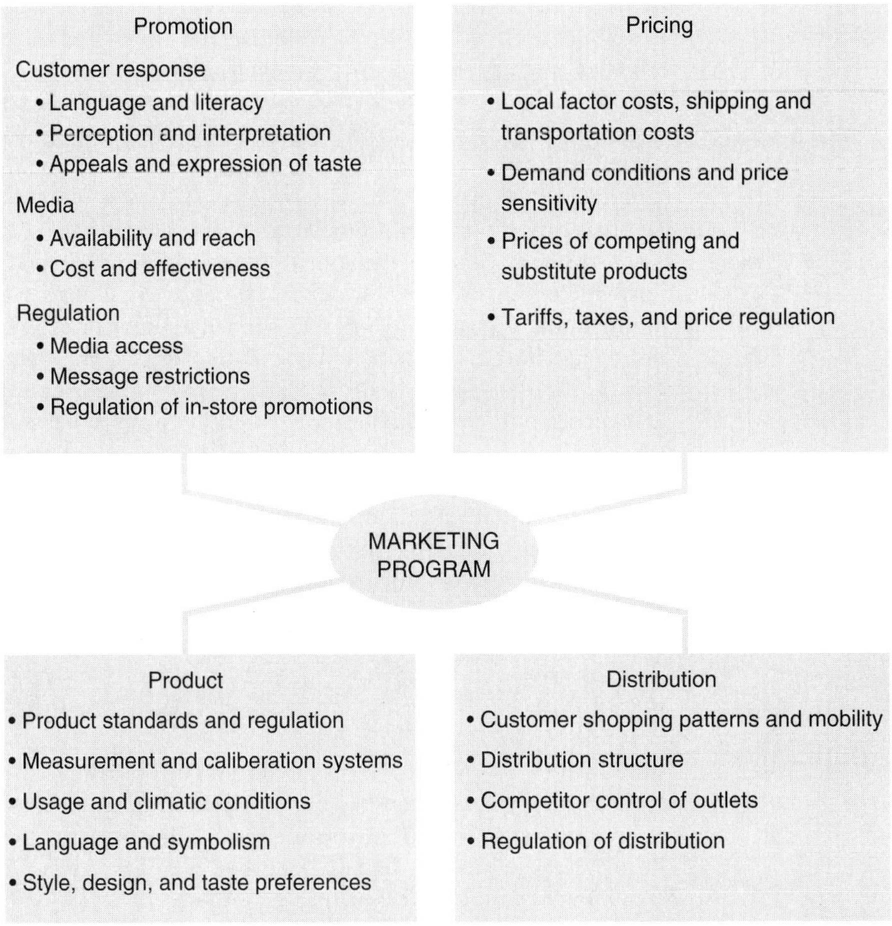

Promotion

Customer response
- Language and literacy
- Perception and interpretation
- Appeals and expression of taste

Media
- Availability and reach
- Cost and effectiveness

Regulation
- Media access
- Message restrictions
- Regulation of in-store promotions

Pricing
- Local factor costs, shipping and transportation costs
- Demand conditions and price sensitivity
- Prices of competing and substitute products
- Tariffs, taxes, and price regulation

MARKETING PROGRAM

Product
- Product standards and regulation
- Measurement and caliberation systems
- Usage and climatic conditions
- Language and symbolism
- Style, design, and taste preferences

Distribution
- Customer shopping patterns and mobility
- Distribution structure
- Competitor control of outlets
- Regulation of distribution

In some instances, where government or regulatory agencies have established regulations or standards, modification of programs is mandatory. In other cases, the extent to which marketing tactics are adapted will depend on how far management is concerned with responding to local market conditions, the cost of making such modifications, and the impact on other elements of the mix.

REFERENCES

1. "Pizza Hut Sliced Evenly in Japan" (1991) *Financial Times,* January 18.
2. Ricks, David A. (1993) *Blunders in International Business,* Cambridge, MA: Blackwell.
3. Henkoff, Ronald (1993) "The Hot New Seal of Quality," *Fortune,* June 28, pp. 116–120.
4. "Apple's Newton Staff Takes To Collecting European Writing" (1993) *Wall Street Journal,* October 9.
5. "Don't Sell Thick Diapers in Tokyo" (1993) *New York Times,* October 3.
6. "Colgate-Palmolive Is Really Cleaning Up in Poland" (1993) *Business Week,* March 15, pp. 54–56.
7. Douglas, Susan P., and C. Samuel Craig (1990) "Achieving Success in Japanese Consumer Markets," *Japan and the World Economy,* pp. 1–21.
8. "Teriyaki McBurger" (1991) *The Economist,* April 28, p. 86.
9. "McDonald's Serves Up Video Games, Clothing" (1993) *Wall Street Journal,* September 17.
10. Skaria, George (1993) "The Coke Challenge," *Business Today,* November 7–21, pp. 50–56.
11. Burton, Jack (1989) "Philip Morris—Puffing Away in Japan," *Journal of Japanese Trade and Industry* 5, pp. 45–47.
12. Wentz, L. (1988) "Europe Opens Wallet: Saatchi," *Advertising Age,* July 4, p. 26.
13. "EC Reviewing Policy on Advertising" (1993) *Business Europe,* April 12–18, pp. 1–3.
14. Foltz, K. (1990) "Agencies Set Sights for Europe," *New York Times,* August 21, p. D19.
15. Boddewyn, Jean (1988) *Premiums, Gifts and Competition,* New York: International Advertising Association.
16. Martin, Beverly (1993) "Machine Dreams," *Brandweek,* April 26, pp. 17–24.
17. "Colgate-Palmolive Is First to Put Ads on Soviet Buses" (1990) *Marketing News,* November 26, p. 5.
18. "Eastern Europe Poses Obstacles for Ads" (1992) *Wall Street Journal,* July 30, p. B6.
19. Kraar, Louis (1994) "TV Is Exploding All Over Asia," *Fortune,* January 24, pp. 98–101.
20. "Euro-Swoosh" (1993) *Brandweek,* August 2, pp. 1–6.

21. *The Leo Burnett Worldwide Advertising and Media Fact Book,* 1994 edition, Chicago, IL, Triumph Books.

22. "Advertisers Seek Global Messages" (1991) *The New York Times,* November 18.

23. "In the Land of Soft Sell" (1990) *Financial Times,* February 9, p. 20.

24. Kishii, Tamotsu (1988) "Message vs Mood—A Look at Some of the Differences Between Japanese and Western TV Commercials," *Deutsu Japan Marketing/Advertising Yearbook.*

25. Kuno, Soichiro (1991), "Rapping the Hammer," *Japan Update,* October, p. 10–11.

26. "Big MacCurrencies" (1994) *The Economist,* April 9, p. 88.

27. Uchitelle, Louis (1992) "That's Funny, Those Pickles Don't Look Russian," *New York Times,* February 27.

28. Jacob, Rahul (1993) "Asia Where the Big Brands Are Blooming," *Fortune,* August 2, p. 55.

29. "P&G Uses Skills it Has Honed at Home to Introduce its Brands to the Russians" (1993) *Wall Street Journal,* April 14, p. B1.

30. "IBM, Apple, Compaq . . . and Vobis and Escom" (1993) *Business Week,* August 2, p. 84.

31. "Brussels Plays Rough with VCR Imports" (1988) *Financial Times,* September 6, p. 24.

32. "Sitting Pretty" (1994) *Business Asia,* January 17, pp. 6–7.

33. AC Nielsen (1990) *The Nielsen European Passport.*

34. "Japan's Distribution System" (1987) *Japan Economic Institute Report,* March 17.

35. "Teaching the Hard Sell of Soap to Eastern Europe" (1993) *New York Times,* February 18, p. D6.

36. "What Will the Market Take? (1994) *Business Asia,* January 17, pp. 6–7.

37. Gogel, Robert, and Jean-Claude Larréché (1989) "The Battlefield for 1992: Product Strength and Geographic Coverage," *European Management Journal,* vol. 7, 2, pp. 132–140.

38. "Silent Enemy Stalks the Aisles" (1993) *Financial Times,* November 30, p. 15.

39. Holyoke, Larry (1993) "What? Everyday Bargains? This Can't be Japan," *Business Week,* September 6, p. 41.

40. Knolton, Christopher (1991) "Europe Cooks Up a Cereal Brawl" *Fortune,* June 3, pp. 175–177.

41. "Dell: Mail Order Was Supposed to Fail" (1992) *Business Week,* January 20, p. 89.

42. "Compaq's European Accent" (1991) *International Management,* March, pp. 50–53.

CHAPTER 11

IMPLEMENTING MARKET EXPANSION STRATEGIES

INTRODUCTION

Success in global markets depends on developing a sound strategy based on a thorough assessment of local market conditions, product market structure, competition, customer interests and behavior patterns, and the market infrastructure. This assessment provides input for determining how products and services should be positioned and how far programs need to be tailored to local market characteristics. However, even the best strategy is doomed to failure if mechanisms to implement it are not put in place. Consequently, once the firm has formulated a strategy, it has to establish appropriate procedures for ensuring that programs are effectively implemented to achieve overall corporate objectives.

While attention to implementation of marketing programs is critical in domestic markets, implementation assumes additional complexity in global markets. The firm needs to establish an organization and tools to implement programs in each local market. At the same time, it has to pay attention to interdependence between markets, and to managing relationships within the overarching corporate structure. In addition, the firm has to manage relations with other organizations that play key roles in helping it implement strategy.

A key parameter in establishing the appropriate organizational structure and operational mechanisms to implement strategy is the extent to which management of programs is directed and controlled centrally, by corporate headquarters in the domestic market, or locally, by the subsidiary. When operations are directed from corporate headquarters, emphasis is likely to be placed on efficiency. If more responsibility is given to local management, more emphasis will be placed on responding to local market needs and exercising minimal control.[1]

Many Japanese companies, such as Hitachi, Sony, and Yamaha, use a centralized approach to international management. Business functions are controlled at corporate headquarters, and most major decisions and final approval are made by the home office.[2] Yamaha, which manufactures motorcycles and other recreational vehicles such as golf carts, snowmobiles, and boats, is run along highly centralized lines. Head office exercises control over the financing of new operations and the development of new products, product specifications, and standards, with little or no input from local managers. The role of local management in markets such as North America and Europe is limited to setting up distribution arrangements and day-to-day management.

Other companies have a more decentralized approach. Corporate headquarters is typically small and focuses on corporate strategy matters. Local country managers are responsible for managing day-to-day operations and for handling issues relating to production and customer service. Atlas Copco, a Swedish manufacturer of compressors, mining and construction machinery, and automation and production equipment, for example, moved towards greater decentralization in the 1980s as it expanded globally. This was intended to reduce layers of management and to place greater emphasis on enhancing customer productivity. Management of production and sales operations has been transferred to local subsidiaries, in order to improve customer service and strengthen exchange of information between marketing and production.[2]

Market characteristics are important factors influencing organizational design. Where product market structure, operating conditions (for example, the market infrastructure), local customs, and codes of conduct governing business differ significantly from one market to another, delegation of responsibility to local management, and flexibility in adjusting to the local market environment, are desirable. Mechanisms to ensure that experience acquired from operating in different environments is transferred across national borders should also be established. If, on the other hand, product markets and operating conditions are highly similar, standardized management processes may effectively be adopted with a high degree of centralization and control from corporate headquarters. P&G, for example, uses its famous brand management system in all countries and coordinates positioning strategies for international brands such as Camay and Mr. Clean across countries. Country managers have considerable autonomy to determine which brands to launch or to emphasize, as well as what promotional and pricing tactics to adopt.

The firm's degree of involvement and experience in international markets also shapes organizational structure and systems. In the initial phase of entry, operations in other countries are likely to be directed from corporate headquarters. A substantial degree of control is exercised, both to ensure that the strategic thrust is executed and to monitor performance. This also provides direct feedback to corporate headquarters, enabling it to make changes in the firm's strategic thrust in international markets and adapt programs accordingly.

As the firm acquires more experience in international operations, it is likely to grant greater autonomy to local subsidiary management. Still, mechanisms to provide effective communication between headquarters and local management, and to ensure the coordination of their activities with the overall operations of the firm, will be required. The organizational structure should also adapt to the evolving nature of the firm's operations as it expands and gains experience in international markets. Central to this design is the balance between achieving cost efficiency in international operations and responsiveness to local market conditions.[3]

Opportunities and mechanisms for innovation and learning across countries should also be created. This in turn requires managing risks arising from fluctuations in local markets and from operating across national borders. The structure should thus allow management and coordination of operations across markets to achieve local objectives, while at the same time furthering its global strategy.

ESTABLISHING ORGANIZATIONAL NETWORKS

A key aspect of the design of an effective organizational structure is the establishment of networks to direct and manage programs in international markets. These networks orchestrate the tangible and intangible activities involved in the flow of goods, materials, and components from sources of supply, through production and distribution, to the final market. This orchestration entails not only organization of sourcing, production, and distribution logistics, but also of financing and information to match supply and demand.

Two types of organizational networks can be identified: *internal* networks, comprising the links within the firm, between various organizational units, such as between corporate headquarters and local subsidiary management; and *external* networks, comprising relations with external organizations such as distributors, advertising agencies, market research companies, and financial institutions.

Internal Networks

The management philosophy underlying the establishment of internal organizational networks typically evolves as the company gains experience in international markets, reflecting different orientations towards the management of international operations. As noted in Chapter 2, four major types of orientation or management philosophy have been identified[4]: ethnocentric, polycentric, regiocentric, and geocentric. An *ethnocentric* orientation is founded in the belief that domestic marketing strategies and procedures can effectively be adopted in foreign markets. A *polycentric* orientation emphasizes the uniqueness of local market characteristics, and management on a country-by-country basis. A *regiocentric* orientation looks for links among markets within a region and organizes operations on a regional basis. A *geocentric* orientation, on the other hand, focuses on global synergies and management on a global scale.

In the initial phases of entry and market expansion, the underlying management philosophy is likely to be ethno- or polycentric. Consequently, in the following section attention is centered on organizational structures associated with these two orientations. Organizational structures emanating from a regiocentric or geocentric orientation are discussed in Chapter 15.

ETHNOCENTRIC ORIENTATION

An ethnocentric orientation is typically associated with direction of international activities from the domestic market, and tight centralized operating and financial controls. Often, products and marketing programs developed in relation to domestic market conditions are "exported" to foreign markets. Local market operations are staffed by expatriates with experience in company operations in the domestic market.

Use of expatriates and tight links with corporate headquarters ensures that strategic objectives are implemented, and that corporate philosophy and operating procedures are transplanted to markets in other countries. Control of resources (capital, skills, information), is retained by corporate headquarters, and resources are allocated to foreign markets based on goals established centrally. (See Figure 11.1.)

Expatriate staffing can also result in insensitivity to idiosyncratic market conditions and difficulties in establishing external relations with local organizations such as distributors and agencies. Such difficulties are especially likely to occur where expatriates lack experience in foreign market operations, or familiarity

FIGURE 11-1

Strategy development under an ethnocenric perspective.

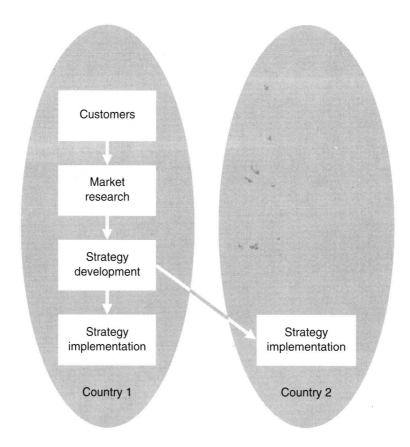

with sociocultural values, customs, and behavior patterns of the particular market. Such inexperience is often further compounded by the belief that strategies and techniques effective in the domestic market will work in other countries and should be applied despite possible evidence to the contrary.

A number of the failures of U.S. companies in the Japanese market have been attributed to efforts to apply mass distribution strategies that are successful in the United States to Japan.[5] Confronted by lengthy distribution channels, some U.S. companies have attempted to short-cut traditional channels and establish direct distribution, ignoring differences in customer demand for service and the importance of establishing strong ties based on mutual trust and support. Often such firms have not only encountered hostility from the trade but also incurred exorbitant costs to maintain the level of service provided by traditional channels. As a result, they have often experienced considerable difficulty in obtaining widespread distribution.

Many of the mistakes made by firms in initial entry into international markets result from lack of sensitivity to differences in market conditions and ways of doing businesses, and failure to recognize the need to adapt to these differences. Even if the firm uses the same product or marketing program it uses in the domestic program, adaptation is often needed in implementation of these programs, for example, negotiating contracts, training employees, and handling external relationships. Some companies run training programs to stimulate greater management awareness and understanding of national cultural differences, and how to adapt to these. At Motorola University in Chicago, one of the academic departments focuses on training Motorola managers in how differences in national culture affect Motorola's ability to export its corporate culture to foreign operations.[6]

Retaining control for implementation of marketing programs at corporate headquarters is most likely to be appropriate in the initial stages of entry, as top management monitors operations closely to assess their success and determine the need for adjustments and additional resources. This also helps to provide direct feedback for planning expansion of international operations.

As, however, international operations evolve and become more complex, and the firm enters into licensing agreements, joint ventures, and other alliances, new types of management skills and experience will be required, and in particular, greater sensitivity to local management practices and customs. As a result, organizational forms providing greater decentralization of responsibility to local operations are required. Often these are governed by a polycentric, or country-by-country, orientation.

POLYCENTRIC ORIENTATION

A polycentric orientation or philosophy emphasizes the importance of understanding local market conditions and is rooted in the belief that only local nationals have that understanding. This philosophy frequently leads a firm to hire local nationals and substantially delegate responsibility to local management. Often these are organized as local profit centers with full responsibility for implementing marketing programs, and in some cases for new product launches and development. (See Figure 11.2.)

Delegating responsibility to local management typically provides maximal local market penetration and development. In contrast to expatriate management, local nationals usually believe that demand, infrastructure, and competitive conditions in their own markets are unique. Consequently, they will frequently advocate the need for adaptation to these conditions and establish goals and priorities based on them. This orientation may lead to variation in the timing of new product launches, as well as differences in product lines, brand identities, and marketing programs from one country to another.[7]

Freedom to make decisions rather than merely executing those of corporate headquarters not only encourages local managers to adapt to local market conditions but also generates a high degree of motivation to achieve and to beat competition. When Parker Pen decided to centralize advertising decisions for its international markets and use a standardized theme, management motivation declined. Local managers resented U.S. corporate headquarters mandating what advertising should be, and which advertising agency they should use. Profits dropped dramatically, and Parker took a $12 million loss.[8] The following year, a group of its British managers bought the pen business, forcing out U.S. senior management. Responsibility for developing advertising copy was given back to local management, resulting in a substantial increase in profitability.

FIGURE 11-2

Strategy development under a polycentric perspective.

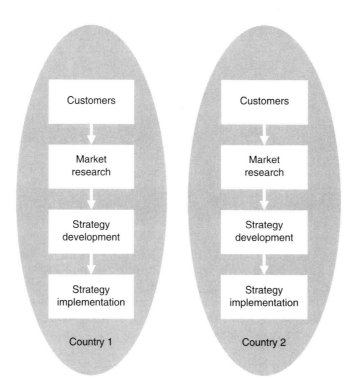

Country managers are also better placed to respond to competitor moves in local markets, especially tactics such as price cutting and trade or customer promotions, which require rapid retaliatory measures. A locally centered management system provides flexibility and avoids many of the administrative delays and costs associated with highly centralized systems.

On the other hand, organization on a country-by-country basis typically leads to a lack of coordination among country operations, as well as poor communication with corporate headquarters. Potential synergies—for example, exporting to a small market from an adjacent market location—are often lost.

Competition between subsidiaries in third-country markets, or unscheduled transborder flows, can also occur. Especially where there are significant differences in ex-factory prices, margins, taxes, or tariffs from one location to another, distribution will seek to import from low-cost locations. Parallel importation of products from the lowest cost location will cause dislocation in production and the development of gray markets. This can generate significant inefficiencies in production and marketing expenditures.

Allocation of effort and resources to different country markets often lacks a strategic focus. Large markets may be emphasized, and small country markets receive little attention. For example, the role of smaller markets such as the Netherlands, Belgium, and Switzerland to provide testing grounds or bases for expansion to other neighboring markets may be ignored.

Poor communication between corporate headquarters and local subsidiary management frequently gives rise to conflict.[9, 10] Local management aims to maximize local market growth and profitability, while corporate headquarters is primarily concerned with achieving the firm's strategic thrust in world markets. Often corporate headquarters views local management as lacking long-run strategic focus and overemphasizing the need for adaptation to the local market.[10] Local management, on the other hand, views corporate headquarters as insensitive to, and lacking understanding of, local market characteristics and competition, while attempting to maintain excessive control over local market operations. Short-run emphasis on profits, and lack of participation by corporate management in local operations, constitute further points of contention.

Organization on a country-by-country basis also results in considerable duplication of effort in terms of R&D, product development, and development of advertising copy and other promotional material. Country managers' concern with local market development and programs tailored to specific local needs often hampers adoption of ideas and experience from the domestic market or other countries and acts as a barrier to improved coordination and integration of operations across national boundaries.

For example, prior to its reorganization in preparation for 1992 and its subsequent acquisition by Philip Morris, Jacobs Suchard, the Swiss chocolate and candy company, was a hodgepodge of national subsidiaries across Europe, extending into Asia and America. Thirteen European factories churned out the entire range of Suchard's confectionery lines, including hundreds of local brands.[11]

Even where the same product was marketed in different countries, it often had a different brand name, as country managers picked a name that was easily pronounced locally. Prices of products also varied from one market to another, opening up the potential for parallel importing or gray markets. This was further compounded by giving subsidiary management responsibility for granting price promotions to wholesalers. As a result, a product promoted in Germany could suddenly become 10–15 percent less expensive than its nonpromoted counterpart in neighboring countries.

Country-centered operations are likely to be most effective in the stage of local market expansion, when acquisition of knowledge relating to the foreign market environment is of key importance.[12] Often the shift from control of international operations in the domestic market to local subsidiary management occurs as a result of mistakes made in initial entry. Where markets are relatively isolated and sufficiently large to be able to operate independently, a country-centered organization may also be desirable. For example, Japan, Brazil, and India are all markets in which the ability to adapt to unique market characteristics and operating conditions is crucial to success. At the same time, they are sufficiently large to warrant the development of programs and an organization specifically geared to their unique needs. For example, Hindustan Lever, Unilever's subsidiary in India, operates autonomously. Unilever's international brands, such as Lux toilet soap and Sunsilk shampoo, are sold in India, but they are produced locally, often in smaller sizes than in Europe, and pricing, promotion, and distribution are the responsibility of Hindustan Lever management.

In the phase of local market expansion, organizational structure should provide input for strategy development relating to specific local market factors and have flexibility in adapting to them. Yet at the same time, such responsiveness should not be at the expense of operating efficiency. Mechanisms for orchestrating operations across national borders should also be developed. While one market may warrant the establishment of an independent organizational unit, another may be served more efficiently from a neighboring market. Hence, structure and operational mechanisms are not necessarily symmetrical but rather should fit market needs and the firm's strategic thrust.

External Relations

In addition to developing an organizational structure to manage internal relationships, and in particular to determine the appropriate balance of responsibility between corporate headquarters and local subsidiaries, the firm has to establish mechanisms to manage the network of external relationships with distributors, advertising agencies, and market research firms. These mechanisms are often closely linked to the nature of the internal organizational structure and its degree of centralization or decentralization.

In the initial stages of entry into international markets, management in the domestic market is typically responsible for establishing and often maintaining relationships with external organizations, until a local sales or marketing organization is established in the foreign market. As a result, the firm often encounters difficulties in selecting and motivating effective distributors and in maintaining communications, obtaining feedback, and monitoring sales.

Once a marketing organization is established in the foreign market and sales begin to build up, responsibility for maintaining relationships with distributors, advertising agencies, and other organizations typically passes to local management. This is particularly likely to occur where there are few links between external organizations across national boundaries, and strategy is developed and adapted to the local market. In these cases, few opportunities or advantages are gained from coordinating relations across national boundaries.

RELATIONS WITH DISTRIBUTORS

In the case of distributor relations, as discussed earlier in Chapter 10, there are significant differences in the structure of distribution from one market or country to another, especially in terms of the degree of concentration and the availability of mass distribution outlets. In addition, relatively few mass distribution organizations are international in scope or span more than a few countries. Consequently, distribution decisions are typically best made by local management, especially where a broad market base is targeted.

In developing local distribution channels, the firm wants to achieve the best coverage of the potential target market. Targeting a broad market base will require intensive distribution through the largest number of intermediaries possible. Focus on a specific target segment, on the other hand, will imply selectively choosing a limited number of intermediaries that effectively tap and provide the service required by that segment. The firm also has to consider coverage of rural areas, particularly in developing countries. While distribution to urban markets can usually be readily obtained in developing countries, distribution to rural areas often poses significant problems. Large distributors may not cover sparsely populated areas where access is difficult, and distribution to scattered areas may be inefficient, entailing high distribution costs.

For example, Beiersdorf, the German skin care and medical products company, had considerable difficulty in penetrating markets and obtaining widespread distribution for its brands in the Indonesian archipelago. Initially, Beiersdorf used Suria Yozani, the distributor for Sara Lee's Prodenta line of female toiletries, medicated skin products, floor care, and other household products. Suria Yozani focused primarily on supermarkets and upscale cosmetic and food product outlets. These did not provide adequate coverage for Beiersdorf's diverse product range, which included Handyplast bandages as well as Nivea brand cosmetics and toiletries. Consequently, Beiersdorf switched to another local distributor, Ultramos Jaya, which had a network of subdistributors, providing broader market reach to the kiosks and *warnungs* (small retailers). Ultramos also enabled Beiersdorf to reach outlying areas such as Kalimantran and Sulawesi. In addition, Ultramos helped Beiersdorf supplement its sales force with *rombong* teams—independent salesmen who use motorcycles or small vans to service outlying retailers.[13]

The firm also has to determine the desired degree of control over channel intermediaries. Direct distribution, through company-owned outlets, to the end consumer provides complete control but is likely to entail higher costs, especially if the sales volume is low. On the other hand, long channels and a large number of intermediaries, provide less control. This may be especially crucial in developing countries, where distribution is fragmented, outmoded, and inefficient, and where distributors do not pursue active promotional and pricing tactics or are not equipped to provide after-sales service.[14]

Differences in legislation relating to distribution contracts can also give rise to difficulties. In a number of countries, the right to terminate a distribution agreement or dismiss a distributor is restricted, and termination can be costly. For example, Nissan fought a costly legal battle to terminate its U.K. distributor, due to disputes over the price of the Primera, its new model built at its plant in Scotland. The distributor claimed the car was overpriced for the U.K. market. While the U.K. distributor had been highly successful in building market share for its imported cars, Nissan decided to terminate the distributor in order to gain greater control over pricing and distribution of its cars.[15] Attention to such issues is important and limits flexibility to make changes or adapt channel relationships.

RELATIONS WITH OTHER SERVICE ORGANIZATIONS

Relations with distributors often require that a firm establish and maintain an infrastructure that is relatively inflexible in the short run. Relations with other service organizations, such as advertising agencies, market research firms, or insurance companies, on the other hand, are often negotiated relative to a given task, such as a concept or market test, or an advertising campaign for a brand or product. While companies tend to continue relations with a given service company over a period of time, in contrast to distributors, the costs associated with switching to another service company are minimal. Some companies, notably large multiproduct businesses such as P&G, purchase services from several different suppliers.

In the initial stages of entry, management located in the domestic market is likely to make decisions relating to the choice of the advertising agency or market research company to handle activities in foreign markets, and may, therefore, prefer branches of suppliers headquartered in the domestic market. As responsibility for strategy implementation evolves to local management, local management is likely to assume responsibility for handling relations with service suppliers and often makes greater use of local companies.

The extent to which local suppliers are used also depends on the standardization of marketing strategy, product lines, positioning, brand identities, and advertising themes across markets. Use of the same advertising themes creates opportunities for centralizing creative advertising functions. The growth of international advertising agency networks, either through the establishment of offices or joint ventures or through acquisitions in foreign markets, and the development of reciprocal agreements with agencies in different countries, further facilitates use of the same agency worldwide.

WWP, which includes Ogilivy & Mather and J. Walter Thompson, is the largest advertising group in the world, followed by Interpublic (McCann-Erickson, Lintas, and Lowe), Omnicom (BBDO and DDB Needham), and Saatchi & Saatchi.[16] Similarly, some media organizations have begun to develop services to coordinate media buying across countries. For example, *The Times of London, Le Monde* (France), *Corriere della Siera* (Italy), and *Frankfurter Allgemeine Zeitchung* (Germany) have developed a service enabling advertisers to buy space in three or all four newspapers at a discounted rate.

Advertising copy can thus be developed in a central location and transmitted via satellite to a local office for adaptation, where necessary. Advertising agencies and, in particular, Saatchi & Saatchi, a leading proponent of global advertising, have in fact often been important catalysts in the standardization of advertising campaigns, since this enables them to secure worldwide advertising budgets for their clients' products or brands.

In general, where external organizations are fragmented and the operations are limited to a single country or region, relations are typically best managed on a local basis. Direct contact and communication are often essential in order to manage relations effectively. On the other hand, where organizations have developed international networks, as, for example, have many advertising agencies and accounting and insurance firms, mechanisms for coordinating relationships across countries may need to be established.

MANAGING THE FLOW OF GOODS AND MATERIALS

The networks of internal and external relationships provide the organizational structure for implementing marketing programs. Central to the implementation task is managing the flow of goods and materials from the various points of supply to the end customer. This requires organizing and managing production and distribution logistics, the flows of financing and payment that parallel those of goods and materials, and the flow of information to direct the flow of both goods and financing. (See Figure 11.3.)

While the same flows need to be managed in domestic markets, in international markets the task is rendered more complex by the distances involved, as well as by cross-border controls and administrative procedures, which add to potential time delays and operating risks. Shipping goods and materials across national boundaries also exposes the firm to currency fluctuations and foreign-exchange risks, and involves additional intermediaries, adding further to management complexity.

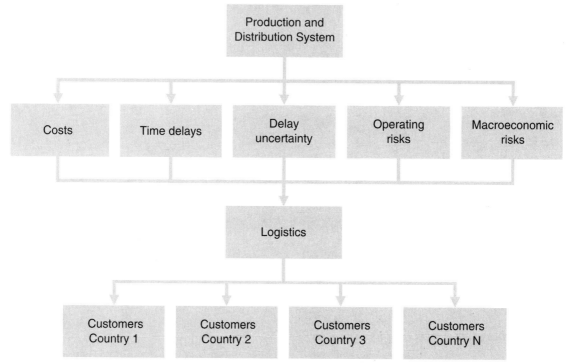

FIGURE 11-3 Production/distribution system.

Management of Production Systems

Decisions about locating production facilities to serve foreign markets provide the basic framework or structure for managing distribution logistics. The firm has to consider whether to service foreign markets from a central location in the domestic market, or alternatively to establish foreign production facilities.

In the initial phase of market entry, market size is often insufficient to warrant establishing foreign production. Consequently, unless a licensing or contract manufacturing agreement is established, markets in other countries are best supplied from a domestic production location. As noted in Chapter 10, this typically results in price escalation, due to freight, documentation, and packaging costs. As demand builds up, it becomes cost effective to supply foreign markets from local production sites. Consequently, management has to weigh the advantages of doing so against continuing to centralize production in the domestic market. In making this decision, a number of aspects have to be considered, including relative costs, time delays and inventory requirements, operating risks, and exposure to macroeconomic risks, as well as market proximity.

Bandai, one of Japan's largest toy makers, for example, decided to relocate production in China. Since toys have relatively low value-added, Bandai had established a manufacturing facility in Hong Kong for export to the United States and Europe. The decision to move into China was motivated in part by competition from Hong Kong manufacturers that had moved to Shenzhen in Southern China. Another important factor was, however, the growth potential of the Chinese market. As a result, Bandai decided to locate in Fuzhou in Fujian province. While the export infrastructure in Fuzhou was not well developed, it was a convenient location for shipping goods to all parts of China, and labor costs were lower than in the special economic zones in Shenzhen.[17]

RELATIVE COSTS

In assessing the costs of centralizing production versus establishing local production, management has to weigh potential economies of scale from centralization against additional freight, packaging, and documentation costs associated with shipping over greater distances. This assessment is rendered more complex by differences in wages, component and raw material costs, and other costs of production or assembly from one location to another, as well as tariff barriers and other import restrictions.

Labor costs, for example, differ significantly from one location to another and result in substantial differences in production costs in labor-intensive industries such as textiles, shoes, and bags. As a result, production in such industries has tended to follow low-cost labor, moving from Taiwan to South Korea, then to Southern China, and more recently to Indonesia. Mattel, for example, has moved production of the Barbie doll from Southern China to Indonesia, and plans to do one-third of worldwide production there by 1995. In 1993, wages for textile workers in Indonesia were $2.50 per day, 10 percent of those in South Korea, and well below the $4.00 daily wage in booming Southern China.[18] Other factor costs such as energy, rent, and capital costs also vary. For example, India benefits from a pool of low-cost engineering skills and hence provides an attractive location for software development.

In the case of manufactured goods, freight costs can often be reduced by shipping components rather than finished goods, and assembling near the point of sale. In addition, as noted in Chapter 7, many countries have lower tariffs for unassembled goods, in order to encourage the establishment of local assembly plants.

The complexity of assessing the costs of serving foreign markets from alternative locations is further compounded by uncertainty with regard to future trends in costs, productivity gains, increased automation, and new product designs, which simplify assembly and reduce direct labor costs. The United States, for example, has now become a low-cost location relative to countries such as Germany, Norway, Sweden, and even Japan.[19]

TIME DELAYS AND DELIVERY UNCERTAINTY

In determining its logistical structure, the firm has to assess the potential time delays and delivery reliability associated with alternative locations. Shipping goods across substantial distances, especially by sea, entailing multiple modes of transportation or transfers, is subject to potential delays and difficulties which are hard to predict.

Such uncertainties are further compounded where goods cross national borders and are subject to lengthy customs formalities and other administrative red tape. This can add considerably to delays, as well as incurring additional costs. Prior to the institution of the single administrative document for trucks crossing national borders within the EU, it was estimated that customs delays, notably at the Italian border, added over 11 hours to the trip from Belgium to Italy and over 7 hours from France to Italy.[20] In addition, border checks and customs formalities were estimated to add around 1.5 percent to the average consignment's value.

In some instances, customs formalities have been used as a means of hampering the entry of foreign goods. For example, the French government required all VCRs imported into France to enter through the southwestern port of Poitiers. The number of customs officials at Poitiers was inadequate to cope with the high volume of imports, predominantly from South Korea and Japan, resulting in lengthy delays. In addition, the VCRs were left on the quays and suffered physical damage.

OPERATING RISKS

In addition to time delays, shipment distances, and cross-border transfers, as well as the number of intermediaries typically involved in such transfers, also give rise to substantial operating risks. Suppliers and intermediaries vary substantially in their efficiency and reliability, thus adding further to delivery uncertainty. Especially where goods are shipped by sea, have to be loaded or unloaded, and may be left exposed on docks, they may suffer damage or loss.

New tracking devices have now been developed that serve as electronic sentries and enable manufacturers and shippers to track goods and their condition.[21] A tracking box installed in the shipping container transmits location to a satellite network, and also registers temperature, humidity, shocks, and other measures in the container. The data are relayed to a tracking center and then forwarded to the manufacturer, shipper, or insurer. While the service is relatively expensive, it is effective for highly valuable cargo or tracking merchandise to areas with high theft losses such as Southern Italy, Argentina, and Peru.

EXPOSURE TO MACROECONOMIC RISKS

A final set of factors to consider in relation to production logistics relates to the firm's exposure to macroeconomic risks. As discussed in Chapter 7, these risks stem from such factors as political instability and insurrection, economic instability and change, and foreign-exchange risk, over which the firm has no control. Political and economic risks imply that a location that initially appeared favorable for supplying foreign markets can rapidly become disadvantageous, as the example of GE's acquisition of Tungsram in Chapter 7 well illustrates.

Closely linked to the issue of economic stability is that of foreign-exchange risk. Decentralizing production to a local site within the foreign market reduces exposure to short-term currency fluctuations that arise in exporting goods from a domestic production base to a foreign market. On the other hand, decentralizing production exposes the firm to foreign-exchange risk in the case of shipments to third-country markets, or where components or raw materials have to be imported. For example, Tatung Industries (Taiwan) purchased the consumer electronics division of Racal in the U.K. in the expectation that this would provide a low-cost site from which to supply other European markets. The subsequent rapid appreciation of the pound sterling, however, put the company at a price disadvantage in competing with French and German producers.

Deciding on the location of production and assembly facilities to serve foreign markets establishes the basic framework and economics of production logistics. While minor adjustments can be made in production volume to accommodate short-run fluctuations in demand, or swings in foreign-exchange rates, location decisions entail commitments and establish a logistical structure that is relatively inflexible in the short run. Changes in economic conditions can have a dramatic impact on the cost effectiveness of a given production location. Consequently, the overall logistical structure needs to be developed with care, and with a view to potential developments in the long run.

Management of Distribution Logistics

As in the domestic markets, the goal of distribution logistics is to manage the flow of goods and materials so as to meet desired customer service levels at minimum cost. However, in international markets, the dispersion of markets and production locations typically implies that goods and materials have to be shipped greater distances. This, coupled with differences in transportation modes, the number of intermodal transfers, and cross-border delays, results in substantial unpredictability and variation in shipment reliability, and renders management of international logistics more complex. At the same time, it offers greater opportunities to acquire a competitive advantage through efficient management of logistics.

Choice of transportation mode is key to efficient management of international distribution logistics. The range of options in the global arena is greater than in domestic markets, especially if use is made of ocean and air freight. The distances that goods often travel to reach international markets, and the number of intermodal transfers, together with possible border and other delays, underscore the importance of a systems or total cost approach when selecting the mode of transportation. For example, while shipping by ocean freight is cheaper per pound or ton than air freight, the transit time is substantially longer, loading and unloading are more cumbersome, and merchandise is more likely to suffer damage and loss. Consequently, better packaging will be required and higher inventory levels will need to be maintained, increasing inventory carrying costs. Ocean freight is also less predictable and more likely to be subject to delays or traffic blockages than air freight, thus further increasing the need for buffer inventory stocks. Consequently, shipping high-value, low-bulk items such as, for example, diamonds and wristwatches, by air freight is likely to be more cost effective.

For example, Acer, the Taiwanese computer manufacturer, used to send fin-ished PCs to its U.S. subsidiary from Taiwan by boat. By the time they landed, the PCs were obsolete or overpriced. In 1992, Acer switched to sending mother-boards by air freight to its California subsidiary for assembly. As a result, sales rose 60 percent.[22] Acer is now moving towards modular assembly, creating PCs from major components that snap together. Ultimately, Acer hopes that dealers will be able to assemble custom PCs with parts from regional distribution centers. Dealers will then be able to custom tailor products cost efficiently, without incur-ring the delays of special orders.

Thus in some instances, efficient distribution logistics can provide a major competitive edge and dramatically improve penetration of international mar-kets. In the case of perishable items, use of air freight and rapid handling has also substantially increased the geographic scope and volume of international sales for products such as fresh flowers, lobsters, and fresh fish.

Similarly, for some products such as fashion goods, or where demand is diffi-cult to predict, order lead times are critical. Development of efficient logistical systems can enable producers to fill orders rapidly, thus preventing stock outs, reducing spoilage and markdowns, and lowering distributor costs. Especially in international markets, this can provide a major competitive advantage.

The development of computerized ordering and inventory systems is often central to efficient international distribution and logistics. Benneton, for exam-ple, was able to improve production scheduling, cut delivery times, and substan-tially reduce distribution costs by developing a computerized international infor-mation system.[23] Cash registers in key stores in markets throughout the world were linked into an international computer network, providing Benneton man-agement at Treviso, near Venice, with up-to-date information on sales of various garments in different colors and sizes at each sales location. As a result, future production could be scheduled based on hot-selling items in each location and reorders filled within 6 weeks. Additional flexibility in filling orders was obtained by delaying dyeing of approximately 10 percent of the season's production until initial sales results were obtained.

Customer expectations with regard to service levels and speed of delivery may also vary from one market to another. In some markets, customers may not expect the same delivery speed as in the domestic market. Consequently, speedy delivery, which adds to costs and increases prices, may not provide a competitive advantage. Conversely, in other markets, customers may lack the storage space or capital to maintain significant inventory levels, and thus require rapid delivery. In Japan, many regional wholesalers and retailers expect high levels of service. In Tokyo, small retailers and kiosks (which lack storage space) selling film or cig-arettes expect delivery within 2 to 3 hours.[24]

Speedy delivery, and delivery reliability, are also important competitive tools in selling to manufacturers who practice "just in time" inventory management or in selling to large-scale distributors. While initially characteristic primarily of Japanese automobile production, the principles of efficient inventory manage-ment have spread to other countries and other industries, for example consumer packaged goods.[25] Establishing efficient logistical systems linking a firm with the customer's network of production or retail outlets may be crucial to developing sales.

Efficiently managing distribution logistics can thus provide an important competitive tool in international markets. While its importance is often neglected, as in domestic markets, the distances that goods travel, and the complexities of international logistics, provide significant opportunities for utilizing distribution to gain an advantage over competition in penetrating international markets.

MANAGING PAYMENT AND FINANCIAL FLOWS

Closely linked to the flow of goods and materials from sources of supply to production and assembly locations, to warehouses and distribution points, and then to the final customer is the parallel or companion flow of payment and financing (see Figure 11.4). Each time title to goods is transferred, arrangements have

FIGURE 11-4

Managing flows in single country vs. multicountry operations.

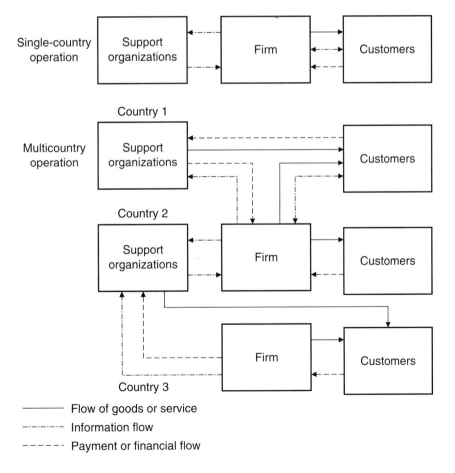

Flow of goods or service
Information flow
Payment or financial flow

to be made for payment of goods, often involving a shift from one currency to another. The underlying strategic importance of payment flows may not be immediately obvious. However, without effective payment mechanisms the firm's ability to implement any strategy is seriously jeopardized. While it may seem obvious, unless the firm is able to arrange some mechanism of payment for its goods and services in a timely manner, it will not be able to continue doing business in the long run. Also, the manner in which payments are made, e.g., currency, accounting transaction, or goods, has important tactical as well as strategic implications. For example, a firm seeking to do business in a country lacking a hard currency may have to make arrangements to market goods received through a barter arrangement.

While such flows also have to be managed in domestic markets, they assume greater strategic significance in international markets due to potential time delays and uncertainties surrounding transit of both goods and payment documentation. Arrangement of payment also involves currency transfers, which expose firms to foreign-exchange risk. Furthermore, distortions occur in payment flows due to restrictions placed by governments on currency movements and convertibility. Distortions also occur since firms may manipulate internal transfer prices between subsidiaries in different countries to minimize the burden of taxation.

The Complexity of Cross-Border Payment Flows

Managing cross-border payment flows is inherently more complex than managing payment in a domestic market. In the first place, use of slower modes of transportation, and border-crossing delays, give rise to considerable uncertainty surrounding the timing of payment, and hence how to manage the payment flow efficiently. Delays can also occur in payment transfers, or in arranging for letters of credit or bills of exchange, thus adding to the uncertainty surrounding the timing of payment.

Potential delays and uncertainty are further compounded by the number of intermediaries involved in cross-border transactions. These include, not only distributors, and import and export agents where indirect channels are used, but also freight forwarders, banks, and insurance agencies. This network of intermediaries adds considerably to the complexity of international payment flows and implies that efficiently managing these flows can have a major impact on costs, as well as playing a key role in pricing strategy and in developing and motivating distribution channels.

Payment in a foreign currency also exposes the firm to foreign-exchange risk. The significance of this risk depends on the specific currencies involved and the time-lag between the negotiation of the sales contract and the date of payment, as well as the size of the sum involved. However, unless currencies are closely linked, as are those of Germany and Austria, fluctuating exchange rates, as well as the possibility of a devaluation or revaluation by a central bank, can expose the firm to substantial risk.

Unlike commercial or transfer risks, exposure to foreign currency risk can be managed through the forward market. The buyer purchases in the forward market, for future delivery, the amount of foreign currency to be paid on receipt of goods, thus protecting itself from possible losses due to a rise in the exchange rate. More recently, markets in foreign exchange options have developed. In this case, the firm purchases the option for delivery of the foreign currency at a specified future date. If the foreign currency appreciates, the firm can then exercise the option to purchase. If the currency depreciates, then it will not be in its interest to do so, and it will buy the currency at the spot rate, forfeiting the cost of the option purchase.

The establishment of the ECU, or European Currency Unit, composed of a basket of the European currencies, provides a means for managing foreign-exchange risks in cross-border transactions between member countries of the European Union. Since the ECU is a weighted average, it fluctuates less than any pair of currencies in the basket. A number of European companies, such as Saint Gobain, use the ECU for cross-border billing within the EEC. This eliminates foreign exchange exposure and, at the same time, simplifies cross-border billing and accounting.

Mattel, the U.S.-based toy manufacturing multinational, also uses the ECU in intercompany pricing in Europe, thus creating a natural hedge for its foreign exchange exposure. Elsewhere, the dollar is used in intracorporate billing, pushing responsibility for foreign-exchange hedging down to local affiliates. This generates greater sensitivity among management to foreign exchange exposure and helps to integrate currency fluctuations with competitive pricing strategies.[26]

Distortions to Payment Flows

In addition to the inherent complexities of managing international payment flows caused by distance delays and currency fluctuations, distortion of flows can arise from restrictions placed by governments on currency movements and convertibility. Firms have to formulate strategies to respond to these restrictions, which often involve engaging in some form of countertrade, a linkage between exports and imports of goods and services in addition to or in lieu of financial settlements. Distortion of payment flows also occurs where firms organize internal pricing flows between subsidiaries in different countries so as to minimize the burden of taxation and other social payments, and maximize overall corporate profitability.

COUNTERTRADE

Governments with balance of payment difficulties, or which lack hard currency, may place restrictions on import of goods or components, or more generally on cross-border financial transactions of all types. These restrictions may take various forms, ranging from blocking convertibility of currency to requiring counterpurchase agreements or establishing clearing accounts or offset purchases.

Initially, many such arrangements arose primarily in transactions by foreign firms in the former Soviet nations and China, whose currencies were not freely convertible. Consequently, corporations interested in doing business with these nations had to engage in countertrade transactions. One of the best-known and most widely publicized was the agreement established by PepsiCo to trade bottles of Pepsi for Russian vodka in 1974, valued at about $3 billion. Other similar deals were signed with Eastern European countries in exchange for wine. Both vodka and wine are sold through a wine and spirits distributor under brand names such as Stolichyna and Premiat. PepsiCo has also extended the agreement to ships that it will help to sell or lease in international markets in return for foreign exchange credits.[27]

As international trade has developed, becoming broader in scope, an increasing number of nations have begun to favor and request the development of countertrade agreements. In 1972, countertrade was used in only 15 countries; by 1989, this had risen to 94, including, not only countries otherwise closed to trade, such as the former Soviet Bloc and China, but also many countries in Latin America, the Middle East, and the Third World (thus providing a means for Western firms to do business in such regions) and even some in Europe.

Countertrade transactions range from pure barter, or exchange of goods, to more complex forms, including switch trading involving third parties and offset agreements requiring local production or assembly. Such transactions also cover a wide range of goods from bananas and toys to toilet seats, aircraft parts, and oil.

A common form of countertrade, a slight variation of a pure barter transaction, is the counterpurchase or parallel barter agreement. Under such an agreement, both parties sign two separate contracts specifying the goods and services to be exchanged. The PepsiCo agreement in the Soviet Union took this form. Similarly, Ford has traded automobiles for sheepskins from Uruguay, potatoes from Spain, toilet seats from Finland, cranes from Norway, and coffee from Colombia.[29]

Another common form is the buy-back or compensation agreement: A company that sells technology or equipment, or establishes a turnkey plant, agrees to take back part of the output produced with the technology or equipment, or by the plant or operation constructed, in partial payment. Occidental Petroleum, for example, negotiated a $20 billion contract in the Soviet Union to build ammonia plants and accepted part of the output in payment. Similarly, the lynchpin of the American Trade Consortium plan to establish joint ventures in the former Soviet Union was the use of dollars earned from oil exports from the drilling venture by Chevron by other members of the consortium to bring in raw materials or other commodities, or to remit their profits.[30]

Another, similar form of countertrade is the offset purchase, which occurs primarily with regard to transactions with governments or other public agencies. In an offset purchase the seller may be required to assemble or purchase components from the purchasing country. Alternatively, imports of components or raw materials have to be "offset" by exports of finished product. For example,

Lockheed helped Hyundai's personal computer division export its products in order to gain aircraft sales in Korea.

A more complex form of countertrade occurs when governments establish a clearing account mechanism. Units of these clearing accounts are given in payment and can be used for purchases within the country but are not freely convertible. Often these units can be sold or transferred to other parties, who use them to purchase goods for their own accounts.

A central problem with regard to countertrade transactions is how to manage them efficiently. While often they provide access to markets that would otherwise be closed, they frequently involve dealing in commodities or products with which management may have little or no experience. Such transactions, therefore, are typically most successful when they involve goods or services similar to those produced by the firm, such as PepsiCo's transactions in wines and spirits or foods. Where goods or services outside these businesses are involved, they are typically best contracted out to brokers or firms specializing in countertrade transactions.

INTERNAL TRANSFER PRICING

Distortions in payment flows also arise as a result of internal or transfer pricing practices between subsidiaries or corporate headquarters and subsidiaries in different countries. Specifically, these practices may be established or manipulated so as to minimize the corporate tax burden or maximize profits worldwide, rather than on the basis of fair market prices.

In establishing the price at which goods are transferred to subsidiaries in different countries, the firm can adopt three alternatives.[31] First, the price can be based on the market price, i.e., "arms-length" pricing, what another buyer would pay. This rate favors the supplying subsidiaries and, hence, is most appropriate if corporate taxes are lower in the shipping country than in the country to which goods are being sent. A second option is to transfer goods at ex-factory or direct cost. This favors the subsidiary receiving the goods and, hence, is most appropriate if management desires to generate profits in this country or location. This option may be preferable, not only if corporate taxes are lower in this location, but also if there are tariffs or *ad valorem* duties on entering the country. For example, Bausch and Lomb set up an Irish subsidiary to manufacture and sell contact lenses under license to the parent. This enabled the company to generate profits in Ireland, a low-tax country, rather than in the United States.[26]

Between these two extremes is a third option, which provides some profit for the supplying subsidiary while at the same time providing a favorable price for the purchasing subsidiary. The compromise price can be reached either on a cost-plus basis, i.e., adding a percentage margin to direct costs, or alternatively, market-based, i.e., offering a discount off market price. Increasingly, however, flexibility to manipulate transfer prices is being restricted by national tax authorities. In the United States, for example, IRS records reveal that more than half the U.S. subsidiaries of foreign firms reported no taxable income. The IRS has assessed penalties against Yamaha Motors and Daewoo International of $31 million and $7 million, respectively, because of alleged inappropriate intracorporate pricing. In many countries, regulations have been introduced requiring intracorporate prices to be established on an "arm's-length" basis.

Transfer prices can be used, not only to minimize the impact of taxation and duties on profitability and to facilitate repatriation of dividends, but also to counterbalance the effects of fluctuating currencies. High transfer prices can be used to recoup R&D and other development costs and to cover expenses incurred in joint venture or other types of collaborative agreements. Conversely, low transfer prices can be used to underwrite the start-up costs of a subsidiary and to develop competitive market position.

Efficient management of transfer pricing can thus be an important element contributing to overall corporate development and profitability. At the same time, the increasing volume and complexity of intracorporate transfers in today's global economy, coupled with fluctuating exchange rates, make effective planning and management of intracorporate pricing even more challenging.

MANAGEMENT OF INFORMATION FLOWS

The second companion flow is that of information. In many respects, the flow of information constitutes the nerve center of operations. Without it, ability to coordinate operations in diverse and far-flung locations, as well as in relation to different functional areas (production, distribution, marketing, and finance), is lost.

Irrespective of the firm's organizational structure, information flows provide the glue to manage and coordinate operations in diverse locations, at different stages in the value chain. Information flows also direct the interplay of the flows of goods and materials, and of payment and financing. At the same time, information flows provide coordination and control links between corporate headquarters and local subsidiary management. The structure of information flows should, therefore, be designed to suit the firm's need for local responsiveness vs. global efficiency.

As international operations begin to develop in the phase of local market expansion, information needs evolve and take on a different character from those of initial market entry. Rather than identifying and tapping specific market opportunities, information flows should shift to emphasize diagnosing and exploring local market trends, and span a broader network of relationships including suppliers, competitors, and customers. At the same time, flows of information between headquarters and local subsidiaries need to be established to facilitate communications and control.

Developing Local Information Networks

As attention focuses on developing local market potential, and information collection needs shift towards identifying and exploring local market trends, greater reliance is placed on conducting primary research rather than utilizing secondary data sources. The firm has to establish links with local research organizations and information suppliers, and develop a capacity to interpret and understand local market behavior patterns.

At the same time, a broader information network needs to be established, linking the firm's operations with those of suppliers and of customers. In industrialized nations characterized by a high level of technological sophistication, the firm should develop computerized information systems linking its production or distribution operations with those of suppliers and other collaborators. As noted earlier, developing such information systems can substantially improve production and distribution efficiency, while at the same time generating increased customer satisfaction.

Establishing Links Between Corporate Headquarters and Local Subsidiaries

At the same time as it is spreading out on a local basis, the firm needs to establish information links between corporate headquarters and local subsidiary management. These should be designed to fit the firm's strategic orientation and its organizational structure, and specifically the degree of autonomy given to each subsidiary operation.

A number of different models to develop information systems can be adopted.[32] In a centralized model, concepts and processes developed at corporate headquarters are rolled out to local subsidiaries. This approach enhances standardization of systems and applications in different countries worldwide, and facilitates tighter control by corporate headquarters over local subsidiary operations.

In a decentralized system, information systems development responsibility is devolved to the local level and adapted to local market conditions. This approach is best suited where a subsidiary is completely autonomous and there is little need for coordination with other parts of the firm. Control by corporate headquarters places primary emphasis on financial performance.

A third option is to establish centers of excellence. Systems development teams in different subsidiary locations are charged with developing specific types of systems in which they have a particular expertise for the entire corporation worldwide. This approach is most likely to be adopted by firms in the global rationalization phase, with extensive operations worldwide.

Irrespective of the specific development processes and organizational structure, new information technologies, such as electronic mail, voice mail, teleconferencing, facsimile, and distributive processing, allow for tighter communication and coordination between headquarters operations and individual subsidiaries, without leading to excessive bureaucratic controls and delays. Systems can be established which enable headquarters to monitor and oversee subsidiary operations, while at the same time allowing subsidiary management considerable autonomy to manage local operations and seize local opportunities. Effective utilization of such systems is however contingent upon the analytical sophistication of managers and on the local communications infrastructure.

SUMMARY

International market expansion requires effective implementation, if the firm is to remain competitive in the various markets in which it competes. While many of the issues the firm faces are not traditionally viewed as marketing related, they are considered here insofar as they have an impact on the firm's marketing strategy.

The first step is to establish appropriate organizational networks to direct and manage programs in international markets. Such networks involve both internal and external linkages. Internal networks link different levels and organizational units within the firm and are essential for proper coordination of marketing activities. External networks link the firm to facilitating organizations that are necessary for successful implementation of marketing strategy (e.g., resellers, advertising agencies, and market research organizations).

Once in place, these internal and external networks are responsible for managing the flows that convey goods and services to customers. These flows are the same as those in the domestic market but are rendered more complex by the spatial separation of markets, the higher costs associated with maintaining the linkages and the different operating environments in which the firm conducts business.

In addition to the flow of goods and services, there are the accompanying financial flows. Each time goods or services are transferred, there is an attendant payment flow. This may involve currency, other goods or services, or simply a bookkeeping entry. International market payment flows are not simple and straightforward, as they are often distorted by the tax consequences of a particular transaction, inflationary risk, or restrictions placed by governments.

As indicated in Chapter 3, an overarching flow is that of information. In addition to the implicit and explicit information contained in the flow of goods, materials, and payment, there is also a need for an information system that integrates and simplifies information, so that it can be used effectively to implement and manage global strategy.

REFERENCES

1. Bartlett, Christopher A., and Sumantra Ghoshal (1989) *Managing Across Border: The Transnational Solution*, Boston, MA: Harvard Business School Press.
2. Business International (1989) *Managing Today's International Corporation*, New York: Business International.
3. Prahalad, C.K., and Yves C. Doz (1987) *The Multinational Mission*, New York: The Free Press.
4. Perlmutter, Howard J. (1969) "The Tortuous Evolution of the Multinational Corporation," *Columbia Journal of World Business*, January–February, pp. 9–18.

5. U.S. Japan Trade Study Group (1983) *Japan: Business Obstacles and Opportunities*, New York: John Wiley.

6. "Motorola Will Be Just Fine, Thanks" (1993) *The New York Times*, Sunday, October 31, p. 3ff.

7. Quelch, John A., and Edward J. Hoff (1986) "Customizing Global Marketing," *Harvard Business Review*, May-June, pp. 59–68.

8. Lipman, Joanne (1988) "Marketers Twin Sons, On Global Sales Pitch Harvard Guru Makes," *Wall Street Journal*, May 12.

9. Hulbert, James M., and William K. Brandt (1980) *Managing the Multinational Subsidiary*, New York: Holt Rinehart and Winston.

10. Sorenson, Ralph Z., and Ulrich Weichman (1975) "How Multinationals View Marketing Standardization," *Harvard Business Review*, May/June p. 39.

11. "Sweet Stuff" (1989) *International Management* September, pp. 32–36.

12. Wind, Yoram, Susan P. Douglas, and Howard J. Perlmutter (1973) "Guidelines for Developing International Marketing Strategy," *Journal of Marketing* 37, April, pp. 14–23.

13. "A Market Too Far" (1994) *Business Asia*, February 16, p. 6–7.

14. Frazier, Gary L., James D. Gill, and Sudhir D. Kale (1989) "Dealer Dependence Levels and Reciprocal Actions in a Channel of Distribution in a Developing Country," *Journal of Marketing*, January, pp. 50–69.

15. "Nissan Gets Back in the Driving Seat" (1990) *Financial Times*, December 31.

16. "World's Top 50 Advertising Organizations" (1994) *Advertising Age*, January 3, p. 22.

17. "Bandai: Making Toys in China" (1989) *Journal of Japanese Trade and Industry*, July/August, p. 52.

18. Kraar, Louis (1993) "Indonesia on the Move," *Fortune*, September 20, pp. 112–116.

19. "U.S. Industry is a World Class Contender Again," (1992) *Business Week*, February 17, p. 28.

20. Cecchini, Paolo (1988) *The European Challenge: The Benefits of a Single Market*, The Commission of the European Communities.

21. "Cargos That Phone Home," (1993) *Fortune*, November 15, p. 143.

22. "Acer: Up From Clones—And then Some," (1993) *Business Week*, June 28, p. 54.

23. Benneton (A) (1982) Harvard Business School Case.

24. Czinkota, Michael R., and Jon Woronoff (1986) *Japan's Market: The Distribution System*, New York: Praeger Publishing.

25. "Clout! More and More Retail Giants Rule the Market Place," (1992) *Business Week*, December 21, pp. 66–73.

26. Business International (1990) *International Transfer Pricing*, New York: Business International.

27. "Pepsi Will be Bartered for Ships and Vodka to Deal with Soviets," (1990) *New York Times*, April 9.

28. "PepsiCo. Signs a 10 Year Trade Accord with Moscow that Includes Soviet Ships" (1990) *The Wall Street Journal*, April 10, p. A8.

29. Aggarwal, Raj (1989) "International Business through Barter and Countertrade," *Long-Range Planning*, 22 no. 3 (June), pp. 75–81.

30. Kraar, Louis (1989) "Top U.S. Companies Move Into Russia," *Fortune*, July 31, pp. 165–169.

31. Shulman, James (1967) "When the Price Is Wrong by Design," *Columbia Journal of World Business*, May-June, pp. 69–76.

32. Roche, Edward M. (1992) *Managing Information Technology in Multinational Corporations*, New York: Macmillan.

PART IV

GLOBAL RATIONALIZATION

CHAPTER 12

GLOBALIZING MARKETING STRATEGY

INTRODUCTION

GE and Whirlpool are two firms that are moving aggressively and boldly into the third phase of global market development. The CEOs of both companies have visions that place the globalization of their companies as the guiding force for growth and survival in the twenty-first century. John F. Welch, CEO of GE, plans to invest over a billion dollars to expand GE's operations globally. His view is that, if the strategy "is wrong, it's a billion—a couple a billion dollars. If it's right, it's the future of the next century for this company."[1] David Whitwam, CEO of Whirlpool, is equally convinced about his firm's need for globalization: "The only way to gain lasting competitive advantage is to leverage your capabilities around the world so that the company as a whole is greater than the sum of its parts."[2]

In implementing these visions, each company has evolved a strategy based on its capabilities, its competitors, and its assessment of global opportunities. GE has moved quickly and decisively into global markets. As a highly diversified $57-billion company, with businesses ranging from appliances, capital, jet engines, plastics, medical equipment, locomotives, and generating plants, GE has decided to move aggressively into India, China, and Mexico.[1] In pursuing the challenges of global expansion, GE has leveraged its knowledge of global markets gained from being a player in plastics and jet engines worldwide. In orchestrating a global strategy, it has relied on its historic strength in technology, joint ventures when appropriate, and the entire range of its capabilities, notably GE Capital, to provide financing.

Faced with modest growth in its domestic market, GE felt it was essential to develop increased sales from outside the United States. China offers potential for GE's jet engines, as the country is moving aggressively to modernize and expand its airlines. GE Capital provided much-needed financing to facilitate the purchase of jet liners with GE engines. GE established a joint venture with Mabe, the Mexican appliance maker, to produce gas ranges and has expanded into refrigerators and washing machines. This provided low-cost labor and greater access to the rapidly growing Mexican market, where GE already has 20 factories. In India GE has a joint venture with Wipro, Ltd., a rapidly growing Indian company that produces CT scanners, applications software, and ultrasound devices. The basic technology for the ultrasound device comes from Yokagawa Medical Systems, Ltd., of Japan, a 75 percent GE-owned joint venture. This has helped GE to compete with Siemens, Philips, and Toshiba in world markets.

Whirlpool's aggressive movement into world markets was prompted in part by the actions of one of its main competitors, the Swedish firm Electrolux. Seeking to improve its position worldwide, Electrolux had made acquisitions in Europe and gained access to the U.S. market by acquiring White Consolidated. Realizing that, if it failed to act, profits and growth would become elusive, Whirlpool moved decisively, spending $1 billion to acquire N.V. Philips's European appliance business in 1989. This immediately made Whirlpool number one worldwide in the appliance business with manufacturing locations in 11 countries (all in the United States, Europe, and Latin America) and marketing operations in 120 locations.[2]

The acquisition provided the scale of operation to allow Whirlpool to be a global player but left it with an organization that lacked the necessary integration to realize global synergies. For example, despite the obvious similarity in function, the washing machines built in Italy and Germany did not have even a screw in common. Rather than imposing draconian cost cutting and organizational changes to absorb Philips, Whirlpool has chosen to transform the two companies "into a unified, consumer-focused organization capable of using its combined talents to achieve breakthrough performance in markets around the world."[2] This customer focus has involved changing the way it thinks about business definitions, from product focused—refrigerators, washing machines, and ranges—to thinking of businesses as "food preservation," "fabric care," and "food preparation." In addition to focusing on cost and quality, Whirlpool has worked hard to differentiate its products through superior design, features, and after-sales support, all aimed at providing greater overall value for the customer.

Whirlpool's overall strategy also involves establishing close relations with suppliers and companies in related businesses, for example, Proctor & Gamble and Unilever. It has reduced the number of its steel suppliers from five to two, and is seeking to gain access to supplier technology to facilitate working together on process improvements. As part of its geographic expansion, Whirlpool has established three regional offices in Asia—Singapore, Hong Kong, and Tokyo. Each office is designed to serve a broader area; Singapore is the base for Southeast Asia, and Hong Kong will serve Greater China. These will also form the basis for their eventual goal of having manufacturing facilities in Asia.

MOVING TOWARD GLOBAL RATIONALIZATION

International expansion, whether through acquisition or adapting existing products and services in response to local demand, can result in market fragmentation and the emergence of a patchwork of diverse national businesses. Particularly with acquisitions, each business markets its own range of products and services adapted to local market characteristics, sometimes targeted to unique customer segments, with nationally oriented promotion, distribution, and pricing strategies. Even where the same or similar products are marketed in different countries, they may not have the same brand name or positioning, utilize the same advertising theme or copy, or coordinate production, pricing, and distribution across national boundaries.

Market fragmentation is further compounded by differences in the mode of operation from one country to another. While in one country products may be marketed through a licensing agreement or distributed through export agents, in another country they may be marketed through a joint venture with a local company. In yet other cases, the firm may have established a wholly-owned production and marketing subsidiary. As a result, the degree of autonomy in managing local operations and control exercised by corporate headquarters can vary considerably.

The piecemeal character of operations, and the lack of coordination between businesses, generate a number of inefficiencies. In the first place, they lead to duplication of effort, as each national business has its own new product development unit and develops its own advertising themes, ad copy, and other aspects of marketing strategy. This duplication generates cost inefficiencies, especially where markets are small and initial development costs are high. Often a multiplicity of national brands and products proliferates, fragmenting markets and marketing efforts further. Secondly, operation on a country-by-country basis with limited communication between subsidiaries does not take advantage of potential synergies arising from operating on a multinational scale. Opportunities for transferring experience from one market environment to another are lost.

Differences in product lines, branding, and promotional themes from one country to another can also result in confused images both at the corporate and product or brand level. This confusion reduces the strength and value of the corporate or brand image across national boundaries. For example, Mars Inc. moved aggressively to rationalize its brands throughout Europe and harmonize them with the names used elsewhere. Raider, Europe's most successful chocolate biscuit was changed to Twix, the name used in the United States. In the U.K., the Marathon bar was changed to Snickers and Bonitos in France were renamed M&Ms. Milky Way and Mars bars present a problem as they already exist around the world, but refer to different products in different countries.[3]

Increased communication and interaction across national boundaries, together with the removal of barriers to trade between nations and improved linkages between national market infrastructures, further compound the inefficiencies of operating on a country-by-country basis. Markets in many areas of the world are becoming increasingly integrated as more and more organizations operate on a transnational basis. In consumer markets, increased travel and the spread of global media, such as satellite TV, generates demand for a product or service in different parts of the world. Similarly, in industrial markets, the spread of multinational corporations creates global customers requiring servicing and delivery of supplies at locations throughout the world. In many markets, competition takes place on a global scale as firms expand international operations to meet the needs of global customers and leverage assets from one market to compete in another.

Such trends suggest a need to reevaluate the firm's strategic thrust and move toward a global perspective, eliminating inefficiencies generated by the existence of a multiplicity of domestic businesses in order to compete more effectively on a global basis. (See Figure 12.1.) This requires reexamination of the business definition and, in particular, its geographic configuration. Redefinition of the business(es) leads to a reevaluation of marketing strategy. This takes place at a number of levels. In the first place, redefinition of the business requires reassessment of opportunities for market expansion and growth as well as for reconfiguration and improved coordination of marketing strategy across national boundaries. Opportunities for expanding into new country markets, consolidating businesses across countries, or targeting global or transnational segments

FIGURE 12-1
Globalizing
marketing strategy.

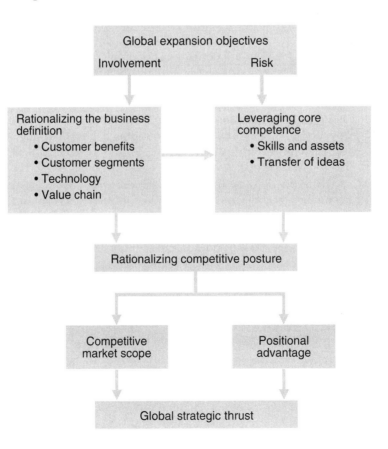

may be identified. Potential for product line and brand standardization across countries can then be exploited, unleashing opportunities for reconfiguring production and distribution logistics, sourcing, product or brand management systems, and consolidating operations across national boundaries.

As discussed in Chapter 3, a key underlying component is the collection of information to guide decisions. Timely information on demand and customer requirements can then be fed into the information system, and production and distribution schedules matched accordingly. Inventory levels and warehousing requirements can be reduced, significantly improving logistical efficiency and lowering costs. Service levels can also be improved, increasing customer satisfaction.

ESTABLISHING GLOBAL GOALS AND OBJECTIVES

The inefficiencies and duplication generated by a system of national businesses, coupled with growing external pressures toward market integration, encourage adoption of a global orientation to strategy development. The dominance of a national domestic market disappears, and markets are viewed as a set of interrelated, interdependent markets that are interlinked worldwide. This perspective does not necessarily imply that the firm adopts a policy of marketing globally standardized products and brands worldwide. Rather, the firm gives greater attention to identifying opportunities for integration and improved coordination of strategy across national boundaries.

Level of Involvement

As GE's and Whirlpool's strategies illustrate, adopting a global perspective implies total commitment to international markets. While both firms are still heavily dependent on the United States, the concept of a domestic market will gradually disappear, as the U.S. market becomes part of a globally interdependent market system. Ultimately, therefore, the home market loses its privileged position as a priority for allocating resources, and as a source of ideas or testing ground for new products and in hiring and promoting senior management.

As an increasing number of firms operate on a global basis, commitment to international markets becomes a sine qua non of competing effectively in these markets. The only exceptions occur where a firm operates in a protected market environment or targets a specific national niche. Operation on a global scale enables a firm to leverage its assets from one market to another in order to attack competitors at their most vulnerable points, to dominate isolated or undefended markets, and to take maximum advantage of changing environmental conditions.

Level of Risk

At the same time, as the firm develops greater familiarity with diverse market environments and experience in international operations, its perceptions of risk will diminish. By establishing regional marketing operations in Asia, Whirlpool is gaining familiarity with the market and reducing the risk when it eventually establishes manufacturing facilities. Entry into new countries may be perceived as less risky, as experience in other similar countries can be extrapolated to make more effective management decisions

In addition, operational risks are diversified insofar as the firm is involved in numerous countries throughout the world. GE is not only diversified geographically but also has an extensive range of businesses throughout the world. If economic or market conditions worsen in one country or region, the effects may be compensated or counterbalanced by results in another country or region. Similarly, if exchange rates fluctuate, production or sourcing can be shifted to more advantageous locations. Thus, while firms still vary in terms of their attitudes towards risk, risk aversion will not necessarily result in a limited geographic scope. Involvement in geographically dispersed markets is viewed as a means of reducing or managing macroenvironmental and operational risks through geographic diversification and by augmenting strategic flexibility.

RATIONALIZING THE BUSINESS DEFINITION

As international operations expand and the firm enters and acquires new products and brands (and new businesses) in different countries, reevaluation of existing business definitions is needed. (See Figure 12.2.) As Whirlpool expanded its global operations through the acquisition of Philip's consumer appliances business, it had to rethink how it defined its core business, shifting from a product focus to a customer benefit orientation. Geographic configuration of activities also becomes important in order to establish the parameters for developing global strategy. Both external forces (increased communication and travel, advances in communications and distribution technology, internationalization of business operations, linkage of businesses across national borders) and internal forces (transfer of R&D, product technology, exchange of ideas between units within the firm) provide opportunities for redrawing or reconfiguring the firm's business definition to extend across national and regional boundaries.

Customer Benefits

The increase in communication and interaction across boundaries has reduced the significance of national differences in desired customer benefits in many product markets and resulted in the emergence of new market configurations. Movement of people, goods, and information across national boundaries has muted specific national preferences and behavior patterns. In some instances, for example, consumer electronics, there is increasing homogeneity in customer

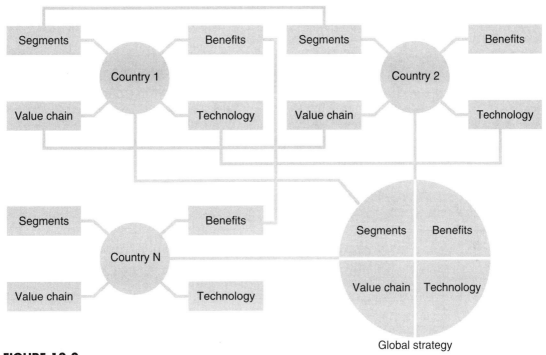

FIGURE 12-2

Rationalizing the global business definition.

tastes and behavior worldwide. In other cases, products or services typical of one country or culture have been transferred or adopted by another. In addition, increased mobility and travel have generated an interest in new types of product benefits, such as compactness, portability, and systems compatibility.

The international expansion of many corporations marketing their products and brands worldwide, together with the growth of international communication links and the spread of international media, have stimulated greater commonality in consumer preferences in a number of product markets. Thus, for example, Sony Walkmans are to be found on the streets of Tokyo, London, Paris, and New York, just as Tupperware containers, Johnson and Johnson baby products, and Band-Aids are to be found in homes worldwide.[4]

At the same time, increased consumer mobility has stimulated interest in light, compact travel-related items—for example, adapter plugs, multidial alarm clocks, synthesized translators, and light luggage with wheels. Similarly, international travellers want to find their favorite brands of soft drinks, cigarettes, tobacco, candy, and even toothpaste available wherever they travel throughout the world, thus stimulating the emergence of global markets.

Parallel to the case of consumer markets, the growth of large multinational corporations with operations throughout the world has created new types of demand for products and services that are compatible with different operating systems in different parts of the world, and readily transferable or transportable across national boundaries, available in multiple locations throughout the world. Demand for services that link markets or operations in different parts of the world has also grown exponentially. Reuters, for example, has now expanded into multimedia and has set up Reuters Financial Television, which pipes live digital TV coverage of major events to currency traders' terminals throughout Europe. Reuters has also started "video on demand" experiments with Bell Atlantic and Nynex.[5]

The business definition should thus specify which, and how many, of these different types of demand it aims to serve in world markets. Often this is closely linked to the definitions of which market segments it intends to target.

Customer Segments

Increased linkages of communication and mobility across national boundaries results in the emergence of more complex patterns of market segmentation. While the first phase resulted in the geographic extension of the domestic market segments, and the second phase in the formation of national patterns of market segmentation, the third phase leads to a cobweb of segmentation patterns, some of which may be national in scope, while others transcend national or regional boundaries.

In essence, patterns of market segmentation are characterized by two facets—the geographic scope of the market, and the degree of market linkage. Segments may be national or even limited to a specific area within a country, or regional, for example, European, North American, or Latin American, or global in scope. Equally, within a geographic area they may be further segmented by age, income, the type of benefits desired, or purchase frequency. Further, the degree of segmentation may vary from one region to another. For example, in Europe, the pet food market is segmented into gourmet, premium, and standard pet foods, and by life cycle. In other markets, only standard pet foods exist.

In some markets, one can also identify segments that are interlinked across countries or markets. As noted earlier, in a number of product markets, companies with worldwide operations source centrally for components, supplies, or equipment to be supplied to their operations worldwide. Thus, global purchasing contracts are negotiated in order to ensure uniformity and consistency in quality of supplies and equipment worldwide. Purchasing power may also be leveraged in order to obtain better purchase terms and service. Banks, for example, frequently develop global contracts for purchasing information-processing equipment, to ensure systems compatibility and to facilitate international data transfer.

Technology

The third component of the business definition concerns the technology used to supply desired customer benefits. The first phase was concerned with the need to adapt technology to international markets and the local market expansion phase, with the ability to leverage technology across products and product lines. In the phase of global rationalization, however, the firm focuses attention on technology that can span national boundaries and enable it to supply multiple markets worldwide.

In the case of the TV industry, for example, attention is focused on TVs that can operate in different existing TV systems, and on developing a new high-definition format, which would be utilized worldwide. Similarly, computer software developers are considering architectures capable of handling Roman alphabet, Arabic script, and Kanji characters. The traditional photography industry is adopting electronic technology for converting film into digital images, enabling rapid transmission of photos through international satellite linkages. Digitized images can also be fed directly into personal computers, to be edited and incorporated into printed documents. Equipment based on this technology could be targeted to global customers.

The advent of modular technology and production techniques has also substantially reduced the cost of minor modifications and customization of products and services to idiosyncratic local tastes. For example, Christofle, the French manufacturer of tableware, produces a basic design and customizes individual pieces to specific market preferences—fish knives and forks and soup spoons for the U.K., salad forks for the United States, soup spoons and sauce spoons for France, and longer prongs for salad forks in Scandinavia.

Value Chain

The final component of the business definition concerns the value chain. In the first phase, the firm centers attention on whether to internalize or externalize participation at different stages in the value chain. This decision will depend on the firm's resources, its commitment to international expansion, and the desired degree of control over international operations, as well as the availability and reliability of organizations capable of performing various functions such as production, distribution, and after-sales service in foreign markets. During the phase of local market expansion, emphasis shifts to concern with economies of scope: spreading fixed costs across a broader product range. In the phase of global rationalization, attention returns to issues of internalization vs. externalization. Now, however, the far-flung character of operations, and the drive for expansion, often imply that even large multinationals will be unable to internalize all phases of operations in all country markets, and that it will increasingly be more cost effective to externalize operations in small country markets or for highly specialized functions. In some instances, strategic alliances with erstwhile competitors will be formed.

In the case of R&D, for example, firms may license technology from other firms in order to devote resources to market development or improve production efficiency. This is particularly likely to occur in industries that rely on a variety of complex and rapidly evolving technologies, such as telecommunications or computer software. In industries such as aerospace or telecommunications, where large investments in R&D are needed to develop new products, firms may enter into alliances to share risk. Equally, firms may enter into alliances for marketing and distribution, or shift to a system of independent distributors in small country markets, in order to obtain more widespread distribution. These different types of alliances are discussed in depth in Chapter 15.

LEVERAGING CORE COMPETENCIES IN GLOBAL MARKETS

As the firm moves towards global rationalization and improved integration and coordination of operations worldwide, it seeks to leverage core competencies across national boundaries and, ultimately, on a worldwide scale. Production, management, and marketing skills, as well as intangible assets such as brand image or reputation, are leveraged across multiple markets. The firm should also investigate opportunities for transferring products, programs, and processes from one market to another, as well as for exchange of knowledge and experience acquired in operating in different market environments.

In addition, in the course of expansion, the firm may begin to acquire new competencies and skills. The global scale of operations will mandate acquisition of specialized skills to manage global operations—skills such as expertise in managing international cash flows, international logistics and distribution, and expatriate training and management. The firm will also accumulate experience from planning and coordinating operations at different levels of the value chain in complex multicountry environments. This experience will contribute to improving the overall efficiency of operations. Thus, potential synergies arising from the global and multinational character of operations can be fully realized.

As in the initial entry phase, attention is centered on leveraging core competencies *across* rather than *within* national markets. GE has developed a core competence in financing in its GE capital group. This has been a key component of GE's global expansion, being highly profitable and working in concert with other divisions. In some cases, a firm may develop a competency in R&D process or production technology in response to specific demand conditions or the competitive climate in a given country. These competencies and skills may then be exchanged and incorporated into new products for specific local markets, or used to develop global products. For example, P&G research technicians in the United States, Japan, and Europe shared their research relating to the use of enzymes, bleach, phosphates, and surfactants in developing liquid detergents. This resulted in the launch of Liquid Tide in the United States, Liquid Cheer in Japan, and Liquid Ariel in Europe, all of which proved highly successful in their respective markets.[6]

In addition to leveraging skills and competencies at different stages of the value chain, opportunities for transferring ideas for new products, marketing strategies, and management processes from one country to another can also be identified. Thus, for example, many ideas for environmentally friendly products and packaging were initially developed in Europe, particularly Germany, in response to environmental concerns in these markets, and have subsequently been transferred to the United States. Biodegradable detergents and refills for fabric softener and liquid detergent bottles were initially launched in Europe and have been subsequently introduced by P&G, Unilever, and Colgate in the United States.

All-purpose cleaners and detergents such as P&G's Cinch and Ariel, developed in response to European demand for high-tech, all-purpose products, are now being marketed in California and Arizona. These brands were initially transferred to Latin America from Europe, and were brought by Mexican immigrants into Southern California.[7] Observing the success of these gray market imports from Tijuana, P&G decided to launch Cinch and Ariel with bilingual packaging in supermarkets on the west coast, targeting Hispanic consumers.

In an attempt to compete more effectively with luxury imports in its home market, General Motors's Cadillac division is trying to leverage the capabilities of the GM German subsidiary, Adam Opel AG. Opel makes the Omega, a luxury car that competes with the Mercedes C class and BMW 3 series. Rather than try to design a car from the ground up, GM is modifying aspects of the Omega to make it more appealing to American tastes while at the same time not compromising its European luxury feel. Cadillac plans to introduce the car into the U.S. market in 1996 and hopes that it will help bring in new buyers, particularly women in their mid-forties.[8]

Marketing skills acquired by operating in different national market environments may also be leveraged. Experience in operating and managing distribution channels in an emerging nation with a poorly developed infrastructure, such as India, may be transferred to other countries with poor infrastructures, such as those in Eastern Europe. Similarly, Indian engineering consulting firms find markets for their services in African nations.

In addition to leveraging existing competencies across countries on a global basis, a company may also acquire new skills and competencies as it expands internationally. In some cases, these may stem from the scale and scope of operations, which permit acquisition of highly specialized skills that would not previously have been economically feasible. In other cases these are skills or resources related to the multinational character of operations, and managing and transferring resources across national boundaries.

COMPETITIVE POSTURE

The growth of competition on a global scale, together with the formation of regional trading blocs and the integration of markets worldwide, suggest the need to adopt a global orientation. Rather than competing on a country-by-country basis, the firm should look for opportunities to utilize its competitive position in one country to compete more effectively in other countries or markets. This may imply using strengths or resources acquired in one market to enter or compete in other markets or, alternatively, maintaining a strong entrenched position in one market while shifting resources to attack competitors in markets where they are most vulnerable.

As competitive pressures intensify worldwide, it becomes increasingly crucial to adopt a proactive stance in developing global competitive strategy. In particular, it becomes important to consider preemptive moves and to build toward a strong competitive position in the long run, in the light of trends toward industry consolidation and market integration in many areas worldwide. National market positions may thus no longer be viable in many industries, unless they target specialized national market niches, which cannot be served efficiently by a global competitor.

Competitive Market Scope

A key aspect of the firm's competitive posture in global markets is the scope of its operations worldwide. Here, as in preceding phases of operations, two dimensions may be identified: the geographic scope of operations, or terrain on which it chooses to compete; and the range of product markets and services in which it will compete. While in the phase of national market expansion attention is frequently focused on expansion along the second dimension of products and services, forces underlying the shift into the phase of global rationalization trigger reexamination of the firm's geographic market scope. The firm needs to consider opportunities for extending product markets into new geographic areas. In addition, managers must seek to integrate and consolidate operations in different countries. (See Figure 12.3.)

FIGURE 12-3
Firm/country relationships as a function of international strategy development.

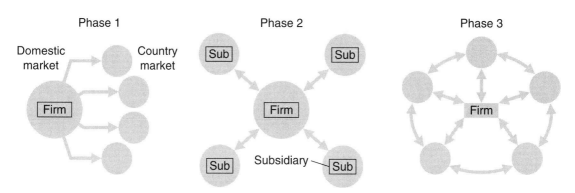

Note: Circles indicate countries

An important consideration underlying this decision is whether the firm identifies and targets global customers. As noted earlier, increased travel and communication across national boundaries suggests that opportunities for identifying such customers are likely to be on the rise. Nowhere is this more evident than in the communications industry. In Europe, efforts are underway to develop the information superhighway. A 2-year effort has begun to tie together 17 incompatible telephone networks. There is a European Union initiative to test broadband services such as financial, medical, and computer-aided design applications. In the U.K., Nynex, Southwestern Bell, U.S. West, Singapore Telecom, and Bell Canada, in conjunction with cable operators, are laying fiber optics.[9] These activities, along with other similar initiatives around the world, begin to lay the foundation for products and services designed to meet the insatiable appetite for technology and communications.

Opportunities to consolidate operations in a given region may also be examined, resulting in competition on a regional rather than a multidomestic basis. A firm may thus be able to consolidate and more effectively utilize its competitive strengths on a regional basis. As noted earlier, the removal of trade barriers, and harmonization of product regulations in the European Union, have encouraged many companies to consolidate production and marketing operations throughout the EU.

Closely linked to decisions about geographic scope are those related to the range and diversity of product lines. Companies with limited resources need to make a trade-off between competing on a global market basis and competing in multiple product businesses. Thus, companies targeting global market segments, such as Body Shop and Benneton, may tend to specialize in a relatively restricted range of product lines. Swatch, on the other hand, targets a specific segment for low-priced fashion watches worldwide, but also markets cellular phones in Europe and has plans with Mercedes-Benz to develop and market a car, the Swatchmobile. In contrast, large multinationals such as General Motors, Toyota, P&G, and Unilever may compete with a broad product line and in multiple product businesses in markets worldwide.

In this context, the firm must decide whether to compete in the same product businesses in different countries throughout the world, or diversify competitive risks by competing in different product businesses. While the latter option diversifies risks, it may also result in dispersion of resources and competitive effort on a worldwide basis. The similarity of demand for the relevant product or service across countries is an important consideration underlying this decision, as well as potential economies of scope and synergies arising from competing in related product businesses.

The major automobile manufacturers, for example, often compete in related product businesses worldwide, due to underlying similarities in the nature of customer demand, and potential economies of scope from leveraging production skills and processes across product lines and countries. However, the specific product businesses in which they compete differ somewhat. For example, GM competes broad-line in the automobile and truck business worldwide, while Ford competes broad-line in automobiles, trucks, and tractors worldwide. Rolls Royce

Motors, on the other hand, targets a global segment of upper-end luxury cars, while Rolls Royce Engines is in the global market for aircraft engines. Mercedes competes in the automobile, truck, and smaller aircraft engine market worldwide. Toyota also competes broad-line worldwide, but only in the automobile market. Honda, on the other hand, competes in a range of product businesses including compact automobiles, motorcycles, lawn mowers, snowmobiles, and marine engines worldwide, leveraging its expertise in the design and production of small engines.

The relative emphasis on different geographic areas, however, varies from one company to another. Fiat, Citroen-Peugeot, and several other European automobile manufacturers compete primarily in Europe, and to a lesser extent, in the United States. Mitsubishi, on the other hand, has focused primarily on joint ventures, in Europe with Daimler Benz and in Asian markets such as Malaysia with government. Companies also vary in terms of the skills they try to leverage. While a common core competence appears to be engine design and production, some firms such as GM and Ford leverage this to related types of vehicles such as trucks and tractors, which may also share similar distribution and marketing skills. Others, such as Rolls-Royce and Mercedes, are concerned with acquiring and sharing research into new lightweight and heat-resistant material with the aerospace business.

At the other end of the spectrum are companies such as Heinz, which compete in different product businesses in different parts of the world. This may be in part because demand for certain product businesses is limited to certain areas of the world, or because the company seeks to diversify its activities geographically. This type of competitive scope seems most likely to occur in product business and companies where core competencies and skills lie downstream in the value chain, that is, in relation to marketing, distribution, and service. As noted earlier, in contrast to R&D and production, competencies in marketing and distribution are less easy to leverage directly across geographic areas, especially where they differ significantly in terms of the nature of customer demand or of the marketing infrastructure. Consequently, where marketing skills, experience, and ideas are transferred across geographic areas, they may need to be adapted to a given environmental context.

Positional Advantage

Another important aspect of the firm's competitive posture is the nature of its positional advantage relative to its competition. Management has to determine how to leverage that advantage to compete more effectively in global markets. This in turn requires identification of key competitors and assessment of their strengths and weaknesses in markets worldwide.

In the phase of national market expansion, the firm centered attention primarily on local competition, and on adapting or extending the product line and marketing tactics to meet local competition. In the phase of global rationalization, emphasis shifts to other global or regional competitors, who are competing in the same or similar geographic and product markets. As discussed in terms of competitive market scope, key competitors may not necessarily be the same in different regions of the world, nor does a firm necessarily compete in the same target segments or mix of product businesses worldwide. For each product business and geographic unit (country, region, or world), a firm has to assess its positional advantages and its strengths and weaknesses relative to competition.

Once the firm has made this assessment, it should determine how to leverage its competitive position in one country or market on a global basis. Management may either emphasize utilizing strengths developed in one country or product business in other countries or product businesses, or, alternatively, attacking weaknesses in another company's position. A central issue here is the aggressiveness of the firm's posture coupled with the degree of industry concentration or market fragmentation.

In some instances, a firm may utilize a strong or entrenched market position in one product business to cross-subsidize entry or growth into another, more competitive business. Profits from a mature or protected domestic business, for example, might be utilized to compete in a new or growing regional or global product business. For example, BiTicino uses profits from its domestic light switch business in Italy to finance R&D in its fiber optics business.

Where, on the other hand, markets are becoming more integrated on a regional or global basis, and industry consolidation is taking place, a firm will have little option but to adopt an aggressive posture, in order to sustain or develop its position in international markets. The strength of its position and its posture, however, may vary from one country or market to another. Market challengers or followers in a major domestic market, such as Sony, have been found to be more aggressive in expanding in international markets.[10] Blocked in their domestic markets, they have focused on expanding and meeting competition in international markets, rather than challenging the domestic market leader.

Market challengers may also attack market leaders in markets where they are most vulnerable, insofar as these provide the basis for their strength in other areas. For example, if a market leader derives a significant proportion of its profits from a single market, it will be particularly vulnerable to attack in that market. For example, Michelin was able to successfully attack Goodyear's position and its profit margins by entering the U.S. market with an aggressive pricing strategy.[11] Such a strategy is susceptible to a counterattack, as Michelin subsequently found when Goodyear counterattacked in Europe. Similarly, Fiat is vulnerable to attack in its domestic market, since it derives over 50 percent of its profits there, and is consequently diversifying into other product businesses in order to counter the impact of such an attack.

In essence, the firm's competitive posture should establish how best to utilize its skills and core competencies as well as its competitive position in different countries and product businesses, so as to compete more effectively in world markets. As with other aspects of its strategy in this phase, a key aspect is how to realize potential synergies through improved coordination, integration, and leveraging of this position across countries and regions throughout the world.

DETERMINING STRATEGIC THRUST

The firm's goals and objectives regarding the globalization of operations, the redefinition of its business, the identification of its core competencies, and its competitive posture, provide the basic parameters for determining its strategic thrust. This establishes the direction of the firm's efforts to achieve stated objectives and provides guidelines for developing global strategy. This thrust should seek to capitalize on potential synergies arising from operating on a global scale and take maximum advantage of the multinational character of its operations. A dual thrust can combine a drive to improve the efficiency of operations worldwide with improved planning and strategy development on a global scale.

Establishing a global strategic thrust entails a number of steps. In the first place, the directions for global expansion in terms of countries, target segments, and products need to be determined. The firm should assess the attractiveness and growth potential of different countries, market segments, and product businesses, and its competitive positions with regard to each of these. This global portfolio in turn provides the basis for allocating resources to different product businesses and geographic areas.

Once the global scope of the firm's operations has been determined, the next step is to develop a blueprint for competing in these markets. This requires identifying target customer segments and developing strategies to meet their specific needs and interests, which leverage the firm's skills and position worldwide.

Finally, opportunities for integration and rationalization of operations across country markets and product lines need to be considered. This includes upstream operations such as R&D, production, and logistics, as well as downstream in marketing, distribution, and service. Communication, control, and coordination mechanisms are needed to monitor and direct these operations and manage relations between different operational units worldwide. Linkages also need to be established with customers and distributors to manage the flow of goods and services throughout the channel. Expansion goals, coupled with competitive pressures, may also suggest the need to develop strategic alliances to expand market scope, acquire needed resources or skills, and ensure that strategies are effectively implemented worldwide.

SUMMARY

While movement into global operations is a gradual process for many firms, it requires that the firm systematically reassess how and why it conducts business in international markets. Marketing operations that have evolved over time to meet needs in individual country markets are likely to result in a diverse patchwork of operations. The firm needs to examine these operations in order to achieve the efficiencies and synergies that will enable it to compete effectively in global markets.

The first step is to reassess the firm's goals and objectives for global markets. This must be done primarily in terms of its level of involvement in global markets and the degree of risk it is willing to accept. As when it made the transition from phase one to phase two, the firm must redefine its business. Again, this must be done in terms of the customer benefits, segments, technology used, and participation in stages in the value chain. The spatial separation of markets, as well as the interlinkages between seemingly disparate markets, make the redefinition of the business essential and quite complex.

A thorough understanding of the appropriate business definition for global markets allows the firm to reevaluate its business strategy. First, reconfiguration of operations to improve coordination and efficiency needs to be considered. With more efficient operations as a starting point, the firm can then begin to examine how its core competencies can be leveraged in global markets.

The firm's competitive posture in global markets is also an important facet of its overall strategy. Competitive posture encompasses the terrain on which the firm chooses to compete, as well as the range of product markets in which it will compete. Related to this is the firm's positional advantage, or how competitive advantages in one market can be used to compete more effectively in global markets.

All these diverse considerations come together in a strategic thrust which determines the firm's direction in global markets. The strategic thrust provides, not only direction, but constancy of purpose. A well conceived strategic thrust will provide the firm with a sustainable competitive advantage and a clear direction to attack global markets.

REFERENCES

1. "GE's Brave New World," (1993) *Business Week*, November 8, pp. 64–70.
2. Maruca, Regina Fazio (1994) "The Right Way to Go Global: An Interview with Whirlpool CEO David Whitwam," *Harvard Business Review*, March-April, vol. 72, pp. 135–145.
3. Browning, E.S. (1992) "In Pursuit of the Elusive Euroconsumer," *Wall Street Journal*, April 23, p. B–1.
4. Ohmae, Kenichi (1985) *Triad Power*, New York: Free Press.
5. "Reuters Dives In—All the Way" (1994) *Business Week*, February 21, pp. 46–47.
6. Bartlett, Christopher A., and Sumantra Ghoshal (1989) *Managing Across Borders*, Boston, MA: Harvard Business School Press.
7. P & G *Annual Report* 1991.
8. Choi, Audrey, and Joseph B. White (1994) "Turning an Opel into a Cadillac, GM Goes Global," *Wall Street Journal*, March 11, pp. B1–ff.
9. Dwyer, Paula, and Jonathan B. Levine (1993) "Britain Races Ahead Down the Superhighway," *Business Week*, September 27, pp. 136–138.

10. Mascarenhas, Briance (1986) "International Strategies of Non-Dominant Firms," *Journal of International Business Studies* Vol. 17, Spring, pp. 1–26.

11. Hamel, Gary, and C.K. Prahalad (1985) "Do You Really Have a Global Strategy?" *Harvard Business Review* July-August, pp. 139–148.

CHAPTER 13

CHARTING DIRECTION IN GLOBAL MARKETS

INTRODUCTION

Charting directions for future growth, and determining how to allocate resources, are important issues confronting management in domestic markets. Decisions have to be made with regard to priorities to be assigned to different product businesses, emphasis to be placed on different market segments, regions within a country, and products or product lines within a business. In addition, the degree of involvement at various stages in the value-chain, and need for forward and backward integration, have to be determined. Priorities for expansion and development also need to be determined, for example, whether to enter new product businesses or market segments or to divest certain product businesses and types of operations.

In international markets, establishing priorities for expansion and growth assumes added complexity due to the significance of the geographic dimension. In the first place, management has to determine in which areas of the world to invest, and where to grow specific businesses. Daewoo Motors, the third largest Korean automobile company, for example, has decided to focus on developing markets in the Third World.[1] Daewoo had been hit by declining market share in the United States, Germany, and Japan, largely due to its image of poor quality and after-sales service. As a result, Daewoo is committing over $8 billion to the production and sales of cars and electronic goods in Eastern Europe, Central Asia, and Latin America. Daewoo has purchased the Romanian car company Oltcit to produce cars for the Eastern European market, and has established joint venture automobile plants in Uzbekistan and Iran.[2] It also expects to begin assembling cars in the Philippines and Vietnam, and is negotiating other projects in Libya, Peru, Pakistan and Tatarstan, and Russia. Daewoo's electronics division is also building a $60 million joint venture plant in Uzbekistan to make cordless phones, television sets, and vacuum cleaners for both local and export markets. Similar plants are under construction in Vietnam and Tatarstan, Russia. Part of the financing for the plants is provided by other Daewoo affiliates, such as Daewoo Telecom.

In addition to deciding which geographic areas to focus on, decisions have to be made with regard to which product businesses, product lines, and segments should be growth priorities within a given country or geographic region, and whether synergies will be obtained from focusing on the same product businesses, product lines, and segments worldwide. While Daewoo focuses on the same businesses, that is, cars and consumer electronics in developing countries, other companies grow different businesses in different geographic areas. CPC, for example, focuses on sauces, soups, and seasonings in European markets, and corn-based products in Latin America. Thus, management has to decide whether or not a given product business or product line should expand into new countries and market segments as new opportunities emerge. At the same time, as markets change and mature in different countries, firms must decide whether to divest product businesses in certain countries, or regions, or worldwide.

Management also has to decide how far the firm should be involved in operations upstream, for example, in R&D, production of components, or sourcing, or alternatively, downstream in distribution and service, and how far such operations need to be expanded or divested in different countries or areas of the world. In addition, it should assess whether greater efficiencies or potential synergies can be realized through coordination or integration of operations across countries and geographic regions. For example, if demand patterns are similar in several countries, new product development costs that would be prohibitive for a single market could be spread across multiple markets. Similarly, a single sales force might be utilized to target customers in neighboring countries, thus reducing promotion costs.

In essence, therefore, management has to establish a global portfolio of countries, product businesses, and market segments that chart its direction for future growth and expansion. First, relevant units and levels of analysis of the global portfolio have to be determined, together with the criteria and procedures by which alternative portfolios are to be evaluated. Next, portfolios are assessed in terms of alternative directions in which the firm might expand and/or should retract, and how resources might be reallocated among various elements of each portfolio. Finally, portfolios that provide the desired balance and direction for growth are selected (see Figure 13-1).

PRINCIPLES OF PORTFOLIO ANALYSIS

In domestic markets, portfolio analysis focuses on examining the business position of the products or SBUs in which the firm is currently involved relative to their market attractiveness and competitive strength. This assessment provides the basis for establishing investment priorities—determining which businesses to invest in and develop, which businesses to harvest, and which to divest.[3,4] At the same time, management can assess whether or not its portfolio of businesses is likely to provide the desired direction or rate of future growth, that is, whether the firm has adequate investment in high-growth businesses. Management can also determine how far risks are diversified, and whether the portfolio contains a well-balanced mix of high-risk/high-return and low-risk businesses.

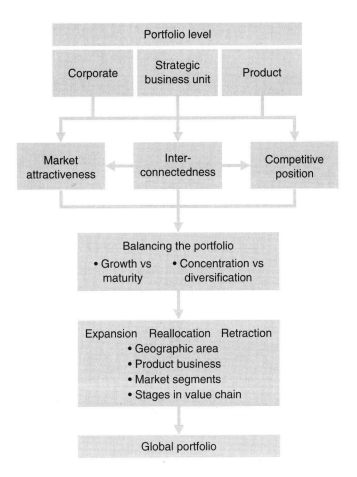

FIGURE 13-1

Developing the global portfolio.

Portfolio analysis can be conducted at several different levels in the organization, from the corporate or product business level to the product line or brand level. At the corporate level, portfolio analysis could focus on resource allocation among product divisions, groups of SBUs, or SBUs. At the product division or SBU level, it might focus on product groups or lines, or individual products and brands. An even finer level of analysis might focus on products or variants targeted to specific customer groups or market segments.

In an early formulation of portfolio analysis, the BCG growth/share matrix, product businesses were assessed on two dimensions: business strength, operationalized in terms of market share; and market attractiveness, measured by rate of market growth. Market growth was viewed as the best indicator of the stage in the product life-cycle. Market share was also likely to be more readily obtained and be more profitable in growth markets. Market share was considered a good indicator of strength insofar as a firm with high market share was likely to enjoy a number of advantages in terms of brand recognition, economies of scale, ability to exploit experience curve effects, and channel dominance. Furthermore, there is substantial empirical evidence from the Profit Impact of Marketing Strategy (PIMS) data base linking market share and profitability.[5] The BCG approach also had the advantage of being simple and easy to understand.

An underlying assumption of this approach is that products or SBUs vary in terms of their resource needs and profitability.[3] SBUs in fast-growing markets will require substantial investment in order to sustain position and realize their potential, but have limited profitability or even losses. Similarly, new products and new product development drain cash, requiring investment in R&D, promotional activities, and development of the distribution system. On the other hand, SBUs or products with strong positions in mature markets require little or no new investment and should generate profits. These can then be channelled into new product development and embryonic SBUs to fuel their growth. A well-balanced portfolio should thus contain both new products and SBUs in emerging markets, and successful products and SBUs in mature markets. The former provides the motor for the firm's future growth, while the latter generates the cash needed to build a strong competitive position in growth markets.

Partly in reaction to the somewhat simplistic nature of the BCG approach, a more comprehensive model was developed by GE planners, based in part on portfolio models developed at McKinsey.[4] This approach proposed using multiple factors to assess both market attractiveness and business position. For example, it was suggested that market attractiveness could be evaluated based on market size, growth, industry profitability, competitive structure, and government regulation. Business strength, on the other hand, could be assessed based on factors such as sales growth, market share, margins, profitability, company image, and reputation.

This approach is much broader and richer than the BCG approach, which emphasizes financial measures and cash flow. It provides a more comprehensive assessment of the industry and environmental conditions in which a business or product group is operating. The specific factors used to evaluate both market attractiveness and business strength can be customized to specific industries or environments and weighted according to their relative importance. The factors included in the analysis, and their weighting, can also be changed, as industry or competitive conditions change.

In addition to providing an assessment of the relative position, strength, and resource needs of various SBUs or product lines, the GE–McKinsey matrix can also be used to guide investment and strategy decisions. Businesses in strong positions in attractive markets provide good candidates for further investment and growth. Those in weak positions in attractive markets will need investment to build this potential, while those in low growth markets are candidates for harvesting or divestment.

Applying this approach to international markets, the units of the portfolio can consist of SBUs, product businesses, or product lines within a given region or country. A portfolio can then be assessed to determine the balance between high-growth and mature country or regional markets, as well as between high-growth vs. mature product businesses, product lines, and market segments. At the same time, management can examine how far risk is diversified across countries or regions, as well as product businesses and market segments.

Balancing Growth and Mature Markets

As in domestic portfolios, the balance between high-growth and mature markets needs to be considered. In international portfolios, management should look at the balance between involvement in mature countries and regions of the world, such as the United States and Western Europe, and rapidly growing geographic areas, such as Southeast Asia, China, and India. It is important to be well positioned and invest in the growth markets of the future as well as the mature markets that offer current returns. Companies that fail to do so risk seeing their sales and world market share gradually erode, and will lose their competitive position in world markets to competitors better positioned for the future.[6] Consequently, even conservative companies that want to limit their risk exposure in international markets need to consider growth potential in different country markets. As noted in Chapter 12, General Electric, for example, plans to invest over $1 billion in ventures in India, China, and Mexico. While these ventures entail substantial risk, they represent the markets of the future for GE's key businesses— jet engines, medical equipment, and power equipment. Furthermore, in each country, the investment is spread across a number of different businesses and ventures to diversify product market risk.

Just as in the case of domestic product businesses, operations in rapidly growing regions and country markets are likely to require considerable investment. Management may need to make substantial expenditures on promotional activities to develop primary demand, corporate or brand awareness and interest, and product modification to meet different market conditions, as well as on building the marketing and distribution infrastructure. Especially in high-growth markets in developing countries, investment in construction of the physical distribution infrastructure, for example, roads, warehousing, or communications, is often needed. For example, Coca-Cola invested over $400 million in developing an infrastructure of five bottling plants and 13 distribution centers in Eastern Germany.[7] It developed a fleet of 370 trucks, 900 cars and vans, and 170 fork lifts, and can deliver orders by the next day. This investment has been well rewarded. In just 3 years, per capita consumption of Coke has surpassed levels in France and the United Kingdom.

Equally, while growth opportunities are greater in emerging country markets, such markets are often characterized by a high degree of economic and financial instability. The risks and costs of operating in such markets are, therefore, often considerably higher than in mature, well-developed markets with an efficient market infrastructure, such as those in Western Europe and North America. Consequently, an appropriate balance between growth and maturity, and the various types of environmental and operating risks, will need to be established.

Concentration versus Diversification

In addition to considering the balance between growth and maturity, management should also consider the diversification of the international portfolio. One aspect of this is risk diversification. This is a particularly important aspect to consider in relation to international portfolios, due to the significance of macroeconomic country risk. In assessing any international portfolio, management should, therefore, consider the level of risk associated with each portfolio unit. As noted above, businesses in emerging countries often entail higher levels of risk. In addition, the impact of the political, economic, and financial situation in a country or region on a given product business needs to be considered. The portfolio should, therefore, be balanced so as to diversify macroeconomic risk and include units in high-risk/high-return areas, as well as low-risk/stable areas.

Management should also consider the geographic diversification of its business portfolio. This may be reflected in the number of regions or country markets in which the firm operates, as well as their similarity and geographic proximity. Management may, for example, decide to concentrate in a geographic region, or in country markets in close geographic proximity, where such markets are characterized by similar demand patterns and the market infrastructures are closely interlinked, for example, the Scandinavian or Benelux countries. Substantial economies can be realized through focusing on such markets. Companies with limited resources relative to competition may also prefer such a strategy in order to focus efforts and cherry pick profitable markets or market segments. It is, however, important to recognize that this strategy is vulnerable to economic and market downturns in the region, as well as entry by other competition.

Diversification, on the other hand, enables management to spread risks across a wider range of markets and geographic areas. Companies can thus counterbalance economic or market fluctuations or foreign exchange risk, as well as competitive risk. For example, companies focusing on baby clothing, toys, or food diversify into countries with differing rates of population growth, to counterbalance demand fluctuations. Mothercare, the U.K. retailer of maternity clothing and baby products, has, for example, diversified into countries such as Mexico and Singapore, with high growth rates. Similarly, Heinz has targeted China and Mexico with its baby food line.

Diversification of operations across country markets or regions also limits vulnerability to competitive threats. If a company has a foothold in a number of different country markets and regions of the world, an attack in one market or region can be countered by channeling resources from another region or market to defend its position, or, alternatively, by focusing on expansion in another geographic region.

Management, therefore, needs to determine the appropriate balance between concentration and diversification based on company goals and objectives, and its resources and competitive position, as well as specific market demand, infrastructure characteristics, and industry structure.

LEVELS AND UNITS OF THE GLOBAL PORTFOLIO

In developing a global portfolio, as with a domestic portfolio, two aspects need to be considered: namely, the *level* of analysis, that is corporate, strategic business unit, or product line, and the *unit* of analysis, such as a country, product, or market segment. In domestic markets, portfolio analysis typically focuses on products and brands at the product line or SBU level, or product businesses at the corporate level. In international markets, however, the addition of the geographic dimension adds further complexity, and extends the combinations of units that can be considered at any level.

The global corporate portfolio provides the most aggregate level of analysis. This portfolio, for example, might consist of operations by geographic region or country, product businesses worldwide or by region, or relevant combinations of both. The next level is the SBU, or product business. Here, relevant portfolio units might consist of regions, countries, product lines or groups, target segments, types of operations, or combinations of these. The product group or line constitutes the most disaggregate level likely to be considered. Again, portfolio analysis might focus on regions, countries, target segments, types of operations, and relevant combinations of these. Alternative portfolio units are shown in Table 13.1. The specific composition of the portfolios considered will depend on the individual company and the nature of its international operations.

The Corporate Portfolio

Corporate portfolio analysis provides an important tool to assess how to allocate resources across geographic regions and countries, as also across product businesses, worldwide, by geographic area, and by type of operation. This analysis can identify the areas of the world and product businesses that appear to offer the most attractive opportunities for growth, or require investment to remain competitive, and those that appear to be maturing and should be harvested or divested.

Various types of corporate portfolios can be examined, depending on the range of product businesses and geographic areas in which the firm is involved, as well as the type of resource allocation or investment decision being considered. As illustrated in Figure 13.2, a diversified consumer goods company with operations in different regions of the world might examine its involvement by region or country to determine where to invest or divest. Equally, it might assess the relative position of its product businesses worldwide, by region, or by country, in order to determine whether to grow or divest a product business worldwide or in a specific region or country.

Corporate portfolio analysis provides a general overview and guidelines for resource allocation, and helps to pinpoint areas for further study or investigation. More detailed analysis is typically required at the SBU or product line level to guide specific planning and strategy decisions.

TABLE 13-1	LEVELS AND UNITS OF PORTFOLIO ANALYSIS

| LEVELS | GEOGRAPHIC SCOPE | | |
	GLOBAL	REGIONAL	COUNTRIES
Corporate	Region/Countries	Countries	Product businesses
	Product businesses worldwide	Product businesses	Product businesses
	Product businesses by region		
	Product businesses by country	Product business by country	Product lines
	Product business/ segment worldwide	Product business by segment	Product business by segment
	Product business/segment by region	Product business/ segment by country	
	Product business/segment by country		
Product Business	Regions/Countries	Countries	Segments
	Product lines worldwide	Product lines	Product lines
	Product lines/by region		
	Product lines/by country	Product lines by country	Brands
	Segments worldwide	Segments	
	Segments by region	Segments by country	
	Segments by country		
Product Line	Regions/Countries	Countries	Segments/ Products
	Segments worldwide	Segments	
	Segments by region	Segments by country	Brands
	Segments by country		
	Brands worldwide	Brands	
	Brands by region	Brands by country	
	Brands by country		

The Strategic Business Unit Portfolio

The SBU portfolio provides a more detailed analysis for a given SBU by geographic regions or countries, target segments, product lines, and involvement in the value chain. Management can assess whether the same target segments or product lines offer growth potential worldwide, or whether this varies with the geographic region or specific country. Product lines and markets that appear to be maturing or in decline can be identified and strategic priorities established. As in the case of the corporate portfolio, SBU portfolios can be composed of different units, depending on the specific allocation decision and the nature of the firm's operations.

Figure 13.3 shows some alternative portfolios for a hypothetical hair care business. Figure 13.3a shows the position of the business by region. While the busi-

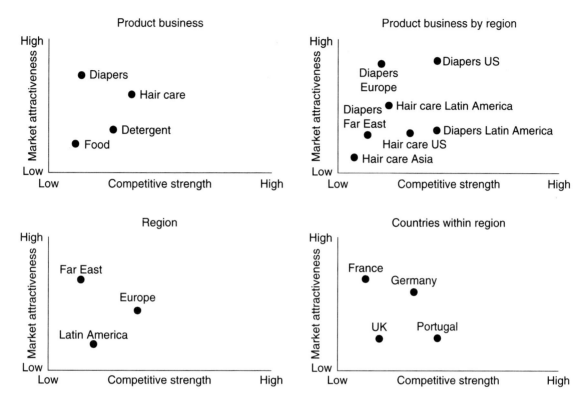

FIGURE 13-2

Alternative corporate level portfolio.

ness is in a strong competitive position in the mature markets in North America and Europe, it is less well positioned in the growing markets of Asia and Latin America. The breakdown by country in Figure 13.3b shows the business is particularly weak in the growing markets of China, Argentina, and Venezuela, suggesting a need to shift resources to improve its position in these markets. Figure 13.3c shows the position of different product lines within the hair care business. Again, while the company has a strong position in the mature shampoo line, it is less well placed in the more attractive hair coloring market. The breakdown of product lines by region provides further insights (Figure 13.3d). The business is in a strong position in shampoos and conditioners in the United States and Europe but needs to improve its position in the rapidly growing hair coloring market in Europe and in the shampoo market in Latin America. As in the analysis of corporate portfolios, examining SBU portfolios helps in assessing the business's position in different geographic areas, whether regions or countries, and in relation to different product lines in these areas.

Ford, for example, analyzed the operations of its tractor division in Europe and in key countries from the rest of the world, based on country attractiveness

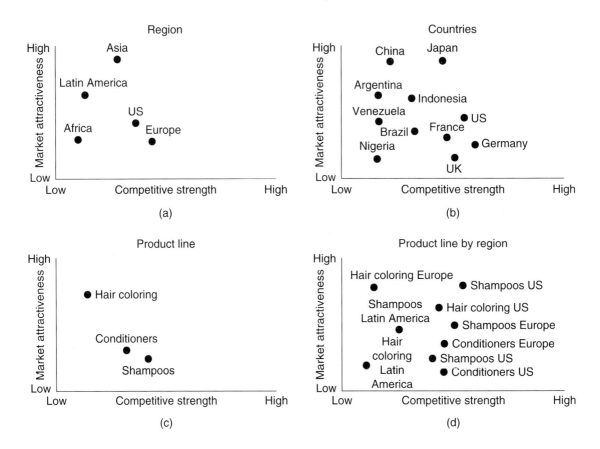

FIGURE 13-3

Alternative SBU portfolio (hair care).

and competitive strength, in order to determine which countries to invest and grow, which to divest or develop through joint ventures, and which to harvest or divest.[8] Examination of the key country markets portfolio in Figure 13.4 suggests that Ford's tractor division is relatively well placed in markets such as Kenya, Pakistan, and Indonesia. Its position in countries such as India and Argentina might, however, be improved. Operations in Spain, a less attractive market, might, for example, be harvested in order to fuel expansion in India and Argentina.

Product Line or Group Portfolios

Where an SBU contains multiple and somewhat diverse product lines, targeted to different customer segments, more detailed and disaggregate portfolio analysis may be conducted. This may be particularly desirable if the product lines or

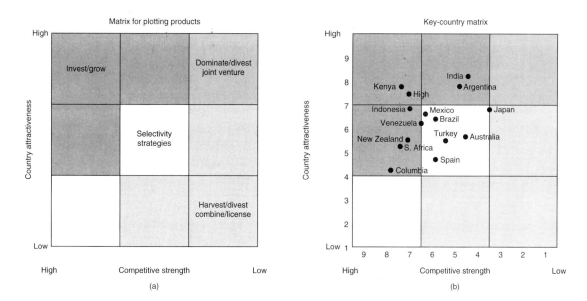

FIGURE 13-4

Portfolio matrices (Source: Harrell, Gilbert D., and Richard Kiefer (1981) "Multinational Strategic Market Portfolios," *MSU Business Topics*, (Winter), pp. 5–15.

groups vary from one part of the world to another. Portfolio analysis can then be conducted by region, country, or distribution channel for a given product line or group.

Figure 13.5 shows some portfolios for the shampoo line of the hypothetical hair care business. Figure 13.5a shows the position of the shampoo line in different regions of the world. While the line is well placed in Europe and the United States, it is in a weak position in Latin America and moderately strong in Asia. Examination of its position in Europe (Figure 13.5b) suggests that the line is in a strong position in the major markets in Western Europe but relatively weak in newly emerging markets in Poland and Hungary. Figure 13.5b shows the line's position in different market segments by region. This suggests that, while it is in a strong position in the baby, family, and dandruff segments in Europe, it is weak in the two segments in Latin America, shampoos/conditioners, and family hair shampoos. Management should therefore examine the importance of these market segments in Latin America, to assess how to improve its position—whether to launch a new brand in these segments or to develop a new market segment such as baby shampoo.

Analysis at the product variant or brand level would provide insights about growth opportunities, and also about transferring or extending a product line or brand from one country or target segment to another, as well as the need for new product development and product line extensions.

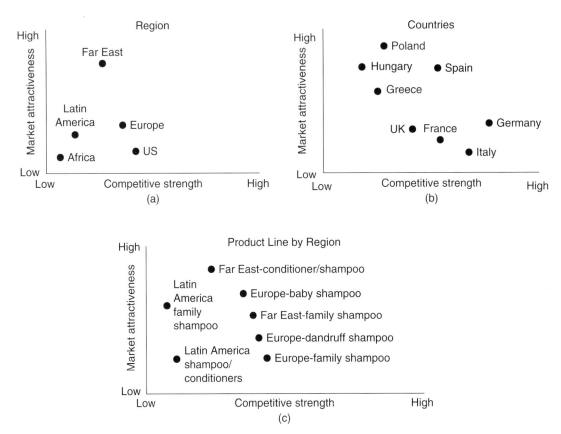

FIGURE 13-5

Alternative product line portfolios (shampoo).

DIMENSIONS FOR EVALUATING THE PORTFOLIO

Once the composition of the portfolio in terms of level and units has been determined, the next step is to identify the criteria on which to evaluate the portfolio based on two key dimensions: *market attractiveness,* and the firm's *competitive position.* In international markets, market attractiveness is a function, not only of the specific industry, product business, or market segment, but also of the region or country in which the business or product line is located. Consequently, macroenvironmental indicators relating to the business climate in the region or country should be included. The specific criteria used will, however, depend on the unit and level of analysis, and the individual firm.

In addition, it is important to assess the interdependence or interconnectedness of the various portfolio units across countries or regions. Markets may be interdependent insofar as a customer may have branches in one or more countries, or a key competitor in one market may also be present in another. Similarly, two product businesses may use a common raw material and buy from the same supplier, or the product lines may share the same distribution network.

Market Attractiveness

The criteria used to assess market attractiveness depend on the composition of the portfolio and the level of analysis. Where the portfolio units relate to a specific geographic area, that is, regions or countries, macroeconomic indicators relating to the general economic, political, or technological environment in a country or region should be included. Similarly, depending on the level of business analysis, that is, SBU, product line, or target segment, indicators relating to the product business, product line, or segment, such as its size, rate of growth, or level of competition, should be included. Where the portfolio units include components of the value chain (R&D, production, and distribution) then relevant criteria include capital and operating costs, importance to success or competitiveness in the industry (see Table 13.2).

The specific criteria used to assess market attractiveness, and the relative importance of each factor need to be determined by management, depending on industry and company characteristics as well as the specific portfolio and level of analysis. For example, in assessing the attractiveness of different country markets for its tractor business, Ford used four indicators: (1) the size of the tractor market in units, (2) the rate of market growth, (3) government regulation, and (4) economic and political stability. The degree of government regulation was determined by the level of price control, homologation or product standards,

TABLE 13-2

ILLUSTRATIVE INDICATORS FOR ASSESSING MARKET ATTRACTIVENESS

MACROECONOMIC INDICATORS

- GNP per capita
- GNP growth
- Population size
- Political stability
- Economic stability
- Tariffs or quotas
- Government regulation

PRODUCT BUSINESS OR PRODUCT LINE

- Market size (sales volume or number of units)
- Market growth
- Product ownership
- Customer concentration
- Number or size of competitors
- Profit margins

INVOLVEMENT IN THE VALUE CHAIN

- Existence of patent protection
- R&D costs
- Importance of service
- Investment intensity
- Key industry success factors
- Availability or efficiency of external suppliers

and local content or compensatory export requirements. Economic and political stability were assessed on the basis of the rate of inflation, the trade balance, and expert ratings of political stability. The scales used to assess each of these indicators are shown in Table 13.3.

Competitive Position

The second key dimension for evaluating a portfolio is the firm's competitive position in the specific geographic region, product business, market segment, or business function. Again, as in assessing market attractiveness, the specific criteria used to assess competitive position will vary depending on the composition of the portfolio and level of analysis. Some illustrative examples of the types of criteria that might be used to assess competitive position for different types of portfolios are shown in Table 13.4. For example, Ford assessed the competitive strength of its tractor business based on four criteria: (1) market share, in terms of percentage of market, as well as market rank; (2) product fit with local market characteristics; (3) contribution margin based on profit per unit, and profit percentage of net dealer cost; and (4) market representation, assessed by the quality of dealer support, and the level of advertising and promotional effort (Table 13.3.)

A key element in assessing the firm's competitive position at the corporate level is the firm's position, rate of growth, and presence in the marketplace. Relevant indicators might include, not only sales volume and assets relative to other firms in the industry worldwide, by region or country, but also involvement in different businesses, including the degree of vertical integration and business diversification, or strength in different industrial sectors. At the regional level, the extent of geographic coverage and presence in multiple country markets is also an important consideration, especially where markets are becoming increasingly integrated.

Competitive strength in various business functions and at different stages in the value chain such as R&D, production, management, marketing, and distribution might also be considered, especially relative to a function which is key to success in the industry. Strength in R&D could be assessed in terms of relative investment in R&D, number of patents, rate of new product introduction, or process innovation, for example. Similarly, production strength might be assessed based on relative production costs and efficiency, capacity utilization, access to raw materials, or rating on total quality management. Marketing strength might be assessed based on promotional and mass merchandising skills, strength and scope of the distribution network, size and experience of the sales force, and level of service provided.

Intangible assets such as corporate, product, or brand image, the impact of country of origin, and distributor or customer loyalty are also important factors impacting competitive position. Depending on the level of analysis, these need to be assessed relative to the specific product business, product line, or market segment as well as the company as a whole.

TABLE 13-3   VALUES USED TO DETERMINE COUNTRY ATTRACTIVENESS AND COMPETITIVE STRENGTH.

COUNTRY ATTRACTIVENESS SCALE WEIGHTS

1) *Market size*

Units	Rating
25,000	10
22,500–24,999	9
20,000–22,499	8
⋅ ⋅ ⋅	
5,000	1

2) *Market growth*

Amount	Rating
5% +	10
4%–4.9	9
3%–3.9	8
⋅ ⋅ ⋅	
Under 3%	1

3) *Government regulation*

a) *Price control*

Type	Rating
None	10
Easy to comply	6
Moderately easy to comply	4
Rigid controls	2

b) *Homologation*

Type	Rating
None	10
Easy	6
Moderate	4
Tough	2

c) *Local content/compensatory exports*

Type	Rating
None	10
Easy to comply	6
Moderately easy to comply	4
Tough	2

4) *Economic and political stability*

a) *Inflation*

Amount	Rating
7% and under	10
⋅ ⋅	
40% and over	1

b) *Trade balance*

Amount	Rating
5% and over	10
0–4.9%	9
– 5–0%	8
⋅ ⋅ ⋅	
–36%	1

c) *Political stability*

Type	Rating
Stable market	10
Moderate	5
Unstable	1

Note: These measurements are indicative of what might be done, rather than concrete examples.

COMPETITIVE STRENGTH WEIGHTS

1) *Market share*

a) *Percentage of market*

Share	Rating
30+	10
27–21	9
⋅ ⋅ ⋅	
4	1

b) *Position*

Rank	Rating
1	10
2	8
3	6
4	4
5	2

2) *Product fit*

Because this scale suggests Ford's competitive product strategy, we decided not to publish it. In general, a 10-point subjective index was created to match product characteristics with key local product needs.

3) *Contribution margin*

Again, this is proprietary, but it reflects two factors.

a) *Profit per unit*

Amount	Rating
$5,000 (example)	10
⋅ ⋅	
$1–400	1

b) *Profit percentage of net dealer cost*

Amount	Rating
40% +	10
⋅ ⋅	
5% –	1

4) *Market support*

a) *Market representation*

Evaluation	Rating
Quantity and quality of Ford distributors and service are clearly "best in country"	10
Ford representation is equal to leading competitor's	8
Ford representation is behind several leading competitors'	2

b) *Market support*

Evaluation	Rating
Ford market support in advertising promotion is clearly "best in country"	10
Ford lead support is equal to leading competitor's	8
Ford support is behind several leading competitors'	2

Note: These measures are indicative of what might be done, rather than concrete examples.
Source: Gilbert Harrell and Richard Kiefer "Multinational Strategic Marker Portfolios," *MSU Business Topics* (Winter, 1981) pp. 5–15

ILLUSTRATIVE INDICATORS FOR ASSESSING COMPETITIVE POSITION

MARKET STRENGTH

- Sales volume
- Market share by industry, product business, or product line
- Market share growth by industry, product business, or product line
- Rank in industry
- Gross/net profits
- Capital assets

MARKET PRESENCE AND COVERAGE

- Geographic market coverage
- Presence in key markets
- Degree of vertical integration

INNOVATIVENESS

- Investment in R&D
- Number of patents
- New product introduction

MANAGEMENT SKILLS

- Production costs and efficiency
- Management expertise
- Marketing skills
- TQM rating
- Strength of the distribution network

LOYALTY AND IMAGE

- Customer loyalty
- Distributor loyalty
- Customer satisfaction
- Corporate image
- Brand strength

Assessing Interconnectedness of Portfolio Units

In addition to assessing each portfolio based on market attractiveness and competitive position, the interconnectedness of portfolio units on these two dimensions needs to be considered. This analysis affects decisions with regard to how portfolio units should be configured, as well as resource allocation and investment or divestment decisions. If, for example, geographic portfolio units, such as two or more countries, are closely interlinked, they might be regrouped as a single unit. Equally, if two countries or product businesses are closely interlinked, a decision to invest or divest one will affect operations in the other. In examining the interconnectedness of portfolio units, management needs to consider two different aspects: the extent to which geographic markets are interlinked, that is, across countries or regions; and the extent to which product businesses or product lines are inter-related.

INTERCONNECTEDNESS OF GEOGRAPHIC MARKETS

As noted earlier in Chapter 7, demand patterns in many industrial markets as well as some consumer markets such as consumer electronics, footwear, and cosmetics are becoming more similar, especially in countries in close proximity. Market segments with similar needs and interests, such as business executives, young adults, or the environmentally conscious, can increasingly be identified in many consumer markets worldwide. The interconnectedness of demand patterns can be assessed based on indicators, such as the similarity of customer behavior patterns, desired benefits, and market segments from one country or geographic region. In industrial markets, presence of the same customer and competitors in different countries or regions could be examined. Where markets appear highly interconnected or similar based on such indicators, portfolio units can be defined on a global or regional basis rather than on a country basis.

Linkages in the market infrastructure between countries and regions have also developed rapidly in recent years, facilitating market integration.[9] These include linkages in the physical transportation infrastructure, as well as the growth of pan-regional and global media and organizational networks of service organizations and distributors. These facilitate implementing strategy on a global or regional basis. Some illustrative indicators for assessing the existence of such interlinkages are shown in Table 13.5.

INTERCONNECTEDNESS OF PRODUCT BUSINESS UNITS

In addition to assessing the interconnectedness of geographic units, the interconnectedness of product businesses and product lines should also be assessed. This is important insofar as investment in, or allocation of, resources to one product business or line will affect other interconnected businesses. Equally, opportunities for potential economies of scope through shared facilities and physical assets, shared experience and knowledge, and shared external relations may be identified.[10]

The interconnectedness of product businesses may be assessed based on the existence of common customers or market segments. Different product businesses may purchase raw materials, components, or services such as information system equipment, from the same supplier. Product businesses or lines may benefit from a strong corporate image, as for example, Kodak or IBM, or family branding. Equally, product businesses may utilize common production facilities or production engineering know-how in such product markets as trucks and automobiles. Similarly, R&D and process technology may benefit multiple product businesses. Businesses or product lines may also share a common sales force and the same distribution facilities. Some illustrative indicators of product business interconnectedness are shown in Table 13.5.

Assessing the interconnectedness of geographic market areas and product businesses is an important step in determining the appropriate configuration of portfolio units and balance of the portfolio. Particularly as markets become increasingly interlinked and integrated worldwide, management should consider how far competitive position in one market or product business affects that in

| TABLE 13-5 | SAMPLE INDICATORS FOR ASSESSING THE INTERCONNECTEDNESS OF PORTFOLIO UNITS |

GEOGRAPHIC MARKET INTERCONNECTEDNESS

- Similarity of customers/customer segments
- Presence of same customer
- Presence of same competitors
- Geographic proximity
- Media overspill
- Pan-regional, global media
- Common distributor/retailer
- Network of service organizations

PRODUCT BUSINESS/LINE INTERCONNECTEDNESS

- Same customers
- Family branding/corporate name
- Common production facilities
- Common suppliers
- Shared R&D expenditure
- Shared warehousing facilities
- Shared marketing expenditure
- Common salesforce
- Shared distribution facilities

another, and how easily operations in one geographic area or product business can be extended to tap other attractive markets.

REBALANCING THE PORTFOLIO

Once the firm's portfolios have been assessed at different levels, based on market attractiveness, competitiveness, and interconnectedness, the next step is to decide whether the firm's current portfolio of countries, product businesses, market segments, and involvement in the value chain is likely to realize corporate objectives. In particular, it is important to determine whether the portfolio charts the desired direction for future expansion, and whether resources are appropriately allocated among portfolio units so as to achieve desired objectives.

Portfolio analysis can be helpful in a number of ways. In the first place, it can aid in determining how to allocate resources within the existing portfolio. As in domestic markets, examination of the balance of the portfolio can suggest which units require investment and which should be harvested. Assessment of the interconnectedness of markets and product businesses can provide insights for improving efficiency through reconfiguring or combining portfolio units, or improving coordination between portfolio units. Secondly, assessment of the dynamics of the firm's portfolio can suggest directions for future growth and expansion within the existing geographic boundaries of the portfolio, or into new geographic areas. Finally, portfolio analysis can pinpoint candidates for divestment, poorly performing businesses or product lines, or operations in high-risk countries or areas.

Reallocating Resources Within the Portfolio

Examination of the firm's portfolios can help in establishing investment priorities relative to regions, countries, and product businesses, product lines, market segments, and businesses operations. As in domestic portfolio analysis, resources should be channeled to more attractive, high-growth businesses and markets, especially where the firm's competitive position needs strengthening. Businesses or operations in mature markets or market segments should be maintained or harvested. In some cases, they may become candidates for divestment.

At the corporate level, the firm should consider whether its portfolio of businesses provides the desired engine for growth. For example, Reuters, the London-based news and financial information services company, has shifted its emphasis from media and financial information products to the more rapidly growing transactions product markets. This includes hardware such as electronic trading terminals, as well as trading systems and screen-based brokerage services.[11] This type of assessment can be made at a global or regional level, or in relation to key countries. Management can then assess the geographic balance of the portfolio and determine whether investment in certain geographic areas should be increased or, alternatively, harvested. For example, VW has a strong position in a number of Latin American markets such as Brazil (36 percent market share) and Argentina (20 percent market share) as well as Mexico, but these countries do not have high priority for investment as they have less strategic importance for Volkswagen than Eastern Europe and the former East Germany.[12]

Firms may also decide to shift emphasis from one business to another in a given country or region due to barriers to entry or entrenched competition. For example, in Europe, AT&T has shifted its efforts away from telecommunications equipment sales into services.[13] Attracted by the opening up of the huge telecommunications market in Europe, AT&T initially attempted to sell public switching equipment. Blocked by government preference for local suppliers and strong European competition such as Ericsson, Siemens, and Alcatel, AT&T decided to move into the more lucrative and expanding market for cutting-edge services.

Similar types of assessments can be made at the product business or product line level to determine investment priorities across different product lines and market segments. Again, this assessment can be made at a global or regional level to determine whether the same lines or market segments should be an investment priority worldwide, or in relation to certain markets or geographic areas.

Portfolio analysis can also be helpful in making decisions relating to the mode of operation,[8] as shown in Figure 13.4b. For example, where a company's position in a product business is relatively weak in a less attractive or small country market, management might decide to sell out or license operations to a local company. If its position were weak but the market attractive, entering into a joint venture or other type of alliance with a local partner to provide knowledge, local contacts, and distribution facilities might help to strengthen its position. If, on the other hand, its competitive position were quite strong, the company might prefer to support and reinforce wholly owned operations in order to ensure control over the management and direction of operations.

Reconfiguring the Portfolio

In addition to establishing guidelines for resource allocation to individual portfolio units, portfolio analysis can also provide insights for reconfiguring portfolio units based on their interconnectedness. For example, the firm might group country units or product lines or businesses targeted to the same customer segments operations within a region, or worldwide. Analyzing the interconnectedness of country or regional markets and product businesses can also suggest how to improve coordination or integration of operations across countries or regions, or across product businesses or product lines at different stages of the value chain. Where product businesses share common high-technology R&D relating to chips or biotechnology, opportunities may exist for consolidating R&D activities either within a region or worldwide.

Equally, examination of interconnectedness across markets may suggest opportunities for improving efficiency through standardizing product lines, brands, and marketing programs across countries. For example, with European market integration, Jacob Suchard, the Swiss chocolate firm, acquired by Philip Morris, decided to restructure operations throughout Europe. Key European accounts for its chocolate lines were handled in a coordinated fashion and quoted a uniform price for a particular line, rather than being quoted different prices by each national subsidiary. Manufacturing was consolidated in six core centers within the European Union, and uniform packing materials, labelling techniques, and production methods adopted, in order to establish a consistent look for their products. At the same time, Suchard moved to transform its stable of predominantly local brands to pan-European brands to strengthen their image.[14]

Improved coordination and standardization of marketing activities across countries facilitates integration and reconfiguration of operations upstream, for example production, R&D and sourcing. Managing interdependence across country markets, and the implications for integrating and reconfiguring operations, are a central theme of Chapter 15.

EXPANDING AND EXTENDING THE PORTFOLIO

Examination of a portfolio also aids in assessing market expansion options. Expansion of the portfolio can take place in either of two directions: within the existing geographic scope, or by extending its geographic scope, entering new countries and regions. Through expansion within the existing geographic scope, the portfolio can focus on targeting new market segments, extending the product line, moving into new product businesses, or adding operations at a given phase of the value chain. Extension of the geographic scope of the portfolio, on the other hand, takes the form of entry into new country markets or regions, with the same or modified product lines, or targeting the same segments worldwide.

Expansion Within Existing Geographic Areas

Examination of the firm's portfolio in different regions or worldwide may suggest opportunities for expansion by targeting new segments or adding product businesses within a given regional or country market. Especially if the business is related to the firm's core business and can be targeted through the same distribution channels, or utilizes the same sales force or the same technology, synergies can be achieved. For example, Reuters has not only moved into multimedia and expanded its transactions products business, but also has acquired VAMP Health to provide computer services to doctors in Britain. VAMP links doctors to hospitals and labs and provides on-line information on lab tests, patient records, and other medical data bases.[15] The business utilizes the same technology as its core financial information services businesses, tapping a new and potentially vast market in health care.

Concern to balance the portfolio may also suggest directions for a portfolio expansion. Especially where the portfolio consists primarily of businesses or products in mature or declining industries; management may want to consider adding or acquiring businesses or products in growth markets to fuel future growth. For example, tobacco companies such as Philip Morris and R.J. Reynolds have been acquiring food businesses such as General Foods, Kraft, and Nabisco, which have higher growth rates in world markets than tobacco. Similarly, P&G and Unilever have both acquired perfume and cosmetic businesses, which share similar skills in marketing and merchandising with their core businesses in household detergents, and have higher rates of growth and margins in world markets. Unilever, for example, acquired Fabergé and Elizabeth Arden,[16] while P&G acquired Cover Girl, Noxell and Max Factor.[17]

Portfolio analysis might also suggest the need for extension into additional stages of the value chain. Examination of a product business with a poor competitive rating may reveal that this is due to poor performance related to some aspect of operations that is contracted out, such as distribution, after-sales service and maintenance, or components production. Hence, management may consider taking over this function in order to exercise greater control and improve its competitive position.

Expanding Into New Geographic Areas

A second direction for expansion is to extend existing product businesses and marketing operations into new geographic areas, or develop new product businesses in new country markets. As more and more markets are opening up worldwide, and communications and linkages between markets are developing, geographic expansion offers increasingly attractive growth opportunities.

Examination of a portfolio, for example, may reveal concentration in mature country markets, or regions of the world with few or no high-growth markets. In this case, management should begin to invest in new rapidly growing markets in order to ensure continued growth. As noted in Chapter 12, GE has invested over a billion dollars in operations in China, India, and Mexico, which it regards as key markets of the future. Similarly, Philip Morris and RJR are moving aggressively into Eastern Europe and Russia. Faced by the growing antismoking lobby and restrictions on advertising in the United States and the European Union, the tobacco companies are tapping into new markets in the former Soviet Union and Eastern Europe created by pent-up demand and tough economic conditions. Previously, both companies' business was limited to hard-currency tourist stores and the power elite. As mass markets are opening up, both Philip Morris and RJR are moving to exploit these opportunities. Market potential is vast. The cigarette market in the Soviet Union is estimated at 430 billion cigarettes a year, and that in Eastern Europe at 270 billion. Philip Morris has invested in tobacco companies in Hungary, the Czech Republic, Lithuania, Russia, and Kazakhstan, while RJR has invested in plants in Hungary, Poland, the Ukraine, and Russia.[18]

Developing new product businesses in new country markets provides the most radical expansion option. If opportunities for extending existing product businesses in other geographic areas are not attractive, then management may prefer to develop new product businesses that utilize the firm's core competence and specific skills, for example, in R&D, production, or marketing. Heinz, for example, has a range of different product businesses in different parts of the world, including ketchup, Weight Watchers, baby food, pet foods, and canned fish. In Italy, since opportunities for canned food are limited, Heinz has acquired and expanded two confectionery businesses and has extended market position by launching new niche products such as Bi-Aghut, gluten-free pasta, Aproteu brand low-protein foods, and Nesura sugar-free candy. In Australia, Heinz has launched a new product category, Kids Cuisine, canned meals for young children, which has proved highly successful. In China, on the other hand, its most important product business is rice-based baby food.[19] Involvement in these different product businesses provides a geographically diversified portfolio, with strong competitive positions in many regions throughout the world. At the same time, these product businesses are all in the food and drink category, and share common emphasis on marketing and mass-merchandising skills.

PORTFOLIO RETRACTION

Parallel to the issue of portfolio expansion is that of portfolio retraction. Following assessment of its portfolio, management might decide to drop a specific product line, divest a product business in one country or worldwide, or discontinue operations or performance of selected business operations in a country or region. Portfolio units with poor competitive positions in less attractive markets are likely to be prime candidates for divestment.

If a product business or specific product line is not successful in international markets, management may decide to divest the business worldwide, or in certain regions, or alternatively drop product lines that are not successful or well adapted to specific markets. For example, American Can decided to divest its can production business worldwide and focus on financial services, changing its name to Primamerica. Similarly, Benetton decided to divest its interests in financial services—banks, insurance, and fund management, to focus on its core business in casual clothing and sportswear.[20]

Companies may also decide to discontinue operations in specific countries or regions of the world. In some cases, this may be prompted by increased political or financial risk, or government regulation of foreign businesses. For example, both IBM and Coca-Cola withdrew from India because they could not accept restrictions placed on product development and pricing and requirements of local equity participation. IBM subsequently returned, establishing a joint venture with Tata, and Coca-Cola did as well through a joint venture with the Parle group. Economic decline or instability, high rates of inflation, threats of insurgency, or growth of local competition may also trigger divestment decisions.

In other cases, divestment may be prompted by low profitability due to aggressive competition, product regulation, price controls, or decline in demand. A number of drug companies, including Hoffman La Roche, GD Searle, and Merck have, for example, withdrawn from the Indian market. In 1993, Hoffman La Roche, decided to divest its stake in Roche Products, a joint venture with an Indian firm, Piramal Enterprises. Roche Products will continue production of Hoffman La Roche drugs under license. Profits from the joint venture were declining, in large measure because its main product, Vitamin B, was subject to price control. In addition, the company has not introduced any new products for some time, as patent protection is limited and allows Indian firms to produce cheaper versions of new drugs.[21]

In evaluating divestment alternatives, it is important to take into consideration the impact on other portfolio units. Divestment of a product business in one country may result in loss of economies of scale or opportunities for shared marketing costs, or be detrimental to brand or product image. Equally, withdrawal from operations in a country or region can have a negative impact on corporate image and generate hostile reactions from governments, trade unions, distributors, or the general public.

Such barriers to exit have thus to be considered in divestment decisions. Costs and difficulties associated with liquidating assets and terminating labor and management contracts, as well as contracts with distribution or other external organizations, all need to be weighed. In some countries, severe restrictions are placed on the termination of employment or distribution contracts.

While each of these types of portfolio options, reallocation, expansion, and retraction, has been discussed independently, they should be examined interactively, as suggested in Figure 13.4. Retraction in one dimension—product line, country, or business activity—should be weighed relative to opportunities for expansion in another direction and in turn trigger consideration of reallocation of resources within the restructured portfolio. In essence, therefore, the array of portfolio options consists of all possible combinations of the expansion, retraction, and reallocation options.

SUMMARY

The task of charting direction in global markets is a complex one. Firms in the third phase of international market development are already committed to global markets. The challenge they face is how to allocate their resources—time, money, and effort—to market opportunities that will maximize returns in the long run. In choosing among competing market opportunities, a portfolio approach is particularly helpful.

Applying portfolio analysis to global markets is not as straightforward as it is in a single domestic market. In addition to determining the appropriate level of analysis (corporate, strategic business unit, or product line), the firm must also assess different geographic markets and varying degrees of involvement in each market. Evaluating the portfolio takes place along two primary dimensions. First, market attractiveness must be assessed in terms of its value to the firm as well as the involvement required to realize that value. Second, the firm must assess its competitive position relative to the competition it faces in each market. In addition, the firm should assess the degree of interdependence of markets and businesses. The added complexity caused by the interdependence of markets means that actions in one market may have repercussions in others.

The evaluation of the portfolio provides the basis for achieving the desired balance between growth and maturity as well as concentration versus diversification. With these objectives firmly in mind, the task of reallocating resources within the portfolio can be performed. This is guided by the overarching goal of achieving better integration and coordination of portfolio units. Within that objective, the firm must reallocate resources and determine the appropriate mode of operation in different markets. Finally, directions for growth or consolidation must be determined as the firm decides whether to expand, extend, or retract the portfolio.

REFERENCES

1. "Daewoo Group Shifts its Focus to Markets in the Third World" (1993) *The New York Times,* October 11, A7.
2. "Daewoo Motor Drives into Untapped Markets" (1994) *Financial Times,* February 2.
3. Day, George S. (1977) "Diagnosing the Product Portfolio," *Journal of Marketing,* 41, April, pp. 29–38.
4. Wind, Yoram, and V.J. Mahajan (1981) "Designing Product and Business Portfolios," *Harvard Business Review,* 59, January-February, pp. 155–165.
5. Buzzell, Robert D., and Bradley T. Gale (1987) *The PIMS Principles: Linking*

Strategy to Performance, New York: The Free Press.

6. Larréché, Jean-Claude (1978) "The International Product Market Portfolio," In: Subhash Jain, ed. *Research Frontiers in Marketing: Dialogues and Directions,* Chicago: American Marketing Association, pp. 276–281.

7. "We Got the Achtung, Baby" (1993) *Brandweek,* January 18, pp. 23–26.

8. Harrell, Gilbert D., and Richard Kiefer (1981) "Multinational Strategic Market Portfolios," *MSU Business Topics,* Winter, pp. 5–15.

9. Douglas, Susan P., and C. Samuel Craig (1991) "Spatial Dimensions of International Markets" In: Charles Ingene and Avijit Ghosh eds. *Research in Marketing,* Suppl. 5, Greenwich, CT: JAI Press.

10. Teece, David J. (1980) "Economies of Scope and the Scope of Enterprise," *Journal of Economic Behavior and Organization,* 1, pp. 233–247.

11. Reuters (1993) *Annual Report.*

12. Birkinshaw, Julian, and Warren Ritchie (1993) "Balancing the Global Portfolio," *Business Quarterly,* Summer, pp. 40–45.

13. "AT&T is No Smooth Operator in Europe" (1994) *Business Week,* April 11, p. 48.

14. "Sweet Stuff" (1989) *International Management,* September, pp. 32–36.

15. "Reuters Dives In—All the Way" (1994) *Business Week,* February 21, pp. 46–47.

16. "Unilever is All Made Up with Everywhere to Go" (1989) *Business Week,* July 31, p. 33.

17. "Procter and Gamble is Following its Nose" (1991) *Business Week,* April 22, p. 28.

18. "Opiate of the Masses" (1994) *Forbes,* April 11, pp. 74–75.

19. Heinz (1990) *Annual Report.*

20. "Benetton Strips Back Down to Sportswear" (1990) *Business Week,* March 5, p. 42.

21. "Wait and Then What?" (1994) *Business Asia,* January 3, pp. 6–7.

CHAPTER 14

DEVELOPING GLOBAL COMPETITIVE STRATEGY

INTRODUCTION

Once the corporate portfolio has been analyzed at different levels in the organization and directions for global expansion have been charted, management should begin to develop competitive marketing strategies. Such strategies translate the firm's strategic thrust into action and enable it to compete effectively in the global market place.

CPC International is aggressively expanding its presence in global markets. Guiding this expansion is a corporate philosophy of "great leading brands, worldwide coverage, global strategies that work, experienced local management and financial strength."[1] As a diversified food company it is engaged in a variety of different businesses in 51 countries throughout the world. For each geographic region, it has slightly different strategies, but there are common themes that run throughout its globalization—introduction of new products, acquisition of products and brands, joint ventures, development of existing brand franchises geographically and to new segments, and realigning manufacturing for maximum efficiency.

In North America, CPC has identified a number of important growth areas. First, it plans to add products that meet consumer preferences for light and cholesterol-free products. This is particularly important in the mayonnaise business, where its Hellmann's and Best Foods brands account for almost 50 percent of the market and are not growing. In January 1993 both brands introduced reduced fat mayonnaise (1/3 the fat of regular mayonnaise). Second, CPC plans to acquire products that fit with its core business. Third, it plans to expand existing brand franchises, notably Knorr and its extensive line of baked goods (Thomas's and Arnold).

In Europe, where CPC has operations in 18 countries, it is responding to the opportunities created by the unification of Western Europe and the opening up of Eastern Europe. It is beginning to extend successful brands and products from one national market to another. For example, Heidelberg salad dressings, which are sourced from Denmark, were introduced in Greece, Ireland, Portugal, and Spain. The Knorr brand (sauces, soups, and boullions) has provided a vehicle to translate product concepts and marketing skills from one country to another. The changes in the European market are also forcing CPC to realign manufacturing to increase its efficiency and competitiveness. It is also extending the geographic scope of its traditional brand franchises into Southern Europe.

CPC's acquisition activity focuses on products and brands that have good potential for internationalization. To accelerate its expansion into Eastern Europe, it has acquired a majority stake in Zabreh, in the Czech Republic, and Amino S.A. in Poland. Both acquisitions fit with CPC's core businesses, as Zabreh makes mayonnaise and tartar sauce, and Amino makes dehydrated soups, bouillons, desserts, pasta, and seasoning. At the same time these acquisitions will facilitate expansion of the Knorr line, which is already being imported into the former Czechoslovakia from Austria and into Poland from Germany.

The European division is also responsible for Africa and the Middle East. The acquisition of a majority interest on TAMI (Israel) provides a platform to expand existing operations in Kenya, Morocco, Saudi Arabia, Tunisia, and Turkey. Again, TAMI fits with CPC's core businesses and has number one brands in soups, sauces, mayonnaise, and desserts.

Latin America is a market where CPC has been for over 60 years. Brazil, Argentina, Mexico, and Colombia form the core of the 15 markets offering the largest growth and market potential. In addition to introducing new product and extending brands that are already successful in these markets, CPC is seeking ways to segment the massive corn starch market. For example, corn starch is sold as Argo in North America; Maizena in North America, Latin America, and Europe; Brown & Polson in Asia and Europe; and Kingsford in North America and Asia. To strengthen its position in Brazil, CPC acquired the Vitamillo business, a precooked corn flour, which complements CPC's existing Maizena, Cremogema, and Arrozina brands.

The Asian market represents a variety of different modes of operation. CPC has joint ventures in seven markets (Hong Kong, Korea, Malaysia, the Philippines, Singapore, Taiwan, and Thailand), a licensing and trademark agreement in Japan, and a presence in India, Indonesia, and Pakistan. In marketing the Knorr line, CPC has been guided by "the concept of 'chefmanship'—the contribution of flavor to basic foods, always consistent with local taste preferences."[1] This has led to Knorr Tom Yam paste for traditional Thai recipes in Malaysia, and Lady's Choice sweet and spicy spaghetti sauce in the Philippines. CPC has also been successful in introducing western-type products into Asia, such as Skippy peanut butter and Lady's Choice mayonnaise.

As CPC's globalization activities illustrate, a good strategy should leverage the firm's core competencies on a global basis, and at the same time achieve potential synergies between specific product businesses and activities in different parts of the world. Further, the key thrust of the firm's global marketing strategy has to be determined in terms of target markets and customers, as well as how resources are mobilized to tap these markets.

CONFIGURING GLOBAL MARKETS

The first step in developing global marketing strategy is to determine the spatial configuration of its target market. Management must first identify firm-specific parameters for global strategy development. The geographic market scope of each product business has to be clearly defined, based on corporate portfolio analysis. Next, the configuration of target market segments has to be identified, and the firm's strategic capabilities and potential operational synergies assessed in a global context. (See Figure 14-1.)

Determining Geographic Market Scope

In the phase of local market expansion, the basic geographic planning unit is typically the country. As linkages between country markets strengthen, and management aims to improve efficiency through greater coordination across country markets, the degree of market integration and interconnectedness across countries and geographic areas needs to be assessed, and geographic units redefined, to reflect these forces.

In general, four types of geographic market areas can be identified: (1) countries, (2) clusters of countries, (3) regions, and (4) global market areas. (See Figure 14-2). The degree of market interconnectedness and integration can be

FIGURE 14-1
Global competitive strategy.

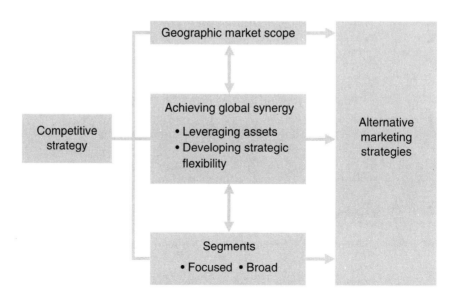

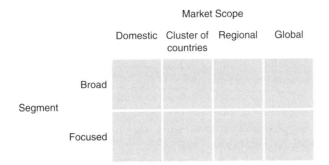

FIGURE 14-2

Configuring target segments.

assessed in terms of the similarity and interconnectedness of demand patterns—that is, the presence of the same customers and of the same competitors. Linkages in organizational, logistics, and communications networks, for example distributor organizations, advertising agencies, physical transportation, and communication systems, and the availability of pan-regional media, all need to be considered.[2] At the same time, the absence of trade barriers facilitates market integration and connectedness.

Country. The country provides an appropriate planning unit, where its market is large, sufficiently different, and isolated from other countries to warrant the establishment of a separate sales and marketing organization. Countries such as Japan, India, China, and to a lesser extent Brazil often fall into this category. In some cases, such countries provide the nexus for marketing and expansion to other neighboring countries. For example, India is used by many pharmaceutical companies such as Pfizer and Ciba-Geigy as a base for exporting to Sri Lanka, Pakistan, Malaysia, and, in some cases, the Gulf States.

Clusters of countries. Where a number of countries are in close proximity, have similar demand patterns, and are too small to provide viable units alone, it may be effective to consolidate marketing operations for these countries. The Scandinavian countries, Spain and Portugal, and Middle Eastern markets tend to form natural market areas of this type for many products.

Similarly, several groups of Latin American countries, such as Colombia, Venezuela, Ecuador, Chile, and Argentina, are beginning to form market areas of this type. Although not fully integrated, demand patterns are similar, and economic and organizational links are developing between these countries.[3]

Region. In some instances, a region is the appropriate geographic market unit. In many areas of the world, such as North America, the EU, Southeast Asia, and Latin America, the movement towards the development of regional trading blocs, and trade agreements to remove barriers and harmonize government regulation—create forces integrating markets. Consequently, even if markets are not fully integrated and there are differences in demand and competition within the region, it may provide an appropriate planning unit. Sony, for example, has established a regional headquarters in Frankfurt, Germany, to plan and coordinate strategy throughout the EU.

Global. In some instances, the relevant market area is global. Where there are relatively few customers worldwide and few suppliers, as, for example, in aerospace or semiconductors, the market is likely to be globally integrated. Some other industries such as fiber optics are moving towards this pattern, but as yet the number is limited.

Geographic market patterns are not necessarily symmetric across product businesses in diversified companies. For example, Unilever has a packaged foods business as well as detergents and chemicals. Market areas are considerably more fragmented and planning more decentralized for packaged foods than for chemicals, and to a lesser extent detergents.[4]

Equally, the appropriate market or planning area may vary for different types of operations. For example, R&D is more likely to be planned at a global level than marketing. Automobile manufacturers such as Ford and GM coordinate production logistics at a global level but plan distribution and sales at the country level.

Configuring Target Segments

Another important step in developing global marketing strategy is to identify target segments and their geographic configuration. Just as market areas are becoming increasingly interconnected, increasing mobility and communication across national boundaries creates opportunities for transnational segmentation. In addition, the breadth of the served market has to be determined. The firm may adopt a broad-line strategy, for example, targeting all segments, or alternatively focus on a specific market niche. This structure is outlined in Figure 14-3.

CONSUMER MARKET SEGMENTATION

In assessing opportunities for transnational segmentation in consumer markets, two types of market linkages, or potential transnational segments, need to be considered. In the first place, increasing communication and interaction across national market boundaries fosters the development of similar interests and response patterns among similar segments in different parts of the world. For example, clothing and footgear fashions, and popular music hits, are highly similar in the youth market around the world. Teens throughout the world spend money on Reebok and Nike sport shoes, Sega and Nintendo videogames, Levi's and Deisel jeans, and Doc Martens and Timberland footware.[5]

Secondly, consumers who travel across national boundaries look for their favorite brands of cigarettes, soft drinks, razor blades, or film. Business travellers often stay in the same hotel chain and use the same car rental agency—especially if they have corporate discounts or can gain frequent flier mileage. Such behavior patterns form the basis for transnational segmentation.

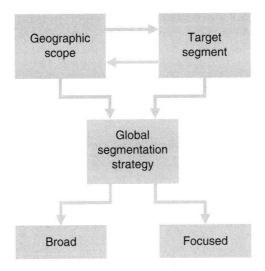

FIGURE 14-3

Configuring global markets.

While both types of behavior lead to opportunities for transnational segmentation, they are somewhat different in character. In the first case, similar subgroups are most likely to lead to a global focused segment strategy focusing on needs of a specific subgroup worldwide. Often, such customers are found primarily in major urban areas and capital cities in developing or emerging countries, resulting in a global linking or network of customer segments. In the case of the mobile customer, however, the products and services are often widely distributed or available in the customer's country of origin. Hence, targeting such customers may provide the basis for expansion into new country markets and developing a broader geographic scope. This strategy has been a key factor fuelling the international expansion of both Hertz and Avis.

Neither type of segmentation is necessarily global in scope. In some cases, transnational segments may be regional (Latin American or European) or focus on the Industrial Triad, depending on the nature of the product or service.

ORGANIZATIONAL MARKET SEGMENTATION

Similar patterns can also be identified in organizational markets. Here, the trend to market interconnectedness is often stronger, due to the growth in international operations of firms in many of these industries. Such firms both impact the behavior of local competitors and are themselves potential global or regional customers.

As more and more firms expand their international operations, ideas for and awareness of new and different production processes and technology; of alternative sources for new materials, parts, and components; and of availability of new equipment and machinery will spread. At the same time, as competition begins to take place on a global level, firms have to keep pace with their competitors in cost efficiency and innovation.

As a result, organizational markets can often be segmented across countries on a similar transnational basis to consumer markets. For example, customers in specialty niche markets such as medical equipment, valves, and precision instruments often have similar needs, interests, and service requirements worldwide and also organize purchasing similarly, as compared with businesses that operate on a larger scale. Volume is often low, margins high, and precision work important. Consequently, they can be targeted on a worldwide basis.

Amertek, a precision instrument manufacturer in Pittsburgh, for example, sells specialty gas-detecting machines to businesses worldwide, and has plants in Italy, Germany, and Denmark. Medtronic, a Minneapolis manufacturer of pacemakers, has developed new technology in micromachining for worldwide markets.[6]

Another type of global segment in organizational markets consists of companies with networks of operations worldwide. For example, international banks, and other financial institutions, need to ensure that information systems equipment and software in different offices or branches throughout the world are compatible, to allow for rapid and efficient data transfer. Consequently, contracts for such equipment are typically negotiated centrally with a single supplier, who then ships and fills orders placed by local subsidiaries in accordance with these terms. Similarly, companies with global operations may negotiate insurance contracts centrally to cover their operations worldwide.

ACHIEVING GLOBAL SYNERGIES

Having determined target markets and their spatial configuration, the firm then has to establish its competitive advantage in those markets. The firm should aim to leverage assets and position in global markets, while at the same time building operational flexibility to respond to changes in market conditions in different parts of the world (see Figure 14-4).

In the initial phase of entry into international markets, the firm emphasizes leveraging assets so as to achieve potential economies of scale in production, R&D, marketing, or other competencies. In the second phase of local market expansion, emphasis shifts to exploiting potential economies of scope in local subsidiary operations. In the third phase, leveraging becomes more complex as the firm seeks to take advantage of interdependencies between local markets. Hence, management needs to leverage resources and assets at different stages of the value chain across markets and product businesses so as to maximize potential synergies from global operations.

Building operational flexibility is also of key importance to compete effectively in world markets. A firm can shift sourcing or production to take advantage of changes in factor costs in different locations, fluctuations in exchange rates, or changes in government policy. Resources can also be shifted in response to competitors' moves, to counter their initiatives, or to attack where they are

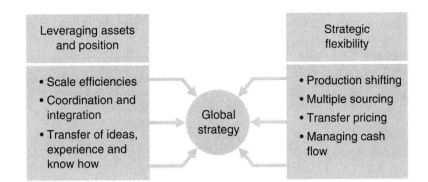

FIGURE 14-4

Achieving global synergies.

most vulnerable, thus taking full advantage of the geographic scope and diversity of the firm's operations.

Leveraging Assets to Compete in Global Markets

As markets become more interdependent, so the firm's ability to leverage assets across product businesses and country markets to achieve global synergies becomes increasingly crucial. Such synergies can arise from the sheer scale of global operations, from improved coordination or integration of operations across country markets or product businesses, and from the transfer of ideas and experience from one market or business to another.

SCALE EFFICIENCIES

While attention is typically focused on economies of scale in production, efficiencies arising from the global scale of operations can be attained at various stages of the value chain, from R&D and sourcing to marketing and distribution, as well as in relation to intangible assets such as reputation and brand image.

In some industries, such as steel, the minimum economic scale is such that a firm can achieve cost economies through producing for world markets. Such efficiencies are especially likely to occur in capital-intensive industries. In addition, as a firm accumulates experience in producing at the volume of world markets, it may become more efficient and introduce improvements in the production process, that are shared by plants throughout the world. Thus, efficiencies may be achieved even without centralization of production. For example, as noted earlier, Japanese companies in consumer electronics have been able to decimate their competition through increased production efficiencies as well as scale economies in producing for world markets.

Economies of scale in R&D can also be obtained by developing products for world markets. This is particularly crucial in industries such as pharmaceuticals, computers, and semiconductors, where R&D expenditure is high relative to sales. For example in the pharmaceutical industry, the costs of developing a new drug are estimated to be around $360 million, and the process often takes 10 years. Consequently, companies need to market drugs globally in order to amortize R&D costs. Drug companies such as Merck and Warner Lambert centralize R&D and production in key markets such as the United States, Japan, India, and Brazil. Marketing and sales are, however, decentralized and adapted to local pharmaceutical regulations, health-care systems, medical practices, and distribution of drugs. In some cases, production of patented drugs may be licensed to local manufacturers where this is less expensive, as it is for example in India.

By operating on a global scale, a firm may be able to utilize specialized skills and resources, or set up dedicated teams and systems, which would not be economic on a smaller scale. Experts with highly specialized skills or knowledge, for example, in assessing foreign exchange risk, or with expertise in a particular technology, might be hired.

Intangible assets such as company reputation, a trademark, or a brand name can also be leveraged in world markets. Brands such as Coca-Cola, Sony, Levi's, and Benneton are household names worldwide. Their high visibility and widespread availability in many countries throughout the world further enhance and reinforce their image. Thus, young adults in markets throughout the world desire the products—the soft drinks, fast food, jeans, and stylish clothing—consumed or worn by their counterparts in other countries. These products become symbols of belonging to the global youth culture.

While these scale economies are in principle similar to those that drive a firm's initial entry into international markets, they differ primarily in magnitude. Operating on a global scale enables a firm to expand and exploit potential scale economies at each phase of the value chain across countries and regions, and achieve cost efficiencies that are not attainable at a smaller scale of operations. Scale efficiencies can also be realized through increased specialization, such as through the employment of highly specialized skills or resources, or through the creation of assets and systems dedicated to specific purposes.

At the same time, as the global scale of operations generates benefits, it can also cause inflexibility and limit the firm's ability to cope with change, or respond to competitors' moves. In particular, the global firm may be vulnerable to nimble-footed local competitors, who can target and cherry-pick profitable niche markets, respond more rapidly to changes in demand or market conditions, or make quick tactical moves—for example, short-term price cuts, promotional deals, or rapidly doubling production output. The global firm must develop strategic flexibility, for example, through establishing flexible manufacturing systems and modular production techniques or improving coordination of global logistics, so as to combine scale advantages with the ability to respond to change, local market needs, and competition.

COORDINATION AND INTEGRATION SYNERGIES

Another source of leverage for the global firm is through the coordination and integration of operations at various stages in the value chain across country markets and product businesses. In some instances this may result in a move toward centralization of operations, but in other cases, benefits are gained where operations remain decentralized.

Coordinating purchasing and sourcing globally for operations worldwide can generate potential synergies. Not only is the firm able to take advantage of economies of bulk purchasing, but also efficiency is improved by eliminating duplication of effort in contacting and maintaining relations with suppliers. In addition, the firm can leverage its bargaining power to negotiate better contract terms such as improved service, better delivery times, higher standards of quality control, and reliability.

Global coordination of production logistics also enables a firm to produce in low-cost locations, close to scarce resources or high weight-to-cost resources, or close to end-user markets, thus generating substantial efficiencies. This is particularly advantageous in industries that are labor-intensive, such as textiles, or where the skills or raw materials required for different components are widely dispersed throughout the world and there are significant differences in comparative production cost advantages in different parts of the world.

Caterpillar, for example, was able to establish a competitive advantage over Komatsu by developing a globally centralized manufacturing system, while building flexibility to add local product features.[7] Product lines were designed to use identical components such as engines, axles, and transmissions, and production of these was centralized in a few large-scale, state-of-the-art manufacturing facilities. Local assembly plants were established close to major markets in Europe, Japan, Brazil, and Australia, which added product features to suit local demand. Caterpillar has been able to achieve a significant cost advantage over competition without sacrificing adaptation to local markets or loss of local value-adding production facilities. In addition, they have gained favor with host governments. In response, Komatsu has entered into an alliance with Cummins Engine to make it more competitive, particularly in large off-road construction equipment.[8]

Coordination of marketing and service operations across national boundaries can also eliminate duplication of effort in developing marketing strategies, advertising or promotional copy, and training procedures. It also facilitates establishing a regionwide or global sales force. This not only improves efficiency but also enables employment of more highly skilled sales or service personnel, which can constitute an important competitive advantage in markets such as supercomputers, turbine engines, and aircraft, where there are relatively few buyers and the sales task is highly complex.

The ability to supply and service multinational customers on a worldwide basis is an important advantage of the global firm. As more and more firms expand internationally, and their operations become interlinked worldwide, availability of products, systems, and services worldwide becomes a key requirement. Again this requires complex coordination of effort across countries, notably with regard to information and logistical systems. Global firms are typically best placed to satisfy the needs of such customers, either through their own operations or through alliances, though increasingly, small firms, notably through the use of advanced communications technology, are developing global networks in order to compete in these markets.

TRANSFER OF IDEAS, EXPERIENCE, AND KNOW-HOW

A third source of leverage is through the transfer of ideas, know-how, and experience from one product business to another, and across country markets and levels. Again, this can have an impact on all levels of the value chain.

R&D units that have developed expertise in a certain area can apply that knowledge to developing and adapting products for different geographic markets or other product businesses. For example, P&G's R&D unit in Japan has developed expertise in surfactants and ultraconcentrate detergents. This has been used in developing products such as Vizir, a heavy duty liquid detergent in the European markets, as well as ultraconcentrate versions of Tide, Cheer, and Bold for the U.S. market.[9] Management and marketing skills acquired in operating under specific environmental conditions can be transferred to similar environmental contexts. For example, Canadian managers from McDonald's operation in Russia went to McDonald's in Brazil to learn tools to manage and operate in a hyperinflationary environment.[10]

Ideas for new products, packaging, advertising, and other marketing tactics developed in response to conditions in one country or region can also be transferred to another country. For example, P&G has transferred Ariel, a presoak detergent effective at low temperatures which was developed in Europe, to India. There, it is marketed in two formulations, one for colored laundry and one for white laundry. It is positioned as an "Eco-system," which eliminates the need to scrub clothes with or without bar soap. Telephone debit cards, which are quite popular in Western Europe, are slowly making their way to the United States. Rather than use coins, the caller inserts the prepaid card into the pay phone and the appropriate amount is deducted. In addition to providing convenience for the consumer, the cards serve as mini billboards for advertisers. An added benefit to the phone companies is that the prepayment feature provides considerable float.[11]

Experience in marketing in diverse competitive and environmental conditions constitutes a key asset and source of potential synergies for the multinational firm. Not only do managers in different countries and product businesses learn from the ideas and strategies developed by other managers in response to their unique operating environments, but also the range and diversity of these environmental contexts provides a much broader learning experience than is available to a domestic firm. Particularly in industries where creative marketing ideas and innovation are at a premium, this constitutes a key advantage for the global firm.

Building Strategic Flexibility

Operational flexibility to shift resources and assets from one market to another is another important competitive weapon in the arsenal of the global firm. The firm can use its network of operations in multiple locations throughout the world to diversify risk, and to hedge against or adapt to fluctuations in market conditions, such as exchange rates, demand, government policy, or regulation, or competitor moves.[12] Cash flows and other resources can also be managed so as to compete more effectively in world markets, using profits from more mature markets to fuel growth in developing areas, and shifting resources to attack competitors where they are most vulnerable. Critical to building this capability, however, is a flexible organizational structure and operational mechanisms to coordinate and implement such moves.[13]

PRODUCTION SHIFTING

Building a global logistical network capable of shifting off-shore production from one site to another to take advantage of exchange rate fluctuations can have a significant impact on production costs. This is particularly likely to occur in situations where labor costs or local raw materials are a significant component of costs. However, production shifting may require investing in excess capacity, or alternatively working additional shifts or overtime, requiring building overtime provisions into labor contracts. Another strategy is to invest in flexible production technologies, which allow adaptation of output or switching from one model to another, to meet needs of different markets and respond to fluctuations in demand. Automobile production lines, for example, can be tooled to produce several different models, and production can be scheduled according to orders for each model. Similarly, in the semiconductor industry, firms can switch rapidly from development of customized chips, which have a higher value added than commodity chips, and vice versa.

The advantages of production shifting depend to some degree on industry cost structure. In industries where there are significant economies of scale or where imports are a major production input, production shifting may not be cost effective. On the other hand, production shifting provides an important buffer and bargaining tool to deal with situations such as labor strikes, work stoppages, civil unrest, and government-imposed embargos or taxes.

MULTIPLE SOURCING

Sourcing raw materials or components from multiple locations reduces dependency on a single source, and production shifting provides a hedge against exchange rate fluctuations, political instability, government restrictions, delivery delays, and supplier unreliability.

Multiple sourcing is only feasible, however, where there is more than one source of supply and no significant scale economies in purchasing. In the semiconductor industry, for example, Intel and a few other suppliers dominate supply of 486 and the new Pentium chips. Consequently, IBM, Toshiba, and Siemens have entered into a joint venture to develop a new-generation chip in order to reduce dependency on Intel.

TRANSFER PRICING

Another potential advantage of a global network of operations is the ability to adjust transfer prices, so as to be competitive in price-sensitive markets, while making profits in protected or price-inelastic markets.[14] For example, transfer prices can be set to cover overhead or investment costs in markets with higher profit margins, and at cost in other markets. For example, in textbook publishing, development costs are typically absorbed in the major markets in the United States or Europe; books are transferred at cost to subsidiaries in price-sensitive markets in other countries.

Transfer pricing can also be utilized to minimize a firm's tax burden. Transfer prices are fixed at cost for low-tax countries, and at arm's length in high-tax countries, so that profits are accumulated in the former. Negative reactions by host governments to such tactics, however, have tended to result in more subtle measures to minimize taxes. For example, in transferring intangible assets such as technology or trademarks, a firm can price (or use different mechanisms such as licensing) so as to shift profits to low-tax subsidiaries, or price aggressively in price-elastic markets. Ability to manipulate price can thus be an important competitive tool for the global firm.

MANAGING CASH FLOWS

Another important source of operational flexibility lies in the management of cash flows and other resources to respond to short-term market fluctuations or changes in market demand. Cash and other transferable resources, for example, can be shifted away from recessionary markets to those with higher rates of growth, or from profitable markets to fund shortfalls in other markets. For example, profits made by Ford of Europe in the late 1980s helped to support its position in the United States. Later, however, the position was reversed, as recession hit Europe and automobile sales plummeted.[15]

Similarly, profits obtained from high-margin mature markets can be funneled into emerging markets or product businesses to stimulate demand and build the market infrastructure. For example, Brooke Bond of India uses profits from mature tea markets in the Gulf States to develop the market and to build the distribution infrastructure for packaged tea in Eastern European countries and Kazakhstan.

GLOBAL MARKETING STRATEGY ALTERNATIVES

Having determined the global configuration of market and customer segments, as well as its competitive strengths and position in global markets, the firm next has to determine its global strategic thrust. This should provide direction for the firm's efforts and establish guidelines for developing marketing strategy, indicating key target markets and customers, as well as how the firm's resources and capabilities should be mobilized to achieve its goals. While the range of strategy options open to the global firm is immense, two major generic types can be identified based on market scope, broad-based vs. focused. Firms pursuing a broad-based marketing strategy target the entire market, or a broad spectrum of it, and attempt to leverage their strengths worldwide. In some instances, they may develop different models or product variants, or marketing strategies, tailored to specific market segments. A focused segment approach, on the other hand, crafts strategy to meet the needs of a single, distinct market segment, to the exclusion of other market segments.

In both cases, firms vary in the extent to which they integrate and coordinate these strategies across country markets and regions, depending on industry characteristics as well as their own capacity to leverage their positions across country markets. Broad-based strategies are more likely to be adapted to country markets and coordinated across product businesses so as to achieve economies of scope. Focused segment strategies, however, are frequently globally integrated as the firm trades off responsiveness to local markets for the benefits of global efficiency and a global image (see Figure 14-5). Potential for economies of scope is often limited.

Broad-Based Marketing Strategies

Broad-based global marketing strategies are common in industries where there are significant economies of scale in production and R&D, and where demand is relatively homogeneous worldwide, providing few opportunities for focused segmentation or niche strategies. In the automobile industry, for example, economies of scale, especially in relation to production logistics and access to distribution channels, are such that opportunities for global niche players are few. Even opportunities which currently exist, such as the upper end of the luxury car market, are rapidly disappearing. Similarly, in markets characterized by a high degree of buyer concentration, such as aircraft, turbine engines, and commodity chemicals, there are few opportunities for differentiation or segmentation strategies.

FIGURE 14-5
Alternative global
marketing strategies.

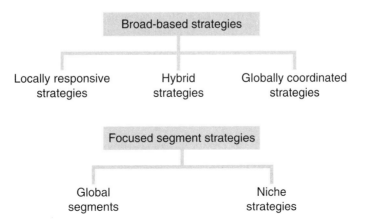

In industries where there are economies of scope, such as consumer packaged goods, high-share firms often tend to pursue broad-based strategies in order to spread marketing and distribution costs across a wide range of products. How far they are able to leverage these strategies globally to obtain cost efficiencies depends on the specific product business and the significance of differences and similarities in customer purchase and response patterns across countries and regions.

Firms that pursue broad-based global marketing strategies vary in the extent to which they coordinate marketing strategies and integrate various phases of their operations across countries or worldwide. Some, for example, in financial services or the aircraft industry, have globally integrated strategies at all phases of the value chain. Others integrate some phases of their operation (production logistics or product design) but not others (marketing and distribution). Yet others emphasize local responsiveness in strategy development and implementation, and only integrate strategy to a very limited extent, for example in relation to intangible assets such as corporate name and logo, brand names, or management and marketing expertise. However, as markets become more interdependent worldwide, increasingly companies are seeking to integrate operations across country markets.

GLOBALLY INTEGRATED STRATEGIES

Global integration of broad-based market strategies at all stages of the value chain is relatively rare except in industries characterized by a high degree of buyer concentration and homogeneity of demand worldwide. For example, there are a relatively limited number of buyers of wide-bodied aircraft and minor differences in purchase criteria and behavior among them. Boeing and Airbus compete for orders from the same buyers in world markets, based on product design, delivery, price, and financing terms.

More common are industries where there are economies of scale in production and R&D, but differences in customer demand or distribution infrastructure across countries or geographic regions, such as the automobile or drug industries. In such industries, firms often integrate R&D and production logistics worldwide, but allow for some local responsiveness and tailoring of products and marketing strategy to meet specific local market characteristics.

As discussed earlier, large drug companies such as Merck, Hoffman La Roche and Ciba-Geigy centralize R&D and production in order to realize cost efficiencies. Often, however, drugs are marketed under different names and may be sold in different forms—powder, tablet, liquid, or suppositories—in each country or region. Marketing and promotional strategies for the different forms differ substantially.

Similarly, in the automobile industry, the major manufacturers, GM, Ford, Toyota, Nissan, and Honda, integrate production logistics on a global scale and are moving toward greater integration of component and model design across regions, especially for markets in the Industrial Triad. Specific models, marketing, and promotional strategies, however, are typically developed or adapted for major country markets or regions, while distribution and dealer networks are set up on a country-by-country basis.

Ford provides an interesting example of an automobile manufacturer's drive towards greater integration of all aspects of operations and strategy worldwide in order to achieve cost efficiencies. Ford's experience also suggests the difficulties a firm can encounter in attempting this. Throughout the 1970s and 1980s, Ford of Europe designed models specifically for the European market. Confronted by strongly entrenched national automobile companies such as Peugeot, Renault, Fiat, and VW, the only way to attain the volume required to meet the minimum efficient scale of operations was by eating into a small piece of each national market. The first Ford models designed for the European market were the Ford Escort, Capri, and Fiesta, which were assembled in the U.K. and Germany from components made at Ford plants in other parts of the world. In the case of the Granada, a common positioning for the car was developed based on fuel economy and reliability—two attributes common to car purchasers throughout Europe.[16] Execution of this theme was carried out locally, with some tailoring to local market characteristics.

With increasing pressures toward market integration and advances in communication technology, Ford, as well as other automobile manufacturers, began to move towards the design of a "world car" in the mid-size range, which could be marketed worldwide. The Ford Escort, for example, was originally planned as a "world car," pooling design, engineering, and manufacturing capabilities on both sides of the Atlantic. However, design engineers in Europe and North America were unable to agree, resulting in two distinctly different models sharing only one common part—a waterpump seal.[15] Ford's new Mondeo, launched in 1993 in Europe (launched a year later in the United States as Ford Contour and Mercury Mystique), was an extremely complex and costly development project taking over 8 years. It is estimated that Ford spent $6 billion on the project, twice the amount spent on the Taurus and Sable in 1985. Development involved 800 engineers in three engineering centers in the United States, U.K., and Germany,[17] and numerous trips back and forth across the Atlantic, as well as costly design changes.

Three different engineering centers took part in the project. Detroit designed the V-6 engine, the automatic transmission, and the heating and air-conditioning units. Dunton, outside London, contributed the interior, the steering, the suspension, the electronics, and the four-cylinder engine. Cologne, Germany, did the basic structural engineering, designing three bodies for the car geared to different markets. Similarly, production involved engine plants in Wales, Cologne, Cleveland, and Chihuahua, Mexico. In addition to creating some complex logistical problems, uniform worldwide engineering standards had to be created, as well as uniform standards for raw materials, design, procurement, and manufacture of individual parts, to ensure compatibility.

In Europe, the Mondeo is the second most expensive Ford, providing a $2,000–$3,000 per unit profit. In the United States, however, due to ferocious competition and fuel economy regulations, Ford is unlikely to break even. Yet despite the complexity and cost of the project, it is considered to be an important component of Ford's future strategy. Economies of scale were achieved, notably in production tools, and better prices were obtained from suppliers. More importantly, superior engineering skills were employed to provide a unique, well-styled, competitive model.

Globally integrated strategies are pursued by firms, not only in order to achieve economies of scale in production and amortize R&D, but also to leverage the power of a strong brand name, and marketing or merchandising expertise, worldwide. P&G, for example, markets Pampers, its disposable diapers, in essentially the same product variants, packaging, and positioning in markets worldwide. Certain minor modifications are made, however. For example, in Asia Pampers are unisex, so that a woman does not have to admit by picking a pink package that her baby is a girl. Similarly, in Japan, Ultra Pampers are thinner and fit into a smaller box adapted to limited storage and living space.[18] Sales promotion tactics and distribution channels are also tailored to specific country characteristics and market infrastructure. Similarly, in its detergents business, R&D know-how is leveraged across regional and country markets. Power brands such as Mr. Clean, Camay, Cheer, Dash, Tide, and Ariel are marketed worldwide, with only minor variations in product formulations and brand names. Again, however, promotion, pricing, and distribution tactics vary from market to market.

Thus, even in businesses where there are substantial differences in customer preferences and purchase behavior between countries or regions, increasingly broad-based marketers are seizing opportunities to integrate strategies across markets so as to leverage strong brand names or good marketing ideas, as well as skills, systems, and expertise in R&D, marketing, and merchandising.

LOCALLY RESPONSIVE STRATEGIES

In contrast to firms that strive to achieve synergies (and greater efficiency) through global integration, other firms place greater emphasis on adaptation and responsiveness to local market opportunities. Such firms are typically in businesses where there are not only marked differences in customer preferences and behavior patterns from one country to another, but also limited opportunities for economies of scale from consolidation of operations across national markets. Packaged food products is one such industry. In these instances, attention is focused on leveraging management and marketing systems, processes, and expertise, rather than on core products and specific strategies.

Nestlé, the Swiss food giant, has traditionally emphasized responsiveness to local markets and, while aiming to build global brands, prefers to tailor brands to local tastes. In addition to a basic research center in Switzerland that focuses on health and food, Nestlé has a network of development research centers investigating local tastes around the world.[19] Product lines and product formulations are typically adapted to local tastes. Unilever follows a similar strategy with regard to its consumer packaged goods businesses, which are often loosely linked on a regional basis. As in the case of Nestlé, much of Unilever's international expansion has been through acquisition of established local brands and companies.

Often these continue to be operated as independent entities, only loosely coordinated with other operations.

For example, Unilever controls 70 percent of the packaged tea business worldwide through its two companies, Brooke Bond Ltd. and Thomas Lipton. Both companies operate independently with some loose coordination. In both companies, some brands are marketed worldwide, while others are national or regional. Brooke Bond's Red Label brand is the largest brand of packaged tea worldwide. In the U.K., however, its number one brand is P.G. Tips, which is sold both loose and in tea bags. In India, in addition to Red Label, Brooke Bond also markets Taj Mahal, a premium brand of high-quality tea, Green Label, lower priced than Red Label, and A1, a dust tea made of crushed tea leaves, which is popular in Southern India and perceived as more economical than regular tea leaves. Lipton also competes worldwide with its Yellow Label brand, which is positioned slightly above Brooke Bond's Red Label. In the Gulf States, in addition to Yellow Label, Lipton's also markets Blue Top, a brand specially blended to local tastes.

In its detergents and cosmetics businesses, as discussed earlier, Unilever markets some brands such as Lux toilet soap and Surf powdered detergent in similar formulations worldwide. Production is typically local, and in some instances contracted out to local manufacturers, thus facilitating adaptation of product size or packaging to the local market. Marketing campaigns are also developed locally, though with increasing attention to coordination of positioning and promotional themes across markets. Some brand formulations are adapted to local markets. For example, in India, Close-Up toothpaste is marketed in three flavors, Tingly Red, Aqua Blue, and Zingy Green. In addition, local management has considerable autonomy to develop new products or acquire existing brands or product businesses. In India, for example, Hindustan Lever is developing an aquaculture business to cultivate shrimp and develop shrimp products. Thus, the key thrust of Unilever's strategy is identification of and response to local market opportunities, rather than global expansion of existing product businesses.

HYBRID STRATEGIES

Midway along the spectrum between companies that emphasize global integration and those that place a premium on responding to specific market needs are those that follow hybrid strategies. Such companies integrate some product businesses and standardize some product lines and brands worldwide, while other product businesses and product lines are regional or country specific. The firm has a portfolio of global, regional, and local product businesses, products, and brands, that enable it to leverage certain products and aspects of its operations globally, while at the same time exploiting specific local market opportunities.

Coca-Cola, although widely cited as an exemplar of the globally standardized brand philosophy, has various local and regional brands in addition to its flagship Coca-Cola brand. In fact only three brands, Coca-Cola, Sprite, and Fanta, are marketed globally. In Latin America and Europe, where lemon-lime and orange sodas are popular, flavors and formulations vary from market to market.[20]

In Brazil, a brand called Guarana Tai is marketed, while in El Salvador and Venezuela, a version of Fanta called Fanta-Kolita, a cream soda type of drink, is a local favorite. In Latin America, the lemon-lime flavor formulations contain more sugar than they do for European markets. Other brands in the category are geared to specific local market tastes. For example, in the U.K., Coca-Cola's number-one-selling soda is Lilt, a pineapple-grapefruit flavor combination sold in diet and regular versions. In Indonesia, on the other hand, Coca-Cola markets strawberry-, pineapple-, and banana-flavored sodas adapted to local tastes.

Heinz also pursues a hybrid strategy, emphasizing a strong portfolio of brands, and product businesses, including global, regional, and national brands. Heinz is geographically diversified, with more than 3,000 varieties in over 200 countries and territories. These include the Heinz line of ketchup and sauces, canned goods, baby foods, Weight Watchers, Starkist tuna, Ore-Ida frozen potatoes, Reward dog food, and 9-Lives cat food, as well as a number of local product businesses.[21]

The company's two strongest global brands are Heinz and Weight Watchers. The geographic scope of these two businesses varies significantly. Weight Watchers is marketed in North America and six European countries with expansion planned in Eastern Europe. Heinz brands, on the other hand, are marketed in North America, throughout Europe and Central Europe, and in Japan, Korea, China, Thailand, Venezuela, Australia, and Botswana.

The specific product lines, product variants, and degree of product adaption, however, vary from one country to another. Heinz's flagship brand of tomato ketchup is sold worldwide in the familiar bottle, whether glass or plastic, but the formulation is often adapted to local customer tastes. In Mexico, Heinz's ketchup is spicier and contains more chili, while in other countries the amount of salt or sugar varies. The range of other sauces varies from country to country. In the United States, for example, Heinz's line of sauces includes chili sauce, barbecue sauce, Worcestershire sauce, traditional steak sauce, and Dijon mustard. In the U.K. it includes various meat sauces, mint sauce, horseradish sauce, and other traditional accompaniments to meat and fish dishes. In other European countries, it focuses primarily on ketchup and tomato sauce.

Again, in canned soups and vegetables, the product line varies from country to country, depending on local preferences and the strength of competition. In the canned soup market in the United States, for example, Heinz falls well behind the market leader, Campbell. In the U.K., on the other hand, Heinz occupies the number one spot and offers a number of varieties adapted to local tastes, such as Oxtail and Mulligatawny. In other European countries, canned soups are less successful due to preferences for dehydrated or packaged soups. For other types of canned goods, while the basic "57 varieties" slogan is still utilized, specific product variants differ widely. In the U.K., where baked beans are highly popular, the line includes curried baked beans as well as chili baked beans, barbecue baked beans, and sausage and beans. Similarly, a wide range of canned spaghetti and noodles is available, including a highly popular range of individual-size servings for children. In Australia, Heinz also has a strong position in baked beans and spaghetti, as well as in ketchup and tomato sauce.

Heinz's global marketing strategy, like Coca-Cola's, is a hybrid and in some respects reflects the historical evolution of the company. Where opportunities for leveraging brands globally exist, these are exploited, though often with adaptation of product formulations and marketing strategies to local market characteristics and competitive conditions. In addition, local products, brands, and businesses are developed or acquired to meet specific local preferences and demand.

Focused Segment Strategies

An alternative approach to broad-based strategies is to focus on catering to the needs of a specific market segment. This type of strategy is often adopted by smaller players that lack the resources to adopt broad-based strategies or compete with the majors. A focused strategy is most effective in industries where there are clearly defined differences in customer needs and interests, and limited potential for economies of scope or economies of scale in R&D, production, or distribution from targeting the entire market. Satisfying the specific needs of a given segment may require use of a particular technology, specialized skills, and know-how that differ from those used in relation to other market segments. Distribution channels or promotional platforms may also need to be tailored to specific segment characteristics. Where such segments are too small to be served economically by a large multinational, they provide an excellent opportunity for firms operating on a smaller scale.

As noted earlier, in some instances the same or similar segments can be identified in different countries and targeted worldwide. As in the case of globally integrated broad-based strategies, a firm can leverage its strategy across national borders to achieve economies in production, design, and sourcing, etc., and take advantage of the potential synergies of a global image or reputation. In other cases, companies adopt a strategy of targeting specific niches in national or regional markets where there is less competition.

GLOBAL SEGMENT STRATEGIES

In many markets global segments can be identified consisting of customers with similar needs, interests, and characteristics in different countries or regions throughout the world. In industrial markets, these segments are most likely to occur where some customers have highly specialized needs, such as for customized product design or specialist services. In consumer markets, global segments are common in markets for personal items such as clothing, watches, and cosmetics, especially at the upper end of the market, or among teenagers and young adults.

In the computer industry, the supercomputer segment, which consists primarily of educational institutions and scientific research operations involved in space technology, has very specific requirements for high-speed capabilities. Cray Computers targeted this segment, developing supercomputers using a vertical processing technology. The sales task is highly complex and requires developing and nurturing a relationship with a potential customer for a period of 1 to 3 years. Consequently, Cray had a virtual monopoly on this segment worldwide. More recently, however, the increased capacity of mainframe computers, together with the development of parallel processing, has threatened Cray's worldwide dominance of this segment, whose needs can now be met by a number of manufacturers, including IBM, Fujitsu, DEC, and others.

Similarly, in the computer software market, small Indian and Israeli companies have targeted specific business applications, such as financial systems, retail distribution, and hotel reservations systems. Since development of applications software is customized and has to be tailored to specific client needs and operating systems, there are few advantages associated with scale. Rather, expertise and experience in a particular type of application, and a reputation for quality, reliability, and speed of delivery are of paramount importance.

Another type of global segment strategy is pursued by a number of Asian high-tech companies. These companies have identified opportunities in high technology industries such as digital communications, automated chip design, and telecommunications, which they are able to supply rapidly at highly competitive prices. Typically, these are segments that do not require substantial investment in R&D or large manufacturing facilities, but rather rely on rapid absorption and application of new technologies to market niches.

Varitronix, for example, a small company in Hong Kong (with about 30 engineers), produces tiny custom-designed LCDs for control panels in automobiles such as Mercedes Benz and Ferrari, and in British Aerospace plane cockpits. Other applications include displays for medical equipment, gas station pumps, cellular phones, and train station and airport signboards. Japanese competitors such as Sharp and Casio, which produce standardized LCDs, are geared up for vast production runs and lack the flexibility to take on small customized orders. Varitronix fills small orders in as little as 2 weeks. As a result, it has little competition in its segment. The company is now moving into innovative end products such as a hand-held terminal for placing gambling bets, primarily targeted at the local Hong Kong market. Telebetting terminals for horse racing authorities in Malaysia and Australia are also being developed.

In consumer products such as fashion or personal items, global segments can often be identified at the upper end of the market. As noted in Chapter 9 more affluent, educated consumers are more likely to be exposed to ideas and trends in other countries, and also to travel more frequently and hence develop similar tastes and interests to their counterparts in other parts of the world. Rolls-Royce Motor Cars, for example, targets the highly affluent consumer worldwide, with its Bentley and Silver Cloud automobiles. Prices for U.S. buyers range from $138,500 for Bentley Brooklands to $319,300 for the Silver Spur II.[22] Each automobile is hand-assembled, requiring about 900 hours of labor. The stainless steel radiator alone requires 12 hours of metal bending and hand soldering—about the time required for Toyota to assemble an entire car. Forty artisans are employed solely to craft the wood veneer for the instrument panel, door trim, and center console. For the higher-end Rolls, fittings are customized to the needs of each buyer—lighting, upholstery, and accessories. Much of the prestige associated with Rolls Royce comes from its stately image of conspicuous consumption.

Similarly, Rolex watches are targeted to the successful businessman or woman worldwide. Identical models, such as the Oyster and the President, are sold in upscale watch and jewelry stores throughout the world, and the same advertising campaign is utilized, focusing on print media, with translation into the appropriate local language. American Express adopts a similar strategy for its Green Card, promoting it for entertainment and travel. The same advertising campaigns, such as the "Do You Know Me?" and "Membership has Its Privileges," have been utilized worldwide. In the "Do You Know Me?" campaign, personalities whose names are known internationally, although their faces are not necessarily familiar, such as Paloma Picasso, were portrayed, to indicate the instant recognition afforded by possession of the American Express Green card. Economies of scale obtained through design standardization and the use of a globally standardized advertising campaign counterbalance the costs of coordinating strategy across country markets. In addition, marketing to customers worldwide conveys an aura of prestige.

In general, in industrial markets, globally focused strategies are most effective where there are market segments with highly specialized needs, which cannot be served efficiently by large multinationals. In consumer markets, on the other hand, global segmentation strategies are effective if there are substantial benefits from leveraging a global image. Given the high costs of reaching such segments and coordinating operations across countries, the segment also has to be large enough to be economically viable, and in many cases is at the premium end of the market.

GLOBAL NICHE STRATEGIES

While global segmentation strategies look to leverage competitive advantage across country markets, global niche players look for opportunities in multiple national markets that are not covered by other major competitors. Although global niche strategies do not appear to be very common, as local niches are often filled by nationally focused companies, such a strategy can provide an effective means for a smaller player to compete in a market dominated by two or three competitors worldwide.

Cadbury Schweppes, for example, has pursued a global niche strategy in the soft drink market, in order to avoid entering into direct competition with Coca-Cola and Pepsi-Cola, which dominate the cola market worldwide. Cadbury Schweppes, the number three soft drink company, has a diverse range of non-colas, including the Canada Dry and Schweppes lines, Hires root beer, and fruit flavored sodas such as Crush and Sunkist.[23] The specific brands and range of flavors vary from country to country, and from one region of the world to another.

In France, Cadbury Schweppes markets Gini tonic water and Atoll and Oasis fruit drinks, as well as Schweppes mixers. In Japan, its Schweppes line includes three flavors of ginger, while in Southeast Asia, the Canada Dry range includes a melon flavor. Recently, it has also acquired A&W Brands in the United States, which include a root beer, cream soda, and Country Time Lemonade, to strengthen its distribution pull.[24] Cadbury Schweppes thus targets specific noncola niches in the soft drink market and adapts the product line to local market tastes, leveraging its marketing skills and bottling expertise to compete against the cola giants.

While industry characteristics and competitive structure play important roles in formulating strategy parameters, and in particular the benefits likely to be gained from integrating operations and leveraging strategy on a global scale, they are not all determinant. Firms in the same industry often pursue markedly different strategies. One firm may exploit the advantages of global integration through centralized production and strategy development, while another focuses on adapting to local markets with integrated but autonomous subsidiaries. Similarly, while some firms opt for a broad-based strategy, others target a specific segment. For example in the beer market, Budweiser pursues a broad market base in its international expansion plans, while Heineken targets the premium segment worldwide.

SUMMARY

Global strategy is more than the sum of the various strategies pursued in all the markets in which a firm is active. While existing operations must be taken into account, global competitive strategy must also consider the interdependence of markets and the ways in which global synergies can be achieved. This assessment suggests alternative strategies that will enable the firm to be successful in global markets.

As indicated in Chapter 13, a necessary prelude to global strategy development is a portfolio analysis that guides market choice decisions. This leads logically to a determination of geographic market scope and target market segmentation. Markets may be defined in terms of countries, clusters of countries, regions, or global market areas. In addition to geographic market scope, strategy has to take into account how customer commonalities cut across different markets, and whether regional or global customer segments can be identified.

After assessing the geographic scope of the market for its products and examining what customer segments exist, the firm is in a position to devise a global strategy that aims to achieve global synergy. This can arise through the leveraging of assets or competitive position from one market to another. Related to how assets and competencies are leveraged is the need to develop strategic flexibility in terms of production, transfer pricing, and managing cash flows.

The firm's global strategic thrust provides direction for developing global marketing strategy. While there is a range of options open to the firm, there are two generic strategic alternatives: (1) broad-based marketing strategies or (2) focused strategies. Firms pursuing a broad-based global marketing strategy target a broad spectrum of the total market. Firms pursuing a focused global marketing strategy, on the other hand, target and tailor strategy to the needs of a distinct market segment. The success of either strategy clearly depends on the underlying market conditions, the capabilities of the firms, and the strategies being pursued by its competitors.

REFERENCES

1. CPC (1992) *Annual Report.*
2. Douglas, Susan P., and C. Samuel Craig (1991) "Spatial Dimensions of International Markets," In Avijit Ghosh and Charles A. Ingene eds. *Research in Marketing,* suppl. 5, Greenwich, CT: JAI Press Inc.
3. Main, Jerry (1991) "How Latin America is Opening Up," *Fortune,* April 8.
4. Bartlett, Christopher A., and Sumantra Ghoshal (1989) *Managing Across Borders: The Transnational Solution,* Boston: MA: Harvard University Press.
5. Tully, Shawn (1994) "Teens, The Most Global Market of All," *Fortune* May 16, pp. 90–97.
6. "Mini-nationals are Making Maximum Impact" (1993) *Business Week,* September 6, pp. 66–69.
7. Hout, Thomas, Michael E. Porter, and Eileen Rudden (1982) "How Global Companies Win Out," *Harvard Business Review,* September/October, 60 pp. 98–108.
8. "Two Diesel Giants Set Alliance" (1993) *New York Times,* February 17, p. D1.
9. Proctor and Gamble (1992) *Annual Report.*
10. "Inflation Lessons Over a Big Mac" (1993) *Financial Times,* February 22, p. 8.
11. Moshavi, Sharon (1993) "Please Deposit No Cents," *Forbes,* August 16, p. 102.
12. Kogut, Bruce (1985) "Designing Global Strategies: Profiting from Operational Flexibility," *Sloan Management Review,* Fall, Vol. 27, pp. 27–38.
13. Prahalad, C.K., and Yves Doz (1987) *The Multinational Mission: Balancing Local Demands and Global Vision,* New York: The Free Press.
14. Arpan, Jeffrey S. (1972) *International Intra-corporate Pricing,* New York: Praeger.
15. "Ford of Europe: Slimmer but Maybe Not Luckier" (1993) *Business Week,* January 18, pp. 44–46.
16. Colvin, Michael, Roger Heeler, and Jim Thorpe (1980) "Developing International Advertising Strategy," *Journal of Marketing,* Vol. 44 Fall, pp. 73–79.
17. Taylor, Alex (1993) "Ford's $6 Billion Baby," *Fortune,* June 28, pp. 76–81.
18. "Don't Sell Thick Diapers in Tokyo" (1993) *New York Times,* October 3.

19. "Nestlé's Approach to Managing a Slow Growth Sector" (1989) *Management Europe,* January 16, pp. 15–17.
20. Coca-Cola (1990) *Annual Report.*
21. Heinz (1991) *Annual Report.*
22. "Where Will Rolls Roll?" (1993) *Fortune,* September 6, p. 66.
23. Bird, Laura (1990) "Flavor by Flavor, Cadbury Builds an Empire of Niches," *Adweek's Marketing Week,* June 16, pp. 18–19.
24. Milbank, Dana (1993) "Cadbury to Buy A&W Brands for $334 Million," *Wall Street Journal,* September 10.

CHAPTER 15

DEVELOPING THE CORPORATE INFRASTRUCTURE FOR GLOBAL MARKETING

INTRODUCTION

A global marketing strategy, however brilliant in concept, will not be successful unless effectively implemented. Once the firm's future direction in global markets has been charted, and a strategy designed to leverage the firm's core competencies in different businesses on a worldwide basis, it becomes critical to put in place the means to execute that strategy and to take measures to ensure that it is carried out.

First, the firm needs to develop a global perspective at all levels of the corporate structure. This requires changing management orientation and attitudes from a national or country-by-country focus to a broader and more integrated view of markets worldwide. This view should stress the importance of linkages and interdependencies between national markets and looking for potential synergies across national boundaries. Management thinking and actions ranging from strategic planning to managing day-to-day operations must be permeated by a philosophy that transcends national, political, economic, and cultural boundaries.

Next, operations at various stages in the value chain need to be managed so as to maximize efficiency and the creation of value for customers and suppliers alike on a worldwide basis. Management must determine the specific location, spatial configuration, and degree of coordination between and within upstream and downstream functions. Management also has to decide whether specific functions can be performed more effectively by the firm or external organizations.

Thirdly, a global management system has to be developed to direct, monitor, and control performance of upstream and downstream functions, and to achieve the desired degree of horizontal and vertical communication and coordination. The stream has to be designed to achieve balance between conflicting pressures for global efficiency and local responsiveness, as well as providing for learning and flexibility to respond to changing competitive market dynamics.

Fourthly, delivery of customer satisfaction should govern the organization and performance of all functions at each stage of the value chain. Customer needs may have been correctly identified and strategy designed to meet these needs, but unless customers are satisfied, the firm is unlikely to be successful in the long run. Often, the firm must establish direct links with customers to manage the flow of goods and services to their operations throughout the world, to provide service and training, as well as feedback on customer needs and satisfaction.

Finally, resources must be effectively mobilized to implement marketing strategy and achieve customer satisfaction. In some cases, strategic alliances with competitors are established to ensure efficient performance of upstream and downstream functions and coverage of customer operations worldwide. (See Figure 15-1.)

ADOPTING A GEOCENTRIC PERSPECTIVE

As the firm moves toward increased integration and coordination of marketing strategy across country markets, adoption of a geocentric perspective in managing operations becomes imperative. The firm must proceed towards a global view and manage operations globally. (See Figure 15-2.) While the implications of adopting this perspective differ depending on the industry, in essence the concept of a domestic base, or lead market, and of nationally focused operations disappears. Rather, the firm focuses on managing operations on a global scale, integrating and coordinating activities at various stages in the value-chain across country markets and regions so as to realize potential synergies from global operations.

FIGURE 15-1

Global
implementation.

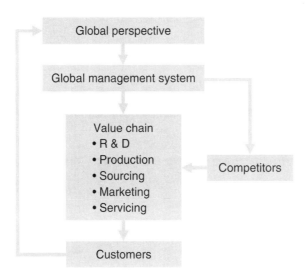

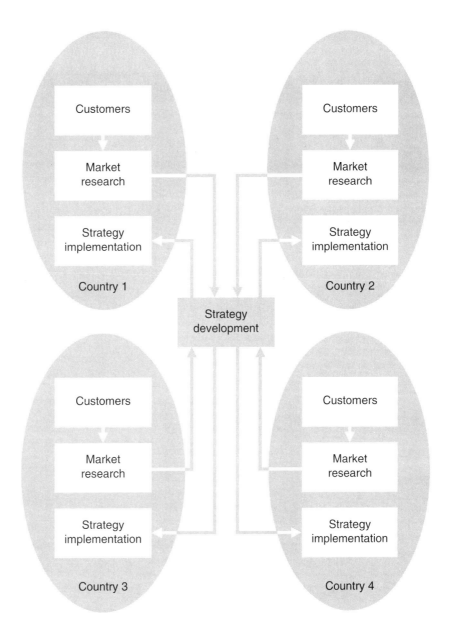

FIGURE 15-2
Strategy development under a geocentric or regiocentric perspective.

In global industries such as aerospace and semiconductors, which are characterized by a relatively small number of customers worldwide, management has to identify, target, and negotiate contracts with such customers, and build a capability to service their operations worldwide. At the same time, sourcing and production logistics should be organized to maximize global efficiency and meet customer quality standards, delivery times, inventory management, and service requirements.

In other industries, such as consumer packaged goods, household appliances, and consumer electronics, which had been regional or multidomestic in character, adoption of a geocentric perspective implies moving toward greater consolidation and integration of operations worldwide. Mechanisms need to be established to facilitate transfer of ideas, experience, and information from one geographic area to another. This also requires the design of management systems and processes to provide improved communication and control between widely dispersed operations, and above all, development of a global mind set.

When Sony initially expanded into international markets in the 1960s and '70s, it focused on the United States, then spread out to Europe and other countries.[1] Sales subsidiaries were established in the United States and Europe that reported directly to headquarters, with little or no communication with each other. By the 1980s price competition in the maturing consumer electronic market had become extremely acute, particularly with the entry of competition from South Korea, Taiwan, and other newly industrialized countries. Sony was especially vulnerable due to its focus on consumer electronic products, and heavy concentration of production in Japan. As a result, Sony substantially revised its business strategy to adjust to the new global dynamics. Operations were reorganized around global product divisions that had responsibility for business worldwide. Control mechanisms and evaluation criteria were established on a global basis, although country sales organizations still retained substantial local autonomy. A global mind-set of cooperative effort between product managers and sales subsidiaries was developed. This is considered to be a key factor underlying the company's success in developing new products and distribution methods for the global marketplace.

MANAGING THE VALUE SYSTEM

In addition to developing a global perspective among managers at all levels, successful implementation of any global marketing strategy also requires determining the appropriate spatial configuration for the performance and management of functions at different stages of the value chain. The firm has to determine whether to perform these functions itself in all locations worldwide, or alternatively, to undertake them in collaboration or contract them out to other organizations or services.

Determining the Spatial Configuration of the Value Chain

A key parameter in achieving global efficiency and maximizing value creation is to determine the appropriate spatial configuration of *upstream* activities such as R&D, production, and sourcing, as well as *downstream* activities such as distribution, sales, and service. This is central to establishing an effective corporate infrastructure and a network of external relationships to implement strategy. (See Figure 15-3.)

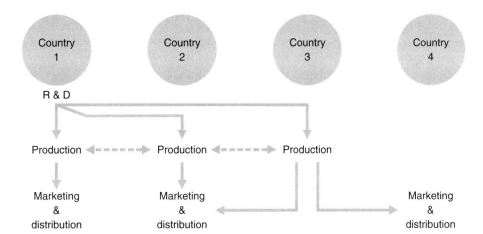

FIGURE 15-3
Configuring the value chain.

In determining the spatial configuration of operations, following Porter,[2] the firm needs to consider two aspects: the degree of centralization or geographic *concentration* of a function, and the degree of *coordination* between activities that are dispersed. First, the specific location where each activity is performed, and how far this function is geographically concentrated or dispersed throughout the world, need to be determined. Production could, for example, be concentrated in a single plant serving the world market, or at the other extreme, a separate production facility could be established to serve each local market.

A highly concentrated spatial configuration of activities allows the firm to take advantage of potential economies of scale in the performance of an activity, and to benefit from potential learning curve or experience effects. (See Figure 15-4.) These are likely to be more significant in relation to upstream than downstream activities. Yet, even in this case, substantial economies can be achieved. For example, centralized production of advertisements, sales promotion materials, and user manuals can generate substantial scale economies. It also facilitates use of advanced state-of-the-art printing or film production technology. Concentration also helps to eliminate potential duplication of effort in relation to activities such as R&D or development of advertising or promotional copy. Hence, a spatially concentrated configuration is likely to maximize performance efficiency of many functions.

Concentration also enables use of highly specialized skills and expertise. For example, a central service support group can employ highly skilled service specialists who can visit local subsidiaries to provide service support and assistance, or alternatively, service customers directly. Defective parts or products can be returned directly to a centralized service department for repair or replacement.

Concentration of activities also facilitates control of performance worldwide. For example, concentration of production in a single or limited number of loca-

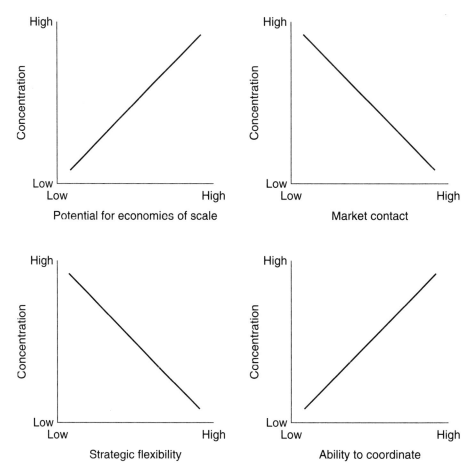

FIGURE 15-4

Relationship of
concentration to key
strategic variables.

tions facilitates application of uniform standards of quality control. Similarly, centralized management training programs, such as those used by McDonald's, help to ensure that similar standards of service and cleanliness are applied in outlets worldwide.

The location of supporting industries and availability of specialized (higher-order) skills and resources such as research facilities, also impacts the configuration of production locations and creates forces towards concentration.[3] For example, Italian shoe production is located close to leather manufacturers to facilitate interaction concerning new textures and manufacturing techniques. Similarly, the ceramic industry is located in the Sarsuolo area, where a pool of skilled workers and technicians, including production specialists and design personnel, has developed.

A dispersed configuration of activities, on the other hand, typically provides greater contact with the market, and hence greater sensitivity and responsiveness to local market conditions and customer needs. This is likely to be more critical for marketing and service activities, especially where customers are dispersed and vary substantially in needs and purchase behavior, as is often the case in consumer packaged goods. Production design and R&D activities can, however, also benefit from proximity to end markets. This stimulates greater awareness of trends in customer needs and usage behavior. Products are more likely to be redesigned or adapted to changing customer needs, and new products designed to meet emerging demand.

Geographic dispersion of activities also provides greater strategic flexibility. As noted earlier, fluctuations in foreign exchange rates; imposition of tariffs, quotas, and other trade restrictions; or events such as wars, insurrections, or labor stoppages can dramatically impact the cost competitiveness or desirability of a given production location or source of raw materials or components. Equally, shifts in demand can impact the desirability of concentration at a given site. Dispersion of activities enables management to counteract the impact of such factors. Sourcing from more favorable locations can be increased in order to remain cost competitive and maintain the flow of parts and components. Dispersion of production also reduces the need to maintain buffer stocks and warehousing facilities, and often enables speedier delivery.

Where activities are dispersed, coordination of activities performed in different locations needs to be considered. Where the firm aims to produce and market a globally standardized product, all plants throughout the world should employ the same production technology, utilize the same parts, and apply the same quality and control standards. Modern communications technology makes it increasingly feasible to link plants and R&D centers in far-flung geographic locations into a global logistics network. Certain plants can, for example, specialize in the production of specific components or models, others in their assembly, and all are linked together through a global information system coordinating production scheduling and logistics. For example, Tiris, a Texas Instruments unit that makes communications devices, is managed from England and develops its products in Germany and the Netherlands, while manufacturing and assembly take place in Germany, the Netherlands, Japan, and Malaysia. The manufacturing and design centers send text, drawings and diagrams over a computer network. Applications for the products are designed in nine other centers.[4]

Management does not, however, make decisions with regard to the spatial configuration of operations within a vacuum, but rather within the context of an existing network of operations worldwide. This may impose certain constraints on the firm's ability to move towards the desired configuration or at least imply high costs in doing so in the short run. Each firm will, therefore, have to determine how best to configure operations to implement strategy in the light of these and other environmental constraints. Such issues are next discussed first in relation to R&D, production, and sourcing, and then in relation to marketing, sales, and service. For a more extensive discussion of sourcing issues, see Kotabe.[5]

CONFIGURING R&D, PRODUCTION, AND SOURCING LOGISTICS

In determining the spatial configuration of upstream operations, three prototypical patterns can be identified: (1) a highly centralized pattern, in which production and R&D from markets worldwide are located in one or two sites, though sourcing for materials and components can either be global or localized; (2) a locationally dispersed but interlinked pattern, where multiple production and assembly sites are centrally interlinked and coordinated into a global logistical system; and (3) a decentralized/dispersed pattern, with multiple sites worldwide and limited interlinking.

Highly centralized patterns are often found in industries where there are significant economies of scale in production and relatively few customers worldwide. In the aerospace industry, for example, Boeing centralizes most production and R&D in Seattle, Washington, and exports aircraft to customers.

Centralized patterns also allow firms to maintain a high degree of control over production, and benefit from synergies between R&D, production, and sourcing. Japanese automobile and consumer electronics firms such as Toyota, Honda, and Sony have traditionally preferred to concentrate production in their domestic market base. This encourages them to maintain high standards of quality control, and production efficiency, and to benefit from "just in time" sourcing.

Highly centralized patterns are vulnerable, however, to sharp swings in foreign exchange rates, as well as to the imposition of tariffs and other trade barriers. Toyota, Honda, and Sony have all begun to develop a more dispersed logistical pattern, establishing assembly plants in the United States and Europe, and sourcing components in lower-wage-cost countries such as Malaysia and South Korea, in order to combat the rising value of the yen, and threats of tariff barriers and other restrictions.[6]

Locationally dispersed but interlinked patterns are most likely to be adopted in industries where production of individual components is best located or sourced from different countries. For example, in the automobile and consumer electronics industries, assembly plants are typically located close to markets, but components are sourced from geographically dispersed locations. Companies can thus take advantage of differences in labor costs and specialized skills in different parts of the world. At the same time, flexibility in sourcing and production can be built into the system to respond to fluctuations in demand, labor, and raw material costs in different countries, and swings in foreign exchange rates.

On the other hand, managing globally dispersed logistical systems is highly complex and costly and can give rise to severe coordination problems. Ford, for example, had to create uniform worldwide engineering standards, with every specification expressed in the metric system, for production of the Mondeo. Renovations and retooling were required at nine big factories including engine plants at Bridgend in Wales; Cologne, Germany; Cleveland, Ohio; and Chihuahua, Mexico, where the Mondeo is produced.[7]

Dispersed unlinked production patterns are most likely to be found in industries where there are few scale economies, or significant differences in the cost of factor inputs and technology from one market to another. Production close to the market may also be mandated by need for product adaptation, perishability, transportation costs, and tariff barriers. Soft drink manufacturers often adopt this type of pattern insofar as there are significant differences in product and packaging from one country to another. This requires modifications in product formulation, new product variants, and different packaging. In addition, packaging and distribution costs are major components of total delivered cost, rendering shipment over large distances uneconomic.

CONFIGURING MARKETING AND SERVICE ACTIVITIES

In configuring marketing and service activities, proximity to customers and responsiveness to customer needs are of key importance. The location of customer operations, and their geographic dispersion, are thus key factors in determining the relative concentration or dispersion of marketing and service functions.

Where the firm targets global customers with worldwide operations, centralized control of marketing and service activities facilitates coordination of distribution, promotion, and service to customer operations in different geographic locations. Information and feedback relating to local customer needs, and customer satisfaction, can also be obtained. Some services companies, such as Saatchi & Saatchi and Citibank, have established global account management systems to handle relations with global customers. Similarly, where customer have regionally coordinated operations, a system of regional account managers can be established.

SKF, the Swedish roller-bearing company, has centralized its distribution network in Europe in order to save costs and shorten delivery times. The number of inventory points has been reduced from 24 to 5 and a new distribution center established in Belgium, close to a well-developed network.[8] This will not only cut costs but also enable the company to be more responsive to customer needs, in most cases providing overnight distribution service.

If, on the other hand, markets are highly fragmented and customers are geographically dispersed, few advantages are likely to be gained from centralizing marketing and service activities. Especially if there are substantial differences in customer characteristics and desired benefits, as well as in the nature of the marketing infrastructure, it will be preferable to perform marketing and service functions on a market-by-market basis. This facilitates greater local responsiveness to customer needs and competitor moves as well as eliminating central administration costs.

Traditionally, IBM's operations, for example, were organized into four geographic divisions, the United States, Europe/Middle East/Africa, Asia/Pacific, and the Americas. Each division has its own manufacturing facilities and strategic planning is developed at the regional level, within the global vision established by top management. Marketing and service functions are, however, decentralized to the country level to ensure customer responsiveness and enhance customer satisfaction.[9] To respond to changing market conditions and increased competition, IBM has abandoned its geographic organizational structure. Marketing and sales have been organized into 14 worldwide industry groups (for example, insurance, banking, and retailing). This allows it to be more responsive to its customers and minimize internal turf wars.[10]

Internal versus External Performance of Activities

A second issue to be considered in managing the value chain is whether various activities are more effectively performed internally by the firm itself or outsourced from other organizations. In addition, where activities are performed externally, management has to determine how much control it should exercise over these operations. Increasingly, many companies are focusing on core activities, for example, designing and marketing computers or copiers and letting outside specialists handle deliveries, servicing, or do the billing and accounting. This holds down the investment needed to turn out new products rapidly and frees up capital for activities and projects where the company has a competitive edge. Attention and energy are focused on what the firm does best, that is its core competence. Other activities and services are outsourced.[11] Reebok and Nike, for example, concentrate on their strengths, designing and marketing high-tech footwear for sports and fitness. Reebok owns no plants and contracts production to suppliers in Taiwan, Indonesia, and other Asian countries. This enables it to keep up with rapidly changing tastes, as its supplier can quickly retool to produce new products and models. In the PC industry, Dell concentrates on marketing and service. It owns no plants and leases two small factories to assemble computers. This gives Dell a major advantage over vertically integrated companies. With no investment in plants and manufacturing, resources are freed up for expenditure on training sales representatives and service technicians, who provide information and support for direct sales to end consumer.

In international markets, the far-flung character and geographic scope of operations make it increasingly imperative to focus on core activities and to outsource noncore operations. Even a large multinational is unlikely to have the resources to perform all functions at all stages in the value chain effectively worldwide. For example, large pharmaceutical companies frequently outsource biotech drugs. They help to fund research by biotech companies for new drugs and then market the drug worldwide, paying the biotech company a royalty.[11] After-sales service may also be contracted out to local organizations, which are better able to respond quickly and effectively to customer needs. This may be particularly desirable in servicing a global customer, where the firm's service network does not match that of its customer.

In some cases, external organizations can perform functions more cost efficiently than the firm itself. Especially where there are substantial differences in technology or cost factors from one market to another, local organizations may be able to operate more effectively and with lower overheads than a global organization. For example, Dr. Reddy Laboratories in India is able to manufacture a number of bulk drugs such as ibuprofen, methyldopa and rantidine, at a third the cost of a large multinational. As a result, companies such as Glaxo have begun to purchase from DRL.[12] Similarly, where an organization specializes in performing a specific function such as, for example, billing or shipping, it can often perform this more efficiently than a multinational. For example, Swiss Air contracts out its billing to a firm in India.

Political considerations may also suggest the desirability of contracting out, or purchasing locally, certain resources, components, or services. In some instances, governments place restrictions on imports, making purchases of components from local suppliers or use of local services mandatory. Equally, in some countries such as Brazil, access to local markets is contingent upon establishment of a joint venture with a local partner and granting of contracts to local firms.

In determining whether or not to outsource a given function, understanding the nature of the firm's core competence is of paramount importance. Contracting out a function that is central to the firm's business may be more cost efficient in the short run, but result in the loss of a significant competitive edge in world markets in the long run. For example, Quantum, a marketer of disk drives, contracts out large-scale manufacturing of standard disk drives to Matsushita-Kotobuki Electronics in Japan, working in close collaboration on design to facilitate easy and rapid manufacture. Quantum remains in close contact with customers and retains control over the design of new products, manufacturing them in-house until they are perfected.[11]

In brief, the decision whether to perform activities internally or contract them out hinges on a number of factors. While cost efficiency is an important consideration, it is not the only issue. In addition, the firm should consider the degree of control it wishes to exercise over a given function or activity and its core competence. It is especially important to retain control of key functions that provide the motor force of its strategic thrust into global markets.

DEVELOPING GLOBAL MANAGEMENT SYSTEMS

The complexity of the management task, and of developing effective management systems in the global corporation, poses a formidable challenge. Management systems should coordinate and control geographically dispersed operations so as to ensure global efficiency, while at the same time providing flexibility to adapt to local market conditions and changes in the global competitive environment.[13, 14] In addition, management systems should facilitate learning and the transfer of skills, ideas, and experience from one geographic area or stage in the value chain to another.

Companies need to evolve towards organizational forms that provide such capabilities. These forms may be characterized by different structural configurations, management processes, and flows of communication and control, depending on specific industry and demand characteristics as well as the company's own administrative heritage.[14] Within this organizational form, mechanisms to provide the desired vertical and horizontal linkages within the firm have to be established. Again, the precise character of these will vary from company to company, depending on the nature of its operations and the desired degree of strategy integration and coordination across markets.

Developing Transnational Organizational Forms

In the initial phase of entry into international markets, the organizational forms or structures adopted by many companies emphasize a single organizational capability such as global efficiency, local responsiveness, or learning. Consequently, they are largely inadequate to meet the new and complex challenges of managing worldwide operations so as to achieve global synergies.

Typical of the organizational form adopted by many companies in initial international market entry is the international division structure. (See Figure 15-5) This provides a high degree of control by corporate headquarters over local subsidiary management. While local subsidiaries are often able to adapt products and strategies to the local market, new products and ideas for marketing strategy originate from corporate headquarters. Strategy is formulated centrally, typically with limited input from local subsidiary management, and focuses on leveraging capabilities and skills developed in the domestic market on an international scale. This organizational form facilitates transfer of knowledge and expertise from the home base to international markets, but provides limited capability to respond to specific local market conditions.

A geographically decentralized structure, on the other hand, provides considerable autonomy to local subsidiary management to develop new products and tailor marketing strategies to local market conditions. It thus allows for much greater local responsiveness than an international divisional structure. Nestlé, for example, has traditionally been organized on this basis. Local managers are allowed considerable autonomy, not only in the day-to-day running of operations, but also in taking initiatives and developing marketing strategies and programs for local markets.[15] Control is exercised by headquarters predominantly through financial mechanisms, i.e., budgeting procedures, profits, capital investment, etc. In some instances this is supplemented by informal contacts and relationships between corporate headquarters and subsidiary management.

While a geographically decentralized form allows for greater responsiveness to local market conditions and is suited to firms in the local expansion phase, it also results in loss of potential economies of scale, duplication of effort, and possible conflict between subsidiaries in third-country markets, as well as slow new product launches and inconsistent brand or product identities across country markets. As a result, many firms that are decentralized have introduced mechanisms to facilitate greater integration of strategy across national boundaries and the development of global brands. Nestlé, which has traditionally given substantial autonomy to local country managers, has, for example, introduced a system of global product directors who interface with country managers to implement global and regional marketing strategies, search for new products, and cross-fertilize ideas and practices internationally. In addition, the company has directly

INTERNATIONAL DIVISION STRUCTURE

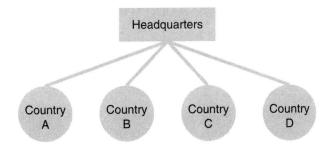

GEOGRAPHIC DECENTRALIZATION

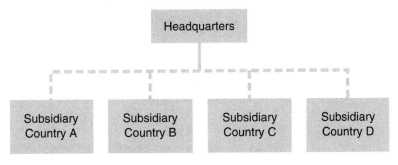

GLOBAL PRODUCT DIVISIONS

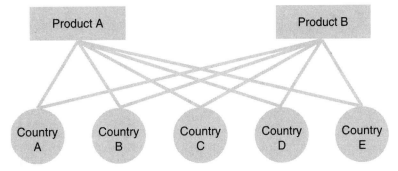

FIGURE 15-5

Alternative
transnational
organizational
forms.

been reorganized into seven "strategic business units" such as milk products, coffee, and ice-cream to facilitate transfer of brands successful in one country to another, and to build global brands.[16]

ICI has also abandoned its traditional country-by-country organization in favor of nine worldwide business units.[17] Each is centered in the country where the company has the strongest capabilities. Advanced materials and specialty chemicals are directed from Wilmington, Delaware, while pharmaceuticals is located in the U.K. R&D labs are also located in the most important market for that business. Advanced materials research is near key clients in the defense industry in Phoenix, Arizona, while leather dye research is located in France. The change facilitated global integration of businesses and substantially reduced the time lag in the introduction of new products to markets around the world. In pharmaceuticals, for example, the time lag in introducing new drugs to different markets throughout the world has been cut from half a dozen years to 1 or 2. The increased mobility of managers across national borders has also encouraged a shift away from strong national loyalties towards a more global orientation.

A third organizational form typically adopted in industries where products are not highly differentiated and there are substantial economies of scale (as for example, chemicals) is the global product division or function structure. International operations are viewed as a means of building the scale of operations and are often tightly linked and coordinated across countries. Local marketing units are primarily concerned with sales and service and provide little input in strategy development. For example, Ford Motor Co. has developed a new organizational structure strengthening global coordination at the functional level. This represents a radical departure from its regionalized structure that provided a high degree of autonomy to Ford North America, Ford of Europe, and Ford Asia/Pacific. The new structure is organized around functions such as product development, sales, and engine/transmissions. The executive in charge of each major function will have the authority to think and act globally.[18] This change is designed to improve global efficiency and underscores Ford's move towards the design and marketing of cars on a global basis. Ford hopes that these changes will result in savings of $3 billion a year.[19]

As a company moves into the third phase of global rationalization, its organizational form should evolve to meet the new demands of implementing a global marketing strategy that relies on a complex network of vertical and horizontal linkages worldwide. Rather than focusing on developing a single strategic capability, this organizational form should provide global efficiency, local responsiveness, and learning simultaneously. The precise form will, however, vary depending on the company's existing organizational structure as well as specific businesses in which it is involved.

Unilever, for example, balances conflicting demands for global efficiency, local responsiveness, and learning with an organizational form tailored to the specific needs of every business, management function, and geographic area.[14] This is illustrated schematically in Figure 15-6. Its chemicals business, for example, is managed globally so as to maximize global efficiency. The packaged goods business, on the other hand, is decentralized to allow for adaptation to local cultural tastes and the distribution infrastructure.

In detergents, the organizational form varies depending on the specific business function. The R&D function is highly centralized and coordinated across geographic areas. Product development combines a high degree of coordination across geographic areas with development of products in response to local market conditions. The sales function, on the other hand, is delegated to local country managers.

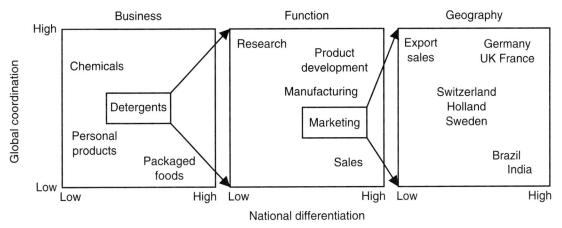

FIGURE 15-6

Unilever's differentiation organization. Modified and reprinted by permission of Harvard Business School Press from *Managing Across Borders: The Transnational Solution* by Christopher A. Bartlett and Sumantra Ghoshal. Boston: 1991, pp. 97. Copyright © 1989, 1991 by the President and Fellows of Harvard College.

Organization of the marketing function varies according to the size of a market and its geographic location. In large proximate markets such as the U.K., France, and Germany, a high degree of coordination is maintained across markets to encourage the marketing of standardized products and brands. At the same time country managers have discretion to adapt promotion and other tactics to local needs. In smaller markets such as Switzerland or Holland, products, ideas, and marketing tactics are borrowed from neighboring markets, as these markets are not sufficiently large to support the development of products or advertising copy specifically tailored to their needs. Large isolated markets, such as Brazil or India, are managed autonomously, with some products and brands imported from other countries, but most products and marketing tactics are tailored to the local market.

The dual challenges of responding to rapidly changing external developments, and meeting the demands of globalization and localization—together with the continued need to rationalize internal operations—creates a drive toward a more flexible and adaptive format for organizing international operations, the network approach. This is based on an adaptive structure of relationships, where information and responsibility are pushed down in the organization. Operations are tied together through a web of information and communication links and personal contacts, supported by advanced systems technology. The network also extends to include external organizations through competitive alliances, outsourcing and licensing arrangements, and tighter logistical and service links with customers.[19]

Managing Headquarters—Subsidiary Relations

Within the context of this organizational form, flows of communication and control need to be established to guide strategy implementation and to ensure effective coordination of operations worldwide. Headquarters–subsidiary relations form the backbone of these links and constitute the nerve center. Here, a delicate balance has to be maintained between directing and focusing the firm's resources so as to achieve corporate goals while at the same time empowering local management to take initiatives and respond creatively to diverse and fast-changing environments.[20]

In many multinationals, traditionally, corporate headquarters have handled relations with all subsidiaries in the same way, applying the same planning procedures, budgeting systems, and controls. This approach ignores inherent differences in the needs and capabilities of different subsidiaries. Often too much attention or emphasis is given to small or less crucial markets, and the needs and potential of larger, more strategically important countries are passed over. Some subsidiaries have, for example, the capability to play a lead role in developing or launching a new product with global potential, or to develop and coordinate strategy for the region. Corporate headquarters also typically has taken the lead in developing and directing global strategy, viewing the role of subsidiaries as primarily one of implementation, with some adaptation when necessary. Relegating subsidiaries to this role underutilizes their capabilities and ignores a crucial need for local input and initiatives in strategy formulation. Excessive control and centralization of strategy development at corporate headquarters is likely to be highly demotivating and stifle the creativity and initiative of local managers.

The complex demands of developing and managing a globally integrated strategy, suggest that responsibility for strategy initiatives and implementation at various stages of the value chain need to be more widely dispersed, rather than centralized and controlled at corporate headquarters. The role played by local subsidiaries should be determined by their specific competencies and skills and the strategic importance of the local market. Highly competent subsidiaries in strategically important markets may, for example, take a lead role in developing and implementing global or regional strategy. P&G's German subsidiary, for example, played a key role in developing Vizir, a highly successful heavy-duty liquid detergent and P&G's first Eurobrand.

At the same time as local initiatives are encouraged, corporate headquarters has to provide direction for global operations. This is especially important where responsibilities are dispersed, to ensure initiatives taken by subsidiaries are consistent with and further the global strategic thrust. At Whirlpool, for example, the company's commitment to globalization is communicated through the vision statement by the chairman, and at annual leadership conferences that bring together senior management from around the world.[21] At the same time, business lines and operating units are responsible for developing their own strategies to respond to regional market conditions.

Corporate headquarters also has to carve out the roles of each subsidiary in the development and implementation of global strategy—who should be responsible for managing a given project or business in a region or worldwide, and who should handle R&D and product development. Resources have to be allocated or redirected according to the roles each is to play in the overall design. In allocating these tasks and resources, it is important to consider, not only the skills and capabilities of a local subsidiary, but also the motivational impact. Giving a small subsidiary a lead role, for example, in a new product development project may help to motivate and energize the unit, which might otherwise only be responsible for implementing strategies developed elsewhere.

The specific management systems and mechanisms adopted to achieve this complex balance between corporate headquarters and local subsidiaries vary widely from company to company, depending on its corporate culture, size, and the specific business or industry it operates in, as well as its strategic thrust. Some companies, such as ABB, operate with a lean corporate headquarters. On merging Brown Boveri and ASEA, Barnevik, the CEO of the new company, ABB, reduced corporate staff at Zurich from 4000 to 200, turning the company into 5000 profit centers run by a corps of 250 global managers.[22] Each center has a country manager as well as a business sector manager who provides coordination for each business, such as transportation or electrical equipment, across national boundaries.[23] Liaison between corporate headquarters and local operations is provided primarily through visits by and personal contacts with Barnevik himself.

Advances in computer technology and the development of "groupware" software that allows information sharing and collaboration by managers in widely diversified geographic locations provide important tools to facilitate global coordination of operations. Compaq, for example, uses groupware to disseminate reseller information regarding technical updates, news releases, and advertising plans. Johnson & Higgins also uses groupware to send its insurance brokers around the world market information, such as price quotes and customer profiles. The company can also gain input from its brokers.[24]

Forging Horizontal Linkages: Eurobrand Teams

In addition to developing effective headquarters–subsidiary relations, a global company also needs to establish mechanisms to coordinate operations across national boundaries. A variety of different linking and coordinating mechanisms can be adopted, depending on how marketing operations are organized, as well as management concern to achieve tighter coordination and integration of activities across national boundaries.

Where strategies are only loosely coordinated across countries, mechanisms focusing primarily on the transfer of ideas and information may be sufficient. Intel, for example, has a companywide electronic mail system linking its 20,000 employees throughout the world. The company has, however, encountered some difficulties in handling the rapid growth in traffic that has risen to over 300,000 messages per day.[25]

Other companies, such as SC Johnson, hold regular meetings of country managers to encourage interaction and sharing of ideas and experience. This is not only limited to new products and programs. Managers can also learn from each other's tactical experiences in dealing with the same competitor or a different marketing environment. For example, managers in countries with restrictions on advertising and mass media, have often developed experience with point-of-purchase tactics that can be useful to others. Similarly, managers in countries such as the U.K. and Germany have experience in dealing with highly concentrated distribution systems and powerful supermarket chains, which can be helpful to other country managers as retail concentration takes place elsewhere.

Where emphasis is placed on identifying opportunities for strategy standardization across countries, and on regional or global product launches, tighter organizational links across countries will be required. P&G has, for example, established a system of Eurobrand teams to coordinate the management of brands sold throughout Europe. P&G initially attempted to coordinate marketing strategy in Europe by assigning coordination responsibility for a brand to a manager at its European headquarters. After encountering resistance from local country managers, this approach was abandoned. P&G then adopted a new approach, co-opting managers from various European subsidiaries as well as managers from the European technical center to build teams to manage brands on a pan-European basis.

This system was first introduced with the launch of Vizir, a liquid heavy-duty laundry detergent. A Eurobrand team, headed by a manager from the largest market, Germany, was set up to develop the launch strategy for Vizir. The team, which consisted of managers from all the countries where Vizir was to be launched, then decided on the positioning, brand name, packaging, and pricing of Vizir for Europe. A common promotional theme was also identified, but specific execution was left to each country manager.

The system proved highly successful and was adopted with some modification for the subsequent launch and management of other pan-European brands. Since Germany was invariably the largest market, the country from which the head manager was selected was rotated to ensure that the team leader was not always German. Greater freedom was also given to country managers to adapt tactics to the local market, particularly in terms of promotion and, to a lesser extent, pricing.

Other companies, such as Scott Paper and Jacob Suchard, have adopted similar types of mechanisms to coordinate marketing strategies regionally or globally. A variety of different organizational structures and linking mechanisms can thus be utilized to coordinate and integrate operations worldwide. The specific form these take will, however, vary with the individual company, depending on the range and character of its product businesses and the desired degree of strategy integration, as well as its corporate culture and history.

DEVELOPING CUSTOMER LINKAGES

In addition to developing a global management system to coordinate and direct operations internally, external linkages with customer and supplier operations need to be established. Development of strong linkages with customers is central to the effective implementation of a global marketing strategy. In the first place, linkages need to be established to manage the flow of goods and services to customers in a timely fashion. This is especially critical where customers have operations worldwide, requiring effective coordination of the supply of goods and services to these various locations throughout the world.

In some instances, companies establish a system of global account managers to handle relations with client corporate headquarters and their operations in different countries throughout the world. This helps in identifying product and service needs, and in coordinating corporate and local subsidiary relations. It also provides a bridge between local firm and customer operations. (See Figure 15-7)

In addition, the firm has to service customer operations and provide training, maintenance, and other facilities on a worldwide basis. Either such services are provided through the firm's own network or through a system of licensed representatives or independent agents. In either case, as discussed in Chapter 3, mechanisms to collect information and feedback from customers, relating to customer satisfaction and need for product or service improvements, are critical to enable the firm to adapt to changing market needs.

Managing the Flow of Goods to Customer Supply Points

As pressures to improve cost efficiency mount and inventory carrying costs increase in markets worldwide, managing the flow of goods and services to customer service points efficiently becomes increasingly important. This is especially critical where production is centralized in a limited number of locations while

FIGURE 15-7

Global account coordination.

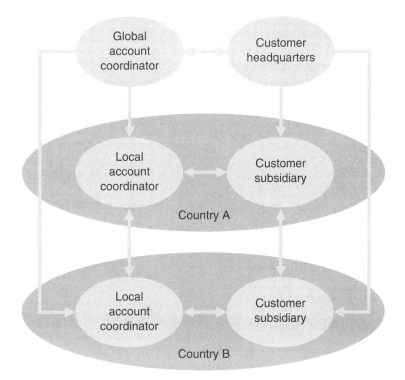

customer operations are widely dispersed throughout the world. It often becomes particularly complex when contracts for the supply of goods and services are negotiated centrally at client headquarters for its operations worldwide. Production and supply from the firm's plants throughout the world have to be coordinated with the requirements of customer operations in different countries and regions.

Customer requirements in terms of order cycle, delivery time, and reliability are key to the efficient management of supply and delivery system. If, for example, a customer practices "just in time" inventory management or requires rapid delivery, the firm may need to establish local warehousing facilities in order to provide the desired level of service. In some instances, maintenance of inventory and delivery can be handled by the local sales office or branch in the country or close to where customer operations are located.

Introduction of EDI computer information and inventory management systems linking customers and supply points is often a key factor in improving response to customer needs. Levi Strauss has, for example, established a Quick Response Program in Europe, linking electronic point-of-sale terminals to its regional headquarters in Brussels. Transactions can be processed rapidly and accurate sales data produced. Orders can then be fed directly to different factories, depending on their work load. Order lead time is substantially reduced, allowing faster response to customer orders and substantial reduction in inventory.[26]

Increasingly, firms are finding it more efficient to establish direct links with customer supply points throughout the world and organize supply directly from the closest production location. Tupperware, for example, has developed a global inventory and order management system that enables it to respond quickly to hot products as they "catch fire" in different parts of the world. The information system not only detects "hot" products rapidly but also enables Tupperware to supplement supply from manufacturing centers in different parts of the world and thus accelerate delivery to distributors in a given country.[27]

In some instances, the firm takes over the management of the reordering and delivery process. In this case, the firm establishes electronic links with the customer's inventory system and/or each supply point, and when stocks fall below an agreed-on level, supplies of the required items are directly shipped wherever they are needed. This approach not only helps to speed up delivery time and shorten the order cycle, but also enables the firm to plan production logistics more efficiently and lower inventory carrying costs.

Global Account Management

Some companies have set up global account management systems to handle and coordinate relations with global customer operations worldwide. Global account management systems are especially prevalent in service industries such as banking, insurance, and advertising. Products and purchasing are not highly routinized and often require tailoring to specific local needs and circumstances.

Typically, an account manager is assigned responsibility for handling relations with the corporate headquarters of a global customer. This includes negotiating contracts, identifying product and service needs, and coordinating marketing activities worldwide to meet these needs. In some cases, local correspondent managers are also appointed to handle relations with local subsidiaries of a customer. These managers report to the global account manager and provide input for planning and coordinating marketing activities, and for developing new products and services, sales, and other activities.

Citibank pioneered one of the early global account management systems in the banking industry. In 1974 a World Corporation Group was established with responsibility for handling relations with major multinational corporate customers, who at the time accounted for about 20 percent of worldwide loans. A parent account manager (PAM) located in the customer's home country was assigned to handle relations with a customer's corporate headquarters. In each country where the customer had a branch or subsidiary, a field account manager (FAM) was appointed to handle local relations. A primary objective of this system was to integrate planning and budgeting for global accounts worldwide and facilitate assessment of their profitability. Each parent account manager prepared an annual marketing plan and budget for the account, with input from the local field account manager. Performance could then be tracked by comparing actual results with those budgeted.

Initially, the system proved highly effective in building business with global customers, and substantial growth was experienced in both the volume of business and the profitability of global accounts. In 1980, however, the World Corporation Group was combined with the domestic Corporate Banking Group and the International Banking Group into a single entity—the Institutional Banking Group. Account managers formerly assigned to global accounts were reassigned to country or regional units. Although the global account management system remained in place, country managers paid greater attention to local profits and were less concerned with global account profitability. Consequently, the service had to be reinforced by appointing a vice president responsible for global accounts. Currently, Citibank is organized into two broad groups, global consumer and global finance, which support the activities of over 3,500 offices in over 90 countries worldwide.[28]

Saatchi & Saatchi also instituted a system of global account management to handle relations with multinational customers and promote the adoption of standardized advertising campaigns worldwide. If a client was interested in a globally standardized campaign, a global manager was assigned to the account. He or she was responsible for handling the planning and development of the campaign in collaboration with corporate staff, as well as promoting its acceptance by customer subsidiaries in different countries. Where local resistance and demand for adaptation were encountered, the global account manager attempted to negotiate and iron out these differences in conjunction with personnel from the local agency branch or office.

The system was intended to promote the adoption of global advertising campaigns and thus enable the agency to capture the local advertising budgets of clients worldwide. However, it proved to be costly, highly cumbersome, and time consuming. Given frequent conflict between corporate staff and local subsidiaries about the need for adaptation or even acceptance of a standardized campaign, account managers frequently spent much of their time trying to mediate or resolve such conflicts. In addition, growth in global accounts fell off, as potential for global advertising campaigns is limited, as discussed in Chapter 10.

Developing Customer Service Linkages

The third type of customer linkage relates to the provision of services, such as training, systems maintenance, and repair, to customer operations worldwide. Here, a variety of options exist, depending on service needs as well as the geographic scope of the firm's own operations. One option is to service customers through a network of company representatives. This is most likely to be feasible where the company has operations in all countries or regions where customers are located. In some cases it can be cost effective to organize the service network on a regional or even global basis, if customer operations are highly concentrated. A company-owned service network enables the firm to control service operations and develop a totally integrated solution to meet customer needs. This type of approach is becoming increasingly popular in some industries such as information systems and software. A customer hotline with a toll-free number can be established to respond to customer questions and trouble-shoot problems.

Another alternative is to rely on distributors to provide service or to develop a network of licensed representatives. In some instances, companies may find that distributors or licensed representatives are better able to provide rapid, high-quality service. This is especially likely to be the case where the company has no, or limited, operations in a region. Often, however, this requires training distributors or representatives to install service or maintain equipment. Caterpillar, for example, has training centers in a number of countries, such as Japan, Brazil, and Germany, as well as in the United States.

Service can also be left to independent agents or companies. This may be effective in a well-developed, mature market, where knowledge and experience with the product and relevant technology are widespread. However, it always incorporates the risk that service and maintenance do not meet company standards, resulting in substandard performance, and subsequent customer dissatisfaction with the product. In addition, use of independent agents provides little information to assess customer satisfaction with the product, to gain ideas for product and service improvement or aspects such as defect ratios and usage problems.

COLLABORATING WITH COMPETITORS

In today's complex world, rare is the firm that has the resources and skills at all stages in the value chain, or the geographic coverage to effectively implement all aspects of its strategy worldwide. As a result, in order to fill these gaps, management often enters into collaborative agreements or strategic alliances with firms in the same or related industries. These firms may, at the same time, be competitors in other markets or at other phases of operations.

Collaborating with competitors offers a number of advantages.[29] In the first place, alliances enable firms to share investment costs and financial risks associated with the R&D, production, or marketing of products. This is often a key motivation underlying alliances in industries such as aerospace, telecommunications, pharmaceuticals, or construction equipment, where development costs can be astronomical. Small competitors aiming to compete in an industry dominated by giants may also enter into alliances to attain critical mass. A number of collaborative agreements among European firms have, for example, been designed to enable them to compete with larger U.S. or Japanese firms. If however, collaboration is undertaken to avoid investment and development costs, it is likely to weaken a firm's long-run ability to compete.[30]

Alliances are also established in order to obtain complementary skills and resources such as, for example, specific technological expertise or manufacturing capability. Entering into an alliance can also enable a firm to gain access to a market that would otherwise require heavy investment in building a distribution network or broadening geographic coverage. Furthermore, collaboration helps to limit competition and can provide a means for a group of small firms to compete more effectively against large firms in an industry.

On the other hand, collaboration with competitors exposes the firm to a number of risks. Both sides will not necessarily benefit equally from the collaboration, especially if one partner is less committed or motivated than another.[31] Collaborative agreements are also difficult to manage, and communication problems often arise, especially if the corporate cultures, management style, and communication systems of the respective partners are widely different. Alliances can also run into difficulties with governments and other regulatory bodies, especially if they are viewed as restricting competition or likely to result in foreign dominance in a strategic industry. The European Union, for example, has established tough antitrust rules, which are being strictly enforced, resulting in close scrutiny of a number of collaborative agreements.[32]

Collaborative agreements with competitors can take a wide range of different forms. Here, three major categories are identified based on the stage in the value chain: (1) collaboration for joint research or new product development (2) collaboration for joint production and logistics, and (3) collaboration on joint marketing and distribution activities. (See Figure 15-8.) In some instances, the collaboration may be multipurpose and combine two or more facets or areas of collaboration. In general, however, the dominant motivation for the alliance lies in one of these three areas.

Collaborating on R&D

Firms typically enter into collaborative ventures for R&D or product development for two main reasons. The firm may not possess certain technological skills or resources needed to undertake a project. In this case the firm looks for a part-

FIGURE 15-8

Alternative strategic alliance configuration.

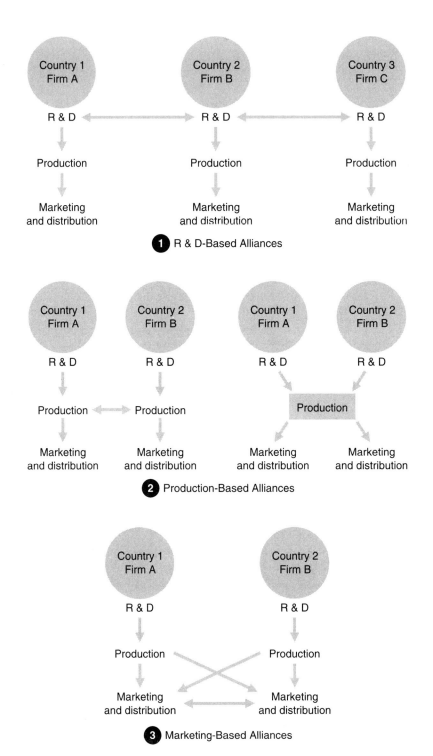

ner with the requisite skills and technological base. This type of collaboration is particularly likely to occur in industries where technology is evolving rapidly, requiring new and different skills, or where the technologies of two industries are converging, as, for example, in computers and telecommunications. Alternatively, in some industries such as aerospace or telecommunications, the costs and financial risks of undertaking basic research or new product development are so great that few firms can afford to do it alone. Collaborative agreements provide a means of pooling resources and sharing financial and, in some cases, marketing risks.

Complementary technologies were a key motivation underlying the ill-fated strategic alliance between AT&T and Olivetti. AT&T possessed the telecommunications and PBX switching technology, while Olivetti had expertise in personal computers and office equipment. A key thrust of the alliance was to develop products that would combine both technologies, incorporating transmission of both voice and data, as, for example, in computerized telephones with the capability to monitor and respond to incoming calls.

In addition, AT&T was to market Olivetti personal computers through its distribution network in the United States, while Olivetti marketed AT&T's Unix software and adapted its PBXs and other telecommunications products to European markets. Olivetti achieved some success in selling Unix software, notably to Philips and some other large European companies. Sales of Olivetti personal computers in the United States were, however, limited principally to internal sales to various AT&T divisions, as AT&T's marketing capabilities were limited. As a result, Olivetti appointed Xerox as a second distributor and sent over Cassoni, a top Olivetti marketing director, to run AT&T's computer division.[33] Some improvement was achieved in AT&T's computer division, but little progress was achieved in new product development, with each side claiming that the other had failed to live up to the terms of the agreement. As a result the alliance was eventually dissolved.[34]

In the aerospace, telecommunications, and semiconductor industries collaboration on R&D and product development is common, particularly among smaller competitors, due to the high costs and risks associated with such projects. Even with large companies, such as Asean Brown Boveri and Rolls Royce have, for example, collaborated on the development of turbine engines for jet aircraft, to share the financial and marketing risks of the project. Another type of venture is that established by IBM, Siemens, and Toshiba to develop 256-megabyte DRAMS, memory chips for the twenty-first century.[35] The three companies will pool their skills and resources. While IBM is generally the first to design and build new generation DRAMS, Toshiba is considered to have the best manufacturing techniques, while Siemens provides input from the European market and financial resources. In addition to sharing huge design costs estimated at over $1 billion, an important function of the collaboration is to reduce their dependence on suppliers of semiconductor chips such as Intel. The alliance is, however, limited to chips. Each partner will use these to build its own computers, which will compete with each other in world markets.

Fujitsu and Hyundai have also established an agreement to share the research and development costs for chips that will enable both firms to compete with their larger competitors. Initially, Hyundai has licensed its design and manufacturing process technology for DRAMS to Fujitsu, which Fujitsu will produce at its Oregon plant. Hyundai will buy these chips to sell in the U.S. market, thus avoiding the 11 percent import duty, while Fujitsu will use them in its own product line. The two companies also plan to explore joint development and production of future generation DRAMS.[36]

Collaborating on Production and Logistics

Another form of collaboration focuses on production and supply logistics. A wave of such ventures has swept the automobile industry in recent years as smaller competitors such as Mazda, Renault, Volvo, and Rover seek to improve global efficiency and geographic coverage to compete with industry giants. The giants, on the other hand, look to acquire specific skills and broaden their product line. As in the case of R&D projects, each partner supplies specialized skills or provides market coverage that complements that of other partners. Alternatively, joint production of models or component and establishing linkages that enable attainment of scale economies provide greater efficiency and, where combined with distribution links, broader market coverage.

Mazda, the number four automobile company in Japan, behind Toyota, Nissan, and Honda, has based its global strategy on forging production and distribution alliances with other automobile companies such as Ford, Citroen, and Suzuki.[37] In Japan, over 12 percent of the cars made and sold by Mazda are Ford models such as the Festiva. Another model, the Carol, is based on an engine, transmission, and chassis from Suzuki. Mazda and Ford have also worked jointly on the design and remodeling of 10 other automobile models, for which Ford was primarily responsible for the styling, and Mazda the engineering. Mazda helped to improve the Ford Escort, the Mercury Tracer, the Mercury Capri, and the Festiva, as well as to design the sporty Ford Probe and the off-road Explorer, while Ford contributed to the MX6, 323, and Protege.[38] Ford and Mazda also collaborated on the development of the Navajo, a modified two-door version of Ford's off-road Explorer, which is produced at Ford's plant in Louisville, Kentucky. Mazda helped to design Ford's plant in Hermosillo, Mexico, which is modelled after Mazda's Hofu (Japan) factory. The plant, which produces the Tracer, has rapidly become one of Ford's most efficient and top-ranking plants for quality.

In addition to collaborating on production, Mazda has also set up the Autorama chain of showrooms in Japan in collaboration with Ford. These display imported Ford cars as well as the Ford models produced by Mazda in Japan. Two other chains of showrooms, Eunos and Autozam, sell Citroen and Fiat models, respectively, as well as Mazda's own models. These collaborative agreements have been highly successful in enabling Mazda to compete with the three Japanese auto giants in Japan while at the same time expanding in the United States and Europe.

Production alliances have also been developed in the personal computer industry. Apple Computer, for example, entered into an alliance with Sony to develop and manufacture the Power Book, a light notebook computer.[39] Apple provided Sony with the basic blueprint and a list of components, from which Sony engineers developed Apple's smallest and lightest notebook computer, applying their skills in miniaturization.

Another successful but highly controversial European collaboration is the Airbus consortium headed by the French company, Aerospatiale, with partners Deutsche Aerospace, British Aerospace, and the Spanish CASA. None of these companies alone had the resources to develop large, wide-bodied aircraft to compete with the market leader, Boeing. A consortium was established with government backing, primarily from France and Germany, to challenge domination of the world market by Boeing.[40, 41] Each partner produces certain components of the Airbus, i.e., fuselage, engines, and wings, which are then assembled in France by Aerospatiale, which directs the project. Substantial government subsidiaries have been needed in order to support the venture and make it financially stable. (This has been a source of considerable controversy.) However, Airbus has been successful in capturing a 30 percent world market share, as well as making substantial inroads into the U.S. market.

The consortium is dominated largely by Aerospatiale, and the director is French, although Deutsche Aerospace has been vying for greater control. Plans announced by Boeing to build a giant airliner of 600–800 seats in partnership with Deutsche Aerospace pose a potential threat to the stability and success of the Airbus consortium, especially since it was already studying plans for a super-jumbo. Financing of the huge $10–15-billion development costs of such an aircraft suggest, however, that broad-based collaboration on the project, including Boeing and other consortium partners, is likely.[40]

Such issues underscore the difficulties of managing cross-national collaborative agreements with competitors. Clashes of culture and management style are likely to occur, especially where one partner dominates the relationship. Numerous failures of collaborative agreements, for example, between Dunlop of the U.K. and Pirelli of Italy, two family businesses, have been attributed to clashes of corporate culture.[31]

Collaborating on Marketing and Distribution

A third type of collaborative agreement focuses primarily on marketing and distribution. In some cases, a competitor may provide access to markets or distribution channels in a geographic area where a firm has no, or limited, coverage. In other cases, a firm may be able to fill gaps in both product lines and distribution coverage through collaborative agreements and cross-selling arrangements.

Links are thus established with competitors to extend the geographic scope of operations and establish a regional or worldwide distribution network.

General Mills and Nestlé (Switzerland), for example, have established an alliance called Cereal Partners Worldwide to market breakfast cereals in Europe, the Far East, and Latin America. The venture makes use of Nestlé's marketing skills and access to distribution channels in these areas, while General Mills provides the product technology, brand names, and experience with breakfast cereals. The venture utilizes Nestlé plants in Europe, and the Nestlé name and logo appear on the packaging together with the General Mills brand name. Nestlé thus gains a new product line in the rapidly growing market for breakfast cereals, while General Mills benefits from Nestlé's marketing strength and powerful distribution network. The venture aims to make inroads into Kellogg's dominance of breakfast cereals in these markets, which neither partner alone was in a position to do.[42]

A number of alliances have also been established between United States and Japanese firms in the construction industry. Deere (U.S.) and Hitachi (Japan), for example, have established a joint venture to produce and distribute hydraulic excavators and have pooled their assembly operations and distribution networks in North America. Caterpillar and Mitsubishi have also merged their hydraulic excavator operations in Japan, while Komatsu and Dresser are pooling their manufacturing and marketing operations in earth-moving equipment in North and South America.[43] These agreements enable the U.S. companies to fill gaps in their product line, notably in heavy equipment such as hydraulic equipment, while the Japanese companies gain access to distribution networks and in some cases production facilities in North America.

A number of pharmaceutical companies have also established global joint ventures in order to broaden distribution coverage and expand in the growing market for OTC drugs.[44] Warner Lambert has, for example, negotiated a joint venture with Welcome, a British OTC drug company, to fuse their nonprescription drugs business worldwide, making it the third largest OTC company after Johnson and Johnson and American Home Products. The OTC market is expected to grow rapidly as governments encourage a switch from prescription to OTC status, for which consumers pay directly. Warner Lambert has also negotiated an alliance with Glaxo, Europe's largest drug company, to sell Glaxo prescription drugs in the United States. This will give Warner Lambert access to Zantac, an antiulcer treatment, one of the top selling drugs in the world, while Glaxo gains access to Warner Lambert's strength in U.S. distribution channels.

With the growth of international travel and increased global competition, airlines have increasingly begun to forge links with foreign competitors and tie into their reservation systems in order to broaden their geographic coverage and gain access to new hubs. KLM Royal Dutch Airlines, for example, paid $400 million for a 49 percent stake in Northwest Airlines; Swissair, the Swiss carrier, established links with Delta to gain access to the U.S. market. Similarly, British Airways bought into ailing US Air to gain access to regional hubs within the United

States. In order to strengthen its European network it acquired a small German carrier, Deutsche BA, and TAT, an independent French airline,[45] as well as buying a 25 percent stake in Quantas, the Australian airline. The Spanish airline, Iberia, on the other hand, has focused on links with Latin America, buying a controlling interest in Aerolineas Argentina and a stake in airlines in Chile and Venezuela.

Many of these alliances appear to be running into difficulties due to cut-throat competition in the airline industry, as well as squabbles over landing rights at different national airports. The projected Alcazar European alliance between SAS, the Swedish airline, Swissair, KLM, and Austrian Airlines has collapsed, as the carrier failed to agree on a U.S. partner.[46] Similarly, British Airways has refused to increase its investment in US Air unless the airline reverses its losses, while KLM has written down its investment in Northwest.[47]

Telecommunications companies on both sides on the Atlantic are also beginning to link up, as state monopolies in Europe break up and technology changes, integrating wire and cellular communications. British Telecom has, for example, bought a stake in MCI, the second largest U.S. carrier. MCI will market phone services to multinationals in North and South America, while B.T. takes on the rest of the world.[48] AT&T has also moved to develop a global network, focusing initially on Asia.

Management of such collaborative agreements is no easy matter, however. In the first place, successful collaborations require the establishment of a common goal or mission.[31] For example, the IBM–Toshiba–Siemens venture has set as its goal the development of a superchip to be used by all partners in building their computers, though they will compete downstream in that market. The Philips and du Pont collaboration on the development and manufacture of compact discs, on the other hand, entails a clear upstream/downstream division of effort, where neither will invade the other's market.

Secondly, the strategy to achieve this goal needs to be clearly articulated. The Cereal Partners venture between Nestlé and General Mills has clearly mapped out their battle plan to conquer Kelloggs in the breakfast cereal market. Finally, collaboration is most likely to be successful where the various partners have complementary needs and skills, or a comparative advantage in a specific aspect of the project, and where they work and interact together on its completion. Thus, for example, in the Airbus consortium, each partner produces a specific part of the aircraft in which it has some technological advantage.

Even with careful planning and common goals, collaborative ventures may fail. An interesting case in point is the Renault/Volvo merger, which took 3 years to plan and fell apart 3 months after it was announced. Renault and Volvo had been cooperating in a strategic alliance, and the two chairmen had a vision of a $40 billion company capable of meeting global competition. Unfortunately, some of the Swedish shareholders and workers did not agree. The following quote from a manager in Volvo's truck division reveals this sentiment: "We gave the French all our ideas, all our plans, and we got nothing in return."[49]

SUMMARY

Ultimately the impact of a global marketing strategy depends on how successfully it is implemented. No matter how well designed, unless a strategy is effectively implemented, its objectives will not be achieved. Managers may wrongly conclude that the strategy was flawed and abandon it prematurely. Successful implementation begins with the adoption of a global perspective at all levels of management. This is essential to ensure that management does not place undue emphasis on a particular part of the world, such as the home market.

Successful implementation of global marketing strategy entails effective management of all activities in the value chain. Management must decide on the degree of geographic concentration, as well as the extent of coordination of activities across countries needed to implement marketing strategy effectively. Successful implementation entails more than attention to marketing, which is the last step in delivering value to the customer. Issues related to location of R&D activities, production, and sourcing logistics are often equally important in order to ensure efficient delivery of customer value. In addition, firms have to decide whether it is more efficient to perform these functions internally or externally.

The global management system must be designed to achieve a balance between global efficiency and responsiveness to local conditions. These potentially conflicting needs may never be fully reconciled. Recognition of this fact requires the development of an organizational structure that is sufficiently flexible to respond to changing market and competitive dynamics. This management system must provide effective linkages within the organization as well as with external organizations. Establishment of linkages with customers is essential to ensure that the firm responds to customer needs for product quality and delivery requirements. In some instances a firm may also need to establish linkages with competitors through various types of strategic alliances to acquire needed skills or geographic market coverage to implement global strategy.

REFERENCES

1. "Sony: Global Management Drives a Global Image" (1991) *Building a Global Image,* New York: Business International.
2. Porter, Michael E. (1986) "Competition in Global Industries: A Conceptual Framework," In: M.E. Porter (ed.) *Competition in Global Industries,* Cambridge, MA: Harvard University Press.
3. Porter, Michael E. (1990) *The Competitive Advantage of Nations,* New York: The Free Press.
4. Magnet, Myron (1992) "Who's Winning the Information Revolution," *Fortune,* November 30, pp. 110–117.
5. Kotabe, Masaaki (1992) *Global Sourcing Strategy,* New York: Quorum Books.
6. Taylor, Alex III (1993) "How Toyota Copes with Hard Times," *Fortune,* January 25, pp. 78–81.

7. Taylor, Alex III (1993) "Ford's $6 Billion Baby," *Fortune,* June 28, pp. 76–81.
8. "SKF to Centralize Distribution" (1993) *Business Europe,* April 12–18, p. 7.
9. Business International (1990) *Managing Today's International Company,* New York: Business International.
10. Byrne, John, Kathleen Kerwin, Amy Cortese, and Paula Dwyer (1994) "Borderless Management," *Business Week,* May 23, pp. 24–26.
11. Tully, Shawn (1993) "The Modular Corporation," *Fortune,* February 8, pp. 106–114.
12. "Quick Growth, Reddy Money," (1993) *Business India,* August 16–29, pp. 82–84.
13. Prahalad, C.K., and Yves Doz (1987) *The Multinational Mission,* New York: The Free Press.
14. Bartlett, Christopher A., and Sumantra Ghoshal (1989) *Managing Across Borders: The Transnational Solution,* Boston: Harvard Business School Press.
15. Quelch, John A., and Edward J. Hoff (1986) "Customizing Global Marketing," *Harvard Business Review,* May-June, pp. 59–68.
16. "Nestlé: A Giant in a Hurry" (1993) *Business Week,* March 22, pp. 50–54.
17. Main, Jeremy (1989) "How to Go Global and Why," *Fortune,* August 28, pp. 70–76.
18. Ingrassia, Paul, and Jacqueline Mitchell (1994) "Ford to Realign with a System of Global Chiefs," *Wall Street Journal* March 31, pp. A-3-ff.
19. Business International (1989) *Managing Today's International Company,* New York: Business International.
20. Bartlett, Christopher A., and Sumantra Ghoshal (1986) "Tap Your Subsidiaries for Global Reach," *Harvard Business Review,* November-December, pp. 87–94.
21. Business International (1991) *Global Strategic Planning,* New York: Business International.
22. Hofheinz, Paul (1993) "Europe's Tough New Managers," *Fortune,* September 6, pp. 111–116.
23. Rapoport, Carla (1992) "A Tough Suede Invades the U.S.," *Fortune,* June 9, pp. 76–79.
24. Manzi, Jim (1994) "Computer Keiretsu: Japanese Idea, U.S. Style," *New York Times* February 6, p. 15.
25. Hadjian, Ani (1993) "Andy Grove: How Intel Makes Spending Pay Off," *Fortune* February 22, pp. 56–61.
26. "How Levi's Works with Retailers . . ." (1993) *Business Europe* July 19–25.
27. Roche, Edward M. (1992) *Managing Information Technology in Multinational Corporations,* New York: Macmillan.
28. "Citicorp: A Unique Global Bank," (1993) New York: Citicorp.
29. Ohmae, Kenichi (1990) *The Borderless World,* New York: Harper Business.
30. Hamel, Gary, Yves Doz, and C.K. Prahalad (1989) "Collaborate with Your Competitors and Win," *Harvard Business Review,* January-February, pp. 133–139.

31. Perlmutter, Howard V., and David A. Heenan (1986) "Cooperate to Compete Globally," *Harvard Business Review,* March-April, pp. 136–152.
32. "The Free Market Enforcer Who's Shaking Up Europe (1991) *Business Week,* November 4, pp. 47–50.
33. Lewis, Geoff, and John J. Keller (1988) "AT&T's Love Affair with Vittorio Cassoni," *Business Week,* February 8, pp. 87–88.
34. "Cross Border Alliances Become Favorite Way to Crack New Markets" (1990) *Wall Street Journal,* March 26, p. A1.
35. "IBM, Toshiba, Siemens Form Venture to Develop DRAM's for the Next Century" (1992) *Wall Street Journal,* July 13, p. B8.
36. "Fujitsu and Hyundai Electronics Form Unusual Joint Venture in Memory Chips" (1993) *Wall Street Journal,* October 7.
37. Rapoport, Carla (1990) "Mazda's Bold New Global Strategy," *Fortune,* December 17, pp. 109–113.
38. "The Partners" (1992) *Business Week,* February 10, pp. 102–107.
39. Schlender, Brenton (1991) "Apple's Japanese Ally," *Fortune,* November 5, pp. 151–152.
40. "Boeing Launches a Stealth Attack on Airbus" (1993) *Business Week,* January 18, pp. 32.
41. "Zoom, Airbus Comes on Strong" (1991) *Business Week,* April 21, pp. 48–50.
42. Knowlton, Christopher (1991) "Europe Cooks Up a Cereal Brawl," *Fortune,* June 3, pp. 175–179.
43. "A Dream Marriage Turns Nightmarish" (1991) *Business Week,* April 29, pp. 94–95.
44. "Drug Groups in Global Links," (1993) *Financial Times,* July 29.
45. Labich, Kenneth (1992) "Europe's Sky Wars," *Fortune,* November 2, pp. 88–94.
46. "Four Airlines Merger Plan Ends in Clash over U.S. Links" (1993) *Financial Times,* November 23.
47. "Sky Anxiety" (1994) *Business Week,* March 21, p. 38.
48. Zeigler, Bart, Mark Lewyn, and Paula Dwyer (1993) "Who's Afraid of AT&T?" *Business Week,* June 14, pp. 32–33.
49. Dwyer, Paula (1993) "Why Volvo Kissed Renault Goodbye," *Business Week,* December 20, p. 54.

PART V

DYNAMICS OF GLOBALIZATION

Chapter 16 The Global Imperative

THE GLOBAL IMPERATIVE

INTRODUCTION

The three phases identified in this book—initial entry, local market expansion, and global rationalization—form a series of successive stages through which the firm passes on its path to globalization. The phases represent a progression, reflecting different levels of involvement and commitment to international markets. Progress through the different phases may be accomplished rapidly or slowly, hesitantly with many false starts, or smoothly and with ease. It may require radical change and new direction for the firm, or be achieved with minimal disruption.

Firms, both large and small, are to be found in each of these phases, as the examples and cases in this book illustrate. Numerous small and medium-sized firms from industrialized nations, as well as large firms from developing countries, or those which are just opening up, such as India and China, are taking their first steps into foreign markets. Many diversified consumer goods companies, such as Nestlé, Unilever, and Kao, are in the second phase, focusing primarily on local market expansion, but at the same time seeking ways to improve coordination of operations across country markets. Yet other companies such as Ford, GE, Caterpillar, and ABB are in the third phase of global rationalization, seeking opportunities to target global customers and target segments worldwide, and devising ways to cope with the complexity of managing operations on a global scale.

The issues and challenges facing firms in each of these phases are characteristically different. Yet the forces that shape the global context in which they do business are the same. These are the forces that determine how markets are defined, and their changing spatial configuration, and fuel the growing intensity of global competition. They mold customer aspirations, tastes, and expectations, and define the nature of opportunities facing the global firm as well as the resources available to formulate and deliver an effective response (see Figure 16-1 for a summary of the forces and challenges).

371

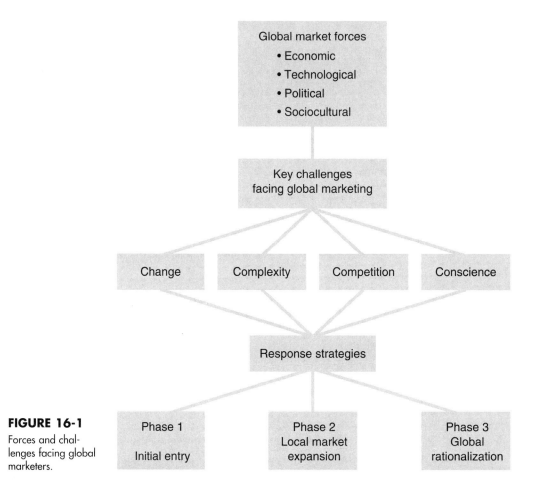

FIGURE 16-1

Forces and challenges facing global marketers.

GLOBAL FORCES FOR CHANGE

A variety of complex forces shape the global marketing environment, establishing the parameters under which global marketing strategy must be formulated. These forces were discussed in detail in Chapter 1 and will only be identified briefly here. They include *macroeconomic* forces driving towards a greater interdependence of nations and country markets, as well as *microeconomic* factors that underpin key elements of marketing strategies and determine the potential for economies of scale and scope. *Technological* advances have radically changed production and distribution logistics and modes of communication, creating rapid knowledge obsolescence and new communication highways interlinking markets. *Political* forces have both lifted and created new barriers to market entry and international trade, and impact the development of industrial policy as well as the regulation or deregulation of markets, products, and terms of competition. *Sociocultural* trends, such as increased travel and communication between countries, the internationalization of life-styles, growing ethnic awareness and fragmentation, heightened social consciousness, and environmental awareness are all key imperatives for the global marketer.

KEY CHALLENGES FACING GLOBAL MARKETERS

The global marketer faces a number of challenges in developing marketing strategies to compete effectively in world markets. The precise nature of these challenges, depends to a substantial degree on the firm's involvement in international operations. Yet, regardless of the stage in its evolution, a firm needs to develop strategies to respond to these rapidly evolving forces. The rapid pace of *change* implies that marketing strategy must be continually monitored and adapted to take into account new economic, technological, political, and social realities. The interplay of these forces in different geographic areas creates a new *complexity* for the global manager as market configurations evolve. This taxes the firm's ability to manage far-flung and diverse operations. The increasing intensity and accelerated speed of *competition,* together with the proliferation of diverse types of competition, constitute yet another hurdle in the path towards success in global markets. In addition, growing awareness and concern with ethical issues, such as environmental protection and conservation, consumer rights and education, social responsibility, and job creation, require that the firm develop a social *conscience,* and heeds this in shaping its global marketing strategy.

Change

Rapid change pervades all aspects of operations in global markets, as well as the context in which they take place. Not only are the rate of technological evolution and knowledge obsolescence, and the intensity of competition, increasing at an alarming pace in many industries, but unforeseen events are dramatically changing the political and economic context in which markets develop and strategies are formulated.

Technological change renders product development, production processes, and experience rapidly obsolete and contributes to escalating investment costs as well as heightened competitive pressures. In the notebook segment of the personal computer industry, for example, the cycle of new model introduction has shrunk to less than 3 months, rendering models rapidly obsolete and requiring constant vigilance to new product development and attention to keeping ahead of the competition.

At the same time, as customers become more mobile and are exposed to new ideas and patterns of behavior through the new global media, the diffusion of new products and innovation takes place more rapidly. Rather than first being adopted by opinion leaders and then trickling down to other members of society, innovations are now spreading horizontally across countries and societies.

No sooner does a new trend or fashion emerge in one country than it spreads rapidly to another. Not only are global marketers agents of change in introducing new and innovative products and services to other countries, but in addition they must respond to the rapid pace at which societies are changing and market trends evolving.

While the pace of change is accelerating, pushed by the engine of technology and global communication, it is becoming increasingly uncertain and unpredictable—occurring in unexpected ways from unexpected sources. Events such as the breakup of the former Soviet Union have had far-reaching, often cataclysmic effects on world markets and on the geopolitics of world trade. Subsequent political and economic events dramatically halted the rate of economic growth and foreign investment in the former Soviet economy. The break up also affected former trading partners such as India, Cuba, Vietnam, and North Korea, forcing them to seek out new markets for their products, and sources for energy, arms, minerals, and other raw materials. It also put a sudden end to the Cold War and ushered in a new political era. Industries such as defense, which fed on the desire to maintain the geopolitical balance, declined, triggering the realignment of related and tributary industries such as aerospace and defense electronics.

The reunification of Germany markedly changed the course of events in Europe, substantially altering the balance of economic power and introducing a new centrifugal pull towards the East. The motor of European unification put in motion by EC 1992 has slowed as positions and economies become realigned in light of a united Germany and the changing face of the new Europe.

Similarly, the explosive rate of China's economic growth, particularly around the Pearl River Delta and the coastal cities, as well as overtures heralding the gradual opening of markets in Vietnam, North Korea, and Myanmar (Burma), are dramatically changing the shape of world markets. A new economic order appears to be emerging, characterized by new players and new and more diverse patterns of trade. Yet all these changing patterns appear fraught with uncertainty, as a surge in one direction is countered by a pull in another.

A new instability has thus crept into world markets, threatening at any moment to tilt the precarious balance of economic forces. Moves toward world economic growth, regional integration, or the empowerment of Third World nations can without warning be thwarted by pressures to retreat behind the bulwark of economic nationalism.

Complexity

A second challenge arises from the increasing complexity of managing international operations. Technological advances enable management to direct, coordinate, and control operations on a much broader and diverse geographic scale and scope than previously possible. Yet at the same time, such advances add further complexity, as management has to master the tools and skills required to handle the burgeoning international infrastructure. As the geographic scope and scale of operations extends further and further, management is faced with the task of directing and controlling diverse and far-flung activities at various stages in the value chain, often in widely divergent environmental contexts. Spatial market patterns of global market development are also becoming more complex, as traditional market boundaries disappear or are bridged by physical and communication links.

Additional layers of organization begin to creep into the corporate infrastructure and further complicate the global management task. With trends toward regional market integration, management systems are established to direct and coordinate marketing operations within a region and to provide an intermediate link between corporate headquarters and local management. At the same time, organizational links between business functions in each stage of the value chain are added at a global level to ensure the transfer of ideas, information, and experience across geographic areas, and to exploit potential synergies worldwide.

In addition, as customer markets become more dispersed, additional layers of organization are needed to collect information from these markets, and at the same time to coordinate rapid and efficient supply and service. As maintaining close relationships with customers and suppliers becomes increasingly critical in order to compete effectively in global markets, developing organizational networks to sustain these relations is crucial to success.

Sometimes links are established with other organizations, in some cases competitors, to exploit newly emerging opportunities in specific product markets or parts of the world. Strategic alliances may be formed with firms to provide desired geographic market coverage, or acquire skills and resources needed to implement a given strategy. In other cases, temporary networks are formed by far-flung partners (suppliers, customers, and competitors) sharing costs, skills, access, and operations in global markets through electronic links, utilizing the latest information technology, to take advantage of a specific market opportunity.[1] These networks are fluid and flexible, evolving in response to changing market conditions. Once an opportunity is met, or disappears, so the network will disband.

Spatial market patterns are also becoming increasingly complex. Once the configuration of markets was predominantly national in character, surrounded by seemingly impenetrable boundaries. However, the gradual breaking down of such boundaries in many parts of the world, together with increasing ability to transcend the remaining barriers, have led to a variety of patterns of global market development.

Markets previously viewed as separate and independent are becoming linked and beginning to function as one. The removal, or impending removal, of trade barriers in various regions such as Europe and North America acts as a catalyst to the formation of regional markets for many products and services. This facilitates increased interaction and communication between national markets in close proximity, and increases the potential for further interaction. For example, harmonization of product and equipment standards in the cellular telephone market allows the emergence of a regional market in Europe rather than 12 national markets.

Market linkage also occurs as customer demand extends spatially across national boundaries. Internationally mobile consumers may require a product or service to be available in multiple locations throughout the world. Similarly, in industrial markets, as companies spread into international markets and develop networks of international operations, they often centralize purchasing for these operations or negotiate contracts for the supply of products and services for their operations worldwide. Corporations anxious to obtain such contracts need to expand their geographic networks to conform to, and service, those of potential customers.

Global markets also develop through mergers, acquisitions, and strategic alliances. Here the resulting pattern of linkages between markets is a product of the preexisting market networks of the various partners and the most rational way to consolidate them. Where mergers and acquisitions were motivated by market access considerations, partners will typically have complementary spatial configurations and minimal duplication of market coverage. This is often the case in acquisitions and strategic alliances in the service sector, for example, advertising agencies or airline companies, and leads to a more extensive spatial network.

Competition

Increasing intensity of competition in global markets constitutes yet another challenge facing companies at all stages of involvement in international markets. As markets open up and become more integrated, the pace of change accelerates, technology shrinks distances between markets and reduces the scale advantages of large firms, new sources of competition emerge, and competitive pressures mount at all levels of the organization.

As more and more firms venture into global markets, competition proliferates, posing new threats and dangers to be reckoned with. In addition to facing competition from well-established multinationals and from domestic firms entrenched in their respective product or service markets, firms face growing competition from firms in newly industrializing countries and previously protected markets in the Third World, as well as emerging global networks or coalitions of organizations of diverse national origins.

Firms from new industrializing nations such as Taiwan, Singapore, Korea, and Hong Kong are increasingly taking the initiative in competing in global markets, rather than acting as low-cost suppliers to firms in the Industrial Triad. Often they target niche markets in consumer electronics, office equipment, and industrial machinery, sometimes utilizing low-cost labor in neighboring countries such as China or Indonesia. The threat of competition from companies in countries such as India, China, Malaysia, and Brazil is also on the rise, as their own domestic markets are opening up to foreign competition, stimulating greater awareness of international market opportunities and of the need to be internationally competitive. Companies that previously focused on protected domestic markets are entering into markets in other countries, creating new sources of competition, often targeted to price-sensitive market segments.

As free market principles become more widely adopted, protection and subsidization of domestic industries is declining. Government contracts and national monopolies in areas such as telecommunications and energy are being opened up to foreign competitors, while state-owned enterprises are privatized, and those that remain state-owned are adopting a market-oriented philosophy. Regulation of industry and of competition is on a downward path, thus allowing competitive market forces to work unfettered.

At the same time, spurred by new advances in communications technology and rapid technological obsolescence, the speed of competitor response is accelerating. No longer does a pioneer in global markets enjoy a substantial lead time over competitors. Nimble-footed competitors, benefiting from lower overhead and operating costs, enter rapidly with clones or low-cost substitutes, and take advantage of the pioneer's investment in R&D and product development. Modern communications and information technology also encourage rapid competitor response to price changes, or new distribution and promotional tactics, and further heighten the pace of competition.

The growth of global market segmentation and the increased segmentation of markets worldwide, coupled with the development of flexible production techniques, make it increasingly feasible to serve small market segments on a regional or global basis. As a result, even small companies are finding that they can compete in global markets by establishing international alliances or participating in global networks to produce, promote to, distribute, and service markets worldwide. Consequently, broad-based market strategies are becoming increasingly vulnerable to cherry-picking by focused or niche strategies.

Conscience

The fourth challenge relates to the firm's moral and social responsibilities in the global marketplace. A host of such responsibilities can be identified, depending on the individual firm and the specific product market, as well as the countries or areas of the world in which it is involved. In the early decades of internationalization, in the '60s and '70s, political issues and responsibilities to host governments were of prime concern. Most governments were alarmed at the economic power wielded by large multinationals in their respective countries and at the potentially subversive effects on the countries' national culture resulting from the introduction of foreign products, ideas, and influence. As a result, they sought to place limits on, and restrict, foreign ownership of business.

Consequently, multinational corporations devoted considerable attention to cultivating their image as responsible corporate citizens, local employers, and tax payers, and to building good relations with host governments. In today's marketplace, as the globalization of business has become an undeniable and all-pervasive motor of economic growth, a broader spectrum of social and corporate issues needs to be addressed.

In the first place, environmental issues have emerged as a key theme in the '90s. Companies have become increasingly aware of the need to take measures to limit destruction of the environment.[2] These include measures to limit pollution of the atmosphere through the emission of gases and other toxic substances, to conserve resources such as paper and pulp, whose production results in environmental destruction, and to produce and design products and packaging which are environmentally friendly.

Such measures need to cover all aspects of the firm's activities from R&D and production to marketing and service, as well as its operations in all parts of the world. Production should be engineered so as to conserve resources and limit toxic waste. Products should be designed to be free of environmentally harmful substances, such as phosphates and fluorocarbons. Use of recyclable packaging and refillable containers also helps reduce environmental pollution.

An important issue in this context is the extent to which a firm plays an active role in initiating environmentally responsible practices, rather than passively conforming to local regulatory standards. Automobile manufacturers, for example, can build automobiles to meet the strictest international pollution standards, rather than only meeting local regulations. Similarly, detergent manufacturers can introduce environmentally friendly packaging developed in response to consumer pressures in one country into other less environmentally conscious climates, as P&G, Colgate, and Unilever have done in the United States.[3]

Another area of social responsibility of particular relevance in international markets is concern with customer education and general well-being. This is often an important issue in marketing in Third World countries, where disadvantaged or poorly educated consumers are less able to judge the merits of a product or service or understand how to use it. Attention to the potential of promotional material or product information to mislead customers is important. While customers in industrialized nations are accustomed to puffery or exaggerated product claims and are typically highly skeptical of manufacturer-originated material, customers in developing countries are often less well equipped or likely to screen such material. Ability to read or understand usage instructions is another issue requiring attention. Hiring support staff to explain appropriate usage and educate consumers is often an effective approach.

Product safety standards should also meet the most exacting international standards, even in countries where no such regulation exists. This is especially critical in the case of products such as pharmaceuticals, where substantial health risks are present. Firms must take the responsibility to provide accurate information to the industry and regulatory bodies, and to educate consumers and distributors to ensure appropriate usage.

RESPONDING TO GLOBAL MARKET CHALLENGES

All firms, regardless of their size or degree of involvement in international markets, are buffeted or benefitted by the forces shaping global markets and face the challenges of change, complexity, competition, and conscience, in developing effective global marketing strategies. The significance of each of these challenges and the strategies companies should adopt in responding to them will depend, however, on the evolution of their global operations.

Phase 1—Response Strategies for Initial Entry

Firms initially venturing into international markets are typically of two types: either they are small or medium-sized firms that have only just begun to sense potential international opportunities and are only recently able to exploit them due to modern communications technology. Sometimes these are entrepreneurial ventures that have developed an innovative product or service with international potential. Alternatively, they are larger firms from developing or newly emerging nations, which have often previously been isolated or insulated from global market pressures and are beginning to feel the impact of foreign competition or are looking to expand.

Faced by entrenched competition from firms in phase 2 and 3, small and medium-sized businesses need to identify niche opportunities in international markets, which are ignored or less easily exploited by large-scale competitors. Often, meeting the needs of such niche markets requires specialized skills, custom-tailoring of product offerings, or provision of personalized service on a level uneconomic for a large-scale organization. Small and medium-sized businesses, by focusing on such customers, can operate at a scale to satisfy their needs efficiently and at a profit. It is, however, crucial for them to remain focused on a niche, keeping overheads and management costs to a minimum, while responding rapidly to customer requirements to retain their competitive edge. Pall, a U.S. manufacturer of filters, has successfully targeted markets for specialty filters worldwide, ranging from blood filters, which laboratories use to strain out viruses such as that which causes AIDS, to filters for the brewing industry, jet engines, and earth-moving equipment.[4] Similarly, Johnson Electric Holdings of Hong Kong has become the second largest manufacturer of micromotors worldwide. A niche player, Johnson manufactures micromotors that power small appliances from door locks to hair dryers for companies such as General Motors, Chrysler, Black and Decker, Philips, and Singer. Johnson has low overhead and administrative costs and is able to respond rapidly to customer requirements, turning a product concept into a prototype within 6 months.[5]

Small entrepreneurial firms with a new and innovative product or service may also be in the initial stages of international market entry. Typically they have developed a new idea or product in response to demand in their domestic market and seek opportunities to leverage their idea internationally to a broader market. For example, Marlow Foods, a subsidiary of the British drug firm

Zeneca, has developed Quorn, a tasteless, meatless, high-protein, low-calorie substance targeted to vegetarians. The product, made from maize and wheat extracts mixed with egg whites, has no cholesterol and little fat, and is tasteless. It soaks up flavor from whatever sauce or flavor is added.[6] Quorn has been highly successful in the U.K. and is now expanding into Europe, with plans to enter the U.S. market.

Large firms from developing and newly emerging economies, on the other hand, will typically find it advantageous to compete primarily on the basis of price. Low labor and operating costs in their domestic market provide a natural platform for developing a cost-oriented strategy that can be exploited in international markets. A number of computer software development companies in India, have, for example, been able to expand internationally, utilizing low-cost Indian engineering talent to develop customized software for large U.S. and European multinationals. Programs can be sent by satellite to the U.S., tested, and then sent back to India for review and debugging.

Other companies target price-sensitive customers and market segments in other countries. The South Korean companies that make automobiles and electronics are expanding their market by targeting price-sensitive segments. Low wage rates and efficient production allow them to produce low-priced high-quality cars and appliances. This strategy, however, often poses problems in international markets as the firms must struggle not to be perceived as producers of cheap, low-quality brands.

Firms in the initial entry stage of international market entry will find it advantageous to make use of sophisticated information systems and communication technology to manage international operations and maintain direct contact with distributors and end-user markets. Companies from developing countries should set up information systems to monitor developments in end-user markets, such as changes in customer tastes and purchasing behavior, emergence of new competition, new technologies, government or industry regulation, etc. Products and marketing strategies can then be fine-tuned to changing market trends. Information technology should also be utilized to monitor sales in different markets worldwide, and to manage distribution logistics more effectively, by cutting down on warehousing costs, spoilage, and excess production or inventory.

Information and communications technology also enables small firms to manage operations on a geographic scope previously unthinkable. Not only are they able to stay abreast of developments in far-flung end-markets but also maintain contact with suppliers in remote parts of the world, and source products or components on a global basis. Opportunities can thus be identified and effectively targeted in international markets, enabling the firm to leverage its specific skills and resource-based advantages on an international scale.

Phase 2—Strategies for International Market Expansion

Companies focusing on developing local markets in different parts of the world are most likely to be in industries where market demand differs substantially from one country or geographic region to another. This suggests that there is limited potential for economies of scale, and that local market responsiveness is of paramount importance. In some cases, these are large diversified companies, pursuing broad-based, country-centered marketing strategies, such as Nestlé, Unilever, Henkel, or Kao. Niche players in these markets, such as Cadbury-Schweppes or Reckitt & Colman, which have strong brands targeted to specific market niches, will also seek to strengthen their position by broadening their market base. Former state-owned or nationalized companies with home-country-centered strategies need to adapt their strategies to deal with the opening up of their markets and the growth of global competition.

Large diversified companies with country-centered strategies need to integrate and coordinate operations and strategies across national and regional markets. A key issue in this context is to leverage the company's core competence across geographic boundaries and different business functions, or product divisions, so as to take advantage of the multinational scope of its operations, rather than competing as a series of domestic businesses.

Product lines can be planned on a multicountry basis so as to eliminate potential duplication of effort in R&D, product or strategy development, and possible competition in third-country markets. Gillette, for example, now markets razors on a global basis. After losing market share to disposable razors marketed by Bic, Gillette decided to invest in the development of a high-technology razor, the Sensor, with blades set on springs to follow the contours of a man's face. The Sensor was the first product Gillette marketed on a global rather than a country-by-country basis, focusing on similarities across markets and the ability of the Sensor to respond to differences in shaving needs from one country to another. Attention was focused on developing a global image for the Sensor and establishing Gillette as the technological leader in the field.[7]

Niche players are also seeking to build their niche brands globally. For example, Reckitt & Colman has acquired a number of small and medium-sized companies with strong national brands such as Boyle Midway, Durkee Foods, and Frenchs. With a number of specialized brands that are market leaders in relatively small product categories, they have sought to expand these globally. For example, their niche brands include, Dettol antiseptic, first introduced in the U.K. in 1933 and now sold in over 70 countries; depilatories sold under the Veet, Neet, and Immac names in over 30 countries; and the Woolite brand of delicate fabric wash.[8]

Lego, the Danish manufacturer of plastic building blocks, is also seeking to strengthen its market base and develop its global brand image by expanding into clothing and theme parks.[9] Lego has operated a theme park in Denmark since 1969 and has plans to open other parks in the United States and Europe. It has also expanded its Dacta line of educational toys for use in schools, promoted by travelling activity centers. This includes miniature computers teaching math and science concepts, as well as Lego building sets. The apparel line features clothes worn by "Jack the Lego Maniac," an older kid featured in advertising of Lego building blocks. All these extensions are designed to broaden the appeal of the Lego brand and its market base.

State-owned and nationalized companies that thrived in markets protected by their governments from international competition, and have country-centered strategies, need to develop strategies to compete effectively in a global market oriented economy. The French Thomson Group is attempting to develop strategies to compete in two global businesses, defense electronics and consumer electronics.[10] While the partially private defense business, Thomson-CSF, has been successful despite a shrinking market, the state-owned consumer electronics business has incurred huge debts, despite capital infusions from the French government. Since European Union rules prohibit further capital infusions, which are needed to develop new products and technology, Thomson has focused on new product design and sales, though with limited success to date.

The drive to improve coordination across national markets and product businesses, while at the same time responding to local market demand and competitive conditions, adds additional complexity to the management task. Another layer is added to the organization structure to link and coordinate national management systems. The challenge is to add this layer without developing a cumbersome, slow-moving, and costly administrative bureaucracy and losing strategic flexibility and ability to respond to local market conditions.

The growing integration of markets worldwide implies that firms in phase 2 will need to move away from country-centered strategies to expand the scope of their operations and strengthen their geographic coverage, as well as their ability to leverage their core competencies in international markets. Specialized skills and resources available at various stages in the value chain in different countries should be utilized on a cross national basis. R&D skills developed in one country should be utilized to design products to be marketed in another country, while production or engineering techniques or management systems designed for one environmental context are applied in another.

Phase 3—Strategies for Global Rationalization

Firms seeking to rationalize operations on a global basis and map out globally integrated strategies are often companies that have been involved in international markets for long periods of time, such as ABB, Caterpillar, Ford, P&G, and IBM. Often such firms are in global industries where competition takes place on a global scale. In some cases, they are shifting away from country-centered strategies and seeking to integrate operations worldwide, to improve efficiency and competitiveness in world markets. In other cases, they are primarily concerned with extending the international scope of their operations to be positioned for the growth markets of the future.

Increasingly, there are a number of small or medium-sized firms, in industrial or service businesses, seeking to operate on a global scale. Faced by growing competition from foreign competitors, benefiting from lower operating costs or customers with worldwide operations, such firms have to globalize operations in order to survive. Developing global networks of relationships with suppliers, customers, and even potential competitors, and employing modern information systems and communications technology, enable them to tap into global markets and sources of supply.

A key challenge for all firms both large and small is to stay ahead of their competition, by anticipating, responding, and adapting to market changes. In particular, they need to be positioned to take advantage of growth opportunities in the markets of the future. This requires developing a global portfolio of countries and product businesses that is not only attractive in the short run, but will sustain growth into the twenty-first century. As markets in China, India, and Southeast Asia open up and expand, often this means shifting focus away from the mature markets of the Industrial Triad to emerging markets in these countries.

At the same time, companies continually need to improve the efficiency of their operations, introducing new technology and streamlining sourcing and organizational links in order to remain competitive in world markets. This is particularly crucial in markets where maintaining cost leadership is a key component of competitiveness. In the automobile market, U.S. manufacturers have restructured operations, establishing plants in low-cost locations and pressuring suppliers to cut prices, as well as redesigning and reengineering models in order to cut costs.[11] As indicated earlier, both Ford and General Motors are attempting to reduce costs by designing cars that are suitable for more than one market. Ford designed its world car, Mondeo (Ford Contour and Mercury Mystique in the United States) to help it achieve scale economies. General Motors' Cadillac Division, on a more modest scale, is modifying aspects of Opel's Omega to make it more appealing to American tastes.

Japanese automakers are also improving efficiency in order to cut costs and regain market share. In particular, they have reduced the number of models and model variants and have started to build more plants in other countries to take advantage of lower costs, develop joint ventures and ties with other firms, and design cars with more common parts.[12] Toyota is reducing the number of model variants and reorganizing product development to operate more efficiently. All vehicles are bunched into three basic groups—front-wheel drive, rear-wheel drive, and trucks—under the control of a chief engineer. Cooperation on model development within each group is encouraged to reduce the number of unique parts, saving money both in engineering and manufacturing.[13]

Where differentiation of the product or image from that of competitors is a focal point of a company's strategy, building a global image is often of key importance. Reebok, for example, is aiming to build a global image comparable to that of such household names as Coca-Cola and Sony, in order to sell its products worldwide. The centerpiece of Reebok's strategy is a global advertising campaign based on Planet Reebok.

Smaller and medium-sized firms, particularly in service industries such as advertising, banking and insurance, or law, often find it advantageous to enter into networking arrangements with firms in other parts of the world, so that they can service customers worldwide. In many cases, such networks can effectively make use of advances in information technology to link up and work together,[1] assemble the needed resources, and respond rapidly to emerging opportunities.

Given the accelerating pace of competition in global markets, even large companies find it advantageous to enter into such alliances. AT&T, for example, used the Japanese trading company Marubeni to link with Matsushita to produce its Safari notebook computer, designed by a small U.S. company, Henry Dreyfuss Associates,[1] and get it into the market ahead of competition.

To compete effectively in global markets, firms need to be able to respond rapidly to emerging opportunities and competitor moves in a myriad of markets throughout the world. The challenge is to bridge time and distance cost effectively, while at the same time maintaining a lean organizational structure. Remaining on the cutting edge of communications technology can provide an important competitive advantage. Price Waterhouse, for example, uses group software to bring together people and information from the four corners of the globe.[14] Managers can access electronic bulletin boards providing information relating to client businesses, regulations, and developments in different parts of the world, as well as messages and queries from other managers. The software can also be used to help managers in different locations work together in writing a proposal for a contract, report, or simply interact and exchange information and views.

The "truly" global firm has thus to face diverse and conflicting demands. On the one hand, it needs to build on local resources and be responsive to local market conditions. On the other hand, it needs to capitalize on a global presence, leveraging skills to other markets worldwide. At the same time, it needs to manage diverse and far-flung operations efficiently and avoid becoming entangled in a web of cumbersome administrative complexity.

SUMMARY

Regardless of where the firm is on the path towards globalization, it must respond to the forces shaping the global environment and the challenges they present. The precise nature of the challenges continues to change, and the form they will take in the twenty-first century remains uncertain. What is clear is that, to be successful, the firm must be an even more astute marketer than in the past.

The firm must have a clear vision of its mission in global markets, as well as the ability to implement this vision successfully. It must understand its core competencies and find ways to leverage them in global markets. This may also involve developing new competencies or entering into strategic alliances to acquire the capabilities necessary to compete effectively in fast-moving global markets.

While the core competencies form the basis for its strategic thrust in global markets, the firm must also be able to mobilize resources worldwide. The necessity to respond quickly and appropriately to opportunities and challenges throughout the world places a premium on developing an effective corporate infrastructure to implement and modify strategy. The firm must become an organic process that continually evolves, adapts, and responds to the changing realities of the global market place. Firms that are able to do this will prosper; firms that do not will wither.

REFERENCES

1. "The Virtual Corporation," (1993) *Business Week*, February 8, pp. 98–102.
2. Gladwin, Thomas N. (1993) "Envisioning the Sustainable Corporation," Smith, Emily T. In: *Managing for Environmental Excellence, the Next Business Frontier*, Washington, DC: Island Press.
3. Tully, Shawn (1989) "What the Greens Mean for Business, *Fortune*, October 23, p. 19.
4. "Mini-nationals Are Making Maximum Impact" (1993) *Business Week*, September 6, p. 66.
5. "Asia's High-Tech Quest" (1992) *Business Week*, December 7, pp. 126–130.
6. Rapoport, Carla (1994) "The Brits Invent a New Food," *Fortune*, January 24, p. 16.
7. Hoffman, Peter (1991) "Gillette Sensor: Global Innovation in Technology and Marketing," *Marketing News*, February 20, pp. 10–29.
8. Reckitt & Colman (1991) *Annual Report*.
9. Applebaum, Cara (1992) "The Next Disney," *Adweek's Marketing Week*, March 9, pp. 22–23.
10. "When You Can't Control History," (1993) *Fortune*, December 13, p. 170.
11. "Cut Costs or Else" (1993) *Business Week*, March 22, pp. 28–29.
12. "Overhaul in Japan" (1992) *Business Week*, December 21, pp. 85–86.
13. Taylor, Alex III (1993) "How Toyota Copes With Hard Times," *Fortune*, January 25, pp. 78–81.
14. Kirkpatrick, David (1993) "Groupware Goes Boom," *Fortune*, December 27, pp. 99–106.

PART VI

CASES

STERLING MARKING PRODUCTS INC.

On November 27, 1988, Jan d'Ailly, the 29-year-old International Marketing manager for Sterling Marking Products of London, Ontario, was reviewing his options with regards to selling the Mark Maker embosser in the United Kingdom. He had identified possibilities for licensing, exporting, joint venture, and acquisition. Jan was expected to make his recommendations at tomorrow's International Marketing Committee meeting.

In addition to the U.K. market, a larger question loomed. The Mark Maker, which had captured over 60 percent of the Canadian embosser market in just two years, was starting to attract attention from dealers around the world. He had received inquiries from firms in Australia, Japan, Sweden, Italy, France, Barbados, Spain, and Indonesia. These firms were interested in selling and in some cases manufacturing the Mark Maker. How, thought Jan, should Sterling move on these worldwide opportunities?

EMBOSSERS AND THE EMBOSSER MARKET

Used to imprint seals on corporate, legal, and certain government documents, (Exhibit 1) embossers had been around for hundreds of years. Since that time, the only significant innovations were the developments of a pocket seal and the Mark Maker. Throughout the world, lawyers, corporations, and consumers had purchased seals for either legal requirements or personal reasons such as embossing their names on books and documents to show ownership or make them look more official. In countries where the legal system was based on English common law, an embosser was frequently a legal requirement for notary publics (lawyers who authenticated documents). Currently 90 percent of Mark Makers were purchased by lawyers and corporations. The fact that embossers appealed to business and nonbusiness consumers alike made any country in the world a potential market for embossers. Exhibit 2 outlines per capita GNP, population, basis of law (common, civil, and so forth), and where available, statistics on lawyers and incorporations for 31 countries.

Case, "Sterling Marking Products, Inc." Jonathan Calof prepared this case under the supervision of Professor Paul Beamish of the Western Business School solely to provide material for class discussion. Copyright © 1989, The University of Western Ontario. Reproduction in any form is prohibited without written consent from the Western Business School.

EXHIBIT 1 Examples of seals and seal impressions.

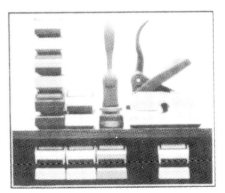

Illustration from an advertisement comparing the Mark Maker to traditional desk seals

MARK MAKER™

NEW

In 1986, the Canadian legal embosser market was estimated to be $1.5 million per year. While an embosser was not a legal requirement for companies, almost all the 70,000 incorporations and 20,000 corporate name changes per year resulted in embosser sales, with the remaining sales accounted for by those new lawyers who decided to become Notary Publics. Most embosser sales were accounted for by the traditional desk seal.

Throughout most of the world, the process of producing and selling embossers was similar (Exhibit 3). The embosser was composed of two parts: a sub-assembly which was the actual body, and a die which contained the text and

EXHIBIT 2 International markets—selected information.

COUNTRY	POPULATION (IN MILLIONS)	PER CAPITA GNP 1987	NOTARY	NUMBER OF LAWYERS	YEARLY INCREASE LAWYERS AND INCORPO- RATIONS	BASIS OF LAW
Argentina	30	2,130	Yes			Civil
Australia	16	10,840	Yes	16,077		Common
Bangladesh	101	150	Yes			Common
Brazil	135	1,640	Yes			Civil
Canada	25	13,670	Yes		82,000	Common
China	1,041	310		12,000		Other
Colombia	28	1,320	Yes			Civil
Egypt	47	680	State*			Civil
France	55	9,550	Yes			Civil
Germany, Fed	61	10,940	Yes	30,510		Civil
India	765	110	Yes	200,000		Common
Indonesia	162	530	Yes			Civil
Iran	45	NA	Yes			Other
Italy	57	6,520				Civil
Japan	121	11,330	Yes	82,042		Both
Kuwait	1	14,270				Other
Mexico	79	2,080	Yes			Civil
Nigeria	100	760	Yes			Both
Norway	4	13,890	State*	2,000		Civil
Pakistan	95	380	Yes			Common
Philippines	55	600	Yes			Both
Poland	37	2,120	State*			Other
South Africa	32	2,010	Yes			Common
Spain	39	4,366	Yes			Civil
Sweden	8	16,421		2,000		Common
Switzerland	10	16,380	Yes			Both
Thailand	51	830				Both
Turkey	49	1,130	Yes			Civil
U.K.	56	8,390	Yes		200,000	Common
U.S.A.	239	16,400	Yes		820,000	Common
U.S.S.R.	277	NA	Yes	127,000		Other

*In these countries, notarization of documents is the responsibility of state bureaucratic officials and not lawyers.

EXHIBIT 3 The
Process of embosser
manufacturing and
sales in the legal
market.

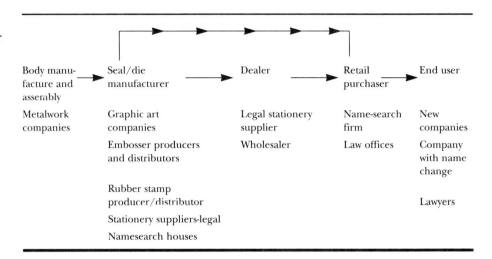

Body manu-facture and assembly	Seal/die manufacturer	Dealer	Retail purchaser	End user
Metalwork companies	Graphic art companies	Legal stationery supplier	Name-search firm	New companies
	Embosser producers and distributors	Wholesaler	Law offices	Company with name change
	Rubber stamp producer/distributor			Lawyers
	Stationery suppliers-legal			
	Namesearch houses			

graphic to be imprinted on documents. The die was then placed in the sub-assembly. Subassemblies were typically manufactured by national firms with metal-working expertise. Within Canada, five firms produced most embosser bodies. Embosser die production was more diffused with a proliferation of small, regional dies manufacturers.

The actual sale of a complete embosser (subassembly and die) occurred through either product suppliers or service firms. Product suppliers (e.g., legal stationery suppliers) stocked products such as incorporation kits and other supplies required by lawyers. Service firms, such as name search houses, were usually employed by lawyers to assist in the incorporation process. Typically, these firms, as part of their service, provided an embosser.

An embosser sale resulted for one of two reasons: (1) a firm approached a lawyer to help them incorporate or (2) a lawyer became a notary public and required a seal. In both cases, the lawyer would then approach either a product supplier or a service firm (if the lawyer was using the particular service) and request an embosser. Product and service firms had two avenues for supplying embossers: they could purchase the subassembly, contract out the die manufac-turing to one of the regional die suppliers, assemble the complete unit and then sell it to the lawyer; or they could purchase the subassembly, produce the die internally, and then assemble the embosser.

Throughout the world, the legal seal industry had remained stagnant. While the number of models had grown, there had been very little innovation for 50 years. Three factors had contributed to this: the legal profession had accepted the problems associated with the seal; most of the die manufacturers were small, without funds for product development; and, for the larger firms, embosser sales were typically not the dominant product, thus there was little incentive for them to undertake embosser research and development. The combination of these factors resulted in a deterioration in the function of embossers such that it ceased to be an image product. The once proud seal became a commodity purchased on the basis of price alone.

In many cases, medium and large manufacturers in the embosser industry also produced rubber stamp products. The rubber stamp industry had higher margins and was more competitive than was the embosser industry. Much innovative product and process R&D had occurred for rubber stamps. While rubber stamps and embossers were both used for marking purposes, until recently the products were complements and not competitors. However, in some countries where corporations did not require an embossing seal, firms were starting to purchase rubber stamps to stamp their corporate seal on documents, rather than the harder-to-use embosser.

THE MARK MAKER

Sterling Marking Products Inc. was founded in 1945 by Warren R. Schram, initially as a one-man rubber stamp company in London, Ontario. Under Warren Schram's leadership and focus on customer service, Sterling developed a committed dealer network almost 1,000 strong. In 1976 Mr. Schram's son, Bob, a University of Western Ontario M.B.A., who had worked at Sterling for 11 years (since he was 19), acquired the business. At that time, Sterling's primary focus was still on the production and sale of rubber stamp products. In 1981, Bob Schram, Sam Hassan (controller), and Cam Fink (general manager) decided that the time was right to strike out into a new area. In the past, Sterling's embosser involvement consisted of supplying customers with assembled embossers. Since the subassembly was not manufactured by Sterling, their only value-adding activity was the actual assembly of the embosser and the manufacturing of the die. In management's view, all Sterling offered was an easily copied service. They decided that getting into embosser production and supply made strategic sense as it increased Sterling's independence. Bob, Sam, and Cam discussed many times whether the new embosser should be a bold, innovative design or the old, traditional desk seal but with some of its flaws corrected.

Bob wanted his firm to bring back prestige to the embosser. The suppliers believed that lawyers wanted to buy the lowest cost items, regardless of utility or prestige. Bob felt that this assumption was inappropriate. "Lawyers buy BMW's and have large offices, prestige must be important to them." However, to try to develop a new, more functional, and prestigious embosser could be dangerous. Failure on an innovative design could damage their credibility with the employees, which the new management team was trying to establish. There were some significant benefits: They would learn about plastic molding and how to manage new product development. Further, if they succeeded, the nature of competition could shift from a commodity-like product dominated by small firms to a differentiated product market dominated by one large firm, Sterling.

As a first step, Sterling applied for and received a $30,000 grant from the Ontario Provincial government to underwrite the Mark Maker's industrial

MARK MAKER: $29.95

ADVANTAGES	DISADVANTAGES
On-line ordering system	Nonchangeable dies
—ease of ordering	Nonreversible dies
—accuracy	Die size limitation
—speed of delivery	
Plastic impression quality	High subassembly cost
Modern appearance	Will not fit in corporate registration
Ease of use	binder
Durability	
Easy to read index system	
Non skid/nonmark pads	
Easy to use handle mechanism	

POCKET SEAL: $19—$30

ADVANTAGES	DISADVANTAGES
Compact—fits in corporate registration	Poor impression quality
binder	Hard to use
Light weight	Looks cheap
Inexpensive	No indexing possible
Proven market acceptance (80% of the	Short throat
U.S. market)	
Rotating die set	
Various die sizes available	

TRADITIONAL DESK SEAL: $25—$35

ADVANTAGES	DISADVANTAGES
Various die sizes available	Impression is inconsistent
Good quality impression	Heavy
Recognized as the classic	Awkward
Special intricate logo capability	Awkward to use
	Noninterchangeable
	Nonreversible
	Frames crack
	Not easily stored
	Hard to transport
	Sharp metal edges

Source: Advantages and disadvantages from Sterling records.

design. To help in the design Bob conducted interviews with lawyers in which they were asked what they would like in a seal. From these discussions, and an analysis of other problems which he had identified with desk and pocket seals, Bob obtained an idea of the product features required in the new seal (Exhibit 4). Sterling then turned the design over to an industrial design consultant.

By the end of 1981, after extensive meetings with Bob and Cam, the consultant returned with the completed design, molds, and tooling required to produce the Mark Maker. A meeting was subsequently held in which the product was shown to Sterling management. Bob assembled the Mark Maker, and to his horror discovered that "it would not even emboss toilet paper."

Employees were already questioning the young management team's initial decision to develop the Mark Maker. At the same time a poor economic climate was affecting Sterling profits. Bob felt that attention was better spent focusing on Sterling's current problems, rather than on developing the Mark Maker. For the next 30 days management discussed possible modifications for the Mark Maker—subsequently the project was shelved.

By the end of 1982, attention started to shift back to the Mark Maker. Management felt that perhaps they were too hasty in their abandonment of the project. Since they already had the basic design and the tooling for Mark Maker, they could develop the product internally. Cam Fink hired Anthony Gentelle (a Fanshawe College industrial design student). Willy Brandt, an independent mold maker, was contracted to help in the mold design, and DuPont Canada Inc. was brought in to help select the appropriate materials for the Mark Maker. Cam and Anthony met after work for over a year, attempting to correct the flaws in the initial Mark Maker. By October 1984 the project which had taken five years and $400,000 to develop was completed. All that was left was to apply for a patent and then enter the new product on the market.

Sterling was proud of the Mark Maker (Exhibit 1). It weighed less than one pound and was trim. The weight and durability arose from using Du Pont "Delrin" acetal resin and glass reinforced "Zytel" nylon resin. It had a collapsible handle in nylon which could lie flat at the push of a button, making the unit 13.5 centimeters long, 7 centimeters high, and 5.4 centimeters wide (small enough to fit into a briefcase). Its impression quality was tested to 25,000 embossing operations and with the handle serving as a lever, the manual force needed to exert pressure on the die and achieve a clear impression was reduced. The parts were injection molded so that the assembly could be quickly snapped together. While Sterling would own the molds and tooling, subassembly production was contracted out to Willy Brandt's firm, Exacu Mould Inc. in London.

In December 1984, Sterling entered the product on the market. The subassembly was priced at $8.05 allowing Sterling a 50 percent profit. Competitor products were sold for $6.50 but Sterling felt that if they met this price, the ensuing 25 percent profit was insufficient to justify the investment. Further, it was felt that the Mark Maker's superior features should allow for a price premium.

Mark Maker orders were encouraging. In the first year (1985) 40,793 Mark Maker subassemblies were sold. Unfortunately, Sterling learned that many Mark Makers were gathering dust on the shelves of the legal stationers and name search houses. Sterling identified two primary reasons for the poor results: changing the image of the embosser from a commodity-like product to a differentiated one required more direct sales than dealers had used in the past; and, as Sterling only sold the subassemblies, they had no control over die production, and unfortunately, most of the dies were not manufactured to the rigorous specifications set out by Sterling. The inferior dies were damaging Mark Maker's credibility in the market.

As dealers were unwilling to change their die production processes, Sterling realized that they had to somehow convince their customers to exit the lucrative seal production aspect of their business and allow Sterling to sell them both the Mark Maker subassembly and the die.

At the same time that this problem was developing, Sterling's computer systems/services division was implementing a program which interfaced the computer with the typesetter. This initiative, started around 1981, was not related to Mark Maker. Rather, it was an attempt to increase the efficiency of stamp making operations by standardizing activities and automating production. Cam, Sam, and Bob realized that with some modifications the program could be used for on-line ordering and production of the Mark Maker. Customers would be supplied with terminals and modems (approximate cost $1,000) which would be used to dial into Sterling's computers in London using telephone lines, and enter the text for their embosser. The host computer could then communicate with the production computer engraving systems which would then output the text for the die. Getting the client to enter the text directly into the system virtually assured error free final text. In the past, some errors had occurred as a result of operators entering the client's text from the order form incorrectly. The on-line text outputting processes would also result in improved quality and lowered production costs. A by-product of the automated text processes could be that as part of the same run, text could be output which could be used to manufacture a brass identification plate. Previously, customers used a piece of paper placed in a plastic window on top of the Mark Maker for identification purposes.

Management felt that increased quality and service would help convince the majority of their customers who manufactured the dies to relinquish die production and make the customer captive to the Sterling system. However, Sterling realized that the major hurdle for getting dealers to relinquish production of the die was the price and speed of delivery. Die production, though only a small part of most of Sterling's customers' business, was none the less extremely profitable with margins of 50 percent. Sterling found a price which maintained most of their customers' old profit. In addition, Sterling endeavored to provide dealers with sales support (marketing literature and sales incentives). The new Mark Maker, which cost Sterling $6.64 in labor and materials ($5.01 for the subassembly and $1.63 for the die), $1.75 for shipping and $2 for selling and computer allocation, was retailed at $34.95 with wholesale volume discounts of up to 55 percent. Direct sales could be made to lawyers at the full list price of $34.95; however, this was not encouraged as it would put Sterling in competition with their primary customers (legal stationers and name search houses). To ensure that dealers did not produce their own dies for the Mark Maker, Sterling limited subassembly sales to 20 percent of a customer's order. Sam Hassan felt that this was a necessary but high-risk decision as it precluded Sterling from selling only subassemblies as they had in the past.

In 1986, 22,948 assembled Mark Makers had been sold ($424,359) and five of Sterling's largest customers were using the on-line ordering system. In 1987, 41,287 units were sold ($712,332). Sales for 1988 were forecasted to be 58,705 ($1,004,415)—67 percent of all Canadian embosser sales. And with its gross margin of $8.63 per unit and a forecasted $6.63 per unit contribution after allocated expenses, Mark Maker was the number one product for Sterling. Mark Maker had become so entrenched in the Canadian market that it was becoming more difficult to find the old metal desk seal subassemblies in Canada. Few sales went to the traditional stationer houses (the bulk of the 1,000 dealer network developed by Warren Schram). Ninety percent of sales went to a new type of customer: the legal stationer and law firm.

True to their initial objectives, Sterling had managed to change the competitive dynamic of the Canadian embosser market. Smaller, regional die manufacturing firms were being pushed out of the business, the product was losing its commodity-like status, and metal subassembly manufacturing (which was dominated by American firms) was dying out. The only competitive reaction had been by Marque D'Or, a rival of Sterling's in Quebec. In response to the introduction of the Mark Maker, Marque D'Or had lowered its price for the old metal seal. However, in the past month, Marque D'Or had begun to place more orders with Sterling because its largest customer had requested the Mark Maker. Sterling management felt that with this latest development in Quebec and recent inroads in western Canada, it was conceivable that Mark Maker would have a 90 percent market share within the next few years.

The innovativeness of the Mark Maker was widely recognized. In 1986, the Mark Maker received two awards: a design Engineering Achievement Award at the Plast-ex show in Toronto; and the Federal Government's Award for Excellence in industrial design.

Despite this success, and lack of competitor reaction, management decided to continually innovate Mark Maker's product and service to discourage competitors. While the product and its design was patented for the next 15 years in Canada, the United States, and the European Economic community, any modification (such as a different handle mechanism) would allow a competitor to legally duplicate the Mark Maker concept. However, the on-line ordering system could be difficult to replicate.

STERLING MARKING PRODUCTS INC.—1988

Sterling operated its production facility and head office in London, Ontario with sales offices in London, Toronto, and Windsor. Directly employing 141 people, Sterling offered a variety of products and services (Exhibit 5) which were divided into four operating segments: (1) Stationer items—Rubber stamps, signs and markers; (2) Industrial marking systems—code dating; (3) Graphics—artwork, commercial printing, and typesetting; and (4) Data management and printing real estate books.

Many of these products were developed by Sterling. However, most of the industrial sales products such as high-speed label makers and line-coding machines had been developed by other firms with Sterling holding the Canadian distribution rights.

EXHIBIT 5 Product overview.

PRODUCTS	DISTRIBUTION	STRENGTHS

Marking device and stationery products
    Legal and consumer
        Markmaker Embosser®
    Rubber and perma stamps
    Dating and numbering devices
    Signage systems
    Desk plates (badges)
	Large consumer customer base
	Direct mail programs
	Major national accounts
		Loyal customers
		Strong customer service
		Unique on-line computer
		Integrated manufacturing
		    system

Industrial products group
    Date coding application (mechanical and
        computer spray jet machines)
    Shipping supplies
    Steel type and punches
    Mechanical presses
	Large consumer customer base
	Regional sales force based in
	    Toronto, London, Windsor and
	    Niagara Peninsula Dealers
		Application responsive sales
		    and manufacturing
		    group
		Worldwide product
		    sourcing

Graphics Product Group
    Commercial Artwork and Typesetting
    Printing plates
        Corrugated cartons
        Tape and label
        Flexo for poly bags
    Bingo plates and computer programs
    Printing
        MLS directories
        Direct mail Brochures
	National sales effort
	Large consumer customer base
	Major national accounts (Labatts)
		Outstanding responsive
		    sales and manufacturing
		    capability to satisfy
		    customer requests
		Superior technical capa-
		    bility

Computer Systems/Services
    Hardware selected from a wide range
        of vendors which support our
        ultimate operating system
    Specialty software
    Bingo programs
    MLS on line system
    Dealer on line system incorporating our
        proprietary computer-integrated
        manufacturing software driving typesetting
        and N/C computerized engraving output
    Real Estate Broker systems for administrative
        function and on-line enquires
	Company wide sales and
	    marketing effort
	Satisfied customers including 11
	    real estate boards
	On-line sales through our consumer
	    customer and dealers
		Superior operating system
		    offering excellent
		    migration flexibility of
		    software
		Creative, responsive sales
		    and programming staff
		Unique programs for type-
		    setting output and data
		    manipulation

This diversified product line arose from the visions of Bob Schram (42), Cam Fink (32), and Sam Hassan (42). Bob Schram's commitment to customer service and desire for innovation led him to seek ways to increase the utility of products. He often discussed new product ideas with customers, suppliers, and employees. Sam's main interests were in computer technology. When he joined Sterling in 1978 he had a vision of a firm with unique computer capabilities. To help realize this, he formed a relationship with Ultimate Computers, a value-added resaler of computer hardware. Cam joined Sterling in 1981 after working for a firm which supplied automotive products to General Motors. Cam brought with him a focus on production efficiency. He saw Sterling making thousands of "somethings" efficiently, thereby reaping the benefits of economies of scale.

One of the by-products of these visions was the development of Sterling's computer skill advantage. The original purpose of the computer technology was to assist in processing and storing transactions. The custom nature of Sterling's marking products activity (e.g., stamps are personalized), created a tremendous paper burden in the organization as each sale generated its own order form. As Sterling grew, so did the number of individual orders. By 1980, it had reached the stage that the processing of transactions had become a costly and time-consuming part of the production process. Sterling realized that without an efficient method of processing transactions, future growth would be limited; thus, they looked toward computers.

In 1980, Sterling bought their computer system. As they spent time developing administrative applications for the system and learned more about the computers' capabilities, they started to realize that the computer could also be used for production and product development purposes. For example, the data manipulation routines used for order information coupled with the typesetting expertise garnished from the production of stamps could also be used to produce data base systems for real estate agents. All that was needed was some efficient searching routines. As well, the on-line production system would, if interfaced with the real-estate database, result in a cost effective method for printing the Real Estate books. In 1986 MLS database products and real-estate book production were added to Sterling's business lines. In September 1988, this lucrative area had attracted contracts from 14 real estate boards in Canada. Other products and services arose from this technological edge such as on-line ordering and production. Another innovative extension was the production of Bingo cards. A program was developed which would design Bingo cards. The program determined the number of cards to produce based on hall sizes, output the printing plates, and designed the Bingo cards such that no card had a higher probability of hitting "BINGO" than any other.

The company also focused attention on improving production processes. Sterling's quality standards were fast being adopted by the larger firms in the industry. However, most firms could not keep up with Sterling's process innovations. Without Sterling's level of expertise, most were unable to progress much beyond the technology and processes of the 1960s.

Product and process innovation were viewed as a principal task for Sterling. The impetus behind this was a desire for growth. Sterling viewed themselves as a potential future IBM in terms of size. But the focus on growth, innovation, and service had to be balanced with management's deep concern for employee well being. Schram felt that employees were the key to Sterling's success.

One of the primary objectives for the organization was to increase the satisfaction of employees and managers. Consideration of these and other intangible benefits was so important, that Sam Hassan's job was not to merely look at return on investment but to rationalize investment on the basis of its long-term benefit to the company. Sterling's investment decision criteria focused on the invest-

EXHIBIT 6
Selected financial
and corporate
information.

	1983	1984	1985	1986	1987	1988*
Mark Maker sales:			*(Subassemblies)*		*(Complete Units)*	
Units			40,793	22,948	41,287	58,705
$000's			343	424	712	1,004
Gross margin ($000's)					428	615
Contribution ($000's)					224	402
Employees:						
Full time	106	103	120	122	130	
Part time		9	11	6	11	
Sales ($000's)	4,598	5,369	6,536	7,285	7,971	
Debt/equity	2.13	1.57	1.24	1.16	1.06	

*Estimate

ment's effect in terms of the learning benefits of the investment, the impact of investment failure on both the employees respect for management and overall operations and what the employees would think of management for undertaking the investment. Financial considerations (e.g., ROI), while being important, were usually of secondary status.

The focus on innovation, service, and employee well-being led to an adaptable, flexible organization, the result of which was dramatic increases in sales and profits. Between 1983 and 1987, sales increased 73 percent going from $4.6 million to $8 million, with 1988 sales estimated to be $10 million (Exhibit 6).

MANAGING GROWTH

Management's primary concern was the management of growth. They felt that what had "made" Sterling was its identity—a focus on innovation and a 40-year-old service ethic. Maintaining the sense of commitment and an environment where "it was fun to come up with something that benefits the customer" would be difficult. In recruiting they sought individuals like themselves. They looked for people who could "share the vision." Salaries were low but Sterling offered would-be employees opportunities for growth. An apprenticeship period was served by most new management employees (with the exception of marketing) where the individual was expected to develop informal leadership in the organization. Titles were meaningless and new hires were expected to work their way slowly into management, gaining respect from other employees and distinguishing themselves as leaders. New hires who were not able to earn the respect of employees would not last long. Management personnel were seldom given a clear role, direction, or authority.

ORGANIZATIONAL STRUCTURE

While Sterling had explored the possibility of many different structures, they maintained the simple structure of the past, with most major decisions being made by Bob Schram after receiving input from various employees. Recently, the three senior managers had begun a process of adding more management employees, thereby removing themselves strictly from day-to-day operations and instead allowing them to focus on longer range strategic issues. Despite this, the three senior managers continued to work six to seven days a week.

The structure was undergoing other transformations. Attempts were being made to divisionalize Sterling's product groups. For example, Jan d'Ailly was put in charge of marketing for all marking devices. However, as one employee stated: "We see ourselves in the longer run going toward a divisional structure, but given the current dynamic of Sterling and its success, it is hard to get any sort of structure, functional or divisional."

Sterling's international activities were coordinated by the international marketing department, and the international marketing committee. The international marketing committee consisted of Jan, Sam, Cam, Bob, Rick Verette (operations manager), Vince Lebano (a representative of the Ontario Provincial government), and was chaired by Mel Dear, an ex-3M sales executive who was now a private consultant. The committee met every two to four weeks to discuss all aspects of international operations. The committee used a broad definition of international which included any sales outside of Ontario.

Jan d'Ailly was hired as the one-man international marketing department in 1986, shortly after completing his M.B.A. at the University of Western Ontario. Jan had worked in France, Taiwan, Australia, and South Africa and spoke English, Dutch, French, and Mandarin. Consistent with Sterling's focus on customer service, Jan was hired more to provide customer support than to make sales. In fact, Jan did not have previous sales experience prior to joining Sterling. It was Jan's job to identify foreign markets for Sterling's products and to help out foreign customers. Since joining Sterling, Jan's time had been devoted to the Mark Maker. He had personally conducted market research trips to the United States and the United Kingdom and was also involved in selecting Blumberg to introduce the Mark Maker into the United States.

THE UNITED KINGDOM TRIPS

Three market research trips had been made to the United Kingdom. These trips yielded information on the U.K. embosser market as well as information on labor availability, and information pertinent to Sterling's other products. Exhibit 7 presents a portion of Sterling's market study. The last trip was in November 1988. Jan, together with Cam, Warren Schram, and a consultant, went to the

EXHIBIT 7 Sterling Marking Products Inc.

MARKET SIZE			RUBBER STAMP MARKET		
Company registrations	100,000 } Range to 170,000		MacFarlane—$22,000,000	35%–50%	
Name changes	50,000 }		Mark C. Brown	? 10%	
Vehicle testing stations	10,000 best guess		William Jones Clifton	? 5%–10%	
Personnel embossers	12,000 Jones Clifton		40–60 smaller firms		
Total market	172,000 seals per year		Said no one is making		
	Work with 680 per day		any money		

STRUCTURE OF THE LEGAL SEAL MARKET

SEAL PRODUCTION			NAME SEARCH HOUSES			END USERS		
Jordans	48,000	28%	Jordans	15,000	26%	Lawyers	60,000	35%
			(A group of small houses)					
Bolsoms	84,000	49%	Stanley Davis	22,500	13%	Accountants	60,000	35%
			London Law	17,200	10%			
Western			Smaller houses	65,300	38%			
Pro Marketing			(All less than Stanley Davis)			Private legal	30,000	17%
City Seals	21,000	12%	Rubber stamp companies					
	153,000	89%		150,000	87%	Vehicle testing		
						stations	10,000	6%
Jones Clifton	18,000	10%	Retailers, wholesalers			Consumers	12,000	7%
			Direct mail					
			Rubber Stamp					
			Man.	22,000	12%			
			MBF Clansman	?				
Totals	172,000	100%		172,000	100%		172,000	100%

Price Competitive.	As a whole, a very fragmented market.
Generally very low quality seals.	Heavy price competition "Cheaper is Better."
Seals delivered to name search houses or mailed direct to end users.	Jordans seen as a leader in the industry, higher priced, and maintains a whole database and reporting business.
	Stanley Davis determined to catch Jordans

Source: Company report on the U.K. market.

United Kingdom for one week. The purpose of this trip was to confirm Sterling's perceptions of the U.K. market, and to investigate alternative modes for competing in the United Kingdom. The information in this section is based on the results of these research trips.

The United Kingdom was the only European country where seals were a legal requirement for corporations. Thus, all of the 100,000–120,000 incorporations, 50,000 corporate name changes and 12,000 new lawyers per year required embossers. This provided a fertile ground for embosser sales. However, the U.K. government had recently indicated that an embossed seal might not be legally required in the future. Similar to Canada, sales were dominated by the traditional desk seal (approximately 50 percent of all sales). The major buyers of seals were lawyers and accountants who purchased some 70 percent of all seals, primarily for their incorporation clients.

Unlike Canada, the major embosser manufacturers were fully integrated. The largest manufacturers of both dies and embosser subassemblies were Jordan and Bolson. Much of Jordan's sales were to their own name search houses. In recent years, some of these were expressing displeasure at this arrangement as they wanted the flexibility to select embossers. The largest market shares of the seal production market were held by Bolson's (50 percent) and Jordan and Sons (28 percent).

Eighty-five percent of legal seals were handled through company formation agents. Similar to the service firms in Canada, formation agents were hired by lawyers to assist in incorporations. These agents also provided an embosser as part of their service; thus, if Sterling was to seriously compete in the U.K. market they would have to either usurp Jordan's production, or supply Bolson's customers. The major agents were Jordan and Sons (26 percent share of seal sales), Stanley Davis (13 percent), and London Law (10 percent).

The relationship between the seal producers and formation agents was one of great loyalty. Jordan and Sons purchased their seals from Jordan's, while Stanley Davis purchased from Bolson's

Pocket seals were priced at 5.50 and desk seals at 7.50 (prices in Pounds Sterling—1 pound sterling = $2.10 Canadian, $1 U.S. = $1.22 Canadian). Similar to the Canadian product, the quality of the seals was poor.

THE CURRENT SITUATION

Jan looked again at his notes on the United Kingdom. Several possibilities existed. They could continue exporting subassemblies to Jordan. In 1984/85 Sterling had sold 5,000 Mark Maker subassemblies to Jordan. They were originally to be a distributor for Mark Maker; however, due to problems in die manufacturing and weak sales efforts, not only were sales low, but there was some concern that the Mark Maker was developing a bad reputation. Jordan had recently improved the quality, developed an effective on-line production system, and were manufacturing high quality dies. This, coupled with placing the Mark Maker prominently in their brochure, resulted in 3,000 Mark Makers being sold in the past year. Jordan was interested in continuing their relationship with Sterling, but they wanted to produce the dies themselves.

Perhaps, thought Jan, Sterling could export the finished product. Duty was only 4.6 percent, the value-added tax (a tax levied at each stage of production) was 15 percent, and overnight courier costs were $7.50 per Mark Maker (the minimum courier charge was $60). Meeting U.K. demands would be no problem. Sterling could produce 168,000 Mark Makers with seals per year out of its London, Ontario plant, 250,000 if they added a third shift.

Alternatively, Sterling could use licensing. MBF McFarlane, a U.K.-based rubber stamp manufacturer, had expressed an interest in this possibility. Maybe, thought Jan, all MBF wants is Sterling's computer technology and to keep Sterling from marketing other products there. In fact, MBF had visited Sterling in the spring of 1988 and in their recent catalogue claimed to have computer ordering capability.

Perhaps, Sterling could purchase one of the seal producers or construct their own branch. Labor availability was not a problem. Martyn Wright, a director of production with Jordan, had expressed a strong interest in leaving Jordan and heading up a Sterling operation in the United Kingdom. Martyn felt that Sterling could purchase Jordan's seal operations and tie the computer typesetting business into Jordan's production facility. Alternatively, Sterling could build their own branch. A 60,000 per year Mark Maker plant required two employees and $50,000 in equipment. This included the on-line ordering and production systems, and the software. Administrative support, rent, and the employee salaries were estimated at $5,000 per month.

Jan tried to elicit management opinion on the various entry mode options. They saw Mark Maker as a product which could open foreign market doors for Sterling, thereby paving the way for the introduction of Sterling's other products. Unfortunately, senior management was not in total agreement on the appropriate entry modes required to attain these objectives. One of the managers believed that great profits could be attained by licensing the product to a U.K. manufacturer. He felt that Sterling should be focusing its attention on developing new products and a stronger sales organization, not spreading resources thinner by getting involved in an overseas branch. Another senior manager felt that providing there was a reasonable chance of success in the United Kingdom, it would be in Sterling's best interest to have a branch there. This manager envisioned creating five branch plants with sales offices each year over the next five years. Each branch would control $1 million in yearly sales. Branch plants in the United States and United Kingdom were essential for the realization of this plan. He also felt that Sterling had developed a culture of innovation and risk taking. Accepting a licensing agreement would send the wrong message to employees.

Management was unsure of Sterling's ability to manage a foreign branch. They had experienced difficulties in managing the Windsor and Toronto offices and thought a branch overseas would pose even greater difficulties. They were considering putting a production and sales branch in Montreal within the next few years as a test of Sterling's ability to manage a foreign operation.

Another more recent experience was Sterling's foray into the United States. On May 1, 1988, Julius Blumberg Inc. (a U.S. legal stationery supplier) was made Sterling's exclusive sales agent for the United States for a seven-month period, after which, Sterling would have the option of appointing other agents. Under this arrangement, Blumberg would not produce the seal; rather, they would send their customers' orders to Sterling who would produce the seal and then ship both the seal and subassembly to the appropriate Blumberg office. It was felt that the market presence of Blumberg, and a guarantee of featuring the Mark Maker in their catalogue would result in substantial U.S. sales. Jan looked back over the past five months. Overall sales had been disappointing (under 100 units per week). However, Sterling had learned much about the U.S. market from this experience. Jan felt that the low sales could have resulted from using the traditional passive approach to selling embossers. A catalogue could not impress upon customers the advantages of the Mark Maker over other embossers. Jan suspected that some direct promotion was required. During the past year, he had traveled to Blumberg offices in Albany, New York, and Texas. During these visits, he had tried to convince the sales people to use a more direct sales approach. As an incentive, he offered them one dollar for each Mark Maker sold. The results of these visits were impressive. For example, in Albany, prior to Jan's visit, Mark Maker sales averaged 5 per week; shortly after his visit, sales increased to 70 per week. Blumberg felt that the direct approach was inappropriate and instructed their sales force to tone down the sales approach. Subsequently, sales dropped to their old levels.

The same problem had occurred in Canada. However, when the legal stationers started using more aggressive sales techniques and Sterling started dropping into legal offices to show them the Mark Maker, sales increased dramatically.

Jan looked over the U.K. market report again. How to decide? And how fast to move? More fundamentally, should they do anything with respect to the United Kingdom without first developing a broad approach to international markets?

MARY KAY COSMETICS: ASIAN MARKET ENTRY

In February 1993, Curran Dandurand, senior vice president of Mary Kay Cosmetics Inc.'s (MKC) global marketing group, was reflecting on the company's international operations. MKC products had been sold outside the United States for over 15 years, but by 1992, international sales represented only 11% of the $1 billion total. In contrast, one of MKC's U.S. competitors, Avon Products Inc., derived over 55% of its $3.6 billion retail sales from international markets in 1992.

Dandurand wondered how MKC could expand international operations and which elements of MKC's culture, philosophy, product line, and marketing programs were transferable. She wanted to define the critical success factors for MKC internationally and establish a marketing strategy for future international expansion. Specifically, she was currently evaluating two market entry opportunities: Japan and China. The first was a mature but lucrative market where cosmetics marketing and direct selling were well-known and accepted. The second was a rapidly growing and changing but relatively unknown market with substantially lower individual purchasing power.

THE COSMETICS AND DIRECT SELLING INDUSTRIES

MKC competed in both the cosmetics and direct selling industries. A decade of mergers, acquisitions, takeovers, buyouts, and sell-offs had dramatically changed the shape of the global cosmetics industry. Powerful multinational marketing companies such as Colgate-Palmolive, Procter & Gamble, Estee Lauder, Gillette, and Unilever (Elizabeth Arden and Chesebrough-Pond's) had increased their market shares, many pharmaceutical companies had exited the industry, and Japanese companies such as Kao and Shiseido were gaining strength internationally.

In 1992, worldwide retail sales of facial treatments and color cosmetics products exceeded $50 billion, with the United States accounting for $16 billion. The top four companies in the U.S. cosmetics market in 1992 were Procter & Gamble with $4.3 billion cosmetics retail sales, Estee Lauder, Avon, and Revlon. L'Oreal, a subsidiary of Nestle, dominated the world market with $5.9 billion in retail sales, followed by Procter & Gamble, Avon, Unilever, Shiseido, Revlon, Colgate-Palmolive, Estee Lauder, SmithKline Beecham, and Gillette.

In 1992, the value of sales to consumers by the U.S. direct selling industry was estimated at $14 billion. Products of all types were sold to consumers in their homes by independent salespeople, many of whom worked on a part-time basis. Retail sales by the U.S. direct selling cosmetics industry were estimated at $5 billion in 1992. Cosmetics companies used two approaches to direct selling: the repetitive person-to-person method, used by Avon, in which a salesperson regularly visited customers in their homes and sold products one to one; and the party plan method, in which a salesperson presented and sold products to a group of customers attending a "party" or "show" in one of the customer's homes. The party plan method was used by MKC.

Other large international direct selling organizations included Amway, which sold a variety of household and personal care products and recorded retail sales of over $3.5 billion in 1992, and Tupperware, which sold household products through the party plan method and had retail sales of over $1 billion. International sales for Amway and Tupperware accounted for 60% and 75% respectively.

MKC OPERATIONS AND PHILOSOPHY

Incorporated in Texas in 1963 by Mary Kay Ash, MKC was a direct selling cosmetics company with 1992 estimated retail sales of $1 billion, net company sales of $624 million,[1] cost of goods sold of $148 million, and earnings before interest and taxes of $110 million. (**Exhibit 1** depicts the growth in MKC net revenues, operating cash flow, and number of consultants between 1986 and 1992.) MKC sold a range of skin care, personal care, and cosmetics products through approximately 275,000 independent salespeople worldwide, known as "beauty consultants," who purchased products from the company and resold them at skin care classes or facials held in homes that were attended by four to six, or one to two potential customers respectively.

The company's powerful culture was based on offering unlimited opportunities for women in business, coupled with a distinctive compensation and recognition plan. Mary Kay Ash's charismatic personality and drive had been central to the company's rapid growth and success, and, for many beauty consultants, she represented a caring and successful role model. In 1993, MKC defined its mission as promoting business opportunities for women, teaching women how to care for their skin and use cosmetics, offering skin care systems as opposed to individual products, and providing unsurpassed personal service to its customers. (**Exhibit 2** outlines what the company considered to be its competitive advantages and points of difference with respect to both potential beauty consultants and cosmetics consumers.)

---

[1] Net company sales were defined as sales of MKC products by the company to its sales consultants. Retail sales are defined as those sales made by consultants to consumers.

Product Line

In 1992, MKC manufactured a relatively narrow line of 225 SKUs (stockkeeping units), including different color shades.[2] Product policy emphasized skin care "systems" that included several related items formulated for specific skin types or skin conditions. (**Table A** reports the number of products—excluding different shades within color product categories—and percentage of 1992 sales for each of the eight product categories in which MKC competed.)

TABLE A

	NUMBER OF PRODUCTS	% SALES (1992)
Skin care (cleansers, creams, moisturizers, foundations)	27	46%
Glamour (lipsticks, eye colors)	24	30
Fragrances	9	10
Nail care	12	5
Body care	5	3
Sun care	7	2
Hair care	5	1
Men's skin care	6	1

MKC regularly involved its sales force in product policy decisions, sending them samples of prospective new products for evaluation. Virtually all MKC products were manufactured in a single plant near Dallas, considered to be the most efficient cosmetics production facility in the world.

Sales Force

Four basic levels of independent contractors were included in the MKC sales force: beauty consultants, sales directors, senior sales directors, and national sales directors. Promotions were made from within and based entirely on performance, as defined by volume sales and recruitment of new salespeople. Virtually all MKC beauty consultants were female, and new consultants were recruited by existing salespeople whose compensation and advancement were partly dependent on their recruiting success.

A new MKC beauty consultant had to purchase a Beauty Consultant Showcase, which cost around $100. Consultants bought MKC products at a 40% to 50% discount off the retail selling price, depending on volume. A minimum wholesale order of $180 had to be placed once every three months for a consultant to remain active. If a consultant terminated her association with MKC, the company would, if requested, buy back all her MKC inventory at 90% of the price she had paid for it.

[2] In 1992, Avon had an estimated 1,500 SKUs.

In addition to the margins made on product sales, salespeople received a 4% to 12% commission on the wholesale prices of products purchased by those beauty consultants they had recruited. This commission, which increased with the number of recruits achieved, encouraged consultants to devote time to recruiting and training other consultants. To be promoted to sales director, a consultant had to recruit 30 active consultants; to become a senior sales director one of the director's recruits had to become a sales director herself; and to become a national sales director, a director had to motivate at least 10 of the consultants in her group to become sales directors. Nonmonetary rewards and recognition incentives, for which MKC was renowned, included pink Cadillacs, diamonds, and furs.

Communications

MKC developed programs, manuals, and sales training aids for its sales force. Since the emphasis was on "teaching skin care and glamour" to consumers, beauty consultants had to be taught how to teach. A new recruit would attend three "classes" given by an experienced consultant, study the "Beauty Consultant's Guide," and sit through an orientation class organized by her unit director prior to her being enrolled as an MKC beauty consultant. Weekly training sessions covered product information, customer service, business organization, and money management. Each year, some 15% of the MKC sales force traveled to Dallas at their own expense for a three-day seminar where sales and recruiting achievements of top-performing consultants were recognized. Queens of Sales and Recruiting were crowned by Mary Kay Ash and well-known entertainers made guest appearances. Workshops on every aspect of building and managing the business were conducted by consultants and directors that had developed a particular expertise. In addition, many national directors held their own yearly "jamborees" patterned after the Dallas event.

MKC also supported its consultant sales force with consumer print advertising, placed in women's magazines. (**Exhibit 3** reproduces some examples of recent MKC print advertisements in the United States.)

Challenges Facing MKC in 1993

In 1993, MKC was facing a mature U.S. cosmetics market, an increasing number of competing direct selling organizations, and potentially maximum historical penetration in some areas of the United States. At the same time, MKC's international subsidiaries' sales growth had been modest. Given that competitors such as Avon and Amway had been very successful internationally, MKC executives could see no reason why MKC could not do the same. They believed that the MKC culture could be transferred internationally and that Mary Kay Ash's charisma, motivation, and philosophy were likely to appeal to women throughout the world.

INTERNATIONAL OPERATIONS

In early 1993, MKC products were sold in 19 countries. The company had 100%-owned subsidiaries in nine countries: Argentina (which also served Uruguay and Chile), Australia (with additional sales to New Zealand), Canada, Germany, Mexico, Taiwan, Spain, Thailand, and Russia. MKC was also planning to enter Italy, Portugal, the United Kingdom, and Japan or China in the near future. In addition, distributors existed in Costa Rica, Singapore, Malaysia, Brunei, Bermuda, Guatemala, Sweden, Norway, and Iceland.

Historically, international expansion had been opportunistic, based largely on personal contacts. The first two markets entered, Australia and Argentina, were not chosen for strategic reasons but in response to approaches to the company from local entrepreneurs. An international division with separate backroom operations, based in Dallas, had evolved to support the international businesses; this ensured the latter received adequate attention but duplicated functions and resources at headquarters.

In 1992, MKC initiated an organizational change that resulted in the formation of global resource groups to support sales subsidiaries worldwide, thereby consolidating the human resource, legal, finance, manufacturing, and marketing functions. (**Exhibit 4** depicts the new organizational structure.) The global marketing group, headed by Dandurand, provided subsidiaries with product development and marketing support, advertising, public relations and consumer promotion materials, and controlled the quality, consistency, and image of the Mary Kay brand around the world. Dandurand anticipated that marketing communication strategies would gradually become more locally driven. She explained:

> Once we have firmly established consistently high quality and clearly communicated the desired image for our company and brand, the local subsidiaries will be given more autonomy to develop their own marketing communication programs.

In addition, regional sales headquarters were established for Asia/Pacific, Europe, and the Americas (excluding the United States) to support the country subsidiaries within those regions more effectively and to facilitate MKC's future international expansion.

To illustrate the challenges MKC faced internationally, the evolution of each of four MKC subsidiaries is briefly described:

Canada. The Canadian market was similar to the United States both in product requirements and organization, and U.S. sales directors were allowed to go to Canada to recruit and build sales areas. The Canadian subsidiary had been operating for 15 years. However, in 1993, market research indicated that MKC was perceived by some Canadian consumers as out of date. A salaried country manager with a marketing and sales staff ensured local contact with the Canadian consultants and the efficient order processing and delivery of MKC products.

Australia. THe Australian subsidiary began with the acquisition of an existing direct selling company in the early 1970s. In 1992, MKC had low brand awareness and a poor image. All products were imported from the United States and the U.S. pricing strategy had been replicated without much adaptation to local market conditions. Nutri-Metics, an Australian competitor, had successfully used a hybrid of party plan and door-to-door direct selling methods, backed by media advertising, catalog sales, and Buying Club sales.[3] Unlike MKC, Nutri-Metics did not hold skin care classes, and salespeople could buy in and remain "active" with lower purchase commitments than were required for MKC consultants.

Mexico. In 1988, MKC established a subsidiary in Mexico headed by a husband-and-wife team who had previously worked for the direct selling party-plan cosmetics company, Jafra. The couple became salaried employees with performance incentives. The new Mexican subsidiary also benefited initially from U.S. sales directors who went to Mexico to recruit consultants. Three thousand new consultants joined the company in the first three months. After four years, brand awareness was high, the brand image was positive, and sales force size exceeded 6,200.

Taiwan. The Taiwan subsidiary, launched in July 1991, emphasized intensive training for new consultants. Chinese women were characterized as typically entrepreneurial, independent, and hardworking, with a strong drive to make money. The local country manager had previous experience in direct selling with both Avon and Tupperware. In 1992, rapid expansion had generated $3.3 million in sales through 1,800 consultants. Sales were expected to triple in 1993. All products were shipped from Dallas.

MKC also had established subsidiaries in Germany, with an estimated 1,500 consultants in 1993, and in Argentina which, despite periodic hyperinflation throughout the 1980s, was profitable in 1992. Poor results in the United Kingdom had resulted in the subsidiary being closed in 1985 after four years of operation, though there were plans to reopen in 1993. (**Exhibit 5** presents data on MKC sales, number of directors, and number of consultants by subsidiary.)

Dandurand believed the MKC's limited international success was due partly to the direct application of the U.S. marketing strategy, products, and communications to different subsidiaries without sufficient local modifications. Other factors constraining growth included low consumer brand awareness and insufficient marketing resources to develop it. Dandurand explained:

---

[3] Buying Clubs enabled women to purchase products such as cosmetics at a discount for their personal consumption rather than for resale. Individuals were not required to purchase a minimum level of inventory to enroll in the club. The most successful clubs offered broad product lines.

In some countries, cultural barriers impede the use of the party plan and door-to-door selling. The size of a typical home may be smaller than in the United States, or a party for unfamiliar guests may be considered an invasion of privacy. In addition, the time required for a two-hour skin care class is sometimes an obstacle.

Future International Expansion

A strategic planning process in 1993 identified a "great teachers" strategy to differentiate MKC worldwide from other retail and direct selling competitors and to build on the company's proven capabilities in this area. Greater emphasis would be placed on sales force training and on adapting MKC's positioning, the product range, and marketing communications mix to local market needs. A standard core product line would be supplemented with products developed specifically for each local market. Products would either be imported from the United States or manufacturing and/or final packaging would be subcontracted in individual country markets as was currently done in Mexico and Argentina. In particular, MKC was currently looking for a European manufacturing site to support its planned market entry into several European countries.

A country manager who wanted products adapted would have to seek the approval of the MKC regional president who, in turn, would meet with the international marketing and manufacturing managers. MKC regional presidents were all equity holders and therefore both advocates for the interests of the countries in their region as well as representatives of the headquarters' perspective.[1]

MKC executives believed that the company's values were transferable. Dandurand elaborated:

> Telling women they can achieve, making them believe in themselves and giving them caring and respect, is an international message. However, the message needs to be tailored to each market and communicated effectively and I'm not sure whether or not additional role models are needed in each foreign market for the company to be successful.

It was recognized that one or two charismatic leaders could generate massive growth in number of consultants and product sales.

Avon's International Strategy

Avon had become a successful international cosmetics company. Each country subsidiary was run by a country manager who had considerable decision-making authority so long as agreed-upon performance objectives were achieved. On

---

[1] As a private company, MKC had a compensation plan for senior executives that worked like a partnership.

average, 60% of the Avon products sold by a foreign subsidiary came from a common core line, while 40% were adapted to local markets. The company placed a heavy emphasis on merchandising with 18 three-week marketing campaigns used to promote specific consumer events such as Mother's Day, and 26 two-week drive periods supported by specific sales brochures each year. Avon sales consultants had to deal with the complexity of a product line of 1,500 SKUs. In contrast to MKC, Avon employed salaried sales managers who oversaw the company's independent salespeople.

In 1992, Avon eliminated its regional headquarters in favor of a single global support group based in New York. Many Avon subsidiaries were large enough to afford their own strong functional staffs and therefore no longer needed back-up from regional headquarters. MKC executives believed that their lower product line turnover ought to permit a more streamlined and lower-cost central support group than Avon's.

Avon had been more willing than MKC to adapt its marketing programs internationally, adjusting prices according to the level of consumer buying power in individual countries. Avon hired strong local nationals as country managers, giving them specific strategic direction, generous resource allocations, and clear profit-and-loss responsibility. The Avon culture was considered "hard-nosed" and numbers-driven—return on equity and return on assets being especially important—but local country managers who delivered enjoyed considerable autonomy. According to some MKC executives, MKC had a more caring orientation and placed greater emphasis on support systems, mentoring, training, and recognition of consultants.

MKC IN ASIA

MKC's Taiwanese subsidiary had, in 1992, become profitable and promised good future sales growth. As part of the recent reorganization, an Asia/Pacific regional manager would shortly establish a base in Hong Kong from which to build MKC sales in Asia.

Asia was evolving as one of the fastest growing and most dynamic regions of the world. Its share of world GDP was scheduled to reach 32% by the year 2000, up from 24% in 1988. The choice between a Japanese or Chinese market entry would, Dandurand believed, impact MKC's long-term market position in Asia. She began to compare the two countries on some key characteristics to help make the decision (**Table B**). She wanted to build on MKC's past international experience and current competitive advantages to develop a market entry strategy that fit with the MKC culture and the local market environment and that would enable MKC to establish a firm base from which to build its Asian operations.

TABLE B	KEY CHARACTERISTICS OF JAPANESE AND CHINESE MARKETS		
		JAPAN	CHINA
Population, 1992		124 million	1,139 million
Estimated population, 2020		137 million	1,541 million
Population distribution (0–24; 25–49; 50 +):			
1993		32%; 37%; 31%	42%; 39%; 19%
2000		29%; 35%; 36%	40%; 39%; 21%
Urban population, 1992		77%	27%
Population/square mile		865	315
Gross domestic product (US$ billion)		3,370	371[a]
1993 GDP growth % (estimated)		2.3%	10.1%
1994 GDP growth % (estimated)		3.2%	9.5%
1990 per capita GNP		$14,311	$325
Average hourly compensation (US$)		$14.41	$0.24
Penetration of:			
Televisions		1 per 1.8 persons	1 per 8 persons
Radios		1 per 1.3	1 per 9
Telephones		1 per 2.3	1 per 66
1992 advertising expenditure per capita		$220	$0.86

[a] In early 1993, China's GDP was reestimated at $1,700 billion by the International Monetary Fund on the basis of purchasing power parity. This meant the Chinese economy was the third largest in the world.

JAPAN

The Cosmetics Industry

In 1992, there were 1,100 cosmetics manufacturers in Japan but five companies accounted for 69% of domestic sales. Domestic production exceeded $9 billion in factory sales in 1991 and included local production by foreign firms, estimated at 18% of total domestic production. Imports represented 5% of total sales in 1991, up from 3% in 1989; over 45% of imports came from France, of which 27% consisted of fragrances and cologne. In addition, Japanese tourists purchased around $500 million of cosmetics at duty-free shops each year. **Table C** summarizes the size of the Japanese cosmetics market and the sources of product.

The Japanese cosmetics market was mature, recording average annual value growth of 3% between 1988 and 1992, compared with a growth rate of 4.4% in the United States. Major consumers of cosmetics were women in their 20s and 30s. Foreign-made cosmetics were considered high-status products. Issues impacting the industry in 1992 included the end of manufacturers' control over the prices at which their products were resold by retailers and a continuing decrease in the number of independent cosmetics retailers. Strict Ministry of Health regulations governing imports and the manufacture of cosmetics

TABLE C	**JAPANESE COSMETICS MARKET SIZE AND SOURCES OF SHIPMENTS**		

$ MILLIONS (MANUFACTURER SHIPMENTS)	1989	1990	1991
Imports:	265	318	460
From the United States	41	57	89
Local production	8,983	8,433	9,072
Exports	128	147	214
Total market	9,119	8,603	9,319

involved lengthy approval processes. In many cases, common ingredients approved for use in cosmetics outside Japan were prohibited by the Ministry of Health, requiring reformulations of most products.

The Direct Selling Industry

In 1992, Japan was the largest direct selling market in the world with an estimated $19.2 billion in retail sales. Direct selling enabled consumers to bypass inefficient wholesale and retail distribution systems which some viewed as inefficient and non-price competitive. Japanese women who left business in order to have children came back into a company with no tenure and had to start up the corporate ladder from scratch. Consequently, direct selling, which could be done part time, was an attractive second career for mothers seeking to reenter the work force. According to the Japan Direct Selling Association, 1,120,000 women engaged in direct selling in 1992.[5]

Amway had been in Japan since 1977 and, by 1991, recorded sales of US$1.2 billion with a product line that included home care, personal care and food products, housewares, cosmetics, and gifts. The company had a sales force of 1,000,000 people, developed primarily through word-of-mouth. Training was conducted by direct distributors who sponsored new distributors. Compensation consisted of a 30% commission and a bonus based on the sales of sponsored distributors. Conventions were held every year for training purposes and to recognize outstanding performance. In 1990, only seven other foreign companies generated more revenues in Japan than Amway. Reasons for this success were: an effective distribution system based on company-owned warehouses; high-quality, value-oriented products; good relations with dedicated distributors; and a philosophy that emphasized human relationships, fulfillment of dreams, and financial freedom.

Consumers

In the 1990s, an increasing percentage of Japanese women were going on to further education and working outside the home. In 1992, over 50% of the 51.8 mil-

[5] In 1992, the total Japanese population was 124 million, of whom 41% were women over 15 years of age.

lion Japanese women aged over 15 years were employed, predominantly on a part-time basis. They earned lower salaries than men and preferred more flexible work schedules. Women's activities outside the home were increasing as were their expectations of equality. Many women were marrying later and having fewer children. (**Exhibit 6** summarizes the results of a 1990 attitude study of 1,000 Japanese women.)

Annual cosmetics expenditures were above US$260.00 per household in 1992. Forty percent of all cosmetics sales were to women in their 20s and 30s (26% of all Japanese women over the age of 15). The heaviest users were 8.8 million women aged between 20 and 29 (14% of all Japanese women over the age of 15). These heavy users were less price sensitive and more interested in high-quality cosmetics. Working women spent, on average, 25% more on cosmetic purchases than women who did not work outside the home. A fair complexion and fine-textured skin were considered hallmarks of beauty in Japan, so skin care products accounted for 40% of all cosmetic sales. The growing sales of skin care products were also fueled by the increasing average age of the Japanese population; 23% of the population would be aged over 65 years by the year 2010, compared with 14% in 1992.

Fifty-four percent of facial skin care users and 40% of shaded makeup users purchased all or some of their products from direct sales companies. Corresponding figures in the United States were 25% and 22% respectively. Nineteen percent of Japanese skin care users and 20% of shaded makeup product users purchased only from direct salespeople. Japanese women purchased, on average, 16.2 skin care items a year at a price of $32.97 per purchase. In the United States, an average 20.1 annual purchases were made at $9.05 per purchase. Thus, the average Japanese woman spent almost three times more on skin care than the average American woman. In the area of shaded makeup, Japanese women made 13 purchases per year compared with 27 in the United States, but price differentials between the two countries resulted in almost equal annual expenditures. (**Exhibit 7** summarizes Japanese consumer buying behavior for skin care and shaded makeup products.) In addition to functional product benefits, Japanese consumers placed a special emphasis on the visual appeal of product packaging.

Japanese consumers believed that they had sensitive skin as MKC confirmed when it ran extensive trials with Japanese women who had recently arrived in the United States. Pink was seen as a color more appropriate for children and teenagers so the classic MKC pink was muted on potential packaging and caps retooled to present a more upscale image. It was felt that redesigned packages might also appeal to U.S. consumers and that the potential existed for a global packaging redesign.

Products

Skin care products accounted for 40% of all cosmetics sales in Japan in 1992. (**Exhibit 8** details sales of major cosmetics product categories over time.) In the skin care category, sales of skin lotion increased by 12%, face wash and cleansing products by 4%, while cold cream, moisture cream, and milky lotion decreased by 1%. In 1992, Kao and Shiseido dominated the Japanese skin care market. Makeup accounted for 23% of cosmetics sales but its share had been declining since 1986. Foundation products accounted for more than 50% of makeup sales.

Foreign manufacturers were more successful in selling makeup than skin care products while the reverse was true for domestic companies. Dandurand explained:

> In Japan, makeup products are associated with status, image, and dreams. Japanese women tend to aspire to look like the Western women on the cosmetics ads and so foreign brands, with the attached status, are more popular for color cosmetics. When it comes to skin care products, Japanese women tend to be more pragmatic. They believe that they have very delicate skins that require highly scientific products especially made for them by Japanese manufacturers who understand their needs better.

Distribution

Cosmetics were distributed in Japan through three main channels: franchise systems; general distributorships; and door-to-door sales.

Franchise systems were based on contracts between manufacturers and retailers, also known as chain stores, whereby a manufacturer's affiliated distribution company provided retailers with a full range of products, marketing support, and product promotions. In addition, trained beauty consultants were provided by manufacturers at each outlet. This enabled manufacturers to maintain control over the selling process and to provide consumers with individualized service. Franchise systems accounted for 40% of cosmetic sales in 1992 but were expected to decline. A variation of the franchise system was the direct selling franchise system whereby manufacturers dealt directly with retail accounts without going through a distribution company. This method was used by many foreign manufacturers who focused their marketing efforts, supported by face-to-face counseling, on a limited number of prestige shops and department stores.

General distributorships were the conventional channels whereby products flowed from manufacturer to wholesaler to retailer, and the manufacturer and retailer were not connected directly. The manufacturer provided full marketing support via advertising and promotion for products that tended to be lower-priced and less sophisticated. The volume share of cosmetics sold through this channel was estimated at 30% in 1992 and expected to increase.

Door-to-door sales or home visiting systems enabled manufacturers to bypass the costly, complex retailing network. This direct selling system, which had worked well in the past, was facing problems in 1992: fewer women were staying at home, and direct selling companies were finding it increasingly difficult to attract sales personnel. In 1982, this channel had represented 25% of cosmetic sales; by 1992, it represented 19%. Some direct selling companies were diversifying into other ways of reaching the consumer. For example, Pola, a major Japanese direct selling cosmetics company, had started marketing its products in variety shops, aesthetic salons, and by mail order. Avon and Noevir, also a large Japanese direct selling cosmetics company, and Menard, had opened retail stores and Salon outlets. Other channels included beauty parlors and barber shops. (Shares of cosmetics sales in Japan by distribution channel and by consumer age group are given in **Exhibit 9**.)

Competitors

The top five domestic cosmetics manufacturers in 1992 were Shiseido with 27% of the market; Kao with 16%; Kanebo with 11%; Pola with 8%; and Kobayashi Kose with 7%. These companies spent, on average, 4% of sales on research and development, double the level spent by the major foreign manufacturers. Shiseido, founded in 1872 as Shiseido Pharmacy, entered the cosmetics business in 1902. Ninety years later, Shiseido products were sold through 25,000 chain stores and 9,000 retail beauty consultants. Kao, Kanebo, and Kobayashi Kose also operated nationwide networks. Foreign companies such as Max Factor, Revlon, and Clinique entered the Japanese market in the early 1980s and pursued selective distribution through a limited number of prestigious department stores. (**Exhibit 10** summarizes sales data for the major Japanese and foreign cosmetics manufacturers, and **Table D** profiles the major direct selling cosmetics companies.)

Pola was established in 1946 and had $740 million in sales in 1991. With 180,000 "Pola Ladies," 20,000 salespeople, and 6,500 retail outlets, Pola ranked third in cosmetics sales and first in direct sales of cosmetics in Japan. Originally targeted at older women, Pola had begun recently to focus on younger women with its moderately priced product line. Pola provided in-depth training for its staff, ranging from one month for a "Pola Lady" to over a year for sales research

TABLE D

MANUFACTURER SALES OF MAJOR DIRECT SELLING COSMETICS COMPANIES IN JAPAN—1990

	SALES GROWTH 1989–90	TOTAL SALES 1990 ($ MILLION)[a]	FACIAL SKIN Care (%)	MAKEUP (%)	HAIR CARE (%)	FRAGRANCES (%)	MEN'S COSMETICS (%)
Pola	2.4%	$704	54%	28%	2%	3%	2%
Nippon Menard	(2.3)	373	67	23	1	1	2
Avon[b]	1.9	304	35	30	4		
Noevir	2.8	292	64	24	4	4	4
Oppen	0.0	213	64	24	3	1	1
Aistar	0.0	185	100				
Naris	12.0	110	58	26		1	2
Yakult	1.7	50	56	22	4	2	2

Total company figures. Some companies were engaged in other businesses in addition to cosmetics; therefore, percentages of cosmetic sales do not add to 100%.
[b]Avon percentages total 69% because Avon also sold jewelry and lingerie.

staff at company headquarters. The compensation structure for Pola Ladies had 21 levels: "Class 1" salespeople who sold up to $370 monthly made a 25% margin and no commission. A "Super Million Lady" salesperson, with monthly sales over $37,000, earned a 35% margin, a $400 jewel allowance, and $800 in bonus. In 1991, Pola spend $28.5 million on media advertising, of which newspaper ads accounted for 9%, magazine ads for 28%, and television commercials for 63%.

Nippon Menard was established in 1959 and had $373 million in sales in 1990, of which 67% was derived from skin care products and 23% from makeup. Organized into 33 sales companies and sold through over 12,000 retail outlets and 160,000 beauty specialists, it ranked eighth among cosmetics companies and second among direct selling cosmetics companies. Main brands included Entals, Delphia, and Ires, positioned at lower price points and targeted at women in their 20s and 30s, and Eporea, positioned at a high price point and targeted at older women. Beauty specialists followed a series of four training classes and could advance through seven levels from "beginner" to "special" depending on their monthly sales. A beginner beauty specialist, who achieved monthly sales of $300 to $450, earned a commission of 30% but no bonus. At the other extreme, a "special" beauty specialist sold over $23,000 per month and earned a 38% commission plus between $350 and $1,000 in bonus. In 1991, Menard spent a total of $25 million on advertising, of which 6% was on newspaper ads, 11% on magazine advertising, and 83% on television commercials.

Noevir was established in 1978 and had $292 million in sales in 1990, of which 64% was derived from skin care products and 24% from makeup. It operated on a consignment basis with 580 sales companies selling to two levels of 109,000 agencies, through 200,000 sales people. It ranked ninth among cosmetic companies and third among direct selling cosmetic companies. In 1992, Noevir had two subsidiaries, Sana and Nov; Sana sold through 5,000 skin care retail outlets and 400 makeup retail outlets, and Nov sold through 2,000 pharmaceutical outlets. Sana targeted younger women while Nov's product line included hypo-allergic cosmetics recommended by dermatologists. In 1991, Noevir spent $8 million on advertising—13% on magazine ads and the remainder on television commercials.

Avon was established in Japan in 1973 and had $325 million in sales in 1991, of which 65% was derived from cosmetics. Avon sold through mail-order catalogs and 350,000 Avon Ladies. In 1992, Avon had successfully floated 40% of the subsidiary's equity on the Tokyo stock exchange. It ranked thirteenth among cosmetics companies and fourth among direct selling cosmetics companies. The company targeted women in their 30s and 40s and, unlike other direct selling companies, Avon's products were not regularly demonstrated to consumers by Avon Ladies.

Avon, Menard, Pola, Noevir, and Amway also offered "buying club" programs. Most recruited salespeople on the basis of providing an opportunity to make extra income, but only Amway heavily stressed advancement into management based on recruiting and sales performance. Most competitors offered thorough product training at little or no cost; the training was more extensive than that provided by most U.S. direct selling organizations. Sales presentations typically were made one-to-one, but other than through catalogs and brochures, little instruction was provided to consumers. (**Exhibit 11** profiles the characteristics of consumers using the principal brands, and **Exhibit 12** reproduces competitor print advertisements.)

MKC in Japan

MKC began assessing the Japanese market in 1988 with a comparative study of products and competition. It was determined that the typical Japanese woman's skin care regimen involved a seven-stage process as opposed to three steps in the United States,[6] and that whitening products, not widely available in the United States, were very popular in Japan. In 1989, a comparative pricing study was undertaken and relationships established with an ingredient supplier and a private-label manufacturer who might produce an estimated 20% of the product line, tailored to the Japanese market, including whitening products and wet/dry foundation cake. In 1992, MKC proceeded with lengthy product approval processes involving the Japanese Ministry of Health. By year end, over $1 million had been invested in preparing to enter the Japanese market.

There was concern that MKC would be a late entrant in a mature, complex, fragmented, and highly competitive market. Dandurand believed that it would take three to five years before MKC would turn a profit and take share from competitors. On the other hand, 1993 might be an opportune time for MKC to launch in Japan since, increasingly, women wished both to raise children and be involved in activities outside the home, and an economic recession created more demand for part-time employment to supplement household incomes. Some MKC executives believed that success in Japan was essential to the company's future in the countries of the Pacific Rim.

CHINA

China covered 3.7 million square miles and was divided into 22 provinces, 3 municipalities (Beijing, Shanghai, and Tianjin), and 5 autonomous regions (Guangxi, Zhuang, Nei Mongol, Ningxia Hui, Xinjiang Uygur, and Tibet). The population was estimated at 1.1 billion in 1992 and was predicted to grow to 1.5 billion by the year 2020. Eight percent lived in the eastern half of the country depicted in **Exhibit 13.** The urban population was estimated at 310 million, the female population at 545 million, and the female population living in urban areas at around 156 million. In the second half of the twentieth century, China experienced one of the fastest demographic transitions in history. Mortality rates decreased and average life expectancy rose from 42 years in 1950 to 70 in 1992.

---

[6] In the United States a typical skin care regimen involved a cleanser, a toner, and a moisturizer. In Japan, several different cleansers and moisturizers were typically used in a single skin care regimen.

Fertility rates fell from an average of 6 children per woman in 1950 to 2.3 in 1992. Trends towards urbanization and a shift in population from the agricultural to the service sector were expected to continue in the 1990s.

In 1979, the "Open Door Policy" heralded a series of wide-ranging economic reforms: agriculture was decollectivized; the development of private and semi-private enterprises to produce goods was permitted; free market pricing and more liberal foreign exchange conversion were introduced; and foreign investment became more acceptable. These economic reforms had the greatest impact on the coastal provinces where economic free zones were established to facilitate foreign investment. Guandong province, for example, had experienced the fastest growth in East Asia in the 1980s. Overall, China's GNP had increased by 9% annually during the 1980s, while consumption had increased by 6.6%. In 1990, 70% of industrial growth was attributed to private, cooperative, and foreign ventures.

Since 1988, a higher-income, urban middle class had emerged with household earnings over $125 a month and saving rates estimated at 35%. By the year 2000, it was estimated that 41 million households would have incomes of over $18,000 per annum. Retail sales had increased nearly fivefold since 1980 with the number of retail outlets increasing from 2 million in 1980 to 12 million in 1992, most being private enterprises. All types of goods were available in the major cities, and the adoption rate of new products was rapid. In 1992, China was viewed as a sellers' market but experts believed that more sophisticated marketing skills and product differentiation would become increasingly important.

In assessing the political and economic risks of investing in China, multinational companies had three main concerns. First, some thought political instability was likely to follow the retirement or death of China's long-standing Premier Deng Xiaoping. Political struggles between conservatives and reformers might delay further economic reforms. Second, the Chinese government was not granting its people political freedom commensurate with their increasing economic freedom. Progress on human rights was essential to China maintaining most-favored nation status as a trading partner with the United States. Third, multinationals importing finished goods into China faced not only high tariffs but also the likely devaluation of the Chinese currency which would further increase the retail prices of their goods.

During the 1980s, cosmetics and toiletries became an important branch of China's light industry, and the number of cosmetics factories in China increased sixfold between 1982 and 1990. In 1992, the cosmetics market was estimated at $825 million (manufacturer sales), with skin care products dominant. There were approximately 3,000 cosmetics producers in China manufacturing limited product lines; about half were located in Shanghai. Many local brands were available as import tariffs on cosmetics averaged 100%. In 1991, the Chinese Ministry of Commerce initiated a professional training program for two million cosmetics managers, purchasers, and sales clerks with the objective of teaching them how to appraise the quality of cosmetics and skin conditions of consumers.

Consumers

There was a growing difference in purchasing power and consumer behavior between the urban and rural populations in China, with the urban population becoming increasingly prosperous and demanding, and the rural consumer evolving less quickly. Consumer habits also varied by region: northerners appeared to be more concerned with clothing and appearance while southerners bought more household products and consumer electronics. Brand names were highly appreciated by Chinese consumers who would pay up to four times more for foreign or joint venture brands, such as Ritz Crackers and Sony televisions, than for the equivalent local products.

Eighty-seven percent of Chinese women worked and many held two jobs: one state job and one independent job. Urban workers were generally employed in factories or workshops, employment assignments being allocated by local labor bureaus. Safety standards in factories were poor but compensation was adequate. The wage range from lowest grade to highest grade was a factor of three, and a sum equal to 10% of total wages was typically available for bonuses. Virtually all housing, medical, and transportation costs and midday meals were subsidized by Chinese government work units. Around 40% of the household income of a two-income urban household was typically spent on food and housing; the remainder was disposable income.

Government-subsidized housing units were small; 200 square feet was the typical size of a one-bedroom urban apartment. A workers' committee still managed each apartment building. A few apartments were also available for purchase; US$5,000 could purchase a two-bedroom apartment in Guangzhou in early 1993. Housing conditions were better in Guangzhou and Beijing than in Shanghai. Young workers, especially women, tended to live with their parents until they married. Once married, they would live with the husbands' parents or take their own apartments.

Female workers were entitled to 56 days of pregnancy leave and most factories had nurseries and kindergarten facilities. The Chinese government wished to encourage women to spend more time at home and therefore established the "Period Employment" system whereby women could elect to take three months maternity leave at 100% pay and/or up to seven years off at 70% of basic pay to aid in childraising. In 1992, an estimated 66% of Chinese women over the age of 25 were married.

A 1991 consumer study concluded that the average Chinese female urban consumer was 32 years old, married with one child, worked in a state factory, and earned the equivalent of $50 a month. She typically controlled the family budget and was concerned about the rising cost of living. Attracted to foreign brands, she considered skin care and cosmetics important, particularly those that prevented freckles and promoted cleanliness.

Chinese women were greatly interested in learning; education was held in very high esteem in Chinese culture. Chinese colleges and universities were increasingly asserting their independence; MKC might be able to sponsor skin

TABLE E

CHARACTERISTICS OF THREE PRINCIPAL REGIONAL MARKETS IN CHINA: 1992

	GUANGZHOU	BEIJING	SHANGHAI
Location	South (100 miles north of Hong Kong)	North (China's capital)	East Coast by Yangtze River
Population	6 million = city 25 million = province	4 million = city 11 million = province	13.5 million = city 60 million = province
Region characteristics	Low-cost manufacturing base for Hong Kong. Most flexible for business approvals and hiring.	Government ministries. Second-largest retail center and strong industrial base.	8.5% of China's industrial output. Cultural and commercial capital.
Foreign companies	Avon, Colgate, P&G and Amway	Shiseido, L'Oreal	Johnson & Johnson, Unilever
Consumer characteristics	Unrefined. Main interest is food and family. But more interested in glamour.	Rigid, bureaucratic. More cerebral.	Elegant, vain, tough negotiators, seek quality.
Typical wage level	$200/month, highest consumer goods spending in China. Flooded by foreign consumer goods.	$80/month but rising level of affluence in the last two years.	Over $100/month. Highest spending on clothing, cosmetics, jewelry. (Estimates = 30% disposable income.)

care courses and sell products to the enrolled students and/or secure product endorsements from medical schools.

By 1992, differences in buying power and buyer behavior were evident across the various regions of China. The three most important regional markets were: Guangzhou, Beijing, and Shanghai. (**Table E** summarizes key characteristics of these three metropolitan markets.)

Guangzhou. Hong Kong's influence was strongly felt in Guangzhou, whose economy was driven by the private sector. More interested in spending their disposable incomes on food, drink, eating out, and entertaining, Guangzhou consumers were wealthier but characterized as less cosmopolitan and sophisticated than other urban Chinese consumers. Described as flashy and ostentatious, Guangzhou consumers were also known as generous and free-spending. Many companies viewed the Guangzhou consumer market as very similar to Hong Kong's and believed that consumer characteristics of the two markets would continue to converge.

Beijing. Beijing consumers were generally characterized as conservative and serious. Less concerned with appearances than Shanghai consumers, they spent less on clothing and personal care products. However, Beijing, being the home of senior government and Party officials, had an elite group of consumers interested in luxury goods and designer labels. Also characterized as straightforward and honest, advertisements based on fact and information were well-received. Before making a major purchase, Beijing consumers would be well-versed on the technical aspects of the product. On the other hand, these consumers also appeared to be more willing to try new products, and new brand launches were often initially more successful than in Shanghai.

Shanghai. Being the largest city, Shanghai was the commercial and cultural center of China. Shanghai consumers were characterized as proud and very concerned about their appearances. While not the wealthiest consumers in China, they were known as the best dressed and smartest looking. Shanghai consumers spend a significantly greater proportion of their disposable income on clothing, jewelry, and personal care products than their counterparts elsewhere in China, and premium-priced products and brands moved better in Shanghai than anywhere else. Shanghainese acknowledged and even took pride in the historical European and Western influences on their city and personal habits. Housing conditions however, were distinctly worse in Shanghai than in most other cities in China.

Shanghai was also the manufacturing center of China, and Shanghai goods were recognized as among the best in China. As a result, Shanghai consumers were more loyal to their local brands than were other Chinese consumers. Considered the most influential market in China, it was believed that a successful launch in Shanghai was likely to be able to be extended to the rest of China, whereas a marketing program which worked in Beijing or Guangzhou would not necessarily work in Shanghai.

Products

Within the skin care category of the Chinese cosmetics market, the main product claims being made were prevention and removal of wrinkles; reduction of premature aging; absorption into and the effect upon functions of the skin; environmental protection; making skin snow-white, smooth and more elastic; healing acne; and purifying pores. Within the makeup category, Avon's Cake Foundation claimed to complement oily skins and give complexions a smooth, matte finish.

Packaging was much more basic than in the United States or Japan. Skin care products were mainly marketed in plastic or glass jars with decorated or colored caps. Labels were applied or jar screened (stamped directly onto the jar) and carried both English and Chinese copy. Outer packaging was less common and varied widely in the quality of carton and liners used. Inserts ranged from instructions on thin paper in Chinese only to color brochures with pictures and illustrations in both English and Chinese.

Distribution

State-owned department stores with 280,000 outlets accounted for 40% of all consumer product retail sales. Collectively owned stores, of which there were 1.2 million, accounted for 32%, while 8 million individually owned stores accounted for 20% of retail sales. The remaining sales were made through 330 joint venture stores (5% of sales) and direct-selling companies (3%). In general, the Chinese distribution system was more accessible to U.S. companies than the Japanese system. However, it was even more fragmented.

Cosmetics displays in stores tended to be confusing and cluttered with many brands. In department stores however, imported brands were sold in separate cases from domestic products. Three price tiers existed: imported brands such as Dior retailed at 8 times the retail prices of China-manufactured brands of Western/Chinese joint ventures and at 15 times those of local brands. Cosmetic companies rented cosmetic cases and shelf space from the department stores and paid the wages of the department store clerks.

Advertising

In 1992, per capita advertising spending in China was less than $1.00 but was expected to increase by 174% between 1992 and 1995. Newspapers were small and fragmented and rarely used for print advertising. Regional or provincial television channels were more popular than the single national channel, and advertising on the national television channel was more liable to censorship. A satellite television channel broadcast from Hong Kong, Star TV could be accessed by 4.8 million households in China and advertising costs through this channel averaged $0.50 per 1,000 people.

The cost of television advertising varied according to the status of the advertiser. The cost of a 30-second prime time advertisement on provincial television in Guangzhou province in May 1993 was $200 for a local company, $500 for a joint venture partnership, and $2,000 for a foreign importer. In Guangzhou City, these costs were about 40% of those for advertising to the entire province. For a foreign importer, the cost of a 30-second prime time advertisement on Chinese national television was $4,000 compared to $9,000 on Hong Kong television.

Competitors

Foreign competitors in China in 1992 included Avon, Johnson & Johnson, Kao, Unilever, L'Oreal, Procter & Gamble, Revlon , and Shiseido. However, their combined sales accounted for only 3% of the market. (**Exhibit 14** lists the main cosmetics products and brands available in China in 1992; **Exhibit 15** provides comparative pricing data for the major cosmetics product segments.)

In 1992, Avon was the first and only direct selling cosmetics company in China. Avon had established a joint venture with the Guangzhou Cosmetics

Factory (GCF) in which it owned 60% of the equity. GCF owned 35%, with the remaining 5% split between two Hong Kong business partners who had provided introductions to Chinese government officials. Avon operated only in the southern province of Guangdong. Sales in 1991 were about $4 million and rose to $8 million in 1992. Avon offered a full product line of 170 items (including a product that was a skin toner, moisturizer, and cleanser all in one), selling for an average of $4.00 each. Sales of skin-whitening products were especially strong. It was estimated that half the items were imported.

In 1993, Avon used television advertising to promote product benefits and print advertising to recruit salespeople. Products were sold by about 15,000 Avon Ladies, mostly part-timers, who kept their regular state jobs to retain their housing subsidies, medical benefits, and pensions. Salespeople sold Avon products for whatever markup they could achieve. On average, they were believed to earn a 30% margin on product sales. Avon distributed its products through 10 branch depots located throughout Guangdong. Two hundred sales managers, who were salaried employees, oversaw 4,500 Franchise Dealers, who in turn managed the sales representatives. A training program for the Franchise Dealers included classes on product benefits, cosmetics and skin care, and general business management.

Avon positioned itself as offering consumers service, quality, reliability, and product guarantees; the latter, in particular, was a new concept for the Chinese consumer. Typical Avon consumers were urban women, aged between 20 and 35 years. Many were thought to live with their parents and spend their wages on Western goods. Compared with other imported brands, Avon was thought to be popular with younger women because Avon products were reasonably priced, and purchase—either at work or at home—was considered convenient. In addition, Avon Ladies gave their good customers a 10% to 20% discount on volume purchases and received "finders fees" for recruiting salespeople.

By 1993, Avon had achieved a beachhead in China, but several problems were evident. Inflation was forcing frequent pay increases for Avon's trained salaried employees, many of whom were receiving attractive job offers from other direct marketing firms. Avon's salaried employees were also demanding that the company provide housing as state-owned enterprises had traditionally done. In addition, Avon executives did not receive the permanent discount off of the standard 30%–40% retail turnover tax and the temporary exclusivity for the direct marketing of cosmetics in Guangzhou that executives believed they had negotiated with the provincial government.[7]

Shiseido had established a joint venture company, Shiseido Liyuan Cosmetics Co., with Beijing Liyuan in 1987. Products were sold under the brand name Huazi and cumulative sales during the first five years after the launch were estimated at $80 million. Shiseido positioned itself as offering high quality, techno-

---

[7] "Avon Calling," *Business China*, Economist Intelligence Unit, July 12, 1993, pp. 1-2.

logically sophisticated products. The company offered 15 items at prices ranging from $4 to $6, in four product categories: eye makeup; hair car; nail care; and skin care.

MKC in China

In addition to choosing a location, MKC could choose to enter the Chinese market either by designating a licensed distributor or negotiating a joint venture agreement with a Chinese partner. Joint ventures were the most common structures Western companies used for entering China. Negotiations always involved government bodies and took an average of two years to complete. Successful joint ventures, such as those set up by Pepsi and Colgate-Palmolive, emphasized a careful search for the right partner, and in-depth market feasibility study, patience and a long-term commitment to the investment, and a strong focus on training and developing local management. MKC could also choose to build a manufacturing facility as Gillette and Amway had, expand and upgrade an existing production facility as Avon had done, subcontract manufacturing, or simply import products from the United States. It was estimated that the construction of a one-million-square-foot manufacturing plant would take two years and cost over $20 million.

Timing was considered critical in the decision to enter the Chinese market: Avon was still marketing only in the South; the number of cosmetics competitors was increasing; and the retail infrastructure was expected to continue to improve substantially.

MARKET ENTRY DECISION

One critical issue in deciding which markets to enter and in what order, was the acceptability and potential success of MKC's party plan approach to sales in the two markets. In Japan, Tupperware had pioneered the use of party plans, which were subsequently successfully used by a number of companies. By 1992, party plans had become an established and accepted sales technique in Japan. On the other hand, to date, no company had attempted the party plan approach in China. In 1992, MKC conducted a number of focus groups to help determine the acceptability and potential success of this sales approach. Initial findings suggested that the party plan method would be well-received in China. However, most homes were small, and in Shanghai living conditions were particularly difficult such that people did not, as a rule, entertain in their homes. In terms of consultant recruiting, results indicated that Chinese women were highly entrepreneurial, placed an emphasis on learning and self-development, and were strongly attracted to a flexible financial opportunity that would enable them to supplement their state salaries. The focus group results indicated that Chinese women were interested in cosmetics and very eager to learn more about products and how best to use them. Dandurand believed that MKC could implement a successful party plan operation in China but that resources would be needed to explain and communicate the concept to both potential consultants and consumers.

Marketing Mix Options

Product line. Dandurand believed that it was essential for MKC to enter any market with both skin care and makeup products. She explained: "The two product groups both depend on consumer education. First, we teach consumers how to care for their skin and demonstrate the available treatments, then how to use glamour products to enhance their natural beauty."

Individual products in both lines would require local adaptation. Developing a product line to meet the exacting government regulations and demanding consumers of Japan would require roughly three times as much time and resources as developing a line for the Chinese market. Some MKC executives argued that the product line should be adapted as little as necessary. They believed that, with the exception of certain shades of makeup, the current product line was already global in appeal.

Positioning. Assuming MKC would be marketing both the skin care and makeup products, Dandurand had to decide whether the company should be positioned as a "glamour provider," offering makeup products and expertise combined with some skin care products, or as a "skin treatment" expert that also provided makeup products. Other decisions would include the level of emphasis to place in MKC communications on the career opportunities and consumer training aspects of the MKC organization, and what messages to use to communicate them. To help with the latter, MKC conducted recruitment research in Taiwan, Japan, and China in early 1993. The results of this study are given in **Exhibit 16.**

In Japan, Dandurand believed that competitive differentiation was key to success but was unsure what the basis of differentiation should be and which age group to target. One suggested modification of MKC's U.S. strategy was a buying club, similar to those offered by Avon, Menard, and Noevir. This would accelerate the recruitment of consultants, would be more consistent with competition, and would offer women the discounts on products and purchase convenience that they wanted. However, some MKC executives argued that this approach was inconsistent with MKC's emphasis on offering consultants a career opportunity and professional consumer training, and that it would not differentiate MKC from other direct selling companies operating in Japan.

Pricing. Even taking product development costs into account, it was estimated that unit margins obtained on products sold in Japan would be twice as high as for corresponding products sold in China. Dandurand, however, pointed out that start-up costs, office overheads, and advertising expenditures, could be somewhat lower in China and that a Chinese market entry was expected to break even within 24 months as opposed to three to five years for Japan.

Dandurand wondered how MKC products should be priced in relation to both domestic and foreign competitors, particularly Avon, to support her positioning decision, and whether to replicate the U.S. consultant compensation scheme or to adopt consultant compensation that matched competitors' programs and local economics.

Promotion. In either market, consultant recruitment programs would have to be developed, backed by print advertising, public relations, and public service workshops on women's issues. In Japan, MKC was considering establishing a toll-free number, distributing videos, organizing career opportunity seminars, and/or developing a traveling showroom to target consumers in the suburbs. Dandurand wondered what the best way to reach potential consultants and consumers in China might be.

To build the necessary level of MKC brand awareness among consumers in Japan would require at least $3 million per year in advertising. To create comparative brand awareness levels in one region of China might require $100,000 in advertising per year for the first three years.

In order to compare the economics of the two market entry options, Dandurand made the preliminary calculations summarized in **Exhibit 17.**

EXHIBIT 1

Mary Kay Cosmetics—net revenues, operating cash flow, and number of consultants, 1986–1992.

Net Revenues

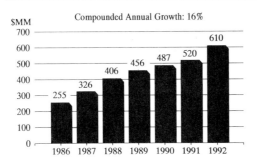

Operating Cash Flow

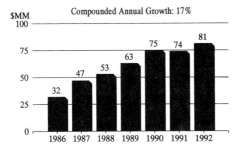

Beauty Consultants

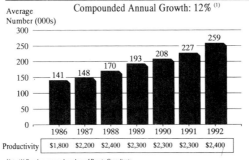

Note: (1) Based on year-end numbers of Beauty Consultants

EXHIBIT 2   The Mary Kay Cosmetics Career and Consumer Program.

THE MARY KAY CAREER

■ The Mary Kay career path allows a woman to advance into a management/training position if she so wishes. She cannot buy her way into these positions, but can earn them based on her proven ability to sell and build a team.

■ The Mary Kay career path provides the opportunity to earn higher part-time and full-time compensation more quickly than other direct sales companies and most corporations.

■ The company does not compete with its Consultants by offering products at retail locations, salons, or via "buying club" discounts.

■ The company provides advanced training and the presentation and sales tools to allow a Consultant to offer her customers value-added services and information. "She is a teacher of skin care and glamour." In addition the Consultant receives training on leadership and aspects of running a successful business.

■ The company supports a Consultant's business by offering business-building programs:
- Direct Support (consumer direct mail program) to retain and increase current customer business.
- Leads for new customers and recruits generated by company advertising, direct mail, and sampling programs.

■ A Mary Kay Consultant is in business for herself, but never by herself. She receives ongoing training (product knowledge, business and leadership skills), recognition, and motivation from the company and her Director. The Director forms a mentorlike relationship and encourages ongoing involvement and success on the part of the Consultant.

■ The unit concept of the sale force organization taps into the Japanese desire to belong to a group and compete with others based on team activities.

THE MARY KAY CONSUMER PROGRAM

■ Mary Kay Cosmetics offers women self-improvement and self-esteem enhancement through skin care and glamour education provided by a certified Beauty Consultant.

■ Consumers are taught how to care for their skin and basic glamour application skills within a unique training class that provides:
- Individualized analysis of their skin type.
- Individual vanity tray and mirror that allows the customer to apply each product as it is explained and demonstrated.
- The ability to try all products prior to purchase via hygienic, single-use samplers.
- Hands-on glamour application training.
- Fun, social interaction and entertainment aspect of a skin care class.

■ Consumers are offered advanced training including the ColorLogic Glamour System, Advanced Glamour, Skin Wellness, Nail Care, etc.

■ On-the-spot delivery of product is provided for most products.

■ Enrollment in a unique gift-with-purchase program (Direct Support)

■ 100% satisfaction guarantee or full refund.

■ Products' packaging are designed to be as environmentally friendly as possible (refillable compacts, recycled/recyclable cartons).

■ Ongoing advice and service from a trained expert.

■ Skin care products designed for particular skin types and skin conditions.

■ Unique glamour system designed to take the guess work out of selecting glamour shades.

■ Customers have the opportunity to earn valuable product discounts or unique gifts by hostessing a skin care class.

■ Value-added services and further education are provided through high-quality brochures, and newsletters given free of charge to customers.

EXHIBIT 3

Reproductions of Mary Kay Cosmetics print advertisements in the United States, 1992.

Viva la Colour

BOLD. BRILLIANT. ANYTHING BUT BASHFUL. THE MOST **DRAMATIC** NEW LOOK IN MAKEUP FOR FALL.

EYES **SMOLDER.** LIPS ARE **OUTSPOKEN.** COLOR MAKES A COMEBACK LIKE NEVER BEFORE.

Model is wearing Plush Pink and Passionate Purple Powder Perfect™ Eye Colors and Vintage Violet Liquid Eyeliner; Wild Rose Powder Perfect™ Cheek Color and Richest Raspberry Lasting Color Lipstick.

MARY KAY

FACE-TO-FACE BEAUTY ADVICE™ FROM THE EXPERTS AT MARY KAY

Quench Your Thirst.

Water. Your skin can't live without it. That's why you need Advanced Moisture Renewal® Treatment Cream. It hydrates. Replenishes. Eases the appearance of fine lines. Has microscopic spheres called liposomes that are designed to help boost the skin's moisture level. Your skin looks firmer. Younger. Alive. Advanced Moisture Renewal® Treatment Cream. For the life of your skin.

Call your Beauty Consultant today. Or to locate one in your area, call 1-800-MARY KAY (1-800-627-9529); Mon.-Fri., 7 a.m.-7 p.m., CST.

MARY KAY

EXHIBIT 4

Mary Kay Cosmetics organization, 1992.

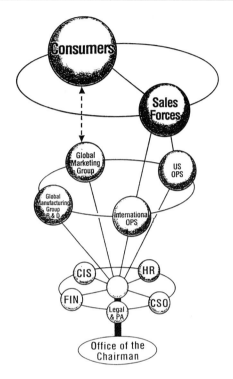

Note: CIS = Customer Information System
CSO = Chief Scientific Officer
OPS = Operations (incl. manufacturing)
FIN = Finance
HR = Human Resources

EXHIBIT 5

Mary Kay Cosmetics net sales and headcount, 1989 and 1992.

	NET SALES ($000s)		CONSULTANT COUNT		DIRECTOR COUNT	
	1989	1992	1989	1992	1989	1992
United States	$404,990	$559,719	171,073	232,692	4,689	5,837
Argentina	3,638	12,450	5,142	6,675	152	152
Australia	9,494	7,812	4,161	4,143	122	116
Canada	24,811	25,386	9,866	10,597	167	283
Germany	1,210	5,131	583	1,306	9	26
Mexico	4,598	8,586	2,640	6,241	25	89
Taiwan	0	3,133	0	1,064	0	13
Distributors	3,333	4,690				

EXHIBIT 6 1990 survey of Japanese women.

AGE GROUP	IMPORTANT JOB ATTRIBUTES	POINTS OF DISSATISFACTION AT WORK
19-24	Realize own potential and develop own capabilities.	Low bonus, too much overtime, inability to display or develop one's capabilities.
25-29	Able to continue after marriage and children, availability of nursery facilities, flexible time schedule to take care of children.	Feel job has no value.
30-39	Availability of nursery facilities, flexible time schedule, contributes to local community.	Low bonus, too many minute duties.
40-43	Job encourages and promotes women.	Inadequate social benefits.
44-49	Within close vicinity.	

Source: Adapted from a survey by *Pola Cultural Center*, 1990.
Note: Data based on a study of 1,000 Japanese women between 15 and 65 years of age.

EXHIBIT 7 Japanese cosmetics consumer buying behavior, April 1991–January 1992.

PRODUCT CATEGORY	PENETRATION: PERCENTAGE PURCHASING	MARKET SHARE (UNIT)	MARKET SHARE (VALUE)	DISTRIBUTION SHARE RETAIL	DISTRIBUTION SHARE DIRECT	AVERAGE $ SPENT PER PURCHASE	AVERAGE FREQUENCY OF PURCHASE (10 MONTHS)
Skin Care							
Cleansing	41.7	10.5	7.2	58.0	42.0	39.13	2.2
Cold and massage	19.1	3.2	3.1	43.1	56.9	36.40	1.6
Clear lotion	81.5	29.5	25.3	53.6	46.1	70.54	2.9
Milky lotion	52.9	10.9	9.9	57.4	42.6	42.29	1.7
Moisture cream	40.4	8.7	14.0	45.2	54.8	78.49	1.7
Mask	23.2	4.5	4.8	50.5	49.5	47.27	1.7
Whitening powder	2.1	0.4	0.6	73.4	26.6	64.72	NA
Essence	31.6	7.4	12.6	56.0	44.0	90.80	1.9
Foundation	78.9	24.8	22.5	66.1	33.9	64.59	2.5
Glamour							
Lipstick	68.9	38.8	47.3	65.5	34.5	33.93	1.7
Eye shadow	21.3	9.8	9.9	76.7	23.3	23.05	1.4
Eyeliner	11.6	4.9	3.9	65.3	34.7	16.58	1.7
Mascara	11..9	4.8	4.8	79.8	20.2	19.99	1.7
Eyebrow	20.6	8.7	6.3	70.7	29.3	20.00	1.5
Blusher	21.5	8.7	9.3	61.4	38.6	21.26	1.4
Manicure	25.9	16.0	6.1	75.6	24.4	11.72	1.9
Fragrance	16.8	8.3	12.4	63.2	36.8	36.38	1.8

Source: Adapted from *Cosmetics and Toiletries Marketing Strategies*, Fuji Keizai, 1991.

EXHIBIT 8   Japanese cosmetics market: growth by subcategory (billion yen).

VALUE OF FACTORY SHIPMENTS	1986	1987	1988	1989	1990	1990/89
Skin Care Products	452.5	430.0	455.2	484.4	500.8	103.4%
Face wash cream/foam	41.4	42.7	46.8	51.0	53.0	
Cleansing cream/foam/gel	27.7	28.7	32.9	35.6	37.2	
Cold cream	22.5	18.2	18.4	16.8	16.7	
Moisture cream	87.9	68.7	79.0	75.9	75.3	
Milky lotion	64.6	60.6	63.0	64.6	62.1	
Skin lotion (freshener)	134.0	142.1	142.5	159.1	178.4	
Face mask	26.1	22.3	22.3	23.2	24.3	
Men's	10.2	10.2	11.6	11.8	10.7	
Other	38.1	36.5	38.7	46.4	43.1	
Makeup Products	306.8	308.8	300.3	301.9	295.8	98.0
Foundation	154.3	157.1	160.0	161.8	158.3	
Powder	19.6	18.2	18.9	18.8	18.5	
Lipstick	44.2	49.3	48.3	46.4	48.2	
Lip cream	9.7	9.2	10.0	8.6	9.1	
Blush	15.5	14.1	11.9	11.4	11.2	
Eye shadow	26.0	27.5	22.3	22.7	19.9	
Eyebrow/eyelash	15.2	15.0	15.1	16.9	15.8	
Nail care	17.8	15.4	11.8	13.5	13.0	
Other	4.5	3.0	2.0	1.8	1.8	
Hair Care Products	335.5	362.2	392.1	403.5	413.4	102.5
Fragrances	22.1	21.1	18.7	18.8	20.9	111.1
Special Use (Suncare, shaving, bath products)	27.3	27.9	30.2	31.1	33.7	108.6
Total	1,144.0	1,146.6	1,196.2	1,239.6	1,263.9	102.0

Source: Adapted from *The Compete Handbook of Cosmetics Marketing 1992*, Shukan Shogyo.

EXHIBIT 9   Japanese cosmetic sales by distribution channel and consumer age group, 1990.

	PERCENTAGE WOMEN 1985	PERCENTAGE WOMEN 1990	CHANGE 1985-1990	1990 TEENS	1990 20s	1990 30s	1990 40s	1990 50s
Department store	22.8	25.2	2.4	37	30	19	19	24
Cosmetic store	44.6	37.5	(7.1)	26	48	33	37	43
Drug/pharmacy	12.7	22.3	9.6	25	20	29	18	18
Door-to-door	19.6	12.0	(7.6)	1	7	19	16	12
Supermarket	15.6	18.1	2.5	22	11	21	22	15
Beauty salon	3.7	6.1	2.4	3	7	4	7	9
Convenience store	NA	2.9		12	2	1	1	1
Variety shop	NA	1.7		5	2	2		
Others	NA	8.4		2	9	13	10	5

Source: Adapted from a survey by Marketing Intelligence Corp.

EXHIBIT 10

Major cosmetics companies in Japan, 1990.

COMPANY	TOTAL SALES $ MILLION	SKIN CARE	MAKEUP	HAIR CARE	FRAGRANCES	MEN'S COSMETICS
Top 5 Cosmetics Companies						
Shiseido	$1,963.3	49%	31%	3%	3%	10%
Kanebo	1,331.2	39	36	5	3	12
Pola	704.1	54	28	2	3	2
Kose	553.8	51	36	5	1	3
Kao	470.8	46	42	2	0	10
Top 5 Foreign Cosmetics Companies						
Max Factor	440.8	37	54	1	2	1
Avon	303.8	35	30	4	0	0
Revlon	92.3	25	52	10	7	0
Clinique	80.7	72	25	1	0	0
Chanel	76.1	21	21	0	58	0

Source: Adapted from *Cosmetics and Toiletries Marketing Strategies,* Fuji Keizai; 1992.

EXHIBIT 11

Customer profiles of MKC's principal potential competitors in Japan, 1992.

	MENARD	POLA	NOEVIR	AVON	AMWAY
Educational Background					
Current student	0.0	2.7	2.0	1.1	2.1
College	11.1	17.3	14.3	32.6	27.7
Senior high school	63.9	62.7	63.3	53.7	63.3
Junior high school	25.0	17.3	20.4	12.6	6.4
Marital and Employment Status					
Married—not working	27.8	32.9	22.9	44.2	39.1
Married—working	69.4	53.4	70.9	40.0	36.7
Unmarried	2.8	13.7	6.2	15.8	23.9
Age					
15-19	0.0	2.7	0.0	2.1	0.0
20-29	8.3	18.7	14.3	15.8	38.3
30-39	11.1	17.3	30.6	28.4	17.0
40-49	41.7	25.3	30.6	32.6	25.5
50-59	38.9	36.0	24.5	21.1	19.1
Occupation					
Not employed	27.8	32.0	22.4	43.2	38.3
Employed	72.2	65.3	75.5	55.8	59.6

Source: Company reports.

EXHIBIT 12
Competitor print advertisements, Japan 1993.

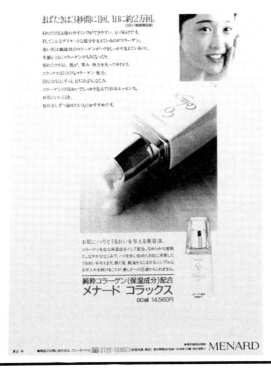

EXHIBIT 13
Map of eastern China.

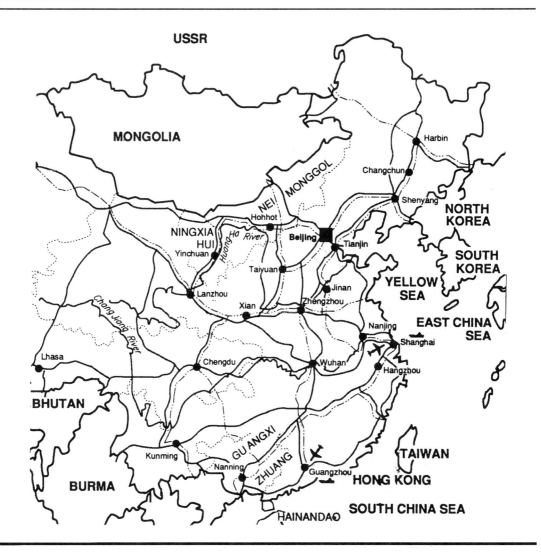

EXHIBIT 14
Partial listing of skin care cosmetics products sold in China, 1992.

BRAND/PRODUCT	MANUFACTURER
Avon Rich Moisture Face Cream	Avon (joint venture)
Avon Skinplicity	Avon (joint venture)
Ballet Pearl Beautifying Cream	Cosmetic Factory of Nanjing China
Ballet Pearl Cream	China Light Industrial Products Import and Export
Ballet Silk Peptide UV Defense Cream	Nanjing Golden Ballet Cosmetic Co. Ltd.
Bong Bao Maifanite Face-Beautifying Honey	Dongyang Mun Cosmetics Works, Zhejiang Provence
Bong Bao Maifanite Pearl Cream	Dongyang Mun Cosmetics Works, Zhejiang Provence
Dabao Instant Anti-Wrinkle Cream	Beijing Sanlu Factory
Lan Normolee Moisturizing Cream	International Gottin Cosmetics
Lorensa U.S.A. Retin-A Nourish Cream	Lorensa Cosmetics U.S.A.
Lychee Brand Pianzihuang Pearl Cream	Made in chemical factory for domestic use, Zhangzhou, Fujian, China Supervised by Pharmacy Industry Corporation, Fujian, China
Maxam Cleansing Lotion	Maxam Cosmetics (joint venture with S.C. Johnson)
Maxam	Maxam Cosmetics (joint venture with S.C. Johnson)
Meidi Beautiful Youth Nourish Cream	Grand Blom Co. Ltd., Hong Kong
Monica Beauty Skin Cleanser	Formulated in France
Montana Anti-Wrinkle Cream	Concord Group U.S.A. (joint venture)
Montana Bleaching Cream	Concord Group U.S.A. (joint venture)
Qinxiang Day Cream	Guangzhou Cosmetic Factory
Rhoure Ulan Cream	Guangzhou First Lab Cosmetics Industry Thailand First Lab Chemical Products Co. Ltd.
Ruby Nourishing Cream	S.C. Johnson (joint venture)
Smiss Natural Silk Cream	Wuxi Novel Daily Chemical Co. Ltd.
Ximi	—
Yue-Sai Protective Moisturizer	—
Ying Fong	Nan Yuan Ying Fong Group Co.

Source: Company research.

EXHIBIT 15   Indexed retail prices of domestic and imported cosmetics in China by product category, 1992.

PRODUCT	DOMESTIC PRODUCTS			IMPORTED PRODUCTS		
	SHANGHAI	GUANGZHOU	BEIJING	SHANGHAI	GUANGZHOU	BEIJING
Moisturizer	100	45	121	703	341	418
Cleanser	163	57	70	459	354	366
Toner	43	72	NA	340	368	NA
Mask	NA	104	NA	NA	400	NA
Day cream	48	55	76	345	351	373
Night cream	57	100	88	354	397	385
Pearl cream	45	84	NA	341	381	NA
Nourishing cream	55	58	83	352	354	380
Hand/body lotion/cream	37	43	68	333	340	364
Eye cream	NA	69	88	NA	366	385
Anti-aging cream	18	23	53	315	320	350
Whitening lotion	39	22	80	335	318	377
Lipstick	85	59	41	381	356	337
Cheek color	NA	72	NA	NA	368	NA
Foundation	71	128	NA	367	425	NA
Nail polish	40	72	32	337	368	328
Perfume	117	98	NA	413	394	NA

Source: Company reports.

EXHIBIT 16 Recruitment study in Taiwan, Japan, and China, 1993.

	TAIWAN	JAPAN	CHINA
Ideal Life Aspirations	Would like to work as long as they can take care of family. Personal fulfillment and increased knowledge are important.	Key aspiration is to get married and be a good mother/wife. Lead fulfilling and satisfying personal lives and enjoy themselves.	Most women have government-sponsored jobs. Would like to reduce the number of nonproductive hours of work, expand their knowledge and feel more productive.
Jobs and Careers	Career: perceived as involving risk, long-term commitment and higher financial rewards. Job: no risk, short-term way to make money. To work is to gain self-confidence.	Career: image of independence not positive. Do not feel that it is possible to combine career and family. Job: Should be enjoyable and flexible, a hobby to pass time. Interest was not in earning an income.	Career: Sounded far fetched, an alien concept. Job: Only vehicle to earn money. Earning money perceived as a way to become independent, gain social acceptance and self-esteem.
Role Model Images	Self-confident, independent but not tough. Good relationship with family. Nice environment and surroundings.	Good mother figure. Happy family. Children playing. Husband and wife.	Pretty, youthful, well dressed. Romantic and relaxing life. Nice environment and surroundings. Career women type only prominent among younger, white-collar workers.

Source: Based on in-depth focus groups.

EXHIBIT 17

Preliminary estimates of the economics of market entry: Japan and China.

	JAPAN	CHINA
Average retail unit price US$	$25.00	$9.00
Average MKC wholesale unit price	$12.50	$4.50
Cost of goods	$ 2.30	$1.20
Freight and duty	$ 0.75	$1.28
Gross margin	$ 9.45	$2.02
Product development costs/year	$ 0.9 million	$0.1 million
Start-up investment costs	$10.0 million	$2.0 million
Promotion and advertising costs/year	$ 3.0 million	$0.1 million

HEINEKEN NV: BUCKLER NONALCOHOLIC BEER

As he spoke, Jerome de Vries, in charge of marketing at Heineken Netherlands, looked first at Hans Brinker, the European corporate marketing manager, and then at the rest of the team sitting around the room. "Since this time last year, Bavaria Malt has grabbed 30% of our market share. Its prices are one-third of ours, but, on top of that, 60% of the customers say that they prefer the taste of Bavaria Malt. So, we either have to change our taste or drop our price."

It was July 1990, and the European brand team was holding its first meeting at Heineken's corporate headquarters in Amsterdam. The function of the group, consisting of two members from Corporate Marketing, one from Export, and six from the operating companies, was to coordinate European activities for Buckler nonalcoholic beer.

Brinker hesitated a moment before answering de Vries. "It would be easy, Jerome, to react on a local level and pull down prices if we're only after market share. But that would lead to other problems. There are bigger things at stake."

For the first time, Heineken had developed and launched a Pan-European product from its very beginning, one that was centrally managed and highly standardized. This was part of a larger corporate goal initiated by Mr. Gerard van Schaik, CEO of Heineken, "to make Heineken a truly European company which happens to have a head office in the Netherlands, rather than a Dutch company which does business in Europe."

Buckler was first introduced into Spain and France in 1988 and then was extended to other European countries. The brand had been highly successful for Heineken. By 1990, only two years after its launch, Buckler had attained a 15% share of the European nonalcoholic beer market even without entering the two largest markets, the United Kingdom and Germany.

"We had a similar problem in France, Jerome, just after we launched Buckler," said Claude Pelletier, responsible for marketing in France. "BSN reacted by offering a one-litre bottle, cutting prices, and repositioning Tourtel. This slowed us down, I can tell you. We didn't even make budget in the first year. But we stuck it out, and now we have over 15% of the segment. I would say we've got a good product here."

De Vries replied, "Well, I can tell you that if we don't do something quickly, we won't be in the Dutch market much longer. We can't just sit back and enjoy a technological advantage the way we used to. Our competitors are too quick to respond. We've got to move fast to hold our share."

Case, "Heineken NV: Buckler Non-Alcoholic Beer M-377" prepared by Research Associate James Henderson under the direction of Professor Sandra Vandermerwe. Copyright © 1991 the International Institute for Management Development (IMD), Lausanne, Switzerland. IMD retains all rights. Not to be reproduced or used without written permission directly from IMD, Lausanne, Switzerland.

"I understand you position, Jerome, but I think you are overemphasizing local market share. The nonalcoholic beer segment is growing as a whole in Europe. Last year alone it jumped by 55%. So, I say that if we stick to our strategy, we should get a 25% growth per year."

"It is all very well for you to say, 'Stick to a European strategy," said Emilio Fernandez, marketing manager in Spain. "But we have to deliver bottom-line results. I am worried, too. At first I thought we would be OK, but in the last few months, three brands have come into Spain, including Tourtel. I also expect a local brand, Laiker Sin, to be launched any day, and it could very well be priced much lower than our brand!"

BACKGROUND: HEINEKEN NV

G. A. Heineken founded Heineken NV in 1864 by purchasing de Hooiberg (the Haystack), a brewer which had been operating in the centre of Amsterdam since 1592. By 1990, Heineken, still in the hands of the Heineken family, had become one of the world's largest international beverages group, producing and distributing leading brands of beer, soft drinks, spirits, and wine. In addition to Heineken, its world-famous brand, there were other well-known names: Amstel, Sourcy, Royal Club, and more recently, Buckler. The company also carried a variety of national and regional brands in several markets.

Heineken, like other international brewing companies, followed several distribution strategies for its global brands: exporting, brewing under license, and, finally, either wholly acquiring or taking a minority position in other breweries.

Exporting. This strategy had the initial advantage of providing the breweries with another market. The product, as an import, could also be marketed as a premium brand. However, with an export strategy, the brewery's transportation costs were increased, and without a substantial distribution network, its market share was limited.

Licensing. Another common strategy was for a brewery to license its recipe to another brewery. In this way, a company could obtain a steady stream of profits and an increased market share through the licensee's distribution network. However, breweries complained about the lack of control over marketing the brand.

Acquisition. With this strategy, beer companies would either take a minority position or would wholly acquire other breweries. The brewers then had the choice of exporting the global brand with the distribution being handled by the operating company or having the product produced locally by the operating company. However, when acquisitions in other countries were made, the brewery added numerous local brands from that company to its portfolio. In addition, the acquired company needed to have a sufficiently wide network to ensure successful distribution of the global brand. In the 1960s and 1970s, several UK beer companies acquired German and Belgian breweries. The strategy failed because these two markets were too fragmented.

The following table shows Heineken's distribution strategy for each European country:

DISTRIBUTION STRATEGIES IN EUROPE

EXPORTING	LICENSING	ACQUISITION (OPERATING COMPANIES)
Belguim	United Kingdom	Spain (El Aguila)
Portugal	Norway	France (Sogebra)
Switzerland	Sweden	Italy (Birra Dreher)
Germany	Finland	Greece (Athenian Brewery)
Austria		Ireland (Murphy Brewery)
Denmark		Netherlands (Heineken Neth.)

With this setup, the company's European strategy was to have a portfolio of international brands such as Heineken and Amstel, along with local brands produced by the operating company, among the leaders in each market segment. For example, Heineken's operating company in France, Sogebra SA, produced a local brand, "33" Export, for the mainstream lager market and imported the Heineken brand for the premium import lager market. The company was most successful with its global brands in the countries where there was an operating company and was less successful in countries where it exported.

The Heineken Organization

The Heineken organization was managed by a five-person executive board which included the president, van Schaik, and the four regional coordinating directors (Europe, Asia/Australia, Africa, and Western Hemisphere). At Heineken Corporate, the organization was divided into six main areas: Marketing and Licensees, Technical Affairs, Social Affairs, Exports, Finance, and finally Regional Coordination. These four regional coordinating directors were given strategy and coordinating responsibilities for the operating companies in their respective regions. (For an organization chart of Heineken NV, refer to Exhibit 1.)

The issue of centralisation versus decentralisation often arose in the company. The executive board realized that the complexity and diversity of the operating companies made central control difficult. As well, they felt that local breweries that were left as autonomous business units rather than incorporated into an overall Heineken structure would be better positioned to exploit domestic market situations. Heineken Corporate, then, had a service and coordinating function: assisting the operating companies with managing operations, technical problems, marketing services, and logistics.

However, certain areas were centralised, for example, policies on finance, technology, and, to a lesser extent, marketing. The amount of centralisation in the marketing function had increased over time. Corporate Marketing, in trying to maintain a consistent international image for the corporate brands, developed stricter marketing guidelines, which reduced the opportunities for local creativity. Operating companies were therefore left to market their own domestic brands and to operate on a day-to-day basis.

EXHIBIT 1A

Organization chart, Heineken corporate.

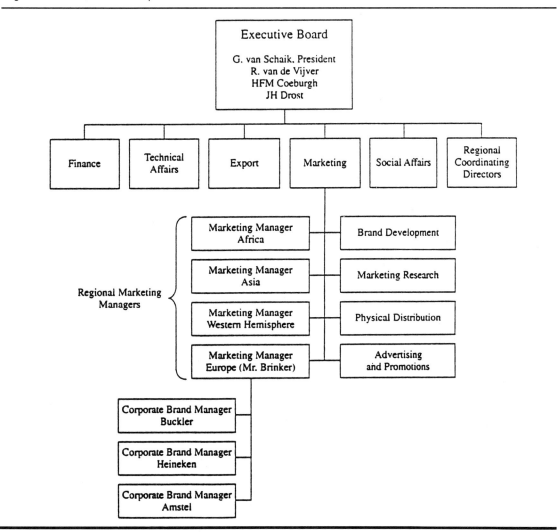

EXHIBIT 1B

Organization chart, regional coordination.

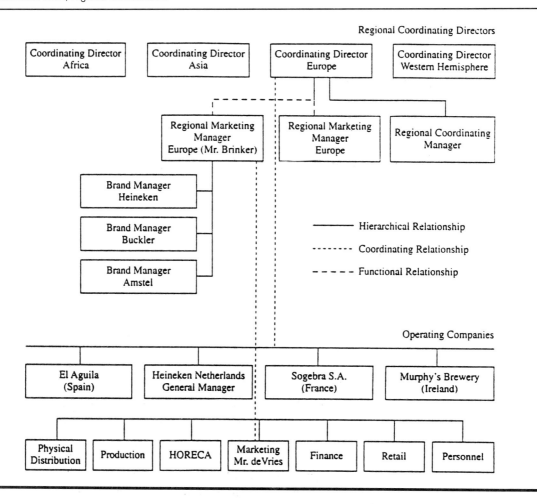

Regional Coordinating Directors

| Coordinating Director Africa | Coordinating Director Asia | Coordinating Director Europe | Coordinating Director Western Hemisphere |

Regional Marketing Manager Europe (Mr. Brinker)

Regional Marketing Manager Europe

Regional Coordinating Manager

Brand Manager Heineken

Brand Manager Buckler

Brand Manager Amstel

——————— Hierarchical Relationship

- - - - - - - Coordinating Relationship

– – – – – Functional Relationship

Operating Companies

| El Aguila (Spain) | Heineken Netherlands General Manager | Sogebra S.A. (France) | Murphy's Brewery (Ireland) |

| Physical Distribution | Production | HORECA | Marketing Mr. deVries | Finance | Retail | Personnel |

Corporate Marketing

Hans Brinker, as the regional marketing manager for Europe, was well aware of the tensions between centralisation and decentralisation. For the corporate brands (Heineken, Amstel, and, more recently, Buckler), Brinker was instrumental in trying to find ways to standardise marketing strategy without dampening local marketing initiatives.

One such example occurred in 1990, when Corporate Marketing appointed one Pan-European advertising agency for the Heineken brand. Historically, each operating company had had its own local agency. Therefore, each communications strategy was developed through discussions with the operating company and Corporate Marketing. With the new arrangement, Brinker set up a European brand team for Heineken consisting of two members from Corporate Marketing, six marketing managers from the operating companies, and an export manager to develop the Pan-European communications strategy. In this way, he could include local ideas and opinions.

THE NONALCOHOLIC BEER INDUSTRY, 1986–1990

The Product

Nonalcoholic beer was part of the $45 billion European beer industry, which in turn fell into the $134 billion European drinks industry. While the beer industry was stagnating and sometimes even declining during the 1980s, nonalcoholic beer was enjoying a moderate to fast growth in sales. (For details on sales volumes of nonalcoholic beer, refer to Exhibit 2.)

The first introductions of nonalcoholic beer took place in Switzerland and Germany after World War II. The production process at that time, called *vacuum distillation,* removed the alcohol after fermentation. Since then, other production methods had been developed, including a special fermentation process where alcohol was not produced.

Nonalcoholic beer usually contained some alcohol; the amount depended on a country's legal limit for alcohol in nonalcoholic drinks. In Germany, for example, nonalcoholic beers could contain up to the legal limit of 0.5% alcohol, whereas in France the limit was 1%. It was often referred to as alcohol-free or low-alcohol, which were simply more specific descriptions. Alcohol-free beer contained traces of alcohol, whereas low-alcohol contained a little less than the legal limit.

EXHIBIT 2

Sales volumes of nonalcoholic beer by region (in hectolitres).

COUNTRIES	1985	1987	1988	1989
Saudi Arabia	400,000	300,000	250,000	225,000
West Germany	400,000	750,000	1,100,000	1,500,000
France	200,000	330,000	450,000	600,000
Spain	180,000	250,000	350,000	600,000
Netherlands	15,000	25,000	50,000	250,000
Belgium	10,000	20,000	50,000	165,000
United Kingdom	150,000	400,000	600,000	800,000
Switzerland	80,000	80,000	85,000	85,000
United States	625,000	750,000	795,000	850,000
World	3,000,000	4,000,000	4,800,000	6,000,000

Source: Heineken estimates.

The Market

The drinkers of nonalcoholic beer were those who liked the taste of beer but were avoiding alcohol for some reason. Most often, the reason was medical (i.e., pregnancy, diabetes, etc.), and some consumers were also concerned about drinking and driving or felt guilty about drinking too much alcohol.

However, the taste of nonalcoholic beers put regular beer drinkers off. Research findings showed that the product had a watered-down negative image among traditional beer drinkers. As one Heineken executive explained, "A person would describe it as a perfect drink for the neighbour who drinks too much beer. And, in return, the neighbour would say that it's the perfect drink for *his* neighbour because he does not know anything about beer!"

During the 1980s, two market trends created more demand for the product: increasing health consciousness and social pressure regarding alcohol abuse. From the statistics, regular beer companies could see the decline in their share of the total drinks market as more "healthy" beverages including nonalcoholic beer were consumed. In Europe, governments were becoming increasingly tougher in their laws against drinking and driving. Fines and police monitoring had increased substantially. For example, in the United Kingdom, fines ranged from $500 to $4,000 with drivers' licenses often being taken away. As a result, police checks, breathalizer tests, and criminal charges all caused the public to shun drinking and driving. Moreover, it had become socially unacceptable to be drunk in a public situation. Therefore, moderate drinking and diluting drinks (for example, beer with lemon-lime) took place more often. Much of the slack in alcohol consumption was replaced by mineral water, soft drinks, and fruit juices.

These trends also affected the proportion of the market who drank nonalcoholic beer because of feeling guilty about consuming too much alcohol. These people consciously gave up some taste in order to not have alcohol in their beer.

THE INTRODUCTION OF BUCKLER BEER

Nonalcoholic beer was nothing new at Heineken. As early as the 1930s, there had been discussions about introducing a product in the United States during the prohibition period. By the 1980s, the company already had two nonalcoholic products, Amstel Brew and Aguila Sin, in the Saudi Arabian and Spanish markets. However, both suffered from poor taste, as did many nonalcoholic beer brands at the time. Therefore, neither one was ever considered for an international rollout.

Top management felt that the nonalcoholic beer market was too small to warrant a full-scale product development effort to make the taste right. Corporate Marketing, however, continually monitored the activities in some of the larger nonalcoholic beer markets, such as Switzerland and the United States, in order to be up-to-date on any new developments. The executive board did not become really interested until 1986, when Guinness introduced Kaliber alcohol-free beer.

Heineken quickly provided financial support for a full-fledged product development and commercialization program. In February 1987, the company formed a working team consisting of the brand development manager from Corporate Marketing, a technical manager from HTB (Heineken Technical Beheer, the research and development arm), and the production and marketing managers from Heineken Netherlands, the Dutch operating company. The objective was to develop, by December of that year, a better tasting non-alcoholic beer than the existing competing brands and to introduce it first in Europe and, later, throughout the world. The time period for development gave the working team a formidable challenge, as such a project usually took around two years to complete.

In April 1987, during a meeting of the general managers of the European operating companies, the general manager of Spain announced, coincidentally, that his organization was going to develop an upgraded version of its nonalcoholic beer, Aguila Sin. The brand's market share had continued to decline at the expense of the only other brand in the country, Cruz Campo Sin. When Heineken's president learned that Spain was interested in a better tasting non-alcoholic beer, he jumped at the opportunity. Because Spain needed a replacement brand urgently and because that country's operating company already had marketing experience with nonalcoholic beer, the president suggested that it be given a "lead country" role, that is, be the "locomotive" for getting the process going. One week later, the marketing manager for Spain joined the working group.

DEVELOPING A MARKETING STRATEGY

The team was excited by the opportunity to launch the brand in several countries. They instinctively believed that nonalcoholic beer drinkers tended to be the same everywhere. They were people who liked the taste of beer but could not or did not want to have alcohol. The consensus was that a standard marketing strategy for the brand could be used with only minor local changes. (Refer to Exhibit 3 for the expected level of standardization in the marketing mix elements for Buckler.)

Product Development

The working group felt that developing a nonalcoholic lager would be most appropriate, as its taste in regular beer was most widely accepted in Europe. They agreed to an alcohol content of around 0.5%, which was the average amount in nonalcoholic beers on the market. During the five months of development, a friendly rivalry grew between the technical manager from HTB and the production manager from Heineken Netherlands as to who could produce the best-

EXHIBIT 3

Level of standardization for Buckler's marketing mix elements.

MARKETING MIX ELEMENTS	LEVEL OF STANDARDIZATION*
Brand name	5
Product name	4
Product	5/4
Design	5
Positioning	5
Packaging	4
Pricing	4
Advertising	5/4
Sponsoring	5/4
Sales promotions	3/2
Public relations	3/2
Customer service	2
Expiry date	5/4

*5 = Highly standardized, 1 = Highly localized.

tasting nonalcoholic beer. The Spanish organization also got involved. Both processes—fermentation without alcohol or removing alcohol after fermentation—were explored. In the end, a special fermentation process was developed and kept a tight-lipped secret.

The group soon realized that the more alcohol the product had, the better it tasted. They had always assumed that nonalcoholic beer drinkers would want the taste to be as close to traditional lager as possible. This product was therefore slightly altered (0.9% alcohol) for the Spanish and French markets, where the legal limit was 1%. For the rest of Europe, the alcohol content was kept at the accepted 0.5%.

Positioning

Previous research findings showed that two positioning strategies were possible for Buckler: to be either a nonalcoholic adult drink or a beer with no alcohol. In both cases the object was to increase the consumption of nonalcoholic beer, only the approach was different. The first implied being a substitute for all soft drinks, and the second offered an alternative beer to beer drinkers.

The group debated the pros and cons of each strategy. As a nonbeer drink, the potential market was enormous. But, the competition for soft drink substitutes was vast; there were colas, mineral water, fruit juices, coffee, and each had its own positioning and marketing strategy. They agreed that using that strategy was too risky.

The group therefore decided to follow the second option. From the market research that had previously been performed in Switzerland, they knew that the majority of the existing nonalcoholic beers were positioned as beer products rather than as nonbeer products.

They also decided to pursue their idea to develop a beer as close to the typical lager beer as possible. They did not want to move too far from a regular beer

EXHIBIT 4

Positioning chart of nonalcoholic beer with other drinks.

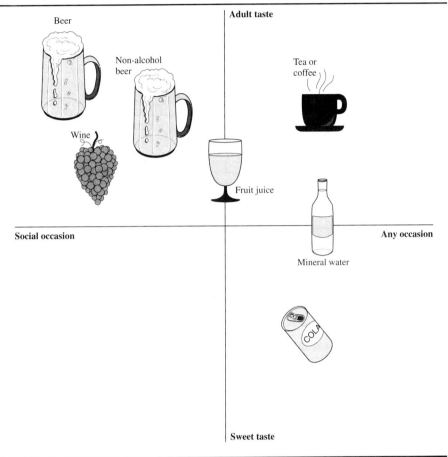

taste or image because they wanted the consumers to feel they were getting the "real thing" without alcohol rather than something inferior. (Refer to Exhibits 4 and 5 for positioning maps used by the company for competitive brands and substitute products.)

Target Group

The aim was to reach the upper- and middle-income class groups because, the group felt, they would be the first to reduce their alcohol intake. Regular Heineken beer drinkers were between 20 and 35 years of age. Buckler, the group decided, would be directed at consumers 25 to 40 years old, the age category where people were more apt to be concerned about alcohol consumption.

EXHIBIT 5

Positioning chart of Buckler and competing beer products.

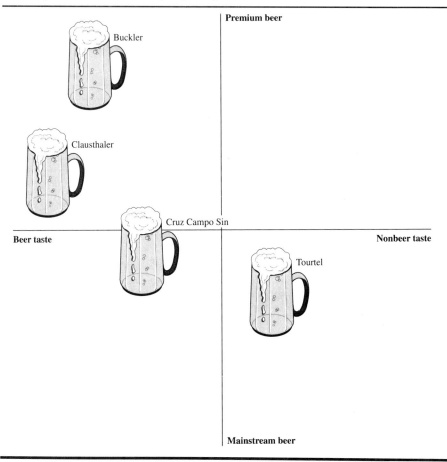

At the beginning, the team did not really know whether they should target the heavy or light drinker. Some believed that heavy drinkers had a greater need. But others disagreed and said lighter users were more rational about alcohol intake. The debate was left unresolved. The final marketing strategy, though, did take heavy users into account.

Pricing

The group decided to introduce Buckler at a premium price even though it cost less to produce due to savings in excise duties. They believed that the product would then have more credibility, and they wanted it to be seen as a premium image brand, especially after the poor quality of nonalcoholic beers in the past.

They also wanted to reinforce the taste quality and make consumers feel as if they were gaining something—taste with no alcohol—instead of making a sacrifice when buying the product.

Branding

A debate also centered around whether the product should be a line extension of an existing brand or have a totally new name. Although the company had extended both the Heineken and Amstel brands (Amstel Gold, Amstel Light, Heineken Old Bruin, etc.), all these extensions contained alcohol. Some argued that nonalcoholic beer had a negative connotation; therefore, by extending an existing brand name, the company would not only jeopardize the success of the standard brand but also confuse the consumer. Others, however, pointed out that some line extensions had performed quite well in their local markets. Swan Special Light, an extension of Swan Export, a mainline lager, took a market

EXHIBIT 6
Examples of the Buckler labels.

share of approximately 40% in the Australian market. Cruz Campo Sin, an extension of Cruz Campo, also enjoyed a 40% market share in the Spanish nonalcoholic beer market.

Having decided to use a new name, the group briefed an international agency, Interbrands, to develop something "beer sounding." After several months of consumer preference tests, as well as language and legal checks on 25 proposed names, the agency came up with two: Buckler and Norlander. Two design agencies were asked to develop different beer labels, some contemporary and some more traditional. (As the illustration in Exhibit 6 shows, the group decided on a more traditional label.)

Market Research

After developing the product, settling on a positioning strategy, and choosing a traditional label, the two names—Norlander and Buckler—were finally tested. Both qualitative and quantitative tests were done in four countries: the Netherlands, Spain, the United States, and France. The qualitative surveys consisted of focus group discussions on the attributes of nonalcoholic beer. The quantitative research asked participants to compare the taste and image of Buckler and Norlander with competing products: in Spain against Cruz Campo Sin, the market leader; in France against Tourtel, also the market leader; in the United States, against an important import called Kaliber; and in the Netherlands against Clausthaler, the imported market leader.

Results of the qualitative test confirmed that nonalcoholic beer was perceived as not tasting very good. However, the participants were pleasantly surprised during the taste tests. In general, both Buckler and Norlander performed better than the competition. Consumer preference did not differ significantly between the two names, so they arbitrarily decided to choose the name *Buckler.*

THE PRODUCT LAUNCH

The brand development manager, from Corporate Marketing, sent a memo to each operating company in early November informing them of the proposed marketing plan for Buckler beer. The paper included reasons why the group had made the various decisions on the different elements of the marketing mix: product, packaging, price, target group, positioning, and communications strategy. (Refer to Exhibit 7 for highlights of the marketing plan.)

The executive board decided to proceed with a product launch in late December 1987. Corporate Marketing was somewhat surprised when the operating companies showed a mixed reaction to the plan. Ideally, they wanted to introduce the product throughout all the operating companies in Europe. However, the divisions in France and Spain were the only ones interested in introducing the product immediately. The Netherlands division stalled because it was introducing a similar product, Amstel Light, on the Dutch market and did

EXHIBIT 7
Highlights of the marketing plan on nonalcoholic beer.

MEMORANDUM

To: Marketing Managers
From: Peter Meijer, Corporate Brand Development
Date: Nov. 11, 1987
Subject: Introduction of Buckler

The objective is to participate in the growing beer market with the recently developed Buckler product as an international brand and to gain a leading role. The priority is to introduce the product in all European countries where we have Operating Companies: introduction is planned April/June, 1988. Furthermore, our aim is to have the product available for export elsewhere and/or license it to other countries.

Product:
The product is a lager type beer with the following characteristics:
Original Gravity: + 5 P°
Alcohol Content: 0.4 vol %-0.9 vol %
Bitterness: 21 EBE
Colour: 7 EBC

The product may vary in alcohol content; this depends on the local situation given by the law. When a higher alcohol content is possible, this is preferred (better taste). The differences in taste, due to the different alcohol content, are small and therefore acceptable. The .5% alcohol beer will be brewed in the Netherlands whereas the .9% alcohol beer will be produced in Spain. The Spanish version will be exported to France and the Dutch version will be exported to all other European countries, first with Operating Companies and then ones without.

Product Benefits:
A nonalcoholic beer (alcohol percentage the same or lower than other nonalcoholic drinks like fruit juices)

- a tasteful (nonsweet) refresher/thirstquencher
- an adult drink
- a healthy drink (natural ingredients)
- low in calories (50% less than regular beers)
- an acceptable alternative for beer
- a better lager beer taste than the competition.

Target Group
The following segmentation has to be made:

1. Nonalcoholic beer as an occasional drink (at lunch/after sport/before driving)
   - medium/heavy beer drinkers
   - male
   - 25–45 years
2. Nonalcoholic beer as a tasteful thirstquencher (in competition with mineral water/soft drinks)
   - light/medium beer drinkers
   - male and female
   - 20–45 years

Positioning
In theory, two concepts are possible: a beer without alcohol concept or a nonalcohol refresher with an adult taste concept. For the time being the beer concept seems to be the most realistic; motivations and drinkers are more or less coming from regular beer. Beer is the reference. However, it is necessary to develop an own identity for the nonalcoholic beer and to avoid a too strong beer-minus approach.

In general, people are very skeptical about the taste of nonalcoholic beer (watery/flat); after tasting, the product appears to be better than expected. The taste of Buckler is better (more lager taste) than the competition. Although nonalcoholic beers try to be similar to regular beers, they won't be the same due to the lack of alcohol. Nonalcohol beers have to be valued in their own nonalcoholic context against other nonalcoholic drinks, not against regular beers.

EXHIBIT 7 (continued)

Brand Name

Since nonalcoholic beer could be considered as beer-unfriendly, it has been decided to develop a new brand name, instead of a line-extension of Heineken/Amstel. But, above all, a new brand name is desired to establish the proper identity which is felt to be important for this new segment.

The criteria for the development of the brand name were: a good lager beer taste (not watery), social, refreshing, healthy, safe, high, quality, international, masculine, not to be ashamed of. To give it authority, it is possible to use Heineken sourcing (a Heineken product).

Packaging/Label

The packaging is a beer bottle (brown/returnable or one way). The label is, in principle, a beer label; however, the colours (blue/yellow and white/silver) give it a character of its own (nonalcoholic). No draught beer will be provided.

Pricing Strategy

The pricing will be a 20% premium above regular beer or more, the latter if exported. When the product is imported it will be higher due to the higher costs of transport. The pricing throughout Europe will be within a range to avoid parallel imports.

Communications Strategy

The communications strategy will be to position the product as a premium brand with a good quality beer taste. An international communication concept is striven for (with possible local adaptation); the reason behind this international concept is that the background for the development of nonalcoholic beer in different countries is felt to be more or less the same for each country.

---

not want to confuse the consumer. In addition, the management did not strongly support the product because the Netherlands had only a small nonalcoholic beer market at that time. In Ireland, the organization was introducing Amstel and felt there were not enough resources to introduce two brands at the same time. The Italian operating company felt there was no market in Italy and so was resistant. In Greece, the company did not feel that the association between healthy living and less alcohol consumption had caught on yet, so they also rejected the brand.

DEVELOPING A COMMUNICATIONS STRATEGY

Corporate Marketing was therefore left with only Spain and France where they could introduce the brand and develop a communications strategy. Despite the fact that France was the only country really interested in having an advertising campaign, Corporate Marketing still wanted to pursue a Pan-European communications strategy, with a consistent message to all Europeans.

The First Campaign

FHV, a Dutch agency used by Heineken Corporate, was briefed on the product. The agency proposed the slogan "Sometimes you drink beer, sometimes you drink Buckler." This concept was shown to the marketing managers of the operating companies in a meeting in Amsterdam. It was not received warmly by anyone, especially the managers from France and Spain. Spain did not like the message because it seemed to focus too much on developing the nonalcoholic beer category and not enough on the brand; the Spanish nonalcoholic beer market was already well established. The meeting ended with no decision being made. The Spanish and French divisions were left to create their own advertising.

These two operating companies discussed their respective proposals for advertising copy before deciding on the French one. In Spain, some changes were made. For example, in a television advertisement using a hang glider, in the French advertisement nothing was written on the sail, whereas the Spanish ad had the word *Buckler* on the sail.

The Second Campaign

The executive board got involved in the fall of 1988. They concluded that the brand required a consistent communications strategy for the whole of Europe. This time, however, the general manager of the Spanish operating company was appointed to develop the Pan-European communications strategy for Buckler beer. With the aid of a selection agency, the general manager and members of Corporate Marketing chose the international advertising agency Lintas, because of the concept they proposed: "So much taste you won't miss the alcohol." (Refer to Exhibit 8 for an illustration of the concept.)

EXHIBIT 8
Example of second advertising concept.

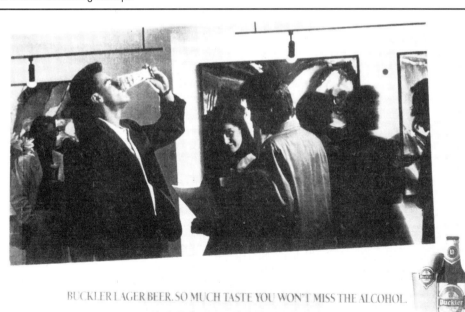

BUCKLER LAGER BEER. SO MUCH TASTE YOU WON'T MISS THE ALCOHOL.

The general manager, along with Corporate Marketing, decided to take a more objective stand with the operating companies. First, they were shown the briefing to the advertising agencies, which they accepted. Then, before discussing the actual campaign with the operating companies, Corporate Market Research tested it in the various countries to determine the response. If positive, the operating companies would have to accept it. If negative, they could run their own campaign. Managers at the French operating company objected because they did not want to give up their original hang glider campaign. Therefore, Corporate Market Research tested both campaigns to show that the second one, a story of a journalist's day on the run, was more successful. In the other countries, Spain, Ireland, and the Netherlands, the tests also proved successful.

One year later, the second campaign with the journalist advertisement was still being used by each operating company, including Spain, France, the Netherlands, Ireland, and then, in 1990, by Italy and Greece (the last two operating companies to take on the product).

BRAND DEVELOPMENTS IN THREE COUNTRIES

The Netherlands

The competitive situation in the Netherlands was quiet before the introduction of Buckler in the fall of 1988. Clausthaler, an imported German brand, virtually owned the market, which was only approximately 20,000 hectolitres.

Because of this small market, the Dutch operating company did not have much faith in the Buckler brand. The management was more interested in Amstel Light, a low-calorie product introduced several months earlier. Therefore, in 1989 the operating company budgeted for only 15,000 hectolitres, with no advertising support. However, in that year, the brand achieved a 60% market share, or 100,000 hectolitres, virtually destroying Clausthaler. When they saw the sales increase so impressively, management at Heineken Netherlands quickly allocated G 13 million[1] for the European advertising campaign.

In the beginning of 1989, the Buckler brand began to notice some competitive activity. At that time, a local brewery called Bavaria started selling Bavaria Malt (originally exported to the Middle East markets) in the Netherlands at discounted prices. Grolsch and Allied, other local breweries, then entered with "me too" products, Stender and Classe Royale, respectively. The Bavaria Malt brand consistently won in blind taste tests. Test participants considered it "milder, less

---

[1] G = Dutch guilders

EXHIBIT 9   Nielsen report on the Dutch nonalcoholic beer segment, 1989, 1990.

	APR./MAY	JUNE/JULY	AUG./SEPT.	OCT./NOV.	DEC./JAN.	FEB./MAR.	APR./MAY
Market Shares Retail							
Buckler (Heineken)	66.3	62.9	62.7	62.2	46.2	33.2	28.0
Clausthaler (Binding)	10.8	9.6	6.0	4.8	3.4	2.2	2.2
Bavaria Malt (Bavaria)	19.8	25.3	28.9	30.4	34.5	43.3	45.8
Birell (Huerlimann)	2.2	1.4	1.0	1.0	0.5	0.4	0.3
Strender (Grolsch)	0.0	0.0	0.0	0.0	14.3	20.1	23.1
Percentage of total							
beer market	2.4	3.8	3.0	4.1	5.2	6.4	7.0
Weighted Distribution°							
Buckler	98%	95%	98%	98%	98%	98%	98%
Clausthaler	94	91	90	88	92	86	89
Bavaria Malt	27	29	44	49	54	71	85
Birell	18	19	17	17	15	13	13
Stender	0	0	0	0	27	76	87
Price per Litre							
(in Guilders)							
Buckler	2.95	2.97	2.99	2.96	2.98	3.00	3.02
Clausthaler	5.38	5.36	5.42	5.38	5.13	5.02	4.71
Bavaria Malt	2.00	1.90	1.94	1.93	1.94	1.95	2.00
Birell	3.24	3.51	3.46	3.51	3.44	3.68	3.63
Stender	n.a.[†]	n.a.	n.a.	n.a.	2.83	2.78	2.79

°Weighted distribution: 20% of the stores carrying the product sell x% of the total product sales.
[†]n.a. - not available.
Source: Nielsen Food Index, the Netherlands.

bitter than the lager taste of Buckler, and easier to drink than regular lagers." In addition, Bavaria Malt was priced 30% lower than the Buckler brand. By the middle of 1990, Bavaria Malt had stolen 40% market share, and Buckler was down to 30%. (Refer to Exhibit 9 for more details about the Dutch market.)

Spain

The competitors in Spain before the introduction of Buckler were Cruz Campo Sin, the market leader with 60% market share, followed by Aguila Sin, with a declining market share. El Aguila's original plan was to introduce Buckler with no advertising support, along with Aguila Sin. The intent was to slowly remove the old brand, but Buckler sold so well both in retail and on-premise that Aguila Sin was removed after only two months.

Despite low advertising and marketing support, Buckler began gaining approximately 1% market share per month, even with the 20% premium over Cruz Campo Sin. No changes had been made to the Cruz Campo Sin brand. However, other competing brands had already appeared in the Spanish market, including Tourtel (BSN), Dansk LA (Carlsberg), and Malt Beer (Grupo Damm, a regional brewery). Soon, Laiker Sin, developed by Mahou, another regional

EXHIBIT 10   Nielsen report on the Spanish nonalcoholic beer segment, 1989, 1990.

	APR./MAY	JUNE/JULY	AUG./SEPT.	OCT./NOV.	DEC./JAN.	FEB./MAR.	APR./MAY
Market Share Retail and Bar							
Buckler	40.6	40.6	41.7	44.5	44.0	46.0	45.9
Aguila Sin	1.7	1.7	1.1	0.8	0.9	1.2	1.2
Cruz Campo	51.4	50.1	46.3	41.8	39.3	37.2	35.7
Other (Tourtel, Dansk LA)	6.3	7.6	10.9	12.9	15.8	15.6	17.2
Numeric and Weighted Distribution*							
Buckler	19%/34%	21%/36%	22%/39%	22%/38%	23%/39%	25%/40%	26%/42%
Aquila Sin	2/3	1/3	1/2	1/2	2/2	1/1	1/1
Cruz Campo	20/34	22/36	21/34	21/34	20/35	20/33	20/34
Average Price per Litre as Index vs. Cruz Campo Sin "Bar" Price (Cruz Campo "Bar" = 100)							
Retail							
Buckler	61	61	62	62	64	66	66
Aquila Sin	58	50	58	53	54	51	51
Cruz Campo Sin	56	56	57	58	58	61	61
Other	60	62	65	64	65	66	68
Bar							
Buckler	107	97	98	102	102	100	100
Aquila Sin	95	102	104	104	108	105	108
Cruz Campo Sin	100	100	100	100	100	100	100
Other	102	106	111	112	110	116	109

*Numeric distribution: % of Nielsen audited stores carrying product.
Weighted distribution: 20% of the stores carrying the product sell x% of total product sales.
Source: Nielson Food and Bar Index.

brewery, would be introduced as well. (Refer to Exhibit 10 for more details about the Spanish market.)

The success of the product sales in Spain also caused some worry. Could the growth be maintained? What would stop another competitor from repeating the same experience that had happened with Bavaria Malt in the Netherlands? The company waited in anticipation.

France

In France, before the introduction of Buckler, there had been only one dominant brand, Tourtel, a product that had been in the market for 20 years.

Positioned as an adult drink rather than a beer, and with an extensive distribution, the brand commanded a 90% market share.

The immediate competitive reaction to Buckler's entry by BSN, the brewers of Tourtel, was to try to block distribution by dropping its prices below Buckler, changing the labeling, revising the product composition, and positioning Tourtel as a beer competitor rather than as a substitute adult drink. Furthermore, BSN offered more types of packaging (a one-litre bottle) and introduced two umbrella brands: Tourtel Brune and Tourtel Amber Gold.

These competitive actions caused the Buckler brand to have a slow start in France relative to the two other countries. Retail chains were hard to penetrate as they demanded huge listing fees and some proof of a successful product. After the first year, sales of Buckler were below budget. Blind taste tests showed a 50% preference for Buckler and 50% for Tourtel. However, by the middle of 1990, the company had attained a 15% market share. (Refer to Exhibit 11 for more details about the French market.)

THE DECISION

Hans Brinker had a problem. The executive board had made a decision to make Buckler Pan-European, and he personally felt that this was a breakthrough for the company. He was convinced that the original Buckler marketing strategy was sound but that the long-term earning potential would be jeopardized if a change were made now in midstream.

He was not particularly worried about the local brands. The real competition, he believed, were the Pan-European brands like Tourtel. Since Buckler's intro-

EXHIBIT 11   Nielsen report on the French nonalcoholic beer segment.

	APR./MAY	JUNE/JULY	AUG./SEPT.	OCT./NOV.	DEC./JAN.	FEB./MAR.	APR./MAY
Market Share Retail							
Buckler	12.4	16.1	16.6	15.4	14.8	16.4	17.3
Tourtel	79.8	76.8	77.0	77.8	78.6	77.5	75.3
Celta	n.a.*	n.a.	4.0	4.9	4.7	4.6	5.1
Other	7.8	7.1	2.4	1.9	1.9	1.5	2.3
Numeric and Weighted							
Distribution°	%	%	%	%	%	%	%
Buckler	23/70	23/74	28/77	27/76	27/77	33/79	37/84
Tourtel	65/96	66/96	70/96	68/97	66/97	66/96	67/96
Average Price in French Francs							
Buckler	9.08	8.90	8.91	8.89	8.93	9.12	9.10
Tourtel	6.90	6.97	7.04	7.12	7.22	7.24	7.48

*n.a. = Not available.
°Numeric distribution: of Nielsen audited stores carrying the product.
Weighted distribution: 20 of the stores carrying the product sell x of total product sales.
Source: Nielson Food Index.

EXHIBIT 12 Marketing mix details, Tourtel.

MARKETING MIX	FRANCE	BELGIUM	UNITED KINGDOM	SPAIN	SWITZERLAND
Brand name	Tourtel	Tourtel	Tourtel	Tourtel	Tourtel
Packaging	Almost the same over the different countries, with slight differences in text: green bottles.				
Product composition	Alcohol: 0.7%	Alcohol: .35%	n.a.*	Alcohol: .75%	Alcohol: .4%
	Wort: 6.9	Wort: 6.9		Wort: 7.0	Wort: 6.9
	Colour: 7.5	Colour: 8.0		Colour: 7.5	Colour: 8.0
	Bitterness: 20	Bitterness: 22		Bitterness: 19	Bitterness: 20
Positioning	Drink more	Drink more	n.a.	Drink more	n.a.
	Personal care	Personal care		Taste	
Price proportion with mainstream beer	106	122	n.a.	153	129
Advertising theme	Tourtel, you can drink it all night long.	Tourtel, you can drink it all night long.	n.a.	Tourtel, you can drink it all night long.	n.a.
Advertising agency	BDDP	Booster/BDDP	n.a.	BDDP	n.a.
Media choice	Television	Television, print billboard	n.a.	Television, print	n.a.
Entry strategy	Locally produced	Import	Import	Import	Import
Distribution intensity	Intensive	Intensive	n.a.	Intensive	Intensive
Target group	n.a.†	Age group: 25–34	n.a.	Age group: 25–34	n.a.
		Sex: male, female			
				Sex: male, female	
		Beer/nonbeer drinker		Beer/nonbeer drinker	
Market share	75%	61%	n.a.	5%	n.a.

†n.a. = Not available.

duction in France, BSN continued to react by introducing Tourtel in other countries such as Belgium, Switzerland, the United Kingdom, Spain, and, more recently, Italy and Greece. BSN also had several operating companies with wide distribution power. In addition, more was being spent for advertising on Tourtel than on Buckler, and Tourtel's price was also lower. (Refer to Exhibit 12 for details about the Tourtel brand.) At the same time, something had to be done for the operating companies, as they were entitled to have a fair share of the market.

LEVI STRAUSS JAPAN K.K.

In May 1993, Mr. A. John Chappell, President and Representative Director, Levi Strauss Japan K.K. (LSJ), was contemplating a conversation he just had with the National Sales Manager and Managing Director, Mr. Masafumi Ohki. They had been discussing the most recent information regarding the size of the jeans market in Japan. It appeared that after two years of market shrinkage in 1990 and 1991, the market contracted further in 1992. Although LSJ was still increasing its share of the market, Mr. Chappell was disturbed by this trend and wondered what new strategies, if any, LSJ should pursue.

In addition, Mr. Ohki had brought up the issue of selection criteria for retailers and sales agents. The distribution channel was undergoing structural changes, and Mr. Ohki believed that LSJ needed to evaluate and possibly revise their distribution strategy. LSJ was very selective in choosing its retailers and had historically focused their distribution on traditional urban jeans specialty shops. However, there were many new, large stores opening in the suburbs which were carrying jeans, amongst other items. Although LSJ did sell their jeans in some of these new stores, they had not pursued this new channel as aggressively as some of their competitors. As a result, their largest competitor, Edwin, was currently represented in twice as many stores as LSJ.

Mr. Chappell realized that increasing the number of stores would improve LSJ's reach and possibly help to stimulate the overall market. However, this could have a serious impact on LSJ's image. LSJ had spent years developing a premium product image which had catapulted them to market leader. Besides their product and advertising strategies, this image had also been cultivated by their selectivity in choosing retail outlets and sales agents. Not only did this ensure that LEVI'S would have a good image with the consumer, but it also was the only way LSJ could influence the retail price. Mr. Chappell feared that a decision to expand the number of retail outlets would have a negative impact on LEVI'S prices and might even result in discounting. This could seriously affect the premium product image LSJ had worked hard to foster over the years.

Mr. Chappell wondered what new strategies he should pursue to deal with these issues, or whether he should continue with the strategy that had made LEVI'S the number one jeans brand in Japan.

LEVI STRAUSS ASSOCIATES

Overview

Levi Strauss invented jeans in San Francisco in the middle of the nineteenth century gold rush. At that time Levi Strauss made pants for the gold miners that would not rip apart when miners filled their pockets with gold. Since then, the company bearing the founder's name has been faithful to the guiding principle—"Quality Never Goes Out of Style"—and has built a strong reputation and broad customer base.

Today, Levi Strauss Associates (Levi Strauss) designs, manufactures, and markets apparel for men, women, and children, including jeans, slacks, jackets, and skirts. Most of its products are marketed under the LEVI'S® and DOCKERS® trademarks and are sold in the United States and throughout North and South America, Europe, Asia, and Australia. In 1992, Levi Strauss was the world's largest brand name apparel manufacturer. Sales of jeans-related products accounted for 73% of its revenues in 1991.

Levi Strauss International

Levi Strauss International (LSI), which market jeans and related apparel outside the United States, is organized along geographic lines consisting of the Europe, Asia Pacific, Canada, and Latin America divisions. In terms of sales and profits, Europe is the largest international division. Asia Pacific is the second largest, particularly due to the strong performance of its Japanese and Australian operations. Sales growth in LSI is faster than in the domestic division. The following table gives the breakdown of domestic and international sales for the recent years.

LEVI STRAUSS—DOMESTIC AND INTERNATIONAL SALES
(IN MILLIONS OF DOLLARS)

	1989		1990		1991	
Domestic	$2,395	66.0%	$2,560	60.3%	$2,997	61.1%
LSI	$1,233	34.0%	$1,686	39.7%	$1,906	38.9%
Total	$3,628		$4,247		$4,903	

ORGANIZATION AND PRODUCTS

In 1991, LSI was more profitable than the domestic operations on a per unit basis. LSI was generally organized by country. Each country's operations within the European division are generally responsible for sales, distribution, finance and marketing activities. With few exceptions, Canada, Latin America, and the Asia Pacific divisions are staffed with their own merchandising, production, sales and finance personnel.

LSI's sales are derived primarily from basic lines of jeans, shirts and jackets. LSI resells directly to retailers in its established markets, although other distribution agreements are made elsewhere in the world. Retail accounts are currently serviced by approximately 310 sales representatives. LSI's manufacturing and distribution activities are independent of domestic operations. However, in 1991, LSI purchased $117.7 million of jeans products from the domestic division.

THE MARKETS, COMPETITION AND STRATEGY

The nature and strength of the jeans market varies from region to region and from country to country. Demand for jeans outside of the US is affected by a variety of factors, each of varying importance in different countries, including general economic conditions such as unemployment, recession, inflation and consumer spending rates. The non-US jeans markets are more sensitive to fashion trends, as well as being more volatile than the US market. In many countries, jeans are generally perceived as a fashion item rather than a basic functional product and are higher priced relative to the US. Sales in Japan have increased in recent years due primarily to increased consumer spending and population growth. Internationally, LSI maintains advertising programs similar to the domestic programs, modified as required by market conditions and applicable laws. Advertising expenditures for LSI were $108.4 million (5.7% of total sales) in 1991, a 21% increase from 1990.

INDUSTRY

The worldwide apparel market is affected by demographic changes in the consumer population, frequent shifts in prevailing fashions and styles, international trade and economic developments, and retailer practices. With the maturation of "the baby boomer" generation, the target market, a company's success will become more dependent on its ability to quickly and effectively respond to changes in fashion and other customer preferences.

JAPANESE JEANS INDUSTRY ENVIRONMENT AND TRENDS

Jeans Market

Jeans were introduced into the Japanese market before World War II. Yet, the first market boom occurred right after the war, when US forces brought a large supply of jeans into the country. The second growth spurt in the market for jeans was in the mid-1970s concurrent with the United States bicentennial. During this time, being American was in vogue, greatly enhancing the demand for American culture and products. The third boom, in 1986, was fueled by the increasing popularity of the casual fashion look among Japanese youth. This fashion trend, along with more leisure time, has greatly increased the market for jeans, resulting in a doubling of output from 26 million pairs in 1985, to more than 50 million pairs in 1990[1] (compound annual growth rate of 14%). However, the trend is towards slower growth, and the market actually shrunk in 1991. The growth in total production of jeans from 1987 to 1991 is given in Exhibit 1.

The financial results of major jeans manufacturers in 1992 indicates that the market continued to shrink following 1991. Yet, towards the end of 1992, some companies started to see the market revive. After the last couple years of market contraction, the jeans industry seems to be revitalized due to the development of new dying techniques (such as antique look jeans), as well as the development of jeans made of new fabrics such as light ounce denim and rayon. In addition, some of the smaller jeans manufacturers which have concentrated on the women's market are experiencing double digit growth in sales.

Competitive Environment

During this period of rapid expansion, LSJ grew 35% annually, more than twice as fast as the market.[2] As a result, LSJ currently enjoys the highest share of any single brand at 16% of total market sales. Still, there is fierce competition for market share with the five other large brands in the jeans market: Lee, Wrangler, Edwin, Big John and Bobson, due to the fact that all of the brands market similar product lines (emphasizing basic blue denim jeans, followed by other basic jeans, fashion jeans and chino pants) targeted at essentially the same customer segment. Also, all the American brands market their products by emphasizing the image of Americana.

---

[1] "Fashions Come and Go, But Blue Jeans Never Fade," *The Nikkei Weekly*, August 17, 1991.
[2] "Fundamentals Lend More-Than-Casual Look," *The Nikkei Weekly*, September 14, 1991.

Sales figures for the six largest jeans manufacturers are given in Exhibit 2. These figures show that the market share of the three large domestic Japanese brands, Edwin, Big John and Bobson is currently declining. LSJ, however, moved up from fifth position in 1986 to second position following Edwin in 1990 with a market share of almost 13%, and in 1991 LSJ became the top selling brand with approximately 15% of total jeans sales.

Following is a brief description of each of LSJ's major competitors.

Edwin—In addition to marketing its own brand of jeans, Edwin, the largest domestic manufacturer, also markets Lee jeans under a license agreement with VF Corporation, the US company which owns the Lee brand. Edwin wants to increase market share of its original brand, however Lee is important for them to compete with Levi's. This is a dilemma for Edwin, since the Lee brand seems to be cannibalizing the Edwin brand. In 1992, for the first time, LSJ exceeded Edwin in the total sales amount as shown in Exhibit 2. The figures for Edwin include revenues from Lee and Liberto brands. Edwin is also planning to sell a new Italian brand called Fiorucci beginning in the autumn of 1992.

Big John—Sales and net income are expected to increase after two consecutive years of decrease. This is due to the success of their new product line, the "antique collection." The company expects the blue jeans market will grow again in 1993. Since blue jeans is Big John's major product line, the company believes it is well positioned for growth in 1993. In May 1993, the company will begin construction of a new headquarters which will enable it to effectively concentrate the cutting, distribution, trading, and kids clothes sections into one location.

Wrangler Japan—Wrangler, also a jeans brand of VF Corp., is produced and sold through a license agreement with Wrangler Japan, a joint venture between Mitsubishi and Toyo Boseki. Sales have begun to pick up in September 1992, especially in the women's jeans market which is growing at double digit rates.

Bobson—Bobson's sales target for 1993 is ¥20,000million. The company has been incredibly successful in the women's jeans market. As a result, from October 1992 to January 1993, sales in that segment have increased 40% over the same period of the previous year. The company expects 1993 to be a growth year.

It is interesting to note that up to this point, Levi Strauss' US competitor, VF Corporation, has chosen to operate in Japan solely under licensing arrangements. However, there is speculation that VF Corporation is planning to shift its marketing strategy from licensing to direct sales. This could drastically change the competitive market in the near future. Market experts predict that the Japanese jeans market will eventually be dominated by the three major American brands: Levi's, Lee, and Wrangler.

New Emerging Markets

In 1990, Wrangler Japan Inc. tried to reinforce their traditional image by marketing "revival jeans," which feature natural dye extracted from the indigo plant. These indigo blue jeans, named Vintage Wrangler, are made of 100% denim and hand dyed. They are priced at ¥30,000 (approx. $240.00), but selling well.[3] LSJ also introduced reproductions of its 5033BSXX and 701SXX styles, popular in the 1950s and 1960s, which are priced at ¥48,000 ($384.00) in September 1991. Yet, it is reported that LSJ cannot make these jeans fast enough to satisfy the demand.[4]

On the other hand, new well-preserved second-hand jeans are in high demand, some of which are being sold for more than ¥500,000 ($4,000.00). About 30 to 40 stores have opened which specialize in selling used jeans from the United States made in the 1940s, 1950s, and 1960s. One store says that the most popular items are priced slightly below ¥100,000 ($800.00).[5] However, the slowing growth in demand seems to indicate that oversupply is becoming a problem and that the market is close to saturation. According to the National Sales Manager of LSJ, this trend is supported primarily by jeans enthusiasts and may not last long.

Sales of women's blue jeans registered a phenomenal 109% growth between 1985 and 1989, increasing from 8.5 million to 17.8 million pairs a year. With the forecast that the young men's market is stabilizing, all the companies are looking at the potential in the market for women's jeans, creating fierce competition in that category.[6]

Changing Distribution Channel

Unlike the US Europe, and other countries in Southeast Asia, jeans sales in Japan are still predominately through jeans specialty stores. In other countries, jeans specialty stores have already lost market share to large national chains (such as Sears and J.C. Penney's) and to discounters (such as Walmart and Kmart). The successful specialty stores in the US are those who have been able to develop their own brands, such as The Gap and The Limited.

Although there has not been a similar shift in the Japanese market (from specialty stores to national chains), the shift is occurring within the jeans specialty shop channel. The structure of this channel seems to be changing with the emergence of a new type of jeans shop. Traditionally, jeans shops were located in urban areas and sold only jeans (both factors placing a constraint on store size). Recently, new chain stores have been built in the suburbs which are usually five to seven times larger and may carry other products besides jeans. These jeans stores have proliferated, increasing their revenue at the expense of the smaller jeans stores. Their success is partly a result of their emphasis on sales promotions, ability to stock a full line of products and the unique store designs. Two such chains, Marutomi and Chiyoda (the two largest shoe store chains), entered

---

[3] "Fashions Come and Go, But Blue Jeans Never Fade," *The Nikkei Weekly,* August 17, 1991.
[4] "Vintage American Products Attract Japanese Rebels," *The Nikkei Weekly,* December 7, 1991
[5] Ibid.
[6] "Fashions Come and Go, But Blue Jeans Never Fade," *The Nikkei Weekly,* August 17, 1991.

the jeans retail market four to five years ago and now boast retail stores in excess of 200 each. This emergence of jeans specialty store chains has saved this category from losing market share following those in other countries.

In 1992, approximately 250 new stores were opened, most of which are large-scale suburban stores of the type described above. Even though the peak is over, an additional 230 stores are likely to open in 1993. This consists mainly of Chiyoda's 75 to 85 "Mac House" stores and Marutomi's 100 "From USA" stores. In some suburban areas, the increasing number of stores has started to stimulate competition for local market share. For example, at the city of Tsukuba, a growing suburban area outside of Tokyo, 10 jeans stores (including those under construction) ranging in size up to 4,500 square feet are clustered in 3.1 square miles. Many retailers, therefore, are attempting to differentiate themselves by increasing customer service and being more selective in what product lines they will carry. Yet, with the slowing down in the jeans market, compounded by the recession, the excessive increase in jeans retail space is worsening the inventory turnover leading to inventory surpluses.

Given this new retail situation, the ability to develop an effective inventory control system and low cost operations is an important competitive advantage. Jeans manufacturers and retailers are entering a new era of competition where capital strength and efficient inventory management and distribution systems will have a significant impact on the success of the company. Moreover, in order to provide extensive customer service, the recruiting and training of employees are becoming increasingly important points of differentiation. In the US, Canada and Europe, the shift in jeans distribution towards the discount stores negatively affected the overall image of jeans. Thus, jeans manufacturers have had to invest heavily in order to revive the former image. The destiny of the Japanese jeans industry will depend on how manufacturers, retailers, and customers react to the changes that are occurring in the retail environment.

POTENTIAL IMPACT ON PRICING

Thus far, most of the distribution channels, including jeans specialty stores, department stores and even national chain stores, have maintained the suggested retail price. National chain stores such as Daiei and Itoh Yokado have discount stores as their affiliates, yet, these discount stores have different supply routes and sell different products. This enables Daiei and Itoh Yokado to maintain the retail price suggested by jeans manufacturers.

A similar change in channel structure has occurred in the distribution of business suits, where sales of department stores and specialty stores in the cities have suffered due to the emergence of larger men's shops in the suburbs. In this case, price competition is increasing between the discount stores (the "category killer"), but not between the national chain stores as has occurred in past. National chain stores have not entered the price war but are stuck in the middle between the discount stores (at the low end) and the specialty and department stores (at the high end).

If this holds true in the jeans industry, national chain stores are not likely to begin competing on price. Also, department stores and traditional jeans specialty stores (with few stores) are unlikely to discount. However, the new jeans specialty stores with many outlets, giving them strong purchasing power against manufacturers, may begin competing on price. These stores, which have expanded rapidly, are experiencing increasing competition and inventory surpluses creating a ripe environment for price competition. The eventual outcome depends somewhat on how jeans manufacturers will react to discounting, should it occur, and on the sales policies of traditional jeans specialty stores.

LEVI STRAUSS JAPAN K.K

Overview

Levi Strauss entered Japan with the opening of a branch office of Levi Strauss (Far East) Limited (Hong Kong) in April of 1971. Prior to this, its presence was limited to a minimal level of sales generated by importers. The Hiratsuka Distribution Center was opened in November of 1973, and in June 1974, Levi Strauss began domestic production of jeans products.

In December of 1975, Levi Strauss began selling through wholesale agencies, in addition to its direct sales to retailers. Levi Strauss also began importing products from the US in 1978. In the same year, the reporting line of the Japanese office was changed from Hong Kong to LSI headquarters in San Francisco.

In 1982, Levi Strauss Japan K.K. (LSJ) was established as an independent operating company. Another important milestone occurred in June of 1989, when 4.1 million shares of LSJ were listed on the Tokyo OTC market in an initial public offering. This sale brought in $80 million, while still leaving Levi Strauss with an 85% share of the Japanese company's equity.

LSJ's strategy has been to maintain consistency and a long-term view. With a heavy emphasis on advertising, constant new product introduction in addition to traditional styles, systems development, good relationships with suppliers, contractors, wholesalers, and retailers, and personnel training, LSJ has successfully built its position in Japan. (See following sections for elaboration on LSJ operations.)

This position is largely due to LSJ's marketing strategy described below.

1. Target young male customers and advertise extensively through TV commercials and men's magazines, creating the image that LEVI'S jeans is cool American casual wear.

2. In order to have extensive accessibility, contract with various kinds of sales outlets from small specialty jeans shops, mainly located in urban areas, to national chain stores which have larger sales space, mainly located in suburbs.

3. Provide not only the traditional jeans imported from the United States, but also new jeans which are in line with current fashion and sewn to fit Japanese physical features.

Performance

LSJ experienced sluggish sales until around 1984. Since then year-on-year sales has been increasing by approximately 35% every year until it slowed down to 20% in 1991. The company expects this slower level of growth to continue in the short term. In 1991, LSJ sales were ¥35.056 billion with profits of ¥7.058 billion. LSJ is planning to raise its market share to over 20% by fiscal 1995.

LSJ experienced a decrease a profit in 1992, due to an increase in indirect marketing costs, including depreciation from investment on the distribution center and system development. Yet, LSJ still posts an impressive 17.4% return on sales, far higher than its competitors, and nearly three times the industry average. In 1993, the company expects sales growth to be moderate, therefore it expects a further decrease in net income.

Employing the strategy described above, LSJ has successfully increased sales volume through stimulating the jeans market. It enjoys constant demand not subject to the whims of fashion or the changing season. LSJ has been successful in establishing the reputation of high quality products and brand image, allowing them to sell higher end products than their competitors. This high quality, premium product strategy was successful since it capitalizes on the Japanese economy (with one of the highest GNP per capita and significant growth).

On the cost side, LSJ is very efficient in the sense that it does not have a factory requiring huge capital expenditure, but instead, contracts out all its production in Japan. As a result, it does not have to worry about potential costs associated with downtime, equipment improvement, and workers compensation both in monetary and non-monetary terms. Moreover, LSJ has a very small sales force to cover all of Japan. As a result, LSJ's sales-to-employee ratio is ¥180 million ($1.4 million), which is roughly three times the average of its rivals.[7] Another strength of LSJ is its no debt strategy to alleviate risk due to interest rate fluctuations. Since its IPO on the Tokyo Stock Exchange, the stock price has been constantly increasing to the current P/E ratio of 50.[8]

Products

Product lines sold by LSJ consist of tops (shirts, jackets and sweatshirts), men's and women's basic jeans, other basic jeans and fashion jeans. There are approx-

[7] "Fundamentals Lend More-Than Casual Look," *The Nikkei Weekly,* September 14, 1991.

[8] Ibid.

imately 18 kinds of men's basic jeans (excluding multiple colors), 10 kinds of women's basic jeans, 20 kinds of other basic jeans (including 5 for women), and several fashion jeans. Other basic jeans consist of trendy jeans products and fashion jeans consist of cotton (non-denim) pants. The sales breakdown is as follows: 20% from tops, 20% from women's jeans, 40% from basic men's jeans and 20% from the remainder.

Belts, accessories, shoes, socks, bags and kid's jeans are sold by another company under a license agreement. In addition, apart from traditional styles, product managers in LSJ design new styles which are in line with the fashion at the time. New products are introduced twice a year in spring and in autumn. Occasionally, product innovations developed for the Japanese market are later introduced into other markets. This was the case for "stone-washed" denim jeans and the Dockers line, which were successfully introduced in the U.S. after being developed and introduced in Japan.[9]

Organization

LSJ currently employs approximately 500 people spread throughout its headquarters, sales offices and distribution center. The company's headquarters is in Tokyo while additional sales offices are located in big cities such as Osaka, Nagoya and Fukuoka. The company operates a large distribution center in Hiratsuka, outside Tokyo in order to store the finished products and to distribute based on orders. Among the 500 employees, 160 people work at the department stores as sales personnel, 150 people work at the distribution center, and the remainder are employed at the headquarters. An organization chart for LSJ is shown in Exhibit 3.

Human Resources

LSJ does not recruit directly from the university. They tend to hire university graduates with one to two years of working experience (not necessarily in the apparel industry). Hiring is done on an as-needed basis. Although U.S. companies often have trouble hiring in Japan, the National Sales Manager of LSJ claims that the company has not had difficulties in recruiting employees. This is due to the fact that LSJ tends to hire from non-traditional sources, i.e., women and experienced hires, therefore they do not directly compete with traditional Japanese companies for labor resources.

Approximately 300 of the 500 employees work under contract to LSJ. Most of these employees work in the distribution center. Although this is not typical of the traditional Japanese system of lifetime employment, it is not uncommon in the apparel industry. In addition, compensation is not determined according to

[9]Geoffrey Duin, "Levi's Won't Fade in the Japanese Market," *Tokyo Business Today,* April 1990, p. 46.

the traditional Japanese system based on seniority. Rather, compensation is determined by the job description covering the activities performed by the employee.

In order to build company loyalty among employees, LSJ provides a complete educational system. The company recognizes training to be one of the most important factors contributing to the overall success of the company in Japan. Education provided by the company ranges from educating new employees on the importance of the customer to developing management skills. Many of the programs are designed to upgrade the skills of each employee. There are five major training systems: a training system for newly entered employees, a correspondence education system, an English education system, various objective training systems, and an overseas training system.

Production

While LSJ does not own its own production facilities in Japan, all its domestically produced clothing is made by contracted factories which produce only Levi Strauss products. These contractors sew jeans products from denim purchased by LSJ from various domestic textile manufacturers and from trading companies. Currently, the domestic production accounts for 50% of the total products sold in Japan, while 30% is imported from the United States and 20% from Southeast Asia, mainly from factories in the Philippines.

It is interesting that until 1978 the company sold only domestic- and Asian-made jeans products in Japan. Then, realizing the importance of having the original U.S.-made jeans, the company started to sell some U.S.-made products (specifically the 501 product line) in Japan. According to Mr. Ohki, it was crucial to send customers a message that LSJ is selling "real" American products. Yet, the domestically made jeans products actually fit Japanese bodies better, which partially contributed to the company's success in the early years.

Distribution

The company first established its distribution center in Hiratsuka, Kanagawa in November 1973, two years after establishing operations in Japan. However, LSJ recently reconstructed its distribution center in order to enhance customer service by improving the quality and quantity of warehouse and shipping facilities. In October 1990, it completed the first stage of reconstruction, including installation of the computer controlled warehouse system named AS/RS (Automated Storage and Retrieval System). Automation of picking and shipping areas, which are controlled along with the automated warehouse, was completed in May 1991. These renovations greatly improved the storage capacity and more than doubled the daily shipping capability. They also enabled the company to handle small quantity, frequent, short-term delivery orders. In addition, LSJ has installed automated ordering systems at some of the national chain stores, allowing for better inventory control and quicker response.

The company has two distribution channels, one is direct sales by sales personnel, and the other is wholesale by sales agencies. Currently, 53% of total sales comes from direct sales made by 40 LSJ sales personnel located in the four sales offices. Using 1991 sales data to calculate the revenue generated by the direct sales force, the average salesperson generated ¥464.5 million (approximately $3.7 million) of revenue in that year. This demonstrates the extraordinary productivity of LSJ's sales force. The remaining 43% comes from 13 domestic sales agencies.

Sales of LSJ products occur through four kinds of sales outlets. LSJ's sales personnel and sales agencies both have contact with these key sales outlets consisting of: (1) major nationwide jeans shops such as Big American and Eiko; (2) major nationwide department stores, from the prestigious Mitsukoshi Department Store to Marui, a department store specifically targeted to the younger generation; (3) national chain stores such as Daiei, Itoh Yokado, and Seiyu; and (4) nation-wide men's shops such as Iseya. Most of LSJ's sales occur in jeans shops (70%), with the remaining sales fairly evenly split among department stores (12%), national chain stores (10%) and other stores (8%). A listing of LSJ's major sales outlets, as well as suppliers and sales agencies is given in Exhibit 4.

Currently, LEVI'S are sold at fewer sales outlets than some of their domestic competitors. For example, 5,000 stores carry the LEVI'S brand, while more than 10,000 stores sell the Edwin brand. Although LSJ receives a higher percentage of its sales through traditional jeans shops (70%) than the market overall (60%), there is very little difference between LSJ distribution patterns and that of the other top brands.

LSJ's effort to be a Japanese company can be observed from its strategy of building good relationships with its sales outlets. LSJ provides various services to each outlet store, from giving advice on product displays and in-store arrangements to organizing seminars and handing out sales manuals. Japanese department stores rely heavily on the manufacturers to provide sales staff, forcing LSJ to place 160 employees in department stores as sales clerks. However, this necessity allows LSJ, and other Japanese manufacturing companies, to gather information regarding customer preferences.

Pricing

Historically, LSJ was positioned as a price leader, charging 15 to 20% higher than competitors for similar jeans products. However, about 10 years ago, competitors raised their prices to match LEVI'S (pricing of LEVI'S remained flat), allowing LSJ to greatly increase their market share. Today, compared to competitive brands such as Edwin, Lee and Wrangler, LSJ has a similar price range for its jeans products. Even so, the average product price which LSJ's customers pay (¥7,900 = approximately $63.20) is about 5 to 10% higher than the average price received by competitors. This is due to the fact that LSJ customers are willing to buy more expensive types of jeans.

Wholesale price varies by distributor due to the rebate scheme. However, the average price charged to sales outlets is 55% of retail, while sales agents pay about 50% of retail on average. LSJ charges a higher wholesale price to the department stores in order to offset the cost of LSJ employees who work as sales personnel in those stores. However, there is no significant difference in retail price across the various distribution channels, since retail outlets so far have maintained the suggested retail price.

Advertising and Promotion

Similar to the strategy employed by Levi Strauss in the US, LSJ emphasizes a pull strategy spending heavily on advertising to increase demand. Since 1976, LSJ has been spending approximately 6% of total sales on advertising (TV and print) compared to an industry average of 4%.[10] It uses James Dean as an advertising character in order to establish the image of the young, active American. Its target customer has traditionally been young men, aged 16 to 29, who have grown up with, and maintain a good image towards, American products.

When LSJ first launched its campaign in 1984 with the slogan, *"Heroes Wear LEVI'S,"* its main purpose was to increase the awareness of the LEVI'S brand. The ads showed movie scenes in which James Dean, John Wayne, Steve McQueen and Marilyn Monroe wore jeans, while a famous movie announcer, Mr. Haruo Mizuno, read the slogan. In 1985, the slogan was changed to *"My Mind, LEVI'S"* and, in 1987, to *"The Original LEVI'S,"* both of which were intended to project traditional American values and a pioneering spirit with a more familiar nuance. The current slogan, *"Re-Origin"* was launched in 1989 to emphasize the revival of traditional jeans. Since the very beginning, the company has recognized the Japanese purchase mentality towards imported goods—Japanese are willing to choose imports and even pay more for these goods—and has been maximizing its marketing by appealing to this psychology.

LSJ focuses on TV commercials and magazine advertisements which accounts for 65% of the total promotional budget. Of this advertising expense, approximately 70% is used for TV commercials, and 30% for magazine advertisements. The company uses mass media effectively based on differences in features. For TV commercials, LSJ uses an advertising agency in order to maximize reach and communicate the company's image to a larger audience. In contrast, the company creates its magazine advertisements mostly in house, since the goal of the magazine ads is to increase consumers' understanding of its products and to appeal strongly to certain target customer segments. In terms of cooperative advertising with sales outlets, LSJ is consistent with other Japanese manufacturing companies which tend not to use this method as much as U.S. companies.

LSJ also publishes seasonal product catalogs named "LEVI'S BOOK" and places them in outlet stores in order to introduce new products. Two million copies of this catalog are produced twice a year accounting for 10% of LSJ's promotional

---

[10] "Fundamentals Lend More-Than Casual Look," *The Nikkei Weekly,* September 14, 1991.

expenditures. The remaining 25% of promotional expense is used for direct communication with customers at the point of purchase. By these consistent advertising and promotional activities, the company is trying to increase (1) awareness of the LEVI'S brand, (2) understanding of its products, and (3) the willingness to buy.

LSJ promotional expenditures.

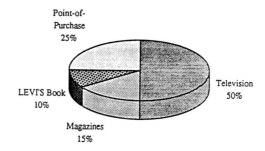

Point-of-
Purchase
25%

LEVI'S Book
10%

Television
50%

Magazines
15%

FUTURE CHALLENGES

LSJ's major challenges, resulting from the changing market and retail environment, are:

■ how to continue to grow faced with a contracting market;
■ how to respond to the changing structure of the distribution channel; and
■ how to develop and implement a pricing strategy given the current retail environment.

First, the traditional market for jeans in Japan has peaked and will likely continue to shrink or remain flat. The number of young people is decreasing due to the lower birth rate, shifting the demographics to an older population. For the last twelve years, the birth rate each year has been the lowest ever recorded, a trend which is expected to continue.[11] Also, the average frequency of jeans purchase per person per year in Japan is a meager 0.5 compared to the 1.5 in the US.[12] This is due to the fact that high schools in Japan require students to wear uniforms so there is significantly less time and chance to wear jeans. These

---

[11] 1992 Statistics Handbook: Statistics Bureau, Management and Coordination Agency; Ministry of Health and Welfare.
[12] "Fundamentals Lend More-Than Casual Look," *The Nikkei Weekly*, September 14, 1991.

trends will further impact the market size of the young male segment, the traditional market which jeans manufacturers (including LSJ) have targeted.

Second, the development of a new type of jeans specialty stores have presented some interesting issues for LSJ. The rapid expansion requires LSJ to develop a strategy for how many and what type of stores (i.e., jeans specialty, department, national chain, etc.) should distribute the LEVI'S brand. Once a strategy is decided on, selection criteria for retailers and sales agents need to be determined. In addition, servicing a growing number of retailers creates challenges in delivery and inventory systems (described in the distribution section), production capacity and sales force expansion.

Finally, with increased competition between both the manufacturers and the retailers, the possibility of discounting cannot be ignored. Price competition may be initiated by manufacturers or certain retail channels may elect not to maintain the suggested retail price. A feasible strategy must address the fact that LSJ has little direct control over retail pricing due to anti-trust laws. Government intervention is also a concern in that, as part of an international company, LSJ must be sensitive to trade policies regarding pricing. In addition, operating in various countries requires a pricing policy which limits the potential for a gray market. Thus, the pricing strategy will significantly impact LSJ's future, since price discounting could negatively affect the premium product image that LSJ has established.

Mr. Chappell wondered how he should deal with these important strategic and marketing issues to ensure LSJ's continued success.

EXHIBIT 1

Size of the Japanese jeans market.

	UNITS OF TOTAL JEANS PRODUCTION					
	BLUE JEANS		COLOR JEANS		TOTAL JEANS	
	UNITS	GROWTH	UNITS	GROWTH	UNITS	GROWTH
1987	36,924		15,186		52,110	
1988	43,274	17.2	12,904	(15.0)	56,178	7.8
1989	45,614	5.4	13,310	3.2	58,924	4.9
1990	45,401	(0.4)	13,238	(0.5)	58,639	(0.5)
1991	43,864	(3.4)	12,946	(2.2)	56,810	(3.1)

Source: Japanese Jeans Manufacturing Association (JJMA)
Notes: These numbers include imports, but not exports, thus are an appropriate proxy for market size. Also, these production quantities are more than LSJ estimates based on annual consumer surveys. For example, in 1991, LSJ estimates the total market size to be 45 million pairs, while the JJMA indicates 25% more. As JJMA's figure is based on self reporting by each of the jeans manufacturers, it is likely to be inflated over the actual sales quantity.

	TOTAL JEANS PRODUCTION IN YEN (¥ MILLIONS)		
	BLUE JEANS	COLOR JEANS	TOTAL
1988	90,660	27,273	117,933
1989	95,562	28,124	123,686
1990	95,115	27,972	123,087
1991	86,992	24,774	111,766

Source: Yano Institute

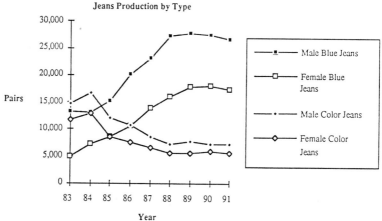

Jeans Production by Type

Source: Yano Institute

EXHIBIT 2

Sales and income data for jeans manufacturers.

SALES OF TOP SIX JEANS BRANDS (¥ MILLION)						
	1988	1989	1990	1991	1992	1993E
LEVI'S	15,425	21,508	28,855	35,056	37,626	38,600
Edwin (incl Lee)	30,342	33,579	38,250	38,534	37,099	
Lee			5,000(e)	6,300(e)	6,500(e)	10,000
Wrangler	11,715	13,550	15,367	16,972	17,847	
Big John	13,939	16,472	18,163	17,684	17,421	18,400
Bobson*	13,190	15,578	18,187	18,277	16,403	
Other	90,439	98,674	103,689	108,363	111,327	
Total	175,050	199,361	222,511	234,886	237,723	

NET INCOME OF TOP FIVE JEANS MANUFACTURERS (¥ MILLION)						
	1988	1989	1990	1991	1992	1993E
LEVI'S	3,585	4,421	6,124	7,058	6,532	6,280
Edwin (incl. Lee)	2,592	3,445	3,365	3,045	3,039	
Wrangler	596	631	1,118	1,127	802	
Big John	881	1,358	827	781	346	1,250
Bobson	531	812	1,413	883	925	
Other	1,814	3,023	2,380	2,416	3,141	
Total	9,999	13,690	15,227	15,310	14,785	

RETURN ON SALES OF TOP FIVE JEANS MANUFACTURERS (%)						
	1988	1989	1990	1991	1992	1993E
LEVI'S	23.2	20.6	21.2	20.1	17.4	16.3
Edwin (incl. Lee)	8.5	10.3	8.8	7.9	8.2	
Wrangler	5.1	4.7	7.3	6.6	4.5	
Big John	6.3	8.2	4.6	4.4	2.0	6.8
Bobson	4.0	5.2	7.8	4.8	5.6	
Other	2.0	3.1	2.3	2.2	2.8	
Total	5.7	6.9	6.8	6.5	6.2	

Source: Company Financial Statements. Yano Institute.
Notes: (1) Includes sales of jeans and tops.
(2) Bobson merged its sales affiliate in 1990, therefore, the financial statement has not be publicized since then. The figures since 1990 are taken from a report by the Yano Institute.
(3) Since Edwin does not break out sales of Lee brand, Lee sales numbers are estimates provided by LSJ.
(4) 1993 estimates for LEVI'S and Lee provided by LSJ. 1993 Big John figures estimated by Big John.

EXHIBIT 3

LSJ Organizational structure.

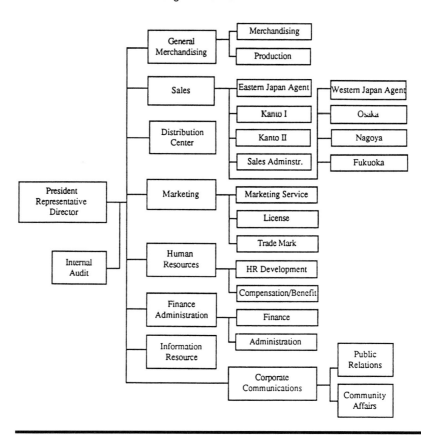

Levi Strauss Japan K.K.
Organization Chart

EXHIBIT 4

Key sales agencies, suppliers and sales outlets.

SALES AGENCIES

K.K. Daiman Shoten
Daimaru K.K.
Daiwa K.K.
Eiko Shoji K.K.
Igarashi K.K.
Ishida Sangyo K.K.
Maruhon K.K.
Mori Iroy K.K.
Morimen K.K.
K.K. Ohno Iryo
Sanwa Iryo K.K.
Takaya Shoji K.K.
K.K. Yamakatsu

KEY SUPPLIERS

C. Itoh & Co., Ltd.
Ihara Kogyo K.K.
K.K. Kasuya Shokai
K.K. Kisugi Sewing Center
K.K. Kurabo Apparel
Kurashiki Boseki K.K.
Levi Strauss & Co. (USA)
Levi Strauss (Far East) Ltd.
Nagao Shoji K.K.
Nishie Denim Co., Ltd.
Nisshin Bouseki K.K.
Scovill Japan Co., Ltd.
Sundia K.K.
Takahata Co., Ltd.
Tentak K.K.

KEY SALES OUTLETS

Jeans Shops:
Big American
Blue mate
Eiko
Goshibo
IB Shoji
Joint
Kyushu Sanshin Group
Marukawa Hachioji
Marukawa Ogawa
Sun Village
Taro's House
US Sanshin

National Chain Stores:
Daiei
Itoh Yokado
Jusco
Nichii
Seiyu
Uni

Department Stores:
Daimaru
Hankyu
Hanshin
Isetan
Kintestu
Matsuya
Matsuzakaya
Maruei
Marui
Mitsukoshi
Odsakyu
Seibu
Sogo
Takashimaya
Tokyu

Men's Shops:
Iseya
Roughox

EXHIBIT 5

LSJ magazine advertising 1991 and 1992.

1991 LSJ MAGAZINE ADVERTISEMENTS			
MAGAZINE	TYPE	READERSHIP PROFILE	NUMBER OF LSJ ADS, 1/91–12/91
Popeye	Fashion	Young Males, 18–23	22
H D Press	Fashion	Young Males, 18–23	24
Men's Non No	Fashion	Young Males, 18–23	20
Fineboys	Fashion	Young Males, 18–23	15

1992 LSJ MAGAZINE ADVERTISEMENTS			
MAGAZINE	TYPE	READERSHIP PROFILE	NUMBER OF LSJ ADS, 1/92–10/92
Popeye	Fashion	Young Males, 18–23	18
H D Press	Fashion	Young Males, 18–23	17
Men's Non No	Fashion	Young Males, 18–23	17
Fineboys	Fashion	Young Males, 18–23	11
Asahi Weekly	News	White collar males, all ages	1
Shincho Weekly	News	White collar males, all ages	1
Bunshun Weekly	News	White collar males, all ages	1
Bart	News	Young, white collar males	1
Non No	Fashion	Young single females	1
Pia	Entertainment	Young males/females, <35	1
Dime	New Product Into	Affluent males, 30–40	1
Sarai	Housekeeping	Married females, 25–35	1
Number	Sports	Males, all ages	1

ICI PAINTS (A) STRATEGY FOR GLOBALIZATION

"We at ICI Paints aspire to the number one position globally in the paint business. Our goal is to make ICI Paints the first choice among paint suppliers to whom a customer anywhere in the world would turn if he were seeking a long-term supply relationship," said Herman Scopes, PEO of ICI Paints. "Now, we are already the world's leader if measured in market share, sales volume, or liters of paint produced. However, we have not yet been able to translate this position into superior financial performance. To get there, we will have to become much better at learning from each other and at transferring best practice from one operation to another."

INDUSTRY PROFILE

The world paint market was estimated at some £20[1] billion at ex. factory level and some 12 billion liters. Growth was expected to average 2–3% through the next decade.

North America accounted for 31% of the market by volume, followed by Europe (29%), Japan (13%), Asia-Pacific (11%), and the rest of the world (16%). In the more mature paint markets of North America and Europe, annual growth was expected to be below GNP growth whereas in the newly industrializing countries growth was expected to be in line with GNP growth. Long term, the three principal paint user areas of Europe, North America, and Asia-Pacific were expected to become of equal size and account for 75% of the world market (*refer to **Exhibit 1***).

Major application segments included decorative uses (50%), industrial uses (37%), coatings for cans (3%), automotive OEM (6%), car repair/refinishing (4%).

There were approximately 10,000 paint manufacturers worldwide. Leading paint companies, aside from ICI, PPG, and BASF, were Sherwin-Williams (US), AKZO (Netherlands), Nippon (Japan), International-Courtaulds (UK), Kansai (Japan), DuPont (US), and Valspar (US). The top 10 companies shared 30% of the world paint market in 1988. That share was expected to increase over the next decade.

Case, "ICI Pai..ts (A): Strategy for Globalization GM-557" prepared by Professor Jean-Pierre Jeannet. Copyright © 1990 IMD, the International Institute for Management Development, Lausanne, Switzerland. IMD retains all rights. Not to be reproduced or used without written permission directly from IMD, Lausanne, Switzerland.

[1]In 1988 £1.00 = $1.50

COMPANY PROFILE

ICI Paints was the world's largest paint manufacturer with a sales volume of £1.5 billion, or 8% of the world market, and an annual output of 800 million liters, or 7% of world volume. The company operated some 64 manufacturing plants in 29 countries. Licensees operated in another 14 countries (*refer to* **Exhibit 3**). ICI was about 70% larger than its next biggest competitor, PPG Industries.

ICI Paints was part of the Consumer and Specialty Products sector of ICI. The division accounted for about 12% of total ICI turnover and 7% of its trading profit. Sales in 1988 (excluding sales by related companies) had reached £1.363 billion with a trading profit of £98 million resulting in a return of 7.2% of sales. ICI Paints' profitability was on a par with BASF, its leading European competitor, and about twice that of its Japanese competitors. ICI Paints had been a consistent performer in an industry that had been characterized by considerable restructuring (*refer to* **Exhibit 4**).

ICI's market position varied considerably by market segment. The company was the world leader in the decorative and can coatings areas, a major player in automotive refinishes, one of the smaller automotive OEM players, and it also held positions in powder, coil coatings, and other industrial coatings. ICI was absent from the marine paints sector (*refer to* **Exhibit 5**).

Decorative Paint Segment

About 57% of ICI Paints' business was accounted for by the decorative segment, which included paints and coatings used for the protection and decoration of industrial, commercial, and residential buildings. ICI was the world's largest producer of decorative paints, both for professional and do-it-yourself (DIY) users. The company marketed its Dulux brands in the UK, Australia, New Zealand and a few other Asian markets, the Valentine brand in France, Ducolux in Germany, and Glidden Spred in the US, which was acquired as part of the acquisition of Glidden in 1986. Glidden was the inventor of waterborne latex paints for popular emulsions. Although trading under different brands, ICI was the leader in most of these markets, particularly in the premium end of the market.

Most decorative paint was used where produced with little cross-shipping due to its low value. ICI tended to meet different local players country by country.

The wholesaling structure and retailing industry as well as the role of the DIY market varied considerably from one country to another. Furthermore, there was little economy of scale effect in this business. Some 500 paint companies competed in this segment in Italy alone. Paint formulations used also had to be adjusted to local use conditions such as prevailing surfaces, building materials, and climate.

Despite these local differences, some commonalities existed. "Attitudes to what consumers want are far more common than different," commented John Thompson, ICI Paints Planning Manager. "We have done market research in Turkey, Italy, and Columbus, Ohio, and the same overall pattern emerges: the woman in a household determines when a surface is to be painted, and she determines the color. The husband selects the brand, usually on the basis of price and technique, although women are increasingly also making this decision. In terms of paint application, it is about evenly split between husbands and wives."

Can Coating Segment

Although the can coating segment with worldwide sales of £800 million accounted for only 3% of the world paint market, it accounted for 11% of ICI business, or £165 million, representing about 28% market share and giving it world leadership. Some 46% of the market was in North America, followed by Europe (24%) and Asia-Pacific (22%). Major competitors were BASF, Midland, and Valspar.

The coatings were used on the inside of tin or aluminum cans for food or beverage containers, making them corrosion resistant. This thin layer on the inside of every can was a crucial part for a successful canning operation. Consequently, this part of the paint industry was viewed as a high technology application.

Customers were concentrated with major use in the hands of four groups and their licensees: Continental Can, Pechiney-Triangle (included former American and National Can), Carnaud-Metal Box, and Crown Cork and Seal. These can manufacturers operated canning lines all over the world, and they expected the suppliers to follow them everywhere with a consistent product insuring same tastes for globally marketed products such as Coca-Cola.

Coating products had to be developed for each application and depended on the particular food or beverage as well as on the type of metal or aluminum container used. Customers were increasingly looking for simplifications and tended to look for a narrower technology range.

In this business, it was important to be able to make the development effort go around. A new product for sardines might be developed in Portugal but might have applications for Norwegian packers as well. Success depended on avoiding duplication of effort in applications development. Although coatings were usually not identical, a considerable part of the concept development could be widely applicable to other customers with the same applications.

ICI had acquired some 11 coatings companies over the years including Holden (Birmingham) with operations in Europe, Marsden (UK), Wiederhold (Germany), Attivilac (Italy), and Glidden (US). In Europe, ICI had strong operations in Rouen, France, where its Holden operation was located near the Carnaud company. The French operation had thus always been strong in food applications. Glidden, on the other hand, enjoyed a 80% market share in the US for beverage cans.

ICI had targeted the can coating segment for major growth and planned to increase its market share to 40% of the world market, up from 28% currently. A new production facility was planned for Taiwan. As part of this expansion strategy, the company combined all of its various can coatings businesses under the same leadership in a single packaging group. Prior to that change, can coatings had been part of the larger group for general industry coatings.

Major changes were also contemplated for development. Work was conducted to transfer Glidden's aluminum can coatings technology to steel and tin plate. Also under review was a decision whether or not to site a new development center in Singapore or Malaysia to service the growing Asia-Pacific markets. Other research initiatives were considered on basic background chemistry and how to develop this for the canning industry.

Automotive OEM Paint Segment

The automotive paint segment consisted of paint sales made to automobile manufacturers for use in their assembly plants. Worldwide, this segment represented 5% of the paint market. Major markets were North America (31%), Europe (32%), and Japan (26%). Leading competitors were PPG, BASF, Kansai, Nippon, DuPont, Hoechst, and ICI, in order of importance.

ICI's market share was about 6% worldwide, ranking it number 7 out of 8 international players. Most of its sales were in Europe, followed by the Asia-Pacific area (exclusive of Japan) and North America, and major local markets in Malaysia, Australia, and Canada. ICI was considered technically good but commercially weak in this segment. The company was a leader in the initial development of electrolytic paint and in the development of waterbased top coat paints (Aquabase) for automotive users. The latest product was first introduced by GM in Canada and was now being introduced by Volvo in Sweden. Other European manufacturers were testing it, and ICI had granted a license to a Japanese company.

"This is an incestuous industry," remarked John Thompson, ICI Paints' Planning Manager. The customer base was largely globally operating companies and technologically very demanding. The technical service requirements of customers required paint suppliers to station technical service personnel permanently on location. As a result, the automotive companies preferred suppliers located at their doorsteps. This led to scattering factories close to assembly plants. In the US, major paint companies would typically have several plants. Trends were away from multiple sourcing, which had kept local players alive, towards single sourcing and worldwide deals. Typically, a customer maintained a major supplier each for top coats and base coats with a second supplier for smaller volume applications "to keep the big ones honest."

This segment was technically very demanding. PPG had reached segment leadership by developing electrolytic techniques key for the important base coating of car bodies. The initial development was actually made by ICI, but it was PPG which had made a commercial success out of the invention. At that time, PPG occasionally achieved single-source status through the installation of "hole-in-the-wall" plants where the company was producing adjacent to the paint shops of the assembly plant.

Although the particular paint applications such as color, etc., were developed for each customer, a substantial part of the basic research had worldwide applications. Technical spin-offs were also possible for other paint segments such as the refinish sector (with modifications in formulations due to the different paint application methods) and for industrial components in areas such as the domestic appliance industry. This was one of the reasons why many players stayed in this segment despite low profitability or losses.

ICI had a very narrow geographic base in this segment and currently lacked platforms for major expansion. As a result, ICI engaged in a joint venture with DuPont called IDAC on a 50:50 basis to supply the Western European automotive market. DuPont had most of its automotive paint business in the US and was therefore relatively weak in Europe. DuPont's area of strength was in the top coat business, with GM and Ford as major customers in the US. The IDAC goal was to reach a 20% market share in Europe during the early 1990s.

Automotive Refinish Paint Segment

The refinish segment included paints and coatings for repairing automobiles. The segment accounted for 4% of world sales and had the highest price per liter (£3.34). It was considered the most profitable paint segment. North America accounted for 36% of the world market, followed by Europe (30%), and Asia-Pacific (25%).

Only 10 paint manufacturers competed significantly in the refinish sector. Among those, only Sherwin-Williams of the US and Rock of Japan did not also compete in the automotive OEM market. No new competitor had entered since the 1950s.

The world leader was BASF as a result of its recent acquisition of Inmont in the US, followed by DuPont and ICI. ICI was the largest refinish supplier outside the US. Its Autocolor brand led in the UK and was well known in Europe. In France, the company was the leader with its Valentine brand. ICI had a color inventory of some 30,000 formulae to match the stock colors of virtually all vehicle manufacturers. ICI's matching capability was developed in the UK market where a wide variety of car models were on the road following the decline of the local UK car industry.

Customers were largely small paint shops who needed quick and frequent deliveries, typically on a daily basis. Paint manufacturers supplied their customers with mixing schemes through local distributors who would combine the basic colors and shades with solvents to obtain the correct color match. There were some 10,000 different shades and some 60 different colors to select from. For ICI, this resulted in some 30,000 different formulae, partly as a result of different application techniques for the same shades and colors. A recent trend was in the direction of color mixing at the end-user location using color systems supplied by the paint manufacturer. Recently, ICI had placed a computerized management system at the disposal of its customers.

To compete in this business, a company had to have access to the color and paint shops of the car manufacturers to obtain the needed information. Automobile manufacturers wanted to make sure that their customers could get their cars repaired wherever they were marketed. As an example, a company like Toyota was interested in worldwide coverage. Refinish paint manufacturers profited if they could have access to all car manufacturers, wherever they were located, so that they could supply the widest possible color range in any geographic market.

Powder Paint Segment

Powder paints was the fastest growing segment and represented an alternative technology for traditional wet paint rather than a particular application segment. Growing 10–20% annually, the segment had attracted many large companies as well as smaller suppliers. Leaders were International-Courtaulds (UK), Ferro (US), ICI, and DSM (Netherlands).

Powder coatings were a precisely formulated mixture of pigment and resin which were sprayed using electrostatic spray guns. The sprayed item, a metal object, was then heated for about 10 minutes to cure the surface. Coatings had been developed for heat resistance or chemical resistance. The major benefits for users were the reduced emissions such as solvents used with wet paints and the reduced need for waste disposal. Major user groups were the automotive component suppliers, the metal furniture industry, and domestic appliance manufacturers. Powder paint could conceivably substitute up to 50% of the paint being applied to metal. In Europe, where the product was pioneered, the substitution already amounted to about 20%, compared to about 10% in the US, an amount that was, however, growing rapidly.

While the technology itself had become basic, there was room to develop many applications. ICI had selected some specific applications for further development, such as domestic appliances and architectural components. ICI had concluded a joint venture with Nippon Oil & Fats of Japan in Malaysia. About half of ICI's powder volume was in the US, about 40% in Europe, and the rest spread over many countries. In the US, ICI was tied for first place with Morton, but was only sixth in Europe.

General Industrial Paint Segment

Some £250 million of ICI Paints' business was part of the general industrial paint category, which included general industrial liquid paints, wood finishes, adhesives, ink, and others. Two-thirds of this segment was allied in some way to its four core business areas, such as adhesives in the US or metal can printing. Another part consisted of stand-alone businesses, not necessarily connected to core sectors, such as inks for screen printing in Germany. In these segments, ICI did not compete consistently throughout the world and had only selected local pockets of excellence.

STRATEGY

ICI Paints aimed at world leadership and profitable growth. The company intended to concentrate on its key paint businesses on a global basis and wanted to exploit particular regional opportunities in the EC and Asia-Pacific regions. ICI believed that a commitment to R&D and innovation was an essential part of industry leadership.

Organizationally, ICI aspired to become a marketing driven organization that was quality and customer focused, health and safety conscious, and environmentally responsible.

Organization

ICI management believed it was essential to have a global organization and management structure which would be both global and territory centered, support R&D centers of excellence in certain locations, and maximize resources and synergy between businesses, operations, and locations.

ICI Paints was organized both along geographic and business lines (*refer to Exhibit 6*). Reporting to the PEO were three regional heads (Chief Executives) for Europe, North America, and Asia-Pacific. Each Chief Executive had P&L responsibility for the entire paint business in his area. The North American Chief Executive was also the head of Glidden, ICI Paints' major US operating unit.

Reporting to each Chief Executive were several managers with country or territorial responsibility, called TGMs (Territorial General Managers) and BAGMs (short for Business Area Managers) for the four core sectors: decorative, can, automotive refinish and OEM, and powder. In some situations, BAGMs were identical with TGMs. In general, P&L results were a joint responsibility of BAGMs and TGMs.

At the territory or country level, BAGMs existed for the core business areas to the extent that each country had business in each of the four core sectors. Each territory also had other paint businesses. The percentage of sales in the latter category varied across territories, with higher percentages reported for some developing markets in Asia and lower percentages in the developed markets of Europe and North America.

Decision Making

Major decisions were always discussed and decided by the International Business Team (IBT) chaired by Herman Scopes, its PEO Eight executives were members of the IBT, including the PEO and the three Chief Executives. The ICI Paints Group was led by Herman Scopes as its PEO and the seven members of the International Business Team (IBT). Part of the IBT were the three Chief Executives for North America, Europe, and Asia/Pacific/Australia regions, as well as four other executives with either functional or segment responsibility (*refer to **Exhibit 7***). The IBT met six to eight times per year at various locations.

Executives were nominated to the IBT because of their ability to contribute broadly to the development of the ICI Paints Group rather than their specialties or specific skills. Once part of the IBT, members were assigned "portfolios" based on their own talents and experience, occasionally resulting in changes when the personnel constellation changed in the IBT.

An important aspect of the way ICI Paints operated was its use of International Leaders (ILs). IL positions existed for each of its four core business areas (decorative, can coatings, automotive, and powder) as well as for five functional areas: finance, information technology, operations, R&D, and management development. The ILs for three of these five areas were members of the IBT.

The ILs of the core sectors had the roles of facilitators or coordinators. These international leaders did not have P&L responsibility. However, they were responsible for the development of global strategies for each of their assigned core sectors. Powder was coordinated out of the US, decorative out of Europe (by the Chief Executive Europe), and automotive and can coatings from Europe (head of that sector for Europe).

Strategies were developed at the business level by the international leaders and their teams, and were then proposed to the International Business Team.

COORDINATING CORE BUSINESS SEGMENTS

The strategy making and coordination process differed considerably across the four core business areas.

The *decorative world strategy* consisted of three major elements. First, ICI Paints was to pursue quality leadership in all markets where the company was competing. It was understood that this meant setting the pace in the sector and pursuing a premium price. Second, there was to be a drive towards running a world brand, Dulux, the only world consumer paint brand in existence. This goal included having a consistent role for Dulux as the aspirational brand in all ICI decorative paint markets. Third, ICI was to use the fact that it was the largest paint producer worldwide and should thus be able to maximize its resources in key functional areas.

Coordination was hampered by the fact that local operating companies considered their competitive situations to be unique. Glidden in the US did not compete in the premium sector at all and its market share was only about 10%, compared to 40% in the UK, or the three-brand product line in Australia. To launch Dulux as a premium brand in the US would entail a marketing investment of about $50 million over 4–5 years with a 7-year payback period for a required 5% market share. Glidden executives were not convinced that this strategy would be successful in the US.

Due to the differences encountered, the IL for the sector had pursued a "consultative mode," meeting about twice annually with the key executives from the various operating companies. In addition, the IL had frequent individual meetings with operating executives and territorial managers.

In the *automotive sector*, the IL positions for the OEM and refinish segments were combined. For refinishes, where ICI had major positions in Europe and Australia only, the strategy was fairly heavily led from the center. Involved were key managers from Europe and Australia with others "mostly along for the ride." A major point of discussion was ICI's future strategy in the US where it had no position at that time. Glidden executives were very interested in entering the refinish sector. However, a "greenfield approach" (i.e., starting up with no previous capability) was considered difficult, and, as yet, no ready candidates for acquisition existed.

In the automotive, OEM segment, the IL role consisted largely of outside contacts with DuPont, ICI's partner for Europe, and frequent negotiations with Japanese companies on technology transfers that might result in obtaining business for ICI from Japanese transplant operations in Canada, Australia, Southeast Asia, India, and Pakistan, all countries where ICI was active in the OEM business.

Coordination in the *can coatings sector* was very close and involved a formal business area review team under the leadership of the IL for can coatings. The team consisted of the key players worldwide in ICI Paints, who met several times each year. A major challenge here was to devise a strategy in view of the increased concentration among customers. Despite ICI's leading market position, the company could not dictate prices. The resulting squeeze on margins had reduced profitability, and a new strategy would have to be devised to lead the company out of this "commodity hole."

For the *general industrial paint sector*, no IL had been appointed. These businesses were led in various ways. Businesses that were closely affiliated with one of the four core areas were attached to the IL teams of those areas. Others were left under the direction of the territorial management. Some businesses not directly tied to the paint business were kept as long as they were meeting required profitability targets.

Coordinating at the Functional Level

The ILs for the five key functions undertook their roles in different ways. For all functional ILs, however, the objectives were similar. ICI wanted to transfer skills, experience, and best practice around its group operating companies. It also wished to accelerate the innovation process (as distinctly different from the invention process). And finally, the desire, as elsewhere in the business, was to simplify and focus on operational aspects, not just "spin wheels."

For the finance area, this largely involved the enforcement of corporate guidelines and practice around the Paint Group. For information technology (IT), the mission was still vague. One of the jobs was to encourage and promote the use of IT where appropriate, often convincing Chief Executives to make the necessary investments. The coordinating activities had led to a policy of using DEC equipment for technical applications, and IBM for commercial and operational tasks.

In operations, efforts were undertaken to spread efficient production procedures across the group. Here, ICI relied on Glidden's skill as a low-cost producer.

In the R&D area, there had been a long-held conviction that technology was driven by the automotive and industrial market, such as coil coatings. ICI Paints was now moving the emphasis of its R&D brainpower to new fields such as decorative, can coatings, and powders, which was beginning to yield exciting results.

Coordinating the various functions was a challenging task since many of its operating companies had different corporate origins, were acquired from various sources, and represented different nationalities and cultures.

Current Organizational Issues for ICI Paints Worldwide

Over the past years, ICI's organization had undergone considerable changes. Aside from its territorial focus, it introduced the idea of ILs for segments and functions. However, the company encountered a major obstacle in the fact that much of its production assets were shared. It was believed that some 50 of its 64 plants were common sites for a number of paint products and segments. This meant that the business segments were largely responsible for business volume, but the BAGMs did not have full asset responsibility. At this time, not more than 75% of the company assets could be clearly attributed to individual business lines.

Aside from the organization issues and the challenges faced by each of the four core sectors, ICI Paints needed to leverage the benefit of its being the largest global player into a superior financial performance.

OPPORTUNITIES FOR ICI PAINTS

ICI Paints faced a number of opportunities in different geographic areas and various paint segments. These opportunities had to be seen in relationship to its own resources. "Although ICI is a very large corporation with considerable financial resources, it is not realistic to expect that we can do everything," said Thompson. "We still need to keep in mind that our profitability, while on a par with the best paint competitors, is below average for ICI as a whole." Some typical opportunities (not an exhaustive list, however) were:

ICI Paints' Opportunities in Japan

ICI Paints, despite its world leadership, did not have a direct presence in the Japanese market. For some time, the company had been considering an opportunity to go beyond licensing but was unsure about the appropriate entry strategy. Considered were approaches ranging from exporting to joint ventures, making an acquisition, or even a greenfield start-up. Furthermore, which paint business to launch first in Japan was an unresolved question. Another question was how to relate any operation to the rest of ICI's business in Japan.

ICI Paints had virtually no direct sales in Japan. From time to time, decorative paint had been supplied by its Southeast Asian factories, for sale as Japanese brands. Dulux Australia had supplied solid emulsion to be sold by Nippon Paints in the small Japanese DIY market.

The company's current presence in Japan consisted of two full-time ICI Japan employees—one long-serving and performing a liaison job with licensees plus color standards collection from Japanese automakers for ICI's refinish business, and the other recently appointed as a technical coordinator for submission of can coatings products for approval by the can manufacturers.

ICI had also concluded a series of licensing agreements, some granting technology to Japanese companies and others gaining access to Japanese technology. ICI granted automotive OEM licensees to Kansai, NOF, and Shinto, while obtaining licensees in the same area from Kansai and NOF. Furthermore, a powder coatings license was granted to Shinto while an industrial electrocoat license was obtained from the same company. A flexible packaging refinish license was granted to Rock which in turn granted ICI a refinish license. A can coatings license, due to expire in 1991, was also granted to Dai Nippon Inks.

ICI Paints considered it inopportune to enter the general paints business. Instead, an entry through one of its key segments was viewed as more promising. Best opportunities appeared in can coatings and powder paints.

Powder paints were viewed as having a major opportunity in Japan due to the high concentration of metal based industries (automobile, appliances) dominated by firms such as Matsushita, Hitachi, and Mitsubishi.

The market for powder coatings was estimated at about 18,000 tons, or 8% of the world market. This was equal to the UK market but smaller than the market for powder coatings for Italy. The cost of building a factory was estimated at about $3 million with break-even volume of about 1,500 tons annually. Some $500,000–750,000 of the original investment might be saved if the investment could be made together with ICI Films, another ICI international business, because the same buildings could be used. However, there were no production or marketing synergies between films and powder coatings.

In the can coatings sector, the opportunity was also tempting. Japan was a major market for metal cans, particularly in the beverage sector with three leading brewers, Kirin, Ashahi, and Sapporo, as well as international soft drink firms such as Coca-Cola and Pepsi Cola. The soft drink firms were global companies which were already indirect customers of ICI Paints elsewhere.

The Japanese can making market was dominated by Toyo Seikan, the second largest can maker in the world, Mitsubishi, and Daiwa. They supplied coated cans directly to major users. Can users, such as beverage companies, often looked for suppliers who could serve them on a worldwide basis. Can coatings were typically formulated to the specific requirements of a customer.

The Japanese market for can coatings was estimated at some 70 million liters, or about 17.5% of the world market. A greenfield investment would cost about $15 million. The annual break-even point depended considerably on the particular product mix achieved. However, annual operating costs would be about $4 million with another $1 million required for technical support. This would result in a break-even volume of about 5 million liters. On the other hand, licensing fees averaged about 3% of sales with a minimum annual payment of $150,000.

ICI Paints needed a presence in Japan as part of its strategy to reach its goal of 40% market share worldwide in the can coatings sector. Major risks were a drain on critical resources such as human resources, capital funds, and the need for "patient money" to do well in Japan.

Present suppliers for can coatings included Dainippon, an old ICI Paints licensee of an earlier generation of coatings technology. Market leaders were Toyo Ink and Dainippon (DNIC), which accounted for about 50% and 40% of the Japanese market, respectively. In the present Japanese market, ICI Paints could compete with superior technology. No other foreign company maintained a base in Japan for can coatings.

The major question remained on how to proceed. A joint-venture with Toyo Sekan appeared possible. It was not clear, however, how to develop a local technology base, how to do the manufacturing and staffing. Another issue was how fast to proceed.

ICI Paints' Decorative Opportunities in the US

ICI Paints had undertaken a recent attempt to investigate the possibilities of entering the premium paint segment in the US. The difficulty of this strategy was underlined by the fact that such a premium segment was very small in the US, amounting to about 12% of the market for DIY paint compared to the UK where it represented almost 40% of the decorative paint market. In the US, regional companies such as Benjamin Moore and Pratt & Lambert were leaders in that segment.

Glidden, acquired in 1986, had pursued a low-price strategy that had resulted in enormous success. Sometimes described as "pile it high and price it low," Glidden was able to expand its business from just 4% market share to 17% currently in the DIY market, expanding its brand into national distribution and reaching the leading brand position in the US market. By contrast, Sears (supplied by De Soto) had dropped from 30% to just 16% market share in the same 15-year time period. Furthermore, Glidden also achieved a 10% share in the contractor market aimed at painters and professionals.

At first, ICI Paints in the UK believed it might pave the way for a launch of a premium decorative brand in the US by sending one of its own people to the US operation. The assignment was to investigate if ICI's premium brand Dulux might be launched in the US at some time in the future. Actually selected by Glidden, this British executive was soon isolated and "cocooned," which rendered his situation untenable, and no progress was achieved in resolving the issue whether a premium strategy might work in the US. "It was like sending a 'Brit' to the 'Colonials'," commented Herman Scopes, ICI Paints PEO. "This experience taught us that some other approach would have to be chosen."

ICI Paints set up a study team consisting of both Glidden and ICI Paints executives. Scopes thought it might be helpful to "park" the idea of a position on global branding around Dulux and to look at the market more objectively. The output of the study was to be fed into a global review of ICI's decorative paint business. In the meantime, ICI's Canadian operation had agreed to launch a premium brand under the Dulux name.

Automotive Refinish Opportunity in the United States

The automotive refinish segment was a very stable market with only four major players: DuPont, BASF/Inmont, PPG, and Sherwin-Williams. These top four accounted for 90% of the market. This segment was highly profitable, with return on sales ranging from 18–24% and return on net assets (RONAs) of around 40%. The market consisted of some 60,000 body shops supplied through local jobbers via company-owned warehouses. Warehouse distributors played a decreasingly important role as they were usually not specialized enough.

The refinish segment in the US was subject to a number of changes. One major factor was the increase in car imports into the US, which tended to increase the range of products requiring refinishing. New top coat technologies adopted by car manufacturers required new refinishes and continued technological improvements on the part of the paint manufacturers. More sophisticated body shop equipment, such as controlled environments to counter solvent emission into the air, constantly forced adjustment in the refinish formulae. Furthermore, there was a trend towards supplying body shops with color mixing schemes rather than factory-packaged colors, shifting the mixing forward into the body shop as each job required it.

In the opinion of John Thompson, ICI Paints Planning Manager, key to success in this segment was color performance, followed by technical service to body shops, then environmental friendliness, training opportunities for paint sprayers and, finally, delivery service. Price was viewed as much less important than any of the above five criteria.

Several theoretical entry options existed. The first was through a major acquisition. "Who would sell such a beautiful business?" John Thompson asked. Acquisitions of a smaller player would not be big enough to make a difference. A greenfield entry was likely to be slow. AKZO, the large Dutch paint manufacturer, had been working at it for ten years and had still only achieved a 3% market share. There was an opportunity to enter regionally with expansion to national distribution later on.

The financial resources required to develop this segment were considerable. Depending on the approach chosen, the pace of expansion, the company's skill and success, a maximum negative accumulated cash flow of about $30–50 million for a national introduction would have to be considered. Thompson considered the necessary volume for break-even to be 5% market share of a significant regional market and 4% market share nationally.

SELECTING A COURSE FOR THE FUTURE

ICI Paints management approached the future with some confidence. 1989 had been another good year for the paints business with total sales of £1,628 million and a trading profit of £100 million. Volume in the major decorative DIY markets of the US and the UK were affected by the depressed housing markets in both countries. Competitively, however, Glidden was able to assume clear brand leadership for decorative paints in the US. Dulux Australia enjoyed record profits following the integration of an acquisition. Sales in Southeast Asia achieved strong growth with the successful introduction of new paint product lines and a joint venture in Hong Kong to develop business with China PRC.

In the can coatings segment, ICI was able to increase its world market share. Its position in Europe was strengthened through an acquisition in Spain (Quimilac SA). Powder paint continued to experience strong growth in Europe.

EXHIBIT 1
World paint industry profile.

By Region

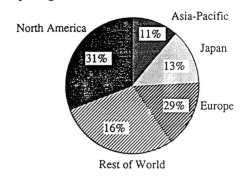

Volume 12,000 ML

EXHIBIT 2
World paint volume by market segment.

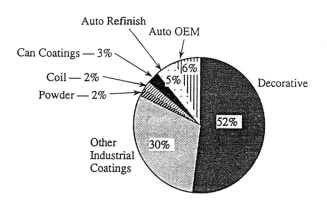

EXHIBIT 3

ICI paints territorial spread.

ICI PAINTS MANUFACTURING COMPANIES

Australia	Malaysia	Taiwan
Canada	Mexico	Thailand
Eire	New Zealand	United Kingdom
Fiji	Pakistan	Uruguay
France	Papua New Guinea	USA
India	Singapore	West Germany
Italy	Spain	
Madagascar	Sri Lanka	

ICI MINORITY HOLDINGS

Botswana	Indonesia	South Africa
Malawi	Nigeria	Zimbabwe

COMPANIES MANUFACTURING UNDER LICENSE

Columbia	Korea	Turkey
Cyprus	Portugal	Venezuela
Japan	Saudi Arabia	Yemen
Jordan	Sudan	
Kenya	Trinidad	

EXHIBIT 4
ICI Paints financial performance
1985–1989.

ICI Paints Financial Performance
1985 - 1989

Turnover £m

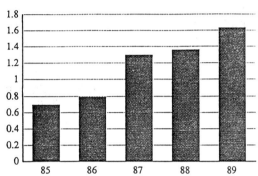

Trading profit

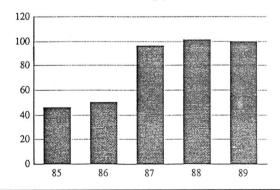

EXHIBIT 5

ICI volume by market segment.

Volume 800 ML

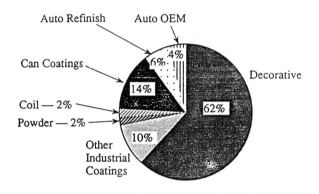

EXHIBIT 6

Organization chart.

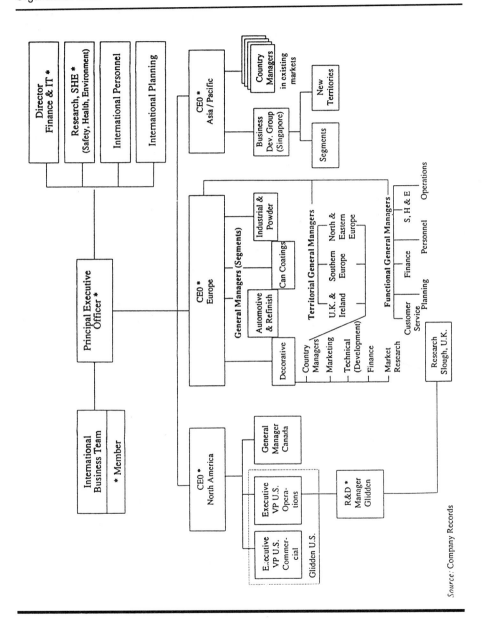

EXHIBIT 7

Members of the International Business Team (IBT).

HERMAN SCOPES	PEO ICI PAINTS
John Dumble	Chief Executive North America, President Glidden
Doug Curlewis	Chief Executive Europe International Leader Decorative Paint
Richard Stillwell	Chief Executive Asia-Pacific/Australia
John Danzeisen	Finance Director International Leader Powder International Leader Finance Function International Leader IT Function
Alex Ramig	International Leader R&D
Brian Letchford	International Leader Automotive Refinish and OEM (designated International Leader Can)
Quintin Knight	International Leader Can Coatings (retiring in March 1990)
Other International Leaders not part of the IBT:	
June Thomason	Operations Manager, Glidden International Leader Operations
Ian Cope	International Leader Management Development

ICI PAINTS (B): CONSIDERING A GLOBAL PRODUCT ORGANIZATION

In the spring of 1993, Herman Scopes, Chief Executive Officer (CEO) of ICI Paints, was having a discussion with the members of the company's International Business Team (IBT) about how the paint industry had changed over the past few years.

> The passage of time has increasingly impressed upon us the rate at which markets are becoming international and global in nature. Over the past few years, ICI Paints has become an agglomeration of companies; global, but not necessarily globally managed. Moreover, as a result of past practices, we have an organizational structure that is, for the most part, based on geographic regions, not global product lines. As I look at the present business environment, however, I wonder whether that is the best arrangement and how the remainder of the IBT views the situation. Specifically, is our regional management structure, which has served us well in the past, appropriate for the rest of the decade?

In contrast to regional executives, who managed several of the company's products in one or more countries, some felt that ICI Paints should appoint worldwide business leaders with global product line responsibility. Doing so, however, raised all kinds of questions—such as the ability to maintain a local image in, say North America and Asia, with a product manager based in the UK. Adopting an organization based on global product lines also raised communication issues; would people feel able to relate to a product line organization that was worldwide in scope? Despite the potential problems, a global product organization offered distinct advantages in terms of allocating resources, deciding priorities, and making investment decisions. For Herman Scopes and his colleagues on the IBT, the question was whether the company should move from a regional to a global product organization and if so, how.

IMPERIAL CHEMICAL INDUSTRIES PLC

The Imperial Chemical Industries (ICI) was formed in 1926 by the merger of Great Britain's four major chemical companies: Nobel Industries Limited, the United Alkali Company, the British Dyestuffs Corporation, and Brunner, Mond,

Case, "ICI Paints (B): Considering Global Product Organization GM-558" prepared by Professor Jean-Pierre Jeannet. Copyright © 1993 IMD, the International Institute for Management Development, Lausanne, Switzerland. IMD retains all rights. Not to be reproduced or used without written permission directly from IMD, Lausanne, Switzerland.

501

and Company Limited. At that time, the newly formed ICI was divided into nine groups: alkalis, cellulose products, dyestuffs, explosives, fertilizers, general chemicals, rubberized fabrics, lime, and metals. Beginning in the 1930s, ICI's dyemakers used their knowledge of chemistry to diversify into plastics, specialty chemicals, and pharmaceuticals—higher margin products that later became ICI's core businesses. In 1991, those core businesses were structured along product and geographic lines into four principal areas: Bioscience Products, Specialty Chemicals and Materials, Industrial Chemicals, and Regional Businesses. In the same year, the ICI Group reported a turnover of $22.1 billion, profits of $1.8 billion, and employed 128,600 persons around the world.

Sometime in the early 1990s, executives began considering breaking up ICI into smaller companies. In doing so, it was proposed, new companies would be better prepared to devote the amount of management attention and resources needed in an industry where the return on investment had gradually declined over the preceding 20 years. Had the reorganization occurred in 1992, ICI would have been split into two companies; one was to retain the company name with interests in industrial chemicals, paints, and explosives, while the other company—with the proposed name of Zeneca—was to include drugs, pesticides, seeds, and specialty chemicals. (***Table 1*** *gives financial data on how the two firms would have looked if they had been split in 1992.*)

Organization of ICI Paints

In 1991, ICI Paints was the largest paint manufacturer in the world and accounted for $2.9 billion, or 13%, of all sales within the ICI Group of companies. In the same year, ICI Paints operated manufacturing plants in 24 countries, had licensees in an additional 16 countries, all of which manufactured and marketed coatings in the company's main application segments: decorative, automotive

| TABLE 1 | 1992 ICI–ZENECA TURNOVER & OPERATING PROFIT (LOSS) |

TURNOVER ($MILLION)	ZENECA	OPERATING PROFIT (LOSS) ($MILLION)
228	Trading & Misc.	(18.2)
1429	Specialties	39.5
1961	Agrochemicals & Seeds	129.2
2447	Pharmaceuticals	741.8
	NEW ICI	
2827	Materials	(38)
5396	Industrial Chemicals	(25.8)
2052	Regional Businesses	12.2
836	Explosives	89.7
2402	Paints	174.8

OEM, automotive refinish, can, powder, and coil. (*Refer to **Exhibit 1** for a list of ICI Paints manufacturing companies, minority holdings, and licensees.*)

Like other multinationals, ICI Paints traditionally structured its operations on the basis of individual markets. That is, executives had profit and loss responsibility for the full range of ICI products within a given market. Following the acquisitions of the 1980s, however, the management of ICI Paints felt that its customers could be better served by managers with a multi-country product line responsibility. To this end, ICI brought the management of Mexico, Canada, and the United States together under a regional CEO who reported to Herman Scopes in the UK. Similarly, regional constructs were devised for Europe and Asia. By 1990, the array of ICI Paints' subsidiaries and licensees was organized along geographic and business lines (*as shown in **Exhibit 2**).

Within their respective regions, each Regional CEO had profit and loss responsibility for the entire paint business. Also, within each region and reporting to the Regional CEO, ICI Paints had country managers, Territorial General Managers (TGMs), and Business Area General Managers (BAGMs). As the name implied, country and territorial managers supervised more than one of ICI Paints' product lines on a geographic basis, while Business Area General Managers concentrated on the products of only one of ICI Paints' application segments. Because the latter were not required unless an individual segment reached a certain size, Territorial General and Business Area General Managers were sometimes one and the same person. In those areas where both existed, profit and loss results were a shared responsibility.

At ICI Paints, major decisions were always discussed and decided upon by an International Business Team (IBT), chaired by Herman Scopes. Additional members included the three Regional CEOs, and four other executives with either functional or segment responsibility (*as shown in **Exhibit 3***). Typically, executives were nominated to the IBT because of their ability to contribute to the development of the ICI Paints Group rather than their specialties or specific skills. Once part of the IBT, members were assigned "portfolios" based on their own talents and experience. Occasionally, these responsibilities changed when there was a change in the composition of the IBT.

Yet another important aspect of the way ICI Paints operated was its use of International Leaders (ILs), persons drawn from each of the company's core business areas as well as three out of five of the following functional areas: finance, information technology, operations, research & development, and management development. Typically, International Leaders drawn from the core businesses acted as facilitators or coordinators. And though they did not have profit and loss responsibility, International Leaders were responsible for developing global strategies in their respective application segment. Most recently, the company had appointed a worldwide Safety, Health, and Environment (SHE) executive whose presence as an IL increased management's awareness of environmental issues.

Though the strategy making and coordination processes differed among ICI's application segments, in general, strategies were developed at the business, or operational, level by the International Leaders and their teams. In turn, these strategies were proposed to the International Business Team which met six to eight times per year in various locations.

THE WORLD PAINT INDUSTRY

In 1991, the world paints and coatings industry was valued at $46 billion at suppliers' prices, corresponding to a volume of 13.5 billion liters. Generally speaking, the industry included a range of products such as pigmented coatings, or paints, as well as unpigmented coatings like stain and varnish, used to decorate and/or protect different substrates. Analysts and participants alike divided coatings sales into two main classes: decorative or architectural paints, used in decorating buildings and homes, and industrial coatings, which provided functional properties and added value to manufactured goods. Typically, decorative coatings were high volume, low priced, and commanded low margins. Industrial coatings, on the other hand, were high priced and focused on niche markets. (*Refer to* **Exhibits 4 and 5,** *respectively, for a breakdown of world paint sales by market sector and region.*)

Decorative Paints

By far, decorative coatings was the largest single segment in the industry. Overall, the potential demand for decorative coatings in any country was influenced by climate, construction methods, and lifestyle, together with the collective successes of the local paint industry in presenting its offering to private and professional consumers in a readily accessible and attractive form. From this baseline, variations in demand were driven primarily by changes in real disposable income and in real interest rates, the latter already being an indicator of the level of construction activity and house moves.

In the decorative segment, paint sales were further classified according to two major user groups, each of which accounted for roughly half the sales in the segment. As the name implied, the professional market consisted of professional painters, further subdivided into restorers, new housing contractors, and commercial contractors. Sales to the professional market were either through small independent stores or branches of manufacturers. The second segment consisted of individual Do-It-Yourself (DIY) users who bought paint through a variety of retail stores.

RETAILING

Traditionally, decorative paints had been sold in small shops or hardware stores, but, recent developments in the DIY segment were substantially changing the retailing process. In recent years, in fact, the DIY segment had increased its share to slightly over half the decorative market. In part, the increased share reflected a change in the way consumers viewed paint. Though once considered a lowly commodity, at the start of the 1990s, domestic paint was beginning to be seen as a household fashion accessory, adding value to the object it coated. In other words, the market for household paint, like that for beans, soap, and fish fingers, had become retail led and susceptible to all the pressures which afflicted grocery producers. While the supermarket's rise to eminence in food and packaged goods took 30 years, the storming of the trade by DIY superstores happened in only 10 years.

Worldwide, these developments were most evident the in Anglo-Saxon countries—the UK, the US, and Australia, to a lesser degree in Northern Europe, and considerably less in Southern Europe. To clarify, in the late 1960s and early 1970s, specialist store chains like High Street in the UK and Sherwin-Williams in the US replaced most small shops. Thereafter, variety department stores and supermarkets such as Woolworth, Sears, JC Penney, and Montgomery Ward in the US, and Tesco in the UK took the lead in retailing decorative paints; at one point, it was reported that Sears had reached a 30% US market share through its own branding. In concert with the growing popularity of variety department stores and supermarkets, however, DIY superstores—i.e., sheds—soon gained importance. In the US, for example, the opening of stores like Home Depot cut Sears' market share in half. In the UK, the number of specialist stores declined from about 20,000 in 1979 to some 11,000 in 1988, and large DIY chains such as B&Q, Texas, and Pay Less accounted for 65% of all sector sales.

Throughout this retailing cycle, the marketing task of the paint manufacturer changed at each turn. In the first cycle, independent distributors and wholesalers gave way to manufacturer-owned stores and outlets. When the chains took over, increased buying power led to bargaining over shelf space. Thereafter, the supermarket or departmentalized variety stores brought private labels. Finally, the super stores narrowed the brand choice by typically carrying just one advertised brand and their own private label, and the reduced number of brands led to the disappearance of many retail paint suppliers.

In 1991, the decorative segment accounted for 50% of the value of all paint sold in the world, or roughly 6.67 billion liters. Geographically, North America accounted for 30% of these sales; Western Europe, 32%; Japan, 9%; and the rest of the world, 29%. One analyst pointed out that, despite the size of Japan's population and economy, decorative paints accounted for a surprisingly small share of the country's coatings sales. He attributed this to the fact that traditional, domestic architecture in Japan, with its paper partitions, meant that millions of square feet of walls were not painted.

Industrial Paints

In contrast to decorative coatings, demand for industrial coatings depended on a country's manufacturing profile, vehicles vs electronics or furniture vs textiles, for example. That is, industrial coatings tended to have more specialized uses than decorative coatings and included paint for cars, ships, planes, boats, white goods, cans, and thousands of other applications. In this segment, properties such as corrosion, abrasion resistance, and the ability to withstand high temperature or wet weather were important purchase criteria. To monitor the market, participants further classified industrial coatings according to application: automotive OEM (original equipment manufacturers), automotive refinish, can coatings, powder, and coil. Each segment had its own particular customer group and usually required its own technology and application base.

AUTOMOTIVE OEM

The automotive paint segment consisted of paint sales to automobile manufacturers—usually global companies—for use in their assembly plants. In this segment, users applied coatings by emersing an entire car body in a "paint bath" in which the paint carried an electric charge, opposite from that of the car body, resulting in a corrosion resistant finish. Because of the service requirements associated with maintaining electrolytic paint baths, as well as the desire to provide a consistent color wherever cars were assembled, automotive OEM customers preferred paint suppliers that were both local and global in nature. That is, customers favored suppliers able to provide a consistent color around the world yet, at the same time, deliver local service. As a result, paint manufacturers tended to locate their factories close to automotive assembly plants and stationed their personnel permanently at automotive sties. When purchasing coatings, automotive OEM customers usually maintained a major supplier for each top coat and base coat, and a second supplier for smaller volume applications "to keep the big ones honest." In 1991, the volume of paint sold to car manufacturers was roughly 791 million liters, or 6% of the industry volume, with sales distributed among North America, 22%; Western Europe, 27%; and Japan, 34%.

AUTOMOBILE VEHICLE REFINISHING

The refinish segment included paints and coatings for repairing automobiles. Although the volume of paint sold in this market was smaller than the automotive OEM segment, it was a larger segment by value due to its higher sales price and was, in fact, the most profitable segment in the industry. Refinish customers were primarily small paint shops which needed quick and frequent deliveries, usually on a daily basis. Typically, paint manufacturers supplied these customers with mixing schemes through local distributors, who combined basic colors and shades with solvents to obtain a correct color match. Because there were some 10,000 different shades and some 60 different colors to select from, a refinish company had to have access to the color and paint shops of car manufacturers. And, because automobile makers wanted to ensure that, if necessary, car owners could get their cars refinished wherever they were purchased, car manufacturers were interested in worldwide coverage. Not surprisingly, refinish paint manufacturers profited when they had access to all locations of a car maker, then they could supply the widest possible color range in any geographic market. Worldwide, the refinish segment accounted for 5% of industry sales, which were distributed among North America, 39%; Western Europe, 23%; and Japan, 13%.

CAN COATINGS

As the name implied, can coatings were applied inside tin and aluminum cans to make them corrosion resistant for use as food or beverage containers. In 1991, can coating sales were concentrated among four groups: Continental Can, Pechiney-Triangle (which included former American and National Can), Carnaud-MetalBox, and Crown Cork and Seal, as well as their licensees, all of which operated canning lines around the globe. Because these canning companies were expected to provide a consistent taste for globally marketed products such as Coca-Cola, they in turn expected their suppliers to provide local service at each of their canning sites. In 1991, the can coating segment accounted for only 3% of the world paint market, with sales distributed among North America, 41%; Europe, 27%, and Japan, 16%.

POWDER PAINTS

In contrast to other coatings, powder paints were 100% solids in the form of pigmented resin powders, usually electrostatically sprayed onto a grounded metal substrate and then cured by heat. Because powder paint could be applied in layers of 50–60 microns—five times as thick as wet paint, it was far more durable, retained its color longer, and resisted abrasions for up to 20 years. As a result, powder paint was ideal for coating domestic appliances such as washing machines or refrigerators, as well as metal surfaces on the outside of buildings which were subject to extreme weather conditions. Despite these advantages, powder paint had two limitations. First, because powder paint left thick layers, it could not be used in applications such as can coating where thin layers of coating were a must. Second, because powder coatings had to be cured by heat, there was an upper limit to the size of an object which could be coated.

Other than the functional properties they imparted to a given substrate, powder paints had a major advantage over solvent borne paints in that they released no toxic fumes into the atmosphere. As well as reducing emissions, powder coatings avoided the problem of waste disposal, as any stray powder was collected and reused. By contrast, wet paint always had a residual waste which had to be disposed of.

Worldwide, the market for powder coatings was growing 10–20% per year and was seen as a possible substitute for up to 50% of paint being applied to metal. In Europe, where the powder process was pioneered, the substitution already amounted to roughly 20% compared to about 10% in the US. Although major user groups included automotive component suppliers, the metal furniture industry, and domestic appliance manufacturers, most powder makers were also looking into applying colored coatings to inferior grades of plastic, thus enabling them to compete with the attractive high-quality plastics used for chairs and garden furniture. As one analyst pointed out, the trick was to develop a paint that could be cured at relatively low temperatures, so that it did not melt the plastic. Other potential new applications included car engine blocks, baskets inside automatic washing machines, and the steel reinforcement bars used in concrete.

One analyst commented that manufacturers were also experimenting with high-gloss powder finishes that could eventually be used for car body work. Worldwide, powder coatings accounted for only 2% of industry sales and were distributed among Europe, 54%; North America, 21%; and Japan, 10%.

COIL COATINGS

The coil-coating segment derived its name from coiled steel or aluminum, which was given a decorative or industrial coating before the main manufacturing step or construction process. Typically, steel or aluminum coils were unrolled on automatic lines and the coating was applied by roller or spray. They were dried and hardened, and then the metal was coiled up again for shipment to manufacturers. Upon receipt, manufacturers could bend or stamp the metal into a required shape—such as a refrigerator cabinet or building cladding—without damaging the painted surface. In Europe, coil-coating customers included major metal producers such as British Steel, Sollac of France, Phoenix (part of the Belgian Cockerill group), Hoesch of Germany, Svenska Stal of Sweden, and La Magona of Italy.

In 1991, roughly 60% of coil-coated steel and 50% of coil-coated aluminum in Europe went to the building sector. Other important outlets were the automotive industry, domestic appliances, and packages. Also in Europe, it was estimated that, although manufacturers produced roughly 2.2 million tons of painted steel per year in the form of car and commercial vehicle bodies, 95% of that steel was painted after assembly. In other words, industry used only 110,000 tons of prepainted coil, and coil coaters hoped that more European manufacturers would follow the example of Nissan's Sunderland, UK, plant which used precoated car body panels. In terms of world paint sales, coil coatings represented less than 1%, or roughly 181 million liters, of industry sales. Geographically, these sales were concentrated in Europe, 34%; North America, 33%; and Japan, 22%.

COMPETITION

Despite the takeover activity of the 1980s, in 1991, roughly 10,000 paint companies remained active around the world. In general, these competitors could be grouped into two categories: large multinational companies and, primarily, domestic manufacturers. In the first category, the 10 largest companies accounted for 35% of industry sales, employed hundreds if not thousands of people, and were sometimes part of larger chemical companies. Typically, these players made and marketed coatings products in all, or almost all, of the industry's market segments, having attained their size by acquiring smaller companies. (*Refer to Exhibit 6 for information on the top 12 paint companies.*)

At the other end of the spectrum, small companies had sales under $10 million and employed fewer than 10 persons. Normally, these smaller manufacturers concentrated production on one or only a few segments, usually in their home markets, and they sometimes augmented their sales by OEM relationships with other specialist paint companies.

ICI PAINTS' COMPETITIVE POSITION

Worldwide, ICI Paints' competitive position varied as a function of region and application segment (*as shown in* **Table 2**).

TABLE 2

BREAKDOWN OF ICI PAINTS SALES BY REGION AND APPLICATION SEGMENT

	% MARKET SHARE BY REGION			APPLICATION SEGMENT'S SHARE (%) OF TOTAL ICI PAINT REVENUES
SEGMENT	EUROPE	N. AMERICA	ASIA PACIFIC	
Decorative	5	13	5	62
Auto OEM	4	0	15	3.4
Auto Ref	11	1	14	13
Can	32	44	19	9
Coil	2	10	6	1.6
Powder	4	14	2	2

Decorative

By far, decorative paints was ICI's strongest product line, accounting for 62% of the company's 1991 sales. Despite ICI Paints' worldwide strength in the decorative segment, however, it was not the biggest in some regional markets, and market shares varied considerably by country. In Western Europe, for example, ICI had only a 5% market share, behind Akzo with 8% and Casco-Nobel with 7%. In the UK, on the other hand, ICI's Dulux product line accounted for an estimated 37% of all retail paint sales and included Dulux Vinyl Silk Emulsion, Dulux Matt Emulsion, Dulux Vinyl Soft Sheen, Dulux Satinwood, Dulux Gloss Finish, Dulux Non-Drip Gloss, Dulux Definitions, Dulux Undercoat, Dulux Options, and Dulux Weathershed. Dulux was also known for its Natural Hints product line, consisting of 9–10 shades of off-white colors.

In North America, ICI Paints, through Glidden, its US subsidiary, had an estimated 13% share of market, second only to Sherwin-Williams with 20% and well ahead of Benjamin Moore with 7%. And, though ICI Paints had no decorative paint sales in Japan, it had a 5% market share in the rest of the Asia Pacific region, second only to Nippon Paint with 6%.

Industrial

AUTOMOTIVE REFINISH

After the decorative segment, the automotive refinish segment was ICI Paints' largest segment, representing roughly 13% of company turnover. Similar to the decorative segment, sales of paint in the automotive refinish segment varied by region. In Western Europe, for example, ICI Paints had an estimated 11% market share, behind Hoechst with 19%; BASF, 18%; and even Akzo at 11%. In North America, ICI had only a 1% share of the refinish market, well behind DuPont with 31%; PPG and Sherwin-Williams with 22% each; BASF, 13%, and Akzo, a 6% market share. Despite having no sales in this segment in Japan, ICI was in first place in the Asia Pacific region with a 14% market share, ahead of Korea Chemical with 13%; Kansai, 6%; and Kunsul and Nippon, each with 5% of the market.

AUTOMOTIVE OEM

With only 3.4% of ICI Paints' total sales, the automotive OEM coatings segment was among the smaller of the company's product lines. In Western Europe, ICI had only a 4% share of this market segment, well behind PPG with 31%; Hoechst, 25%; BASF, 18%; and Akzo, 8%. In 1991, ICI sold the Canadian portion of its automotive OEM business to PPG. Thereafter, in North America and Japan, ICI was not present in the automotive OEM segment. In the rest of the Asia Pacific region, though, the company had a 15% market share in this segment, second to Korea Chemical with 23%, but well ahead of Dong Ju with 9%; Goodlas Nerolac, with 7%; and Daihan and Shen Yan, with 5% each.

CAN

Worldwide, can coatings accounted for roughly 9% of ICI Paints' sales. Geographically, ICI was a distant leader in Western Europe with a 32% market share, well ahead of BASF with 16%; Dexter with 15% and Courtaulds with 11%. ICI was also a formidable competitor in can coatings in North America with 44% of the market, more than twice the share of its closest rival—Valspar with 20%, and considerably ahead of BASF and Dexter with 12% and 10% of the market segment, respectively. Despite a strong presence in Western Europe and North America in can coatings, ICI had no sales in this segment in Japan. It was, however, by far the leader in the rest of the Asia Pacific region with 19% of that market. In terms of market shares, its closest rivals in that part of the world were Courtaulds and Kunsul, each with a 9% share of market.

COIL

In 1991, sales of coil coatings by ICI accounted for a mere 1.6% of all sales; in Western Europe, several competitors led in this segment. In decreasing order of market share, these competitors were Becker, 18%; Sigma, 13%; Casco-Nobel,

12%; PPG, 9%; Akzo and Courtaulds, 7% each; Kemira, 3%; and BASF, Dexter, Grebe, Hoechst, Salchi, and ICI, 2% each. In the North American coil-coating segment, ICI was tied for fourth place with Lilly at a 10% market share; Valspar was the leader with 21%, followed by Morton, 19%; and Akzo, 16%. As with its other coatings, ICI had no sales in Japan but did have 6% of the Asia Pacific market for coil coatings, behind Nippon, 22%; Kansai, 17%; Korea Chemical, 13%; and Daihan, 10%.

POWDER

Powder coatings represented approximately 2% of ICI Paints' 1991 sales and, in Western Europe, accounted for 4% of all sales in that segment. Powder competitors with greater market shares were DSM, 13%; Becker, 11%; Courtaulds, 9%; and Hoechst, 6%. In North America, ICI's powder paints had a 14% market share, second only to Morton with 17%, yet still ahead of Ferro with 13%; Valspar, 12%; and Fuller O'Brien, 9%. In the Asia Pacific region, ICI's powder coatings had only a 2% share of market; there, leading competitors and their market shares were Daihan and Korea Chemical, 15% each; Jotun, 9%; Chokwang, 4%; and Kunsul, 3%. To bolster its presence in the powder segment, in 1991 ICI began merger discussions with Ferro. Though the deal was never concluded, a merger of Ferro and ICI would have made that company the worldwide leader in powder coatings.

DESIGNING AN ORGANIZATION FOR THE 1990S

At ICI Paints, Management sought to have an organization in the 1990s that was both global and territory oriented, that supported R&D centers of excellence in certain locations, and maximized resources among the company's different operations and locations. At the same time, the company intended to concentrate on its key application segments on a global basis, and wanted to exploit opportunities in the European Community and Asia Pacific regions.

ICI Paints' organization had already evolved over time and, by 1992, several changes had been made (*refer to **Exhibit 7***). In both the North American and European regions, territorial general managers had been eliminated, moving the entire organization away from a territorial approach to more brand-oriented structure.

Upon review, some of ICI Paints' executives felt that, in order to succeed in the future, the company needed to focus more directly on and better coordinate the activities of its main application segments. To this end, executives cited four advantages in moving towards a global product organization. First, it was believed that a global product organization would enhance ICI's ability to serve a customer base that was itself becoming increasingly global. For customers with global operations—such as can coating companies and automobile makers, a single product and service package that was applicable worldwide was bound to be appealing.

Second, executives cited the substantial cost benefits of standardizing ICI's products. To emphasize this point, it was mentioned that reducing the number of the company's refinish top coats from 24 to 10 would save upwards of $17 million on a product line with an annual turnover of approximately $300 million.

Third, executives believed that a global product organization would have additional benefits in terms of resource allocation. As an example, one manager mentioned that, with increasingly expensive pollution abatement equipment, it did not make sense to have as many manufacturing plants. Rather, he stressed, the company should consider consolidating the number of plants and upgrading the remainder to world-class manufacturing standards. In fact, it was believed that some 30 of the company's 64 plants were common sites for a number of paint products.

Lastly, the executive mentioned that, in a truly global product organization, there would be a much greater chance to transfer experience from one market to another. For example, he described how an application developed for a can coating customer in North America, while not identical, had a number of parallels to the needs faced by can coating customers in Europe.

In contrast to these advantages, another group of executives pointed out that, although some of ICI Paints' customer needs had become global, there were still substantial differences among individual markets. In the US decorative segment, for example, Glidden had a 13% market share, was priced below other brands, and distributed to DIY customers through mass merchandising outlets such as Walmart. Because Glidden did not compete in the premium sector, it was seldom purchased by small-scale professional users like interior decorators. In contrast to Glidden in the US, ICI's premium brand—Dulux—had a 37% market share in the UK. As a result, in 1993 ICI launched the Glidden brand in the UK, aiming it toward commercial contractors—a segment in which Dulux had been weak. John Thompson commented further.

> To establish Dulux as a global brand, the US market might be the next logical step. However, we estimated that a country-wide launch would cost ICI Paints $50 million over four to five years. An important issue would be not only determining the timing of such a large-scale project, but also resolving the positioning of Glidden versus Dulux.

In conjunction with trying to establish a global brand, the group went on to say that reducing the number of paint formulations and standards might well yield savings, but at the risk of jeopardizing ICI's sensitivity to local market conditions. "How would you feel," he asked, "if you worked at Anheuser-Busch and your 'local' can coating salesman was in fact based in the UK?" Then too, the executives pointed out that, in theory, it was easy to reduce the number of manufacturing plants. In practice, however, local management and governments would hardly be receptive to the unemployment created due to such restructuring. As well, the executives mentioned that, because many of ICI Paints' production assets were shared, Business Area General Managers were largely responsible for business volume in an application segment, yet did not have full asset responsibility. In fact, no more than 75% of the company's assets could be clearly attributed to individual product lines.

SUMMARY

Before meeting with the IBT again, Scopes reviewed in his mind how his industry had changed and, in particular, what those changes implied for the organizational structure of ICI Paints. He recalled the words of one industry analyst who said that the worldwide merger and acquisition activities of the 1980s were merely part of the ongoing globalization of the paint industry. At the start of the 1990s, the analyst believed that the globalization process was driven by three factors. First, the need to service customers with international manufacturing operations such as can makers, vehicle assembly, and domestic appliances. Secondly, the need to service customers dealing with the aftercare of internationally traded products such as vehicles and ships. Lastly, the need to amortize the ever growing costs of research, product development, and marketing over a broad volume base. With these thoughts in mind, Scopes turned to the IBT to renew the discussion on developing a new organizational structure at ICI Paints and the role of the Territorial General Managers, the Business Area General Managers and, particularly, the International Leaders in the 1990s.

EXHIBIT 1

ICI paints territorial spread.

ICI PAINTS MANUFACTURING COMPANIES

Australia	Italy	Spain
Canada	Malaysia	Taiwan
Ireland	Mexico	Thailand
Fiji	New Zealand	United Kingdom
France	Pakistan	United States
India	Papua New Guinea	West Germany
Indonesia	Singapore	

ICI MINORITY HOLDINGS

Botswana	South Africa
Malawi	Zimbabwe

COMPANIES MANUFACTURING UNDER LICENSE

Brazil	Kenya	Sudan
Columbia	Korea	Trinidad
Cyprus	Madagascar	Turkey
Ecuador	Portugal	Venezuela
Japan	Saudi Arabia	Yemen
Jordan		

EXHIBIT 2

Previous organization chart (1988–1990).

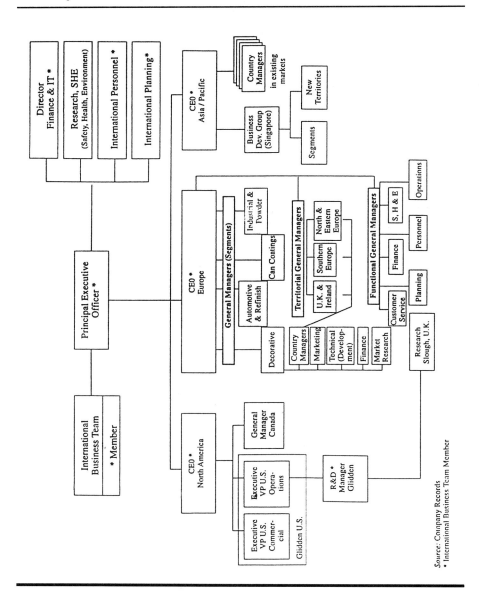

Source: Company Records
* International Business Team Member

EXHIBIT 3

Members of the International Business Team (IBT).

Herman Scopes	CEO Paints
John Danzeisen	Chief Executive North America
Peter Kirby	Chief Executive Asia Pacific
Denis Wright	Chief Executive Europe International Leader Decorative
Adrian Auer	Chief Financial Officer
Nigel Clark	International Leader, Operations and Personnel
Brian Letchford	International Leader, Automotive and Can Coatings
Alex Ramig	International Leader, R&D
John Thompson	Chief Planner

EXHIBIT 4

World paints by market sector.

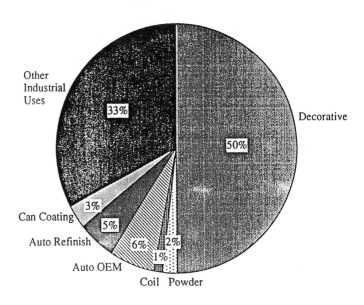

1991
13,500 ML

Note: Excludes Central and Eastern Europe, the Middle East, and the African Continent

EXHIBIT 5

World paint markets by region.

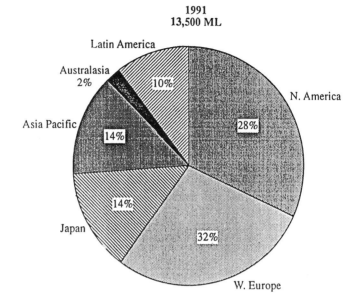

1991
13,500 ML

Region definitions:
1. Western Europe = The UK, France, Germany (including former East Germany), Italy, Spain, Portugal, Belgium, the Netherlands, Denmark, Finland, Norway, Sweden, Austria, Ireland, Greece, and Turkey.
2. North America = USA and Canada
3. Asia Pacific = India, Pakistan, Sri Lanka, Thailand, Malaysia, Singapore, Indonesia, Taiwan, Hong Kong, China, and Korea
4. Australasia = Australia and New Zealand
5. Latin America = Brazil, Argentina, Mexico, Ecuador, Uruguay, Colombia, and Chile
6. Excludes Commonwealth of independent states, Eastern Europe, the Middle East and Africa

EXHIBIT 6
ICI's principal paint competitors.

	COATINGS AS % OF GROUP SALES	1990 M.LITRES	SALES $ MILLION	R.O.N.A. AVE 1987-90	KEY MARKET SECTORS	SIGNIFICANT DIRECT COMPETITION WITH ICI
International						
PPG	38%	515	1,963	26%	Motors, Refinish Dec-USA	Refinish Decorative-USA
BASF	7%	485	c.1,945	<15%	Motors, Refinish, Can	Refinish, Can
AKZO	23%	485	2,160	15%	Dec-Europe Refinish, Motors	Decorative-Europe Refinish
Courtaulds	31%	300	1,767	25%	Marine, Can, Powders, Dec	Can, Powders Decorative-Australia
Regional—Americas						
Sherwin-Williams	100%	535	2,338	26%	Dec, Refinish	Decorative
Dupont	3%	265	c.1,160	?	Motors, Refinish	
Valspar	100%	230	539	24%	Dec, Can, Wood, Coil	Can
Regional—Europe						
Casco Nobel	37%	250	892	20%	Dec, Coil, Wood Gen Industrial	Decorative-UK
Hoechst	4%	220	1,160	c.10%	Motors, Refinish	Refinish
Regional—Asia						
Nippon	100%	350	1,374	20%	Motors, Refinish Marine, Dec, Coil	Decorative Refinish, Motors
Kansai	100%	275	1,080	19%	Motors, Refinish, Dec Marine, Can, Coil	Refinish, Motors
ICI	13%	805	2,927	17%	Dec, Refinish, Can Powders	

EXHIBIT 7
Present organization chart (1992).

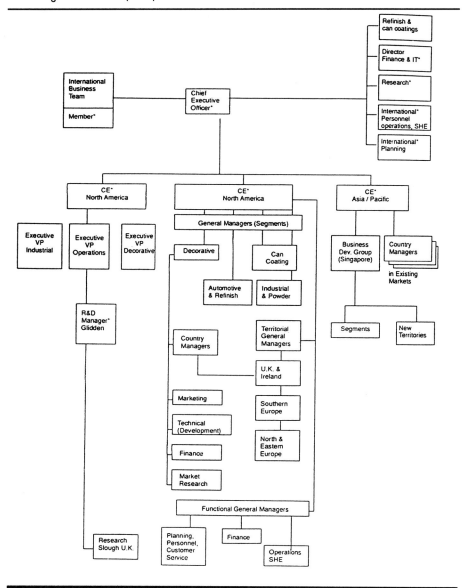

AIR BP: AVIATION SERVICE CENTRES

Graham Evans finished reading the last memo, returned it to the file, and shook his head. "How did we get ourselves into this pickle?" he asked himself. Based not far from London's Heathrow Airport, Evans was the newly appointed strategic planning manager for Air BP—the aviation fuel operations of British Petroleum. He had just spent several hours reading through a series of memos dating back five years to June 1986, when Air BP had taken its first steps toward developing a chain of company-owned business aviation service centres around the world. The tone of the memos, originally enthusiastic and optimistic, had become steadily more cautious over the years as both progress and setbacks were recorded.

Aviation service centres were commonly known in the industry by the American term of FBOs (fixed base operations), were airport-based fueling, maintenance, and terminal service facilities for corporate aircraft, although not all FBOs provided all services. One BP executive had described FBOs as "truck-stops for executive jets." In the mid-1980s, the outlook for continued increases in the demand for jet fuel for such aircraft had seemed encouraging. However, competition from other oil companies was stiff, and jet fuel itself was a commodity. BP wanted to defend market share and increase its margins. Investing in FBOs that provided added-value services had seemed an attractive strategy.

Pursuing this strategy, Air BP had made significant investment on three continents, creating FBOs at Cleveland, Ohio and Atlanta, Georgia, (USA), at Melbourne (Australia), Cologne (Germany), and at two of Britain's major airports, London-Heathrow and London-Stansted. Other locations under review in Europe included Paris-Le Bourget, Rome, and Budapest. But, by June 1991, the mixed results achieved to date had led the CEO of Air BP to request a thorough review. He had asked Evans:

> Should we continue our global strategy of spending $80 million to purchase FBOs in various parts of the world or come up with a different approach?[1] I find myself wondering whether there may be other, better ways to achieve our goals!

[1] Currency exchange rates varied widely between 1986 and 1991; for instance, the value of the US dollar against the British pound ranged from US$ = £0.51 to £0.70. For simplicity, financial data will be reported first in the currency in which they were originally stated, and then converted to US dollars at the following exchange rates: US$1.00 = £0.57 = A$1.33 = DM1.77.

CORPORATE AVIATION

Air traffic comprised commercial, general, and military aviation. Commercial traffic involved scheduled passenger airlines, airfreight and certain charter operations. General aviation, by contrast, consisted of privately owned aircraft flying for business or recreational purposes, together with small charters and air taxi operations.

The most important segment of the general aviation fleet consisted of aircraft owned by corporations (or wealthy individuals) and used for business travel. By 1991, there were almost 6,900 jets and some 8,000 turboprops in corporate service around the world. Two-thirds of corporate aircraft were based in the United States; other key regions included Europe and South America. There seemed to be little relationship between national wealth and executive jet ownership on a country-by-country basis, with Japan having a surprisingly small number (*refer to Exhibit 1*).

For much of the 1980s, the number of corporate aircraft had grown at an annual rate of around 3%. Growth was higher outside the United States, which had become a fairly mature market. Worldwide, corporate aircraft consumed over 5 million tonnes (1.65 billion US gallons) of jet fuel each year.[2]

Executive jets were expensive to own and operate. Purchase prices ranged from $2 million for a Learjet which could fly six people up to 3,000 km (1,900 miles) to $24 million for a 19-seat Gulfstream IV, capable of flying from Chicago to Paris nonstop. But, few aircraft were capable of transoceanic flight. Turboprops were slower than jets and often had a smaller range, but were also cheaper. Companies needing more seat capacity sometimes purchased used airliners, which they refitted to suit their needs.

A small executive jet had a fuel capacity of some 3–4,000 litres—double that of a twin-engined turboprop. By contrast, a Gulfstream IV could load over 16,000 litres of jet fuel. But, even this volume paled by comparison to the fuel needs of a Boeing 747-400, which might load 140,000 litres for the 13-hour flight from Singapore to London.

The major rationale for purchasing a corporate aircraft was travel time savings over commercial airline services. Another key advantage was flexibility. Executives were freed from the constraints of airline schedules, did not have to change flights at intermediate airports, and could land at small airfields not served by passenger airlines. Other perceived benefits included security and secrecy.

The average jet flew only about 400 hours a year. Shareholders often criticized these aircraft as unjustified perks for top management. Still, more corporations were making seats available to any employee whose need to get somewhere

---

[2] Both jets and turboprops consumed jet fuel (kerosine). Piston-engined aircraft used avgas, a high-octane leaded petrol (gasoline). Jetfuel was sold in litres or US gallons (USG), but ex-refinery prices tended to be quoted worldwide in US dollars per metric tonne. Conversion: one USG = 0.8 imperial gallons = 3.78 litres; one metric tonne = 1,250 litres.

quickly was important to the firm, provided that the journey could not be completed more efficiently by other means. Pilots of corporate aircraft were responsible for more than just flying—economic pressures to cut costs meant that they had to be good business managers, too, and seek operating economies without compromising safety.

AIRCRAFT SERVICING NEEDS

Corporate aircraft destinations ranged from major international airports—where there was a trend to restrict small corporate aircraft—to unpaved airfields in remote locations. Rugged turboprops, such as the Twin Otter, could land on short, rough runways that would be unsuitable for executive jets. General aviation airports received no commercial airlines—their focus was on corporate transports (including chartered air taxis) and recreational flying. At commercial airports, corporate aircraft were usually directed to areas reserved for general aviation.

When flying away from home, the pilot would call ahead to arrange ground services. Speed was of the essence for busy corporate executives; to save time they sometimes even held business meetings in a private lounge at the airport before departing on the next stage of their journey. While waiting, the aircraft might need refueling and cleaning, and to be kept in a secure location. Occasionally, diagnostic tests or emergency maintenance were required, but most aircraft maintenance was undertaken on a scheduled, preventive basis at the home base. Food and beverages might be requested for the upcoming flight. Pilots—who often complained that they spent more time waiting at airports than actually flying—might want a quiet space to plan the next flight segment or attend to management issues. Access to a fax machine, telephones, weather forecasts and air traffic control briefings was also important.

At small airfields, a pilot might find just a handling agent who could arrange for fueling and find independent suppliers for other services. But, at airports where several aircraft had their home base, there was often a fixed base operation (FBO) with a small terminal and hangar offering storage, maintenance, avionics (aviation electronics), and other services. Some American airports were served by several FBOs, and the pilot would select one based on the range and level of services offered, the quality of facilities, and which oil company credit cards were accepted. Price cutting was not generally used as a competitive tool by FBOs. However, the European and American markets took very different approaches to pricing fuel and other services.

FBOs in Europe

Europe had some 200 commercial airports and 200 general aviation fields accessible to corporate jets. In total, there were about 120 FBOs (often referred to as aviation service centres), of which only 12 ran large full-service operations. Some competition came from handling agents who could coordinate delivery of various services that they did not actually provide themselves. Commercial airlines sometimes offered handling services for corporate aircraft, as well as use of terminal lounges and other facilities for passengers and crew.

Once an oil company had acquired the right to sell fuel at an airport served by commercial airlines, it could sell directly to any type of customer. However, at small airfields, a single FBO or fuelling service generally enjoyed a monopoly. European retail margins on fuel sales to corporate aircraft were the equivalent $0.15 per US gallon (as compared with $0.02 for airline fuel sales). FBOs in Europe billed pilots on an itemized basis for services such as hangaring, cleaning, local transportation, use of office facilities, and so on.

FBOs in the United States

There were over 1,200 airports in the US accessible to corporate jets (plus many smaller airfields). And the nation accounted for more than 90% of the world's FBOs. Over 3,000 FBOs sold fuel (another 400 sold no fuel but provided other aviation-related activities). Some busy general aviation airports boasted three or four FBOs; pilots would choose among competing operators primarily on the range and level of services offered, the quality of facilities, and which oil company credit cards were accepted. However, price cutting had not traditionally been used as a competitive weapon.

The great majority of fuel-selling FBOs were individual businesses—often family-owned—and many were said to be undercapitalized. Most FBOs, in fact, provided nothing but fuelling services. Their physical facilities might be limited to a small office, plus underground storage tanks and a couple of fuel tankers. Annual revenues for a small American FBO ranged from $100,000 to $1,000,000. Only about 500 FBOs had revenues over $1 million, usually achieved by combining fuel sales with maintenance and other services. Of these, only 100 were large, full-service operations offering sophisticated maintenance and avionics services, as well as achieving annual turnovers above $5 million.

Some 150 FBOs were part of a chain. During the second half of the 1980s, interest in purchasing FBOs by corporate buyers who wished to form chains had led to sharp increases in selling prices. By 1991, the principal chains were Page Avjet with 20 FBOs, Butler with 19, and AMR-Combs (a subsidiary of American Airlines) with 10.

About 2,200 FBOs were branded with the name and colours of a major oil company (*refer to* **Exhibit 2**). Other FBOs sold regional brands or were unbranded, purchasing from third-party resellers who bought jet fuel on the spot market. Oil companies provided various services, including credit cards and promotional support designed to enhance brand loyalty for their dealers. Most fuel contracts ran for one year at a time, and were normally renewed automatically. But, a lower fuel price or the offer of extra services might encourage an FBO to change brands and switch to a different supplier. Fuel prices varied from one airport to another.

At most airports, FBOs were licensed only to sell to general aviation aircraft. But, some operators augmented their income by acting as subcontractors to oil companies and refuelling commercial aircraft with fuel drawn from oil company tanks. For this service, FBOs negotiated a fee ranging from one to five cents per gallon. When oil companies sold directly to commercial airlines, they obtained a margin of as little as $0.005 per gallon; when they sold at wholesale to FBOs, their margin was typically $0.05–0.10.

American FBOs provided many services free of charge, including use of their parking areas, hangars, and terminal facilities. Larger FBOs went to great lengths to appeal to pilots, offering such extras as aircraft cleaning, weather briefings, and use of conference rooms and showers free of charge in the hope of obtaining their fuel business. The FBO added a margin of $0.80–1.00 per gallon (plus relevant taxes) to the wholesale price to cover the cost of all these other services. Separate charges were made for maintenance work, catering, and long-distance phone calls or faxes.

BRITISH PETROLEUM COMPANY

BP was the third largest oil company in the world (after Royal Dutch Shell and Exxon), conducting business in 70 countries on six continents. On a 1990 turnover of £33 billion ($58 billion), BP achieved pretax profits of £2.8 billion. It had four businesses: exploration, oil, chemicals, and nutrition. BP Exploration was responsible for upstream activities, including oil and gas production. About one third of its oil came from the North Sea and 55% from the US, chiefly Alaska.

With a turnover of over £20 billion, BP Oil was responsible for activities in the downstream oil sector. It operated five refineries in Europe, five in the US, two in Australia, and one in Singapore, plus a large shipping fleet. BP sold branded oil products and services in over 50 countries. The brand was strongly represented in Europe, Australasia, parts of Africa and Southeast Asia. In the United States, where BP had purchased the Standard Oil Company of Ohio (the legendary company founded by John D. Rockefeller) and renamed it BP America in 1987, building awareness of the new brand name was a major objective. However, the company had almost no presence in Canada.

Key markets for fuel and lubricants included road vehicles, ships and aircraft. BP boasted almost 20,000 retail service stations worldwide, of which 38% were located in the USs, 45% in Europe, and 10% in Australia/Asia. Some were company owned, others were operated by independent franchisees. The goal was to focus on large, strategically sited stations offering 24-hour self-service fuel plus an array of other motorist services, including (at some sites) a car wash and a convenience store. All stations were being "re-imaged" to feature a new design treatment using the BP green with yellow lettering. In 1990 the company had begun rebranding its US stations from Sohio, Gulf (and other names) to feature the distinctive BP shield.

To better serve the road freight industry, BP Oil was developing a network of company-owned BP truckstops. They offered fast refuelling, full maintenance and repair services, a shop, and facilities where drivers could eat, relax and shower. There were video games and TV, a self-service laundry, telephones, and fax. Since fuel was priced competitively to encourage drivers to stop, profitability depended heavily on achieving good sales of other services. BP had opened 14 purposely built truckstops in Europe and would soon have 10 in Australia. It operated 43 company-owned sites in the US under the name "Truckstops of America." More were planned.

As a division of BP Oil, Air BP supplied fuel and services to some 400 airline customers at over 600 locations worldwide, as well as to corporate aircraft and to individuals who flew small aircraft for pleasure. Air BP's annual turnover was around £1.4 billion ($2.5 billion) and it sold some 13 billion litres (3.5 billion USG) of aviation fuel worldwide. Over 95% of this total was jetfuel.

Aviation fuel was first shipped from BP's refineries to its own terminals, where there were two distribution alternatives. One was for Air BP to transport the fuel to its own airport-based tank farms, from where the company could transport it to aircraft parking bays and pump it directly "into-plane." A variant of this strategy was to subcontract the actual into-plane activity to independent intermediaries (such as FBO operators) who would draw fuel as needed from the Air BP tank farm. A second alternative was to sell the fuel wholesale to FBOs and other airport-based dealers, who then stored it in their own underground tanks for resale under the Air BP brand name to retail customers. Any refined fuel not sold through BP's own outlets was sold unbranded to traders (jobbers) at the currently prevailing prices. Competition came from many other oil companies, notably Exxon (Esso in some countries), Shell, Mobil, Texaco/Caltex, Chevron (in the US), and Total (Mainly in Europe).

Air BP and the FBO Industry

Traditionally, large oil companies had not been especially interested in selling fuel to general aviation customers. An Air BP executive explained why:

> During the 1970s, the aviation business was growing so quickly—particularly international aviation—that we thought we'd have our arms full just selling to the major airlines. And we'd organized our assets around this business. At a time when everyone was going from 707s to 747s, everything kept getting bigger.
>
> The small customer on an airfield was a nuisance. There was no schedule. We didn't know when they were coming in or when they were leaving. Our operations were geared around the schedules of international airlines. Our contracts said we had to meet them on time and turn them around in, say, 45 minutes. Our whole staffing and equipment was designed to meet that requirement. Small customers were simply served as and when we had the availability. At an airport like Heathrow, where small aircraft were based at the far side of the field, it could be four to five hours before we got a tanker over there. General aviation represented about 10% of all aircraft movements there and less than 1/2% of fuel sales.

Evolution of a European FBO Strategy

Following the recession of 1980–81, airlines became desperate to get fuel prices down. Finding its margins squeezed, Air BP started to look more closely at small customers who were paying substantially higher prices for the same fuel. Around 1983, Field Aviation Ltd., owner of the Executive Jet Centre, the large FBO at Heathrow, started to complain about the slow fuelling service provided by BP and other oil companies. An Air BP executive recalled his company's response:

> We said to Field "If you could deliver all your customers to us, we would be willing to base a vehicle over at your facilities." Our interest was sharpened by concern that a competitor, Total, might be about to make similar overtures. Fortunately, Field agreed to work with us and so we developed a relationship. Not only was the margin attractive, but now we had the volume to justify dedicating a vehicle to their operation.

By the mid-1980s, the general aviation market in the United Kingdom accounted for only 7% of Air BP's British sales but close to a third of its profits. In mid-1986, Air BP and Field (which was a subsidiary of a large holding company) agreed to form a 50–50 joint venture called Field Aviation Enterprises Ltd (FAEL) to develop an international chain of FBOs. BP would supply experience in fuelling and in international operations, and Field would contribute its operational experience and personnel. The flagship of the new chain would be Field's Executive Jet Centre, described as one of the best FBOs in Europe. Air BP agreed to pay £1 million ($1.7 million) for its 50% share in FAEL, projecting an internal rate of return of 16.9% on its investment.

The Executive Jet Centre (EJC) was close to Heathrow's new Terminal 4 complex. It comprised offices, a reception area and lounges, a large modern hangar and a state-of-the-art maintenance facility. FAEL rented these facilities, constructed in 1983 at a cost of £4.5 million ($7.5 million). The EJC had 24 "resident" aircraft—mostly large and medium-sized jets—whose owners paid a fixed annual fee that covered hangaring, a certain level of maintenance, and various other services. Fuel was not included. Pilots of visiting aircraft paid for services as they were consumed. The EJC's main competition came from British Airways, which offered handling services and terminal facilities for corporate aircraft, passengers and crew.

Heathrow was vulnerable to a possible future ban on corporate aircraft as commercial airline traffic continued to build. The government had already designated Stansted, north of London, as the capital's long-term general aviation airport, so FAEL decided to develop a second FBO at Stansted, where Air BP already had a fuelling operation. In August 1987, it purchased an existing FBO at this airport; Air BP's 50% investment amounted to £500,000 ($850,000).

FAEL wanted to create a chain of five FBOs to serve Europe and the Middle East. After reviewing corporate air travel patterns, Air BP planners identified several key sites for investigation, including Paris, Brussels, Geneva, Milan, and Madrid. But further study revealed that Jet Aviation, which operated 10 FBOs in Europe and the US, had a dominant position at both the Geneva and Zurich airports, which eliminated Switzerland. The idea of developing an FBO at Abu Dhabi in the Persian Gulf was dropped when research showed that most corporate jet owners from that region liked to have their aircraft serviced on their frequent visits to Europe.

Then Germany was suggested. Air BP already had a large contract with the German national carrier, Lufthansa. It had also developed contracts to supply fuel to a number of general aviation airports. Among the larger airports where BP had a fuelling service was Cologne (Köln) which also served Bonn. Learning that the entrepreneur who ran the FBO at Cologne was looking for a buyer and that Total had expressed interest, BP decided that it had to protect its fuel sales there and so made an offer. A price was agreed upon and for an investment of DM 2.9 million ($1.6 million), FAEL took over the Cologne FBO in early 1988.

Much of the business at Cologne involved service to visiting aircraft. There was no resident corporate fleet. Most corporate jets in Germany were based in the big industrial cities like Frankfurt and Dusseldorf. But the FBO's new managing director soon came up with a promising opportunity. UPS (United Parcel Service), the large American package delivery firm, was busy expanding its international services and was seeking both a base and a contractor to run a European airfreight operation on its behalf. Negotiations were initiated, went well, and FAEL-Cologne obtained not just a resident fleet but the challenge of running a small freight airline as well.

Activities in the United States

Through its purchase of Standard Oil (Sohio), BP could trace its involvement in FBO activities back to 1955, when Sohio had obtained an operating lease at the Cleveland Hopkins Airport, had built an FBO, and leased it to an independent dealer. In 1971, when the dealer experienced financial problems, Sohio decided to run this FBO with its own employees. The facilities were leased from the airport, so Sohio's investment was mainly in vehicles. This model of an oil company owning an FBO was unique at that time, and it enjoyed substantial sales from refuelling commercial aircraft. Sohio decided to focus on this "into-plane" business, which provided a margin of $0.05-0.15 per gallon. It discouraged maintenance, eventually "de-certifying" the mechanics, and eliminated high service activities for executive jets. The other FBOs at Hopkins chose to concentrate on the general aviation business and did not aggressively pursue the commercial into-plane business.

The Cleveland operation proved to be very profitable, consistently earning half a million dollars a year. A number of BP executives became familiar with the Hopkins FBO, since Cleveland was the headquarters city for Standard Oil and its successor, BP America. In 1987, James E. Timmons, whose previous assignment had included management of the Hopkins facility, was transferred to Texas as manager of general aviation at Air BP's head office in Houston.

At this time, one of Air BP's largest west coast customers was Chuckair, a profitable, family-owned business. It operated FBOs at two mid-sized California airports, both widely used by executive jets. At the busy San Felipe airport, Chuckair enjoyed a monopoly as the only FBO on the field.[3] Its general aviation fuel sales at San Felipe totalled $6 million a year; other activities, including maintenance, a restaurant, and various ground services, yielded a further $4.2 million. When the owner's son took over the business, he proposed that Chuckair and Air BP form a joint venture to operate two new FBOs. One of them would require building a new facility at an airfield in Nevada, but the other could be acquired by buying an existing FBO at a big airport in Arizona.

Attracted by the opportunity to share in the large retail margins, BP agreed in June 1987 to a 50–50 joint venture and to contribute its share of the investment, estimated at $2 million. Plans for development of the two new FBOs went ahead, but soon Chuckair confessed that it was having trouble coming up with its full share of the money: the banks questioned its ability to meet principal repayments and interest out of projected income. When Chuckair fell heavily behind the payments to BP for fuel purchases, Air BP decided to sell out its share, dissolve the partnership, and to avoid future joint ventures in the US. But the company remained interested in operating new FBOs.

CREATING A GLOBAL STRATEGY

With interest in FBO acquisitions increasing on both sides of the Atlantic, the suggestion was made that Air BP should be thinking globally. Based on the experience of FAEL-Heathrow and knowledge of the finances of selected American FBOs—such as Chuckair's operation in San Felipe, the business development group in London drew up a proposal for presentation to Air BP's Executive Committee. This called for a total investment over five years of $80 million to develop 15 new sites: $50 million would be allocated to the US, and another $30 million for four in Europe and two in Australia, where BP had a very strong presence. The base case financial analysis projected an internal rate of return of 18%. In November 1988, the plan was approved, and $13 million allocated for capital expenditures in 1989.

From a worldwide perspective, Air BP's strategy was to establish an international network of FBOs with a strong image of quality fuel and service. Specific goals were to secure BP's market position at existing locations, to expand into high volume/high growth locations, and to erect entry barriers. But, there were also different emphases on different continents. In the US, the priority was to gain access to the large retail margins available, instead of just selling at wholesale. In Europe and Australia, it was to secure Air BP's retail market share at current retail margins.

In its search to add value through better service, Air BP developed enhanced information systems to help FBOs receive faster payment on credit card sales.

---

[3]Chuckair and San Felipe are both disguised names.

But, the company recognized that this innovation would be relatively easy for competitors to copy. Looking to the future, Air BP hoped to develop systems to help corporate pilots improve flight planning and cost management.

Expansion in the United States

Since the American market for FBOs was close to saturation, Air BP saw little opportunity to build any new FBOs in the United States. So, the Houston office set to work looking for possible acquisitions. Jim Timmons and his staff identified several key selection criteria.

Critical success factors for an FBO were that it should be conveniently located on the airfield, with a site lease of at least 15 years, have annual retail fuel sales of more than one million gallons, and good facilities. To avoid excessive competition, BP would not invest at airports with more than three FBOs. Timmons categorized FBO activities into three types: (1) mostly fuel with very limited maintenance services; (2) a full-service FBO deriving 25–50% of its revenues from maintenance and avionics; and (3) FBOs where maintenance and avionics accounted for 50% of the revenues. The intent was to purchase a mix of all three types, with an emphasis on type 1.

The company came close to purchasing an FBO at John Wayne Airport in Orange County, south of Los Angeles. The business included a charter airline, thus guaranteeing sufficient maintenance business. But, Air BP had to withdraw when it could not get around the federal regulation that prohibited a non-American company from owning more than 25% of an American-certified charter operation.

Then Timmons found a very attractive new FBO for sale at the Peachtree-De Kalb airport (PDK) in Atlanta, Georgia. It was one of three FBOs at this site. PDK served as an official reliever airport to attract general aviation customers away from Atlanta's Hartsfield International Airport. The facility comprised a recently built two-story terminal with 1,150 m² (12,000 ft²) of floor space offering lounges, conference rooms, office space, flight planning, weather service, and a canteen. Its most distinctive feature was a huge exterior canopy with room below for two executive jets to park out of the sun or rain. Other elements included an executive hangar, and well-equipped maintenance and avionics departments capable of a wide variety of projects.

BP made an offer, hoping for quick agreement but, because of legal and financial problems faced by the seller, the deal (for $5.2 million) was not struck until April 1990. Timmons believed that the delay had hurt business, because some customers had lost confidence in the future of this operation and had taken their business to other FBOs. He retained the highly regarded staff, changed the name from Texaco to Air BP, and began an aggressive promotional effort, emphasizing the quality of both the physical facilities and the services. (*refer to **Exhibit 3***).

The Atlanta FBO had won much favourable publicity for Air BP in the US, including awards from two magazines, *Aviation International News* and *Professional*

Pilot, for superior performance as evaluated by corporate pilots. A much repeated story told of a corporation that switched its business to Air BP after its chairman, soaked to the skin while running from his jet to a competing FBO in a downpour, had angrily told his captain to park under the Air BP canopy on future occasions. But, despite significant marketing activities and effective cost control, the facility reported a small loss for the year 1990. In contrast, the Cleveland FBO continued to be profitable, netting $400,000 a year, primarily from commercial into-plane fueling.

Entry into Australia

Although Australia was a much smaller market than either the US or Europe, it was seen as having significant potential. The distances between cities were considerable, business activity in Australia was expanding, and the number of aircraft was growing. An opportunity was soon identified at Melbourne's main airport, Tullamarine. Thirteen executive jets were based in Melbourne, most of them at the old municipal airport, which was threatened with closure.

Elders IXL, a major corporation, had just acquired a Boeing 737, bringing its fleet of corporate aircraft to three. In partnership with the Australia New Zealand Bank (ANZ), which based an aircraft of its own at Melbourne, Elders was building the Melbourne Jet Base (MJB). When finished, this large and beautifully equipped facility would contain three executive suites—one each for Elders and ANZ, plus a third for an undetermined future client of the MJB. There would also be a dedicated customs facility, rental office space—notoriously short at Tullamarine—for airport suppliers, and an executive hangar and maintenance facility. Air BP was invited to take an equity share of up to 30% in return for the fuel rights.

Examining the market, Air BP saw opportunities to service the VIP fleet of the Royal Australian Air Force and perhaps to build a pipeline to distribute fuel to a new maintenance base that Qantas (Australia's international airline) planned to build nearby. In 1989, BP agreed to take 10% of the equity with the balance split between Elders and ANZ. After constructing fuel tanks and related facilities, BP's investment totalled A$3.3 million (US$2.5 million).

But, then, a serious blow struck the Jet Base, even before completion. Discontented with Elder's financial performance, the board dismissed its chief executive. His successor promptly instituted major cost-cutting moves, including elimination of the corporate fleet. ANZ had to take on Elder's share in the MJB. By September 1990, BP's accumulated losses amounted to A$1.5 million (US$1.2 million).

Activities in Europe

Air BP continued to look for new FBOs on the Continent while trying to make its existing ones profitable. Heathrow made a profit, yet Stansted barely broke even, and Cologne was losing money. The view was that Stansted would turn the corner once a resident fleet was attracted, which would justify construction of a hangar and maintenance facilities and, in turn, attract more business.

The Cologne FBO was having trouble running UPS's freight airline. Margins were squeezed as UPS sought to reduce its costs and as the aircraft lessor pushed for higher leasing fees. Losses in 1990 amounted to DM 1.4 million ($790,000). The managing director kept predicting profits but the losses continued. Finally, he was replaced by a new man hired from Deutsche Bank. In early 1991, a task force reviewed the operations. Identifying the major problem as the UPS airline, it suggested that consideration be given to scaling down or eliminating this side of the business. Other options were seen as selling the FBO, upgrading it, or continuing to subsidize operations in the hope of future improvements.

REASSESSMENT

By mid-1991, many industrialized countries remained stuck in recession. Sales and utilization of corporate aircraft had slowed or declined in many parts of the world as companies tightened their belts. The margins on FBO fuel sales in the US were under pressure due to increased price competition in a soft market.

Meanwhile, BP had redefined its strategic goals to emphasize secure placement of company-produced aviation fuels under the Air BP brand. The company wanted to sell all the fuel it refined under its own brand name, capturing as much margin as possible, rather than selling surplus fuel to traders who would then resell it through another distribution channel. Future investments, declared the CEO of Air BP, would be evaluated with reference to the sales volume secured relative to the amount invested. At the same time, renewed emphasis was to be placed on achieving "quality service and customer responsiveness second to none."

Other developments concerned individual FBOs. BP had decided to move its own corporate fleet of three aircraft from another field in southern England to the more conveniently located Stansted. This would provide FAEL-Stansted with the resident fleet it needed to justify leasing hangar space and adding additional services. In Cologne, the German managing director had found a prospective buyer for the facility if the company wanted to sell that FBO. Meanwhile, Melbourne's situation had stabilized and there was a prospect of new resident aircraft moving to MJB.

In the US, sentiment was moving away from acquisition of company-owned FBOs towards increasing the number of Air BP branded FBOs that were owned and operated by other parties. Jim Timmons told the London office that recent federal legislation had created some interesting opportunities:

The Environmental Protection Act focussed on underground storage tanks as a potential source of contamination. The new law says that tanks over a certain age must be upgraded or removed and replaced by new ones. This could be very expensive for FBOs. Most have several tanks for jet fuel and avgas. Upgrading and adding leak detection devices will cost a few thousand, but replacing a whole system could run more than $100,000.

Fuel trucks, too, are getting more expensive because of new environmental requirements. One 2,000 gallon truck today costs maybe $70,000, a 5,000 gallon [19,000 litre] model will run you $100,000 to $125,000. It's getting to the point where FBOs are facing a real capital crunch.

Timmons urged that Air BP offer loans at competitive rates to help FBOs upgrade their fuel farms (storage facilities), in return for a fuel supply contract covering the 5–7 year duration of the loan. Exxon and Phillips already had very limited programmes of this nature. Timmons felt that it would be unwise for BP to share ownership of a dealer's fuel farm, since that would increase the company's exposure to legal liability in the event of a spill or accident. He also suggested that BP expand its truck-leasing operation to offer dealers the chance to lease new fuel trucks on a monthly basis—a service already available from Exxon, Phillips, and Texaco. The bottom line, declared Timmons, was that Air BP could use its capital to secure fuel sales far more effectively in this way than by spending millions to buy a single FBO.

In Europe, there was still interest in buying more FBOs. A handsome new facility at Paris-Le Bourget (a location coveted by Air BP since it was at the centre of European business aviation) was nearing completion. The project even included a hotel. The developer had gone bankrupt and prospective buyers were being courted. New opportunities were opening up in Central Europe. Berlin was seen as an increasingly important destination for executive jets, but no one could forecast which of Berlin's airports would be designated for general aviation. In Hungary, the Budapest airport already handled five corporate jets a day. The recently privatized airport authority had awarded general aviation fuel rights to Air BP, but, Field's and BP thought the authority might be prepared to contract out many other services, too, as part of a general upgrading and repositioning of the airport. Further west, Rome, Milan, and Madrid remained under consideration.

Evaluation

Evans reviewed his notes again. He had prepared a summary of the situation at each of Air BP's six existing FBOs (*refer to **Exhibit 4***). Taking a clean pad, he wrote "NOW WHAT?" and then jotted down some questions:

- Goals and priorities—the same worldwide or vary by continent?
- Investment criteria: volume versus margins—or can we have both?
- What do we mean by "service" and "quality"? How do they add value?
- Hold, expand, or sell our own FBO network? What percentage share?
- How to build up the number of Air BP branded dealers in the States?
- Strategies for Europe, Australia, rest of world?
- Lessons from experience to date? For Air BP? BP in general?
- Actions: what to do and when?

EXHIBIT 1

Corporate aircraft in use around the world, 1991.

	JETS	T/PROPS	TOTAL		JETS	T/PROPS	TOTAL
AFRICA				**EUROPE**			
Libya	7	14	21	Austria	39	31	60
Morocco	9	13	22	Belgium	13	19	32
Nigeria	25	19	44	Denmark	20	33	53
South Africa	59	129	188	Finland	13	15	28
All other	72	117	189	France	179	292	471
TOTAL	172	292	464	Germany	91	182	273
				Italy	181	75	256
ASIA				Netherlands	18	23	41
India	3	31	34	Norway	9	22	31
Indonesia	16	26	42	Spain	38	43	81
Iran	9	20	29	Sweden	31	56	87
Japan	18	56	74	Switzerland	87	52	139
Philippines	9	48	57	United Kingdom	188	112	278
Saudi Arabia	76	9	85	Yugoslavia	15	7	22
All other	105	42	147	All other	45	26	71
TOTAL	236	232	488	TOTAL	945	978	1,923
AUSTRALIA & OCEANIA				**NORTH-AMERICA & CARIBBEAN**			
Australia	84	148	232	Bermuda	20	2	22
All other	7	18	25	Canada	182	334	516
TOTAL	91	166	257	Mexico	286	175	461
				United States	4,591	5,052	9,643
				All other	17	23	40
				TOTAL	5,096	5,586	10,682
CENTRAL & SOUTH AMERICA							
Argentina	24	76	100				
Brazil	225	230	455				
Colombia	8	188	196				
Peru	9	19	28				
Venezuela	52	187	239				
All other	16	52	68				
TOTAL	334	752	1,086	*WORLD TOTAL*	6,882	8,035	14,917

Note: Figures are shown for individual countries only when total corporate aircraft in use amount to 20 or more.
Source: Reorganized from information in *Flight International* 29 May–4 June 1991, page 54

EXHIBIT 2

Number of branded FBOs contracted with specific oil companies in the United States, 1985 vs. 1990.

BRAND	1985	1990
Phillips	800	825
Exxon	400	340
Chevron	350	360
Texaco	300	315
Air BP (and predecessor brands)*	300	260
Shell**	275	50
Mobil**	125	45
Pride/Avfuel	50	155
Triton	—	200
Other brands	200	175
Unbranded	700	590
TOTAL FBOS Selling fuel in USA	**3,500**	**3,350**

*In 1985 Air BP sold primarily through predecessor brands such as Sohio, Gulf, and Boron; By 1990, most had been rebranded as Air BP.

**Shell and Mobil had made a strategic decision to withdraw from branded FBO outlets and were selling their franchises to minor brands such as Pride/Avfuel and Triton.

EXHIBIT 3

Picture Perfect.

Air BP

Even a thousand words can't describe our dramatic airside canopy. It keeps dry things dry and cool things cool. Like passengers and planes. And unless you've experienced

Air BP Atlanta, words aren't enough. And neither are pictures. Twenty-four hours a day, we're at your service. Get the picture?

Line Service

- 8,000 square foot convenience canopy
- UVair Facility at PDK
- BP Jet Fuel pre-blended with additive
- BP 100LL
- Crew cars
- Courtesy van

Maintenance

- Authorized Learjet Service Station
- Turbine airframes, Including:
  Learjet
  Citation
  King Air
- GE CJ-610
  Garrett TFE-731
  P&W JT 15 D
  P&W PT 6

Avionics

- State-of-the-art avionics shop
- Full Capability for:
  Design,
  Engineering,
  Installation,
  Retrofit and
  Repair
- Dealer/ distributor for all major manufacturers

Facilities

- Luxurious Passenger Lounges
- Pilot lounge with 'Snooze Room'
- BP Jet Fuel pre-blended with additive
- On site Hertz rental cars
- Executive conference room with full a/v

AIR BP ATLANTA

PDK• DeKalb Peachtree Airport
One Corsair Drive • Atlanta, Ga 30341
(404) 452-0010 • Fax (404) 457-1775
UNICOM 122.95 • ARINC 128.97

GENERAL AVIATION

EXHIBIT 4

FBO strategy review.

	AIR BP EQUITY	YEAR ACQUIRED	AIR BP INVESTMENT US$000	ASSESSED PRE-TAX ROI	FUEL VOLUME MUSG	NET FUEL MARGIN* US CENT/USG	AIR BP INCOME** US$000	NOTES
USA								
—Cleveland	100%	1972	n/a***	n/a	85.00	0.47	400	
—Atlanta	100%	1990	6,300	9.0%	0.95	0.93	9	
EUROPE								
—Heathrow	50%	1986	1,750	34.0%	2.70	n/a	114	Dividend on JV equity
—Stansted	50%	1987	850	-6.8%	0.70	n/a	0	Commission from fuelling
—Cologne	51%	1988	650	-56.0%	1.20	n/a	0	Commission from fuelling
AUSTRALIA								
—Melbourne	10%	1990	2,500	-0.4%	2.30	7.00	161	Investment excludes fuel farm

*Net Fuel Margin is margin direct to Air BP from fuel sales, this excludes any wholesale margin (which Air BP would earn irrespective of whether it owned the FBO or not).

**Air BP Income is net income directly received by Air BP from its investment, and excludes any wholesale fuel margin.

***Includes $1,100,000 in working capital injected by Air BP

COMPANY/NAME INDEX

SUBJECT INDEX

Page numbers followed by *f* indicate illustrations.
Page numbers followed by *t* indicate tables.